THE NEW ROUTLEDGE COMPANION TO SCIENCE FICTION

The New Routledge Companion to Science Fiction provides an overview of the study of science fiction across multiple academic fields. It offers a new conceptualisation of the field today, marking the significant changes that have taken place in sf studies over the past 15 years.

Building on the pioneering research in the first edition, the collection reorganises historical coverage of the genre to emphasise new geographical areas of cultural production and the growing importance of media beyond print. It also updates and expands the range of frameworks that are relevant to the study of science fiction. The periodisation has been reframed to include new chapters focusing on science fiction produced outside the Anglophone context, including South Asian, Latin American, Chinese and African diasporic science fiction. The contributors use both well-established critical and theoretical approaches and embrace a range of new ones, including biopolitics, climate crisis, critical ethnic studies, disability studies, energy humanities, game studies, medical humanities, new materialisms and sonic studies.

This book is an invaluable resource for students and established scholars seeking to understand the vast range of engagements with science fiction in scholarship today.

Mark Bould (he/him) is Professor of Film and Literature at the University of the West of England. He is the recipient of the Science Fiction Research Association's Lifetime Achievement Award and the International Association of the Fantastic in the Arts' Distinguished Scholarship Award. His books include *This Is Not A Science Fiction Textbook* (with Steven Shaviro; 2024), *The Anthropocene Unconscious: Climate Catastrophe Culture* (2021), *M. John Harrison: Critical Essays* (with Rhys Williams 2019), *Solaris* (2014), *SF Now* (with Rhys Williams 2014), *Africa SF* (2013), *Science Fiction: The Routledge Film Guidebook* (2012) and *The Routledge Concise History of Science Fiction* (with Sherryl Vint; 2011).

Andrew M. Butler (he/him) is the author of *Eternal Sunshine of the Spotless Mind* (2019) and *Solar Flares: Science Fiction in the 1970s* (2012). He is Managing Editor of *Extrapolation* and chair of judges for the Arthur C. Clarke Award.

Sherryl Vint (she/her) is Professor of Media and Cultural Studies and Chair of English at the University of California, Riverside. She is the recipient of the Science Fiction Research Association's Innovative Scholarship and Lifetime Achievement Awards. Her books include *Programming the Future: Politics, Resistance, and Utopia in Contemporary Speculative TV* (with Jonathan Alexander; 2022), *Biopolitical Futures in Twenty-First-Century Speculative Fiction* (2021), *Science Fiction: The Essential Knowledge* (2021), *After the Human: Culture, Theory and Criticism in the 21st Century* (2020), *The Futures Industry* (2015), *Science Fiction and Cultural Theory: A Reader* (2015) and *Science Fiction: A Guide for the Perplexed* (2014).

ROUTLEDGE LITERATURE COMPANIONS

ALSO AVAILABLE IN THIS SERIES:

THE ROUTLEDGE COMPANION TO ECOPOETICS
Edited by Julia Fiedorczuk, Mary Newell, Bernard Quetchenbach and Orchid Tierney

THE ROUTLEDGE COMPANION TO LITERATURE AND THE GLOBAL SOUTH
Edited by Alfred J. López and Ricardo Quintana-Vallejo

THE ROUTLEDGE COMPANION TO CHILDREN'S LITERATURE AND CULTURE
Edited by Claudia Nelson, Elisabeth Wesseling, and Andrea Mei-Ying Wu

THE ROUTLEDGE COMPANION TO LITERATURE AND SOCIAL JUSTICE
Edited by Masood Ashraf Raja and Nick T. C. Lu

THE ROUTLEDGE COMPANION TO LITERATURE AND FEMINISM
Edited by Rachel Carroll and Fiona Tolan

THE ROUTLEDGE COMPANION TO LITERATURE AND ART
Edited by Neil Murphy, W. Michelle Wang, and Cheryl Julia Lee

THE ROUTLEDGE COMPANION TO EIGHTEENTH-CENTURY LITERATURES IN ENGLISH
Edited by Sarah Eron, Nicole N. Aljoe, and Suvir Kaul

THE ROUTLEDGE COMPANION TO PUBLIC HUMANITIES SCHOLARSHIP
Edited by Daniel Fisher-Livne and Michelle May-Curry

THE ROUTLEDGE COMPANION TO ABSURDIST LITERATURE
Edited by Michael Y. Bennett

THE NEW ROUTLEDGE COMPANION TO SCIENCE FICTION
Edited by Mark Bould, Andrew M. Butler and Sherryl Vint

For more information on this series, please visit: www.routledge.com/Routledge-Literature-Companions/book-series/RC4444

THE NEW ROUTLEDGE COMPANION TO SCIENCE FICTION

Edited by Mark Bould, Andrew M. Butler and Sherryl Vint

Routledge
Taylor & Francis Group
LONDON AND NEW YORK

Designed cover image: Sepia Times / Contributor, Getty

Second edition published 2024
by Routledge
4 Park Square, Milton Park, Abingdon, Oxon, OX14 4RN

and by Routledge
605 Third Avenue, New York, NY 10158

Routledge is an imprint of the Taylor & Francis Group, an informa business

First edition published by Routledge 2009

British Library Cataloguing-in-Publication Data
A catalogue record for this book is available from the British Library

Library of Congress Cataloging-in-Publication Data
Names: Bould, Mark, editor. | Butler, Andrew M., editor. | Vint, Sherryl, 1969– editor.
Title: The new Routledge companion to science fiction / edited by Mark Bould, Andrew M. Butler and Sherryl Vint.
Description: Second edition. | Abingdon, Oxon ; New York, NY : Routledge, 2024. | Series: Routledge literature companions | "First edition published by Routledge 2009." | Includes bibliographical references and index. |
Identifiers: LCCN 2023059332 (print) | LCCN 2023059333 (ebook) | ISBN 9780367690533 (hardback) | ISBN 9780367690687 (paperback) | ISBN 9781003140269 (ebook)
Subjects: LCSH: Science fiction–History and criticism.
Classification: LCC PN3433.5 .R685 2024 (print) | LCC PN3433.5 (ebook) | DDC 809.3/8762–dc23/eng/20240226
LC record available at https://lccn.loc.gov/2023059332
LC ebook record available at https://lccn.loc.gov/2023059333

ISBN: 978-0-367-69053-3 (hbk)
ISBN: 978-0-367-69068-7 (pbk)
ISBN: 978-1-003-14026-9 (ebk)

DOI: 10.4324/9781003140269

Typeset in Times New Roman
by Newgen Publishing UK

CONTENTS

CONTRIBUTORS

Ibtisam Ahmed (he/him) is an independent scholar who works as the Head of Research at LGBT Foundation. He completed an MPhil at the University of Nottingham with a thesis that explored decolonial utopianism. He is currently completing a project exploring community building through queer performance houses, funded by the BA/Leverhulme Small Research grant. He has been published on multiple platforms on queer culture and history, including *The Politics of Culture* (2020), which he co-edited.

Jonathan Alexander (he/him) is Chancellor's Professor of English and Informatics at the University of California, Irvine. The author, co-author or co-editor of twenty-two books, his most recent is *Writing and Desire: Queer Ways of Composing* (2023).

Rebecca McWilliams Ojala Ballard (she/her) is an assistant professor in the Department of English at Florida State University, where she researches and teaches contemporary US literature and culture, speculative fiction and film, and environmental humanities. Her scholarship, including her current book project, *Genre Frictions*, explores how the political and the literary inform each other in the contemporary world, tracing how social movements take narrative shape and how fiction responds to social justice. Her essays (also under Rebecca Evans) have appeared in *ISLE, American Literature*, *ASAP/J*, *Science Fiction Studies*, *Resilience* and elsewhere.

Beyond Gender Research Group see Ibtisam Ahmed, Avery Delany, Tom Dillon, Sasha Myerson, Eleonora Rossi, Smin Smith, Katie Stone and Josephine Taylor.

Mark Bould (he/him) is Professor of Film and Literature at the University of the West of England. A founding editor of the *Science Fiction Film and Television* journal and the *Studies in Global Science Fiction* monograph series, he is the recipient of the Science Fiction Research Association's Lifetime Achievement Award (2016) and the International Association of the Fantastic in the Arts' Distinguished Scholarship Award (2019). His most recent books are *The Anthropocene Unconscious: Climate Catastrophe Culture* (2021) and, coedited with Steven Shaviro, *This Is Not A Science Fiction Textbook* (2024).

Amy Brookes (she/her; formerly Amy Butt) is an architect and lecturer in architecture at the University of Reading with a specialisation in architectural representation and communication. Her research explores the way the fictional worlds we construct influence and reflect the world we inhabit, writing about the imaginary in architecture through sf literature and film. Recent publications include 'Made up Ground: Architecture, Science Fiction, and the Surface of Imagined Worlds' in *Architecture and Culture*, and 'The Present as Past: Science Fiction and the Museum' in the *Open Library of Humanities*, which won the Science Fiction Research Association Innovative Research Award 2022.

Andrew M. Butler (he/him) wrote *Solar Flares: Science Fiction in the 1970s* (2011), *Eternal Sunshine of the Spotless Mind* (2014), 'Human Subjects/Alien Objects? Abjection and the Constructions of Race and Racism in *District 9*' in *Alien Imaginations* (2015), 'Sleeping/Waking: Politicizing the Sublime in Science Fiction Film Special Effects' in *Endangering Science Fiction Film* (2015), as well as books on Philip K. Dick, cyberpunk, Terry Pratchett, postmodernism, and film studies, and articles or chapters on Cornish folk horror films, futurology, millennial British sf film, Philip Pullman, Mary Doria Russell and Jack Womack. Currently he is working on science fiction art, folk horror and John Wyndham film adaptations. He was co-editor of *The Routledge Companion to Science Fiction* (2009) and *Fifty Key Figures in Science Fiction* (2009) and is managing editor of the journal *Extrapolation*. He is the non-voting chair of judges for the Arthur C. Clarke Award. In his spare time, he investigates real ale and collects shiny trousers.

Dan Byrne-Smith (he/him) was formerly a senior lecturer at Chelsea College of Arts, University of the Arts London. He now lives in the New Forest and is training to become an existential psychotherapist, studying for a DProf at NSPC in London. His published work includes writings on art, sf and critical utopianism. He is the author (as Dan Smith) of *Traces of Modernity* (2012) and the editor of *Science Fiction: Documents of Contemporary Art* (2020). More recently, he has been working on a book that explores Tangerine Dream's album *Phaedra* as a form of sf.

Elizabeth Callaway (she/her) is an assistant professor in the Department of English at the University of Utah and affiliated faculty with the Environmental Humanities Graduate Program. Her *Eden's Endemics: Narratives of Biodiversity on Earth and Beyond* (2020) investigates the stories we tell in literature and science about the multiplicity of life on Earth. Her current book project looks at the relationship between artificial intelligence and the natural environment. She has published articles on digital humanities, climate change, and the speculative ecosystems of sf.

Christos Callow, Jr. (he/him) is Senior Lecturer in Creative Writing at the University of Derby, a playwright and a fiction writer. He founded the *Talos: Science Fiction Theatre Festival* of London and is the artistic director of Cyborphic, an sf theatre and Greek theatre company. He has written several sf plays (including *Posthuman Meditation* and *Mayuri*), which were presented at Being Human Festival, the Kensington and Chelsea Festival and the Edinburgh Fringe. He has also co-written a reconstructed version of Euripides' lost tragedy *Melanippe Wise* with Dr Andriana Domouzi (based on her PhD research of the play), first presented at the Hope Theatre in London in 2019. His monograph *Science Fiction Theatre: The Theatre of the Future* is forthcoming.

Gerry Canavan (he/him) is a professor and chair of the English Department at Marquette University. He is co-editor of *The Cambridge History of Science Fiction* (2019) and *Uneven*

Futures: Strategies for Community Survival from Speculative Fiction (2020) and the journals *Extrapolation* and *Science Fiction Film and Television.* He is also the author of *Octavia E. Butler* (2016).

Jordan S. Carroll (he/him) is the author of *Reading the Obscene: Transgressive Editors and the Class Politics of US Literature* (2021) and *Speculative Whiteness: Race, Science Fiction, and the Alt-Right* (forthcoming). He received his PhD in English Literature from the University of California, Davis. He was awarded the David G. Hartwell Emerging Scholar Award by the International Association for the Fantastic in the Arts, and his first book won the MLA Prize for Independent Scholars. Carroll's writing has appeared in *American Literature, Post45, The Nation* and the *Los Angeles Review of Books.*

Bodhisattva Chattopadhyay (he/him) is Associate Professor in Global Culture Studies at the Department of Culture Studies and Oriental Languages, University of Oslo, Norway. He leads the international research group CoFUTURES, works on contemporary futurisms and leads several major research projects funded by the European and Norwegian Research Council. He is the recipient of numerous awards, including the World Fantasy Award (2020). He has also exhibited in six transnational art projects and produced the award-winning film *Kalpavigyan: A Speculative Journey* (2021), the first documentary on sf from India and Bengal. His research website is https://cofutures.org

Avery Delany (they/them) is a disabled, queer, non-binary and polyamorous writer, activist, educator and worldbuilder from South London. They are an ESRC funded PhD student in the Department of Anthropology at Goldsmiths, University of London, whose thesis explores questions of 'what it means to be human (and non-human)' vis-a-vis sf video game narratives about artificial intelligence. They are a podcaster for Lore Party Media, and a former co-director of the London Science Fiction Research Community

Tom Dillon (he/him/they/them) looks after the Science Fiction Collections at the University of Liverpool, where they care for a wide array of sf materials and aid researchers in accessing the collections. Their research focuses on the material contexts of sf magazines and completed a thesis on *New Worlds* magazine at Birkbeck, University of London. They are a former co-director of the London Science Fiction Research Community.

Arthur B. Evans (he/him) is Professor Emeritus of French at DePauw University and managing editor of *Science Fiction Studies*. He has authored numerous books and articles on Jules Verne and early French sf, including the award-winning monograph *Jules Verne Rediscovered* (1988), as well as co-editing the popular classroom text *The Wesleyan Anthology of Science Fiction* (2010). For many years he served as general editor of Wesleyan University Press's *Early Classics of Science Fiction* book series, a notable collection that features more than two dozen fictional and non-fictional sf titles.

Christopher T. Fan (he/him) is Assistant Professor of English at the University of California, Irvine with courtesy appointments in the Departments of Asian American Studies and of East Asian Studies. He is the author of *Asian American Fiction after 1965: Transnational Fantasies of Economic Mobility* (2024) and co-editor, with David S. Roh, Betsy Huang and Greta A. Niu, of

Techno-Orientalism 2.0: New Forms and Formulations (2025). He is also a co-founder of *Hyphen* magazine.

Paweł Frelik (he/him) is Associate Professor and the Leader of Speculative Texts and Media Research Group at the American Studies Center, University of Warsaw. His interests include cultures of speculation, sf, video games and fantastic visualities. He has published widely in these fields, serves on the advisory boards of *Science Fiction Studies*, *Extrapolation* and *Journal of Gaming and Virtual Worlds*, and is the co-editor of the *New Dimensions in Science Fiction* book series (University of Wales Press). He is a recipient of Science Fiction Research Association's Thomas D. Clareson Award for Distinguished Service (2017) and Innovative Research Award (2023).

Nicole Ku'uleinapuananioliko'awapuhimelemeleolani Furtado (she/her) is a Kanaka Maoli scholar from Nānākuli, Hawaii. She works at the intersection of Critical Oceanic Studies, Visual Culture, Indigenous Feminisms and Speculative Aesthetics to examine the work of Native Hawaiians and other Indigenous artists who use visual art as a means to disrupt colonial notions of time and knowledge production. Her work aims at centring how Indigenous digital arts restore kinship relations, develop land-based pedagogies that challenge the settler commercialisation of land and landscapes, and emphasise the need for ethical networks of relations for how we encounter social technologies into the future.

Lincoln Geraghty (he/him) is Professor of Media Cultures in the School of Film, Media and Communication at the University of Portsmouth. He serves as editorial advisor for *The Journal of Popular Culture*, *Transformative Works and Culture*, *Journal of Fandom Studies* and *Journal of Popular Television*. His books include *Living with Star Trek: American Culture and the Star Trek Universe* (2007), *American Science Fiction Film and Television* (2009) and *Cult Collectors: Nostalgia, Fandom and Collecting Popular Culture* (2014).

Michael Goodrum (he/him) is Reader in Cultural History at Canterbury Christ Church University. Goodrum has published widely on superheroes, sf and horror narratives across a range of media, chiefly comics and film. His most recent book is *Printing Terror* (2021), co-authored with Philip Smith, and his work has appeared in journals such as *Gender & History*, *Horror Studies* and *Literature Compass*, as well as in a number of edited volumes.

Barry Keith Grant (he/him) is Professor Emeritus of Film Studies and Popular Culture at Brock University, Ontario, Canada. A Fellow of the Royal Society of Canada, he is the author or editor of many books, including *Film Genre: From Iconography to Ideology* (2007), *100 American Science Fiction Films* (2013) and *100 American Horror Films* (2022). His most recent books are the newly expanded *Voyages of Discovery: The Cinema of Frederick Wiseman* (2023) and *Film Genre: The Basics* (2023).

Anna Maria Grzybowska (she/her) is a PhD student at the University of Warsaw. With her dedication to understanding various (not-only-)human ways of experiencing the world, her research focuses on representations of the human psyche – her recent article 'Invisible Cuts: Psychological

Violence and Hermeneutical Injustice in *Tau* (2018) and *Upstream Color* (2013)' explores the confluence of psychological violence and sf film – as well as its formation in collision with the complexity of nonhuman beings within the realms of speculative fiction. Her dissertation-in-progress examines speculative visions of human-animal futures, with a particular focus on narrative transformations (or consolidations) of the animal-industrial complex within literature, film and video games.

Dan Hassler-Forest (he/him) works as Assistant Professor of Media and Cultural Studies at Utrecht University. He has published books and articles on superhero movies, comics, transmedia storytelling, critical theory and zombies. He has recently completed two books on race and global media, focused on the creative work of performing artist Janelle Monáe, and is currently writing a monograph on the *Fast & Furious* franchise.

Karen Hellekson (she/her) is an independent scholar based in Maine who has published on *Doctor Who*, fandom, Cordwainer Smith, alternate histories and audio dramas.

Rebecca J. Holden (she/her) is a fan and scholar of feminist, African American and YA science fiction. She earned her PhD in English Literature from the University of Wisconsin-Madison and is currently a Principal Lecturer at the University of Maryland, College Park. She has published essays and reviews on topics ranging from young adult Afrofuturism to feminist cyberpunk, and points in between, in *Foundation, Science Fiction Studies, Oxford Bibliographies in American Literature, Los Angeles Review of Books, Literary Afrofuturism in the Twenty-First Century* and others. With Nisi Shawl, she co-edited and contributed to the Locus-nominated *Strange Matings: Science Fiction, Feminism, African American Voices, and Octavia E. Butler* (2013).

Veronica Hollinger (she/her) is Emerita Professor of Cultural Studies at Trent University in Canada. A long-time co-editor of *Science Fiction Studies*, she has also co-edited four academic collections. Her earliest research focused on cyberpunk and her latest has considered posthumanism and its entanglements with the ecological crisis. She is also intensely interested in contemporary Chinese sf. A committed queer-feminist, she admires the sheer diversity of sf's worldbuilding and its potential to imagine differently. She is a recipient of the SFRA's Innovative Research Award, Thomas B. Clareson Award and the Award for Lifetime Contributions to Science Fiction Scholarship.

Nicola Hunte (she/her) lectures in the Literatures in English discipline at the Cave Hill campus of the University of the West Indies. She has published on popular culture, specific to Barbadian expression on and offline in the *Journal of West Indian Literature* (*JWIL*). Her research interests include the critical texts of Guyanese writer/theorist Wilson Harris as well as speculative fiction, particularly from the Caribbean and the African cultural diaspora. Her work on Caribbean speculative fiction can be found in *JWIL*, the *SFRA Review* and *Uneven Futures: Strategies for Community Survival from Science Fiction* (2022).

Melody Jue (she/her) is Associate Professor of English at the University of California, Santa Barbara. Her research and teaching focus on the ocean and environmental humanities, sf, STS and media studies. She is the author of *Wild Blue Media: Thinking Through Seawater* (2020) and *Coralations* (2024). She is the co-editor, with Rafico Ruiz, of *Saturation: An Elemental Politics* (2021) and, with Zach Blas and Jennifer Rhee, of *Informatics of Domination* (2025).

Brooks Landon (he/him) teaches in the English Department at the University of Iowa. He is the author of *The Aesthetics of Ambivalence: Rethinking Science Fiction Film in the Age of Electronic (Re)Production* (1992), *Science Fiction After 1900: From the Steam Man to the Stars* (2002) and numerous essays on sf and technoculture.

Martin Lund (he/him) holds a PhD in Jewish studies from Lund University and is a senior lecturer in religious studies at the Department of Society, Culture and Identity at Malmö University, Sweden. His main research interest is comics. His research is particularly focused on urban cultural formation, racial formation and identification, religion and politics. He has published widely and edited several collections in comics studies, including the monograph *Re-Constructing the Man of Steel: Superman 1938–1941, Jewish American History, and the Invention of the Jewish–Comics Connection* (2016). He is also co-editor, with Julia Round, of the *Encapsulations: Critical Comics Studies* book series.

Anna McFarlane (she/her) is Lecturer in Medical Humanities at the University of Leeds and a Visiting Collaborator on the Wellcome Trust-funded Future of Human Reproduction project at the University of Lancaster. She is the author of a monograph on William Gibson, *Cyberpunk Culture and Psychology: Seeing Through the Mirrorshades* (2021). She is co-editor, with Graham J. Murphy and Lars Schmeink, of *The Routledge Companion to Cyberpunk Culture* (2019) and *Fifty Key Figures in Cyberpunk Culture* (2022) and, with Gavin Miller and Donna McCormack, of *The Edinburgh Companion to Science Fiction and the Medical Humanities* (2024).

Rubén R. Mendoza (he/him) is Associate Professor of Chicana/o Studies at East Los Angeles College, where he has taught since 2009. He holds an MA in Chicana/o Studies and a PhD in English/Rhetoric Studies from University of California, Riverside. His work applies rhetoric studies in development of critical pedagogy through focus on contemporary Chicana/o art, Latin American cultural production, and speculative fiction. He has presented at conferences throughout the Americas in Latinx Studies, Rhetoric, Latin American Studies, Comparative Literature and Science Fiction Studies, and has published in *Paradoxa*, *Science Fiction Studies*, *Confluencia* and *Science Fiction Film and Television*.

Emily Midkiff (she/her) is Assistant Professor at the University of North Dakota, where she teaches courses on children's literature and literacy. Before getting her PhD, she spent 9 years working in children's theatre, and now researches sf and fantasy for children with attention to what children have to say for themselves. She is the author of *Equipping Space Cadets: Primary Science Fiction for Young Children* (2022), an interdisciplinary case study of sf for children and winner of the Science Fiction Research Association's New Book Award.

Gavin Miller (he/him) is Reader in Contemporary Literature and Medical Humanities at the University of Glasgow, where he co-directed the Medical Humanities Research Centre. He is the author of *Science Fiction and Psychology* (2020), and Lead Editor of the Edinburgh University Press's book series *Contemporary Cultural Studies in Illness, Health and Medicine*). His research interests include the cultural history of the psychological disciplines, book history and UFO practices.

Glyn Morgan (he/him) was the curatorial lead for the *Science Fiction: Voyage to the Edge of Imagination* exhibition at the Science Museum, London. A former editor of *Vector: The Critical Journal of the British Science Fiction Association*, he frequently contributes to journals, including the *Los Angeles Review of Books*, *Science Fiction Studies Review* and *European History Quarterly*. He is the author of *Imagining the Unimaginable: Speculative Fiction and the Holocaust* (2020) editor of *Sideways in Time: Critical Essays on Alternate History Fiction* (2019) and *Science Fiction: Voyage to the Edge of Imagination* (2022).

Upumanyu Pablo Mukherjee (he/him) is Professor of Anglophone World-Literature at University of Oxford. His research involves four inter-related fields: colonial and postcolonial literatures, environmental humanities, world-literary studies, and Victorian studies. He is the author of five monographs – *Crime Fiction and Empire* (2003), *Postcolonial Environments: Nature, Culture and Contemporary Indian Novel in English* (2010), *Natural Disasters and Victorian Imperial Culture* (2013), *Final Frontiers: Science Fiction and Techno-Science in Non-Aligned India* (2020), which won the Science Fiction Research Association's Book Award in 2021, and with the Warwick Research Collective (WReC) *Combined and Uneven Development: Towards a New Theory of World-Literature* (2015). He has also edited three essay collections and anthologies, and co-edits Palgrave Macmillan's book series *New Comparisons in World Literature*. He was elected Fellow of British Academy in 2022.

Sinéad Murphy (she/her) is an independent researcher focused on Arabfuturisms, theories of world literature, and principles and practices of community-building. She also works and writes collaboratively as part of the interdisciplinary research collective Beyond Gender. She holds an AHRC LAHP-funded PhD in Comparative Literature from King's College London. She has publications forthcoming with Routledge and Palgrave, and her writing can be found in places like *Science Fiction Studies*, *Strange Horizons*, *Wasafiri* and *The Literary Encyclopedia*. She currently works as Policy Engagement Coordinator at University College London Public Policy.

Sasha Myerson (she/her) is an independent researcher with a PhD in English and Humanities. Her doctoral thesis explored the collective subjects and communities of second wave feminist cyberpunk fiction. She has published articles and chapters on Japanese cyberpunk film, the poetry of Sun Ra and queer sf. Her other research interests include feminist and queer theory, postmodernism, urban studies, critical theory, postcolonial thought and utopian studies. She is a former co-director of the London Science Fiction Research Community.

Hugh C. O'Connell (he/him) is an associate professor of English at the University of Massachusetts Boston. His current research examines the relationship between speculative fiction and speculative finance. He is the co-editor with David M. Higgins of *Speculative Finance/Speculative Fiction*, a 2019 special issue of *CR: The New Centennial Review*. Essays on contemporary and postcolonial sf have appeared in *The Cambridge History of Science Fiction* (2019), *Extrapolation, Utopian Studies, Postcolonial Literary Inquiry, Modern Fiction Studies, Paradoxa, Science Fiction Film and Television, Literary Geographies* and *Los Angeles Review of Books*.

Sunyoung Park (she/her) is Associate Professor in the departments of East Asian Languages and Cultures and of Gender and Sexuality Studies at the University of Southern California. She is the author of *The Proletarian Wave: Literature and Leftist Culture in Colonial Korea, 1910–1945* (2015) and has edited and/or translated several volumes, including *Revisiting Minjung: New Perspectives on the Cultural History of 1980s South Korea* (2019) and *Readymade Bodhisattva: The Kaya Anthology of Science Fiction from South Korea* (2019). She is currently writing a monograph on sf, politics and modernization in South Korea from the 1960s through the 2010s.

Baryon Tensor Posadas (he/him) is Associate Professor at the Hong Kong University of Science and Technology. Prior to joining HKUST, he taught at the University of Minnesota, Twin Cities and was a Postdoctoral Fellow at McGill University. He is the author *Double Visions, Double Fictions: The Doppelganger in Japanese Film and Literature* (2018) and the translator of Aramaki Yoshio's *The Sacred Era: A Novel* (2017). His current research revolves around Japanese sf and empire, animation and posthuman bodies, and techno-orientalism and transnational fan culture.

Robin Anne Reid (she/her) retired from Texas A&M–Commerce in 2020 and can now enjoy time to work on her scholarship. She draws on queer, feminist and critical race theories to analyse speculative fiction and fantasy, specifically feminist sf and J.R.R. Tolkien's legendarium, its adaptations and its fandom. She edited *Greenwood's Women in Science Fiction and Fantasy* (2008) and is currently working on two anthologies (one on queer approaches to Tolkien, another on race, racisms and Tolkien). In recent years, she has also focused on racisms in online fandom in the wake of Racefail '09.

John Rieder (he/him) is Emeritus Professor of English at the University of Hawai'i at Mānoa. Recipient of the Science Fiction Research Association's Innovative Research Award in 2012 and Lifetime Achievement Award in 2019, he is the author of *Colonialism and the Emergence of Science Fiction* (2008), *Science Fiction and the Mass Cultural Genre System* (2017) and *Speculative Epistemologies* (2021), as well as many essays on sf and other topics. In retirement he remains active as a scholar of sf studies and a member of the editorial board of *Extrapolation*.

Adam Roberts (he/him) is Professor of 19th-Century Literature and Culture at Royal Holloway, University of London, and the author of *The History of Science Fiction* (second edition, 2016) and *History of Fantasy* (2024). He is also the author of 22 science fiction novels and a great many short stories, none of which are covered in the present volume.

Brittany R. Roberts (she/her) is Lecturer in World Literature at Appalachian State University. She researches twentieth- and twenty-first-century Russian and American speculative fiction, particularly horror and sf, with additional interests in the environmental humanities, animal studies and critical plant studies. Her work has appeared in *The Irish Journal of Gothic and Horror Studies*, *The Spaces and Places of Horror* (2019), *Plants in Science Fiction: Speculative Vegetation* (2020), *Fear and Nature: Ecohorror Studies in the Anthropocene* (2023) and *Contemporary Slavic Horror Across Media: Cursed Zones* (forthcoming).

Eleonora Rossi (she/her) recently completed her doctorate in English at Birkbeck College, University of London. Her academic work to date looks at the intersection between posthuman theory and contemporary art and fiction by female, queer, Black and Indigenous authors. Throughout her PhD, she focused on the hybridisation of human and nonhuman bodies of water. In her future research, she hopes to combine her literary and analytical training with qualitative methods of sociological analysis, bridging the gap between the imagined and lived realities of anthropogenic environmental change.

Patrick B. Sharp (he/him) is Professor of Liberal Studies at California State University, Los Angeles. His scholarship explores the complex relationships between colonial formulations of race, gender, evolutionary science and the history of sf. His co-edited anthology *Sisters of Tomorrow* (2016) recovered major contributions women made to sf magazines from the 1920s to the 1940s. His most recent monograph, *Darwinian Feminism and Early Science Fiction* (2018), shows how first-wave feminist sf was deeply influenced by evolutionary science; it received the Choice Outstanding Academic Title Award from the Association of College and Research Libraries.

Sharon Sharp (she/her) is Professor of Film, Television, and Media at California State University, Dominguez Hills. Her research interests include speculative media, human animal studies, and media industries. She has published essays on speculative media in *Science Fiction Film and Television*, *Women's Studies* and *Fear and Nature: Ecohorror Studies in the Anthropocene* (2023). Her current research is on interspecies labour in film and television.

Rone Shavers (he/him) is a writer and literary critic. He is the author of the experimental Afrofuturist novel *Silverfish* (2020), a finalist for the Council of Literary Magazines and Presses Firecracker Award, and Fiction and Hybrid Genre Editor at *Obsidian: Literature and Art of the African Diaspora*. He is also co-editor, with Joseph Tabbi, of *Paper Empire: William Gaddis and the World System* (2007) and, with Mark Bould, of the 2007 Afrofuturism special issue of *Science Fiction Studies*. He is Associate Professor of English at the University of Utah.

Smin Smith (they/them) is an sf artist and researcher. They are the founder and editor of *Science Fiction Art & Fashion* (FKA *Vagina Dentata Zine*), a publication celebrating still-image sf from marginalised artists. Smin is also a Lecturer in Digital Art within UCA's School of Games and Creative Technology, and a PhD candidate at University of the Arts London. Their academic research contextualises contemporary queer/trans/feminist artworks within sf traditions, communities and discourses.

Alison Sperling (she/her) is Assistant Professor of English at Florida State University, a freelance artistic researcher in Berlin, Germany, and the Vice President of the Sunshine State Biodiversity Group, an environmental non-profit in Tallahassee, Florida.

Eric Steinskog (he/him) is an associate professor in musicology at the Department of Arts and Cultural Studies, University of Copenhagen, Denmark. The author of *Afrofuturism and Black Sound Studies: Culture, Technology, and Things to Come* (2018), his latest publications include 'Ljom: A Meditation' (2023), 'A Young, Black, Queer Woman in Metropolis: Janelle Monáe and Sci-Fi Queerness' (2023) and 'Sounding Horror: Ballads, Ring Shouts, and the Power of Music in Black Horror' (2023).

Katie Stone (she/her) is an independent researcher working on childhood, feminist utopianism and sf. She has a PhD from the Department of English, Theatre and Creative Writing at Birkbeck College, University of London. She is a founding member of the Beyond Gender Research Collective and the Utopian Acts research network. She has published research on anti-work politics and vampirism, time travel and colonialism, and James Tiptree Jr. and trans feminism. Her most recent article, 'Hollow Children: Utopianism and Disability Justice', was published in *Textual Practice*. She has been working on the accessible educational series *Welcome To... Dystopia* and is currently writing a book about *Frankenstein.*

Shelley Streeby (she/her) is Professor of Literature and Ethnic Studies at the University of California, San Diego. She is the author of *American Sensations: Class, Empire, and the Production of Popular Culture* (2002), which received the American Studies Association's Lora Romero First Book Prize, *Radical Sensations: World Movements, Violence, and Visual Culture* (2013) and *Imagining the Future of Climate Change: World-Making through Science Fiction and Activism* (2018). She received a 2021 American Council of Learned Society Faculty Fellowship to support the writing of her latest book on feminist ecologies, memory-work, and world-making in the published writings and archives of Judith Merril, Ursula K. Le Guin and Octavia E. Butler, which is forthcoming.

Josephine Taylor (she/her) is Assistant Professor in English Literature at Northeastern University London. Her doctoral work examined petrocultures and animal studies, focusing on the nonhuman narratives of energy. She is currently revising this work into a monograph for Palgrave's Animal and Literature Series. Her research sits broadly in the area of environmental humanities and cultural studies, and she is also working on artistic responses to urban breathlessness and air pollution.

Taryne Jade Taylor (she/her) is Advanced Assistant Professor of Science Fiction Studies at Florida Atlantic Universit and co-editor, with Grace L. Dillon, Isiah Lavender III and Bodhisattva Chattopadhyay, of the *Routledge Handbook to CoFuturisms* (2023). Her research focuses on the politics of representation in speculative fiction, particularly Latinx Futurisms and feminist sf. She is currently working on a monograph on Latinx Futurisms. She is the submissions and reviews editor for the Americas for *Journal of the Fantastic in the Arts*, editor of the Routledge book series *Studies in Global Genre Fiction* and a juror for the Theodore Sturgeon Memorial Award.

J.P. Telotte (he/him) is Professor Emeritus of Film and Media Studies and former Chair of Georgia Tech's School of Literature, Media, and Communication. Co-editor of the journal *Post Script*, he taught courses in film history, film genres, animation and sf film and television, and has published widely in these areas. He has authored more than 200 scholarly articles and written or edited nineteen books. His latest publications are *The Oxford Handbook of New Science Fiction Cinemas* (2023), *Selling Science Fiction Cinema: Making and Marketing a Genre* (2023) and *Science Fiction Theatre* (2024).

John Timberlake (he/him) is the author of *Landscape and the Science Fiction Imaginary* (2018). A practicing artist, and a passionate devotee of sf illustration from an early age, he studied Fine Art at Brighton Polytechnic, England, The Whitney Museum of American Art Independent Study Program, New York City and Goldsmiths, University of London. He lives in London with his wife and an ever-changing pile of second-hand sf paperbacks, which he unabashedly judges by their covers.

Sherryl Vint (she/her) is Professor of Media and Cultural Studies and of English at the University of California, Riverside. She has received the Science Fiction Research Association's Innovative

Research, Service, and Lifetime Achievement awards. She has published widely on sf, most recently *Biopolitical Futures in Twenty-First Century Speculative Fiction* (2021).

Josefine Walivaara (she/her) is a researcher at Umeå University, Sweden and conducts research concerning normativity, temporality, (dis)ability, gender, sexuality, mental illness and storytelling in speculative and fantastic fiction. She completed her PhD in drama-theatre-film on (hetero) normativity, sexuality and queer potential in sf film and television in 2016 and has published work on *Torchwood, Star Trek, The Handmaid's Tale, Star Wars, Buffy the Vampire Slayer* and *Aniara.* She is currently working on eugenic discourses and genetic augmentation in *Star Trek* and an attempt to understand narratives about clones and artificial intelligence in terms of crip time.

Rhys Williams (he/him) is Senior Lecturer in Energy and Environmental Humanities at the University of Glasgow and director of the Infrastructure Humanities Group. He works on the narratives, aesthetics, poetics, politics and infrastructures of sustainable and just futures, with a focus on energy. He has work published and forthcoming in *South Atlantic Quarterly*, *Open Library of the Humanities* and *Critique*, as well as chapters in *Routledge Handbook of the Energy Humanities* (2024) and *Energized: 101 Keywords*. A core contributor to the After Oil Collective, he is a co-author of their second book, *Solarities: Seeking Energy Justice* (2022).

Wu Yan (he/him) is an sf writer and professor in the School of Humanities and Social Science at Southern University of Science and Technology. He serves as the Director of Science and Human Imagination Research Center under the university since 2017. He has written many works of fiction, including *Spiritual Quest* (1994), *Life and Death of the Sixth Day* (1996) and *China Orbit* (2020). He has also been engaged in academic writing, including *Outline of Science Fiction Literature* (2011) and *History of Chinese Science Fiction of 20th Century* (2022). He is the founder of sf education in China. He has received many awards including the Science Fiction Research Association's Thomas D. Clareson Award, the National Outstanding Children's Literature Award of China, Bing Xin Literature Award, the Xingyun Award (Chinese Nebula), Yinghe Award (Chinese Galaxy), as well as Sci-fi Educator Achievement Award at Fishing Fortress Science Fiction Awards. He is the Deputy Chairman of the Science Fiction Committee of the Chinese Writers Association, Vice Chairman of China Science Writers Association, and was the Founding President of World Chinese Science Fiction Association.

INTRODUCTION

Mark Bould, Andrew M. Butler and Sherryl Vint

We all live in science fiction times.

The genre is everywhere, even as it bleeds into all other kinds of cultural production. At the same time, the border between reality and sf grows increasingly porous, a tenuous proposition at best.

When we, along with Adam Roberts, assembled the first version of this volume in the late 2000s, we were still getting to grips with social media. Facebook, Twitter and their ilk were making more immediate connections between more people than any communications platforms had before. Broadsheet op-eds might have argued that these were not real communities, but discussions about sf (and sf studies) could suddenly expand beyond academics, students, conferences, conventions, festivals, libraries, magazines and fanzines to a much greater extent. Formally trained academics could converse with and learn from informed fans and vice versa, enriching the conversations (and fuelling arguments). The various camps had never been distinct – as the pages of *Foundation: The International Review of Science Fiction* and *The New York Review of Science Fiction* have long demonstrated – but these new social media enabled exchanges between them to unfold into new areas and cross-fertilise at a more rapid pace.

Even then, though, sf was already too big to encompass in a single volume: the genre and the conversations around it were global, if unevenly distributed. The magisterial second edition of Peter Nicholls and John Clute's *The Encyclopedia of Science Fiction* (1993; with addenda 1995) did a pretty good job of digesting the field, especially if you were interested in prose fiction and, to a lesser extent, film and television, and albeit with a predominantly Anglophone and Euro-American focus and perspective. After *The Routledge Companion to Science Fiction* appeared in 2009, the *Encyclopedia* went online so it could be continually updated and expanded. Its hyperlinks make for a pleasurable dérive through the genre, but it remains a little atomised and, inevitably, in a constant race to keep up. The fixed parameters of a physical book exacerbate these problems even as they relieve its editors of much of that burden.

The first section of the 2009 *Companion* contained historical surveys of prose fiction, film, television, comics and sf tourism. Since most previous histories of sf had been dominated by prose fiction, we were keen to see that other media and modes were taken just as seriously. The second section took 14 critical and theoretical lenses, dominant in sf studies since the 1970s, and explicated such approaches, applying them to individual examples. The next section added a dozen further theories and paradigms, which we felt to be emerging in the field at the time or deserved more investigation. The final section offered brief examinations of major subgenres.

DOI: 10.4324/9781003140269-1

A decade later, Routledge invited us to update the book. One solution might have been to return to the original chapters and update them, within the same word count, but that seemed like a wasted opportunity. There was a clear tension in the 2009 *Companion* between our desire to include numerous voices and viewpoints, without privileging any particular one, and a perhaps inevitable clustering around the Western traditions with which many of our readers would likely be familiar and wish to explore. In the introduction, we wrote that we were

> conscious of [the *Companion*'s] bias toward Anglophone sf from the US, the UK, and to a lesser extent Canada and Australia. Although some materials from other nations are discussed, these are mostly from northwestern Europe, the former Soviet Union, and Japan. One of the slowly emerging trends in sf scholarship is a sense of the genre as a global phenomenon, not merely in terms of the consumption of texts and practices produced in or by the First World, but also in its ability to express the experience of modernity among peoples excluded from the economic and geopolitical core.
>
> (xxi)

We still recognise this judgement, but Indigenous sf and sf from the Global South have been major success stories in the 15 years since we wrote those words, even if far too little of it is available in translation and the examples written in English tend to be published only by small presses.

Much of this sf challenges our ideas about the nature and shape of the field, rewiring cyberpunk, planetary romance, space opera, utopia, dystopia, the technothriller and so on, or doing its own beautiful, exciting and exhilarating thing. Indefatigable anthologists have compiled impressive collections of short works and online book dealers and e-editions make such works more readily available. Traditional accounts of sf might begin with the 1926 launch of Hugo Gernsback's pulp magazine *Astounding Stories* (Westfahl), even if he reprinted earlier work, had previously written and published an sf novel, *Ralph 124C41+* (1911), and did not use the term until a couple of years later; others trace sf back to writers from classical antiquity or the first century CE, such as Euripides, Cicero, Plutarch, Diogenes and Lucian (Roberts). Brian Aldiss's suggestion in 1973 that Mary Shelley's *Frankenstein, or, the Modern Prometheus* (1818) was the first sf novel remains influential, while others have championed the fiction of Edgar Allan Poe in the 1830s and 1840s, Jules Verne from the 1860s onwards, and H.G. Wells from the 1890s onwards. Even extending Aldiss's history backwards to take account of the long arc from the Copernican revolution (Roberts) to Mary Shelley to H.G. Wells, or sideways to allow for the significance of the French *roman scientifique* (Stableford) or the Russian *nauchnaia fantastika* (Bannerjee), is – however important – still too narrow, too Eurocentric. It seems to us to be a cultural chauvinism to overplay the Gernsback–Campbell continuum of a founding moment in magazines that led to a golden age that was challenged by New Wave and feminist sf that in turn created a moment for cyberpunk to emerge before giving way to new space opera, new hard sf, biopunk, mundane sf, and so on and so on. However, it remains a potent, localised narrative, albeit at the expense of sf from a wider set of traditions.

Such important expansions and equally important shifts of perspective have begun to proliferate in sf studies, including *Science Fiction Studies*' special issues on globalisation (2012), Chinese sf (2013), Indian sf (2013) and the work of Liu Cixin (2019); Grace L. Dillon's work and *Extrapolation*'s special issue on Indigenous futurisms (2016); new articulations of Afrofuturism (Anderson; Brown; Carrington; Lavender; Lavender and Yaszek); *Paradoxa*'s 'Africa Sf'

(2013) special issue; Geoff Ryman's interviews with 100 African sf writers and the emergence of Africanfuturism (Cleveland); Palgrave Macmillan's *Studies in Global Science Fiction* (since 2016) and Peter Lang's *World Science Fiction Studies* (since 2017) monograph series; and the CoFutures project (www.cofutures.org) and related publications (Taylor et al.).

The view from now is very different from 15 years ago. Any new *Companion* had to devote as much space as possible to a wider array of national and linguistic traditions, Sisyphean as such a task must be. We are painfully aware of the gaps in our coverage, resulting from restrictions on space, a relative dearth of Anglophone scholarship in some areas and the limitations of our own expertise, as well as from the world events and other pressures that ultimately thwarted a number of contributions.

We did 'not regard *The Routledge Companion to Science Fiction* as The One-and-Only True History of Sf' (xxi), and we certainly do not regard *The New Routledge Companion to Science Fiction* as The One-and-Only True History of Sf (Revised). We have made no attempt to reconcile the contradictions between these two accounts, nor would we wish to erase or devalue the chapters in the 2009 *Companion*. The 'History' section has been renamed 'Histories' and is longer. Dividing the account of Anglophone prose sf into fewer and longer periods, and contextualising them with more chapters on other histories, de-emphasises and complicates the hitherto dominant narrative of sf's development and allows others to emerge. We have organised the 'Histories' section in rough chronology according to the earliest significant exemplar each chapter mentions (even if its overall emphasis is on a later period). This relocates sf's origins outside of Western Europe, while also to some extent challenging the dominance of the written word. Acknowledging versions of the genre that emerged before Western definitions of 'science' is part of the ongoing conversations about what the term means and what kinds of speculation constitutes 'speculative fiction'. In any case, what were once key texts now seem less central, while previously neglected works take on new significance.

Since almost all of the single volume histories of sf have been written by men, and since most of them underplay the contributions of female and nonbinary writers, we invited our writers to reflect the diversity of the field. We commissioned new histories of comics, film, music, television and tourism, and on sf in other modes, such as art, theatre, radio and podcasts; fandom moved from a theoretical framework to a more historical approach. The 'Histories' section offers a historical sweep from several centuries ago to the present day, made more complex by these parallel and intersecting narratives.

When revisiting the 'Theory' and 'Issues and Challenges' sections, we found that distinction far less clear cut than it had once seemed. Sf discourse is more polyphonic than in earlier decades and even the 'traditional' approaches, such as Marxism and feminism, are asking new questions. Some theoretical frameworks felt less crucial than they once did and some of the 'challenges' we once identified have become mainstream or even taken for granted. Therefore, we re-envisaged key interventions in the field in terms of 'Praxis', frequently bowing to the contributor's expertise on a chapter's title and scope. Some areas were retained (e.g., Animal Studies, Empire), others are new additions (e.g., Biopolitics, Disability Studies, Medical Humanities), but most of the section is by new authors. And even where we asked an author to revisit the theme of their 2009 chapter, a decade more of reading and thinking transformed their approach. The one thing we did retain was our decision to arrange these chapters in alphabetical order so as to avoid any implied hierarchy and to thwart any sense of historical progression from one to the next. These chapters – indeed the whole volume – can be read in any order.

The 2009 'Subgenres' section no longer felt so relevant as a way of mapping of the field, and some of that material is now covered in the 'Histories' section. But those chapters still exist out there and do useful work, and as editors we certainly do not disown them. *The New Routledge Companion to Science Fiction* is a different beast; it does not supersede the 2009 *Companion* but instead extends, complements and complexifies it.

Fifteen years ago, we were unable and unwilling to define sf – we pointed to a 'dozen main contenders identified by Clute and Nicholls (1993) and the 30 listed by Wikipedia' (ix) – and that remains the case, although Wikipedia is now closer to 40. Rick Altman argues that genres 'are not inert categories shared by all [...] but discursive claims made by real speakers for particular purposes in specific situations' (101), and Sherryl Vint and Mark Bould argue that genres are 'fluid and tenuous constructions made by the interaction of various claims and practices by writers, producers, distributors, marketers, readers, fans, critics and other discursive agents' (48). Any attempts at definition have more to do with various commentators establishing their relationships to others within the conversation than with a serious attempt to delimit a mode.

Gary K. Wolfe suggests that American genre sf was formalised much later than we might think, if indeed it ever was, and that it may no longer exist. But nonetheless, there are works that look like sf, swim like sf and quack like sf – and it is helpful to consider them in the company of whatever we might just about agree upon as being sf. We have attempted to extend this open-ness in all directions so that we are encouraged constantly to question what we mean by sf, and to embrace nuance, complexity and contradiction over the pithiness of a (necessarily) contestable and unsatisfactory definition.

There has been at least one generation of sf critics since the 2009 *Companion* and their experience will be different from our own (and each other's). The field is simply too big for any one person to consume. There is not enough time to read all the books, watch all the films, stream all the shows, attend all the performances, play all the games... At the same time, sf has become less distinct from the rest of culture, less dismissed by mainstream commentators (although such hostility is still sometimes expressed). Musicians have grown up reading Octavia E. Butler, and filmmakers reading comic books, while many sf authors now look not to the previously hallowed genre 'greats' but elsewhere for inspiration. And reviewers, critics and academics have lived through these same cultural shifts.

The Shape of Water (del Toro 2017) and *Everything Everywhere All at Once* (Kwan and Scheinert 2022) were the first sf films to win the Academy Award for Best Picture, demonstrating that one more prejudice against the genre's acceptance has faded. Marvel has released almost three dozen interrelated superhero films, both before and after Disney bought the company, while that studio's purchase of Lucasfilm means that we have not only seen the STAR WARS prequel trilogy promised as far back as 1977, but a sequel trilogy and several other spinoff films. Disney has also released Marvel and STAR WARS television series. Streaming services – Amazon Prime, Apple+, HBO, Netflix, Paramount+ and others – have added new versions of STAR TREK and other familiar sf properties, although their pockets no longer seem quite so bottomless. The pandemic-era demand for domestic entertainment fuelled this boom while also undercutting cinema, which still has not recovered to 2019 attendance levels. And, just as the Academy of Motion Picture Arts and Science had ignored sf, so some sf academics and readers still have a prejudice against film, television, comics, music, games and other such 'product'. But again, we need to maintain an expanded sense of what constitutes sf.

As noted above, we began work on the 2009 *Companion* in the early era of social media, and sf then had little conception of how it might transform our world. But we are not convinced that the genre has ever had much to say seriously about the future. It has always, via estrangement, allegory, metaphor or whatever, been more about the situation in which its creators have found themselves – environmental crises, geopolitics, personal identity, new technologies, scientific developments, and so on. As readers, viewers, listeners and participants, we find ourselves attracted to those texts which speak to our priorities and concerns. We consume the genre with a knowledge both of our present and our pasts, filtered through our own perceptions and preconceptions. Therefore, we have attempted to bring together as many disparate voices on as wide a body of sf as possible, so that we all might be challenged to think more deeply and to see the genre – and the world – anew.

We first came together online in May 2019 to develop a vision for the *New Companion* and to begin thrashing out a contents page and a list of potential contributors. By Christmas that year – as far as we can make out from our many immense email chains – we started assigning chapters. Soon after, we entered into the subgenre of the apocalypse and channelled 1950s John Wyndham novels, only with less toilet paper and many more video calls. Academia was already in a period of greater precarity, so some authors simply did not have the time to contribute within the envisaged schedule, or the energy, or were, sadly, leaving the profession. All too often, the obvious choices, were already spread too thin, juggling increased workloads and deteriorating working conditions or holding down multiple short-term contracts. And then came Covid-19. It delivered just too many blows to too many talented scholars within the neoliberal university sector. All of which gave us plentiful opportunities to move out of our comfort zones and familiar networks to find new voices, for which we are profoundly grateful – we learned from them as they transformed what this book could become. At some point, one of our original quadrumvirate, Adam Roberts, had reluctantly to step down from editorial duties. And as the pandemic stretched into a seemingly endless future, so this project inched along.

Our deepest thanks, then, to the patience of our contributors – especially as they were all balancing multiple responsibilities and more and new kinds of work in an impossible era – and to our editors at Routledge for their seemingly infinite forbearance.

Works cited

Aldiss, Brian W. *Billion Year Spree*. Weidenfeld & Nicolson, 1973.
Altman, Rick. *Film/Genre*. BFI, 1999.
Anderson, Reynaldo and Charles E. Jones. *Afrofuturism 2.0: The Rise of Astro-Blackness*. Lexington, 2015.
Bannerjee, Anindita. *We Modern People: Science Fiction and the Making of Russian Modernity*. Wesleyan UP, 2013.
Bould, Mark, Andrew M. Butler, Adam Roberts and Sherryl Vint. 'Introduction'. *The Routledge Companion to Science Fiction*. Ed. Mark Bould, Andrew M. Butler, Adam Roberts and Sherryl Vint. Routledge, 2009. ix–xxii.
Brown, Jayna. *Black Utopias: Speculative Life and the Music of Other Worlds*. Duke UP, 2021.
carrington, andré m. *Speculative Blackness: The Future of Race in Science Fiction*. U of Minnesota P, 2016.
Cleveland, Kimberly. *Afrofuturism: African Imagining and Other Times, Spaces, and Worlds*. Ohio UP, 2024.
Dillon, Grace L. *Walking the Clouds: An Anthology of Indigenous Science Fiction*. U of Arizona P, 2012.
Lavender III, Isiah and Lisa Yaszek, eds. *Literary Afrofuturism in the Twenty-First Century*. Ohio State UP, 2020.
Lavender III, Isiah. *Afrofuturism Rising: The Literary Prehistory of a Movement*. Ohio State UP, 2019.
Roberts, Adam. *The History of Science Fiction*, second edition. Palgrave, 2016.
Ryman, Geoff. '100 African Writers of SFF'. *Strange Horizons*. http://strangehoriz ons.com/100-african-writers-of-sff/

Stableford, Brian. *The Plurality of Imaginary Worlds: The Evolution of the French Roman Scientifique*. Blackcoat, 2016.
Taylor, Taryne Jade, Isiah Lavender III, Grace L. Dillon and Bodhisattva Chattopadhyay, eds. *The Routledge Handbook of CoFuturisms*. Routledge, 2023.
Vint, Sherryl and Mark Bould. 'There is No Such Thing as Science Fiction'. *Reading Science Fiction*. Ed. James Gunn, Marleen S. Barr and Matthew Candelaria. Palgrave, 2008. 43–51.
Westfahl, Gary. *The Mechanics of Wonder: The Creation of the Idea of Science Fiction*. Liverpool UP, 1998.
Wolfe, Gary K. *Evaporating Genres: Essays on Fantastic Genres*. Wesleyan UP, 2011.

PART I

Science fiction histories

1

NORTH AFRICAN, MIDDLE EASTERN, ARABIC AND DIASPORIC SCIENCE FICTION

Sinéad Murphy

Introduction: Locating Arab sf in time, space and place

Arab sf, as Ada Barbaro states, 'was not born all of a sudden' (Qualey n.p.), but over the last 20 years there has been increasing interest in the 'rapidly evolving face of Arabic science fiction literature' (Green n.p.) in both scholarly and popular contexts, and accounts of the 'subversive futures' (Mucci n.p.) found in contemporary Arabic sf in both Arabic- and English-language outlets. A string of Arabic sf narratives has recently attracted the attention of prestigious literary and translation awards, demonstrating the wide marketability of the genre and its appeal across different readerships. In 2014, for example, Hassan Blasim's *The Iraqi Christ And Other Stories* (2013) won the *Independent* Foreign Fiction Prize – the first time it has been awarded to an Arab and to a short story collection – and Ahmed Saadawi, with *Frankenstein in Baghdad* (2013), became the first Iraqi writer to win the International Prize for Arabic Fiction (Jonathan Wright's 2018 English translation was shortlisted for the Man Booker International Prize).

The fantastic has a long-standing history in Arabic literature, and contemporary sf material is underpinned by a rich tradition of utopian imagining and mythical folklore. Ian Campbell describes utopia in Arabic literature as past-oriented, with the utopian society envisioned generally modelled on the community in Madina where the prophet Muhammad ruled both as political and spiritual leader from 622 to 630 CE (*Arabic* 8). Similarly, Barbaro identifies al-Farabi's (c. 872–950/951 CE) *Mabadi 'Ara' Ahl al-Madina al-Fadila* ('The Principles of the Views of the Citizens of the Virtuous/Best City') as 'the urtext of the Arabic utopia', and suggests that Arabic texts written in the utopian tradition offer 'a flight from reality, often in order to criticize it in an open manner' (qtd Campbell *Arabic* 67, 44). While dystopian writing is a more recent trend in Arabic literature, it remains closely conversant with this utopian tradition. As Zeina Halabi indicates, for example, contemporary works of dystopian fiction by Egyptian authors can be connected to the utopian imaginaries of writers Jurji Zeidan and Hafez Mahmoud, whose work dates back to the early 1900s and was similarly driven by an interest in reimagining social and political realities (Mounzer n.p.). We see a convergence of these utopian and dystopian impulses intensified in contemporary speculative fictions, as in the stories collected in *Iraq +100: Stories from a Century After the Invasion* (2016) and *Palestine +100: Stories from a Century After the Nakba* (2019), edited by Hassan Blasim and Basma Ghalayini, respectively. Both volumes espouse science fictional futurity as

DOI: 10.4324/9781003140269-3

a 'space to breathe' (Blasim v), a liberating creative and critical 'blank canvas' (Ghalayini xii) through which to interrogate social issues and authoritarian political structures in the present.

Comprehensively accounting for North African, Middle Eastern, Arabic and diasporic sf requires wrestling with each of these terms as the heterogeneous signifiers that they are – a heterogeneity implied by the variety of terms by which such material is described. Campbell, for instance, argues that Arabic sf is 'by definition a postcolonial literature, but differs from most of the works studied as postcolonial literature' (*Arabic* viii), and his conceptualisation of the genre excludes material written in a language other than Arabic (for example, by diasporic Arab writers working in English or French). The contemporary Arabic term for sf, *al-khayyal al-'ilmi*, is a semantically ambiguous expression which dates from around the 1970s, and remains inconsistently used or understood by Arabic speakers generally (*'ilmi* can imply both scientific knowledge and religious scholarship (*Arabic* 12, 47–8)). Barbaro argues that 'for texts that were attributed to *al-khayyal al-'ilmi*, the definition of "impure genre" that so often distinguishes SF applies' (54, Arabic in original, citing Clute and Nicholls 567). Given the degree to which Iraqi author Ahmed Saadawi's material draws on personal experience and real events, he has described *Frankenstein in Baghdad* as 'reportage', even as the text conspicuously refers to Mary Shelley's novel that many consider to be foundational to sf (Saadawi and Wright n.p.). The contributors and editor of the *Strange Horizons* special issue on 'the palestinian speculative' describe the speculative register as a place of rest, a space of future imagination, a means of rupture, and a method of 'unflattening' (Abdulhadi, Mansour and Tbakhi n.p.), while Sophia Azeb's response to the call for contributions was that 'all palestinian writing is speculative' (Abdulhadi n.p.).

Some scholars describe recent forms of cultural production as Arabfuturist, locating 'complications of the sort that already featured in Afrofuturism too: articulating histories of dispossession as part of imaginary futures' (Parrika 41). In both Afrofuturist and Arabfuturist material, 'corresponding themes of the city, technological temporalities, media cultures of sounds and visuals are mobilised in different ways and to create an alternative infrastructuring of time as part of the artistic discourse' (40–1). Alongside these evolving conceptions of the genre in Arabic, however, is a persistent and often orientalising tendency in both scholarly and mainstream commentary to suggest a relationship of equivalence between Arabic and anglophone sf (Ayed). Arab authors' resistance to this propensity is explicit in the challenges they articulate to the ways in which works of sf are categorised. For example, Nael el-Toukhy, whose fantastical novel *Nisa'al-Karantina* (2013), translated as *Women of Karantina* (2014), has been well-received in both its original Arabic and its translation, voices discomfort with his work being categorised as dystopian because 'it is something that Western critics do' (Mounzer n.p.), while Yassin Adnan wonders why Salim Barakat, 'a pioneer in the narrative genre of the fantastic, finds himself completely marginalised' by prestigious awards like the International Prize for Arabic Fiction (Adnan 15).

Fantastical centres of gravity

The literary history of fantastika in Arabic is perhaps most ubiquitously associated with *The Thousand and One Nights* (*alf layla wa layla*). The circumstances of its production are themselves somewhat science fictional; the *Nights* is 'an authorless text' with no definitive single edition, and no consistency in its canon or collection (Lemos Horta 6). In its reach and influence on fantastical storytelling, the *Nights* can be considered a 'centre of gravity' (Vint 57) for Arabic sf, and it exemplifies sf's self-reflexivity, capturing the ways in which symbolic meaning is enriched rather than restricted through repetition across texts. Scheherezade demonstrates that at its core, creating fantastic tales is about reanimating and rearranging tropes and patterns in ways that captivate and intrigue – and that doing so is a question of survival.

Scheherezade's storytelling for survival inspired Iraqi writer Anoud's 'Kahramana' (2016) in *Iraq +100*, whose eponymous protagonist is an Arab refugee struggling against the injustices of a hostile immigration process. More generally, this technique of narrating one's way into the future is a key feature of 'Gulf Futurism', a term coined by Qatari-American artist Sophia al-Maria and Senegalese-born Kuwaiti artist and musician Fatima al-Qadiri to describe works focused on understanding and interrogating the effects of hypermodern, but ultimately destructive, petrocapitalist development in the region. The *Nights*' cyclical narrative structure drives the plot of American Muslim author G. Willow Wilson's *Alif the Unseen* (2012), which revolves around a mysterious set of tales, the *Alf Yeom* ('thousand days'), written by jinn who 'think about the world differently, and [...] inhabit it at an angle' and described as 'the inverse, the overturning' of the *Thousand and One Nights* (96). Like the *Nights*, Wilson's *Alf Yeom* is revealed to be a palimpsestic amalgamation of meanings and interpretations, analogous to the ways in which sf 'explicitly refers back to earlier instances of itself' (Vint 57).

As Gasser Ali has stated, however, 'we've surpassed the point of having to assert potential by looking back to *One Thousand and One Nights* or [Zakariya] al-Qazwini's tales to prove anything. The basis of suspending reality to tell a narrative has never lacked in Arab stories' (n.p.). So rather than provide an exhaustive record or linear historiography, this chapter celebrates the variety encoded in North African, Middle Eastern, Arabic and diasporic sf as an assemblage, locating commonalities and distinctions in the literary–cultural traditions and socio-political events upon which they draw. The *Nights*, considered here not as a point of origin or validation but as a source of worldbuilding, is just one of many related and overlapping 'centres of gravity', and this chapter examines Arabfuturist creations from the vantage point of a different one: Larissa Sansour's audiovisual 'sci-fi trilogy', comprised of *A Space Exodus* (video 2009), *Nation Estate* (video and photography 2012) and *In the Future They Ate from the Finest Porcelain* (video 2016). Her science fictional innovations are unmistakably Palestinian in their iconography while emblematic of several themes shared across and reinvented in Arabfuturist works: space, nationhood and futurity. Invoking an 'alternative infrastructuring of time', and emphasising the importance of speculative storytelling as a matter of survival, Sansour's sf creations serve as a portal to Arabfuturist conceptions of time, space, scale and imagined community.

Space: Inner space, outer space, astrophobia

Sansour's short film *A Space Exodus* explicitly refers to *2001: A Space Odyssey* (Kubrick 1968), with Sansour playing a 'Palestinaut' through whom the moon landing is reimagined as 'one small step for a Palestinian, one giant leap for mankind'. Kubrick's film, organised around 'the play of identity and difference in the colonial encounter between the civilised and the primitive' (Rieder 'Spectacle' 90), depicts 'the essential passivity of the human recipients of the gift of development' (91). Sansour riffs on both of these themes, critiquing both the imperialist domination of the state of Israel in Palestine and the apathy and factionalism of the Palestinian Authority that have debilitated organised political resistance to ongoing occupation. Similar critiques of the techno-scientific subjugation of Palestinians echo throughout *Palestine +100*. For example, Saleem Haddad's 'Song of the Birds' (2019) imagines the Palestinian right to return as a simulation, a virtual reality covertly generated by the state of Israel by harvesting the collective memories of Palestinians under occupation. The simulation captures how 'Gaza – our home – is like a laboratory for all that experimentation' (10–11), where one who discovers they are inhabiting a simulation feels 'a prisoner of both history and time' (2). In Selma Dabbagh's 'Sleep it Off, Dr Schott' (2019), with the siege of Gaza ongoing, in Israel a referendum has been passed legalising the expulsion of anyone whose DNA is found to be less than 50% Jewish. Playing on the presumed clinical rationality of its high-tech setting, Dabbagh highlights the volatile ways in which occupation is maintained, and gestures to the eugenicist fears underpinning apartheid logic.

As a site, Jerusalem is a nucleus of contested identities, with cultural and historical significance for several different communities as well as the three major monotheistic faiths (Christianity, Judaism, Islam). By casting Jerusalem as the territory with which to 'claim' the moon landing in *A Space Exodus* (2009), Sansour captures this dense history of place and the overwhelm of competing individual and collective attachments to it, concluding with her protagonist free-falling in outer space while calling out for 'Jerusalem? Jerusalem?'. In centring the collective Palestinian struggle, while also emphasising the Palestinaut as a disconnected and isolated figure, Sansour's film recalls that most well-known of extraterrestrial characters from modern Arabic literature: the space creature in Emile Habibi's *The Secret Life of Saeed the Pessoptimist* (1974). The space creature is a deeply ambiguous character and a fantastical counterpoint to the eponymous hapless anti-hero, through whom Habibi critiques both the crimes and oppressions of the state of Israel and the shortcomings of Palestinian social and political elites. The space creature's intermittent appearances facilitate 'a series of reversals in the novel, underscoring themes of space, exile, and the absurdities of Sa'id's everyday life' (Wanberg 188). In the Arabic text, Saeed refers to the space creature as *al-fada'i*, which suggests a possible play on words with the term *fida-i* (guerrilla fighter). The space creature is an icon of resistance, like Sansour's Palestinaut, and a vital figure through which Habibi estranges the irrationalities of the Israeli occupation of Palestine.

The sense of alienation expressed by the Palestinaut's drift through space resonates with a similar motif in Sophia al-Maria's portrayal of her diasporic identity in *The Girl Who Fell to Earth: A Memoir* (2012). Science fictional estrangements pervade this text, in which al-Maria depicts herself as gripped by a sense of 'astrophobia' (67), persistently anxious about 'falling up' (32) and 'plunging up into the sky' (63). This notion of being pulled unbidden into an unmooring exploration of outer space contrasts with colonial framings of outer space as territory to be conquered. Similarly, al-Maria's 'Sci-Fi Wahabi', after whom her eponymous 2008 manifesto is named, emphasises exploring the 'inner reaches of inner space' (n.p.) in an explicit rejection of petrocaptialist expansion and hypermodern territorial appropriation in the Gulf. Sci-Fi Wahabi is a key figure in Gulf Futurism, which maps the 'connection between luxury consumerism and the geopolitics of Middle East oil-producer countries turned banking and financial hubs, and spatially [...] the desert-realities and mega-architectures that have emerged there since the 1970s' (Parikka 46). Both Sansour and al-Maria invoke the neocolonial gaze underpinning this expansionism built on extractivism, demonstrating that '"narratives of colonial history and ideology" persist in the genre as one of its structuring fictions, whether such narratives be reproduced or resisted' (Vint 145, qting Rieder *Colonialism* 15). al-Maria relatedly observes, for instance, that 'just as Orientalists were seduced and subsequently obsessed by what lay beyond the veil/garden-wall/ Mecca, now we court speculation over what lays beyond reality' ('Gaze' n.p.), with Gulf Futurism articulating and interrogating in science fictional and futuristic terms the rapid economic-spatial transformations taking place in Gulf countries.

Nation: 'Now it's the space race for skyscrapers' (al-Maria qtd in Orton)

Arabfuturist works often use sf imagery to craft and define a national self-image, while also threading these national imaginaries into a broader schema of fantastical worldbuilding. National imaginaries are refracted through sf visions of ecocatastrophe in *In Vitro* (Sansour 2019) and Tasnim Abutabikh's 'Vengeance' (2019), of ever-intensifying neoliberal capitalism in Ahmed Khaled Towfik's *Utopia* (2008) and Mohammad Rabie's *Otared; A Novel* (2014), of structural inequalities and violence wrought by racist ideologies and sectarian divisions in Saadawi's *Frankenstein in Baghdad*, Saud Alsanousi's *Mama Hissa's Mice* (2015) and Mazen Maarouf's 'The Curse of the Mud Ball Kid' (2019), and of other world-systemic realities and imagined realities. The eponymous structure at the centre of Sansour's *Nation Estate* is a dense signifier of several of these themes. This nine-minute film tracks the protagonist (played by Sansour) travelling via the Amman Express to her apartment in the Nation Estate, a towering skyscraper in which Palestinians have access to various sites in the Occupied Territories while 'living the high life'. In the elevator, a poster advertises that Gaza Shore features the 'Best Sushi on the Block', a sardonic gesture to the restrictions imposed upon actual Gaza's water supplies and access to fishing. A recurrent motif that 'restrictions may apply' highlights not only the state of Israel's ever-increasing topographical control of Palestine, but also the processes of exclusion and exploitation so intrinsic to neoliberal capitalism. The autonomy afforded by the Nation Estate is shown to be highly circumscribed: as Sansour waters an olive tree – a prominent symbol of Palestinian *sumud* ('steadfastness') – that struggles to crack through the sheer edges of the nation estate, the Separation Wall creeps slowly into the frame, remaining firmly *in situ* at the outskirts of the estate.

In 'The Curse of the Mud Ball Kid', the reassembled regime of spatial control in Gaza is evoked through the carceral logic of the cube in which the protagonist is confined. He possesses a unique resistance to the genocidal bioweapon deployed to kill all Palestinians in 2037; his immunity derives from his capacity to store the cells of dying Palestinians as 'pure energy' (189), which will be released upon his death. The institute responsible for the weapon adopts an approach of strategic debilitation, containing the Mud Ball Kid within a glass cube and managing his energy emissions by shooting him with a single bullet on a monthly basis. The well-worn trope of striving to achieve immortal life features in several earlier Arabfuturist works – perhaps most notably in Nihad Sherif's *Qāhir al-Zaman* (*The Conqueror of Time*, 1974), which depicts a rogue scientist's ill-fated attempts to extend human life through cryogenesis – but is here inverted in dystopian fashion to express the horror of 'debilitated life' (Puar 2) and narrowly fictionalise the Israel Defence Forces' well-documented practices of pre-emptive assault. The grim surrealism of Maarouf's story resonates strongly with the register of contemporary Iraqi sf authors such as Sinan Antoon, Ali Bader and Hassan Blasim. These authors' bleak fantastical narratives focus primarily on the consequences of the 2003 US invasion of Iraq, including the loss of a unified literary culture through displacement and exile which Ali Bader describes as 'a long phantasmagorical dream' (37).

The use of estranging spatial imaginaries to express oppressed freedoms – and particularly, forms of exclusion arising from the nation as a category – is also a prominent feature of recent Egyptian dystopian fiction. Towfik's *Utopia*, Rabie's *Otared*, Basma Abdel Aziz's *The Queue* (2013) and Ahmed Naji's *Using Life* (2014) each express the social and political dynamics leading to and resulting from the Arab Spring uprisings through science-fictional reconfigurations of space. Towfik's *Utopia* depicts a near-future Egypt devastated by economic neoliberalism, in which a small minority of wealthy Utopians live in a gated community, monopolising every available economic, educational and medical resource while segregated from the dispossessed majority of Others. Towfik's use of the gated community motif is very different in register to that of his contemporaries; Sherif's short story *Imra'a fi Tabaq Ta'ir* ('A Woman in a Flying Saucer', 1981), for example, frames a retreat from city life into seclusion as a shift which heralds a mystical vision. Towfik imagines a post-petroleum era, which is nonetheless not a post-petrocapitalist one: Egyptian officials have exchanged the country's national antiquities for a 50-year supply of biroil, a synthetic fuel developed exclusively in the US. Presciently foreshadowing the development of gated compounds in the deserts around Cairo, *Utopia* allegorises the manner in which the seemingly explosive moment of collective resistance of January 2011 arose from the slow violence of neoliberal economic policies inflicted on the majority of Egyptian citizens from the later part of the twentieth century onwards. Although Towfik was one of Egypt's most prolific and well-loved writers of sf and fantasy, *Utopia* is the first of his works to be translated to English. Its relative success adds weight to the notion held by a number of Arab authors that 'it's not far-fetched to think that part of the fascination [among anglophone readers] for this dystopian fiction is due to the fact that it somehow fulfils people's expectations of what they think the Arab world is like: a place of chaos, authoritarianism, and violence' (Mounzer n.p.).

Published after the uprisings and in the wake of Mohamed Morsi's reactionary coup, the spatial imaginary of *The Queue* was inspired by an actual queue outside a government building, spotted by the author in 2012, which did not seem to progress or change throughout the course of an entire day. In the novel, an authoritarian body known as 'The Gate' issues decrees and regulations which gradually envelop every aspect of the lives of Egyptian citizens, while an ever-increasing number of people wait in the queue for The Gate to open and process their documentation. While the stasis of The Queue captures 'the cul-de-sacs where unrealized possibilities were stranded' (Gallagher and Greenblatt 60) following the revolution in Egypt, The Gate in many ways recalls the dynamics of power encoded in the Separation Wall, as both a physical boundary and a system of control. Like the Separation Wall, the power of The Gate derives from what Eyal Weizman calls the Wall's 'elasticity' – elasticity not in the sense of 'physical softness or pliability, but rather that the outline of the project has continuously accommodated political pressures of various kinds into its changing path' (162–3). The Gate is almost animate, imposing its own circadian rhythm:

> The old man said the area had changed a great deal since the Gate appeared, and even more so after it had closed and the queue formed nearby. As time passed, he told them, people said the weather in the area was always strangely stifling – but only around the Gate – and that sometimes the sun both rose *and set* over the Northern Building, perhaps bowing to whatever went on in there.
>
> (Abdel-Aziz 48)

The Gate is less a barrier than an enclosure, and as with Towfik's segregated society in *Utopia*, its structure stages 'the performative structuring of societies on the basis of an assimilationist/outcast logic, a categorical imposition that aims to determine reality while it is one that is divorced from the reality it purports to represent' (146).

Future: 'palestine is a futurism' (Tbakhi n.p.)

As well as interrogating the nation as a concept and unit, Arabfuturist creators interrogate the language of science fictional futurity, and notions of who normatively speaks this language: as Palestinian author Fargo Tbakhi explains, questions and claims of futurity are part of building a 'grammar of freedom [...] This is a not only a vitally important concern, but a speculative one: to wonder, to commit to the exploration of what we might be that we are not yet' (Abdulhadi, Mansour and Tbakhi n.p.). Sansour's video essay *In the Future They Ate from the Finest Porcelain* exemplifies this idea of speculative fiction as creating and narrating a grammar of freedom. Describing herself as a 'narrative terrorist', Sansour's protagonist has undertaken to bury porcelain plates, whose age has been scientifically altered, throughout Palestine, the goal being to plant archaeological material to act as an intervention into future narratives of the Occupied Territories that seek to occlude their Palestinian inhabitants. Since 'our lives are already determined by a fiction imposed on us', the protagonist muses, it is possible to stage a resistance through a counter-narrative, an alternative fiction. Throughout the video essay and its accompanying installation *Archaeology in Absentia* (2016), Sansour juxtaposes archival photographs with highly stylised CGI material to estrange and critique the effects of colonial intervention on the narration of sovereignty and belonging; this technique gestures to conceptions of archiving, future-proofing, and collective memory, which loom large in Arabfuturist fictions.

Sansour's emphasis on historical counter-narratives calls al-Maria's Sci-Fi Wahabi to mind once more: as a 'latter-day Scheherazade… a fearless myth-correspondent, she relays images and video to us from the edge of time: right now' ('Gaze' n.p.). Drawing on both Sheherazade's storytelling-for-survival and Donna J. Haraway's conception of 'the cyborg as a fiction mapping our social and bodily reality and as an imaginative resource' (150), the Sci-Fi Wahabi figure interrogates resource imperialism in a way that resonates with Sansour's more recent work, *In Vitro* (2019). In this short film, an eco-catastrophic oil spill has destroyed historical Palestine and its (re)establishment depends on a clone engineered from what is described as 'the remains of those we left behind'.

Egyptian artist Heba Y. Amin takes up this relationship between historiography and extractivism in another way in *Operation Sunken Sea* (2018–ongoing), one of her several projects which illuminate the irrationalities underlying various geoengineering schemes proposed to alter the landscape of the Middle East and North Africa to facilitate colonial trading routes. Amin's mixed media piece (performance, installation and video) reimagines the mid-nineteenth century German geographer Herman Sorgel's 'Atlantropa' project, which proposed to drain the Mediterranean Sea and divert the water into the Sahara, thus opening North Africa to trade with the French, as a possible solution to the ongoing migrant crisis. Amin's work is infused with a keen interest in the ways in which surveillance and communication technologies have been deployed in support of these and other colonial projects, manifesting most prominently in her efforts to estrange the algorithmic gaze. 'The idea', she explains, 'is to completely plagiarize all his material and claim it as my own – in the way that you know these projects are about consuming other peoples' content, belongings and land – and to erase him out of history. So when you look up Herman Sörgel, all my images come up' (F. Campbell n.p.).

In conclusion: An *other* to realism

'Reality in some cases could become so fictional', Sansour states, 'that the only way to address it is to make work that exaggerates it even more – when one's experience of reality approaches fiction, how can it be apprehended?' (Gabsi 115). This perspective echoes Seo-Young Chu's conception of the poetics of sf as an intensification of realism – she argues that 'what most people call "science fiction" is actually a high-intensity variety of realism' (7). For Chu, making a referent available for representation is to make that referent 'knowable' (75), and differentiating between sf and realist texts can be understood as the 'intensity' (9) required to do so. While Towfik's *Utopia* introduces biroil as a science fictional device of defamiliarisation, for example, 'the low-income inequality of contemporary Egypt is only exaggerated, not invented' (I. Campbell 'Prefiguring' 543). Across these and other Arabfuturist works, exaggeration and intensification are strategies to draw us closer to lived reality by estranging, capturing Ursula K. Le Guin's conviction that 'what science fiction does is enlarge the here and now' (5).

Drawing on a recognisable megatext of sf tropes, symbols and images, Arabfuturism intertextually engages with a genre that is not only considered Eurowestern in its tendencies and history, but which has often relied on colonial histories and ideologies in its presentations of strangeness. Thus, rather than being definitively *post*colonial, Arabfuturism expresses the continuities of colonialism, imperialism and orientalism within sf, in terms not only of content and aesthetics, but also of how this material circulates in an increasingly globalised marketplace. Engaging with and intervening in the shared vocabulary of sf, Arabfuturism challenges Western delineations of genre, of strangeness, of temporalities and of what futurities look like.

Works cited

Abdulhadi, Rasha. 'The Future is a Palestine of the Dreaming'. *Strange Horizons* (2021). http://strangehorizons.com/non-fiction/azimuth/editorials/the-future-is-a-palestine-of-the-dreaming/

Abdulhadi, Rasha, N.A. Mansour and Fargo Tbakhi. 'Roundtable: The Palestinian Speculative'. *Strange Horizons* (2021). http://strangehorizons.com/non-fiction/articles/roundtable-the-palestinian-speculative

Adnan, Yassin. 'A Season of Migration to the Novel: Transformations and Manifestations'. *The Middle East in London* 15.1 (2018–9): 14–15.

Ali, Gasser. 'Ancient Aliens, Gulf Futurism, and Social Justice: The Liberating Visions of Arab Science Fiction'. *Scene Arabia* (28 May 2020). https://scenearabia.com/Culture/Ancient-Aliens-Gulf-Futurism-and-Social-Justice-The-Liberating-Visions-of-Arab-Science-Fiction

Ayed, Kawthar. 'Convention Review. Lucien de Samosate le Syrien: The First (Unofficial) Arab Science Fiction Conference'. Concatenation.org (undated). www.concatenation.org/conrev/lucien.html

Bader, Ali. 'Iraq: A Long Phantasmagorical Dream'. *Shahadat: Witnessing Iraq's Transformation after 2003*. Ed. uncredited. Friedrich Ebert Foundation, 2007. 37–47.

Barbaro, Ada. *La fantascienza nella litteratura araba*. Carocci editore, 2013.

Blasim, Hassan. 'Introduction'. *Iraq +100: Stories from a Century after the Invasion.* Ed. Hassan Blasim. Comma, 2016. v–x.

Campbell, Faye. 'Heba Y. Amin'. *BerlinArtLink* (20 December 2019) www.berlinartlink.com/2019/12/20/heba-y-amin/

Campbell, Ian. *Arabic Science Fiction*. Palgrave Macmillan, 2018.

——. 'Prefiguring Egypt's Arab Spring: Allegory and Allusion in Ahmad Khalid Tawfiq's *Utopia*'. *Science Fiction Studies* 127 (2015): 541–56.

Chu, Seo-Young. *Do Metaphors Dream of Literal Sheep? A Science-Fictional Theory of Representation*. Harvard UP, 2010.

Clute, John and Peter Nicholls, eds. *The Encyclopedia of Science Fiction*, second edition. Orbit, 1993.

Dabbagh, Selma. 'Sleep it Off, Dr Schott'. *Palestine +100: Stories from a Century After the Nakba*. Ed. Basma Ghalayini. Comma, 2019. 21–42.

Gabsi, Wafa. 'Fiction and Art Practice: Interview Larissa Sansour "A Space Exodus"'. *Contemporary Practices* 10 (2012): 114–9.

Gallagher, Catherine and Stephen Greenblatt. *Practicing New Historicism*. U of Chicago P, 2000.

Ghalayini, Basma. 'Introduction'. *Palestine +100: Stories from a Century after the Nakba*. Ed. Basma Ghalayini. Comma, 2019. vii–xii.

Green, Lydia. 'Close Encounters of the Arab kind'. *BBC Arabic* (9 October 2013). www.bbc.co.uk/news/world-middle-east-24403002

Haddad, Saleem. 'Song of the Birds'. *Palestine +100: Stories from a Century after the Nakba*. Ed. Basma Ghalayini. Comma, 2019. 1–19.

Haraway, Donna J. 'A Cyborg Manifesto: Science, Technology, and Socialist Feminism in the Late Twentieth Century'. *Simians, Cyborgs and Women: The Reinvention of Nature*. Routledge, 1991. 149–81.

Le Guin, Ursula K. 'Introduction'. *A Fisherman of the Inland Sea: Science Fiction Stories*. Victor Gollancz, 1996. 1–11.

Lemos Horta, Paulo. *Marvellous Thieves: Secret Authors of the Arabian Nights*. Harvard UP, 2017.

Maarouf, Mazen. 'The Curse of the Mud Ball Kid'. *Palestine +100: Stories from a Century after the Nakba*. Ed. Basma Ghalayini. Comma, 2019. 171–214.

al-Maria, Sophia. 'The Gaze of Sci-Fi Wahabi', scifiwahabi.blogspot.com (7 September 2008). http://scifiwahabi.blogspot.com/
——. *The Girl Who Fell to Earth: A Memoir*. Harper Perennial, 2012.
Mounzer, Lina. 'Apocalypse Now: Why Arab Authors Are Really Writing about The End of The World'. *Middle East Eye* (1 April 2019). www.middleeasteye.net/discover/apocalypse-now-dystopia-why-arab-authors-are-really-writing-about-end-world-egypt
Mucci, Alberto. 'Arabic SF – Subversive Futures'. *LA Review of Books* (20 June 2014). https://lareviewofbooks.org/article/arabic-sf-subversive-futures/
Orton, Karen. 'The Desert of the Unreal', *Dazed Digital* (9 November 2012). www.dazeddigital.com/artsandculture/article/15040/1/the-desert-of-the-unreal
Parikka, Jussi. 'Middle East and Other Futurisms: Imaginary Temporalities in Contemporary Art and Visual Culture'. *Culture, Theory and Critique* 59.1 (2017): 40–58.
Puar, John. 'The "Right" to Maim: Disablement and Inhumanist Biopolitics in Palestine'. *Borderlands* 14.1 (2015): 1–27.
Qualey, Marcia L. 'ArabLit Re-Runs: Science Fiction in Arabic Was Not Born All of a Sudden'. *ArabLit & ArabLit Quarterly* (17 June 2014). https://arablit.org/2014/06/17/arablit-re-runs-science-fiction-in-arabic-was-not-born-all-of-a-sudden/
Rieder, John. *Colonialism and the Emergence of Science Fiction*. Wesleyan UP, 2012.
——. 'Spectacle, Technology and Colonialism in SF Cinema: The Case of Wim Wenders' *Until The End of the World*'. *Red Planets: Marxism and Science Fiction*. Ed. Mark Bould and China Miéville. Pluto, 2009. 83–99.
Saadawi, Ahmed and Jonathan Wright. 'Frankenstein in Baghdad: An Evening with Ahmed Saadawi and Jonathan Wright, in Conversation with Professor Wen-chin Ouyang and Annie Webster'. SOAS University of London, 23 May 2018.
Tbakhi, Fargo. 'Palestine is a Futurism: The Dream', *Strange Horizons* (2021). http://strangehorizons.com/poetry/palestine-is-a-futurism-the-dream/
Vint, Sherryl. *Science Fiction: A Guide for the Perplexed*. Bloomsbury, 2014.
Wanberg, Kyle. 'Secrecy, Lies, and the Exilic Imagination in *The Pessoptimist*'. *Middle Eastern Literatures* 18.2 (2015): 184–201.
Weizman, Eyal. *Hollow Land: Israel's Architecture of Occupation*. Verso, 2007.
Wilson, Willow G. *Alif the Unseen*. Corvus, 2012.

2
THE COPERNICAN REVOLUTION

Adam Roberts

This chapter is a small example of 'long history' sf. The 'long history' assumes, as its name might suggest, that sf is a cultural mode of relative antiquity, a view held by some commentators, though not, it should be noted, by most. The majority of critics are more comfortable with a 'short history' model, seeing sf as a relatively *recent* development in human culture, beginning (according to some) with Gothic Romanticism – Mary Shelley's *Frankenstein, or The Modern Prometheus* (1818) is sometimes cited as the 'first sf novel' – or (others say) beginning later still, with the work of Jules Verne and H.G. Wells in the later nineteenth century, or (according to yet others) even later than that, with Hugo Gernsback in the 1920s (respectively, Aldiss with Wingrove; Luckhurst; Westfahl). These various accounts chime for many with the sense that sf is a characteristically modern phenomenon, one that does not truly flourish until the twentieth century.

But the 'short history' leaves commentators with the problem of accounting for a large body of work of much greater antiquity that contains many of the features and tropes we all recognise as sf: travel to other planets, encounters with extraterrestrial lifeforms, utopian social speculation and futuristic extrapolation. To call such works 'proto-sf', 'ur-sf' or 'precursors to the genre' may be thought to beg the question (as if one decided that sculpture began with the work of Henry Moore, and so classified all earlier sculptural work as 'proto-sculpture'). A simpler approach would be to note that if something walks like a cyberduck, and quacks like a cyberduck, then we might as well include it in our science-fictional aviary. That is a flippant way of putting it; but, as this chapter will try to show, there are in fact more important issues at stake in identifying the origins of sf with the Copernican revolution. To read the genre in that light is to see it as being determined by the forces present at its birth: the rapid and conceptually dizzying expansion of the cosmos, the encounter with alienness, a new way of thinking about time and, above all, a cleavage between longstanding religious ways of understanding existence – which is, in essence, a magical apprehension of the cosmos – and the newer materialist, non-magical discourses of science.

Certainly it makes sense to separate out '*science* fiction' from 'fantasy' on the grounds that the latter is magical; it always includes an excess that cannot be reconciled with or explained in terms of the world as we know it really to be. The consensus as to how the world actually works is called 'science'; and just as 'fantasy' exists in some sort of defining relationship with magic, so 'sf' exists in some sort of defining relationship with science. This is true, even insofar as sf

DOI: 10.4324/9781003140269-4

is in the business of exploring, and often transgressing, the boundary between what counts as science and what goes beyond (variously called 'pseudoscience', 'parascience', 'mumbo-jumbo' and so on). Of course, this boundary has not remained stable over the last few centuries; discourses now seen as pseudoscientific such as 'mesmerism' or 'spiritualism' were once counted as science but are no longer. But broadly speaking we can argue that sf begins at the time that science, as we understand the term today, begins. Copernicus has become emblematic of this sea-change in Western science. Howard Margolis lists nine 'fundamental scientific discoveries' made around the year 1600 (including the laws of planetary motion, the magnetism of the earth, and the distinction between magnetism and electricity) that together represent an unprecedented advance in scientific understanding. The title of his history of science sums up his thesis: *It Started with Copernicus*.

What was the Copernican Revolution?

The first-century Alexandrian astronomer Claudius Ptolemy argued that the Earth lies at the centre of the solar system, and that the Sun, Moon, five planets, and a sphere of fixed stars revolve diurnally about us, all of them embedded in transparent, crystalline, perfectly spherical shells. Medieval Europe found this model consonant both with people's common sense and with the Biblical account of the cosmos. It is in this universe that early stories of interplanetary travel take place: for instance, Roman writer Cicero's *Dream of Scipio* (51 BCE), in which the narrator dreams of roaming through the solar system, or Italian poet Dante Alighieri's epic poem *Paradise* (*c*.1307–21), in which the narrator moves outwards from the Earth to the Moon, planets and finally to the sphere of the fixed stars. Dante's poem makes plain that this Ptolemaic cosmos is a spiritual, and indeed *theological*, rather than a material place. Italian poet Ludovico Ariosto's poetical romance *Orlando Furioso* (1532) includes the journey of a chivalric hero to the Moon (helped up by John the Baptist) that makes no concessions to plausibility.

In fact the Ptolemaic model cannot explain all the observable astronomical data; but because this model was endorsed by the Church, challenging it was considered heresy. Mikołaj Kopernik, better known by his Latin name Nicolaus Copernicus, was a Catholic churchman and astronomer from Ermland (now part of Poland). His *On the Revolution of the Celestial Orbs* (1543) argued on the basis of careful astronomical observation that the Sun, not the Earth, is at the centre of the cosmos. He was not the first to argue this – the medieval philosopher Nicholas of Cusa had suggested it in *On Learned Ignorance* (1440) – but Copernicus was the first to make the case on the back of properly collated scientific data, and it was his book that changed the way scientific culture conceptualised humanity's place in the universe.

Talk of a 'Copernican revolution' is, perhaps, misleading; few 'revolutions' in human affairs have been so cautious and, in some senses, conservative. Copernicus believed, for instance, that the planets moved in *circles* about the Sun, not because there was any observational evidence to this effect but because circles were assumed to be more 'perfect' than any other shape, and Copernicus had not shaken off the medieval notion that idealised perfection was the true idiom of the heavens. Similarly, he believed like Ptolemy that the planets were embedded in crystalline spheres, rather than being bodies in ballistic motion. Again, where we might expect a *revolution* to happen rapidly, Copernicus's theories spread only very slowly, hampered by the Church's hostility, the small print run of his book and the inertia of the learned scholastic traditions. By the end of the sixteenth century most European scholars, whether they accepted or rejected it, knew about the theory, although the Catholic Church continued persecuting the theory well into the seventeenth century. So, for example, when Italian astronomer Galileo Galilei published a scientific work arguing in Copernicus's favour in 1632, he was condemned by the inquisition and compelled to recant. Johannes Kepler, as a Protestant, avoided the direct fury of the Catholic Church, although he faced other obstacles and hostility as he refined Copernicus's model, proving many things, not least (in *New Astronomy* (1609)) that planetary orbits follow ellipses rather than circles. By the end of the seventeenth century, English scientist Isaac Newton supplied, with his laws of motion and gravitation, the theoretical and mathematical necessities to make the fullest sense of Copernicus's cosmos. By Newton's time, science had become much more recognisably modern. In the words of A.R. Hall, Copernican science was 'a growth, an intensification of the trend of medieval science, rather than a deflection from it. Almost everything that happens in the history of science in the 16th century has a medieval precedent, and would have been comprehensible, if repugnant, to earlier generations in a way that the science of the age of Newton was not' (449–50).

We might wonder, then, why it is conventional to talk of a Copernican revolution, rather than (say) a Keplerian or Newtonian one? In part, Copernicus gets credit as the first individual to advance heliocentrism on the basis of detailed research. But more importantly, it was Copernicus's theory that became the locus of opposition to the Church's domination of knowledge. The Copernican revolution is bound up with the ways in which science supplanted religion and myth in the imaginative economy of European thought; and sf emerges from, and is shaped by, precisely that struggle. Contemporaries certainly saw the new cosmology in these terms, and many of the earlier writers of sf were Protestants. John Donne's satirical novel *Ignatius his Conclave* (1611) mocks the Pope for continuing to persecute the new science: Donne is surprised to meet Copernicus in Hell ('For though I had never heard ill of his life, and therefore might wonder to find him there; yet when I remembered, that the *Papists* have extended the name, & the punishment of Heresie, almost to every thing' (188)), but this is revealed to be a symptom of Ignatius Loyola's Jesuitical bigotry rather than Divine displeasure. Copernicus, on the other hand, is unfazed; when baited by Lucifer, he retorts that Lucifer is only a sort of alien lifeform ('I thought thee of the race of the starre *Lucifer*, with which I am so well acquainted' (188)). At the end of this satire Copernicus goes free and the Jesuits are all sent off to colonise the Moon, where, the narrator suggests, they can do less mischief.

Seventeenth-century interplanetary tales

Donne's speculative tale of lunar colonisation was one of the earliest examples of what became a vigorous strand of seventeenth-century interplanetary romances (Marjorie Hope Nicolson lists some 200 of these, and hers is an incomplete list). Copernicus had opened up the cosmos, and writers rushed to fill the imaginative vista in radically new and materialist ways. The solidly science-based imaginative extrapolation of Johannes Kepler's *A Dream, or Lunar Astronomy* (1634; written *c.*1600) captures exactly the shift in sensibility that enabled sf to come into being. It starts fantastically enough, with the narrator dreaming of meeting a witch, who in turn summons a demon to carry them both to the Moon; but once there, the story is given over to detailed scientific speculation about what life might actually be like in that place, where each day and each night lasts a fortnight. Kepler imagines weird utterly inhuman alien lifeforms, serpentine and estranging, forced to hide from the heat of the day in caves; and he backs up his speculation with detailed and carefully researched scientific appendices. Indeed, the appendices are four times the size of the brief prose narrative, a ratio which articulates a sense of the respective importance of the scientific and the imaginative in this work. This is the first genuine attempt at imagining alien life in terms of radical otherness, and some see *A Dream* as the first true sf novel (Roberts 42–5).

More commercially successful was Francis Godwin's space-journey adventure *The Man in the Moone: or, a Discourse of a Voyage Thither by Domingo Gonsales, the Speedy Messenger* (1638). The first bestseller of this new sort of Copernican fantastic voyage, it went through 25 editions in the remainder of the century and was translated into several languages. It is not hard to see why it was so successful, for it combines a solid narrative drive with a nicely handled apprehension of the marvellous. Godwin's Spanish protagonist flies up from the island of St Helena to the Moon by harnessing a flock of geese – no ordinary geese, these, but an unusual breed that migrates into outer space. On the Moon, he encounters a utopian society of humanoid creatures, before returning to Earth, landing in China. The whole thing is told with verve and a winning attention to detail, with enough verisimilitude that some contemporary readers believed it a true account.

Cyrano de Bergerac read the French translation of Godwin's book before writing his own sprightly and witty lunar-voyage, *The Other World, or the States and Empires of the Moon* (1657). Cyrano's protagonist flies from France to Canada and thence to the Moon by employing a series of imaginative modes of transportation, including one craft powered by the evaporation of dew and another by fireworks – this last device, effectively a rocket, moves the logic of spaceflight from fantastical into plausibly *technical* idioms. Cyrano's lunarians, huge four-legged beings, refuse to believe that this tiny biped is a man (they eventually classify him as a kind of bird). In a sequel, *Comical History of Mr Cyrano Bergerac, Containing the States and Empires of the Sun* (1662), Cyrano builds yet another spaceship, this time using mirrors to focus the Sun's rays into hot blasts, and visits the Sun.

The Moon was a common destination. The anonymous Spanish work *Crotalón* (1552) looks down upon the Earth from the Moon in order satirically to critique human stupidity. In the anonymous manuscript tale *Selenographia: the Lunarian* (1690), the Moon is reached with a giant kite. Daniel Defoe's *The Consolidator, or, Memoirs of Sundry Transactions from the World in the Moon* (1705) is similarly satirical. Other worlds were also approached. The female protagonist of Margaret Cavendish's *The Description of a New World, Called the Blazing World* (1666) finds a new planet attached to the Earth at the North Pole, and, exploring it, is eventually made its empress. Edmund Spenser's epic poem *The Faerie Queene* (1590–6) is set in 'Fairyland'; but the second book opens with a rebuke to those who had read the first book and claimed not to know where 'Fairyland' is. Previously, Spenser insists, nobody had heard of Peru or America. Fairyland might be a similar case, perhaps located on the Moon or on another star ('What if within the Moones faire shining spheare?/What if in euery other starre vnseene?' (71)). Imagining human travel to the Moon inevitably suggests reciprocation: lunar aliens coming to Earth. French writer Charles Sorel's novel *The True Comic History of Francion* (1623), perhaps the bestselling French novel of the century, wonders if there might be 'a prince like Alexander the Great up there, planning to come down and subdue this world of ours', and speculates about the 'engines for descending to our world' such an invader might be assembling (425).

All the works so far mentioned are 'scientific' romances in the sense that they try, with varying degrees of attention, to ground their speculation in the science of the day. But those very theories of science were deeply implicated in new theories of religion, such that the Renaissance (associated with the former) and the Reformation (associated with the latter) can be considered aspects of the same underlying cultural logic. This fact shapes the sf of the seventeenth century, just as it continues to shape the sf of the twenty-first. Certainly none of the earliest interplanetary stories were what we might call 'secular'. On arriving on the Moon and seeing its inhabitants, the hero of Godwin's *The Man in the Moone* cries out 'Jesus Maria', which causes the lunarians to 'fall all down upon their knees, at which I not a little rejoiced' (96). John Wilkins's *The Discovery of a World in the Moone. Or, A Discourse Tending To Prove that 'tis Probable There May be Another Habitable World in that Planet* (1638) likewise discusses whether extraterrestrials 'are the seed of Adam' and therefore 'liable to the same misery [of original sin] with us, out of which, perhaps, they were delivered by the same means as we, the death of Christ' (186–92).

The problem for these authors was that imaginatively populating other planets with alien life undermined the uniqueness of Christ's atonement for original sin. The crucifixion was taken to be a unique event that saved the inhabitants of the Earth from damnation; but what about inhabitants of other planets? Either they had been abandoned by God, or else they each had their own individual Christ. Neither of these options appealed to seventeenth-century thinkers: the former implied an uncaring God, the latter degraded the uniqueness of Christ's sacrifice. Lambert Daneau's *The Wonderfull Woorkmanship of the World* (1578) rejects the idea that there could be 'another world like unto ours' precisely because nobody can determine 'what is their state, order, condition, fall, constancy, Saviour, and Jesus' or say 'what likewise is their life everlasting, and from whence cometh the salvation of this second or third world' (qtd Empson 201). Similarly, the first person Cyrano meets on the Moon is the Biblical Elijah, who tells him 'this land is indeed the same moon that you can see from your own globe, and this place in which you are walking is Paradise, but it is the Earthly Paradise' (44). Cyrano's Eden was high enough, as it were, to have avoided inundation by Noah's flood. Wilkins makes a similar case in *Discovery of a World in the Moone*, describing the Moon as a 'celestiall earth, answerable, as I conceive, to the paradise of the Schoolemen [...] this place was not overflowed by the flood, since there were no sinners there which might draw the curse upon it' (203–5).

By the middle of the seventeenth century, this anxiety was, broadly, giving way to a belief that not only that there were many other stars and worlds, but, as English philosopher James Howell put it his *Epistolæ Ho-Elianæ* (1647), that 'every Star in Heaven [...] is coloniz'd and replenish'd with Astrean Inhabitants' (530). But in fact this belief was just as theologically determined, based upon the idea that God would not create so vast a cosmic space to no purpose, and that therefore all planets *must* contain life. Two popular French works, Pierre Borel's *New Discourse Proving the Plurality of Worlds* (1657) and Bernard de Fontenelle's bestselling *Dialogue on the Plurality of Worlds* (1686), expatiated on this new idea, and Dutchman Christaan Huygens's *Cosmotheoros* (1698) zips around the Copernican universe to find not only that everywhere is inhabited but also that Justice, Honesty, Kindness and Gratitude are omnipresent. These issues – the anxieties generated by Copernicus's undermining of our special place in the universe; questions of transcendence and atonement; and a sense of the purposiveness and profusion of cosmic life – still haunt sf. For instance, 'saviour' figures occur and reoccur in sf: the 'chosen ones' of Robert A. Heinlein's *Stranger in a Strange Land* (1961), Frank Herbert's *Dune* (1965), the STAR WARS and MATRIX franchises, as well as superheroes like Superman and Spider-Man who carry the burden of having to 'save' the world. I would argue that the reason why sf keeps returning to this figure concerns the forces that determined the origins of the genre. This is not, of course, to suggest that twentieth- and twenty-first-century sf is written in self-conscious dialogue with seventeenth-century theological debates of which few modern-day writers are even aware, but rather that these cultural forces, present at the birth of the genre, determined and gave shape to sf as whole, and indirectly affected those writers who took their places in the tradition of sf by following 'generic' conventions. More to the point those questions are more than narrowly theological; they connect with broadly human-existential anxieties and uncertainties.

Time

Despite these and many other seventeenth-century stories about travelling into space, many critics remain unpersuaded that a 'long history' is the best way of understanding sf's origins. To speak broadly, an important debate in sf criticism is whether the 'voyage in space' is the genre's defining feature, or whether it is better to see sf as embodying a *temporal* imagination. This is not to say that sf novels must be 'set in the future'. Rather, what critics who see sf as temporally determined articulate is a sense that sf is a *counterfactual* literature: not things as they actually are but as they *might be*, whether in the future, an alternative past or present or a parallel dimension.

One of the axioms of sf criticism is that this 'counterfactual' element enters the picture much later than Copernicus. For example, Paul K. Alkon insists that 'the impossibility of writing stories about the future' was 'widely taken for granted until the 18th-century' (4), while Darko Suvin locates the '*central watershed*' of the development of sf as a specifically futuristic fiction '*around 1800, when space loses its monopoly upon the location of estrangement and the alternative horizons shift from space to time*' (89 italics in original). However, the case can be made that *time* was a determinant of sf long before this – that, in fact, the Copernican revolution unshackled the creative imagination from Biblical rectitude in temporal, as well as spatial, terms. By opening up cosmological *spatial* scales, Copernican beliefs also challenged the chronological assumptions of European culture. The Biblical Old Testament dates the creation a few thousand years ago (famously, Irish Archbishop James Ussher's *Annals of the World* (1650) calculated from Biblical genealogies that the creation occurred at the sunset preceding Sunday 23 October, 4004 BC); and the New Testament promises that the end of the universe is imminent. Neither claim is factually accurate. In the seventeenth and early eighteenth centuries, understanding of 'long time' underwent a radical shift. French writer Jean de La Bruyère's *Characters* (1688) looks forward into enormous gulfs of time:

> Even if the world is only to last for a hundred million years, it is still in its first freshness and has barely begun; we ourselves are close to primitive man, and are likely to be confused with them in the remote future. But if one can judge of the future by the past, how much is still unknown to us in the arts, in the sciences, in nature and indeed in history! what discoveries are still to be made! what various revolutions will surely take place in States and Empires! (107)

Benoit de Maillet's post-humously published *Telliamed* (1748) argues that humankind is half a billion years old, and much of its story is given over to a future-extrapolation (of the world desiccating, flaring up to burn as a star and then dying away to a dead and inert body) that takes billions of years more. Smaller-scale future extrapolations were commonplace. John Dryden's long poem *Annus Mirabilis* (1667) describes the Great Fire of London in detail and then ends with a lengthy future vision of the city that, he was sure, would rise from the ashes. Indeed, Alkon himself notes several seventeenth-century future histories, among them the anonymous *Aulicus his Dream of the Kings Sudden Comming to London* (1644), which narrates a possible political future, and French writer Jacques Guttin's popular *Epigone, the History of a Future Century* (1659); and it is easy enough to find even earlier counterfactuals than these. For example, the anonymous English play *A Larum for London* (1602) dramatises the recent Spanish sack of Antwerp in order, explicitly, to present London with a possible future narrative of Spanish invasion. Time itself appears as a character on stage, exhorting the audience to consider how the future might play out and claiming that he 'doth wish to see/No heavy or disastrous chaunce befall/The Sonnes of men, if they will warned be' (Anon. 51).

Politics

By challenging the authority of scripture, Copernicus challenged the authority of the Church, and this, in an era when it was a prime axis of political power, makes the Copernican revolution a political phenomenon. This is reflected in the seventeenth-century flourishing of that more obviously political mode of speculative fiction, utopia. Thomas More inaugurated this sub-genre with his short prose tale *Utopia* (1516), in which a traveller reports visiting a distant island upon which society is ordered in immeasurably better ways than in our corner of the world. The name 'utopia' parses a double-meaning (in Greek *eu-topia* means 'good place' and *ou-topia* means 'no-place' – a place both ideal and fictional). More's new genre caught on fairly quickly. Juan Luis Vives borrowed explicitly from More to plan a utopian welfare state in his native Spain in *Subventions for the Poor* (1526). Italian churchman Tommaso Campanella's *The City of the Sun* (1602) is closer to More's premise in imagining a fictional utopian city. Speaking broadly, it was this emphasis on *place* (good-place/no-place) that shaped imaginative engagement with utopian thought. Joseph Hall's *A World Other and the Same* (1605) and Charles Sorel's *The True Courier* (1632) both locate rather jolly utopias in an imaginary land to the south of Australia. Hans von Grimmelshausen's German picaresque novel *Simplicissimus* (1668) includes among its many adventures a sojourn in a utopia populated by sylphs in the middle of the Earth. As actual explorers mapped the globe, so writers found idealised worlds in all manner of places. French writer Gabriel de Foigny returned to the southern hemisphere for his utopia, *The Australian Land* (1676); Joshua Barnes's *Gerania* (1675) describes a kingdom of miniature humans 'on the utmost Borders of India' (1); Richard Head's *O-Brazile: or The Inchanted Island* (1675) is set in South America.

But this is not to say that utopia, any more than other seventeenth-century sf, was purely a spatial mode of writing. It is easy for utopia, insofar as it represents an idealising commentary upon present-day concerns, to project its alternative into a notional future world. Englishman Samuel Hartlib dedicated his utopian fiction, *Description of Macaria* (1641), to the British Parliament as a model future development for the country as a whole ('Macaria was a kind of prismatic mirage which shone before the zealous projector to the end of his life' (qtd Bush 266)). Some writers, like John Milton in his *The Ready and Easy Way to Establish a Free Commonwealth* (1660), preferred directly to address the actual possibilities of social change in the mode of political tract or polemic; but many others decided that their aspirations for the future of the country would be best embodied in fictional form. Samuel Gott's *Nova Solyma* (1648), imagining England's possible future as a religious republic (its title means 'New Jerusalem') and Gerard Winstanley's dry *Oceana* (1656), an account of a possible future-Britain, are two examples among many. Francis Harding's Latin poem, *On the Arts of Flying* (1692), concerns an idealised future British Empire predicated upon the invention of flying machines: the rich leave Earth for the other planets, bequeathing their estates to the poor, with a new British aerial navy establishing peace on the Moon.

Conclusion

There is always the danger that an essay such as this will degenerate into a dry list of titles and dates. I have tried to show that whatever variety of sf it is that interests us (interplanetary travel, counterfactuals, alien encounters, utopias), there are many examples of it during the period immediately after Copernicus. I hope to have suggested, moreover, that this is no mere coincidence but rather a specific reaction to the imaginative expansion the Copernican revolution entailed. The continuing relevance of these tropes connects profoundly with the new ways of thinking about the world that came with the changes of the Copernican revolution. The seventeenth century was that period when science, as we understand the term, first began to impinge upon culture more generally; and the anxieties and exhilarations of that interaction, inflected through a number of religious discourses, are still shaping sf today.

Works Cited

Aldiss, Brian W. with David Wingrove. *Trillion Year Spree: The History of Science Fiction.* Gollancz, 1986.
Alkon, Paul K. *Origins of Futuristic Fiction.* U of Georgia P, 1987.
Anon. *A Larum for London, or the Siedge of Antwerpe with the Vertuous Actes and Valorous Deedes of the Lame Soldier*. Ed. W.W. Greg. Malone Society, 1913.
Barnes, Joshua. *Gerania: A New Discovery of a Little Sort of People Anciently Discoursed of, Called Pygmies. With a Lively Description of Their Stature, Habit, Manners, Buildings, Knowledge, and Government, Being Very Delightful and Profitable*. Obadiah Blagrave, 1675.
Bush, Douglas. *The Oxford History of English Literature: The Early 17th-century 1600–1660*, second revised edition. Oxford UP, 1962.
Cyrano de Bergerac, Savinien de. *L'Autre Monde ou les Etats et Empires de la Lune*. Garnier-Flammarion, 1970.
Donne, John. *Ignatius his Conclave*. Ed. T.S. Healey. Oxford UP, 1969.
Empson, William. *Essays on Renaissance Literature*, volume one. Ed. John Haffenden. Cambridge UP. 1993.
Godwin, Francis. *The Man in the Moone: or, a Discourse of a Voyage Thither by Domingo Gonsales, the Speedy Messenger*. Ed. J.A. Butler. Dovehouse, 1995.
Hall, A.R. 'Intellectual Tendencies: Science'. *The New Cambridge Modern History: The Reformation 1520–1559*. Ed. G.E. Elton. Cambridge UP, 1990. 422–51.
Howell, James. *The Familiar Letters of James Howell*. Ed. Joseph Jacobs. Kessinger, 2005.
La Bruyère, Jean de. *Oeuvres Completes*. Gallimard, 1935.
Luckhurst, Roger. *Science Fiction*. Polity, 2005.
Margolis, Howard. *It Started with Copernicus*. McGraw-Hill, 2002.
Nicolson, Marjorie Hope. *Voyages to the Moon*. Macmillan, 1948.
Roberts, Adam. *The History of Science Fiction*. Palgrave, 2006.
Sorel, Charles. *La Vraie Histoire Comique de Francion*. Ed. E. Colombey. Garnier, 1909.
Spenser, Edmund. *Poetical Works*. Ed. Ernest de Selincourt and James Cruickshank Smith. Oxford UP, 1970.
Suvin, Darko. *Metamorphoses of Science Fiction: On the Poetics and History of a Literary Genre*. Yale UP, 1979.
Westfahl, Gary. *The Mechanics of Wonder: The Creation of the Idea of Science Fiction*. Liverpool UP, 1998.
Wilkins, John. *The Discovery of a World in the Moone. Or, A Discourse Tending To Prove that 'tis Probable There May Be Another Habitable World in that Planet*. Scholar's Facsimiles and Reprints, 1973.

3
INDIGENOUS FUTURISMS

Nicole Ku'uleinapuananioliko'awapuhimelemeleolani Furtado

Indigenous speculative fiction has continued to grow in popularity inside and outside academic circles over the last two decades. Grace L. Dillon coined, and outlined the tenets of, 'Indigenous futurisms' in the introduction to *Walking the Clouds: An Anthology of Indigenous Science Fiction* (2012); in the years since, the production of Indigenous sf created by writers and artists has gained vast momentum. Indigenous speculative fiction is significantly related to traditional forms of sf but has also expanded and evolved into varied art forms that emphasise relationality through technological dynamism and Indigenous cultural knowledge production. Indigenous speculative aesthetics span across classic sf forms, including literature, comics, film, video games, virtual reality, Artificial Intelligence and experimental artistic projects. However, it is not limited to purely aesthetic or artistic expression. By affirming that Indigenous peoples will be in the future, by situating Indigenous cultural knowledge in futuristic settings, and by asserting that these knowledges will continue to be told to the next generations to come, Indigenous speculative fiction constitutes a political act. Western notions of modernity cast Indigenous peoples and cultures as primitive, savage and out-of-time. They feed settler-colonial logics of elimination that falsely assert that Indigenous cultures and Native communities will 'disappear' so as to make way for 'advanced' civilisations (Wolfe). It is political for Native artists to create futuristic projects of cultural expression that reimagine uses for technology that is not predicated upon continued modes of capitalist and settler-colonial extractivism. Indigenous futurisms and Native sf affirm that ancestral technology and knowledges *are* indeed technologies and knowledge, and that they are both vital forms that need to be learned and extended in the present and into the future.

This chapter uses Indigenous futurisms as an umbrella term for the ways in which Native cultures utilise traditional knowledges to expand, remix and continue to engage in cultural revitalisation and reclamation within contemporary contexts. Under this umbrella, Indigenous speculative fiction signifies literary forms of expression, while Indigenous speculative aesthetics describes a broad range of projects infused with future-oriented aspects that Native artists create and pursue. Indigenous futurity can be used to think through political projects of land activism and sovereignty to revolutionise and challenge violent settler-colonial actions of land dispossession and pollution. These terms are not fixed, but fluid definitions that are still 'in-motion'. Each Indigenous culture has its own distinct contexts and histories that inform its own specific movements and

DOI: 10.4324/9781003140269-5

conversations within the overall field of Indigenous futurisms. Therefore, Indigenous futurisms becomes a transitive mode that is useful for Native peoples to think through and address the problems of the present, while being in close consultation with the knowledge and protocols of our ancestors, and keeping in mind future generations who must contend with the actions we make in the here-and-now.

In academia, Indigenous futurism is considered a new field of research. Yet the future-oriented analytics, ancestral knowledges and cultural values at the heart of these projects of futurity and futurisms are embodied practices of Indigenous peoples that existed long before the term gained popular traction. The technologies used and the stories told in projects of Indigenous futurisms may be 'new' but the cultural relationality which Indigenous artists and writers infuse these artistic expressions within come from traditions that honour and cite the practices and worldviews of our ancestors. Indigenous artists working within this burgeoning field centre legacies of land literacy and emphasise the need for ethical/responsible networks of relations for advancing social technologies into the future. Indigenous sf across global geographical contexts project, imagine and speculate about future(s) where Native peoples and cultures are not only surviving, but thriving.

Indigenous knowledges and epistemologies have their own conceptions of futurity that are antithetical to Western modes of thinking/philosophies. While the framework of advanced technology being central to navigating the problems of contemporary life remains, Indigenous futurisms emphasise the dynamism of technology to allow Western science to finally catch-up to Indigenous knowledge systems in order to continue sustaining ancestral cultural practices. According to Kānaka Maoli artists Nicole Naone and her collaborators, advanced Western science theories like 'The Hydrologic Cycle, Evolution and The Big Bang Theory' are all 'terms used to explain processes that have already been described in intricate detail [...] for centuries' by Native people (n.p.). Indigenous futurisms are about 'Indigenising' Western processes that our ancestors already knew and allowing Native peoples to imagine themselves continuing that knowledge into the future. The future, through a colonial lens, is always relegated to the continuation of settler-colonial power structures. Indigenous futurisms call on us to change this outcome from the knowledge that our elders or ancestors have given us.

Maile Arvin views a productive definition of Indigeneity as an *analytic*. Viewing Indigeneity in this way

> enable[s] both a critique of how Indigenous peoples are always seen as vanishing as well as opening up the boundaries of Indigenous identity, culture, politics, and futures to new, productive possibilities [... and] allows us to deeply engage the various power relations that continue to write Indigenous peoples as always vanishing.
>
> ('Analytics' 126)

Being Indigenous calls upon 'historical and contemporary effects of colonialism and anticolonial demands and desires related to a certain land or territory and the various displacements of that place's original or longtime inhabitants' (121). As an analytic, Indigeneity is in constant processes of social formation that are separate but interlinked with complex histories involving decolonial, anticolonial, anticapitalist and feminist movements. A definition of Indigeneity must address shared legacies of colonialism and imperialism and move beyond identity politics. As Aileen Moreton-Robinson notes when referencing the writing of Daniel Heath Justice,

> Although the history, contexts, and cultures of Native peoples are all vibrantly unique, Indigenous peoples are united through ethical relations that are enabled by obligations,

legacies, loyalties, languages, community, truth, commitment, multiplicity, complexity, and the need to enact honor toward each other and our nonhuman kin.

(10)

Addressing these complex co-determined processes as an analytic of Indigeneity opens up space for a system of alliances through the global movement of Indigenous futurisms and the expansive writings and projects of Indigenous sf.

As an artistic and literary formation, Indigenous futurisms closely coincide with sf, embodying an engagement with the genre's critical future-oriented analytics as a form of cultural and social critique. Based heavily in the aesthetics and literary practices of sf, Indigenous futurisms also flow from the groundwork of Afrofuturism and the movements of Black critical thinkers, such as Octavia E. Butler, Samuel R. Delany and Nalo Hopkinson. Afrofuturism utilises sf to imagine and evaluate the past and future and to build a better *tomorrow* in the present. Sf imagines futures through worldbuilding, inventing new realities, and through its ability to be a 'thought-experiment' on what can/will/could take place. However, like Indigenous futurisms, neither sf nor Afrofuturism are limited to being just an aesthetic or literary form. As adrienne maree brown states, 'I would call our work to change the world "science fictional behavior" – being concerned with the way our actions and beliefs now, today, will shape the future, tomorrow, the next generations' (16). Like Afrofuturism, Indigenous futurisms are about hope: these movements are invested in letting us be in charge of our own narratives to build better futures. In reference to Afro-Indigenous Futurisms, our conceptions must stretch 'beyond a mere understanding of the history of colonisation' and address 'how a system of white supremacy, superiority, and privilege has seeped into our own mindsets – from colorism to white guilt, from privilege to access. It is a process of constant learning and unlearning, and of cultivating pleasure where we can' (Enright n.p.). These movements unravel colonial paradigms and move towards collective healing and catalysing decolonial and abolitionist futures for ourselves.

As a Kanaka Maoli scholar, I recognise that imagining just futures is necessary as a 'regenerative refusal' so that we, as Indigenous peoples, can voice dissent from colonial hierarchies of being and relating to the world and enable transformed and liberatory futures (Arvin). Within Critical Indigenous Studies, Leanne Betasamosake Simpson calls for working together in 'constellations of coresistance' (10) to form a radical resurgent/alternative present for ourselves. Activations of different futures in these contexts has led to even more critical-future oriented movements appearing in our present moments. 'Gulf futurism' was coined in 2012 by Sophia Al-Maria, in response to the unprecedented technological and urban development of places like Dubai and Doha, to critique 'conspicuous consumption and the embrace of technology as well as the concomitant issues of inequality, labor, and environmental devastation' (Lew). 'Chicana futurism'/'Latinx futurism' also emerged in the early 2000s as a movement to interrogate colonial structures and conceptions of borders, dislocation and identity, and to advocate for a revitalisation of Mesoamerican ancestral worldviews. The imagined space of the future becomes an ideological battleground with consequences for our cultures, the planet and the next generations to come at stake. As brown writes, catalysing abolitionist, decolonial, anticolonial and anticapitalist futurities is a battle of the imagination to 'ideate – image and conceive – together' beyond late-capitalism, settler-colonialism, and the afterlives of chattel slavery (18). Imagining diverse futures for marginalised peoples offers a way to navigate the problems of the time-period in which we find ourselves.

Indigenous futurisms seek to combat 'settler futurity' by intervening in the logics of neocolonialism, the military-industrial complex, neoliberalism and late-stage capitalism. Settler futurity invokes the 'whitestream knowledge' (Grande 73) that forces White colonial histories and norms to be the dominant mode of knowledge production. Eve Tuck and Rubén Gaztambide-Fernández call for anticolonial strategies in education to disrupt 'whitestream knowledge' induced by a 'settler futurity' that aims to stake claim to Indigenous cultures, lands, bodies and resources. They write:

> Anything that seeks to recuperate and not interrupt settler colonialism to reform the settlement and incorporate Indigenous peoples into the multicultural settler colonial nation state is fettered to settler futurity. To be clear, our commitments are to what might be called an Indigenous futurity, which does not foreclose the inhabitation of Indigenous land by nonIndigenous peoples, but does foreclose settler colonialism and settler epistemologies. (80)

The term 'settler futurity' illustrates how settler-colonialism forecloses futures for Indigenous people. Settler futurity cannot be divorced from the Western conception of *modernity*. Through colonial lenses of culture and identity, modernity perpetuates images of Native cultures as static and relegates Indigenous people outside of time. Therefore, this falsehood is combatted through Indigenous futurisms and the stories we tell that engage decolonial speculative forms. By continuing to tell our ancestral stories and lived experiences, and by engaging the space of the past in the present, Indigenous futurisms create a temporal reactivation of Indigenous visual, cultural and intellectual sovereignties.

Indigenous science fiction and speculative aesthetics

Sf texts usually contain at least one element of our reality made different. A form of speculative storytelling, the genre envisions scenarios to interrogate ethical matters concerning advanced technologies and encourages readers to (re)think why society is the way it is. Darko Suvin saw sf as a literature of revolt that 'show[ed] how things could be different' (Nodelman 24). It is a genre of imagination that critically analyses the consequences of social, scientific and technological aspects of society and ideates alternatives to create a better present-time for ourselves and build better futures for those to come. A generative sf reading practice means looking at what expression of reality the author has written within their story and what relevance and connections it has to us today. Indigenous futurisms help us to theorise through sf praxis to (re)world our present realities, and offer ways to engage the knowledge of our ancestors that challenges colonial forms of knowledge-making and to speculate about what a decolonial or anticolonial future could and can be.

Colonial processes of improvement through progress mean moving away from 'primitiveness' and into a linear conception of the future. This ideological assumption is manifest throughout the hegemonic Western perspective in sf, but Indigenous futurisms dispute the linearity of technological 'progress', calling this teleology into question, playing with and changing it. Many of Western sf's plots revolve around apocalyptic scenarios in which the planet becomes no longer habitable, whether because of alien invasion, capitalist extractivism and exploitation or climate catastrophe. Indigenous futurisms trouble this presumption of a Western past, present and future, call into question the role and relevance of technology, and question how to create sustainable and abundant forms of relations to ourselves, nonhuman entities and the planet at large. In the age of climate disasters, Indigenous futurisms offer a vital, critical *otherwise* to capitalist and neocolonial forms of relation driven by profit, extractivism and exploitation, while elaborating our specific cultural worldviews as forms of cultural reclamation and revitalisation.

Indigenous authors have contributed a plethora of speculative fictions, covering a wide breadth of issues facing our communities and contributing a larger conversation on what decolonial and anticolonial futures could look like. Cherie Dimaline's *The Marrow Thieves* (2017) features an Earth faced with climate devastation in which no one in North America can dream, apart from Indigenous peoples, who are hunted for their bone marrow as a cure for dreamlessness. The novel, which follows a teenage protagonist, critiques the residential school system and government betrayal, as well as climate change, to address current and past legacies of colonialism in Canada. In the dystopian near future of Louise Erdrich's *Future Home of the Living God* (2017), human evolution has stopped and humanity can no longer reproduce. The protagonist, Cedar Hawk Songmaker is a pregnant Ojibwe woman, fighting for survival as she navigates the dismantling of women's reproductive rights. Claire G. Coleman's *Terra Nullius* (2017), set in an apocalyptic late twenty-first century world divided between 'Natives' and 'Settlers', critiques Australia's colonial/imperial history and present. Stephen Graham Jones engages with horror and experimental writing, as well as sf, to explore speculative themes of identity, temporality and ancestral connections. *Mapping the Interior* (2017), for example, features a teenage Native American protagonist grappling with a spectral figure reminiscent of his father, who passed away before his family left the reservation. With such stories, Jones's readers experience 'loops, glitches, and the constant experience of Indigenous time travel: living in the past, future, and present simultaneously' (Cornum n.p.). These writers represent Indigenous protagonists surviving apocalyptic colonial conditions that parallel the genocide experienced during first contact and call on readers to reflect the subsequent and present-day aftermaths we are experiencing. Rather than fight a colonial reproduction of an exotic Other, these characters must work through and survive the very real conditions we face now. The futures told in these stories have leaky temporal boundaries – what can be read as 'the past' could also be read as a critique of our colonial present – and operate as a meditation on what futures are to come from the current conditions of the societies in which we live.

In addition to the many Indigenous sf novels and novellas, there are also a number of anthologies, such as Hope Nicholson's *Love Beyond Body, Space, and Time: An Indigenous LGBT Sci-Fi Anthology* (2016) and Joshua Whitehead's *Love After the End: An Anthology of Two-Spirit and Indigiqueer Speculative Fiction* (2020), in which symphonies of Native writers engage with sf's much-loved short story format. They represent a continuously expanding movement of artists and writers who remix sf to create rich, generative cultural expressions specific to our individual Native cultures and identities.

There is also a growing field of Indigenous speculative film. *?E? ANX (The Cave)* (Haig-Brown 2009) retells a Tsilhqot'in story about a man who discovers a portal to the spirit world where past, present and future collide and intermix. *Waikiki* (Kahunahana 2020) critiques tourism and US imperialism and poses poignant questions about Hawaiian identity through the story of Kea, a houseless cultural teacher and bar hostess living in the modern dystopia of overdeveloped Honolulu. While many of these films are independent and/or experimental, *Prey* (Trachtenberg 2022) is part of the PREDATOR franchise (1987–). It features a skilled young Comanche woman proving herself as a hunter in the eighteenth century as she battles the dangerous alien. While the film was generally well-received, it was nonetheless attacked over its storyline and casting. Responding to such intersecting colonialist and misogynist views as 'How can the "primitive" Comanche Nation battle a technologically-advanced extra-terrestrial hunter, or how can a woman overpower a 7-foot monster?', its star, Amber Midthunder, responded that the film's importance lay in its representation of 'Indigenous people and what that might mean or how people might receive that or feel about being represented by it' (Chhikara n.p.). Indigenous futurisms undo such colonial 'common sense' notions of what constitutes history and truth, and what counts as technology; by doing so, Indigenous futurisms emphasise the importance of continuing to tell diverse stories/perspectives.

Indigenous futurity as political praxis

Indigenous futurisms are not limited to works of fiction; they are also about actualising the processes of decolonial worldmaking in the here and now, including creating and using technology with Indigenous worldviews at their core. Indigenous led and created digital spaces, such as Aboriginal Territories in Cyberspace (AbTeC) – co-founded in 2005 by co-directors Skawennati and Jason Edward Lewis as a successor to their CyberPowWow, founded in 1996 – represents the need to decolonise the technologies we use. AbTeC Island, their online headquarters situated in the 3D virtual world platform Second Life, is a decolonial digital realm featuring an art exhibition and virtual studio where user avatars can interact.

In the mid-1990s, multimedia director and artist Loretta Todd was also speculating about a decolonial use of technology. She is currently creative director of the Indigenous Matriarchs 4 (IM4) lab, which cultivates Indigenous virtual reality projects addressing issues faced by Native communities and promoting Indigenous epistemologies through the technology's use of full-scale embodiment and immersion. Lisa Jackson's Indigenous VR project *Biidaaban: First Light* (2018) utilises speculative themes for users to interact with a highly realistic alternative future 'Toronto of tomorrow'. An official summary of the project foregrounds its science-fictional premise:

> Nathan Phillips Square is flooded. Its infrastructure has merged with the local fauna; mature trees grow through cracks in the sidewalks and vines cover south-facing walls. People commute via canoe and grow vegetables on skyscraper roofs. Urban life is thriving.
>
> (National Film Board n.p.)

Jackson's use of VR represents a fully immersive interaction with an sf storyline and, according to *Biidaaban*, centres the idea of how 'the original languages of this land can provide a framework for understanding our place in a reconciled version of Canada's largest urban environment'. As large-scale use of open Artificial Intelligence systems are on the rise, Indigenous theorists have been speculating on what a decolonial use could be. The 'Indigenous Protocol and Artificial Intelligence Position Paper', based on meetings that occurred in 2019 and released through the Indigenous Protocol and Artificial Intelligence Working Group, can be used as a framework for thinking through the ethical implications of creating and utilising AI. Indigenous digital projects are artistic expressions of speculative sovereignty, which also foreground concerns about sustainability and the use of technology. By asking such questions as 'How can we create technology that is decolonial in use?' or 'What would this kind of experience with technology entail?', the speculative, the virtual and the real all coincide.

Critical Indigenous Studies offers different ways to frame and conceptualise the leaky boundaries between the real and unreal in sf. Daniel Heath Justice's term 'wonderworks' dismantle such codetermining 'dualistic presumptions [...] that don't take seriously or leave legitimate space for other meaningful ways of experiencing [...]: through lived encounter and engagement, through ceremony and ritual, through dream' (n.p.). Wonderworks offer hope for better futures through the possibility of creating relations that are very different from the present time that we are experiencing and the futures that we face.

Lou Cornum describes Indigenous futurism as an 'extension of already-existing relationships to time, technology, and worlds' as 'we are always going back to the origin, our creation stories, as a starting point for moving forward, or up, or sideways' (n.p.). As Yvonne N. Tiger notes, 'ancient stories envisage for Indigenous listeners a future that is deeply connected to their past and embedded in their cultural memory' (147). Danika Medak-Saltzman echoes these sentiments; 'the complexities of our social engagement, and the variety of our narrative traditions have always incorporated elements of futurity, prophecy, and responsibility-rooted strategies for bringing forth better futures' (139). Therefore, connecting the past to the future is an essential creative and political expression of actualising sf forms and catalysing decolonial futurities.

Indigenous cultures often 'speculate on how our ancestors and our future generations would interpret today's situations and what recommendations they would make for us as guidance for our individual and collective actions' (Whyte 229). Kyle P. Whyte's conception of 'spiraling time' offers an account of Indigenous narrative-making that can be seen as living sf, especially in relation to environmental justice work, since we already inhabit what our ancestors would have understood as a dystopian future: as Native peoples, we are already living Indigenous sf.

My concluding example represents the actualisation of sf pedagogy as political praxis to teach students how to enact more equitable and sustainable world(s). Noelani Goodyear-Ka'ōpua is a Kanaka Maoli educator whose teachings and influence spans across different community, activist and academic sectors throughout Hawai'i. She has written extensively on Indigenous Oceanic Futures with a central question on 'How can Indigenous and settler peoples work together to unmake relations of settler colonialism and instead imagine and move urgently toward decolonial futures?' (82). For over a decade during her tenure in the Political Science Department at the University of Hawai'i at Mānoa, she taught a Decolonial Futures course, focusing on the importance of training students for worlds that could be different from settler-colonial systems and to be active agents of change especially in the face of imminent climate catastrophes (Lewis). The students would read speculative and visionary fiction that mediated social transformation and collapse, such as Octavia E. Butler's *Wild Seed* (1980) or Daniel Heath Justice's KYNSHIP CHRONICLES (2005–7), alongside conventional Indigenous Studies and Indigenous Politics texts; they would then travel to community sites around Hawai'i to meet with community groups, to learn place-based history and Indigenous forms of relationality to land, to carry out restoration work and to create responsible food networks. Goodyear-Ka'ōpua notes that the decolonial future-making elucidated through sf, coupled with the 'embodied experiences on the land', ensured that students left with the feeling that 'another world is possible' (Lewis). In such 'science-fictional behavior' (brown 16), speculation and imagination are a praxis to actualise and project the futures we want, and the worldbuilding inherent to sf becomes worldmaking.

Works cited

Arvin, Maile. 'Analytics of Indigeneity'. *Native Studies Keywords*. Ed. Stephanie Nohelani Teves, Andrea Smith and Michelle H. Raheja. U of Arizona P, 2015. 119–29.

Arvin, Maile. *Possessing Polynesians: The Science of Settler Colonial Whiteness in Hawai'i and Oceania*. Duke UP, 2019.

brown, adrienne maree. *Emergent Strategy: Shaping Change, Changing Worlds*. AK Press, 2017.

Chhikara, Mudit. 'Amber Midthunder Blasts "Haters" Who Called Prey "Super Woke": "That's Not What It's About"'. *MovieWeb* (28 August 2022). https://movieweb.com/amber-midthunder-blasts-haters-who-called-prey-super-woke/

Cornum, Lou. 'The Creation Story is a Spaceship: Indigenous Futurism and Decolonial Deep Space'. n.d. http://mathewarthur.com/pdf/cornum-creation-story-is-a-spaceship.pdf

Cornum, Lou. 'The Space NDN's Star Map'. *The New Inquiry* (26 January 2015). https://thenewinquiry.com/the-space-ndns-star-map/

Enright, Juleana. 'Afro-Indigenous Futurisms and Decolonizing Our Minds'. *Mn Artists* (28 August 2020). https://mnartists.walkerart.org/afro-indigenous-futurisms-and-decolonizing-our-minds

Goodyear-Ka'ōpua, Noelani. 'Indigenous Oceanic Futures: Challenging Settler Colonialisms and Militarization'. *Indigenous and Decolonizing Studies in Education: Mapping the Long View*. Ed. Linda Tuhiwai Smith, Eve Tuck and K. Wayne Yang. Routledge, 2019. 82–102.

Grande, Sandy. *Red Pedagogy: Native American Social and Political Thought*. Rowman & Littlefield, 2015.

Justice, Daniel Heath. 'Indigenous Wonderworks and the Settler-Colonial Imaginary'. *Apex* (10 August 2017). https://apex-magazine.com/nonfiction/indigenous-wonderworks-and-the-settler-colonial-imginary/

Lew, Christopher Y. 'Back to the Futurist'. *Whitney Museum of American Art*. n.d. https://whitney.org/essays/sophia-al-maria

Lewis, Jason Edward. 'Future Imaginary Dialogues: Noelani Goodyear-Ka'ōpua'. (26 July 2017). https://indigenousfutures.net/wp-content/uploads/2018/01/Future-Imaginary-Dialogues_-Noelani-Goodyear-Kaopua.pdf

Medak-Saltzman, Danika. 'Coming to You from the Indigenous Future: Native Women, Speculative Film Shorts, and the Art of the Possible'. *Studies in American Indian Literatures* 29.1 (2017): 139–71.

Moreton-Robinson, Aileen. 'Introduction'. *Critical Indigenous Studies: Engagements in First World Locations*. Ed. Aileen Moreton-Robinson. U of Arizona P, 2016. 3–16.

Naone, Nicole, Chris Kahunahana and Lanakila Mangauil. 'Artist Statement'. *PIKO* (n.d.). https://pikovirtualreality.com/artists

National Film Board of Canada. *Biidaaban: First Light*. www.nfb.ca/interactive/biidaaban_first_light/

Nodelman, Perry. 'The Cognitive Estrangement of Darko Suvin'. *Children's Literature Association Quarterly* 5.4 (1981): 24–7.

Simpson, Leanne Betasamosake. *As We Have Always Done: Indigenous Freedom through Radical Resistance*. U of Minnesota P, 2017.

Tiger, Yvonne N. 'Indigenizing the (Final) Frontier: The Art of Indigenous Storytelling through Graphic Novels'. *World Art* 9.2 (2019): 145–60.

Todd, Loretta. 'Aboriginal Narratives in Cyberspace'. *Immersed in Technology: Art and Virtual Environments*. Ed. Mary Anne Moser and Douglas MacLeod. MIT Press, 1996. 179–94.

Tuck, Eve and Rubén A Gaztambide-Fernández. 'Curriculum, Replacement, and Settler Futurity'. *Journal of Curriculum Theorizing* 29.1 (2013): 72–89.

Whyte, Kyle P. 'Indigenous Science (Fiction) for the Anthropocene: Ancestral Dystopias and Fantasies of Climate Change Crises'. *Environment and Planning E: Nature and Space* 1.1–2 (2018). 224–42.

Wolfe, Patrick. 'Settler Colonialism and the Elimination of the Native'. *Journal of Genocide Research* 8.4 (2006): 387–409.

4
ART AS SCIENCE FICTION

Andrew M. Butler

There is a moment in painter John Constable's 1836 lecture to the Royal Institution when he asserts that 'Painting is a science, and should be pursued as an inquiry into the laws of nature. Why then may not landscape painting be considered as a branch of natural philosophy, of which pictures are but the experiments?' (69). Art is thus always an experiment, a reified thought experiment. Not that all art is sf, but there is a science fictionality to several strands of painting. The intrusion of imagined beings or novums into some works – Hieronymus Bosch's *The Garden of Earthly Delights* triptych (1490–1510), Pieter Bruegel's *The Fall of the Rebel Angels* (1562) – may depict the fantastic, inflected by mythology, religion or folklore, or constitute sf if they are interpretable as machines or aliens. This chapter outlines a history of such pieces, with a bias to the industrialised British, the American and the Parisian, but excludes sf illustration.

Brian W. Aldiss, positioning sf as a branch of the gothic, beginning with Mary Shelley's *Frankenstein* (1818), argues that it represents '*the search for a definition of man and his status in the universe which will stand in our advanced but confused state of knowledge (science)*' (xx); art is on an equivalent quest but the science has often been invisible. At that time, the cultures of art and science still overlapped in Britain, with artists, scientists and patrons interacting in coffee houses, salons, learned societies, philosophical societies and periodicals. In 1765, the Lunar Circle (later the Lunar Society) brought together such industrialists, scientists and intellectuals as Erasmus Darwin, Josiah Wedgwood, James Watt, Joseph Priestley and the artist Joseph Wright. Somerset House, and then Burlington House, provided London bases for the Royal Academy of Arts, the Royal Society, the Society of Antiquaries, the Geological Society and the Royal Astronomical Society. Artists could learn about paint pigments from chemists as well as from suppliers. The Great Exhibition of the Works of Industry of All Nations (1851) in Hyde Park promoted art, craft and technology, with the profits funding the construction of the Victoria and Albert Museum, the Science Museum, the Natural History Museum, Imperial College and the Royal Albert Hall in an area known as 'Albertopolis'. Constable's landscape paintings, formed from layered mixtures of pigments on flat surfaces, represent three-dimensional topographies, which exist in time and follow the conventions of perspective. Whether he was painting in a studio or outside, he depicts a moment in time created over a long period. He might distort, invent or omit for the sake of a particular aesthetic, but he drew on the latest ideas from climatology for his clouds.

 DOI: 10.4324/9781003140269-6

A painting, whether landscape, portrait, still life, history or abstract, can produce an estranging effect due to its colour choices, from photorealist verisimilitude to abstraction, and in its deviations from reality. Viktor Shklovsky, writing about poetry, argues that 'the device of art is the "enstrangement" [*sic*] of things and the complication of the form, which increases the duration and complexity of perception, as the process of perception is, in art, an end in itself and must be prolonged' (20). The geometry of perspective and composition guides and controls the viewer's cognitive navigation of image, while they may experience beauty, pity, the sublime and so on.

Industrial art: Sublimity, 1766–1850

Eighteenth-century developments in physics, chemistry, biology, astronomy and other sciences increased understanding of the universe, offering new materials and subject matter for art. Alongside this, in the writings of Joseph Addison, Edmund Burke, Immanuel Kant and others, the experience of the sublime was expanded from a rhetorical device to visual experiences of landscapes, such as mountains, valleys, passes, waterfalls, erupting volcanos and ice floes, whether witnessed in person or via art. The sublime offers a 'pleasure in pain' (Robu 22), and such landscapes might overwhelm the viewer, despite attempts to master their infinities through the gaze. Scott Bukatman argues that 'The breadth of nature proves ideal in stimulating the dynamic cognitive processes that exalt the mind that engages with it' (94) and locates the sublime in a range of nineteenth-century paintings – especially those which include a viewer as an identificatory substitute for the extradiegetic onlooker – and in the film special effects of Douglas Trumbull.

Joseph Wright of Derby creates the feeling of the sublime by depicting volcanic eruptions, although he had not witnessed them in person and was copying the paintings of his contemporaries. He also creates striking tenebristic effects of light and dark in interior settings. His *A Philosopher Lecturing on the Orrery* (1766) foregrounds a mechanical model of the solar system, with the lecturer pointing to the moons of Jupiter and a girl pointing to the moons of Saturn, celestial bodies which would be used to calculate longitude. Wright omits part of the orrery to avoid obscuring details and instead shows a range of reactions on the onlookers' faces, from the boredom of the teenaged boy and young man to the rapt attention of the girl. The onlookers' heads, positioned around the central lamp, enact the phases of the moon. Wright dramatises and creates a sense of wonder. His *An Experiment on a Bird in the Air Pump* (1768) again foregrounds display as a cockatoo is starved of air in a glass jar; on the right, two young girls are clearly distressed; on the left, two lovers seem more interested in each other.

The industrial revolution, already underway in Wright's lifetime, irrevocably altered British society and topography in the nineteenth century, through the building of mines, factories, canals, railways, telegraph networks, cities and so on; natural resources and slave labour were exploited globally. New industrialists became patrons for contemporary artists, commissioning or buying depictions of factories, foundries and the worked landscape. An emerging industrial sublime straddled excitement and anxiety.

The English J.M.W. Turner looked for scenes in Britain and Europe which might appeal to this new elite and aristocrats (as paintings) and to an emerging middle class (as prints). His patron, Lord Egremont, invested in canals and new agricultural methods; Egremont's lover and later wife Elizabeth Ilive, a scientist and engineer, assisted Turner with pigments. Turner consulted with Michael Faraday about the durability of pigments, drew on William Herschel's observations of the surface of the sun and Mary Somerville's ideas about the spectrum, read Johann Wolfgang von Goethe's *Theory of Colours* (1810, trans. 1840), and made his own colour circles. His landscapes and seascapes edge towards the abstract, laying the foundations for Impressionism and twentieth-century art, although they were initially found bewildering. There is sometimes a sense of ambivalence in Turner's work. *The Fighting Temeraire* (1839) depicts the sailing ship being towed up the Thames estuary by a steam tug to a breakers' yard; the setting sun marks a melancholic passing of an era, but the Sun does not set in the east. His *The Slave Ship* (1840) shows the sublimity of a sea storm, but features enslaved people, probably thrown overboard so that insurance could be claimed, drowning. A steam train, its front glowing demonically red, dominates *Rain, Steam and Speed – The Great Western Railway* (1844), balancing the marvels of technology with a degree of fear.

William Blake detested slavery and industrialisation, rejecting the rationality and logic of science – which brought inequality and suffering – in favour of his own cosmology with religious, mythological, literary and political resonances. His *The Ancient of Days* (1794) depicts the figure of Urizen (Blake's avatar for reason), measuring and limiting the Earth with a pair of compasses; in *Newton* (1795–c.1805) a version of the scientist draws a circle with a compass, oblivious to the ocean bed or star field behind him, seemingly fused with the heel-like rock he is sitting upon. Two centuries later, Scottish-Italian sculptor Eduardo Paolozzi took this composition as the basis for *Newton after Blake* (1995), located outside London's British Library.

The English artist John Martin was also an engineer and an early member of the British Association for the Advancement of Science. While his plans for a sewage extraction system and railway network for London were rejected, he advertised himself as a designer and inventor at the 1851 Great Exhibition. But he is better known for such sublimely apocalyptic canvases as *The Destruction of Pompei and Herculaneum* (c.1821), *The Destruction of Sodom and Gomorrah* (1852), and the triptych *The Last Judgement* (c.1849–53), *The Great Day of His Wrath* (1851–3) and *The Plains of Heaven* (c.1851–3); among the damned in *The Last Judgement*, a steam train hurtles into the abyss. Some of these paintings were toured around the world and may have been seen by a million people. Martin was not the only artist of the era to depict ruins – Constable, Turner and Richard Wilson all recorded the crumbling architecture of the classical and medieval eras – but he was looking to future disasters, somewhat like Sir John Soane's commission of Joseph Michael Gandy's watercolour *A Bird's-eye view of the Bank of England* (1830). Martin's interest in deep time was enriched by advances in geology and palaeontology; he added dinosaurs to his mezzotint of *Adam and Eve Driven Out of Paradise* (1824–7) and *The Deluge* (1828), produced a watercolour and engraving of the hypothesised iguanodon for English geologist Gideon Mantell's *The Wonders of Geology* (1838) and illustrated sea-dragons (presumably ichthyosaurs) for English fossil collector Thomas Hawkins's *The Book of the Great Sea-Dragons* (1840).

Thomas Cole, who emigrated to the US as a young man and became part of the Hudson Bay school, argues that 'Poetry and Painting sublime and purify thought, by grasping the past, the present, and the future – they give the mind a foretaste of its immortality' (1). His THE COURSE OF EMPIRE cycle (1833–6) – *The Savage State, or, The Commencement of the Empire*; *The Arcadian or Pastoral State*; *The Consummation of Empire*; *Destruction*; *Desolation* – depicts the same area over millennia, from the hunter–gatherer era to a future city in ruins. The paintings warn against the President Andrew Jackson's democratising ambitions, which Cole saw as undermining the Republican values of the elite. Having witnessed public disorder in Ohio and New York, Cole feared social breakdown, later writing *Verdura, or a Tale after Time* (c.1845), an unpublished bloody dystopia set at the end of the twentieth century. At first glance, Cole's idyllic *River in the Catskills* (1843) is pastoral, but it contains a steam train. Such depictions of American landscape downplayed Indigenous intervention in nature and largely presented the topography as pristine, ready for Western exploitation. Mountains might be distorted to echo the sublimity of the Alps and artists such as Frederic Edwin Church and German-born Albert Bierstadt encoded patriotic messages into their paintings. Perry Miller suggests that American society was created by and ruled by the machine: the nation 'positively lusted for the chance to yield itself to the gratifications of technology' (54), setting the ground for two centuries of the technological sublime.

Imperial art: Colour experiments, 1850–1900

In Europe, professionalised painting academies replaced apprenticeships, their orthodoxies creating rebels who formed movements which looked back to prior styles or embraced new art materials, aesthetics and subject matter. The Pre-Raphaelite Brotherhood (formed 1848) of Dante Gabriel Rossetti, William Holman Hunt, John Everett Millais, William Morris and Edward Burne-Jones, who looked to earlier Italian and mediaeval art for inspiration, are best viewed as fantasy. The Impressionists (1863), including Berthe Morisot, Édouard Manet, Claude Monet, Pierre-Auguste Renoir and Alfred Sisley, used new brushes and oil paints in tubes to depict both metropolitan Paris and a countryside easily accessible by railways, copying the looser brushwork of Turner and Constable. Monet's dozen paintings of Gare Saint-Lazare in 1877 increasingly focused on the trains, architecture, steam and smoke rather than the passengers. In London, he painted Waterloo Bridge and the Houses of Parliament, with more of a sense of melancholy than sublime; from 1866–76, the American-born but Paris-trained James McNeill Whistler painted a series of nocturnes featuring the Thames and the Cremorne Gardens pleasure ground. The Franco-Prussian War (1870–1) sent several French artists and their main dealer, Paul Durand-Ruel, into exile in Britain; Durand-Ruel set up galleries and exhibitions in Berlin, London and New York. Artists in Australia, Britain, the Netherlands, Scandinavia, the US and beyond were inspired by Impressionism.

The Neo-Impressionists and Post-Impressionists – Paul Cezanne, Camille Pissarro, Georges Seurat and others – were more radical in their palettes, compositions and colour science. Seurat's pointillism fragmented landscapes into dots, creating optical illusions of colours. His *A Sunday on La Grande Jatte* (1884–6) uses coloured dots to present a utopian image of a range of social classes at leisure on an island in the Seine, deleting industrial Paris. Paul Cezanne uses planes, diagonals and diamonds of colour in his still lives, landscapes and groups of dancers and bathers. The aesthetics reflected developments in particle physics, electromagnetism and X-rays, such as James Clerk Maxwell's *A Treatise on Electricity and Magnetism* (1873). Some scientists embraced spiritualism, mesmerism, clairvoyance and religious beliefs, and several generations of artists were influenced by Helene Blavatsky's Theosophical Society, which was founded in New York in 1875 and posited a secret brotherhood of masters of scientific knowledge with access to an underlying divine Absolute being.

The Norwegian Edvard Munch was interested in spiritualism but, having briefly trained at an engineering school, was fascinated by photography, radio, X-rays and electricity. Pascal Rousseau argues that 'Munch realises that the eye can perceive beyond the limited scope of its organology, why the new rays seem to be evidence of far subtler states of matter, making the boundaries between the physics of the "infinitely small" and psychic life more permeable' (161). Munch moved between Naturalist, Impressionist, Fauvist and Pointillist aesthetics, but his *The Scream* (1893, 1895, 1910) is Symbolist, striving to depict emotions beyond visible reality. In several paintings and woodblocks, an asexual figure – possibly inspired by a Peruvian mummy Munch saw at the 1889 Exposition Universelle in Paris – stands, mouth open, with hands over its ears, surrounded by red, yellow and orange swirls of sky. Munch asserted that, while walking through the outskirts of Oslo, he had witnessed a scream passing through nature and the changing colour of the sky; more scientific explanations credit an eruption of Krakatoa or nacreous clouds lit from below during twilight. Munch's images document the angst and alienation of the individual, whether alone, in a relationship or in a crowd. He also conducted experiments on his canvases by leaving finished paintings outside, exposed to the weather.

Modern movements: Time, space and the machine, 1900–45

Late nineteenth- and early twentieth-century technological developments – cinema, radio, cars, aeroplanes and so on – were changing everyday life as industrialised European countries headed towards war over competing empires. Whilst Einstein was working on special relativity and other physicists were developing our understanding of the behaviour and nature of the subatomic world, art documented the impact of machines on humanity, especially with the First World War's trench warfare, poison gas, tanks, planes and Zeppelins, and this new physics.

The Austrian Rudolf Steiner established a German branch of the Theosophical Society in 1904 and then his own Anthroposophical Society from 1912. He believed that art might awaken humanity's true nature. The Swedish Hilma af Klint thought her paintings of cosmogonies, geometries, flowers and different layers of reality would do this, but Steiner and the art critics were unimpressed; she withdrew her work from view until 20 years after her death in 1944. Wassily Kandinsky, who may have been shown her work by Steiner, broke with objective painting in favour of abstraction and transformative use of colour. Piet Mondrian, who joined the Theosophical Society in 1909, experimented with canvases of yellow, blue, red and black squares and rectangles, with white backgrounds, divided by black lines. With Theo van Doesburg, he founded the De Stijl movement, offering a new vision of life via painting, architecture and interior design. Kyiv-born Kazimir Malevich may have come to Theosophy via Pyotr Ouspenskii, but his Suprematist art, which embraces geometry and time as a fourth dimension, was more likely inspired by the non-Euclidean ideas of Nikolai Lobachevsky, who argued that 'geometry needs to have no connection to the real world, but could define spaces that existed only as mental constructs, as long as the geometry was logically consistent' (Luecking 92). Malevich's *Black Square* (1915) attempts to communicate emotion with no connection to the natural world.

Malevich met a number of artists in Paris who had been developing Cezanne's aesthetics since 1907. Georges Braque and Pablo Picasso received the most public hostility; other practitioners included Albert Gleizes, Robert Delaunay, Henri le Fauconnier, Jean Metzinger, Fernand Léger and Thorvald Hellesen. Cubism, being aware of the idea of a fourth dimension or applying Henri Bergson's philosophy of time perception, breaks with the idea of painting representing a single moment in space and time from one viewpoint. It attempts to represent four dimensions in two, as in Marcel Duchamp's *Nude Descending a Staircase No. 2* (1912). Léger, traumatised by the First World War, depicted the fusion of humans or cities with machines, beginning with *The Card Players* (1917). The tone is estranging if not alienating; a similar aesthetic is to be found in the Norwegian Hellesen's cubist paintings produced in Paris.

Based in Paris in 1909, the Italian Futurist poet F.T. Marinetti insisted 'that the world's magnificence has been enriched by a new beauty: the beauty of speed' (21). Futurism included painters in France and Italy. Umberto Boccioni's *The Laugh* (1911) depicts a woman, possibly in a cabaret bar; the background drinkers shifting to the foreground breaks any settled sense of perspective. In *The Boulevard* (1913), Gino Severini painted groups of people overlaid by triangles and other shapes, fragmenting reality. The second wave Futurist, Tullio Crali, caught a racing car's speed in the distorted curves of red metal in *The Forces of the Bend* (1930) and the movement of planes in *Nose-Diving on the City* (1939), in which the city seems as much inside as outside the aircraft.

In the 1960s, he was to paint the COSMIC IMAGE series and write the Orbital Art Manifesto (1969), which called for the use of satellites and asteroids as artworks, the manipulation of clouds by electromagnetism and the sending of poetry into space.

Canadian–British Percy Wyndham Lewis, who kickstarted Vorticism in his magazine *Blast* in Summer 1914, often featured a slanted set of perspectives and blocks of colour in his paintings. *The Crowd* (1915) features small, brown, barely recognisable figures against an abstracted metropolis and possibly a parade. The few female Vorticists, such as Helen Saunders and Jessica Dismorr, hid human features within geometric forms. While British David Bomberg was never a Vorticist, his marrying of Cubist and Futurist styles produced works such as *In the Hold* (1913–4), which locks dock workers within a grid of squares and triangles representing the hold of a ship.

From the mid-1920s, Surrealism built upon the irrationalism and nonsense of the Dadaist movement and retreated from such geometric excesses to create seemingly realist images which uncannily echoed other images or juxtaposed unlikely objects. It took the insights of Freudian psychoanalysis and attempted to forge a new cognition through its estrangements. Evdokia Stefanopoulou notes how the imagery of Salvador Dalí 'reflect[s] on the fluidity of time, the texture of objects, and the fabric of reality' (150) and cites the apocalyptic landscapes of Yves Tanguy, the uncanny works of René Magritte and the biomorphic forms of Jean Miró. Such forms also characterise the works of psychoanalyst Grace Pailthorpe and her husband and patient Reuben Mednikoff, drawing upon and titled after the dates of their dreams.

Cold War art: Machine images, 1945–90

The rise of totalitarian regimes in the lead up to World War II saw an exodus of many European artists to the US and Mexico, with New York becoming the art market's new centre. The Abstract Expressionism of Jackson Pollock, Barnett Newman, Clyfford Still, Mark Rothko and others removed any obvious representation of reality or sense of three-dimensional space from painting. Robert Rosenblum tagged these four as masters of the Abstract Sublime: we are 'standing silently and contemplatively before these huge and soundless pictures as if we were looking at a sunset or a moonlit night' (242). The movement was weaponised in the 1950s, with the CIA covertly funding the Museum of Modern Art's International Program to tempt Eastern European artists away from Soviet-sponsored realism to a more radical style.

America popular images, in the form of films, comics and music, impacted on a Europe under reconstruction. Paolozzi grunted along to his 1952 live epidiascope presentation *BUNK!* at the Institute for Contemporary Arts, featuring the cover for Don Wilcox's 'The Iron Men of Venus' from *Amazing* (February 1952), magazine cuttings, publicity stills and images of machines and circuit boards. His use of the word 'pop' may have influenced Lawrence Alloway's naming of Pop Art. Paolozzi's series of prints, such as *General Dynamic F.U.N.* (1965–70) and *Moonstrips Empire News* (1967), were also collages, and his sculptures combine human or animal forms with the apparently mechanical. A post-apocalyptic installation made with the photographer Nigel Henderson and architects Alison and Peter Smithson was part of the *This is Tomorrow* exhibition (Whitechapel Art Gallery, 1956). Michael Moorcock and J.G. Ballard both visited the exhibition and Paolozzi later appeared on *New Worlds's* masthead as its 'aeronautics advisor'. Other artists appropriated images such as King Kong, Robbie the Robot from *Forbidden Planet* (Wilcox 1956), Vincent Van Gogh's *Sunflowers*, Marlon Brando and Marilyn Monroe. The British artist Allen Jones attempted to critique the eroticism of art and popular culture through his rubber-clad fibreglass mannequins *Hatstand, Table* and *Chair* (1970), but women posed as furniture seem to reinforce objectification instead. Stanley Kubrick asked Jones to design *A Clockwork Orange* (1971) but was unwilling to pay him.

British pop art largely celebrated such imagery, although it might be open to ironic readings, but American pop art was more critical. Roy Lichtenstein selected, altered and enlarged panels from war, superhero and Disney comics, foregrounding the Ben-Day dots, which were used in their original printing. Andy Warhol's silkscreens of Marilyn Monroe, Elizabeth Taylor, Elvis Presley, news photographs, electric chairs, Campbell's Soup Cans and Coca-Cola are certainly estranging, as a variety of colours distort what began as photographic realism. There is a death of affect in Warhol's art – he even stated that 'I want to be a machine' (Svenson 26) – and it is never clear whether a print was made by him or an assistant in his studio, the Factory. Other American pop artists were more explicitly political. Robert Rauschenberg, inspired by a visit to the Factory, produced silkscreens such as *Retroactive I* (1963), which juxtaposed John F. Kennedy, an astronaut and other images, reflecting his sense of being bombarded by the media. Rauschenberg worked alongside Bell Laboratories's Billy Klüver to encourage artists to work with engineers and, after NASA invited him to witness the launch of Apollo 11, produced the STONED MOON lithographs (1969–70). James Rosenquist's monumental *F-111* (1964–5) depicts a fighter-bomber alongside spaghetti, lightbulbs, a tyre, an umbrella in front of a mushroom cloud, a girl under a hair dryer and other images on 59 panels, connecting the military-industrial complex with the rest of the American economy.

The sense of the disappearance of the artist can be found in the early experiments with computers in the 1960s. Charles Csuri created his first picture via computer in 1964 and his film *Hummingbird* (1967), made with James Shaffer, transferred thousands of computer-generated images via punchcards onto 16 mm film. Csuri anticipated a future when computers could think for themselves and he would be an editor or curator rather than an artist. In parallel, Harold Cohen developed various computer programs called AARON between 1972 and his death in 2016, to draw geometries and basic objects via various predetermined codes. The prints he produced were monochrome, sometimes augmented with hand-colouring.

Other artists insisted on the importance of the body. Yves Klein, known for his all-blue canvases, used naked women as brushes in the early 1960s, while performance art, happenings, conceptual art, walking and land art took art out of the gallery into live experiences within the mundane world. Collectives such as Fluxus identified with shamanism rather than the history of art; co-founder Ben Patterson's *Stand Erect* (1961) is a set of instructions for walking which offer an algorithm for the participant.

From the late 1940s, the Austrian Maria Lassnig explored 'body awareness' – the relationship between her body and her surroundings, as well as asking what it would feel like to be an extra-terrestrial – but limited her work outside the canvas to experimental films. Her paintings are portraits in bright colours, often with missing body parts and minimal backgrounds: *Woman Power* (1979) depicts a woman towering above a city; *Hard and Soft Machine/Small Science Fiction* (1988) features two unidentifiable machines: *Lady with Brain* (1990) is a self-portrait with an external brain; *Small Science Fiction Self-Portrait* (1995) is a nude wearing VR goggles. Her self-cyborgisation parallels Helen Chadwick's IN THE KITCHEN series (1977), in which the photographer dresses up as kitchen sink, oven, refrigerator and washing machine, the appliance emphasising her body parts and satirising gender stereotypes of women as household slaves.

Post-colonial art: New cosmologies, 1990–2114

Sf permeates contemporary art. Dominique Gonzalez-Foerste's installation *TH.2058* (2008–9) half-filled the Tate Modern Turbine Hall with bunkbeds, sf novels and clips from sf films, reimagining the space as a shelter from a perpetual rainstorm. The joint 2019 winner of the Turner Prize, Tai Shani, fused sculpture, video and live performance in *DC: Semiramis*, set in a womxn's city inspired by Christine de Pizan's *The Book of the City of Ladies* (1405). The 2022 Turner Prize shortlist featured Sin Wai Kin's virtual boyband, Heather Phillipson's post-apocalyptic landscape, Ingrid Pollard's anthropomorphic machines and Victoria Ryan's estranging seeds and vegetables, with the artists citing the influence of Octavia E. Butler and Samuel R. Delany.

For *Earth-Moon-Sonata (Moonlight Sonata Reflected from the Moon)* (2007), Katie Paterson translated Beethoven's sonata into a Morse code and bounced it off the Moon with radio waves, using this signal to program an automated grand piano. *Timepieces (Solar System)* (2014) consists of nine clocks which record the current time on the Moon and the eight planets of the solar system. Her most ambitious work is *Future Library* (2014–2114), a forest planted in Norway which will supply the wood for a hundred novels to be printed in 2114; each year for a century, an unpublished manuscript will be deposited in Oslo's Deichman Bjørvika public library, with Margaret Atwood, David Mitchell, Karl Ove Knausgård and Tsitsi Dangarembga all contributing so far.

Astronauts feature in series by the Spanish Cristina de Middel, the British-Nigerian Yinka Shonibare CBE, and British–Ghanaian Larry Achiampong. de Middel reconstructed the 1964 Zambian space programme which aimed to send humans (and a cat) to the Moon and Mars in her self-published *The Afronauts* (2012). Previously a photojournalist, she offers an alternative history to Cold War space exploration. Shonibare CBE has repeatedly dressed mannequins and other sculptures in Batik, a wax printed cotton cloth in bright colours, originally made in the Netherlands and distributed to Indonesia, but sold more successfully in Nigeria and bought by him from London's Brixton Market. His REFUGEE ASTRONAUTS (2015–9) dress life-sized figures in Batik with a space helmet and a netted rucksack, showing post-apocalyptic escapees from colonialism and climate disaster. Achiampong's astronauts are a response to the splintering impact of Brexit and the developing African Union. They wear green flight suits with fictional Pan African Union flags, and appear both as mannequins and in his RELIC series of five films and animations (2017–20). Since 2017, his PAN AFRICAN FLAGS FOR THE RELIC TRAVELLERS' ALLIANCE and other flags have flown at various locations in the UK.

The American artist Ellen Gallagher also works in series, usually building images up either by defacing images from such Black magazines as *Ebony*, *Our World*, *Sepia* and *Black Stars* or by building up layers of found images, Plasticine, gold leaf, newspaper cuttings and coloured paper on penmanship paper. *Bird in Hand* (2006) features an ambiguously gendered piratical figure with a peg leg and an Afro which swirls into what might be subterranean species or plant life. It is unclear whether the figure is underwater or on land, and is part inspired by Captain Ahab from Herman Melville's *Moby-Dick* (1851) and the Oankali from Octavia E. Butler's LILITH'S BROOD trilogy (1987–9). Pegleg appears in other works by Gallagher, such as *Bone-Brite* (2009), in which a suited man with a prosthetic arm seems to merge with a skeleton. Her recent practice includes the series WATERY ECSTATIC (2001–) and ECSTATIC DRAFT OF FISHES (2020–), which began with a series of Medusan heads apparently underwater and developed into depictions of submarine life and gold leaf busts. Collectively, they imagine a utopian society of descendants of slaves who were thrown off the slave ship *Zong* (one of Turner's inspirations for *The Slave Ship*). Techno duo Drexciya had produced the album *The Quest* (1997) based on this incident and the imagined aftermath – Gallagher titled a picture *Drexciya* in 1997 – and went onto inspire music by clipping., Rivers Solomon's *The Deep* (2019) and Abdul Qadim Haqq's graphic novel *The Book of Drexciya* (2020). Gallagher's work estranges through its co-optation of sometime racist imagery, questioning fixed identities and histories.

Conclusion

It seems likely that art will continue to produce sf which alters our sense of perception. Csuri's legacy might include generative AI and programs such as DeepDream, DALL-E and NightCafe. Contemporary art, meanwhile, breaks auction records, as do some NFTs (Non-Fungible Tokens), which link data files to a digital or physical artwork. Beginning with *Cold Monument Dark* (2000), the digital artist Pak produced NFTs to be sold, netting $91.8 million for *Merge* (2021). Beeple's *Everydays: The First 5000 Days* (2021), consisting of five thousand collaged images created since 1 May 2007, was auctioned for $69.3 million and was paid for with cryptocurrency. Both bubbles may burst.

Social media is one means of working outside and within the traditional structures of training and gallery representation. Decades of imagery from album covers, comics, films and television are available for inspiration. Afrofuturism has already featured in exhibitions in London, Leiden and Washington; the New York Metropolitan Museum of Art even has an Afrofuturist period room, *Before Yesterday We Could Fly* (2021). The art of sf helps artists and their viewers to cognitively think through the contemporary debates and crises around climate catastrophe, the legacies of colonialism, geopolitics and gender identity, via the tactics of estrangement rather than didacticism. Painting remains an inquiry into the laws of nature and how these interact with humanity, and will continue to make us look at the world in a new way.

Works cited

Aldiss, Brian W. *Billion Year Spree*. Weidenfeld and Nicolson, 1973.

Bukatman, Scott. *Matters of Gravity: Special Effects and Supermen in the 20th Century*. Duke UP, 2003.

Byrne-Smith, Dan, ed. *Science Fiction*. Whitechapel/MIT Press, 2020.

Cole, Thomas. 'Essay on American Scenery'. *American Monthly Magazine* 1 (1836): 1–12.

Constable, John. 'Lectures on Landscape'. *John Constable's Discourses*. Ed. R.B. Beckett. Suffolk Records Society, 1970. 39–74.

Luecking, Stephen. 'A Man and His Square: Kasimir Malevich and the Visualization of the Fourth Dimension'. *Journal of Mathematics and the Arts* 4.2 (2010): 87–100.

Marinetti, F.T. 'The Founding and Manifesto of Futurism'. *Futurist Manifestos*. Ed. Umbro Apollonio. Tate, 2009. 19–24.

Miller, Perry. 'The Responsibility of Mind in a Civilization of Machines'. *The American Scholar* 31.1 (1961–2): 51–69.

Robu, Cornel. 'A Key to Science Fiction: The Sublime'. *Foundation* 40 (1988): 21–37.

Rosenbaum, Robert. 'The Abstract Sublime'. *Reading Abstract Expressionism: Context and Critique*. Ed. Ellen G. Langau. Yale UP. 239–44.

Rousseau, Pascal. 'Radiation: Metabolising the "New Rays"'. *Edvard Munch: The Modern Eye*. Ed. Angela Lampe and Clément Chéroux. Tate, 2012. 161–9.

Shklovsky, Viktor. 'Art, as Device'. *Poetics Today* 36.3 (2015): 151–74.

Stefanopoulou, Evdokia. 'Modern Art and Sf Iconography: An Introduction'. *Science Fiction Film and Television* 16.1–2 (2023): 139–63.

Swenson. Gene 'What is Pop Art? Answers from 8 Painters, Part 1'. *Art News* 62 (1963): 24–7, 60–4.

5
NINETEENTH-CENTURY WESTERN SCIENCE FICTION

Arthur B. Evans

It is often said that sf obtained its name and its social identity from the American pulp magazines in the early decades of the twentieth century. But many critics also maintain that a recognisable literary tradition of sf had already begun to emerge in Europe during the seventeenth and eighteenth centuries, eventually achieving worldwide popularity during the nineteenth century thanks to writers such as Jules Verne and H.G. Wells. It might even be argued that the two sf variants pioneered by Verne in his *voyages extraordinaires* (1863–1905) and by Wells in his 'scientific romances' (1895–1914) established the two primary narrative modes – hard/didactic versus speculative/fantastic – that have dominated the genre ever since.

The sudden upsurge of sf-type narratives during the nineteenth century can only be understood within the historical context of the Industrial Revolution and the transformative (and often alienating) social changes that accompanied it. The generally positive and positivist outlook in certain 'enlightened' works, such as Bernard le Bovier de Fontenelle's *Discussions on the Plurality of Worlds* (1686), Louis-Sébastien Mercier's futurist utopia *The Year 2440* (1771) and the Marquis de Condorcet's optimistic *Sketch for a Historical Picture of the Progress of the Human Mind* (1795), soon metamorphosed into their dark counterparts in novels such as Mary Shelley's *Frankenstein, or a Modern Prometheus* (1818). Moving the source of terror from the supernatural to the scientific, Shelley's Gothic sf tale exemplified the Romantic rejection of the eighteenth-century Cartesian belief in the scientist as hero and in technology as inherently good. *Frankenstein* expressed the fears of an entire *mal-du-siècle* generation caught in a sudden paradigm shift between tradition and modernity. As such, it became highly influential and popularised the archetype of the mad scientist who, in his hubris-filled pursuit of knowledge and power, betrays basic human values. Notable works after *Frankenstein* featuring such Faustian scientists include Honoré de Balzac's *The Centenarian* (1822) and *The Search for the Absolute* (1834), Nathaniel Hawthorne's 'The Birthmark' (1845) and 'Rappaccini's Daughter' (1846), Robert Louis Stevenson's *Strange Case of Dr Jekyll and Mr Hyde* (1886), Robert Cromie's *The Crack of Doom* (1895), H.G. Wells's *The Island of Doctor Moreau* (1896) and Jules Verne's *Master of the World* (1904). Finally, although some sf historians have proclaimed Mary Shelley's novel the 'ur-text' for the entire sf genre (Aldiss), other scholars disagree, insisting that sf's origins can be traced back to ancient Greece

DOI: 10.4324/9781003140269-7

(Roberts), or to the 'technologically saturated societies' of the 1880s (Luckhurst 3) or to Hugo Gernsback and the American pulp magazines of the 1920s and 1930s (Westfahl).

As Western society continued to grapple with rapid industrial growth and the spread of modern technologies, a new and radical idea began to take hold – that the future could be very different from the past. From this simple notion emerged a second major strand of sf that soon proliferated throughout the nineteenth century: futuristic fiction. Félix Bodin's novel/manifesto *The Novel of the Future* (1834) argued for the importance of this new genre and described how such narratives, filled with the wonders of the scientific age, would constitute the 'epic literature of tomorrow' (Alkon *Origins* 245–89). About three decades earlier, Jean-Baptiste Cousin de Grainville had already broken new cognitive ground with *The Last Man* (1805) by visualising the Christian apocalypse in secular terms (an approach adopted by Mary Shelley in 1826 in a novel of the same name where she imagines a plague wiping out humanity). And, near the close of the century, Camille Flammarion's *Omega: The Last Days of the World* (1894) posited a kind of astronomical-cum-spiritualist apocalypse caused by the heat death of our solar system. Other future-catastrophe (though not necessarily end-of-the-world) fictions from this period include Richard Jeffries's *After London* (1885), a post-holocaust novel where England reverts to barbarism, and numerous cautionary future-war stories beginning with George Chesney's highly influential invasion tale *The Battle of Dorking* (1871) (Clarke).

Many of these nineteenth-century tales of the future sought to portray, either positively or negatively, humanity's social 'progress' in the years to come. One imaginative and light-hearted example was Jane Webb-Loudon's *The Mummy! A Tale of the Twenty-Second Century* (1827), an elaborate science fantasy that pokes fun at her own society's foibles by means of an eccentric scientist's resuscitation of the mummy of Egyptian pharaoh Cheops, who promptly travels to London by dirigible and begins to take an active role in the political affairs of the day. Other satiric works about the future in this vein include Émile Souvestre's comically dystopian *The World as It Shall Be* (1846), which depicts a world in the year 3000 that has air conditioning, designer drinking waters, steam-driven submarines and phrenology-based education. Also full of humour and wonderfully illustrated by its author is Albert Robida's *The Twentieth Century* (1883), which recounts the adventures of Hélène, a young woman who is attempting to find a career in an extrapolated (and surprisingly feminist) Paris of 1952. The French capital is teeming with flying aircabs and high-tech pneumatic tubes to transport citizens around the city; each home has a 'telephonoscope' to broadcast the latest news and entertainment; and the government is swept out of office every 10 years in a planned 'decennial revolution'. Robida's other illustrated futuristic novels include *War in the Twentieth Century* (1887), *The Electric Life* (1892) and a unique time-reversal fantasy *The Clock of the Ages* (1902).

Other less satiric and more serious utopias of the future were also plentiful during the nineteenth century, each one offering new speculations on scientific technology and radical political experimentation. Consider, for example, Julius von Voss's *Ini, A Novel from the Twenty-first Century* (1810), which is viewed by some as the first German sf novel; Samuel Butler's *Erewhon* (1872), which visualises an anti-technology paradise where machines have been banned from society for fear that they will evolve and eventually replace humans; Edward Maitland's *By and By: An Historical Romance of the Future* (1873), a Victorian 'three-decker' novel that portrays an advanced pro-science society existing in a future Africa where, among its other technological feats, it has successfully irrigated the Sahara Desert; or W.H. Hudson's *A Crystal Age* (1887), which depicts an ecological utopia whose citizens live in total harmony with nature. Probably the most important example of this sf subgenre is Edward Bellamy's hugely popular *Looking Backward 2000–1887* (1888), which imagines an industry-based and technology-driven socialist utopia in

Boston in the year 2000. Bellamy's novel became an international bestseller, and 'Bellamy Clubs' began to spring up across America to discuss Bellamy's political ideas. *Looking Backward* also sparked the publication of many other futuristic utopias and dystopias during the *fin-de-siècle* period of 1890–1900. Notable among these were William Morris's dreamily pastoral *News from Nowhere* (1890); Ignatius Donnelly's *Caesar's Column* (1890), a grim tale of an ultra-capitalistic New York City that ends up being destroyed from within by its poor and disenfranchised lower classes; and Italian anthropologist Paolo Mantegazza's *The Year 3000: A Dream* (1897), with its vision of a host of technological advances, such as flying machines, artificial intelligence and even credit cards.

Toward the end of the century, another popular strain of futuristic utopias sought to portray pseudo-feminist matriarchal societies, such as the one in Mary E. Bradley Lane's *Mizora: A World of Women* (1880), an all-female hollow-Earth community where children are produced by parthenogenesis; or Elizabeth Corbett's *New Amazonia: A Foretaste of the Future* (1889), where women control all aspects of political and social life; or Henri Demarest's *Women of the Future* (1890), where men are second-class citizens and forced into arranged marriages; or Lady Florence Dixie's *Gloriana, or the Revolution of 1900* (1890), which imagines the successful emancipation of women in Great Britain, leading to a society of peace and prosperity under female rule.

Another important sf 'placeholder' (Harpold 51) that emerged during the nineteenth century took the form of fictional explorations of the distant past and the discovery of 'lost' worlds. Edward Page Mitchell's protagonists travel back to a pivotal historical moment in sixteenth-century Holland in 'The Clock that Went Backward' (1881); Enrique Gaspard's 1887 *The Time Ship: A Chrononautical Journey* features the first machine in Western literature engineered for calibrated time travel (eight years earlier than Wells's *The Time Machine*); Mark Twain's *A Connecticut Yankee in King Arthur's Court* (1889) visits sixth-century Arthurian England in this satire on humanity's endless capacity for violence and folly; and in Grant Allen's *The British Barbarians* (1895), an anthropologist from the future travels back in time to study present-day England. Paleoanthropology is the main focus of the new subgenre of prehistoric fiction in Pierre Boitard's *Paris before Man* (1861), Jules Verne's *Journey to the Centre of the Earth* (1864), Stanley Waterloo's *The Story of Ab: A Tale of the Time of the Cave Men* (1897), and in the novels *Vamireh* (1892), *Eyrimah* (1896) and *Quest for Fire* (1911) by the prolific French sf writer J.-H. Rosny aîné. An entire civilisation living deep inside our Earth is discovered by Captain Adam Seaborn (aka John Cleves Symmes) in his *Symzonia: A Voyage of Discovery* (1820), the first of many nineteenth-century 'hollow Earth' narratives describing an unknown race or alien species inhabiting the interior of our globe. Other subterranean beings include Edward Bulwer-Lytton's Vril-ya in *The Coming Race* (1871), James DeMille's Antarctic race of Kosekin in *Strange Manuscript Found in a Copper Cylinder* (1888), William R. Bradshaw's Plutusians and Calnogorians in *The Goddess of Atvatabar* (1892), and those found in several lost-race short stories by Rosny, including 'Nymphea' (1893), 'The Depths of Kyamo' (1896) and 'The Prodigious Country of the Caverns' (1896). But it was the Victorian novelist H. Rider Haggard who would prove to be the master of this brand of lost-world fiction with his internationally best-selling adventure tales *King Solomon's Mines* (1885), *She* (1887), *Allan Quatermain* (1887) and *The People of the Mist* (1894).

The growing popularity of 'hard' sf – exemplified by the huge success of Jules Verne during the latter third of the century – may be traced (somewhat ironically given his reputation in his homeland as mostly a writer of horror) to the work of American poet, writer and critic Edgar Allan Poe. Identified by Hugo Gernsback in the inaugural 1926 issue of *Amazing Stories* as one of the three founders of the new genre of 'scientifiction' (along with Verne and Wells), Poe pioneered the use of scientific detail to enhance the verisimilitude of his fantastic stories. His admittedly tongue-in-cheek footnote added to the lunar voyage of 'The Unparalleled Adventure of One Hans Pfaal' (1835), for example, could almost stand as a first manifesto for hard sf as he urges 'the application of scientific principles' to increase 'the *plausibility* of the details of the voyage itself' (41). The status of Poe as an early originator of the genre is directly proportional to the variety of sf themes and 'narrative frameworks for bold scientific speculations' (Stableford 'Science Fiction' 19) that he incorporated into his tales: the mechanics of balloon flight in 'The Balloon Hoax' (1844), mesmerism in 'A Tale of the Ragged Mountains' (1844) and 'The Facts in the Case of M. Valdemar' (1845), the future destruction of Earth by a comet in 'The Conversation of Eiros and Charmion' (1839), the discovery of lost worlds in 'MS Found in a Bottle' (1833) and *The Narrative of Arthur Gordon Pym* (1838), and a futuristic utopia in 'Mellonta Tauta' (1849). From his first published poems 'Sonnet to Science' (1829) and 'Al Aaraaf' (1829) to his last published philosophical essay *Eureka* (1848), Poe repeatedly attempted to reconcile a scientific outlook with a kind of sentimental religious mysticism, a *Weltanschauung* that, later in the century, would permeate the work of writers such as Flammarion and Rosny aîné.

Poe's influence on Verne at the beginning of the latter's writing career was pivotal. After reading Baudelaire's translation of Poe's stories (titled, interestingly, *Histoires extraordinaires*), Verne penned in 1864 his only piece of literary criticism, an essay called 'Edgar Poe and his Works', published in the popular French magazine *Musée des familles* (1833–1900). Verne begins his article by praising Poe, explaining some aspects of his life and analysing lengthy excerpts from his stories. Verne then goes on to say that 'they occupy an important place in the history of imaginative works because Poe created a distinct literary genre all his own' (194; my translation). Verne makes clear that it was not Poe's taste for the macabre, nor his odd penchant for hoax-humour, nor his technophobia that attracted him. It was rather Poe's attention to detail and his ability to make the bizarre believable and the extraordinary ordinary. In other words, it was his use of scientific verisimilitude that impressed Verne. Although Verne went on to borrow extensively from Poe's oeuvre (balloons, cryptograms, maelstroms, airships, comets, even the entire story of *The Narrative of Arthur Gordon Pym*), it was actually Poe's style that had the greatest impact on the future author of the *Extraordinary Voyages*.

Sometimes dubbed the 'Father of Science Fiction', Verne popularised in the 1860s and 1870s a new hybrid fictional genre called the *roman scientifique* (the scientific novel). Developed under the strict tutelage of his editor/publisher Pierre-Jules Hetzel, Verne's narrative recipe was unique: start with an educational and fast-paced adventure tale heavily flavoured with scientific didacticism, mix into it equal parts of drama, humour and 'sense of wonder', and then season it with a large pinch of positivistic Saint-Simonian ideology. After the publication and success of his first scientific novel, *Five Weeks in a Balloon* (1863), about an aerial trek across Africa, Verne told his friends at the Paris Stock Market where he had been working: 'My friends, I bid you adieu. I've had an idea [...] an idea that should make me rich. I've just written a novel in a new style [...] If it succeeds, it will be a gold mine' (Evans *Jules* 21). And a gold mine it soon proved to be, not only for Verne and his publisher but also for the history of speculative fiction. Verne went on to write more than 50 novels from 1864 until his death in 1905. Most first appeared in serial format in Hetzel's family periodical the *Magasin d'éducation et de récréation* (1864–1916) and then as luxury, fully illustrated octavo editions. Collectively, Verne's novels were called the *Voyages extraordinaires*, and they also had a specific educative purpose: to help compensate for the lack of science instruction in France's Catholic–controlled schools. As Hetzel explained in his 1866 editorial preface to the collection: 'The goal of this series is, in fact, to outline all the geographical, geological, physical, and astronomical knowledge amassed by modern science and to recount, in an entertaining and picturesque format that is his own, the history of the universe' (Evans *Jules* 30).

Marketing hyperbole aside, Hetzel's preface makes explicit at least one goal that Verne was expected to satisfy in his scientific novels: to teach the natural sciences through the medium of fictional 'arm-chair voyages'. According to some critics, it was partly this social function that allowed Verne's hard/didactic sf to establish a successful 'institutional "landing point" and ideological model' for the genre itself (Angenot 64). From the geology and paleontology of *Journey to the Centre of the Earth* to the physics of space flight in *From the Earth to the Moon* (1865), and from the oceanography and marine biology of *Twenty Thousand Leagues Under the Seas* (1870) to the chemistry and applied engineering of *The Mysterious Island* (1875), Verne's narratives sought to teach science through fiction, not to develop fiction through science (or, in many instances, pseudoscience), as in the case of Wells, Rosny and other early practitioners of the genre.

Counterbalancing the sometimes heavy doses of scientific didacticism in Verne's *romans scientifiques*, three other aspects enhanced their appeal: their epic scope and visions of unlimited mobility, their *Bildungsroman* initiatory plot structures, and their evocative portrayals of technology. As imaginative voyages to places 'where no man had gone before', Verne's novels transported readers to the far ends of the Earth – richly mythic locales such as the North Pole in *The Adventures of Captain Hatteras* (1866), the South Pole in *The Ice Sphinx* (1897), the Amazon jungles in *The Jangada* (1881), the hidden depths of the oceans in *Twenty Thousand Leagues under the Seas*, the dark side of the Moon in *Around the Moon* (1870), and even the distant planets of our solar system in *Hector Servadac* (1877). Most such fictional journeys in Verne's oeuvre involve a quest: to find a missing family member, as in *The Children of Captain Grant* (1867) and *Mistress Branican* (1891); to map an unexplored region of Africa, as in *The Adventures of Three Russians and Three English* (1872); or to survive as castaways on a deserted island, as in *The Mysterious Island* or *A Two-Year Vacation* (1888). Many novels feature pairings of scientist/acolyte characters such as Lidenbrock/Axel in *Journey to the Centre of the Earth* and Marcel/Octave in *The Begum's Millions* (1879). And most foreground a truly memorable piece of technology – Verne's famous 'dream machines'. From Captain Nemo's hi-tech submarine *Nautilus*, to Barbicane's aluminum space-bullet (so similar to Apollo 8), to Robur's powerful helicopter airship *Albatross*, to the steam-powered overland locomotive (fashioned to resemble an Indian elephant) of *The Steam House* (1880), to the many different modes of transport used by Phileas Fogg in his circumnavigation of the globe in *Around the World in 80 Days* (1873), these fictional people-movers represented a new Industrial-age utopian ideal: facility of movement in a moving world – or 'Mobilis in mobile', as Captain Nemo would say.

It is important to note that Verne's post-1887 novels, written after Hetzel's death, sometimes reflect a dramatic change of tone when compared to his earlier and more celebrated works. They tend more often to be pessimistic, nostalgic and even fiercely anti-Progress, recalling some of Verne's pre-Hetzel short stories such as 'Master Zacharius' (1854) or his 'lost' novel, the dystopian *Paris in the Twentieth Century* (1994), rejected by Hetzel in 1863. As might be expected, the scientific pedagogy in these later texts is severely abridged, watered down or cut out altogether. Themes of environmental concern, human morality and social responsibility grow more prevalent. Non-scientists are more often chosen as the stories' heroes, and those scientists who remain are increasingly portrayed as crazed megalomaniacs who use their special knowledge for purposes of world domination and/or unlimited riches. A striking example of these changes can be seen in the final volumes of Verne's 'serial' novels: the trilogy of *From the Earth to the Moon*, *Around the Moon* and *The World Turned Upside Down* (1889) and the two-novel series of *Robur the Conqueror* (1886) and *Master of the World* (1904). In *The World Turned Upside Down*, the heroic feats of ballistic engineering by Barbicane's Gun Club become (quite literally, at least in ambition) Earth-shaking when, instead of shooting a manned capsule around the Moon, they now seek to alter the angle of the Earth's axis with the blast of a gigantic cannon. Wholly indifferent to the catastrophic environmental and human damage that would result from such a project, their scheme is to melt the Earth's polar icecap in order to uncover vast mineral wealth for themselves. Similarly, in *Master of the World* the genius aviator Robur is brought back into the limelight, but it soon becomes evident that the once-heroic *Übermensch* of the skies has degenerated into a maniacal madman who now threatens global terrorism with his high-tech vehicles. Other post-1887 Verne novels target an array of social and environmental issues, such as the cruel oppression of the Québécois people in Canada in *Family without a Name* (1889), the plague of politicians and missionaries destroying Polynesian island cultures in *Propeller Island* (1895), the environmental pollution caused by the oil industry in *The Last Will of an Eccentric* (1899) and the slaughter of elephants for their ivory in *The Village in the Treetops* (1901), among others.

Verne's impact on the developing sf genre during the nineteenth century was both deep and lasting. Because of his unprecedented success, writers from around the world soon began to imitate his hard/didactic *romans scientifiques* and their emphasis on travel, science and technology: in France, Louis Boussenard's *The Secrets of Mr. Synthesis* (1888), Henry de Graffigny and Georges Le Faure's multi-volumed *Extraordinary Adventures of a Russian Scientist* (1889–96) and Paul d'Ivoi's action-packed series of novels collectively called the VOYAGES EXCENTRIQUES (1894–1914); in England and Germany, the many fictional works of Francis Henry Atkins (a.k.a. Frank Aubrey) and Robert Kraft; in Russia, the 'geographic fantasies' of Vladimir Obruchev; in America, Edward S. Ellis's frontier sf western *The Steam Man of the Prairies* (1868), Edward E. Hale's satellite story *The Brick Moon* (1869), Frank R. Stockton's *The Great War Syndicate* (1889), and the many FRANK READE JR and THOMAS EDISON JR 'invention' stories by Luis Senarens and other pulp 'dime-novel' writers that flourished toward the end of the century.

Following his death in 1905, Jules Verne's literary reputation underwent many changes within the French literary canon, among English-language readers and in contemporary scholarship. In his native France beginning in the 1960s and 1970s, Verne's oeuvre finally shed its stigma of paraliterature and joined the respectable literary mainstream; today his novels are taught in French universities. Verne's literary status in the UK and the US, however, continues to suffer from poor English translations, sensationalistic Hollywood adaptations and a cultural mythology that persists in portraying him as an icon of 'sci-fi' futurism. Fortunately, the past three decades have witnessed a growing renaissance of Anglophone interest in Verne, one which has resulted in many improved translations, several new and more accurate biographies, an online international fanbase and a dramatic upsurge in the number of academic studies devoted to his fiction (Evans 'Jules').

An important strand of non-Vernian speculative/fantastic sf that continued to develop throughout the nineteenth century, and surged after the publication of Charles Darwin's *On the Origin of Species* (1859), involves encounters with aliens and extra-terrestrials. Imagining life on other worlds as a means for creating an 'estranged' view of society had been an important theme in sf at least since Francis Godwin's *The Man in the Moone* (1638), Cyrano de Bergerac's *States and Empires of the Moon* (1657) and Marie-Anne de Roumier-Robert's *Voyage of Lord Seton Among the Seven Planets* (1765). In the nineteenth century, this rich tradition continued with Joseph Atterley's (George Tucker) lunar romance *A Voyage to the Moon* (1827); Charles Defontenay's *Star, or Psi Cassiopeia* (1854), which portrays an entire 'Starian' civilisation inhabiting the planet Psi in the constellation of Cassiopeia; Percy Greg's *Across the Zodiac* (1880), Robert Cromie's *Plunge into Space* (1891) and Gustavus Pope's *Journey to Mars* (1894), which all locate their alien societies on Mars (and sometimes manage to find romance on the red planet); the German novelist Kurd Lasswitz's *On Two Planets* (1897), which imagines a thriving Martian colony at the Earth's North Pole; and John Jacob Astor's *A Journey in Other Worlds* (1894), which portrays an interplanetary tour of our solar system where the protagonists encounter – among other oddities – Earth-like dinosaurs on Jupiter and spirits of the dead on Saturn. In this latter vein of mystical alien encounters, special mention must be made of French astronomer Camille Flammarion whose oeuvre oscillates curiously among several different poles: the solidly scientific (his enormously successful *Popular Astronomy*, first published in 1875), the non-fictional but highly speculative *The Plurality of Inhabited Worlds* (1862), in which he describes the types of alien life that might exist on other planets in our solar system and the profoundly spiritualist and *Lumen* (1872), which depicts conversations with a spirit who, travelling faster than the speed of light, encounters different alien lifeforms throughout the cosmos. Other sf tales about alien lifeforms who occupy the interstices of different dimensions include Fitz-James O'Brien's 'The Diamond Lens' (1858), in which a man experiences a doomed love affair with a microscopic woman living in a drop of water; Edwin A. Abbott's mathematical fable *Flatland* (1884), whose narrator, A. Square, lives in a two-dimensional world; and several *fin-de-siècle* sf stories by Rosny such as 'Another World' (1895), where interdimensional alien species, wholly invisible to our limited senses, coexist with humanity on Earth. Also notable is Rosny's short story 'The Xipehuz' (1887), which chronicles an encounter between a nomadic tribe in Mesopotamia and a geometric-shaped and intelligent – yet totally inscrutable – race of alien energy-beings. Many years later, Rosny would transpose this xenobiological theme to an end-of-the-world narrative format in *The Death of the Earth* (1910), where homo sapiens is finally superseded by a mineral-based alien species called the *ferromagnétaux*. Finally, Auguste Villiers de l'Isle-Adam's *Future Eve* (1886) initiated yet another – presciently postmodern – variant of 'alien-encounter' sf with his wondrous android Hadaly, a self-aware robot invented by Thomas Alva Edison as the perfect female but whose very existence raises a host of aesthetic and ontological questions about the 'artificiality of contemporary existence' (Roberts 123). Whether expressed as a utopian society on the Moon, a non-human civilisation inhabiting a distant planet or another dimension of space/time, or a synthetic lifeform created as a simulacrum of ourselves, the recurring theme of the alien in nineteenth-century sf encapsulates one of the core values of the genre: the confrontation with alterity.

As the final years of the nineteenth century approached, this developing mode of speculative/fantastic sf grew to full maturity with the 'scientific romances' of H.G. Wells. It might be argued that Wells bridged the nineteenth and twentieth centuries both literally and symbolically: although his writing career was long and prolific, the visionary novels that would inspire generations of sf writers were written during the relatively brief period of 1895 to 1914. His brand of sf differs from Verne's *romans scientifiques* in at least two fundamental ways. First, his fictions do not seek to teach science *per se* but rather to view the universe through scientific eyes. As Brian Stableford summarises it, the Wellsian scientific romance 'is a story which is built around something glimpsed through a window of possibility from which scientific discovery has drawn back the curtain' (*Scientific* 8). Second, Wells uses science as an enabling literary device to enhance the verisimilitude and deepen the emotional impact of his fantastic tales. As the author himself said, 'Hitherto [...] the fantastic element was brought in by magic [...] But by the end of last century it had become difficult to squeeze even a momentary belief out of magic any longer. It occurred to me that [...] an ingenious use of scientific patter might with advantage be substituted' (viii). In other words, 'scientific patter' served to make the fantastic more plausible, allowing readers to focus more fully on the *human* ramifications of the story: 'So soon as the hypothesis is launched, the whole interest becomes the interest of looking at human feelings and human ways, from the new angle that has been acquired' (viii).

Wells's creative genius breathed new life into the many sf topoi that he inherited from the sf tradition that preceded him, pushing them toward new cognitive and aesthetic frontiers. For example, in his first sf novel, *The Time Machine* (1895), he gave an innovative twist to the time-travel tale by offering a chilling portrayal of humanity evolving into Eloi and Morlocks by the year 802,701 and, millions of years beyond that, of the end of the human species on a dying planet Earth. *The Island of Doctor Moreau* (1896) was a powerful reworking of the Frankenstein motif that dared to satirise organised religion; Wells later described it as an 'exercise in youthful blasphemy' (ix). Another moralistic mad-scientist tale followed, *The Invisible Man* (1897), in which the physicist Griffin's discovery of the secret of invisibility transforms him into an insane megalomaniac who must be hunted down and killed. A brilliant interplanetary adaptation of the Chesney future-war novel, *The War of the Worlds* (1898) and its imagined Martian invasion took advantage of the public's heightened interest in the red planet following the publication of Percival Lowell's provocative book *Mars* (1895). Wells also dabbled in the sf subgenres of prehistoric fiction, planetary disaster fiction and lost-race fiction in 'The Grisly Folk' (1896), 'A Story of the Stone Age' (1897), 'The Star' (1897) and 'The Country of the Blind' (1904). He tried his hand at a Vernian lunar voyage in *The First Men in the Moon* (1901), using an anti-gravity substance called 'cavorite' (which prompted some disapproving scolds from Verne). And he produced several futuristic utopias such as *A Modern Utopia* (1905) and *In the Days of the Comet* (1906), as well as a number of prescient future-war fictions such as *The War in the Air* (1908) and *The World Set Free* (1914).

Wells soon turned away from what he called his early 'fantasies' (vii) toward more realistic novels and the often estranging world of international politics. But in his wake, an identifiable literary tradition had been established. Wells had taken Verne's popular formula of scientific fiction, modernised its thematic repertoire and its hermeneutic breadth, and transformed it into a powerful instrument of speculation and social critique. As the twentieth century dawned, this new type of literature had already earned its *lettres de noblesse*, but it would still be years before it would receive its permanent genre name of 'science fiction'.

Works cited

Aldiss, Brian W. *Billion Year Spree: The True History of Science Fiction*. Doubleday, 1973.
Alkon, Paul K. *Origins of Futuristic Fiction*. U of Georgia P, 1987.
Angenot, Marc. 'Science Fiction in France before Verne'. *Science Fiction Studies* 14 (1978): 58–66.
Clarke, I.F. *Voices Prophesying War: 1763–1984*. Oxford UP, 1966.
Evans, Arthur B. 'Jules Verne in English: A Bibliography of Modern Editions and Scholarly Studies'. *Verniana* 1 (2008): 9–22.
——. *Jules Verne Rediscovered: Didacticism and the Scientific Novel*. Greenwood, 1988.
Harpold, Terry. 'European Science Fiction in the Nineteenth Century'. *The Cambridge History of Science Fiction*. Ed. Gerry Canavan and Eric Carl Link. Cambridge UP, 2019. 50–68.
Luckhurst, Roger. *Science Fiction*. Polity, 2005.
Poe, Edgar Allan. 'The Unparalleled Adventure of One Hans Pfaal'. *The Complete Tales and Poems of Edgar Allan Poe*. The Modern Library, 1938. 3–41.
Roberts, Adam. *The History of Science Fiction*. Palgrave, 2006.
Stableford, Brian. 'Science Fiction Before the Genre'. *The Cambridge Companion to Science Fiction*. Ed. Edward James and Farah Mendlesohn. Cambridge UP, 2003. 15–31.
——. *Scientific Romance in Britain, 1890–1950*. Fourth Estate, 1985.
Verne, Jules, 'Edgar Poe et ses oeuvres'. *Musée des familles* 31.7 (April 1864): 193–208.
Wells, H.G. 'Preface'. *Seven Novels by H.G. Wells*. Knopf, 1934. vii–xi.
Westfahl, Gary. *Hugo Gernsback and the Century of Science Fiction*. McFarland, 2007.

6

LATIN AMERICAN SCIENCE FICTION

Rubén R. Mendoza

While Latin American sf's long, rich history goes back to at least the mid-1800s, the past three decades have been some of its most exciting. From the late 1990s into the mid-2000s, a wave of English-language bibliographical studies developed from increasing Spanish- and Portuguese-language critical work and dovetailed with explosions in Latin American sf production. As a 'period of recovery of neglected texts', this initial '"archeological" phase' (Brown and Ginway 2) reflects what Rachel Haywood Ferreira identifies as a 'desire for evidence that science fiction has been a global genre from its earliest days and that Latin America has participated in this genre using local appropriations and local adaptations' (*Emergence* 1). Numerous recovery, rediscovery and retro-labelling efforts addressed such desires with firm establishment of a Latin American sf genealogy.

These English-language bibliographic efforts were built initially on limited foundational Spanish- and Portuguese-language critical work, mostly from the 1960s, such as Pablo Capanna's *El sentido de la ciencia ficción* (1966) and André Carneiro's *Introdução ao estudio da 'science-fiction'* (1967); on mid-century 'Golden Age' work of sf magazines such as Argentina's *Más Allá* (1953–57) and Brazil's *Fantastic* (1955–60); on fan-based amateur networks and small publications throughout the second half of the twentieth century; and, on growing bodies of more recent Spanish- and Portuguese-language critical studies and fiction anthologies, including Marcial Souto's *La ciencia ficción en la argentina* (1985), Gabriel Trujillo Muñoz's *La ciencia ficción: Literatura y conocimiento* (1991) and *Los Confines: Crónica de la ciencia ficción mexicana* (1999), Horacio Moreno's *Lo fantástico: Cuentos de realidad e imaginación* (1993), José Manuel Morais's *O Atlantico tem duas margens: antologia da novíssima ficção cientifica portuguesa e brasileira* (1993), Paco Ignacio Taibo II's *Fronteras de espejos rotos* (1994), Jorge A. Sánchez's *Los universos vislumbrados: Antología de ciencia-ficción argentina* (1978, revised 1996), Gerson Lodi-Ribeiro's and Carlos Orsi Martinho's *Phantástica Brasiliana: 500 Anos de Histórias Deste e Doutros Brasis* (2000), Miguel Ángel Frenández Delgado's *Visiones periféricas – Antología de la ciencia ficción mexicana* (2001) and Roberto de Sousa Causo's *Ficção científica, fantasia e horror no Brasil 1875–1950* (2003). Many English-language efforts, in fact, had origins in directly translated recovery projects with similar genealogical aims. Scholars such as Yolanda Molina-Gavilán and Andrea L. Bell were uniquely positioned to work across language and theoretical

DOI: 10.4324/9781003140269-8

divides (e.g., sf studies, cultural studies, postcolonial studies and Latin American critical studies). Along with others similarly positioned, they laid important Spanish-language recovery groundwork while translating much of this same work themselves in germinal texts, including their *Cosmos Latinos: An Anthology of Sf from Latin America and Spain* (2003) and, collaborating with others, 'A Chronology of Latin American Sf, 1775–2005', whose introductory materials reflect prior work in Spanish by the editors/authors. Initially published in the Spanish *Chasqui* in 2000, it was translated and expanded for *Science Fiction Studies* in 2007 by the original authors (along with M. Elizabeth Ginway).

The significance of this translational, transnational recovery work cannot be overstated. 'Chronology' is an exhaustive account with more than a thousand primary and secondary sources. Reaching back to Mexican friar Manuel Antonio de Rivas's 'Sizigias y cuadraturas lunares…' (1775), the chronology makes clear that Latin American sf has been produced more widely, with greater diversity, and for much longer than previously recognised by most sf theorists and audiences in the North. This includes work from throughout Latin America, not just powerhouse sf producers Mexico, Argentina, Brazil and, to some extent, Cuba, which typically garner the most attention and recognition, leading to distorted exclusions of other countries' sf. *Cosmos Latinos* demonstrates these same points as well through nationally diverse selections of fiction from the mid-nineteenth to the early twenty-first centuries. Along with its introduction and substantial selected bibliographies, *Cosmos Latinos* thus provided English-language readers an unprecedented demonstration of Latin American sf through exposure to key works and authors. This includes Juan Nepomuceno Adorno's excerpted 'The Distant Future' ('El remoto porvenir') from his techno-utopian *Harmony of the Universe, or Principles of Physico-Harmonic Geometry* (*Armonía del universe: Sobre les principios de la armonía física y matemática*; Mexico 1862); Ernesto Silva Román's cataclysmic account of a rogue planet in 'The Death Star' ('El astro de la Muerte'; Chile 1929); Juan José Arreola's satirical 'Baby H.P.' (Mexico 1952), about harvesting energy from babies; Ángel Arango's darkly humorous account of alien contact in 'The Cosmonaut' ('El cosmonauta'; Cuba 1964); sf critic and author Pablo Capanna's critique of mechanised corporate culture, 'Acronia' (Argentina 1966); Magdalena Mouján Otaño's examination of myth, nationalism and identity through time-travel in 'Gu Tai Gutarrak (We and Our Own)' ('Gu ta gutarrak (nostros y los nuestros)'; Argentina 1968); Angelica Gorodischer's 'The Violet's Embryos' ('Los embriones del violeta'; Argentina 1973), a literarily complex exploration of gender and sexuality; 'Brain Transplant' ('Transplante do cérebro'; Brazil 1978) by André Carneiro, another key sf critic and author, whose story focuses on sensory perception, ideology and understandings of reality; 'The Annunciation' ('Los Anunciación'; Cuba 1983), a hybrid blending of sf, erotica and Biblical scripture by one of Cuba's most celebrated sf authors, Diana Chaviano; Guillermo Lavín's NAFTA-era critique of labour exploitation, the US/Mexico border and cyborgian technologies, in 'Reaching the Shore' ('Llegar a la orilla'; Mexico 1994); and Pablo Castro's consideration of authoritarianism and the lingering traumatisation of post-dictatorship Chile through cyberpunk tropes and video games in 'Exerion' ('Exerión'; Chile 2000). Such examples apply local socio-political and historical contexts to typical sf themes and tropes, including alien contact, robots, cyborgs, utopia, dystopia and alternate history. Through them, Bell and Molina-Gavilán map a geo-historical framework that exemplifies three areas they argue thematically distinguish Latin American from anglophone sf: 'Latin American and Spanish sf's generally "soft" nature and social sciences orientation; its examination of Christian symbols and motifs; and its uses of humor' (14).

These recovery period texts were instrumental in providing the kind of 'much-needed correction to our vision' (*Emergence* 7) of sf production and theory that Haywood Ferreira identifies in the context of the North's more general 'myopia in our perception of the world and its literatures'

(*Emergence* 6). Her points echo Bell and Molina-Gavilán's assessment of the misperceptions of Latin America's relationship to technology and science and how they connect to lack of awareness of Latin American sf: 'Latin American [...] countries are often perceived as being mostly consumers, if not victims, of technology', which dovetails with the 'common and prejudicial corollary...that SF "speaks English" and can only be weakly imitated in other languages' (1). Similar works produced during this initial recovery phase also include editor Darrell B. Lockhart's *Latin American Sf Writers: An A-to-Z Guide* (2004), Ginway's *Brazilian Science Fiction: Cultural Myths and Nationhood in the Land of the Future* (2004) and Haywood Ferreira's historical tracing in 'Back to the Future: The Expanding Field of Latin-American Science Fiction' (2008), which includes an account of this recovery process itself.

Equally important to bibliographical recovery was development of appropriate theoretical lenses. In 2004, Lockhart contended that 'to date there have been only scant critical analyses of this literature' and that the 'overwhelming amount of new information on [Latin American] SF writing has thus far served the useful purpose of identifying authors and texts and tracing the historical development of the genre in Latin America' (xv); this led him to conclude that 'the time has come to advance the study of Latin American SF to a more theoretical level [...] and [...] develop a deeper critical understanding of the phenomenon of SF writing in its uniquely Latin American configurations' (xv–xvi). Similarly, eight years later, Brown and Ginway identify a prevailing critical 'tendency to document rather analyze' (2) and argue that 'it is time to turn from historicizing to theorizing' (7). However, these earlier recovery works must be recognised for more than their historicising and bibliographic dimensions. Reflecting a Latin American critical approach, both 'Chronology' and *Cosmos Latinos* used introductory materials to systematise thematic orientations around continental/hemispheric frameworks counterweighted with nation- and region-centred geographical structuring. This national/regional/continental approach is intertwined with historical timelines produced through the painstaking labour of rediscovery, retro-labelling and republication of often obscure and 'lost' texts. The result is a multi-layered bibliographic-theoretical schematic reflective of the unique complexities characteristic of the region(s) and work.

This intertwining of history, geography and thematics, is not just an effective method of bibliographically organising materials. It does help distinguish Latin American from Anglophone sf production while challenging and avoiding continental generalisations through nation- and region-centred specificity. In so doing, it certainly works to establish corrective legitimacy of the field 'as part of a more global science-fiction continuum' (Haywood Ferreira *Emergence* 13). More than this, however, this framing outlines specific theoretical, historical and geopolitical concerns pertinent to the distinctive ways that authors in specific regions of Latin America have engaged sf throughout particular historical periods, thus establishing essential frameworks for subsequent critical studies.

These works' theoretical dimensions can be seen, for example, in the 'Themes of Theory' section of the introduction to *Cosmos Latinos*, in which Bell and Molina focus attention on Latin American sf's 'emphasis on the sociopolitical' (14) – as demonstrated, for example, in the 'social orientations' of 'Marxism, feminism, nationalism, and ecology' (15) in narratives such as Cuban Agustín de Rojas's *The Year 200* (*El año 200*; 1990, trans. 2016). They can also be seen in Haywood Ferreira's contextualisation of significant early texts, including Fósforo-Cerillos' 'México en el año 1970' (1844), Joaquin Felício dos Santos' *Páginas da história do Brasil escrita no anno de 2000* (1868–72) and Argentine Eduardo Ladislao Holmberg's *Viaje maravilloso del Señor Nic-Nac* (1875–76). As she notes, these works exemplify nineteenth century Latin American sf that emerged 'during periods of political change or unrest [...] but when, at the same time, processes of national consolidation, economic development, and/or advances in science also made for optimism regarding the future' ('Back' 355). Similarly, but with explicit focus on developing critical approaches, Ginway's 'A Working Model for Analyzing Third World Science Fiction: The Case of Brazil' (2005) – partly a condensation of her *Brazilian Science Fiction* – outlines effective models for 'writing about science fiction of the Third World' (467). Ginway addresses the 'lack of a cogent critical model or approach' for assessing 'science fiction of the Third World', which 'requires critical tools different from those typically applied to European and Anglo-American sf, because the shift in geographical and cultural contexts can force a reinterpretation of the genre's basic premises' (467). Ginway develops her methodology from 'perspectives of cultural myths, ecofeminist studies, postcolonial studies, and theories of globalization', and 'from the Latin American critical tradition' (467), which she applies to numerous examples of Brazilian sf and sf subgenres including hard sf, cyberpunk, dystopian fiction, alternate history and robot and alien stories. Examples include Guido Wilmar Sassi's 'Estranha simbiose' (1963); Levy Meneze's 'Terra Prometida' (1965) and 'Ukk' (1965); the 1970s dystopian work of Murilo Rubião and José J. Veiga; Andre Carneiro's utopian/dystopian *Piscina livre* (1980); Jorge Luiz Calife's hard sf 'A morte do cometa' (1985); Braulio Tavares's cyberpunk 'Jogo rápido' (1989); José J. Veiga's alternate history *A casca da serpente* (1989); Cid Fernandez' robot-cyborg 'Julgamentos' (1993); and Adriana Simon's 'Dainara' (2002), which explores women's sexuality through human–alien symbiosis. In developing her methodology, Ginway traces a history of Brazilian sf that simultaneously outlines and applies interdisciplinary critical models essential for appropriately approaching Brazilian and Latin American sf, and sf from the broader Global South.

This phase of recovery work and establishment of critical frameworks was vital in correcting lack of awareness and misperceptions among English-language audiences and critics. Simultaneously, important corrective groundwork was laid for understanding internal reasons for sf's lack of attention and awareness within Latin America itself. Lockhart argues that Latin American sf's 'position as a marginal discourse' reflects how 'it has been eclipsed by the major trends in Latin American literature' (xi), such as magical realism and the fantastic more generally. However, the generic evolutionary development of these forms is more complicated than simply one eclipsing another. It involves a history of mislabelling that Haywood Ferreira examines, for example, as well as related misunderstandings of how Latin American authors have engaged with sf. Analysing this complex phenomenon, Brown and Ginway cite historical perceptions by Latin Americans of sf as 'foreign or inauthentic' (1), a point Roberto de Sousa Causo echoes via Roberto Schwarz' observation that post-WWII, sf 'is associated with *American modernization*, which is frequently denounced as an imperialist tool' (148 italics in the original). Similarly, Haywood Ferreira notes how even recent Latin American sf writers 'often draw charges of being a party to cultural imperialism and of failing to reflect local realities' (*Emergence* 3). She argues that this is partly a consequence of how Latin American literatures of the fantastic evolved – particularly in Argentina – alongside both sf and the literary movement of Spanish American Modernismo (6, 8–10). Latin American authors who emerged during and immediately after Modernismo (c.1890–1920), such as Leopoldo Lugones, Macedonio Fernandez, Jorge Luis Borges, Adolfo Bioy Casares and Silvina Ocampo, engaged sf to varying degrees as one generic tool among many. Examples such as Lugones's 'An Inexplicable Phenomenon' ('Un fenómeno inexplicable'), 'Psychon' ('El Psychon') and 'Yzur' (all 1906, trans. 2001), Fernandez' 'The Squash that Became the Cosmos' ('El zapallo que se hizo cosmos') and 'The Surgery of Psychic Removal' ('Cirugía psíquica de extirpación'; both 1961, trans. 1984), Bioy Casares's *The Invention of Morel* (*La invención de Morel*; 1940, trans. 2003) and Ocampo's 'The Waves' ('Las ondas'; 1959, trans. 2016), demonstrate experimental utilisations of sf specifically and genre more generally. In these and similar examples, fluid, hybridic engagements with sf exemplify John Rieder's argument that sf 'is not a set of texts, but rather a way of using texts and of drawing relationships among them' ('On' 191). These and similar works indicate that their authors were self-reflexively working through precisely such generic rethinking – about sf and other genres – in a rich literary milieu of 'intersubjective, discursive constructs, full of contradictions and constantly in flux' (Vint and Bould 51).

However, as Haywood Ferreira, Causo and Brown and Ginway suggest, the complexity of this evolutionary process involved more than aesthetics. In addition to market impacts on Latin American literary production and reception (Haywood Ferreira *Emergence* 3, 9), it also involved unique political dimensions. These developments occurred in the midst of intertwined facets and tensions of mid- to late-nineteenth and early-twentieth century postcolonial nation-building on one hand, and neo-imperialist/neocolonial industrialisation and modernisation on another. Even as Latin American societies worked to sustain the postcolonial formation of nations and national-cultural identities that had begun largely around the 1820s, the US empire's mid-nineteenth century expansion into Latin America significantly complicated these processes. Mapping quite precisely to the same period (c.1850–1920) that Haywood Ferreira designates the 'first wave' of Latin American sf (*Emergence* 11–12), US expansionism in Latin America began with invasion and colonisation of Mexico's northern half in 1846–8, which actually commenced only a few years after Mexico's 1821 independence. Later, it included US neo-colonial war and occupation in Cuba and Puerto Rico through the Spanish–American War (1898). Thus, local development of Latin American sf took place in complex relation to general aesthetic development, including active engagement with literature from outside Latin America (as evinced, for example, in the outsize influence of Edgar Allan Poe's and Mary Shelley's Gothic aesthetics, alongside European writers of the fantastic such as Camille Flammarion and Jules Verne). But at the same time, such development unfolded within complicated regional histories of prior and lingering European colonial influence and emergent neo-imperialist influence. Latin American authors developed their own postcolonial identities and local literary modes, often contributing directly to nation-building projects through writing and direct involvement in politics, even as 'political independence from European colonial powers did not completely divorce Latin Americans, especially Latin American elites, from their European roots' (Haywood Ferreira *Emergence* 6).

Replacement of European colonial power with US neo-colonial power thus had significant impacts on cultural development – with particular ramifications for development of sf in Latin America (and in the North as well; see Rieder *Colonialism*). This overlap of imperialisms old and new, postcoloniality, neo-colonialism, industrialisation and modernisation reflected a convoluted matrix of tensions around national identity, culture and aesthetic production. Given its intimate relation to industrialisation, colonialism, technoscientific discourse and ideologies of progress and modernisation, sf was therefore one of the key areas of aesthetic production in which these tensions played out (Haywood Ferreira *Emergence* 3). As Haywood Ferreira notes of mid-nineteenth century texts,

> The sociocultural, political, and literary influences of Europe and the United States are central to the form and content of these works. All of the authors portray the estranged, utopian versions of their own nations as strong, politically independent, culturally rich, and globally important, yet each text betrays in some way the legacy of the deeply ingrained culture of dependency.
>
> (Emergence 17)

The dynamics of these tensions and their aesthetic results are well-demonstrated in Haywood Ferreira's study of how such nineteenth century texts 'employ strategies of cognitive estrangement in order to comment upon modernisation, national identity, and political and sociocultural issues of the day' (*Emergence* 12). Similarly, her focus on 'the frequent attempts to amend, challenge, or reverse the tenets of Darwin's theory of evolution by proponents of Lamarckian evolution and Spencerian Social Darwinism' (*Emergence* 13) traces these tensions through analysis of complex engagements with Western scientific discourse in works such as Holmberg's *Two Factions Struggle for Life: A Scientific Fantasy* (*Dos partidos en lucha: Fantastica científica*; Argentina 1875) and Augusto Emilio Zaluar's *Doctor Benignus* (*O Doutor Benignus*; Brazil 1875), as well as Lugones's sf meditation on devolution in 'Yzur' (1906).

Examination of Latin American sf beyond Haywood Ferreira's focus on this particularly significant period of nineteenth century emergence reveals similar tensions in ongoing neo-imperialist influence into and throughout the twentieth century. A key period for development of sf in Latin America, for example, was the 'Golden Age' of the 1950s and 1960s, which reflected aesthetic responses not just to the explosion of Northern sf production from the 1930s onward, but to sociopolitical dimensions of the atomic- and space-age Cold War era. Similarly, Latin American sf during the 1970s and 1980s often reflected responses to the local violence of civil wars and dictatorships, itself largely a consequence of US neoliberal neocolonialism developing and expanding from the late 1960s and into the early 1990s once neoliberal regimes had been installed, usually violently, in countries such as Chile and Argentina. The trauma of the transition to neoliberalism, and of subsequent economic disparities under neoliberal policies, are reflected in the ongoing resurgence of sf that began in the 1990s. This is exemplified in stories such as Castro's 'Exerion', Brazilian Pedro Aguilera's dystopian television series *3%* (Netflix 2016), and Samanta Schweblin's *Fever Dream* (*Distancia de rescate*; Argentina 2014, trans. 2017) and Agustina Bazterrica's *Tender is the Flesh* (*Cadáver exquisite*; Argentina 2017, trans. 2020), both of which presciently use pandemics to construct dystopian worlds.

From its earliest iterations, then, Latin American sf has indeed involved critical-aesthetic engagement with geopolitical developments. It would appear to have thus earned its reputation of an 'emphasis on the sociopolitical', particularly '[i]n times of political repression' when, as Bell and Molina-Gavilán argue, it has 'proven to be an excellent tool to foreground a particular ideological position or to disguise social criticism from government censors' (14) or to 'subvert the status quo' (15). However, while such assessments and their related points about a 'soft' sciences orientation in Latin American sf have become commonplace, they must be re-examined and tempered.

This is not because these points are necessarily untrue, but because they typically are framed through a problematic contrast to Northern anglophone sf's supposed 'hard' science orientation and, most importantly, its purported relative lack of 'a particular discipline, position, or movement used as a main ideological ingredient' (Bell and Molina-Gavilán 15). The contrast here positions Latin American sf as more 'political' than the relatively 'apolitical' sf from the North, which then maps onto 'soft' and 'hard' science orientations. But this framework replicates a very old imperialist–colonialist structure – one which has functioned to normalise imperialist–colonial dominance through disavowal of the ideologies and 'soft' social and psychological sciences driving centuries of imperialism and colonialism and their discourses of progress and modernisation. Rieder's *Colonialism and the Emergence of Science Fiction* demonstrates how sf has not only intimately imbricated with imperialist–colonialist projects, but how its recourse to a veneer of 'hard' technoscientific discourse has often paralleled and fed into the use of 'science' in such projects of 'civilising' and 'modernising' domination, in contrast to the 'backward', 'irrational' and, most importantly, 'unscientific' victims of those projects. Such discourses have mapped onto long-standing misperceptions of Latin American sf as derivative, behind the curve of general sf development, and somehow compromised by its general 'political' and 'non-scientific' orientations.

To put it another way: Latin American sf is no more or less 'political' than Northern sf. Nor is it any more or less 'scientific'. The political distinction is, perhaps, more about the implicit maintenance and normalisation of the imperial–colonial status quo versus the explicit subversion of it. And the 'scientific' distinction is, perhaps, more about different – but equally valid – ways of understanding and knowing in relation to the material world. This includes, for example, what Jessica Langer points to as 'Indigenous scientific literacies', which involve 'practices used by indigenous native peoples to manipulate the natural environment [...] to improve existence in areas including medicine, agriculture, and sustainability. The term stands in contrast to more invasive (and potentially destructive) western scientific method' (Grace L. Dillon qtd in Langer 130). As Joanna Page notes, this 'suggest[s] a different way of thinking about science fiction in a postcolonial context [...] that *includes* both a scientific and spiritual worldview' (130 italics in original).

This is not to suggest that incorporation of spiritist elements into sf stories such as Leopoldo Lugones's should be read as examples of Indigenous scientific literacies (among other things, Lugones's embrace of fascism would preclude such an argument). What it does point to, however, is the need to read Latin American sf's engagement with science – indeed, Latin America's engagement with sf – with appropriate lenses that do not reproduce imperialist–colonialist hierarchies through disavowal of anglophone sf's *very* political (but normalised and thus invisible) mobilisation of 'particular discipline[s], position[s], or movement[s] used as [...] main ideological ingredient[s]' (Bell and Molina-Gavilán 15). Such ingredients include (fantastical) fictions of superiority constructed through discourses of Western technoscience, progress and modernisation. In this light, the generic fluidity with which Latin American authors have engaged sf takes on additional complexity involving the expression and development of different ways of knowing and understanding that reflect distinct evolving positions within imperial–colonial power differential matrices.

This is why critical works that incorporate a postcolonial approach in their methodology, alongside Latin American critical studies, are essential in mapping out the current and next phases of critical studies in Latin American sf. Even Haywood Ferreira's study, which does not explicitly apply a postcolonial lens, nevertheless reflects underlying postcolonialist approaches. This is apparent in her description of her study's period of c.1850–1920 as one that does not just encompass 'the emergence of early Latin American science-fictional texts in the industrial era', but also reflects 'approximately the first hundred years after the abolition of colonial rule in each nation' (*Emergence* 12). Here, Haywood Ferreira demonstrates in passing an important point. Scholars have rightly focused much attention on recent explosions in postcolonial sf, exemplified by Nalo Hopkinson and Uppinder Mehan's groundbreaking anthology *So Long Been Dreaming: Postcolonial Science Fiction and Fantasy* (2004), but such analysis is generally framed within the field's standardised structuring around twentieth century postcoloniality. However, as Haywood Ferreira suggests, this reflects only *one* particular wave of postcoloniality, occluding such precedents as the one that swept Latin America in the nineteenth century.

It should therefore be apparent why postcolonial lenses are essential for Latin American sf. Examples of critical works that employ postcolonial analysis include Ginway's studies of Brazilian sf and Miguel López-Lozano's *Utopian Dreams, Apocalyptic Nightmares: Globalization in Recent Mexican and Chicano Narrative* (2008), which includes examination of Carmen Bullosa's depiction of failed utopia in *Cielos de la tierra* (1997) and Homero Aridjis' dystopian depictions of 2027 Mexico City in *La leyenda de los soles* (1993) and *¿En quién piensas cuando hace el amor?* (1995). More recently, Brown and Ginway's *Latin American Science Fiction: Theory and Practice* (2012) includes relevant critical essays on a wide array of Latin American sf works. Furthermore, while many recent works on postcolonial sf include little if any direct analysis of sf from Latin America, their theoretical frameworks nevertheless provide methodological strategies applicable for Latin American sf, such as Jessica Langer's *Postcolonialism and Science Fiction* (2011); Jason W. Ellis and Swaralipi Nandi's *The Postnational Fantasy: Essays on Postcolonialism, Cosmopolitics and Science Fiction* (2011), which includes Stacy Schmitt Rusnak's analysis of Mexican national identity in *Children of Men* (Cuarón 2006); and Ericka Hoagland and Reema Sarwal's *Science Fiction, Imperialism and the Third World: Essays on Postcolonial Literature and Film* (2010), which includes Juan Ignacio Muñoz Zapata's examination of Mexican author Gerardo Horacio Porcayo's critical dystopian cyberpunk *La Primera Calle de la Soledad* (1993). Matthew David Goodwin's doctoral dissertation, *The Fusion of Migration and Science Fiction in Mexico, Puerto Rico and the United States* (2013), forwards innovative postcolonial analysis of sf treatments of migration through 'space exploration, space aliens and alien invasions, dystopian states, and virtual reality' (24), with analysis of works such as Gabriel Trujillo Muñoz' 'Cajunia' (Mexico 1994), Puerto Rican ADÁL's *Out of Focus Nuyoricans* (2004) and *Coconauts in Space* (2004), Bef's 'Bajo un Cielo Ajeno' (Mexico 2008) and Peruvian-American filmmaker Alex Rivera's *Sleep Dealer* (2008). Postcolonialist concerns underly Page's understanding of how 'composing science fiction from the postcolonial periphery often brings an ironic and parodic perspective to bear on familiar stories of alien invasion and conquest' (6). This informs her new-materialist reading of metafictional reflexivity and with 'a critique of modernity from a postcolonial perspective' (11) in the Argentine sf films *La sonámbula* (Spiner 1998), *Condor Crux, la leyenda del futuro* (Buscarini, Glecer and Holcer 2000), *Estrellas* (León and Martinez 2007) and *La antena* (Sapir 2007).

Drawing on postcolonial studies, sf studies and Latin American critical studies to analyse Latin American sf enriches and expands all of these fields. More than this, such an approach helps develop understanding of how Latin American sf fits within what Walter Mignolo theorises as *The Idea of Latin America* (2005). Along the lines of Edward Said's *Orientalism* (1978) as well as Edmundo O'Gorman's *The Invention of America: An Inquiry into the Historical Nature of the New World and the Meaning of its History* (1958, trans. 1961) and Enrique Dussel's *The Invention of the Americas: Eclipse of the 'Other' and the Myth of Modernity* (1998), Mignolo centres Indigenous epistemologies in analysing the construction of Latin America, through discourses of modernity and coloniality, as a kind of fictionalising projective invention. This invention includes the European utopian fantasy of 'alien' contact and domination in the perceived *terra nullius* which drove Spanish and subsequent European colonialism – and the consequent dystopian experiences of Indigenous Americans. Such a reading suggests, perhaps, that the first 'work' of sf in Latin America is, in some ways, Latin America itself. Rather than being behind the sf curve, then, perhaps Latin American sf has always been – for better and worse – well ahead of it.

Works cited

Bell, Andrea L. and Yolanda Molina-Gavilán. 'Introduction: Science Fiction in Latin America and Spain'. *Cosmos Latinos: An Anthology of Science Fiction from Latin America and Spain*. Ed. Andrea L. Bell and Yolanda Molina-Gavilán, Wesleyan UP, 2003. 1–19.

Brown, Andrew J. and Elizabeth M. Ginway. 'Introduction'. *Latin American Science Fiction: Theory and Practice*. Ed. J. Andrew Brown and M. Elizabeth Ginway. Palgrave Macmillan, 2012. 1–15.
Causo, Roberto de Sousa. 'Encountering International Science Fiction through a Latin American Lens'. *Reading Science Fiction*. Ed. James Gunn, Marleen S. Barr and Matthew Candelaria. Palgrave Macmillan, 2009. 142–54.
Ginway, Elizabeth M. 'A Working Model for Analyzing Third World Science Fiction: The Case of Brazil'. *Science Fiction Studies* 97 (2005): 467–94.
Goodwin, Matthew David. *The Fusion of Migration and Science Fiction in Mexico, Puerto Rico and the United States*. ProQuest Dissertations Publishing, 2013.
Haywood Ferreira, Rachel. 'Back to the Future: The Expanding Field of Latin-American Science Fiction'. *Hispania* 91.2 (2008): 352–62.
——. *The Emergence of Latin American Science Fiction*. Wesleyan UP, 2011.
Langer, Jessica. *Postcolonialism and Science Fiction*. Palgrave Macmillan, 2011.
Lockhart, Darrell B. *Latin American Science Fiction Writers an A-to-Z Guide*. Greenwood, 2004.
Molina-Gavilán, Yolanda. Andrea Bell, Miguel Fernández-Delgado, M. Elizabeth Ginway, Luis Pestarini and Juan Carlos Toledano Redondo. 'A Chronology of Latin-American Science Fiction, 1775–2005'. *Science Fiction Studies* 103 (2007): 369–431.
Page, Joanna. *Science Fiction in Argentina: Technologies of the Text in a Material Multiverse*. U of Michigan P, 2016.
Rieder, John. *Colonialism and the Emergence of Science Fiction*. Wesleyan UP, 2008.
——. 'On Defining SF, or Not: Genre Theory, SF, and History'. *Science Fiction Studies* 111 (2010): 191–209.
Vint, Sherryl and Mark Bould. 'There Is No Such Thing As Science Fiction'. *Reading Science Fiction*. Ed. James Gunn, Marleen S. Barr and Matthew Candelaria. Palgrave Macmillan, 2009. 43–51.

7

RUSSIAN-LANGUAGE SCIENCE FICTION

Brittany R. Roberts

In Russia, literature has long served as a critical vehicle for discussing social and scientific developments (Csicsery-Ronay, Jr 340; Howell 'Introduction' 7; Marsh 297, 309; Reese 161; Shneidman 209; Pukallus 260). With its 'relative freedom of allegory and displacement' (Maguire and Rogatchevski 123), sf has been especially important. This chapter covers eighteenth- to twenty-first-century Russian-language sf. For clarity, parenthetical remarks indicating city of birth are provided for authors born outside present-day Russia. Cyrillic is transliterated according to Library of Congress guidelines, but without diacritics.

Tsarist-era sf: 1784–1917

The roots of Russian sf lie in tsarist-era utopian literature (Britikov 23). These utopias were often conservative (Stites 24), like Mikhail Shcherbatov's *Voyage to the Land of Ofir* (*Puteshestvie v zemliu Ofirskuiu*; 1784, published 1807), *Plausible Fables: Wandering the World in the Twenty-Ninth Century* (*Pravdopodobnye nebylitsy, ili Stranstvovanie po svetu v dvadtsat' deviatom veke*; 1824) by Thaddeus Bulgarin (born in Minsk, present-day Belarus) and Vladimir Odoevskii's *Year 4338* (*4338-i god*; 1840, published 1921). The most influential tsarist-era utopia is Nikolai Chernyshevskii's *What Is to Be Done?* (*Chto delat'?*; 1863, published 1905), which envisions a socialist society founded on women's liberation and the 'rational' (Levitsky 13) division of labour. Fedor Dostoevskii's *Notes from Underground* (*Zapiski iz podpol'ia*; 1864) implicitly critiqued its ideas while Vladimir Lenin praised it as his 'favorite book as a young man' (Stites 42). Some consider it Soviet sf's predecessor (Brandis 7).

The scientific revolution of the 1890s gave rise to another wave of sf (Britikov 25; McGuire *Red* 6 and 'Russian' 427). Advances in science and technology signalled the arrival of modernity in Russia (Siddiqi 19, 367; Krementsov *Martian* 8). Translations of Jules Verne and H.G. Wells became popular (Stites 30), and with them came enthusiasm for stories of 'scientific fantasy' (*nauchnaia fantastika*), which became a premier participant in shaping 'a uniquely Russian vision of modernity' (Banerjee *We* 6).

Some writers embraced scientific advances, such as Konstantin Tsiolkovskii, whose 'On the Moon' ('Na lune'; 1893), *Dreams of Earth and Sky* (*Grezy o zemle i o nebe*; 1897) and 'Outside the Earth' ('Vne zemli'; 1916) depict visions of spaceflight and human-machine co-evolution.

 DOI: 10.4324/9781003140269-9

Others expressed concerns, as in the depictions of destructive experiments in Aleksandr Kuprin's 'Liquid Sun' ('Zhidkoe solntse'; 1913) and devolution in Vladislav Uminskii's *The Unknowable World: Mars and Its Inhabitants* (*V mire nevedomogo: Mars i ego zhiteli*; 1896), Valerii Briusov's 'Republic of the Southern Cross' ('Respublika Iuzhnogo Kresta'; 1905) and Nikolai Fedorov's *An Evening in the Year 2217* (*Vecher v 2217 godu*; 1906).

Some saw the scientific revolution and the 1905 political revolution, which weakened the tsar, as necessary. Aleksandr Bogdanov's *Red Star* (*Krasnaia zvezda*; 1908) and *Engineer Menni* (*Inzhener Menni*; 1912) draw upon scientific developments to present a Martian communist utopia united by blood transfusion. Along with Chernyshevskii, Bogdanov is often considered the founder of Soviet sf (Stites 252).

Early Soviet sf: 1918–27

The 1917 revolution introduced a ferment of utopian activity (Stites 172). Although the immediate post-revolutionary period saw sf's disappearance as the USSR grappled with war (Glad *Extrapolations* 186), it re-emerged in the 1920s (Revich 11), marking the beginning of what would become a 'boom/bust cycle' in Soviet sf (Glad 'Brave' 72).

Russian sf exhibited various responses to post-revolutionary culture, including a revival of anti-utopias (Britikov 94). The best-known is Evgenii Zamiatin's *We* (*My*; 1922, published abroad 1924), a response to Bogdanov that critiques the Proletkult movement and the contemporary enthusiasm for Taylorism (Banerjee *We* 87–8; Laursen 13–4; Suvin 12–3). Zamiatin's novel was not published in Russia until 1989, but it influenced dystopias abroad, including George Orwell's *Nineteen Eighty-four* (1949) (Banerjee 'Introduction' xiii).

Others depicted utopias. Some were anti-Bolshevik, such as *The Journey of My Brother Aleksei to the Land of Peasant Utopia* (*Puteshestvie moego brata Alekseia v stranu krest'ianskoi utopii*; 1920) by Ivan Kremnev (pen name of Aleksandr Chaianov). Others were pro-Bolshevik, such as Andrei Platonov's trilogy 'Descendants of the Sun' ('Potomki solntsa'; 1922), 'The Lunar Bomb' ('Lunnaia bomba'; 1926) and 'The Ethereal Path' ('Efirnyi trakt'; 1926–7), which depicts the taming of nature in accordance with Marxist-Leninist ideals. However, Platonov's ambiguous language suggests some reticence (Clowes 14; Howell 'Introduction' 19; Levitsky 538), unlike Iakov Okunev's and Vadim Nikol'skii's pro-communist utopias, *The Coming World* (*Griadushchii mir*; 1923) and *In a Thousand Years* (*Cherez tysiachu let*; 1927), respectively.

More common was the sf that grew out of popular adventure novels. These tales flourished in periodicals like *World of Adventures* (*Mir prikliuchenii*), *Around the World* (*Vokrug sveta*), *Worldwide Pathfinder* (*Vsemirnyi sledopyt*) and *Knowledge Is Power* (*Znanie – Sila*) (Britikov 135–6; Schwartz 229). Coinciding with the contemporary 'space fad', these were sometimes set in space, such as Aleksei Tolstoi's pro-revolution Martian tale *Aelita* (1923), which also includes mystical resonances with Cosmism (Siddiqi 74, 99). Iakov Protazanov's 1924 adaptation of *Aelita*, one of the earliest sf feature films, premiered to monumental hype (Christie 81–2; Leyda 186; Siddiqi 100–2) but was criticised on ideological grounds, despite its popularity (Youngblood 109–10).

'Red detective' and 'catastrophe' tales also reflect revolutionary zeal. In these sub-genres, socialism confronts capitalist scientists and saboteurs, leading to global revolutions (Nudelman 40–2; Revich 60–1). The sub-genres are exemplified by Marietta Shaginian's *Mess-Mend* (1924), adapted as the three-part movie serial *Miss Mend* (Boris Barnet and Fedor Otsep 1926), in which proletariats struggle against fascists, and Aleksei Tolstoi's *Engineer Garin's Death Ray* (*Giperboloid inzhenera Garina*; 1925), adapted as feature-length film *Engineer Garin's Death*

Ray (*Giperboloid inzhenera Garina*; Gintsburg 1965) and four-part television film *The Collapse of Engineer Garin* (*Krakh inzhenera Garina*; Kvinikhidze 1973), in which an engineer attempts to seize global power, anticipating the villainous engineers that populate later Soviet literature (Marsh 68; Maguire 248, 255, 265). Other examples include *Trust, D.E.* (*Trest, D.E.*; 1923) by Il'ia Ehrenburg (born in Kyiv, present-day Ukraine), Vsevelod Ivanov and Viktor Shklovskii's *Mustard Gas* (*Iprit*; 1925), Vladimir Orlovskii's 'Revolt of the Atoms' ('Bunt atomov'; 1927) and the film *The Death Ray* (*Luch smert'*; Kuleshov 1925).

Other 1920s works blend sf with fantasy. Aleksander Grin set his sf-fantasy tales, such as 'Scarlet Sails' ('Alye parusa'; 1923), in a fictional land where new and old technologies coexist with magic. The works of Sigizmund Krzhizhanovskii (born in Kyiv, present-day Ukraine) feature a blend of sf, fantastic realism and the grotesque, as in his novella *Memories of the Future* (*Vospominaniia o budushchem*; 1929, published 1989). The fusion of sf and fantasy popular in pre-revolutionary literature also appeared in the works of Vladimir Obruchev, whose novels *Plutonia* (1924) and *Sannikov-Land* (*Zemlia Sannikova*; 1926), adapted as *Zemlia Sannikova* (Mkrtchian, born in Yerevan, present-day Republic of Armenia, and Popov, born in Poltava Oblast, present-day Ukraine, 1973), depict exciting expeditions, hollow earths and prehistoric beings.

Recent scientific advances also fuelled sf as writers critiqued the confluence of science and Soviet power (Krementsov *Stalinist* 17–23, *Revolutionary* 175–6, 192). In *The Fatal Eggs* (*Rokovye iaitsa*; 1925) and *Heart of a Dog* (*Sobach'e serdtse*; 1925, published 1989), Mikhail Bulgakov (born in Kyiv, present-day Ukraine) satirises the Bolsheviks's misuse of science (Gomel 'Gods' 373; Howell 'Eugenics' 200; Krementsov *Revolutionary* 34, 176). Biological transformation is also a recurrent theme for Aleksandr Beliaev, whom several critics name the true founder of Soviet sf (Gakov xiii; Revich 117). Beliaev's fiction mixes biological themes and adventure, as in his best-known works 'Professor Dowell's Head' ('Golova professora Douelia'; story published 1925, novelised 1937) and *Amphibian Man* (*Chelovek-amfibiia*; 1928), adapted as *Professor Dowell's Testament* (*Zaveshchaniye professora Douelya*; Menaker 1984) and *Amphibian Man* (*Chelovek-amfibiia*; Chebotarev and Kazanskii 1961), respectively.

Stalinist-era Soviet sf: 1928–55

During Iosif Stalin's first Five-Year Plan (1928–33), almost no sf appeared (Glad *Extrapolations* 193; Stites 235; Suvin 19). Beliaev released *War in the Air* (*Bor'ba v efire*; 1928), and Ian Larri (born in Riga, present-day Latvia) released *The Land of the Happy* (*Strana schastlivykh*; 1931), the last utopia until 1957. By 1932, most sf publishers had been shuttered or nationalised, few foreign translations appeared and censors heavily scrutinised new publications (Griffiths 45–6; Nudelman 48; Schwartz 236).

Sf re-emerged in the mid-1930s. In line with Socialist Realism, mandated in 1934, authors focused on safe topics, such as conflicts between socialism and capitalism and 'near-future' extrapolations (Britikov 170; Gomel 'Gods' 361; Revich 141, 237; Howell 'Introduction' 13; Krementsov *Revolutionary* 197). Ideological depictions of science became common (Schwartz 241; Suvin 18), as reflected in 'Generator of Miracles' ('Generator chudes', 1938) by Iurii Dolgushin (born in Zestaponi, present-day Georgia), about reviving the dead. Despite the repressive atmosphere, several sf films debuted, including an adaptation of Russian-Ukrainian author Volodomyr Vladko's *The Robots Are Coming* (*Idut' robotari*; 1931, written in Ukrainian) titled *The Death of a Sensation* (*Gibel' sensatsii*; Andrievskii 1935) and *Cosmic Voyage* (*Cosmicheskii reis*; Zhuravlev, 1936), for which Tsiolkovsky consulted on zero-gravity effects.

Sf disappeared during World War II (McGuire *Red* 15; Revich 156–7). When it returned, 'near-future' sf was mandated (McGuire *Red* 15), resulting in works resembling popular science (Britikov 199; Gakov xiii), as best exemplified by Aleksandr Kazantsev's and Vladimir Nemtsov's Stalin-era fiction, such as Kazantsev's *Arctic Bridge* (*Arkticheskii most*; fragment released in 1941, fully published 1946), about the construction of a 'friendship bridge' in the Arctic between nations, and Nemtsov's *Seven Colours of the Rainbow* (*Sem' tsvetov radugi*; 1950), about the modernisation of a Soviet collective farm. Exceptions include *Patent AV* (1947) by Lazar Lagin (pen name of Lazar Ginzburg, born in Vitebsk, present-day Belarus), about a growth-accelerating elixir, and *In the Land of Dense Herbs* (*V Strane Dremuchikh Trav*; 1948) by Vladimir Bragin (born in Krasnapolle, present-day Belarus), a rewriting of Larri's 'The Extraordinary Adventures of Karik and Vali' ('Neobyknovennye prikliucheniia Karika i Vali'; 1937) about a shrinking potion. However, by the 1950s, censorship separated sf from global developments (McGuire 'Russian' 432). Little new sf was published until after Stalin's death in 1953 (Revich 88; Schwartz 245).

Thaw-era Soviet sf: 1956–65

Several circumstances led to sf's revival. In 1956, Stalin's successor Nikita Khrushchev denounced Stalin's 'cult of personality', beginning the 'Thaw' era. Ivan Efremov's far-future utopia *Andromeda Nebula* (*Tumannost' Andromedy*), the first in his GREAT RING series, appeared in 1957. Later that year, the USSR launched Sputnik, increasing Soviet prestige and inaugurating the 'Space Race'. These events renewed hope in science and the USSR (Csicsery-Ronay, Jr 338; Gomel 'Gods' 359; Howell 'Introduction' 16; Siddiqi 302), laying the foundation for Soviet sf's second 'Golden Age' (Arbitman 408; Gomel 'Gods' 361; Revich 6–7; Simon 379; Suvin 20).

Andromeda had a monumental impact on Soviet sf. It repopularised cosmic themes and far-future speculations, allowing new writers to explore topics foreclosed under Stalin (Britikov 220, 272; Glad 'Brave' 74–5; Revich 198; Simon 380; Schwartz 245; Suvin 21), as in the space-age tales of Georgii Martynov (born in Grodno, present-day Belarus) collected in the multi-part novels *Starfarers* (*Zvezdoplavateli*; 1960) and *Callisto* (*Kallisto*; 1960), among other places, and films like *The Heavens Call* (*Nebo zovet*; 1959) by Aleksandr Kozyr and Mikhail Kariukov (born in Odessa, present-day Ukraine), *Planet of Storms* (*Planeta bur'*; Klushantsev 1962), adapted from Kazantsev's 1959 story 'Planet of Storms' (later reworked into the 1962 novella *Grandchildren of Mars* [*Vnuki Marsa*]), and the adaptation of *Andromeda* (*Tumannost' Andromedy*; Sherstobytov 1968). *Andromeda* also displayed an interiority and humanism absent from recent sf (Britikov 89, 220–2; Nudelman 54–5; Arbitman 408; Csicsery-Ronay, Jr 343). This humanist shift is evident in Efremov's post-*Andromeda* works, as well as those of Gennadii Gor, Abram Terts (pen name of Andrei Siniavsky), Valentina Zhuravleva (born in Baku, present-day Republic of Azerbaijan), Lidiia Obukhova (born in Kutaisi, present-day Georgia), and Ol'ga Larionova. For instance, in Terts's 'Phkents' (1959, published 1967), an alien living incognito keeps a diary recording his isolation, while in Larionova's *The Leopard from the Summit of Kilimanjaro* (*Leopard s vershiny Kilimandzharo*; 1965), people contemplate life's meaning after learning when they will die. *Leopard* was, along with Arkadii and Boris Strugatskii's *Far Rainbow* (*Dalekaia raduga*; 1963), the first book to be read in space (Arbitman 409).

The Strugatskii brothers are the most influential Thaw-era writers. Regarded as 'spokesmen' of the intelligentsia (Gomel 'Poetics' 94; Howell *Apocalyptic* 5; Revich 286) and representatives of Soviet sf's 'new wave', their oeuvre responds to the call for socially conscious sf issued by writer-critics Ariadna Gromova and Rafail Nudel'man (Glad *Extrapolations* 196). The Strugatskiis helped transform sf into the centre of progressive discourse (Arbitman 412; Glad *Extrapolations*

196, 'Brave' 77; Nudelman 50; Revich 166). In their fiction, particularly their NOON UNIVERSE series, they offered critiques aimed at humanising social and technological progress in the USSR (Csicsery-Ronay 343), as in their most famous NOON UNIVERSE novel, *Hard to Be a God* (*Trudno byt' bogom*; 1964), adapted twice, first in the German Democratic Republic (*Es ist nicht leicht ein Gott zu sein*; Fleischmann 1999) and again by Aleksei German (*Trudno byt' bogom*; begun 2000, released 2013).

Some writers, such as Georgii Gurevich, Dmitrii Bilenkin, Anatolii Dneprov, Mikhail Emtsev and Eremei Parnov, Genrikh Al'tov (pen name of Genrikh Al'tshuller, born in Tashkent, present-day Uzbekistan), Aleksandr Meerov (born in Kharkiv, present-day Ukraine) and Sever Gansovsky (born in Kyiv, present-day Ukraine), explore the human costs of science and technology. For instance, in Dneprov's 'Crabs Walk the Island' ('Kraby idut po ostrovu'; 1958), an experiment unexpectedly produces horrific, self-replicating robots. Gansovsky's 'Day of Wrath' ('Den' gneva'; 1964) depicts super-intelligent human–bear hybrids who terrorise the countryside. Meanwhile, in Emtsev and Parnov's *World Soul* (*Dusha mira*; 1964), an accidental fusion of human biology and cybernetics links humans through telepathy.

In addition to social criticism, another hallmark of Thaw-era sf is optimism and humour (Tucker 197). The Strugatskiis' humour is especially evident in their sf-fantasy satire *Monday Begins on Saturday* (*Ponedel'nik nachinaetsia v subbotu*; 1965). Poet and fiction writer Vadim Shefner blends sf, parody, fantasy and fairy tales, as in 'The Girl at the Cliff, or Kovrigin's Notes' ('Devushka u obryva, ili Zapiski Kovrigina'; 1964). Il'ia Varshavskii (born in Kyiv, present-day Ukraine) serves as another example of the irony and humour of some of the era's sf; Varshavskii's stories are characterised by insights into technology, ironic humour and explorations of scientific and logical paradoxes, as in the short story collection *The Molecular Café* (*Molekuliarnoe kafe*; 1964).

The Thaw era also witnessed a boom in sf anthologies, almanacs and translations (Britikov 269). Soviet works were published abroad and foreign works were translated into Russian, culminating in a twenty-five-volume sf anthology that included Japanese, Western and Soviet authors (Myers 46; Levitsky 34). However, by the mid-1960s, the political climate shifted. Iulii Daniel' and Abram Terts, authors respectively of the 'meta-utopian' novels (Clowes 4) *Moscow Speaking* (*Govorit Moskva*; 1959) and *Liubimov* (1964), were arrested and tried for their fiction. Ideological attacks on sf became frequent (Nudelman 51; Csicsery-Ronay, Jr 337; Arbitman 412–3), driving sf underground once more (Glad 'Brave' 78).

Stagnation-era Soviet sf: 1966–85

Sf attracted suspicion during the second half of Soviet leader Leonid Brezhnev's rule, often described as the 'Stagnation' era due to its repressive atmosphere, lowered living standards and sense of stalled progress (Reese 103). During Stagnation, less sf was published (McGuire *Red* 20; Simon 392–3). Simultaneously, an increasingly permissive state attitude toward religion registered as an 'internal retreat' in Soviet culture and a turn toward personal concerns (Brown 187; McGuire 'Russian' 436; Marsh 10, 147, 238–9; Peterson 23).

This manifested in sf as increased attention to philosophical and cosmological themes (McGuire 'Russian' 436). The Strugatskiis' published Stagnation-era works reflect this shift, such as *The Snail on the Slope* (*Ulitka na sklone*; 1968), *Roadside Picnic* (*Piknik na obochine*; 1972) and *One Billion Years to the End of the World* (*Za milliard let do kontsa sveta*; serialised 1976–7, translated as *Definitely, Maybe*). The sf films of Andrei Tarkovskii also reflect this internal shift: in *Solaris* (*Soliaris* 1972), adapted from Polish author Stanisław Lem's 1961 novel of the same name, a psychologist processes his guilt and grief over his wife's death, and in *Stalker* (1979), adapted from the Strugatskiis' *Roadside Picnic*, a modern-day 'holy fool' endures tests of faith.

Increased attention to psychology is also palpable in Stagnation-era sf. For example, in *Self-Discovery* (*Otkyrtie sebia*; 1967) by Vladimir (Volodymyr) Savchenko (born in Poltava, present-day Ukraine), cybernetic cloning facilitates the exploration of conflicting selves. In Vladimir Mikhailov's *The Door from the Other Side* (*Dver s drugoi storony*; 1974), a marooned space crew contemplates their fate. Meanwhile, Dmitrii Romanovskii's 'Presenting Anna Karenina' ('Chest' imeiu predstavit' – Anna Kareninina'; 1977) highlights a Soviet woman's dilemma after being reprogrammed with the memory matrix of Lev Tolstoi's eponymous heroine.

Other themes also appeared. Relationships with aliens are the subject of Sergei Snegov's *People Like Gods* (*Liudi kak bogi*; serialised 1966–74), regarded as 'the first Soviet space opera since the 1920s' (McGuire 'Russian' 443), Aleksandr Mirer's *Wanderers' Home* (*Dom skital'tsev*; 1975), and the FIRST CONTACT short story cycle (PERVYI KONTAKT; 1978–1997) of Sergei Drugal' (born in Dzhambay, present-day Republic of Kazakhstan). Drugal' also explores relationships between humans and nonhuman animals in his INSTITUTE FOR NATURE RESTORATION short story cycle (INSTITUT RESTAVRATSII PRIRODY; 1966–89). Hard-sf writer Pavel (Pasekh) Amnuel' (born in Baku, present-day Republic of Azerbaijan) foregrounds scientific quandaries, as in his popular story 'Archery' ('Strel'ba iz luka'; 1981).

Kir Bulychev, the best-known Stagnation-era sf writer, produced a long-running (1968–2003) YA cycle of stories and novels about the adventures of futuristic heroine Alisa Selezneva, some of which were adapted for the popular five-part television miniseries *A Guest from the Future* (*Gost'ia iz budushchego*; 1985), the children's film *Lilac Ball* (*Lilovyi shar*; 1988) and the teen sf *One Hundred Years Ahead* (*Sto let tomu vpered*, also known as *Guest from the Future*; Andriushchenko, 2024). Bulychev also wrote cosmic sf tales distinguished by lyricism and humour, such as *People Like People* (*Liudi kak liudi*; 1975). With Richard Viktorov, director of the popular sf films *Moscow – Cassiopeia* (*Moskva – Kassiopeia*; 1974) and *Teens in Space* (*Otroki vo vselennoi*; 1975), Bulychev also co-wrote the films *To the Stars by Hard Ways* (*Cherez ternii k zvezdam*; 1981) and *Comet* (*Kometa*; 1983).

Underground seminars headed by established authors formed the 'Fourth Wave', which included Vitalii Babenko, Eduard Gevorkian, Andrei Izmailov (born in Baku, present-day Republic of Azerbaijan), Andrei Lazarchuk, Liubov' and Evgenii Lukin, Viktor Pelevin, Vladimir Pokrovskii (born in Odessa, present-day Ukraine), Viacheslav Rybakov, Aleksandr Siletskii, Boris Stern (born in Kyiv, present-day Ukraine), Andrei Stoliarov, Mikhail Uspenskii and Mikhail Veller (born in Kamianets-Podilskyi, present-day Ukraine), among others (Shickarev 226; Vladimirskii). These writers aimed to elevate the literary status of sf. Their work circulated in self-published manuscripts and regional sf club magazines (Shickarev 226; Simon 394; Vladimirskii), with the exception of the *Glasnost*-era anthologies *The Blue Road* (*Siniaia doroga*; 1984) and *The Day of Accomplishments* (*Den' svershenii*; 1988).

While sf was rare during Stagnation, the fantastic gained prominence, part of a broader post-Stalin decompartmentalisation of genres (Brown 187–8; Peterson 20, 84, 192; Rougle 308–10; Shneidman 191). Mainstream writers used sf for political critique, blending it with legends and myths, like Nodar Dombadze (born in Tbilisi, present-day Georgia) in *The Law of Eternity* (*Zakon vechnosti*; 1978), Chingiz Aitmatov (born in Sheker, present-day Kyrgyz Republic) in *The Day Lasts More Than a Hundred Years* (*I dol'she veka dlitsia den'*; 1980) and Evgenii Evtushenko in *Wild Berries* (*Iagodnye mesta*; 1981), or with 'meta-utopia' (Clowes 4), as in the Strugatskiis' *The Ugly Swans* (*Gadkie lebedi*; 1967, published 1972; filmed as *Gadkie lebedi* (Lopushanskii 2006)), Aleksandr Zinov'ev's *Yawning Heights* (*Ziiaiushchie vysoty*; 1974, published 1976) and

The Radiant Future (*Svetloe budushchee*; 1976, published 1978), and Vasilii Aksenov's *The Island of Crimea* (*Ostrov Krym*; 1979, published 1981). Meanwhile, like the fantastic realism of nineteenth-century writer Nikolai Gogol (born in Poltava, present-day Ukraine), 'alternative literature' (*al'ternativnaia literatura*) writers Vladimir Makanin, Anatolii Kim (born in Sergievka, present-day Republic of Kazakhstan) and Tat'iana Tolstaia aim to disorient readers' perceptions (Peterson 63–4).

***Glasnost'*-era Soviet sf: 1986–91**

By the mid-1980s, some argued that Soviet sf had stagnated due to genre mixing, censorship and isolation from global trends (Nudelman 53; Pukallus 260–1). However, the introduction of Mikhail Gorbachev's policies of *glasnost'* (openness) allowed contemporary authors to issue more direct criticisms of the myths that supported the state, particularly Socialist Realism (Clowes 25; Dalton-Brown 111, 118; Peterson 1–2, 114). It also allowed previously banned authors to be published (Shneidman 7). Zamiatin's *We* and Bulgakov's *Heart of a Dog* officially reached Soviet readers and suppressed works were rediscovered (Banerjee 'Introduction' xiii; Peterson 24; Simon 402).

Dystopias and 'meta-utopias' were popular (Clowes 4; Dalton-Brown 103, 107; Khagi 'Afterword' 647–8). Vladimir Voinovich's *Moscow 2042* (*Moskva 2042*; 1982, published 1986) depicts a future Moscow where neo-Stalinist and neo-Slavophilic forces vie for control. In the comedy-satire film *Kin-Dza-Dza!* (1986), directed by Georgii Daneliia (born in Tbilisi, present-day Georgia), Soviet Earthlings visit a dystopian planet whose chronic shortages and stratified classes recall Soviet society. Aleksandr Kabakov's novella *Defector* (*Nevozvrashchenets*; 1988, published 1989), translated as *No Return* (1990) and adapted as *Defector* (*Nevozvrashchenets*; Snezhkin 1991), describes a near-future Moscow where Perestroika has failed. In the Strugatskiis' *The Doomed City* (*Grad obrechennyi*; 1970–2; published 1989), survivors of historical atrocities are forced to partake in an 'experiment', while Anatolii Kurchatkin's *Notes of an Extremist* (*Zapiski ekstremista*; 1990) depicts a fanatical group of subway designers who, after a lifetime of work, discover that their city has abandoned metros.

Post-apocalyptic tales also flourished. Konstantin Lopushanskii's film *Letters from a Dead Man* (*Pis'ma mertvogo cheloveka*; 1986), whose screenplay was co-written by 'Fourth Wave' sf writer Viacheslav Rybakov, Boris Strugatskii and fellow director Aleksei German, depicts a society forced underground by nuclear war. Similarly, in Lopushanskii's film *Visitor to a Museum* (*Posetitel' museia*; 1989), survivors of a global environmental catastrophe turn to religion and mindless entertainments. Finally, Liudmila Petrushevskaia's near-future 'The New Robinsons' ('Novye Robinzony'; 1989) depicts a family's struggle for survival in the woods after fleeing from an unnamed terror in Moscow.

Post-soviet sf: After 1991

The transformations triggered by the USSR's 1991 collapse brought immense changes to the post-Soviet states. The newly reader-driven marketplace and the difficult 1990s gave rise to a desire for 'light entertainment' (Peterson 1) and a nostalgia for Russia's history (Howell 'Introduction' 19; Khagi 'Afterword' 648). This, in turn, fuelled a demand for high fantasy, forbidden in the USSR (Gomel 'Science' 437; Krementsov *Revolutionary* 254 n.51; Levitsky 35), and led to a decline in traditional sf (Gomel 'Science' 439–40), with genre-bending becoming more common (Khagi 'One' 268).

Some writers responded to readers' interest in the past with sf-fantasy works, like *Knights of the Forty Islands* (*Rytsari Soroka Ostrovov*; 1992) by Sergei Luk'ianenko (born in Karatau, present-day Republic of Kazakhstan), in which teenagers are compelled by aliens to battle. Luk'ianenko's sf-fantasy series PATROLS (DOZORY 1998–2014) was partially adapted for cinema by Timur Bekmambetov (born in Atyrau, present-day Republic of Kazakhstan) beginning with *Night Watch* (*Nochnoi dozor*; 2004).

Others responded with alternative histories (Gomel 'Science' 440; Khagi 'Afterword' 649), such as Lopushanskii in his film *Russian Symphony* (*Russkaia simfoniia*; 1994), as well as fiction by Kir Bulychev, and 'Fourth Wave' writers Viacheslav Rybakov and Andrei Lazarchuk. Some of the most popular works in this sub-genre include Bulychev's *River Chronos* (*Reka Khronos*; 1992), Rybakov's *Gravity Aircraft 'Tsesarevich'* (*Gravilet 'Tsesarevich'*; 1993), *Pull the Rope* (*Derni za verevochku*; 1996) and *Next Year in Moscow* (*Na budushchii god v Moskve*; 2003), and Lazarchuk's *Another Sky* (*Inoe nebo*; 1993) and co-authored series LOOK INTO THE EYES OF MONSTERS (POSMOTRI V GLAZA CHUDOVISHCH, 1997–2006), written with fellow 'Fourth Wave' writer Mikhail Uspenskii and, later, Irina Andronati (born in Odessa, present-day Ukraine).

Some authors have also used sf for political critique. For example, Tat'iana Tolstaia's *The Slynx* (*Kys'*; 2000) interrogates Russian literature and history through grotesque, apocalyptic imagery. Others target Russia's corruption and authoritarianism under leader Vladimir Putin. Co-authors Aleksandr Garros (born in Novopolotsk, present-day Belarus) and Aleksei Evdokimov critique corporate technocracy in their cyberpunk-thrillers *Headcrusher* (*[Golovo]lokma*; 2002) and *Gray Goo* (*Seraia sliz'*; 2005). Dmitrii Bykov's *Tow Truck* (*Evakuator* 2005) and *Living Souls* (*ZhD*; 2006) envision a dystopian Moscow plagued by religious, ethnic and political tensions. Vladimir Sorokin critiques recent Russian politics in his controversial *Blue Lard* (*Goluboe salo*; 1999), his ICE trilogy (LEDIANAIA TRILOGIIA; also just called TRILOGY (TRILOGIIA); 2002–5) about the 1908 Tunguska explosion, and his HISTORY OF THE FUTURE cycle (ISTORIIA BUDUSHCHEGO; 2006–13), in which Russia returns to tsarism.

'Fourth Wave' and Turborealist sf author Viktor Pelevin, the 'spokesman' for the 1990s intelligentsia (Khagi 'One' 278), has also incorporated sf into his uniquely postmodern fiction (Gomel 'Viktor' 291–2, 305). Pelevin covers many themes, especially the marriage of politics, capitalism and media in late Soviet and post-Soviet Russia, as in *Omon Ra* (1992), *Homo Zapiens* (*Generation 'П'*; 1999), *Empire V: A Novella About a Real Superman* (*Ampir V. Povest' o nastoiashchem sverkhcheloveke*; 2006), *S.N.U.F.F.* (2011), *TRANSHUMANISM INC.* (2021) and *KGBT+* (2022), among others.

The late 2000s birthed the 'Colour Wave' (*tsvetnaia volna*), including Dmitrii Kolodan, Karina Shainian, Iuliia Ostapenko (born in Lviv, present-day Ukraine), Larisa Bortnikova, Tat'iana Tomakh, Natal'ia Fedina, K.A. Terina (pen name of Katerina Bachilo), Vladimir Danikhnov, Shimun Vrochek (pen name of Dmitrii Ovchinnikov), Iuliia Zonis (born in Rostovi, present-day Georgia), Ekaterina Cherniavskaia, Maksim Dubrovin (born in Donetsk, present-day Ukraine), Ivan Naumov, and the members of 'Ethnogenesis' (*Etnogenez*). The Colour Wave writers avoid politics, instead foregrounding emotion, intertextuality and genre mixing (Shickarev 213, 216, 220, 229). They debuted online (Shickarev 211, 218), although the movement officially launched with the anthologies *Premonition of the 'Sixth Wave'* (*Predchuvstvie 'shestoi volny'*; 2007), compiled by Lazarchuk, and *Colour Day* (*Tsvetnoi den'*; 2008), edited by Minsk-based writer Arkadii Rukh (Shickarev 210). The group-authored steampunk novel *Cetopolis* (*Ketopolis*; 2012) is considered the movement's 'magnum opus' (Shickarev 219).

The Colour Wave is the most recent movement in Russian-language sf. Although sf has 'fragmented' (Forrester 205), some noteworthy authors remain active, such as Elena Khaetskaia, who blends sf, fantasy and realism; Oleg Divov, who mixes sf, thriller and fantasy; Anna Starobinets, who produces sf, horror and children's fiction; Ol'ga Onoiko, who favours sf war stories; Vladimir Arenev (pen name of Volodomyr Puzii, born in Kyiv, present-day Ukraine), who writes sf, fantasy and children's fiction; Nikolai Kalinichenko, author of sf and fairy tales; Ol'ga Chigirinskaia (born in Kryvyi Rih, present-day Ukraine), whose fiction blends sf and fantasy; and co-authors Aleksandra Davydova and Viktor Koliuzhniak (penname Aleksei Vert), who write cyberpunk and fantasy. The rich history of Russian-language sf and its varied manifestations today suggest new movements may soon rise.

Works cited

Arbitman, Roman. 'Back in the 1960s: Notes by a Man Who Wasn't There'. *Science Fiction Studies* 94 (2004): 407–14.

Banerjee, Anindita. 'Introduction'. *Russian Science Fiction Literature and Cinema: A Critical Reader*. Ed. Anindita Banerjee. Academic Studies, 2018. viii–xvii.

——. *We Modern People: Science Fiction and the Making of Russian Modernity*. Wesleyan UP, 2012.

Brandis, Evgenii. *Sovetskii nauchno-fantasticheskii roman*. No publisher details available, 1959.

Britikov, A.F. *Russkii sovetskii nauchno-fantasticheskii roman*. Izdatel'stvo 'Nauka', 1970.

Brown, Deming. *The Last Years of Soviet Russian Literature: Prose Fiction 1975–1991*, Cambridge UP, 1993.

Christie, Ian. 'Down to Earth: *Aelita* Relocated'. *Inside the Film Factory: New Approaches to Russian* and Soviet Cinema. Ed. Richard Taylor and Ian Christie. Routledge, 1991. 80–102.

Clowes, Edith W. *Russian Experimental Fiction: Resisting Ideology after Utopia*. Princeton UP, 1993.

Csicsery-Ronay, Istvan, Jr. 'Science Fiction and the Thaw'. *Science Fiction Studies* 94 (2004): 337–44.

Dalton-Brown, Sally. 'Signposting the Way to the City of Night: Recent Russian Dystopian Fiction'. *The Modern Language Review* 90.1 (1995): 103–19.

Forrester, Sibelan. 'Fantastika: An Update on Science Fiction and Fantasy in Russia'. *Russian Studies in Literature* 52.3–4 (2016): 205–8.

Gakov, Vladimir. 'Introduction'. *World's Spring*. Ed. Vladimir Gakov. MacMillan, 1981. ix–xiv.

Glad, John. 'Brave New Worlds'. *The Wilson Quarterly* 7.4 (1983): 68–78.

——. *Extrapolations from Dystopia: A Critical Study of Soviet Science Fiction*. Kingston, 1982.

Gomel, Elana. 'Gods Like Men: Soviet Science Fiction and the Utopian Self'. *Science Fiction Studies* 94 (2004): 358–77.

——. 'Science Fiction in Russia: From Utopia to New Age'. *Science Fiction Studies* 79 (1999): 435–41.

——. 'Viktor Pelevin and Literary Postmodernism in Soviet Russia'. *Russian Science Fiction Literature and Cinema: A Critical Reader*. Ed. Anindita Banerjee. Academic Studies, 2018. 290–305.

Griffiths, John. *Three Tomorrows: American, British, and Soviet Science Fiction*. Macmillan, 1980.

Howell, Yvonne. *Apocalyptic Realism: The Science Fiction of Arkady and Boris Strugatsky*. Peter Lang, 1994.

——. 'Eugenics, Rejuvenation, and Bulgakov's Journey into the Heart of Dogness'. *Russian Science Fiction Literature and Cinema: A Critical Reader*. Ed. Anindita Banerjee. Academic Studies, 2018. 178–200.

——. 'Introduction'. *Red Star Tales: A Century of Russian and Soviet Science Fiction*. Ed. Yvonne Howell. Russian Life Books, 2015. 7–20.

Khagi, Sofya. 'Afterword'. *Worlds Apart: An Anthology of Russian Fantasy and Science Fiction*. Ed. Alexander Levitsky. Overlook Duckworth, 2007. 647–50.

——. 'One Billion Years after the End of the World: Historical Deadlock, Contemporary Dystopia, and the Continuing Legacy of the Strugatskii Brothers'. *Slavic Review* 72.2 (2013): 267–86.

Krementsov, Nikolai. *A Martian Stranded on Earth: Alexander Bogdanov, Blood Transfusions, and Proletarian Science*. U of Chicago P, 2011.

——. *Revolutionary Experiments: The Quest for Immortality in Bolshevik Science and Fiction*. Oxford UP, 2014.

——. *Stalinist Science*. Princeton UP, 1997.

Laursen, Eric. *Toxic Voices: The Villain from Early Soviet Literature to Socialist Realism*. Northwestern UP, 2013.

Levitsky, Alexander. 'Worlds of Russian Fantasy (In lieu of an introduction)'. *Worlds Apart: An Anthology of Russian Fantasy and Science Fiction*. Ed. Alexander Levitsky. Overlook Duckworth, 2007. 9–36.

Leyda, Jay. *Kino: A History of the Russian and Soviet Film*, third edition. Princeton UP, 1983.
Maguire, Muireann. 'Aleksei N. Tolstoi and the Enigmatic Engineer: A Case of Vicarious Revisionism'. *Slavic Review* 72. 2 (2013): 247–66.
Maguire, Muireann and Andrei Rogatchevski. 'Introduction: Filming the Strugatskiis'. *Science Fiction Film and Television* 8.2 (2015): 123–6.
Marsh, Rosalind J. *Soviet Fiction Since Stalin: Science, Politics and Literature*. Croom Helm, 1986.
McGuire, Patrick L. *Red Stars: Political Aspects of Soviet Science Fiction*. UMI Research, 1985.
——. 'Russian SF'. *Anatomy of Wonder: A Critical Guide to Science Fiction*, second edition. Ed. Neil Barron. R.R. Bowker, 1981. 426–54.
Myers, Alan. 'Some Developments in Soviet SF Since 1966'. *Foundation* 19 (1980): 38–47.
Nudelman, Rafail. 'Soviet Science Fiction and the Ideology of Soviet Society'. *Science Fiction Studies* 47 (1989): 38–66.
Peterson, Nadya L. *Subversive Imaginations: Fantastic Prose and the End of Soviet Literature, 1970s–1990s*. Westview, 1997.
——. 'The Poetics of Censorship: Allegory as Form and Ideology in the Novels of Arkady and Boris Strugatsky'. *Science Fiction Studies* 65 (1995): 87–105.
Pukallus, Horst. 'An Interview with Darko Suvin'. *Science Fiction Studies* 54 (1991): 253–61.
Reese, Kevin. *Celestial Hellscapes: Cosmology As the Key to the Strugatskiis' Science Fictions*. Academic Studies, 2019.
Revich, Vsevolod. *Perekrestok utopii. Sud'by fantastiki na fone sudeb strany*. Institut vostokovedeniia RAN, 1998.
Rougle, Charles. 'On the "Fantastic" Trend in Recent Soviet Prose'. *The Slavic and East European Journal* 34.3 (1990): 308–21.
Schwartz, Matthias. 'How *Nauchnaia Fantastika* Was Made: The Debates About the Genre of Fiction from NEP to High Stalinism'. *Slavic Review* 72.2 (2013): 224–46.
Shickarev, Sergei. 'High Waves, Quiet Backwaters'. *Russian Studies in Literature* 52.3–4 (2016): 209–34.
Shneidman, N.N. *Soviet Literature in the 1980s: Decade of Transition*. U of Toronto P, 1989.
Siddiqi, Asif A. *The Red Rockets' Glare: Spaceflight and the Soviet Imagination, 1857–1957*. Cambridge UP, 2010.
Simon, Erik. 'The Strugatskys in Political Context'. *Science Fiction Studies* 94 (2004): 378–406.
Stites, Richard. *Revolutionary Dreams: Utopian Vision and Experimental Life in the Russian Revolution*. Oxford UP, 1989.
Suvin, Darko. 'The Utopian Tradition of Russian Science Fiction'. *Russian Science Fiction Literature and Cinema: A Critical Reader*. Ed. Anindita Banerjee. Academic Studies, 2018. 1–29.
Tucker, Frank H. 'Soviet Science Fiction: Recent Development and Outlook'. *The Russian Review* 33.2 (1974): 189–200.
Vladimirskii, Vasilii. 'Kto prishel na smenu Strugatskim'. *Gor'kii* (8 May 2020). https://gorky.media/context/kto-prishel-na-smenu-strugatskim/.
Youngblood, Denise J. *Movies for the Masses: Popular Cinema and Soviet Society in the 1920s*. Cambridge UP, 1992.

8
SOUTH ASIAN SCIENCE FICTION

Bodhisattva Chattopadhyay

South Asian sf is a difficult domain to address, partly because several regions with their specific languages themselves constitute relatively large bodies of work, much of which is local to the context, untranslated, unread and often unknown outside the area. What is generally presented as South Asian sf, especially in international arenas, thus consists of Anglophone and translated sf, which represent only a small proportion of the field. The only notable exception to the regional language rule is sf in Bangla (Bengali) language, which is the source of most sf from India available in English translation and, alongside South Asian Anglophone sf, has attracted the most scholarly and critical attention (Chattopadhyay; Chattopadhyay et al.). (There are small bodies of work translated into English from Marathi, Hindi, Tamil, Urdu and other languages). The picture is further complicated by the fact that sf production in other languages, as well as their translations, often makes classification of specific works as sf a somewhat arbitrary, and often academic, exercise once variations in genre and aesthetic sensibility are taken into account. This chapter focuses primarily on Anglophone sf, while gesturing towards these other bodies of work, and takes a broad view of what sf is in this context.

Modern sf in South Asia arguably begins with two English language future histories written in Bengal, Kylas Chunder Dutt's 'A Journal of Forty Eight Hours of the Year 1945' (*The Calcutta Literary Gazette*, 6 June 1835) and Shoshee Chunder Dutt's 'The Republic of Orissa: A Page From the Annals of the Twentieth Century' (*The Saturday Evening Harakuru*, 25 May 1845). Both had a strong anticolonial theme. A later alternate history, Bhudev Mukhopadhyay's *Swapnalabdha Bharatbarsher Itihas* ('India's History Revealed in a Dream'; 1862) is also widely known, along with such technofictions as Hemlal Dutta's 'Rahasya' ('Mystery'; *Bigyan Darpan*, 1882). Other early works, such as Jagadananda Ra's 'Shukra Bhraman' ('Voyage to Venus'; *Bharati*, 1895), sometimes regarded as the first proper sf work from India, or 'Begum' Rokeya Sakhawat Hossain's 'Sultana's Dream' (*Indian Ladies' Magazine*, 1905), one of the earliest feminist utopias, took the form of dream narratives. Another widely known work, scientist polymath Jagadish Chandra Bose's 'Niruddesher Kahini' ('The Story of the Missing One'; 1896; republished as 'Palatak Toofan' ('The Runaway Cyclone'; 1921) offers a fascinating view of the relations between metropolitan and Indigenous science. Notable early examples in Hindi include Pandit Ambika Dutt Vyas's 'Ascharya Vrittant' ('Marvellous Tale'; *Piyush Pravaha*, 1884) and Babu Keshav Prasad's 'Chandra Lok Ki Yatra' ('The Lunar Voyage'; *Saraswat*, 1900). The influence of *tilism* literature,

 DOI: 10.4324/9781003140269-10

particularly the Hamzanama and the Hoshruba narratives, is particularly visible in the early Hindi fantastic; they inform, for example, several speculative elements in Devaki Nandan Khatri's *Chandrakanta* (1888). Another notable early writer from Bengal, Trailokyanath Mukhopadhyay, who wrote fiction primarily in the 1890s and 1910s at the end of a long career as a civil servant in the British Empire, created the genre-defying and genre-defining cycle of stories *Damarucharit* (*The Epic of Damarudhar*; 1910–7), where fantastic elements blend seamlessly with horror, folklore and scientific speculation. Common themes in many of these works include anti-colonial resistance, extraplanetary or extradimensional travel, and a strong but critical use of both scientific knowledge and technology. Colonial contact undoubtedly played a role in shaping South Asian sf, as science and technology, especially colonial science and technology, were seen as a double-edged sword: useful and beneficial in a modern context, they enabled a form of global scientific exchange but were also responsible for the problems and ills arising from that exchange.

While anti-colonial sentiments became stronger with the dawn of the twentieth century, scientific elements also become much more pronounced. Writers such as Jules Verne, H.G. Wells, H. Rider Haggard, Robert Louis Stevenson, Arthur Conan Doyle and Edgar Rice Burroughs, as well as many other pulp writers, were widely read and translated into many languages, including Hindi, Marathi, Bangla, Urdu, Tamil, Telugu, Kannada, Malayalam and Odia. In addition to such translations, numerous inspired and derivative works can be found in the literary and cultural magazines across South Asia and, as in other parts of the world, sf was just one genre among many in this mix. By the 1920s and 1930s, a large number of sf or science-fictional works, some of which were well received and reviewed, could be found in many languages. Particularly in Bangla, which had one of the most developed publishing industries in the eastern part of the country, one finds a larger number of writers and a wide range of sf in the same vein as in the UK and US at that point, with lost world adventures, aliens, time travel, underwater and outer space romps, utopias and technological marvels. Writers such as Manoranjan Bhattacharya, Sukumar Roy, Lila Majumdar, Kshitindranarayan Bhattacharya, Hemendrakumar Ray and Premendra Mitra deserve special mention due to the volume and quality of their work, some of which is only now being translated and read outside Bengal. Bangla sf continued to thrive in India in the 1940s and the post-independence 1950s, and is perhaps the only unbroken line of sf in India. There were fewer and more sporadic publications in other languages, but works such as Munshi Nadim Sehbai Ferozpuri's *Naqli Rais* (*The Fraud Aristocrat*; 1938) in Urdu, featuring a brain transplant plot, was well received. In Hindi, probably the most famous of several early twentieth-century examples is Rahul Sankrityayan's socialist utopia, *Baisvee Sadi* (*The 22nd Century*; 1924); in Telugu, Tekumalla Raja Gopala Rao's *Vihanga Yanam* (*The Flight of the Birds*; 1906), which features a female protagonist in a submarine adventure, is also notable.

But it is not until the 1960s–1990s that sf really takes off in South Asia in most languages. The years immediately before and after independence in India saw an enlarged and renewed investment in science and technology, and this began to bear fruit in literature and other media, including film. Adrish Bardhan launched the first proper sf magazine in India, *Ascharjya* (*Strange*), which appeared from 1963–8, and together with Ranen Ghosh, Amitananda Das and Sujit Dhar he was responsible for several others, including the short-lived *Fantastic* (1975–6) and the sporadic *Bismay* (*Wonder*; 1982–), as well as *Kishor Gyan-Bigyan* (*Youth Science and Knowledge*; 1981). Bardhan used the term 'kalpavigyan' to refer to Bangla sf, reversing, literally, the term 'science fiction' to 'fiction science'. Part of this transformation had to do with relatively flexible notion of science or 'vigyan' in Bangla and various other South Asian languages. Science was knowledge, but only in a material sense, while knowledge (or 'gyan') transcended the limitations of a purely material perspective. By emphasising fiction, Bardhan did not however mean that science was unimportant, or that fantasy or folklore were to be emphasised, only that storytelling was the priority. This flexible definition lent to the sf aesthetic foregrounded in these magazines. In addition to being a prolific sf writer and editor, Bardhan was also an avid translator and one of the three people, along with Satyajit Ray and Premendra Mitra, to make sf respectable in Bangla. Mitra, however, wrote far less pulp-ish sf in the years after Indian independence, and is now more well known for his fiction featuring the character Ghanada. In these stories, Mitra produced some of the sharpest critiques of colonialism, and satirised, even if sympathetically, Bengali society. The GHANADA stories with their cheeky humour have served as an inspiration to other sf writers in the subcontinent, including writers such as Vandana Singh, as well as produced imitators. Ray is best known as a filmmaker, but he also wrote sf stories, the most famous being his PROFESSOR SHONKU stories, which feature the other most famous sf character from Bengal and South Asian sf more generally. On the other side of Bengal, in Bangladesh, authors such as Muhammad Zafar Iqbal, who wrote more straightforward sf, and Humayun Ahmad, who wrote weird fiction with science-fictional undertones, both started writing in the 1970s.

Marathi sf also took off in the 1970s and 1980s, with the work of astrophysicist Jayant Narlikar, who wrote sf stories and novels alongside his academic research and popular science articles and books. Narlikar, a student of British physicist and sf writer Fred Hoyle, was one of several writers encouraged to work with the genre in Marathi, with the support of the Marathi Vidnyan Parishad. Other writers, such as Bal Phondke, Niranjan Ghate and Laxman Londhe, also enriched the general space of sf, but most of their work remains untranslated and unavailable to non-Anglophone audiences. Unsurprisingly, Narlikar's work has received the widest critical attention, and several novels and stories have been translated, including *Vaman Parat Na Ala* (*The Return of the Vaman*; 1986) and *Virus* (1996).

There are also many sf writers in Hindi from the 1960s onward, including Naval Bihari Mishra, Kailash Shah, Maya Prasad Tripathi, Shukdev Prasad, Rajeshwar Gangavar, Devendra Mawadi, Arvind Mishra, Harish Goyal and Kalpana Kulshrestha, but again most of their work remains untranslated and largely unknown outside the local context. However, writers such as Arvind Mishra have also been custodians of scholarship as well as development of the genre, such as founding The Indian Science Fiction Writers' Association in 1995, largely as an initiative with writers in Hindi; in 1998, a second organisation, the Indian Association for Science Fiction Studies, was also established in Karnataka. A selection of Mishra's work has recently been translated into English, in the collection *The Space Cuckoo and Other Stories* (2021).

The renowned writer Izhar Asar wrote a larger number of sf works from the 1950s onwards, mostly in the pulp mode, but they remain largely unknown to readers unfamiliar with the Urdu in which they were written. Similar unfortunate cases include the Sinhalese writer K.A. Lionel Perera, who started his career in the late 1950s and is often regarded as one of the first sf writers from Sri Lanka, and the Tamil writer Sujatha, who produced major works in the 1960s and 1970s; both authors remain untranslated and their work is largely unknown among those who do not read their languages.

Anglophone sf from South Asia began to become more available and distributed outside the region following the success of Amitav Ghosh's *The Calcutta Chromosome* (1995), which won the Arthur C. Clarke Award, and Manjula Padmanabhan's *Harvest* (1997), which won the Onassis Prize. Padmanabhan had been an active writer of sf in English from the 1980s, and continues to produce some of the finest sf from the region, including *Escape* (2008) and *Island of Lost Girls* (2015). By the mid-2000s, Anglophone sf from the subcontinent had begun to shine. Samit Basu enjoyed breakout success with his GAMEWORLD Trilogy (2004–7), a genre-blending series that is as original and South Asian in its ethos as it is science-fictional. Rimi B. Chatterjee's prescient, near-future novel *Signal Red* (2005) anticipated the concerns of some of the next decade's political future fiction from South Asia.

Furthermore, in the twenty-first century, writers with South Asian heritage or belonging to South Asian diaspora have actively contributed to the global sf community. Perhaps the most notable example is the weekly online magazine *Strange Horizons*, founded in the US in 2000 by Mary Anne Mohanraj (who also served as its first editor-in-chief, from 2000–3). Having published new and established writers, and notable for the diversity of its vision, it remains one of the leading online venues for publication of Anglophone sf worldwide. In 2017, *Strange Horizons* founded a sister magazine, *Samovar*, which publishes sf in its original language and English translation. Both venues are crowdfunded.

Other writers whose works move seamlessly between the South Asia and the Anglo-American context, such as Vandana Singh and Anil Menon, also began writing in the new millennium. Singh, who has produced a small but exquisite body of short fiction, much of it collected *The Woman Who Thought She Was a Planet and Other Stories* (2008) and *The Ambiguity Machines and Other Stories* (2018), is unarguably one of the finest writers in the genre, as well as an urgent, critical voice. Her short fiction, novellas and critical work reflect a deep engagement with issues faced by the marginalised in society, and with the disastrous consequences of climate change. Menon has published two novels, the quite straightforwardly science-fictional *The Beast With Nine Billion Feet* (2009) and the more genre-twisting work, *Half of What I Say* (2015), but as with Singh, his sf short stories are the true delight, some of which are collected in *The Inconceivable Idea of the Sun* (2022). Menon's works are simultaneously playful, acerbic and serious. Another key writer from the region who began his career in the same period, but whose major work did not appear until the 2010s, is the Pakistani writer Usman Tanveer Malik (Sadaf and Kanwal). He has written sf, fantasy and horror in various forms, including short stories, chapbooks and poetry. His widely acclaimed 'The Vaporization Enthalpy of a Peculiar Pakistani Family' (2014) won the Bram Stoker Award, as well as being nominated for Locus and Nebula awards, and his most recent collection, *Midnight Doorways: Fables from Pakistan* (2021), won the World Fantasy Award. Indrapramit Das's fiction, such as the *The Last Dragons of Bowbazar* (2023), is often set in Kolkata and utilises the city's unique colonial and multicultural history alongside South Asian myth; his brutal debut novel, *The Devourers* (2015), won the Lambda Award.

Several of these more contemporary writers, including Menon, Malik and Das, have participated in international workshops for sf writing, such as Clarion West, sometimes as students, sometimes as instructors. These international exchanges have had ripple effects. For example, the first Indian sf writer's workshop, which was held in 2009 at Indian Institute of Technology Kanpur, was modelled on Clarion West. It was organised by Anil Menon (who had attended Clarion West in 2004), Vandana Singh and Suchitra Mathur, and aimed to train Indian writers, most with little or no experience with sf, to write in the genre. The workshop led to the ground-breaking anthology of Indian sf, *Breaking the Bow: Speculative Fiction Inspired by the Ramayana* (2012), edited by Menon and Singh. Led by Menon in the subsequent years, the workshop itself has evolved in different guises and with a much broader approach to genre, and several of its alumni have gone on to published careers. Usman T. Malik, who attended in 2013, has been key to recent developments in the sf community in Pakistan, serving as an advisor for the Salam Award for Pakistani sf (founded 2017). The Salam Award organised its first workshop to train writers in sf in 2023, with Mohanraj serving as an instructor. Exchanges between the two sides of the Bangla speaking community in India and in Bangladesh have also been quite productive and fertile, with the online magazine *Kalpabiswa*, launched in 2016, being the only active, purely genre sf publisher in any non-Anglophone South Asian languages; a key player and hub for the region, it has since 2017 branched out into sf book publishing. Furthermore, while many South Asian writers, such as Singh, Menon, Malik and Das, have been nominated for or won major awards, the Salam Award for Pakistani sf and *Kalpabiswa*'s two awards for sf writers (established in 2022) are the only sf awards from the subcontinent to date.

The last decade of Anglophone sf and fantasy from South Asia has seen more published work and names than all the previous decades put together. The Bangladeshi Saad Z. Hossain's *Djinn City* (2017), *The Gurkha and the Lord of Tuesday* (2019), *Cyber Mage* (2021) and *Kundo Wakes Up* (2022) are hilarious yet poignant, setting issues such as the ongoing climate catastrophe and extreme poverty against the madness of South Asian history, myth and mind-boggling diversity. India, which also boasts a stronger local Anglophone readership, has become a hub for regional sf and fantasy publishing, with international publishers, such as HarperCollins, Hachette, Simon & Schuster and Gollancz working alongside such regional players as Blaft, Rupa, Zubaan and Niyogi in the local publishing ecosystem. Priya Sarukkai Chabria's *Generation 14* (2008; revised as *The Clone* (2019), Shovon Chowdhury's *The Competent Authority* (2013), Prayaag Akbar's *Leila* (2017), Sami Ahmad Khan's *Red Jihad* (2012) and *Aliens in Delhi* (2017), Tashan Mehta's *The Liar's Weave* (2017) and *The Mad Sisters of Esi* (2023), Samit Basu's *Chosen Spirits* (2020; aka *The City Inside*) and *The Jinn-Bot of Shantiport* (2023), Yudhanjaya Wijeratne's *NumberCaste* (2018) and *The Salvage Crew* (2020), S.B. Divya's *Machinehood* (2021) and *Meru* (2023) and Gautam Bhatia's *The Wall* (2020) and *The Horizon* (2021) are among the best recent novels.

Short fiction remains a dominant form for many new sf and fantasy writers from South Asia, partly due to the increased demand from online magazines, such as *Strange Horizons*, *Lightspeed* and *Clarkesworld*. Writers such as Swapna Kishore, Mimi (Monidipa) Mondal, Kehkeshan Khalid, Lavanya Lakshminarayan, Vajra Chandrasekera and Soham Guha have written sf short fiction to wide acclaim. Anglophone writers often bridge worlds, moving seamlessly between genres as they move between countries (and sometimes, their other languages), even as they project futures. Other than writers in the diaspora, many of these Anglophone writers have lived in the US or UK, or have degrees from these countries, which facilitates their movement between the international and regional space, even while much of the fiction they write has clear South Asian tonalities or referents.

South Asian sf and fantasy authors have also straddled a fine line between genre fiction and mainstream literary fiction, such as magical realism. While Salman Rushdie, Arundhati Roy, I. Allan Sealy and others have achieved sufficient name recognition for their work to be consider 'non-genre' by the literary establishment, other writers whose work has utilised similarly satirical or fantastical tropes, including Kuzhali Manickavel's *Insects Are Just Like You and Me Except Some of Them Have Wings* (2008), Shubhangi Swarup's *Latitudes Of Longing* (2018), Numair Atif Choudhury's *Babu Bangladesh* (2019) and S. Hareesh's *Moustache* (2020; originally in Malayalam), can also be read as sf, fantasy, weird fiction or magical realism, depending on the critical lens.

Work in other media has also flourished in more recent years, with sf graphic novels, games and fine arts also finding a place. Some notable recent contributions in this space include Bishakh Som's graphic novel, *Apsara Engine* (202), and *Journeys through the Radiant Citadel*, a contribution to the DUNGEONS & DRAGONS franchise conceived by Ajit George, which includes Mimi Mondal's own adventure 'Maniversha'. Sf visual and sonic arts from South Asia have also boomed in recent years; however, it is primarily international and tends to work in a sphere of its own, with little cross-fertilisation with textual sf. The work of artists such as Chitra Ganesh, Saks Afridi, Osheen Siva, Himal Singh Soin and Rohini Devashar are noticeable in this boom. Several key exhibitions of 'South Asian Futurism' have been held in the last few years, including *The Missing One* (2016 and 2017; curated by Nada Raza for the Dhaka Art Summit 2016 in Bangladesh, and The Office for Contemporary Art in Norway), and *A Lost Future* (2018; curated by Beth Citron for The Rubin Museum of Art, New York). Subash Thebe Limbu, a Yakthung (Limbu) artist from Yakthung Nation (Limbuwan) in what we currently know as eastern Nepal, has also contributed to a short manifesto on Adivasi Futurism (modelled on Indigenous Futurisms), and produced *Ningwasum* (2022), the first consciously sf film in Yakthungpan. Also notable here is Arunava Gangopadhyay' *Kalpavigyan: A Speculative Journey* (2021), the first feature-length documentary on Indian sf, with a special focus on Bengal.

Indian audiovisual sf has a long history, with early alien films and television series often adapted from US or British sources, such as *Space City Sigma* (DD National 1989), which fused *Blake's 7* (BBC 1979–81) and *Star Trek* (NBC 1966–9). Bollywood produced a small but notable number of sf films during the 1950s–90s, and there has been a significant increase in the number of sf films in the new millennium (Langer and Alessio) across various languages, including *Patalghar* (Chaudhuri 2003), *Koi... Mil Gaya* (Roshan 2003) and its Kriish (2006–) sequel series of superhero movies, *Enthiran* (Shankar 2010) and its sequel *2.0* (Shankarrom 2018), *Love Story 2050* (Baweja 2013), *Cargo* (Kadav 2019) and *Leila* (Deepa Mehta 2019), adapted from Prayaag Akbar's 2017 novel of the same name.

Even if Anglophone sf is most well-known, regional language sf continues to coexist and thrive. For example, Kalpabiswa, which began as an online Bangla language sf magazine, turned into a publishing house for reprinting classic and contemporary sf and fantasy, collecting and anthologising the works of older authors, and engaging in archival research and critical work, also played an important role in supporting and shaping the next generation of Bangla sf and fantasy writers. Recent anthologies of South Asian sf, such as the two volume *The Gollancz Book of South Asian Science Fiction* (2019 and 2021) edited by Tarun Saint, and *Kalicalypse* (2022), edited by Saint and Francesco Verso, have also featured some work in translation. It is also important to note that anthologies, such as these, which feature writers who come from different language traditions, regions and cultures, also infuse the Anglophone works with a variety of words, ideas, idioms and aesthetics of different parts of South Asia.

Thematically, then, there are hardly any proper ways to sort and classify the heterogeneity of South Asian sf, although there have been some attempts, especially for Indian sf. Both Suparno Banerjee's *Indian Science Fiction: Patterns, History and Hybridity* (2020) and Upamanyu Pablo Mukherjee's *Final Frontiers: Science Fiction and Techno-Science in Non-Aligned India* (2020) try to capture work in multiple languages but are stronger in their historical understanding than in their engagement with contemporary materials. Banerjee's work is perhaps more comprehensive, but sf and fantasy publishing is accelerating at a pace with which it is hard for critical work to keep up. Sami Ahmad Khan's *Star Warriors of the Modern Raj: Materiality, Mythology and Technology of Indian Science Fiction* (2021) and Urvashi Kuhad's *Science Fiction and Indian Women Writers: Exploring Radical Potentials* (2021) do a better job in this respect, but it is largely because they both focus solely on Anglophone sf. There have been some scattered critical reflections on Pakistani sf as well on the futurisms discourse, with local variations including Desi Futurism, South Asian Futurism, Dalit Futurism/Dalitfuturism, Tamil Futurism and so on. Several manifestoes, such as Vandana Singh's 'A Speculative Manifesto' (2008) and Yudhanjaya Wijeratne's 'The Ricepunk Manifesto' (2020), have tried to capture and express some of the characteristics of South Asian sf.

Overall, South Asian sf in the present is part of a growing body of sf worldwide, and part of the same marketplace of ideas. Many of these works are published with the same publishing houses, awarded or nominated for the same awards, and even read by the same audiences outside the region. This is particularly true of Anglophone sf. However, the relatively large number of local readers, and a growing interest, both in the publishing market and scholarship, means that the works have to negotiate and balance the local, with its histories and myths, as well as its specific political needs and genre aesthetics, with the global requirements and expectations of genre classification and readership.

Works cited

Banerjee, Suparno. *Indian Science Fiction: Patterns, History and Hybridity*. University of Wales Press, 2020.

Chattopadhyay, Bodhisattva. *Bangla Kalpabigyan: Science Fiction in a Transcultural Context*. PhD Dissertation. University of Oslo, 2013.

Chattopadhyay, Bodhisattva, Aakriti Mandhwani and Anwesha Maity, eds. *Indian Genre Fiction: Past and Future Histories*. Routledge, 2023.

Khan, Sami Ahmad. *Star Warriors of the Modern Raj: Materiality, Mythology and Technology of Indian Science Fiction*. University of Wales Press, 2021.

Kuhad, Urvashi. *Science Fiction and Indian Women Writers: Exploring Radical Potentials*. Routledge, 2020.

Langer, Jessica and Dominic Alessio. 'Indian Science Fiction: An Overview'. *The Liverpool Companion to World Science Fiction Film*. Ed. Sonja Fritzsche. Liverpool UP, 2014. 56–68.

Mukherjee, Upamanyu Pablo. *Final Frontiers: Science Fiction and Techno-Science in Non-Aligned India*. Liverpool UP, 2020.

Sadaf, Shazia and Aroosa Kanwal. *Contemporary Pakistani Speculative Fiction and the Global Imaginary Democratizing Human Futures*. Routledge, 2023.

9
AFRODIASPORIC SPECULATIVE FICTION

Nicola Hunte

The field of Afrodiasporic speculative fiction is as vast and diverse as the conceptual, aesthetic and cultural frames used to talk about Blackness and African-centred expressions beyond the African continent. This field has a significant presence in the United Kingdom, the Caribbean and the Americas, with burgeoning communities in Australia and Europe. Afrodiasporic writing is positioned as always culturally marked, in its relations to both Afro-descendant/African practices and the specific localised contexts within diaspora. This kind of awareness, when negotiated through the subversive nature of speculative fiction, offers fertile possibilities for alternatives: alternative forms of storytelling, alternative voices, alternative realities, alternative visions of the future. (Given the heterogeneous quality of diasporic experiences, 'alternative' should be understood as 'alongside' not 'instead of'.)

The growing *visibility* of Afrodiasporic speculative fiction in the twenty-first century is partly a consequence of late-twentieth-century social, political and cultural movements concerned with articulations of identity in the face of oppression, alongside the 1990s upsurge in 'new wave' aesthetic movements in popular, well-circulated Anglo sf. According to Paul Kincaid, the latter trend signalled 'growing uncertainty about the role, nature, and future of the genre' (174). Arguably, therefore, the increasing attention paid to Afrodiasporic speculative fiction is due, in part, to its capacity to revision sf tropes and themes.

It is undeniable that this creative energy speaks to the value of relationships across communities dedicated to exploring the wondrous potential of sf and speculative fiction more broadly. The dialogue between Anglo sf and Afrodiasporic sf means that much of the conversation is happening in English. There are, for example, African Brazilian sf writers, such as Aline França, Alê Santos, Sandra Menezes and Fabio Kabral, and Afro-Latin writers, including Linda Raquel Nieves Pérez and Circe Moskowitz, as well as the French Caribbean author Bertène Juminer, who do not work primarily in English but have had some of their work translated into, or have opted to write in, English as well; this highlights the fact that the sphere of visibility primarily covers Anglophone works, which tends to be the entry point into Afrodiasporic sf. Fiction (and critical responses) from Britain, Canada, the US and to some extent the Anglophone Caribbean feature prominently in discussions about Afrodiasporic engagements with speculative fiction. Such work is concerned with imperialism, colonialism, slavery, otherness and time, addressed through

DOI: 10.4324/9781003140269-11

science and spirituality as sometimes competing, sometimes complementary, forms of technology. This nexus of ideas springs from shared but not necessarily similar experiences with forms of oppression and alienation and from the forms of creative redress offered by the rhizomatic nature of Afro-descendant cultures.

All Afro-everything

Sheree Renée Thomas's watershed *Dark Matter: A Century of Speculative Fiction from the African Diaspora* (2000) signalled the presence of Afrodiasporic speculative fiction throughout the twentieth century. Two decades later, Sheree Renée Thomas, Zelda Knight and Oghenechovwe Donald Ekpeki's *African Risen* (2022) declared a new era of speculative fiction from across Africa and its diaspora, its introduction outlining the growth of such work in the new millennium and presenting a constellation of anthologies, publishing houses, literary journals and editors dedicated to the exploration of this field. These two anthologies are vital contributions to the dynamic dialogue concerning the emergence and cultural significance of African-descendant speculative imaginations.

Dark Matter demonstrated that speculative narratives from the diaspora and their theoretical underpinnings have been around for at least a century. Thomas points to three early African American texts – Martin Delany's *Blake; Or the Huts of America* (1859–61), Sutton E. Griggs's *Imperium in Imperio* (1899) and Pauline Elizabeth Hopkins's *Of One Blood: Or, The Hidden Self* (1902) as 'proto-SF work [...] in the service of liberating and improving the real, lived lives of Black people' (5). Mark Bould argues that they and other novels by African Americans, appearing up to the eve of World War II, are a mode of revolutionary sf, and that if such texts had earlier been included in the sf canon,

> we might now have a very different genre, perhaps one that throughout the last century was more centered on promoting social justice and speculating about alternative social arrangements than on championing capitalist-imperialist expansion, technological fixes and gee-whizz bits of kit. Imagining sf as it otherwise might have been helps us to understand the sf that we have and opens up the possibility of radically reconstituting it.
>
> (1)

Both Delany's *Blake* and Mary Shelley's *Frankenstein* (1818), arguably the foundational text of Anglo sf, use speculative modes to address social concerns and anxieties arising from imperialism and slavery. *Frankenstein* is threaded with the dread of imperial masters produced by the monstrosity of their own desires for exploitation and violence (Ball 31), while *Blake* confronts the necessity for the enslaved Black subject to achieve agency, not grudgingly through political compromise but through revolution. Delany's utopic Black futurity is especially poignant given that chattel slavery and its attendant dehumanisation of Afro-descendant peoples was still openly practiced in North America. It is not surprising that one of the significant threads in African American literature is the repeated apprehension of slavery and racism, nor that speculative modes would play an important role in what Guyanese writer/critic Wilson Harris would term such 'creative rehearsals' ('History' 160). Joining the then-small but crucial vanguard of Octavia E. Butler, Samuel R. Delany, Charles R. Saunders, Steven Barnes, Jewelle Gomez and Tananarive Due, the new voices in Thomas's collection and its sequel, *Dark Matter: Reading the Bones* (2004), offered diverse speculative narratives of alternate realities, first contact with aliens, postapocalyptic events, fabulist encounters, the supernatural, robots and posthuman bodies.

Several anthologies after *Dark Matter* are attentive to diasporic voices, including Bill Campbell and Edward Austin Hall's *Mothership: Tales from Afrofuturism and Beyond* (2013), Nisi Shawl's *New Suns: Original Speculative Fiction by People of Color* (2019), Oghenechovwe Donald Ekpeki and Zelda Knight's *Dominion: An Anthology of Speculative Fiction from Africa and the African Diaspora* (2020) and Ekpeki's *The Year's Best African Speculative Fiction* (2021). These collections highlight cross-culturality within African diasporas and between Afrodiasporic and other diasporic expressions. In *Mothership*, for example, links can be drawn between Ernest Hogan's 'Skin Dragons Talk' (1998), with its alien invaders in the form of dragon tattoos, and C. Renee Stephens's 'Culling the Herd' (2013), about possession by an ancient god. Both protagonists, once inhabited by more powerful beings, receive preternatural insight into the flawed nature of their society. Both were already aware of their marginalised status – as a refugee migrant of Peruvian/Japanese ancestry, as a young Black girl – and their stories concern the decision to claim agency through being possessed. In *New Suns*, Steven Barnes's 'Come Home to Atropos' (2019) and Tobias S. Buckell's 'The Galactic Tourist Industrial Complex' (2019) highlight a cross-cultural conversation between African American and Afro-Caribbean communities. Barnes addresses the pall cast by the imperial gaze over less powerful island nations. In his futuristic vision of ubiquitous corporate capitalism, the vocabulary of marketing campaigns is used to elide the brutalities of plantation slavery. The attitude towards Caribbean islands in this future (which feels so much like the present) is that everything – their location, peoples, history – is in service to more powerful, external societies. Nonetheless, the end of the story suggests that there is resistance to this way of thinking. Exploitative business and systemic disempowerment also figure in Buckell's imagined future of global tourism, in which aliens visiting the Earth for 'authentic primitive world experience' (Buckell 25) treat the entire planet like the Caribbean islands in Barnes's story.

The sharing of imageries and socio-cultural concerns is a key feature of Afrodiasporic speculative fiction, which acknowledges such connections across forms of storytelling and of knowing, and interrogates established limits, structures of power and modes of relation in human society. Hence, there is a prevailing attention to destabilisation and revisioning. As Eugen Bacon observes about the stories in *Dominion*, 'such miscellany [highlights] the urgency to decolonize language, while deconstructing and reconstructing the selves and identities of people of colour' (8).

Africa Risen signposts not only the enduring presence of stories from Africa and the diaspora but the greater visibility of diversity within Anglophone Afrodiasporic sf, with African writers in diaspora as well as African American, Afro-British and Afro-Caribbean writers. This diversity, and the range of narrative forms and concerns, can also be demonstrated by novels published since the turn of the millennium. In the US, Maurice Broaddus's *I Can Transform You* (2013) blends sf noir and police procedural in a dystopian future, Victor LaValle's *The Changeling* (2017) moves through folklore to fairy tale to address familial trauma, Rivers Solomon's *An Unkindness of Ghosts* (2017) takes race and class oppression into outer space, and Tomi Adeyemi's *Children of Blood and Bone* (2018) roots magic in Yoruba Orisha as context and catalyst for a world defined by discrimination and marginalisation. In the UK, Bernardine Evaristo's *Blonde Roots* (2008) offers an alternate reality in which Europe, not Africa, is plundered for the transatlantic slave trade, and Courttia Newland's *River of Time* (2022) explores African cosmology and alternate realities in a rendering of what seems like a human addiction to hierarchies of power. The Canadian Minister Faust's *From the Notebooks of Dr. Brain* (2007) deploys the conventions of comic book superheroes in a satirical treatment of power dynamics across capitalism, race and sexuality, while the Australian Eugen Bacon combines magic with interplanetary settings for an exploration of gender in *Claiming T-Mo* (2019). Human and non-human concerns with negotiations of trauma, power and time are touchstones for storytellers of the African diaspora.

Another anthology that helped to widen the field of sf and Afrodiasporic speculative writing was Nalo Hopkinon's *Whispers from the Cotton Root Tree: Caribbean Fabulist Fiction* (2000). Its stories are not organised according to the notion of Afro-descendant cultures, but emerge from the heterogeneity of (Anglophone) Caribbean identities, including writers from the diaspora working within Afrodiasporic traditions. Addressing presumptions about how the speculative is defined, Hopkinson's 'fabulist fiction' is characterised by the porosity of such categories as sf, the supernatural, folklore, spirituality, horror and the fantastic. Hopkinson notes that 'fabulist' acknowledges the unknown, the unquantifiable, and in fiction this operates to unsettle our familiar views, whether these be about the past, the present or the future (Hopkinson and Batty 183). She also points out that the stories in the anthology are not 'inherently Caribbean' so much as they are stories told the world over but 'we just find different paradigms in which to express them' (Hopkinson and Batty 183). For example, Geoffrey Philp's 'Uncle Obadiah and the Alien' (1996) contextualises alien visitation as a mission of healing, an interplanetary undertaking in which ganja and Haile Selassie figure prominently; the spiritual and ideological practices of Rastafarianism are acknowledged as powerful tools of redress across the cosmos. In Pamela Mordecai's 'Once on the Shores of the Stream Senegambia' (2000), a surreal, fragmented narrative perspective reveals the dehumanising, alienating experience of technology used to target and absolutely control Black women's reproductive processes; a climactic epiphany surprisingly suggests an avenue of resistance connected to the protagonist's ancestry. The significance of the cotton root tree as a site of ancestral rootedness – as spiritual resource and as haunting – captures the main engagement of Afro-Caribbean speculative writing with trauma, diaspora and time.

Hopkinson is herself a diasporic writer from the Caribbean who has made her home in Canada and the US. Her first novel, *Brown Girl in the Ring* (1998), incorporated linguistic, spiritual and sociocultural features rooted in Caribbean experiences, opening up for larger sf communities, and other readerships, the fluid possibilities of the genre. Although the Caribbean is a site of multiple diasporas, it is possible to identify tropes recognisable across its communities. Antonio Gaztambide-Géigel observes the region's shared cultural responses to the 'presence and irradiation of the plantation and counterplantation' as a unifying factor that has made it possible to identify the Caribbean as 'those parts [...] which stand between the United States and Brazil [and] include the Caribbean migrant communities in the United States and Europe' (148). The plantation metaphor encapsulates the region's legacy of colonialism and slavery. It is not an exaggeration to claim that the Great House – the iconic building of the plantation owner – and its surrounding villages haunts Caribbean imaginative expression, especially in the twentieth century. In more recent speculative fiction, there are noticeable manifestations of the metaphorical cotton root tree – to express the ways in which the past and present are acknowledged in speculative realities, alternate timelines and futuristic societies.

Key contemporary Anglophone Caribbean speculative fiction writers include Tobias S. Buckell, R.S.A. Garcia, Karen Lord, Stephanie Saulter (long resident in the UK) and Caldwell Turnbull. In the foreword to Lord's anthology *New Worlds, Old Ways: Speculative Tales from the Caribbean* (2016), she points out that there is 'a longstanding tradition of Caribbean literature with fantastical or speculative elements' hidden in plain sight even as newer works are gaining visibility ('Foreword' 7). These newer works also seek out connections between alternative ways of knowing: between folklore and technology in Brian Franklin's 'Quaka-Hadja' (2016), for example, or between hypothetical science and grief in Damion Wilson's 'Daddy' (2016). *Reclaim, Restore, Return: Futurist Tales from the Caribbean* (2020), co-edited with Buckell, signals the trend towards exploring nascent futures. Lord explains the ethos of the collection: 'reclaim' expresses its revolutionary tone; 'restore' identifies healing redress and 'return' is a commitment to creating home for 'both those who leave and those who stay' ('Our' 6). This vision is encapsulated in 'The Mighty Slinger', co-written by Lord and Buckell, which she summarises thus

> a long-view future with Caribbean roots and a multiplanetary scope. Saving an environmentally degraded Earth from demolition and gentrification by the super-rich takes time, influence and money. We gave our revolutionary kaiso band plenty of both with periodic suspended animation, the support of generations of a Caribbean dynasty dedicated to politics and service, and the riches of bestselling calypso tunes with conscious lyrics.
> ('Our' 4)

Recent Anglophone Caribbean speculative novels locate Caribbean peoples and their experiences in technology-driven futures concerned with collective agency in a way that takes account of the region's 'conquistadorial legacies' (Harris 'Some' 99). Buckell's XENOWEALTH series (2006–12), set in a sprawling galaxy of wormholes, human colonies and power-obsessed aliens, pits resistance across diasporic communities against imperialism and slavery. Lord's *The Best of All Possible Worlds* (2013) and *The Galaxy Game* (2014) confront the tensions produced by dislocation and discrimination across planets, with threads of hope created by building family and community. Saulter's ®EVOLUTION series (2013–6) tackles exploitative social hierarchies and marginalisation with a view toward communal redress. This is just one of the observable trends; other concerns are also articulated through Caribbean paradigms. For example, Turnbull's 'Loneliness Is in Your Blood' (2017) focuses on isolation and marginalisation expressed by the folklore figure of the soucouyant, while Garcia's '12 Things a Trini Should Know Before Travelling to a Back in Times Fete™' (2022) takes the theme of nostalgia parties to the level of time travel, enabling partygoers from a utopic Caribbean future to participate in the original masquerades on slave plantations.

Contemporary Black Canadian writing also demonstrates speculative elements. Maureen Moynagh attempts to account for the 'revenant, mythical and otherwise spectral figures that burst through realist narratives' (105) by exploring how these 'generic f(r)ictions' highlight gaps in the national imaginary and dominant historiography around Blackness (87). As with African American and Anglophone Caribbean speculative writing, she links this attention to the uncanny legacies of slavery and colonialism at work in Canada, specifically, how the systemic efforts to suppress these legacies have turned them into a haunting presence (86). She points to David Chariandhy, Suzette Mayr and Esu Edugyan as Afrodiasporic Canadian writers who lean into the gothic and magical realism to produce 'afro-fabulation or retro-speculation, [...] mobilizations of the "past that is not past" [to] confront the present political arrangements in Canada and the diaspora with the trace of history that is anti-blackness' (105). Sifton Tracey Anipare's *Yume* (2021) features two marginalised characters who must navigate between the waking world and the dream world of the yokai (supernatural beings) in Japan, thus exploring concerns with cultural consumption and belonging in the face of globalisation. Jael Richardson's *Gutter Child* (2021) is a coming-of-age story for a young girl within a dystopian society built on social inequality and systemic exploitation. These newer novels approach constructions of Blackness and negotiations of subjectivity through speculative frames, and are part of a recent movement to explore the relevance of Black speculative arts in Canada.

Black British speculative imagination is presented in Leone Ross's *Glimpse: An Anthology of Black British Speculative Fiction* (2022). Reynaldo Anderson's foreword and Ross's introduction respectively outline the roots of a Black British speculative tradition and its contemporary literary manifestations. Anderson locates the context for this tradition in the slave narratives of eighteenth century Black British literature, Afro-Caribbean literature from the Windrush generation and early African American speculative fiction. He argues for an interconnected outgrowth of ideas and interventions devoted to Black speculative art that 'integrates African or African diasporic worldviews with science or technology and seeks to interpret, engage, design or alter reality for the re-imagination of the past, the contested present, and as a catalyst for the future' (Anderson 13). Ross observes that Black British speculative writing feels very recent compared to continental African and diasporic Caribbean expressions, which may be due to significant migrations of African and Afro-descendant people to the UK only happening after World War II. Geoff Ryman makes a similar observation, suggesting that the growing significance and popularity of African sf and fantasy is due to the diasporic condition:

> A break with old culture opens up new possibilities in the present and for the future. Diasporans often dream of a better personal future, and it's a short step to dream of other futures for everyone else. The loss of culture draws the gaze backwards in time, to other values. Diasporas make you the Other. You know better what it is like to be an alien.
>
> ('Introduction' n.p.)

By being both forward and backward looking while creating community elsewhere, writers in diaspora can access fertile possibilities for storytelling, for imaginative re-creation, for making connections.

Ryman spotlights several African writers who have made their home, permanently or temporarily, in the UK. Among them are Chikodili Emelumadu whose 'Candy Girl' (2014) features a bewitched umbrella, a literally and figuratively all-consuming relationship, and the significance of a rooted as opposed to cosmetic connection to the gods. Ryman also discusses Leye Adenle's 'Anatomy of Mermaid' as an exploration of a multilayered intersection of 'sex, whiteness, diaspora, traditional belief, and science [and] the image of the mermaid [as] an image of hybrid diasporan culture' ('Leye' n.p.). The story balances scientific observation of marine life, the European myth of the mermaid and the pan-African folkloric/spiritual figure of water, Mami Wata, to underscore multiple ways of framing reality. Ryman also highlights the significance of hybridity in his interview with Jennifer Nansubuga Makumbi about her novel, *Kintu* (2018), returning to the importance of cultural engagement in sf and its deployment for, on the one hand, specifically localised concerns and, on the other, as a conversation with other communities, other influences. Nick Wood's *Azanian Bridges* (2016) illustrates how sf frames can be used to explore not-so-distant past traumas. It depicts the dystopia of apartheid South Africa, supported by a technology devoted to totalitarian control, but includes the distinctively African feature of a significant role being given to traditional belief systems (Ryman 'Nick' n.p.). Technologically-mediated totalitarianism also features in Wood's 'The Paragon of Knowledge' (2015), in which everyone is in service to what seems like a digital data deity. The protagonist is initiated into a community of resistance by an impossibly old Black man whose desire to be remembered creates the first chink in the god-like hold of the information network numen.

It is apparent, even from this small sample of writers in diaspora, that African imaginaries are being mapped through speculative fiction. Some shared contours are negotiations of trauma and of cultural identity, and the (re)turn to traditional ways of knowing, which can clearly be connected to the diasporic condition. And, as Ryman argues, diaspora can also be experienced without migration:

> Colonialism, and then internalized colonialism, both have wrenched African cultures away from home without the people having to physically move. Globalization, new technology, new media continue to do the same. This is a different kind of scattering, but a scattering all the same.
>
> ('Introduction' n.p.)

The dynamic field of Afrodiasporic speculative fiction extends far beyond this brief sketch, which does not address with the scattering of Afro-descendant and African peoples across Asia and Europe. However, it is clear that this speculative tradition reaches back before the twentieth century and it looks toward the creative promise and potential of the current century. The field is shaped by colonialism, racism and diaspora, but what imaginative expression is not? What is distinctive here is Afrodiasporic speculative fiction's tendency to respond usefully to the estrangement and alienation produced by these legacies. By disrupting stasis and/or offering redress, its speculative treatment of past, present and future can be understood as therapeutic.

From ancestors to futures

There are various different, if related, ways to critically read Afrodiasporic sf. Perhaps the most widespread approach is Afrofuturism. Its initial definition in 1993 unequivocally focused on the US: 'speculative fiction that treats African-American themes and addresses African-American concerns in the context of twentieth-century technoculture and, more generally, African-American signification that appropriates images of technology and a prosthetically enhanced future' (Dery 8). However, it has also been discussed in relation to Afrodiasporic cultures, genre diversity and the significance of 'non-Western' belief systems (Womack 9, 191), and defined in terms of 'enigmatic returns to the constitutive trauma of slavery in the light of science fiction' to help imagine counter-futures (Eshun 299). Afrofuturism is primarily concerned with technology, diverse belief systems, constructions of Blackness that acknowledge traumatic legacies, counter-futures, diaspora to some extent and, very importantly, the inter-relationship of these phenomena.

Whereas Afrofuturism 1.0 is concerned with the development of technoculture over the twentieth century and its relationship to constructions of Blackness, and with the experience of Afro-descendant peoples and liberatory futures as points of intervention into the present, Afrofuturism 2.0 or Astro-Blackness looks to these concerns for the twenty-first century through a Pan-Africanist lens. It acknowledges 'regional differences such as, and not limited to, Caribbean Futurism, African Futurism and Black futurism' (Anderson and Jones x). Two significant features of Astro-Blackness are the relationship between emerging/changing technologies and racialised identities – specifically Black identities – and the development of futuristic visions through the past. The main contours here are, necessarily, shared with Afrofuturism, but open on to the diversity of the diaspora.

Africanfuturism distinguishes itself from Afrofuturism, focusing on 'African culture, history, mythology and point-of-view as it then branches into the Black Diaspora, and it does not privilege or center the West' (Okorafor n.p.). It is concerned with Black people, their relationship to technology and their visions of the future, as expressed in sf: 'its default/center is African' and it is 'more concerned with "what is and can/will be". It acknowledges, grapples with and carries "what has been"' (n.p.). Africanjujuism is focused on fantasy rather than sf. It explores the imaginative treatment of African spiritualties and cosmologies, presenting them as legitimate, not made-up elements of the world, thus challenging the fictive nature of the supernatural typical of European and American fantasy. It offers an alternate way of approaching reality through 'guided imagery' to explore the potential of one's own culture (Rutledge and Hopkinson 593).

Afropantheology refers to works of fiction that combine fantasy elements with African spiritual realities. It is distinguished from Africanjujuism through its focus on not only African but also Afro-descendant cosmologies. It emphasises the importance of diaspora when it enables connections across communities, and the relationship between the present and the future.

The Afrospeculative is concerned with the relationship between speculative and historical narratives, such as neo-slave narratives. Its focus is the reinvention of the past, using sf and fantasy elements to construct alternate histories with attention to the mutuality between African folk spirituality and twentieth-century technologies.

Macumbapunk combines fantasy, sf and African cultural elements; it treats technology and nature as mutually supportive and science and magic as coeval, and it accepts the fluidity of gender identities (Brock 21). Its primary contours are the significance of the past, the recourse to African cultures, and – in a manner akin to Africanjujuism – the shared value of science and magic understood in African contexts.

Black Canadian speculative discourse and innerstandings identify pan-African, pan-Caribbean, Black diasporic cultural expressions in co-existence with those of Indigenous communities, with the objective of 'retelling and reimagining of our futurities while stabilising our presence' (Hudson and Lindsay iii). The value of Afro-descendant spirituality to this approach is signalled by its use of 'innerstandings', a Rastafarian term for coming to a realisation through one's soul.

Black quantum futurism blends quantum physics with 'Black/African cultural traditions of consciousness, time and space' (Phillips qtd in Chattopadhyay 18–9) to articulate a non-linear, non-causal approach to time. This layered, cyclical treatment of time allows for casting different futures, re-imagining the present and rehabilitating the past so as to locate ways of healing for the trauma produced by current social inequalities.

Caribbean futurism re-imagines futures and offers healing through imaginative redress. It claims agency in imagining the future for the region with narratives that project current social concerns through various speculative frames. This agency tends to be expressed in three main ways: collective action/communal links in the face of crisis; the use of technology to generate hope; and the presence of love and/or compassion.

These varied responses to Afrodiasporic speculative imaginations are linked through the shared contours of technology, spirituality, futures, trauma, healing, cultural expression and connections. They intersect, compete, diverge and stretch to shape worlds, galaxies and realities. The resulting diversity makes this growing field difficult to pin down, but it works to widen sf communities and redress the 'uncertainty about the role, nature, and future of the genre' (Kincaid 174).

Works cited

Anderson, Reynaldo. 'The Rise of the Black British Speculative Tradition'. *Glimpse: A Black British Anthology of Speculative Fiction.* Ed. Leone Ross. Peepal Tree, 2022. 7–14.

Anderson, Reynaldo and Charles E. Jones. 'The Rise of Astro-Blackness'. *Afrofuturism 2.0: The Rise of Astro-Blackness.* Ed. Reynaldo Anderson and Charles E. Jones. Lexington, 2016. vii–xviii.

Bacon, Eugen. 'Trends in Black Speculative Fiction'. *Fafnir: Nordic Journal of Science Fiction and Fantasy Research* 8.2 (2021): 7–13.

Ball, Clement John. 'Imperial Monstrosities, "Frankenstein," the West Indies and V. S. Naipaul'. *Ariel: A Review of International English Literature* 32. 3 (2001): 31–58.

Bould, Mark. 'Revolutionary African-American Sf before Black Power SF'. *Extrapolation* 51.1 (2010): 1–20.

Brock, Patrick. 'Brazilian Afrofuturism, Heuristic Function, and the Mass Cultural Genre System'. *SFRA Review* 53.3 (2023): 18–27.

Buckell, Tobias S. 'The Galactic Tourist Industrial Complex'. *New Suns: Original Speculative Fiction by People of Color*. Ed. Nisi Shawl. Solaris, 2019. 13–26.

Chattopadhyay, Bodhisattva. 'Manifestos of Futurisms'. *Foundation: The International Review of Science Fiction* 139 (2021): 8–23.

Dery, Mark. 'Black to the Future: Afro-Futurism 1.0'. *Afro-Future Females: Black Writers Chart Science Fiction's Newest New-Wave Trajectory*. Ed. Marleen S. Barr. Ohio State UP, 2008. 6–13.

Eshun, Kodwo. 'Further Considerations on Afrofuturism'. *CR: The New Centennial Review* 3.2 (2003): 287–302.

Gaztambide-Géigel, Antonio. 'The Invention of the Caribbean in the Twentieth Century: The Definitions of the Caribbean as a Historical and Methodological Problem'. *Social and Economic Studies* 53.3 (2004): 127–57.

Harris, Wilson. 'History, Fable and Myth in the Caribbean and Guianas'. *Selected Essays of Wilson Harris: The Unfinished Genesis of the Imagination*. Ed. Andrew J.M. Bundy. Routledge, 1999. 152–66.

——. 'Some Aspects of Myth and the Intuitive Imagination'. *Explorations: A Selection of Talks and Articles 1966–1981*. Ed. Hena Maes-Jelinek. Dangaroo, 1981. 97–106.

Hopkinson, Nalo and Nancy Batty. '"Caught by a … genre": An Interview with Nalo Hopkinson'. *Ariel: A Review of International English Literature* 33.1 (2002): 175–201.

Hudson, Audrey and Quentin Lindsay. 'The Northside'. *Cosmic Underground Northside: An Incantation of Black Canadian Speculative Discourse and Innerstandings*. Ed. Quentin Vercetty and Audrey Hudson. Cedar Grove, 2020. iii–viii.

Kincaid, Paul. 'Fiction since 1992'. *The Routledge Companion to Science Fiction*. Ed. Mark Bould, Andrew M. Butler, Adam Roberts and Sherryl Vint. Routledge, 2009. 174–82.

Lord, Karen, 'Foreword'. *New Worlds, Old Ways: Speculative* Tales from the Caribbean. Ed. Karen Lord. Peekash, 2016. 7–9.

——. 'Our Sanctury Sea'. *Reclaim, Restore, Return: Futurist Tales from the Caribbean*. Ed. Karen Lord and Tobias S. Buckell. Caribbean Futures Institute, 2020. 1–7.

Moynagh, Maureen. 'Gothic Realism and other Genre F(r)ictions in Contemporary Black Canadian Writing'. *Ariel: A Review of International English Literature* 53.3 (2022): 81–111.

Okorafor, Ndedi. 'Africanfuturism Defined'. *Africanfuturism: An Anthology*. Ed. Wole Talabi. Brittle Paper, 2020. Unpaginated.

Rutledge, Gregory E. and Nalo Hopkinson. 'Speaking in Tongues: An Interview with Science Fiction Writer Nalo Hopkinson'. *African American Review* 33.4 (1999): 589–601.

Ryman, Geoff. 'Introduction: On Diaspora'. 'One Hundred African Writers of SFF – Part Two: Writers in the U.K'. *Strange Horizons* (2017). http://strangehorizons.com/non-fiction/100african/introduction-on-diaspora/

——. 'Jennifer Nansubuga Makumbi'. 'One Hundred African Writers of SFF – Part Two: Writers in the U.K'. *Strange Horizons* (2017). http://strangehorizons.com/non-fiction/100african/jennifer-nansubuga-makumbi/

——. 'Leye Adenle'. 'One Hundred African Writers of SFF – Part Two: Writers in the U.K'. *Strange Horizons* (2017). http://strangehorizons.com/non-fiction/100african/leye-adenle/

——. 'Nick Wood'. 'One Hundred African Writers of SFF – Part Two: Writers in the U.K'. *Strange Horizons* (2017). http://strangehorizons.com/non-fiction/100african/nick-wood/

Thomas, Sheree Renée. 'And So Shaped the World'. *Obsidian: Literature and Arts in the African Diaspora* 42.1 (2016): 3–10.

Womack, Ytasha L. *Afrofuturism: The World of Black Sci-Fi and Fantasy Culture*. Lawrence Hill, 2013.

10
ANGLOPHONE PRINT FICTION
Children's and young adult

Emily Midkiff

Young adult sf (YASF) refers to sf intended for young people, usually from 12–18 years old. Sf for younger children, or primary sf, refers to sf for readers under 12. The significance of the intended audience for both YASF and primary sf cannot be overstated, as it plays into the design, content, themes and cultural context of the books. YA and children's literature are among the few publishing categories, along with new adult literature, that are named after the target audience. Nevertheless, YA and children's literature, including and perhaps especially sf texts, are not exclusively for or about young people.

Recent decades have seen many more texts for young people being consumed outside of their supposed target audience. While evident in many genres, this 'crossover phenomenon' (Falconer *Crossover*, 'Young Adult') is strongly associated with speculative fiction since its origins are often attributed to three bestselling series: J.K. Rowlings's HARRY POTTER (1997–2007), Stephenie Meyer's TWILIGHT (2005–8) and Suzanne Collins's THE HUNGER GAMES (2008–10). While the former series are, respectively, children's fantasy and YA paranormal romance, the latter is YASF and, given the deluge of popular YASF crossover series that followed in its wake, it would seem that YASF is especially well-suited to crossover readership.

The crossover phenomenon provides a useful way to think about sf for young people and how it has changed over time as the categories have been defined and redefined by marketing strategies and different beliefs about adulthood, adolescence and childhood. Given that publishers are very aware of their crossover audiences, the current use of terms like 'YA' and 'children's literature' are not meant to prescribe who can read the books, but instead they serve as a signal to readers young and old that books with these labels can be expected to share certain features and themes, including many that resonate with more than just young audiences.

To long-time sf readers, the current crossover phenomenon may seem familiar, but reversed. As recently as the early 2000s, 'crossover readers' was more likely to refer to adolescents who read adult novels, rather than the other way around. The prevailing wisdom has been that budding sf readers will discover sf around age 12 and then skip over YASF in favour of general sf books (Levy; Fichtelberg). This view implies that YASF is so different from general sf that they appeal to different readers, and that primary sf does not exist. These implications indicate the unique challenges facing sf for young people. However, the recent reversal of the crossover reader also suggests how it is rising to meet those challenges.

 DOI: 10.4324/9781003140269-12

A brief history of primary sf

There is not always a clear demarcation between YASF and primary sf – especially in books intended for the 10- to 14-year-olds that sit at the edge of both categories – but contemporary books for children often feature formatting differences. For readers on the upper end of the age range, these differences include modifications like extra space between lines, shorter chapters to help young readers develop print skills, and content differences such as more explanations of the plot to help ease children into the sf genre's particular emphasis on inferencing comprehension skills. Books for the youngest readers and pre-literate children are often heavily illustrated and savvy authors and illustrators utilise these pictures to expand the scope of sf content. The detailed illustrations in David Wiesner's picturebook *Flotsam* (2006) deliver the speculative questions of the story, hiding details to amaze young readers and inspire curiosity, while Jason Shiga's graphic novel *Meanwhile* (2010) uses panels and arrows to depict complex alternative timelines, helping young readers grasp this mind-boggling sf concept through their visual literacy.

In older books, the distinction between children and teens is harder to identify. Throughout the late nineteenth and early twentieth centuries, children and adolescents consumed the same sf in the form of dime novels, penny dreadfuls, storypapers and comic books. These early serialised stories, such as the popular gadget-based adventures in the FRANKE READ, JR. (1879–99) and TOM EDISON, JR. (1891–2) series, made way for the publication of novels like Victor Appleton's *Tom Swift and His Airship* (1910), one of the earliest sf novels specifically marketed for children younger than 12 years old. Another early title is L. Frank Baum's *The Master Key: An Electrical Fairy Tale* (1901), which grew out of the children's fantasy tradition rather than gadget adventures.

Early examples of sf in formats specifically designed for children, such as chapter books and early readers, include Ellen MacGregor's *Miss Pickerell Goes to Mars* (1951), Ruthven Todd's *Space Cat* (1952) and Eleanor Cameron's *The Wonderful Flight to the Mushroom Planet* (1954). These three, like many sf books intended for the youngest readers, were written by authors who defined themselves as children's authors rather than sf authors. Illustrator Mary Liddell's *Little Machinery* (1926) is the first picturebook for modern children (op de Beeck), but it is also the first sf picturebook. Following this early example, sf picturebooks were not commonly produced until the 1970s, when Bill Peet's *The Wump World* (1970), Gertrude Moore's *Mrs. Moore in Space* (1974) and others appeared. Sf is now produced regularly in all children's formats, but at a slower rate than other genres for children (Midkiff 110).

Overall, primary sf is not new but is often subsumed into general children's fiction rather than distinguished as sf. Some librarians and educators even avoid the term 'science fiction' when promoting these books, in favour of 'humour' or other descriptors (Midkiff 128). Contemporary primary sf books are still often written by children's authors rather than sf authors, with a few notable exceptions, such as Terry Pratchett's *Only You Can Save Mankind* (2005) and Yoon Ha Lee's *Dragon Pearl* (2019).

A brief history of YASF

According to Lee A. Talley, the earliest distinction between children and adolescents as readers can be attributed to the 1802 edition of Sarah Trimmer's periodical *The Guardian of Education*. However, it was not until Stanley Hall's influential *Adolescence: Its Psychology and Its Relation to Physiology, Anthropology, Sociology, Sex, Crime, Religion and Education* (1905) that the current concepts of rebellious adolescents became popular (Trites), leading to increasing separation between literature for adolescents and younger children as YA literature became an institutional force for supporting teens.

While children's books are printed in formats and trim sizes that make their target audience clearly identifiable, much contemporary YA fiction is at first glance indistinguishable from general fiction. YA is sometimes defined by the presence of adolescent protagonists, but there is debate as to whether any book with an adolescent protagonist is YA or only those written specifically with young readers in mind. Some authors reject the YA label, such as Nnedi Okorafor, who stated that her *Binti* novella (2015) is not YA despite being included in many YA lists (@Nnedi). However, this debate is mostly relevant in the less common case of books like Orson Scott Card's *Ender's Game* (1985) that were originally written for a general audience but have been retrospectively labelled as YA due to young protagonists and/or popularity among young readers or high school teachers. In contemporary practice, YA is first and foremost a publishing category. The target audience is decided by the time of a book's acquisition by a publisher, if not earlier, and this choice guides editorial and marketing decisions throughout the publication process.

The first significant examples of sf written specifically for adolescents were not far removed from adult sf. In the late 1940s, Scribner's commissioned Robert A. Heinlein, who was already a popular sf author, to write a series intended specifically for adolescent audiences. These novels were called Juveniles (YA was not a widely used label until the 1960s). While there were sf stories for young people before Heinlein began his series, this marks the beginning of sf for young people as a valuable and distinct publishing category. C.W. Sullivan III ('American') and Karen Sands-O'Connor and Marietta Frank argue that the first of Heinlein's Juveniles, *Rocket Ship Galileo* (1947), was a particularly notable turning point in the history of adolescent sf because it was published in a hardcover edition at a time when much sf came out in highly-criticised pulp magazines (and sometimes, then, as paperbacks). While this publishing choice circumvented criticism and allowed for immediate shelving in libraries, Sullivan also notes that Heinlein's serious attention to science and speculation about cultural assumptions also set his Juveniles apart from what was seen as the low-brow content of popular sf ('American'). Heinlein was followed into the adolescent market by several other established sf writers who wrote for adults, such as Isaac Asimov with *David Starr: Space Ranger* (1952) and Arthur C. Clarke with *Islands in the Sky* (1952). Andre Norton, another landmark author for Juvenile sf, started with *Star Man's Son, 2250 A.D.* (1952) and went on to become better-known for her books for young people than for her other work. During the 1970s, some sf authors begin to specialise in writing for adolescents rather than writing across ages.

Meanwhile, the YA label developed separately before being applied to sf. YA scholars often point to one of three turning points: Maureen Daley's *Seventeenth Summer* (1942), J.D. Salinger's *The Catcher in the Rye* (1951) or S.E. Hinton's *The Outsiders* (1967). All three of these contemporary realistic novels focus on the maturation of the adolescent characters against the backdrop of adolescent culture at the time. Hinton specifically called for realism in YA literature, heralding the problem novels of the 1970s that emphasised gritty stories about the realistic issues faced by young people. Once YA literature became a distinct and profitable publishing category by the end of the 1960s, sf written for adolescents began to be marketed under and possibly even changed by the YA label.

These historical trends in sf for young people follow larger cultural attitudes toward science and young people. Rebecca Onion explains that the 1940s and 1950s were defined – in the US, at least – by a concern that science-loving youth were becoming rare and needed support and encouragement. However, by the 1960s and 1970s, growing apocalyptic fears and general disillusionment with science led adults to want to immerse children in the wonder of science while protecting them from the consequences of science. This shift corresponds with the move from Juvenile sf to YASF and the associated changes in tone and content.

Farah Mendlesohn argues that Juveniles and YA are not interchangeable terms because the shift in terminology corresponds with a change in emphasis. Juvenile sf books by authors like Heinlein and Norton, she says, conclude with a focus on the consequences of the sf premise for the larger world – more like sf for adults – while contemporary YASF books often conclude on a smaller scale, with an inward focus on the protagonist's emotions and relationships. Joseph W. Campbell also writes that YASF turned from a scientific and technological focus as early as 1962, although he argues that this increasing social orientation is a feature rather than a flaw.

Overall, the shift in marketing labels and author specialisation in the 1960s and 1970s led to YASF being a distinct category from general sf, distinguishable by marketing labels and strategies as well as a tendency toward certain themes and issues.

Critical concerns

Primary sf and YASF are not always considered a significant area of speculative fiction studies. Sullivan notes that sf 'written specifically for the young reader has been, by and large, ignored or treated only in passing', perhaps because both sf and children's literature at the time were each new and fairly risky fields on their own, never mind as a combination ('Preface' xiv). Notably, Sullivan's edited collection, *Science Fiction for Young Readers* (1993), goes on to focus on YASF, with only one essay on a picturebook. YASF has gained more critical traction since then, but sf for the even younger reader is often still overlooked.

YASF and primary sf are often criticised through contrast with sf for adults. Sands-O'Connor and Frank, Donald Palumbo and A. Waller Hastings all argue that sf for young people disregards the scientific plausibility deemed valuable in sf for adults. Noga Applebaum writes that YASF tends to portray technology negatively while sf for adults is more nuanced. Mendlesohn and Perry Nodelman both criticise YASF for ending with an inward focus and children's books for ending back at home in security and without any consequences. Nodelman concludes that there are generic differences between values and standards: YA and children's fiction are suspicious of change, while sf embraces it. These critical concerns about primary sf in particular, have even led to the question of whether sf for young children is truly sf or just fantasy in disguise. Mendlesohn's answer to this question is that there are some good titles out there that hold to general sf genre standards, but not enough. Hastings wonders whether children's sf is its own separate genre. The most recent *Encyclopedia of Science Fiction* entry on 'Children's SF' by John Clute, David Langford and Peter Nicholls provocatively wonders whether clean genre distinctions are even valuable when it comes to children's sf.

Meanwhile, Joe Sutliff Sanders argues that it is not the books with different values, but the critics; while sf scholars are likely to evaluate books for scientific rigour and firm genre boundaries, children's literature scholars focus more on the story's relationship with the young target audience. This distinction in the criticism can perhaps be seen most clearly in awards. Most major speculative fiction awards like the Hugo Awards and the Nebula Awards have affiliated awards for YA and children's fiction, although these often group sf and fantasy together into one award category. Yet the books that win YA and children's awards from speculative fiction organisations are rarely the same books that win awards from librarian and children's literature organisations.

In the end, the interpretation and evaluation of YASF and primary sf must be considered in light of the difference between the adults and the young people involved. With very few exceptions, books are written, distributed, stocked and criticised by adults. As a result, these texts often reveal adult anxieties and assumptions about youth. In the case of sf, they reveal adult beliefs about youth in connection with technology and science.

Applebaum and Mendlesohn both argue that many YASF texts express technophobia that runs contrary to the young audience's interests due to the adult writers' fears that when young people have increased technological access – especially access to knowledge – they grow up too quickly. Applebaum and Mendlesohn express concern that YASF with this attitude will ultimately not turn adolescents against technology, but rather will turn them against reading sf. Since adolescents do not have the ability to define themselves or their interests in the literature that is supposedly intended for them, YA embodies a conflict between adult power and adolescent identity. Roberta Seelinger Trites proposes that YA novels are all inherently about power. Thematically, the young protagonists must define themselves in contrast to the institutions that surround and control them but – due to adults controlling the narratives – these rebellions always take place in sanctioned ways that eventually lead to the young character finding a place within the system. Rebekah Fitzsimmons and Casey Alane Wilson note that while the YA category began with relatively young writers, that original 'teen voice' was soon co-opted by adults, and YA literature became one of many adult institutions intended to 'prevent teens from living up to society's worst expectations' (xii). In the case of YASF, those worst expectations are teens using technology to access information beyond what has been granted to them.

Meanwhile, primary sf is heavily influenced by adult beliefs about the age at which children can understand science, technology and their potential consequences. While YA fiction is generally expected to have some element of rebellion and questioning society's rules, which corresponds well with the speculative interests of sf, children's literature is often expected to be more Romantic, which does not fit the ideals of sf nearly as neatly. An idealised, pastoral child would not seem to be a good fit for serious questions about science and technology, especially since the 1960s when adults started to shield children from the consequences of science (Onion) and the twenty-first century when adults have come to fear that technology spoils childhood innocence (Applebaum). The result of these beliefs are primary sf stories that engage in adventures with robots and aliens without ever posing any speculative questions or exploring any consequences of science. However, as Mendlesohn and I both argue, adult beliefs about children's innocence and scientific understanding do not reflect real children's abilities or interests; instead, they point to the cultural legacy of Jean-Jacques Rousseau's 'natural' child who develops reasoning skills at the age of twelve – a long-lasting concept that shows most clearly in the common recommendation that it is the prime age to start reading sf.

Recent directions in YASF and primary sf

The crossover phenomenon is changing sf's treatment of young people. Rachel Falconer attributes the phenomenon to themes of transition and thresholds in YA stories that speak to adults who have come of age in a time when distinct stages of life are no longer the norm. This might explain the sudden surge in crossover readership, but YASF has always had crossover readers. Over a decade ago, Michael Levy argued that YASF themes have been of interest to readers both young and old since at least the 1980s. The growing popularity of sf with crossover audiences, however, has forced this crossover readership into the open and perhaps encouraged more of it. As the audience becomes more mixed – and the publishing industry rises to meet this new demand – the adult beliefs about adolescence and childhood that have influenced sf production are impacted by this destabilisation of target audience age categories. Authors wield these changes in audience and popularity to shatter the traditional adult/child divisions that cause so much critical concern.

Many contemporary primary sf books respect their young readers by offering complex sf speculation in ways that do not clash with developing reading and comprehension skills. Even simple stories can expand outward at the end to imply large changes in the world, but in small ways. In the end of Scott Santoro's picturebook *Farm Fresh Cats* (2006), the narrator asks the audience to consider how the world has changed and offers a clue in the picture. The Fan Brothers' picturebook *The Barnabus Project* (2021) speculates about the ethics of genetic engineering in simple language and through the familiar topic of pets while offering complex pictures to peruse.

Contemporary YASF looks inward in order to speculate outward and treats technology as neutral or an extension of the self rather than an external concept to fear or embrace. Empowered by popularity and its own shifting audience, YASF is likely to utilise the thematic interests and genre strengths of both YA and sf to turn its speculative powers inward and ask powerful questions about the age categories, technology and systems of power that once controlled it. Writing on The Hunger Games, Mary F. Pharr and Leisa A. Clark argue that post-9/11 YASF no longer focuses just on personal survival, but also on social change, while Tom Henthorne suggests that the tight inward focus on Katniss Everdeen's emotions is exactly what fuels the story's most potent extrapolation about the impact she has on her world, and that the story's attention to emotion and relationships does not stop it from expanding outward at the end. Angela S. Insenga argues that Marissa Meyer's Lunar Chronicles series (2012–5) starts with an inwardly-focused sf retelling of Cinderella that gradually becomes a broad exploration of material embodiment and the decentralisation of the biological body. Rebekah Fitzsimmons goes so far as to argue that the overall trend of YASF dystopian trilogies over the last two decades has been 'instructing young readers in a pedagogy of resistance, overthrow, and utopian hope' (16) and that this education has put young people in the right mindset to engage in real political action. In addition, Ferne Merrylees argues that contemporary YASF is depicting its heroes – rather than its villains – as posthuman in order to explore the modern adolescent's hybrid existence with technology and the power that adults wield over adolescent access to technology. Merrylees concludes that these books might even be 'suggesting there has been a shift in our society regarding adolescents' use of technology to one that is more positive' (91).

These movements toward resisting the adult controlling influences on YASF are especially apparent in recent YASF focusing on climate change, an issue that is particularly relevant to contemporary young people and their imagined futures. As Alice Curry writes, young adult readers 'are faced with the prospect of growing up in a post-natural world. This crisis is reflected in the contentious relationships between the young protagonists of the novels and their social and ecological surroundings, relationships that are enacted on the discursive sites of their own bodies' (15–6). Books such as Paolo Bacigalupi's *The Windup Girl* (2009) and Joan He's *The Ones We're Meant to Find* (2021) depict bleak futures in which adults ruin the environment due to politics, greed and personal motives until misused young people – and in both cases post-human young people – take power over the future in open-ended conclusions. Recent YASF has also seen an increase in exploring the impact of environmental destruction on non-Western cultures, as in Cherie Dimaline's The Marrow Thieves (2017–) and Tochi Onyebuchi's War Girls (2019–20) series.

As these two series demonstrate, recent sf for young people not only explores questions of age and power, but also the intersections of age, identity and power. Given that The Hunger Games can be credited for the recent boom in YASF, it is significant that Collins's character Rue features significantly as an example in Ebony Elizabeth Thomas's argument that speculative fiction texts have demonstrated an 'imagination gap' in representations of race. Fortunately, the increase in YASF popularity in the wake of the crossover phenomenon has also made room for greater representation. S.R. Toliver argues that due to the recent popularity of YA dystopias, young women can find far more valuable heroines and that – while not as widespread – there are more heroines of colour, too. Marie Lu's *Legend* (2011), Sherri Smith's *Orleans* (2013) and Dan Wells's *Bluescreen* (2015), among others, highlight how YASF stories can utilise the protagonist's age to explore the intersections of race and youth in the context of technology and the future.

Even the love triangle dynamic of THE HUNGER GAMES, which defines many copycat series, has been questioned and updated through a queer lens in recent YASF series that set up similar expectations only to reverse them as the protagonists work to dismantle related injustices in their societies. Rosiee Thor's *Tarnished Are the Stars* (2009) supplants the love triangle dynamic with a queer romance and an asexual protagonist alongside themes about technology and its relationship to disability and eugenics. In Xiran Jay Zhao's *Iron Widow* by (2021), the protagonist seizes the mechanical power that was denied to her on the basis of biological determinism, gender norms and sex shaming, and her rejection of these limitations culminates in a queer, polyamorous relationship that fuels her control over the machines.

In primary sf, the increasing representation in children's literature due to the We Need Diverse Books movement has also encouraged more sf stories featuring protagonists of colour in the future and in scientific roles, demonstrating to readers from a young age that they belong in sf, the future and the sciences. Many high-quality examples of contemporary primary sf feature minority and queer characters as scientists, as in Brian Pinkney's *Cosmo and the Robot* (2000), or as programmers, as in Gene Luen Yang and Mike Holmes's *Secret Coders* (2015), or as engineers, as in Tom Siddell's webcomic *Gunnerkrigg Court* (2005–). Several books go beyond representation to celebrate and explore culture, difference and ability through sf, such as the celebration of lowrider culture and Spanish language in Cathy Camper and Raúl the Third's *Lowriders in Space* (2014) and the exploration of sf inventions for accessibility in James Patterson, Chris Grabenstein and Juliana Neufeld's *House of Robots* (2014).

Overall, when the age of the target audience is brought into relief through labels like YA and children's literature, sf is subject to the cultural associations and assumptions about those ages, and this can interact with the content of sf in fascinating and even productive ways. The best of YASF and primary sf mobilises its position at the crossroads of sf and age-specific fiction to question age-related systems of power. YASF and primary sf are influenced by their intended audience – or at least adult perceptions of that young audience – but these stories offer worthwhile sf experiences to all readers.

Works cited

@Nnedi. 'The Binti Novella Trilogy is not a YA Series. Who Fears Death is not a YA Novel. The Akata Series is a YA Series. Zahrah the Windseeker is a YA Novel. [YA stands for "young adult"] Sincerely, The Author of These Books'. *Twitter* (08:40 22 December 2017). https://twitter.com/Nnedi/status/944216172429496320

Applebaum, Noga. *Representations of Technology in Science Fiction for Young People*. Routledge, 2009.

Campbell, Joseph W. *The Order and the Other: Young Adult Dystopian Literature and Science Fiction*. UP of Mississippi, 2019.

Clute, John, David Langford and Peter Nicholls. 'Children's SF'. *The Encyclopedia of Science Fiction*. Ed. Peter Nicholls, John Clute, David Langford and Graham Sleight. https://sf-encyclopedia.com/entry/childrens_sf

Curry, Alice. *Environmental Crisis in Young Adult Fiction: A Poetics of Earth*. Palgrave Macmillan, 2013.

Falconer, Rachel. *The Crossover Novel: Contemporary Children's Fiction and Its Adult Readership*. Routledge, 2008.

——. 'Young Adult Fiction and the Crossover Phenomenon'. *The Routledge Companion to Children's Literature*. Routledge, 2010. 87–99.

Fichtelberg, Susan. *Encountering Enchantment: A Guide to Speculative Fiction for Teens*. Libraries Unlimited, 2006.

Fitzsimmons, Rebekah. 'Exploring the Genre Conventions of the YA Dystopian Trilogy as Twenty-First-Century Utopian Dreaming'. *Beyond the Blockbusters: Themes and Trends in Contemporary Young Adult Fiction*. Ed. Rebekah Fitzsimmons and Casey Alane Wilson, UP of Mississippi, 2020. 13–9.

Fitzsimmons, Rebekah and Casey Alane Wilson. 'Introduction'. *Beyond the Blockbusters: Themes and Trends in Contemporary Young Adult Fiction*. Ed. Rebekah Fitzsimmons and Casey Alane Wilson. UP of Mississippi, 2020. ix–xvi.

Hastings, Waller A. 'Science Fiction'. *Keywords for Children's Literature*. Ed. Philip Nel and Lissa Paul. New York UP, 2011. 202–7.

Henthorne, Tom. *Approaching the Hunger Games Trilogy: A Literary and Cultural Analysis*. McFarland, 2012.

Hinton, S.E. 'Teen-Agers are for Real'. *New York Times Book Review* (27 August 1967). https://readingyalit com.files.wordpress.com/2016/09/teenagers-are-for-real-susan-hinton.pdf

Insenga, Angela S. 'Once Upon a Cyborg: *Cinder* as Posthuman Fairytale'. *Posthumanism in Young Adult Fiction: Finding Humanity in a Posthuman World*. Ed. Anita Tarr and Donna R. White. UP of Mississippi, 2018. 55–73.

Levy, Michael. 'Science Fiction'. *Oxford Encyclopedia of Children's Literature*. Ed. Jack Zipes. Oxford UP, 2006. 417–22.

Mendlesohn, Farah. *The Intergalactic Playground: A Critical Study of Children's and Teens' Science Fiction*. McFarland, 2009.

Merrylees, Ferne. 'The Adolescent Posthuman: Reimagining Body Image and Identity in Marissa Meyer's *Cinder* and Julianna Baggott's *Pure*'. *Posthumanism in Young Adult Fiction: Finding Humanity in a Posthuman World*. Ed. Anita Tarr and Donna R. White. UP of Mississippi, 2018. 75–95.

Midkiff, Emily. *Equipping Space Cadets: Primary Science Fiction for Children*. UP of Mississippi, 2022.

Nodelman, Perry. 'Out There in Children's Science Fiction: Forward into the Past'. *Science Fiction Studies* 37 (1995): 285–96.

Onion, Rebecca. *Innocent Experiments: Childhood and the Culture of Popular Science in the United States*. UNC Press, 2016.

op de Beeck, Nathalie. 'The First Picture Book for Modern Children: Mary Liddell's *Little Machinery* and the Fairy Tale of Modernity'. *Little Machinery: A Critical Facsimile Edition* by Mary Liddell. Wayne State UP, 2009: 63–99.

Palumbo, Donald. 'Science Fiction in Comic Books: Science Fiction Colonizes a Fantasy Medium'. *Young Adult Science Fiction*. Ed. C.W. Sullivan III. Greenwood, 1999. 161–82.

Pharr, Mary F. and Leisa A. Clark. 'Introduction'. *Of Bread, Blood, and the Hunger Games: Critical Essays on the Suzanne Collins Trilogy*. Ed. Mary F. Pharr and Leisa A. Clark. McFarland, 2012. 5–19.

Sanders, Joe Sutliff. 'Young Adult Sf'. *The Routledge Companion to Science Fiction*. Ed. Mark Bould, Andrew M. Butler, Adam Roberts and Sherryl Vint. Routledge, 2011. 442–50.

Sands-O'Connor, Karen and Marietta Frank. *Back in the Spaceship Again: Juvenile Science Fiction Series Since 1945*. Praeger, 1999.

Sullivan III, C.W. 'American Young Adult Science Fiction since 1947'. *Young Adult Science Fiction*. Ed. C.W. Sullivan III. Greenwood, 1999. 21–35.

——. 'Preface'. *Science Fiction for Young Readers*. Ed. C.W. Sullivan III. Praeger, 1993. xiii–xv.

Talley, Lee A. 'Young Adult'. *Keywords for Children's Literature*. Ed. Philip Nel and Lissa Paul. New York UP, 2011. 228–32.

Thomas, Ebony Elizabeth. *The Dark Fantastic: Race and the Imagination from Harry Potter to the Hunger Games*. New York UP, 2019.

Toliver, S.R. 'Eliminating Extermination, Fostering Existence: Diverse Dystopian Fiction and Female Adolescent Identity'. *Beyond the Blockbusters: Themes and Trends in Contemporary Young Adult Fiction*. Ed. Rebekah Fitzsimmons and Casey Alane Wilson. UP of Mississippi, 2020. 187–202.

Trites, Roberta Seelinger. *Disturbing the Universe: Power and Repression in Adolescent Literature*. U of Iowa P, 2000.

11
AFROFUTURISM

Rone Shavers

Often, when one hears the term 'Afrofuturism', the image that immediately springs to mind is of *Black Panther* (Coogler 2018) or of a Black nerd cosplaying into Elvish oblivion or an Afro-style hairdo crammed into a space helmet. While these images do portray a certain style or strain of Afrofuturism, it is actually a lot much more than just Blacks in space, Black geeks or a Disney blockbuster. However, Afrofuturism resists easy definition, mainly because it is not only a field of critical enquiry but also an artistic and cultural aesthetic. Broadly, Afrofuturism is a critical and creative aesthetic that combines elements of sf, speculative fiction, magic realism and technoculture with aspects of Afrocentric and non-Occidental cosmologies to highlight the present-day dilemmas of Blacks in the West, as well as to refute, revise and re-examine the past and future social (and subject) positions of Black people. More simply, Afrofuturism is an intellectual and artistic movement that speaks to the contemporary dilemmas of Black people but mediates them through a technological or science-fictional lens. And because it uses sf tropes to illustrate how Western metanarratives are especially problematic when it comes to the intersection of history, identity and race, Afrofuturism is a useful tool with which to examine and interrogate issues of race, technology and social identity.

The term 'Afrofuturism' was coined by Mark Dery in 1993. Inspired by interviews and conversations with Greg Tate, Tricia Rose and Samuel R. Delany, among others, he forged a link between the Black body as technological instrument and the proliferation of 'cyber-culture' and computer technology. He articulated how hip-hop and Black culture in general often reappropriates and repurposes technology as a way of resisting greater cultural hegemony, and emphasised how Black people, often treated as machines, creatively reclaim the machine metaphor for themselves. From the forced breeding of slaves, to the notion that Black athletes should just 'shut up and dribble!', the idea of the Black body as a tool, a complex machine to be studied, used, controlled and mastered, has long occupied a pernicious place in Western culture.

From the mid-1990s onwards, many scholars, artists and public intellectuals seized upon Dery's term and began to expand its conceptual parameters. That they all had different ends and goals in mind is important to note because while we tend to say 'Afrofuturism', what we are often referring to is actually one of three distinct branches of Afrofuturism. Although all three branches are interrelated and interconnected, it is necessary to realise that, despite their similarities, in many

DOI: 10.4324/9781003140269-13

respects they differ. Each resembles a distinct circle in a Venn diagram, overlapping the others but also diverging from them.

The earliest branch could be called 'theoretical Afrofuturism', since it uses philosophical depictions of Black identity (or identities) as a way to analyse and interrogate Blackness as an historical, cultural and, ultimately, ontological construction. Kodwo Eshun's *More Brilliant than the Sun: Adventures in Sonic Fiction* (1998) began to describe Afrofuturism as but one mode – a specifically Black diasporic mode – of postmodernity, mapping and connecting Afrofuturism to a long list of aesthetic and cultural traditions that define contemporary Western and Black Atlantic culture. Yet, as influential as Eshun was to the burgeoning field, he himself – and theoretical Afrofuturism in general – was influenced by the ideas of such US writers as Delany, Tate and Toni Morrison, and by such UK theorists as Paul Gilroy, Stuart Hall and the later members of the Birmingham School (based at the University of Birmingham's Centre for Contemporary Cultural Studies).

Scholars such as Anna Everett and Alondra Nelson (and their fellow members of the Apogee group) began using theoretical Afrofuturist concepts as a way to examine the role race plays in discussions of techno-culture. They made a point of publicly raising questions about the digital divide, including who has access to technology and the resources to use it, and what role does (or should) technology play in everyday Black life (Nelson 1). This 'critical Afrofuturism' differs from theoretical Afrofuturism in that it uses the ideas present in the former as a starting point from which to address contemporary Black problems and, equally as important, present results and possible solutions. In other words, theoretical Afrofuturism is more concerned with what defines and makes up Afrofuturism, while critical Afrofuturism is more pragmatic, centred on using ideas as a basis for achieving some actual goals in the real world. It is a mode of praxis, and as such is currently very much in vogue.

The term 'Afrofuturism' also resonated with a great number of creative artists who serve as influential public intellectuals in their own right. It offered a succinct and powerfully apt way to describe the ideas and intentions of their myriad works. This 'aesthetic Afrofuturism' includes any work that depicts an alternate (or alternately realised) version of Black culture, be it past, present or future. Aesthetic Afrofuturism is more or less synonymous with Black speculative culture. It can support the weight of any project that aims to push back against the racist notions of Blackness or dominant culture stereotypes regarding who, what and how Black people are. Basically, the artifacts of aesthetic Afrofuturism serve as evidence of Black creativity: it is *Get Out* (Peele 2017), Wakanda, pretty much every Janelle Monáe album and the Black nerd who speaks Belter creole because Klingon is just too damn easy, *keyá*? Its focus is more on the production than the analysis of creative works, although it does tend to deconstruct what were previously White-identified spaces.

Among aesthetic Afrofuturism's many luminaries – too numerous to list here – one of the most notable is Sheree Renée Thomas, editor of the two *Dark Matter* anthologies (2000, 2004) that completely changed public perception regarding Black interest in sf and served as an important early venue for many of the twenty-first century's major Afrofuturist thinkers and practitioners, including Tananarive Due, Andrea Hairston, Nalo Hopkinson, Honorée Fanonne Jeffers, Nnedi Okorafor and Nisi Shawl. Thomas can best be described as aesthetic Afrofuturism's grand ambassador, for over the span of decades, she has gone to great pains to bring Afrofuturism to as many audiences as possible.

Yet despite the distinct and at times disparate styles, approaches and end-goals of Afrofuturism's three branches, they nonetheless share several significant themes including, but not necessarily limited to, alienation and estrangement, contesting the future, revisiting and revising the past, and new conceptions of identity.

Alienation and estrangement

Afrofuturist material often hints at a deep-seated sense of alienation and estrangement, a permanent and uncanny sense of otherness. The reason is because Black people have historically been 'othered' in the West, meaning that Blacks have traditionally been treated as if they existed adjacent to or outside of Western history and culture, instead of being integral to it. (A straightforward example of this indisputable fact is that Black Americans were both literally and figuratively excluded – sometimes violently – from many of the common social programmes and opportunities other, more melanin-deficient groups used to achieve the 'American Dream'.) Therefore, Afrofuturism takes the metaphor of displacement, of alienation both from and within the West, and literalises it, often through the sf trope of the alien. In the light of the transatlantic slave trade, the image and idea of Blacks as aliens is not far-fetched. After all, as Eshun suggests in *The Last Angel of History* (Akomfrah 1996), there is nothing more science-fictional than an invasion of weird-skinned beings who kidnap you and your people, cram them onto strange ships, transport them to a new world, forcibly erase their identity, and make them learn new tongues and labour under pain of death for generations. Variations of this premise are worked through in, for example, Delany's *Return to Nevèrÿon* series (1979–87), Octavia E. Butler's Lilith's Brood trilogy (1987–9), Derrick Bell's 'The Space Traders' (1992), Rivers Solomon's *The Deep* (2019), such films as *Get Out* and *Sorry to Bother You* (Riley 2018), and the music, performances and astroblack mythology of Sun Ra, all of which demonstrate that, as Isiah Lavender III argues, Afrofuturism has emerged to understand the science-fictional existence that Blacks have always experienced living in the New World – an unreality driven by economic demands, would-be science, and skin color' (9). Given the centuries-long history and practice of discrimination and 'othering' in Western Atlantic cultures, being Black runs the gamut from, at best, a totally surreal experience to, at worst, an unreal, dystopian experience. Such a distinct, particularised type of subject position begets the overarching sense of social dissociation that appears throughout most Afrofuturist material, manifested in themes that ultimately posit that if anything, Blackness is in itself a science-fictional state of being.

Contesting the future

What would you think about the future if you rarely saw depictions of someone like yourself in it? How would you think about the future if people who looked like you only appeared in support roles? These questions help to explain why Afrofuturism puts issues of race and racial relations front and centre. Most sf depictions of the future tend to treat the idea of racism as something belonging to a bygone age, or simply act as if the history of strife arising from racial difference does not exist; Afrofuturism does the opposite. In fact, it does something quite radical: it specifically draws attention to the Black figure. More than simply relying on outdated tropes, Afrofuturism often injects discussions of race into (or contests) what are supposedly 'race-neutral' environments. By highlighting the concept of a racial (and in some cases, racialised) body as the source of any future representation and conception of 'the figure', Afrofuturist material not only disrupts the very idea of what the future looks like, but it also illustrates the tensions that revolve around what and how the ideal figure appears in dominant culture discourse. In other words, Afrofuturist material seeks to re-configure the very idea of what any sort of idealised future looks like, challenging the metanarrative at work when one assumes that the populace of the future will somehow automatically be Western, liberal and White. Afrofuturism allows one to see that race does indeed matter, because it highlights just how often a bland, Westernised version of Whiteness is used as a default when portraying future societies.

Afrofuturism unpacks and highlights the tension that has always existed in the West towards the Black body. By deliberately drawing attention to the Black body as simultaneous subject and object of the Western imaginary, Afrofuturism both represents and re-presents perspectives of Blackness and the Black body in heretofore unexpected and unfamiliar places. There are numerous allusions to this idea in critical Afrofuturist writing, and countless examples in aesthetic Afrofuturism: from the music and imagery of George Clinton/Parliament–Funkadelic, LaBelle and Janelle Monáe, through such high-tech superheroes as Cyborg and the Sojourner Mullein Green Lantern, to such novels as Hopkinson's *Midnight Robber* (2000) and Okorafor's BINTI trilogy (2015–8). In other words, aesthetic Afrofuturism exemplifies the 'appeals that Black artists, musicians, critics, and writers have made to the future, in moments where any future was difficult to imagine' (Eshun 'Further' 294).

Revisiting and revising the past

Because Blacks in the Americas were completely denied access to knowledge of the past, as well as the histories of their specific African ancestry, it should come as no surprise that when given the opportunity, they would invent what history they could not recover. Therefore, many Afrofuturist artists go to great pains to establish direct connections between depictions of an altered present (or alternate future) and multiple references to past Black histories – whether it is Egyptian civilisation, the Dahomey empire or something entirely fictional.

Afrofuturists make these connections because sf permits – encourages – one to re-imagine the world and one's place in it. In embracing what can best be described as the science-fictional nature of Blackness, Afrofuturist material becomes a tool for looking at past events in a new light. It must also be said that Afrofuturism's excavations of the past help to bolster contemporary Afrofuturist work. By establishing direct linkages to past histories and artefacts, Afrofuturists slyly make observers aware that their creative work already exists within its own ready-made canonical and historical context. Indeed, an early Afrofuturist concern was with recovering and reconceptualising older, often forgotten or otherwise labelled texts, including the music of Duke Ellington and Anthony Braxton, and such fiction as Charles W. Chesnutt's 'The Goophered Grapevine' (1887), Pauline Hopkins's *Of One Blood* (1903), W.E.B. Du Bois's 'The Comet' (1920), George S. Schuyler's *Black No More* (1931) and *Black Empire* (1936–8), Amos Tutuola's *The Palm-Wine Drinkard* (1952), Ralph Ellison's *Invisible Man* (1952), Ishmael Reed's *Mumbo Jumbo* (1972), as well as John Faucette's space operas and a number of Black militant thrillers and blaxploitation films from the 1960s and 1970s (Bould, 'Come', 'Paying' 'Revolutionary' and 'Space'; Lavender; Lock; Tal; Yaszek).

Moreover, attention to excavating past events of particular importance or significance to Blacks (including those that have been deliberately erased or forgotten) – as in Shawl's *Everfair* (2016), an White supremacist of the Congo, and the counterfactual history of *C.S.A.: The Confederate States of America* (Willmott 2004) – often challenge White supremacist and Eurocentric notions of what and how we determine which personages and events are 'worth' historical consideration. In fact, some aesthetic Afrofuturists go so far as to argue that since so much of Black history has been overlooked or ignored, these connections to real and imagined histories are a necessary corrective to the 'whitewashing' of history.

Thus, it requires no great leap to say that Afrofuturism highlights how dominant culture narratives tend to cherry-pick events from history so that those in power can use it to see what they want to see and confirm what they already know; that so much 'official' Western history is actually just glorified myth. Afrofuturism defamiliarises the casual observer, putting them in a strange situation or world so that the tension between contrasting historical accounts can be understood metaphorically as well as literally. And in this way, we can say that Afrofuturism is both forward- and backward-looking – or transhistorical – because by deconstructing and recontextualising the past, Afrofuturism helps to revise our present. This preoccupation with an intentionally obfuscated past and a dangerously tenuous future is found within all three branches of Afrofuturism, and is their crucial, existential theme.

Furthermore, Afrofuturism's obsession with re-envisioning both the future and past of Black people has given it a specific vocabulary that allows it to serve as the lingua franca of twenty-first century Black identity concerns. From this position, Afrofuturist ideas and approaches have taken a distinctive, dominant place in the Black public sphere.

New conceptions of identity

Afrofuturism is over 30 years old and, in an inchoate form and fashion, many Afrofuturist ideas have been around for even longer. While many of the themes commonly identified with Afrofuturism are still in play, there are potent new thematic concepts that have taken hold in the past decade. With the rise of mobile technology and social networking as a means by which to connect and unify what were once disparate and geographically distinct groups, the syncretic field of Afrofuturism has grown even more syncretic. It has expanded its reach, both influencing and being influenced by the dissemination of popular Black Atlantic art and culture on a global scale. Scholars such as Reynaldo Anderson and Charles E. Jones have begun to refer to the current moment as 'Afrofuturism 2.0' – a new iteration, updated for the digital age. It represents a transition from twentieth-century anxieties regarding Black people's relation to technology and culture, and from the myriad nation-state conceptions and representations of Blackness toward a digital, transnational response to the challenges facing Black life wherever Black people happen to be (Anderson and Jones viii).

Regardless of whether one accepts this 2.0 nomenclature, such attempts to expend Afrofuturism beyond its Black Atlantic borders points to an interesting evolution of the genre. Black people are utilising new ways to express their identities in the twenty-first century, and Afrofuturism has taken on the mantle of examining the hows, whys, and ways twenty-first century Blackness can be viewed as an intersectional identity, one that is not necessarily bound by old(er) contours and constrictions of geographic location, birthplace or gender politics. At the same time, Okorafor and others propose that, rather than being subsumed into an Americo-centric model of Afrofuturism, her work and that of others either from or with close ties to the African continent, such as Mame Bougouma Diene, Dilman Dila, T.L. Huchu, Wole Talabi and Tlotlo Tsamaase, should be described by two other terms: Africanfuturism, that is, future-oriented, primarily Black-authored sf, centred in Africa and reaching out into the diaspora, that does not privilege the West; and its fantasy equivalent, Africanjujuism, which draws on African cosmologies and spiritualities (Okorafor). Others have spoken of Caribbean Futurisms, while Latinx Futurisms have increasingly recognised the Black heritage and identities of many Latinx peoples.

Thus, current Afrofuturist discourse shifts Black identity away from the *either/or* binary oppositions that defined much of the past century's discourse on identity (e.g., either Black nationalist *or* American assimilationist, either rap aficionado *or* Anime fanboy) to Black identity conceptions that function as *both/and* – especially in terms of cultural, geopolitical, and sexual and gender identification. For example, one need only think of the sizable number of young, politically-active Black Americans who now celebrate and listen to K-Pop music; it signifies both an acceptance of a decidedly Black identity *and* an embrace of something that, while rooted in African American popular music styles, is definitely not Black by any sort of metric. As this suggests, Afrofuturism has turned towards expressing and encompassing an intersectional, global identity that is nonetheless rooted in Black diasporic worldviews. And in this way, Afrofuturism's themes appear more political and less fantastical, and say surprisingly more about *us*, circa now, than any previous exploration of the Other.

In lieu of a conclusion: Notes on Afrofuturism's future

Given that Afrofuturism is both a field of enquiry and a movement, and given that movements of all kinds are known to have a beginning and end, there remains a fundamental question to be considered: what is the future of Afrofuturism?

Despite Afrofuturism's perhaps oversized role in contemporary Black cultural discourse, without a thorough recognition and occasional re-evaluation of the aesthetic and ideological contours of the field, it does run the risk of becoming, for lack of a better word, 'stale'. After all, we can look as far back as 2013 to find evidence of frustration with Afrofuturism's rising popularity. That was the year when the visual artist Martine Syms threw down a gauntlet of sorts with the publication of 'The Mundane Afrofuturist Manifesto'. Claiming to 'rejoice in [...] piling up unexamined and hackneyed tropes, and setting them alight' (n.p.), Syms challenged individuals to not rely on oversaturated (i.e., mundane) Afrofuturist tropes and instead to think *beyond* them in order to create and make meaning. She acknowledges how familiar Afrofuturist themes can serve as a creative catalyst, but stressed the importance of not solely relying on what has been said and done before; to look to the *here and now* in order to make meaning out of – and for – the here and now. However, after the success of Disney's *Black Panther*, it is unclear how many artists heeded her call to infuse more theoretical, intellectual and philosophical positions into the extremely public-facing aesthetic branch of Afrofuturism. This is a key problem with a category as broad as aesthetic Afrofuturism; it runs the risk of stultifying innovation in the name of establishing genre bona fides. Thus, it may be better to say aesthetic Afrofuturisms, to emphasise how the genre-cum-movement now encompasses various subgenres and subsets of Black identity speculations, such as Afropunk and Afro-Surrealism, and is still evolving, while critical Afrofuturism explicates how and what these subcategories add to a broader understanding of Afrofuturist identity.

Even though 'postmodernism' had its heyday before falling out of use, its deeply influential ideas persist; the same is – or will be – true of 'Afrofuturism'. It will live on, even if the term fades away. There is an intellectual and creative rigour to each of Afrofuturism's branches and, like postmodernism before it, practitioners of Afrofuturism tend to privilege its more formal elements than its allegiance to any particular personage, movement or event. If one believes Afrofuturism to be a response to a particular moment in history, then of course it would peter out; but if one views it as adhering to a set of dialectic explorations and creative formal elements that address ongoing and enduring legacies of anti-Black racism, then like the Energizer Bunny, Afrofuturism is going to keep on going and going and going...

Ultimately, then, what makes Afrofuturism successful as both a cultural movement and an academic field of study is that all three branches, despite their differences, tend to work together. Aesthetic Afrofuturism, even at its most basic and popular, is redeemed by critical Afrofuturism's use of the aesthetic branch's works to illustrate precisely why and how Afrofuturism can be used as a tool for racial equity, decolonisation and liberation. Critical Afrofuturism's claims are often only taken seriously when bolstered and supported, grounded in the philosophical and logical arguments present in theoretical Afrofuturism. Thus, the three complement each other and form a solid basis from which to launch any sort of creative or critical enquiry. And no matter how one defines it, no matter whether or not it continues to be called Afrofuturism, its future is as strong as it ever was and always has been.

Works cited

Anderson, Reynaldo and Charles E. Jones. 'Introduction: The Rise of Astro-Blackness'. *Afrofuturism 2.0: The Rise of Astro-Blackness*. Ed. Reynaldo Anderson and Charles E. Jones. Lexington, 2016. vii–xvii.

Bould, Mark. 'Come Alive By Saying No: An Introduction to Black Power Sf'. *Science Fiction Studies* 102 (2007): 220–40.

——. 'Paying Freedom Dues: Marxism, Black Radicalism, and Blaxploitation Sf'. *Red Alert: Marxist Approaches to Science Fiction Cinema*. Ed. Ewa Mazierska and Alfredo Suppia. Wayne State UP, 2016. 72–97.

——. 'Revolutionary African-American Sf Before Black Power'. *Extrapolation* 51.1 (2010): 53–81.

——. 'Space/Race: Recovering John M. Faucette'. *Literary Afrofuturism in the Twenty-First Century*. Ed. Isiah Lavender III and Lisa Yaszek. Ohio State UP, 2020. 109–27.

Dery, Mark. 'Black to the Future: Interviews with Samuel R. Delany, Greg Tate, and Tricia Rose'. *Flame Wars: The Discourse of Cyberculture*, special issue of *South Atlantic Quarterly* 92.4 (1993): 735–78.

Eshun, Kodwo. 'Further Considerations on Afrofuturism'. *CR: The New Centennial Review* 3.2 (2003): 287–302.

——. *More Brilliant than the Sun: Adventures in Sonic Fiction*. Quartet, 1998.

Everett, Anna. 'The Revolution Will Be Digitized: Afrocentricity and the Digital Public Sphere'. *Afrofuturism*, special issue of *Social Text* 20.2 (2002): 127–46.

Lavender, Isiah III. *Afrofuturism Rising: The Literary Prehistory of a Movement*. Ohio State UP, 2019.

Lock, Graham. *Blutopia: Visions of the Future and Revisions of the Past in the Work of Sun Ra, Duke Ellington, and Anthony Braxton*. Duke UP, 1999.

Nelson, Alondra. 'Introduction: Future Texts'. *Afrofuturism*, special issue of *Social Text* 20.2 (2002): 1–15.

Okorafor, Nnedi. 'Africanfuturism Defined'. *Africanfuturism: An Anthology*. Ed. Wole Talabi. Brittle Paper, 2020. Unpaginated.

Syms, Martine. 'The Mundane Afrofuturist Manifesto'. *Rhizome* (17 December 2013). https://rhizome.org/editorial/2013/dec/17/mundane-afrofuturist-manifesto/

Tal, Kalil. '"That Just Kills Me": Black Militant Near-Future Fiction'. *Afrofuturism*, special issue of *Social Text* 20.2 (2002): 65–91.

Thomas, Sheree R., ed. *Dark Matter: A Century of Speculative Fiction from the African Diaspora*. Warner Books, 2000.

Yaszek, Lisa. 'An Afrofuturist Reading of Ralph Ellison's *Invisible Man*'. *Rethinking History: The Journal of Theory and Practice* 9.2–3 (2007): 297–313.

12
SCIENCE FICTION ILLUSTRATION

John Timberlake

Definitions and historiographies

The impulse to visualise is particularly strong in sf. Throughout the genre's evolution, depiction has been a constitutive element and many sf subgenres might not exist were it not for this vibrant visual culture. In other kinds of fiction illustration arguably functions as merely an occasional supplement to the story's text. But in sf, illustration is originary and, has, since the genre's inception, invariably accompanied textual forms.

There is much debate about the conditions of visualisation in the mid- to late-nineteenth century (Willis 1–9), a period characterised, in Europe at least, by the oppositional binary of Romanticism and Realism, a complex entanglement that conditioned thinking around artistic sensibility, seeing and representation. The broader context of this binary included advances in scientific knowledge and the advent of photography and reprographics, technologies which spread throughout the world with remarkable speed. The need to see, and *how*, underpinned both the natural sciences and the fictions produced around and in response to them.

Within wider histories of fantastic imagery, there are various genealogies that, by dint of some iconic resemblance, are deemed to be progenitors to sf illustration. A typically Eurocentric history might begin with the later paintings of Hieronymus Bosch (which are often thought of as inventive and fantastical, although to a large extent they merely represent the consensus view of Mediaeval Christian theologians) or Leonardo da Vinci's diagrams of war machines and helicopters. From there, such an account might progress through Giovanni Battista Piranesi's *carcere* etchings to the engravings of Gustave Doré, Albert Robida and Warwick Goble, before crossing the Atlantic to discuss the rise of pulp magazine illustration, typified by Frank R. Paul, or the astronautical extrapolations of Chesley Bonestell. Yet any such chronology is problematic, as invidious as it is unhelpful: very few of these artists produced illustrations for sf per se, indeed at least one – Bonestell – actively disavowed sf as a genre. In some cases, their work was subsequently re-used for sf book covers, but that is a different matter. Simply because, by way of a sort of convergent visual evolution, a particular work of art *appears* in retrospect to bear a resemblance to sf illustration does not mean it was or is. All sf illustration is art, but not all art containing science fictional elements was or is produced as illustration. However, prior to any canon of sf illustration, there

DOI: 10.4324/9781003140269-14

were extant elements expressive of a need to visualise things not seen, and in some cases those elements persist now as fragments embedded within the canon.

Timothy F. Mitchell sought to identify the 'when' of what he termed 'sf art' once and for all by focusing on US magazines, asserting that 'The history of science fiction art begins with *Amazing Stories* of April 1926 [...] From that point a distinct and unbroken tradition of sf art has developed, marked by the expansion of the magazine field and the appearance of science fiction in paperback and hard-cover books' (121). This claim erases several alternative time frames, many 'wheres' and thousands of 'whos', producing a canon with significant temporal and geographic exclusions. Just as any history of prose sf that begins with Jules Verne overlooks the sf that emerged in India with Kylas Chunder Dutt in 1835 (Bannerjee), so Mitchell's account ignores the work of, among others, the British illustrators Paul Hardy (in *Cassell's Magazine* in the 1870s) and John Frederick Thomas Jane, better known as Fred T. Jane, who wrote speculative stories and made drawings to accompany them in the 1890s. It also glosses over, for example, the sf culture that emerged in China towards the end of the Qing Dynasty, which saw Huang Jiang's *Lunar Colony* (*Xiuxiang Xiaoshuo*; 1904–5), Lao She's *Cat Country* (*Mao cheng ji*; 1933) and Gu Junzheng's *Underneath the Arctic Pole* (*Zai Bei Ji Di Xia*; 1940), as well as Liang Qichao's and Lu Xun's translations of European sf, all of which were published with illustrations. One could go on.

The second problem with Mitchell's account is more subtle, and hinges on his use of the term 'art' rather than 'illustration', despite it being the latter (and within that, a particular form of pulp imagery) that he focuses on. It is not uncommon for histories of sf illustration to blur the differentiations between illustration and other forms of visual art, but in insisting upon the expansive 'art', Mitchell undermines his attempt to establish a canon confined to magazine illustration beginning in 1926.

Mitchell is more successful at typifying the form and function of sf cover illustration, in this case through Frank R. Paul's cover for the November 1928 of *Amazing*: 'With strong color contrasts, simple compositions, and realism, Paul achieves the two prerequisites of a successful pulp cover: to establish immediately the nature of the publication and to attract a buyer' (121). Paul's work is undoubtedly wonderful, and the elements of his style Mitchell identifies continue to resonate in numerous areas of sf visual culture, including cover illustration, but they are in no way universal. Works of this type tend to make the cut in retrospective coffee table books. However, the majority of magazine illustration was not colour but linework produced for interior pages, which means colour was the exception, not the rule. Where the formal qualities Mitchell describes became more typical was in the paperback market, which rapidly expanded in the second half of the twentieth century.

Perhaps on firmer ground, Vincent Di Fate notes the first publication of *paperback* sf (56), with the 1943 appearance of Donald A. Wollheim's *The Pocket Book of Science-Fiction*, which included stories by such leading magazine authors as John W. Campbell, Jr, Robert A. Heinlein and Theodore Sturgeon. *The Pocket Book*'s cover rewards close study insofar as its content and form are not only indicative of the genre's preoccupations but also of the commercial and reprographic imperatives to which it was subject. It features a deep perspective formed by the opposition of three-quarter views of modernist buildings, set upon a half-tone spectrum that fades downwards from a blue sky, through green and yellow to a red ground. As such, it follows tropes identified by Mitchell, which have persisted across the genre: garish colours, a combination of recognisable particulars and estranged generalities, deep perspective, and some sense of risk or precarity (in this case, the proximity of the speeding aircraft to the building). The style of the buildings owes something to *Metropolis* (Lang 1927) but the futuristic aircraft, which, streaming vapour, swoops steeply from the right-hand portion of the image, past the façade of buildings, downwards towards the receding landing strip formed by the causeway between the buildings, is rather different from Lang's turboprop monoplanes and biplanes.

The cover captures one half of the major schism in sf illustration's subject matter – between an 'anti-humanist' focus on architecture and machines, and the depiction of human or humanoid bodies. Through the depiction of movement and action, both modes present a specific sense of agency to the viewer: in anti-humanist work (for example, Paul, Robert T. McCall, David A. Hardy, Chris Foss) this action is the preserve of machines, buildings, even planetary landscapes and the stars themselves; in humanist work (typified by Margaret Brundage, Frank Kelley Freas, Leo and Diane Dillon, Michael Whelan, Jill Bauman, Victoria Poyser, Jim Burns) humanoid facial expression and biomorphic difference both become signifiers of an embodied sublime.

The artist responsible for the *The Pocket Book* image and the designer of the cover are, as is still too often the case, uncredited. The reasons for such omissions are varied. They can include the working conditions under which the illustration was produced and the development of the genre as a recognised and respected cultural form. In some cases, an artist might not wish to be associated either with book jacket illustration in general, or with a particular genre, widely regarded as pulp, in particular. The illustration and design might have been produced as contracted or in-house design teamwork where industry convention does not normally attribute individual names. In sf, the artist as *name* emerges at the point where it is important either to the artist, the author or the publisher: either the illustrator feels confident enough to demand credit, or, in some cases, their naming is beneficial to the sale of the book. Outside of these pressures, an artist may remain unnamed and their work unattributed. The history of sf illustration is replete with such cases. At the same time, there are cases where the artist becomes so important to that process that not only publishers and authors seek them out, but on some rare occasions publishers actually commission books to be written for particular images (Frank 218), as was the case with very successful paintings of Frank Frazetta. Within sf, recognition of the contribution of illustrators steadily improved during the 1970s and 1980s, with Welsh illustrator Jim Burns, arguably a key influence in the visualisation of sf baroque, winning the first Hugo Award for Best Professional Artist in 1987.

Form and function

The Concise Oxford English Dictionary defines 'to illustrate' as 'provid[ing] a book, newspaper etc, with pictures' and an 'illustration' as 'a drawing or picture illustrating a book, magazine article and so on'. In this light, illustration is specifically associated with the printed text. As a result of this relation between image and text, sf illustration can be as much about misreading and misinterpretation as about any putative direct visual transcription. Through accident or design, there are often disjunctures between image and story. These are about form as well as content: text, however edited, abridged or otherwise bowdlerised, is still text, but we do not encounter the actual textured surface of the painting or drawing as we would in a gallery – we see only a mediated image of it.

Moreover, a visual misinterpretation might come to haunt the text. As Andy Sawyer's annotations point out, H.G. Wells disliked Warwick Goble's rendering of the Martian war machines in *The War of the Worlds* (1897), and Goble's tripods, swaying like dockyard cranes, are unfaithful to Wells's vision of the lithe, whiplash mechanised speeds humans witness for the first time on Horsell Common (Wells 195). Yet the two are often associated, and, as the story's first visual manifestation, Goble's work might mistakenly be read as authoritative.

The two elements of an illustrated publication – the image, and the text – constitute a cultural object. With very few exceptions, the two elements are composed by different people, and, in most cases the story predates the illustration. The image is therefore responsive to the story, but often only partially. The illustration, even if one of a series, represents only a tiny portion of the story, and the manner in which it does so is conditional, since the pressures under which it was produced are distinct to those which dictated the form and length of the story. Here, also, is to be found a constitutive link between sf as romance, and the illustration as *scene*. As Fredric Jameson argues, 'in romance the Scene tends to capture and to appropriate the attributes of Agency and Act, making the "hero" over into something like a registering apparatus for transformed states of being' (99). Although his point is a literary one, it helps us understand how the normative form for book and magazine sf illustration (alien or estranged environments) are themselves agents, characters almost, and how sf illustration itself both reflects and engenders this.

As a form, the paperback has key differences to the illustrated magazine: there is usually only one image, on the cover, and the illustration is surmounted by words. If the image was created by hand with paints, inks or pencils, we cannot appreciate the precise tones or textures created by the artist since they are distorted by reproduction. As with magazines, the image is overlaid with text: the title, blurbs and so on. The original image therefore comes to us partly occluded, perhaps fragmented.

We often encounter the illustration before we know the contents of a book. On those occasions when we know the story already, the illustration might come as a surprise or jarring reminder: 'I'd forgotten the heroine was green', and so on. Reading a story accompanied by an illustration is simultaneously an act of unfolding, and cross referencing. Many refer back to the illustration as they read, or wait, perhaps in vain, for the precise moment illustrated, then note its variances. In sf, this might seem particularly pressing. In the reader, the illustration might evoke distrust or disappointment.

Nevertheless, the illustration does not effectively undermine the authority of the author's voice: as the book is read, the story undermines the illustration, highlighting any omissions or misrepresentations as faults of the artist, not the author. We might enjoy an illustration's transgressions, its ludic infidelities, but ultimately we judge its representative capacity according to the word of the writer; we do not judge the word of the writer by the illustration.

Sf illustration speaks to the persistent desire within sf to *visualise*, not just describe – a desire often also manifest in the writing and reading of sf stories. As Wells's Time Traveller says, in a brilliant moment of reflection, 'If only I had thought of a Kodak! I could have flashed that glimpse of the Underworld in a second, and examined it at leisure' (49). Written after the mid-nineteenth-century emergence and rapid ascendancy of photography, with its indexical relation to the objects it records, these words attest to a desire not only to *see* documentary proof but also to imagine what such visual evidence might look like, were it to be recorded by a camera.

Where there are observable phenomena – the colour of a star, the atmosphere of a planet – we might consider a 'suppositional realism' on the part of the artist. In this sense, the artist might extrapolate extant scientific knowledge to depict something not yet evidenced by photography. This approach is typified by the work of David A. Hardy. 'I do take into account available knowledge about the subjects I depict' (96), he wrote, before commenting on the trend within mid-1970s sf publishing: 'In Britain during the past few years much science fiction art has been expressed in highly "realistic" representations – one might say photographs of the unphotographable' (98).

Hardy's use of 'realistic' as opposed to 'realist' is telling in this context. In his own work, he distinguishes between astronomical and sf illustration, although they are clearly interrelated, but what is important here is the differentiation between realism (with its focus on the quotidian commonplace experiences of society, often foregrounding socio-political concerns) and naturalism (intent on replicating credible visual aspects of things, such as convincing metal surfaces or authentic representations of movement). One can paint or draw a *naturalist* image of our devolved troglodytic descendants from the year 802,701, but one cannot paint a *realist* one. The need to visualise, to establish correlative detail, to examine the artist's glimpse of another world 'at leisure' is an integral aspect of sf's multifarious ocularities that are also evident within the written text. Because of the genre's speculative character, what constitutes realism or naturalism does not proceed in a straight line, nor can it be perceived without its constitutive negative: the realism of sf is made visible through its unrealities. This is not to say there are not elements of *both* realism and naturalism in sf illustration. Indeed, the need for recognisable details, the need for naturalistic affect, are predicated on the void left by that impossible camera to which Wells and Hardy allude.

As noted above, it is not always the case that the illustration accurately represents the contents of the story. This is obviously the case when the book cover features an abstract work, as appeared on some Pan Books in the UK in the 1960s and 1970s, and in the increasingly abstract work of Richard M. Powers for Doubleday, Ballantine, Berkley and others in the US from the 1950s to the 1980s. It is also notable in the trend for British sf paperbacks to completely ignore the details of the story in favour of, for example, an attention-grabbing spaceship by a popular artist such as Chris Foss. This deliberate disjuncture might seem a provocation or an act of visual transgression, or perhaps just commercial chicanery, but it represents a fundamental break with the supposed function of illustration. At the same time, though, it also tells us something about the subaltern character of illustration itself. Normatively, an illustration is a visual interpretation overwritten by its original source. On book jackets, the work of the artist is surmounted in bold letters with the name of another, namely the writer, and the image is overlaid and obscured by textual clutter title, publisher, endorsements, a synopsis, a barcode, the price in various currencies. Illustrations that are printed as wrap arounds frequently allow for this: the majority of interesting details (such as the aforementioned spaceship) occupy the right-hand side of the painting, whilst the left hand, destined for the back cover, might comprise little more than a field of stars, an airbrushed cloudbank, rugged hills or distant city lights. Nevertheless, the overprinting of text in all its forms effectively qualifies the voice of the artist, whose name, if it appears at all, is at the reverse and in the smallest possible font. This may be a point of bifurcation – two readings, the illustrator's and the writer's, now appear simultaneously – but it is also a moment of occlusion. What details are hidden behind the barcode? How much better would that barren expanse of lunar surface be, were it not half hidden behind some quote from the *Telegraph*? There is a veiling here: the particular imagetext hybrid to be found in sf (whether a paperback or an illustrated short story) is itself a novum (Suvin), and, as such, performs a utopian function: the gap between the image and the text, the occlusions and ellipses, all gesture towards a desire for something yet to be seen.

Typical techniques

With a few notable exceptions, an overview of the techniques of sf illustration reveals clearly discernible – and persistent – trends. They are embodied in, and affected by the common tools of the studio, as well as the possibilities and limitations of production budgets and reprographics. Analogue tools and media of the mid- to late-twentieth century sf illustrator were typically watercolours, gouache, casein (latterly replaced by acrylic) applied by hand with brushes (usually a combination of filberts, flats and rounds) or the airbrush, that quintessential tool of Modernity's ocular projections (magazine and book illustration) and redactions (photo re-touching). Indeed, the airbrush established itself as paradigmatic of sf illustration and it remains dominant, albeit superseded by digital software packages that emulate its effect. Despite the costly tendency of water-based paints to rust the spring and clog the needle retraction mechanism, for a large number of sf illustrators, the airbrush became the go-to studio tool for rendering vapour trails and dust clouds, and for imparting the required reflective sheen to curved and polished surfaces common to visualisations of spaceships and robots. As a painting tool, the reason for its ubiquity is probably best summarised in the words of one of its prominent exponents, Chris Foss: it was 'the only way I could see to get smooth gradations of pigment quickly' (7).

The pragmatics of that function, and the airbrush's wider associations as a twentieth-century commercial *design* tool, captures something of sf illustration as a distinct cultural form. Where airbrush work occasionally appears in the output of fine artists, it is only as a structural citation or 'quote' within a work. The use of airbrushing in the custom car fad of the late 1970s, and its cosmetic use in acrylic nails and spray tanning booths are both applications well outside the field of illustration. To a greater or lesser extent, then, the use of the airbrush in painting per se (as opposed to photo re-touching work or blending in a layout) is peculiar to a few modes of illustration, of which sf is by far the most common and has had the greatest cultural longevity.

Even at the height of the airbrush's presence within sf studio practice, a significant number of artists, perhaps deliberately, chose not to use it: Robert T. McCall, Vincent Di Fate, Bruce Pennington and John Harris are high-profile examples. As a result, the styles of these artists are often immediately distinguishable – looser, more expressive paint handling, in which the marks of flats and filbert brushes rather than rounds is more evident in the finished work. Similar, some artists opted for oil paints rather than acrylics, gouache or inks, although the drying times of oils – which is lengthy and varies across different colours – brought additional problems for the commercial artist working to deadlines unless a siccative was used.

Whether executed on line board, paper, designer's film or in some cases, such as the British illustrator Peter Elson, pieces of ordinary cardboard, paintings were generally executed larger than the size at which they would be reproduced. Camera-ready artwork would then be replicated by a photo-mechanical transfer machine and made into a plate for printing. As a result, colour balance varied dramatically. Images could be radically transformed during reproduction, and colours vibrant in the original could be prone to 'drop out' or exaggeration.

Another persistent element is fine brush detail, and fine brushes – whether analogue or digital – are part of the stock in trade of many sf illustrators. Fine detail is a particular form of truth telling. It is found in other cultural forms, such as model-making, where the accuracy of a model is often dependent upon its details, and the more detail a model has, the more it is regarded as truthful. The use of detail as a sign of 'good' painting in sf illustration is concomitant with the idea that the accumulation of empirical evidence by the senses is what constitutes truth and value. Sf illustration plays with this, creating the effect of authentic detail as a verifier of something fantastical, or, indeed, something that might otherwise be deemed completely improbable. The relationship between model-making and illustration does not end there of course – even prior to digital 3D rendering, many sf illustrators, such as Chesley Bonestell and Tim White, constructed models of the objects they sought to illustrate.

It is worth noting the extent to which the advent of digitalisation has not changed analogue-era paradigms. Many digital illustrator apps seek to emulate, rather than replace, the painterly effects and textures of airbrush, pencil, paintbrush and so on. The advantage to working digitally is principally the degree of fine control it affords: digital airbrushes do not clog or cough as their metal and Bakelite predecessors did, erasures are clean and smearless, and digital files can be saved and reproduced without loss of tone, chromatic range or other distortions. The contemporary illustrator might still work initially with pencil and sketchbook, before digitising roughs for approval by an art director, and then proceeding to work up the finished piece using software such as Adobe Creative Cloud.

Economic factors: Boom, bust, marginalisation, then repeat

The field of sf illustration undergoes cyclical expansions and contractions with the booms and slumps of the market for sf fiction itself. A well-known example is the growth and subsequent rapid decline of the British sf paperback market during the 1970s. Various aspects of this process should be of note to any historian of sf illustration. Contractions in markets have a 'winner takes all' effect: those illustrators who managed to consolidate their market position within the field during boom periods continued to be sought for what remaining work there was during a less favourable climate. For an illustrator, this process of consolidation is contingent upon a range of factors, including a popular and distinctive signature style, which enhances book sales, a resilient professional network, and good agency representation focused on building on the illustrator's reputation by procuring commissions with high-profile imprints. However, the nature of freelance work means that illustration is subject to centrifugal as well as centripetal forces: artists are compelled to take work wherever they can and may often have several defined styles for different client groups. This is particularly the case where a neophyte is attempting to break into a market and establish a viable freelance career. In times of economic decline within publishing, an illustrator attempting to consolidate around one particular style and one particular genre may find it simply impossible to find sufficient work. Similarly, they may be compelled to adapt or change their style to meet the demands of a changing market. For example, in early 1970s Britain, the needle nosed V-2 missile extrapolations (that had characterised the astronautical optimism of *Colliers Magazine*'s in the 1950s) were subverted and replaced by images of collapsing and dysfunctional spaceships. The success of E.E. 'Doc' Smith and A.E. van Vogt reissues with striking new covers by Chris Foss and other artists who emulated him meant that hardware – in the form of detailed renderings of lumpy, brightly coloured but battered spaceships, produced with a combination of brush and airbrush – dominated to the point of saturation. Thus, the work of a relatively narrow school of young male illustrators around the Sarah Brown Agency and Young Artists (most born between 1944 and 1952) came to define both a genre and a market, even if spaceships only featured tangentially in the actual content of the story. Illustrators whose work might have been more suited to a given novel but favoured a different style had to look elsewhere, frequently outside the genre, to find work. As the market contracted in the 1980s, many of the illustrators who had been inundated with commissions in the mid- to late-1970s found themselves unable to maintain full-time work in the genre. Even exponents of the lumpy spaceship had to adapt. Some abandoned book illustration altogether for other forms of visual practice, developing their work as fine artists or painting murals for theme parks. Some higher-profile names obtained work in Hollywood film productions, and some were able to successfully market their work in posters and cards. A significant few found work in the nascent gaming industry, initially producing packaging illustrations for early computer games. In time, this has evolved into concept work, developing characters, locations and machines for online gaming. Some, such as Peter Elson, never made it that far, although their 1970s work has subsequently been acknowledged as an inspiration.

In recent decades, the internet has shifted the economy of sf illustration profoundly. A multitude of artists has created an embarrassment of riches and dissolved some of the contexts in which individual illustrators could once command large sums for their work. As with any expanding field, styles of representation once the preserve of a couple of well-known names, have expanded into entire subgenres. The book and magazine, as analogue forms, are no longer centre stage but there is nothing to suggest their total demise is imminent. Rather, as music streaming has changed the status of vinyl, and digital photography that of film, the sense of analogue value is in some ways heightened, and so it may prove with illustration.

Works cited

Banerjee, Suparno. *Indian Science Fiction: Patterns, History and Hybridity*. U of Wales P, 2020.
Di Fate, Vincent. *Infinite Worlds: The Fantastic Visions of Science Fiction Art*. Virgin, 1997.
Foss, Chris. *21st Century Foss*. Dragon's Dream, 1978.
Frank, Jane. *Science Fiction and Fantasy Artists of the Twentieth Century*. McFarland, 2009.
Hardy, David A. 'The Impact of Astronautics and Science Fiction on My Work'. *Leonardo* 9.2 (1976): 95–8.
Jameson, Fredric. *The Political Unconscious: Narrative as a Socially Symbolic Act*. Routledge, 2002.
Mitchell, Timothy F. 'Science Fiction Illustration'. *The Missouri Review*, 7.2 (1984): 121–32.
Suvin, Darko. *Metamorphoses of Science Fiction: On the Poetics and History of a Literary Genre*. Yale UP, 1979.
Wells, H.G. *The Time Machine*. Everyman, 1995.
——. *The War of the Worlds*. Penguin, 2005.
Willis, Martin. *Vision, Science and Literature, 1870–1920: Ocular Horizons*. Pickering & Chatto, 2011.

13
JAPANESE SCIENCE FICTION

Baryon Tensor Posadas

In their magisterial account of the history of the sf, *Trillion Year Spree* (1986), Brian W. Aldiss and David Wingrove mention Japan only once in passing: 'the Japanese have yet to write a science fiction which the world will embrace as an essential part of its vocabulary' (100). Undoubtedly they can be criticised for being overly dismissive of Japanese sf, but their statement should not really come as a surprise given that, at the time (and for most of the twentieth century), there were very few English translations of Japanese literary sf, and they often went quickly out of print.

Consequently, Japanese sf has tended to occupy a peripheral position within histories of global sf. In Andrew Milner's study of sf from a world-systems perspective, which follows Franco Moretti's diffusionist account of literary history, Japanese sf emerged in the early twentieth century out of translations of European scientific romances, leading to domestic productions that were little more than imitations of the European core. Only after the Second World War did it develop its own local particularities as it shifted away from European to American sources to become a more semi-peripheral sf lineage (Milner 166–7). However, such a classification easily becomes self-fulfilling: the perception of Japanese sf as largely peripheral leads to less interest in making English translations available, which, in turn, reinforces its peripheral position. Of course, the case of Japanese sf is but one manifestation of the broader asymmetry in the translation of Japanese texts to English and vice versa, with a ratio of one to thirty at the end of the twentieth century (Fowler 4). This asymmetry, along with the ideological and commercial considerations shaping translation practices, constitute 'Technologies of recognition that selectively and often arbitrarily confer world membership on literatures' (Shih 118–9), and Aldiss and Wingrove can therefore be seen to demonstrate the limits of a conception of world literature (and by extension, global sf) primarily organised on the basis of Anglophone reception.

What makes the case of Japanese sf peculiar though is how the very imagination of 'Japan' is arguably already wrapped up in the language of sf. Indeed, it is frequently observed that a plethora of science-fictional 'Japans' populate the worlds of Anglophone sf texts, tracking the shifting historical dynamics of power in the US–Japan relationship (LaBare 22). Perhaps the most visible manifestation of this is the rise of 'techno-orientalist' imagery, a characteristic feature of such cyberpunk sf as *Blade Runner* (Scott 1982) and William Gibson's *Neuromancer* (1984). The term was coined by David Morley and Kevin Robbins, for whom the tendency to juxtapose images of

DOI: 10.4324/9781003140269-15

high-tech urban spaces marked by the proliferation of cybernetics and information networks with racialised images of a futuristic exoticism coincided with the emergence of Japan as a perceived economic threat to US hegemony during the 1980s (141). Others have developed the idea further to discuss the transnational popularisation of Japanese animation at the end of twentieth century (Ueno 'Japanimation' 228–9) or its significance for approaching sf from the Asian diaspora (Roh et al. 2).

Stephen Hong Sohn argues that the techno-orientalist turn is properly understood not simply as a contemporary development, but more of a revival of earlier yellow peril discourses from the beginning of the twentieth century. For Sohn, it was Japan's rise as an imperial power that could challenge European colonial interests in East Asia that fuelled the popularisation of all manner of future war and alien invasion narratives, including Philip Francis Nowlan's 'Armageddon – 2419 A.D.' (1928) and Robert A. Heinlein's *Sixth Column* (1941), that positioned an imagined 'Asia' as a signifier of absolute alienness. Such writings were in the service of a 'reorientation and reconsideration of Asia more broadly as a location from which to mold futuristic representations and alternative temporalities' (Sohn 5). As such, despite appearing to occupy a peripheral position within the coordinates of global sf's Anglocentric imaginary, Japan arguably plays a more formative role in the historical development of the genre since its beginnings than is usually acknowledged. It therefore seems only proper that greater attention be paid to the development of Japanese sf itself.

Scientific nationalism

The formation of sf as a genre is intimately intertwined with the history of empire, and 'early science fiction lives and breathes in the atmosphere of colonial history and its discourses' (Rieder 3). Indeed, the alignment of yellow peril narratives and future war stories presents one manifestation of this linkage specific to the Japanese case. This, however, is only one part of the equation as Japan too was an imperial power, indeed the only non-Western colonial empire. And much like the historical experience elsewhere, Japanese sf also emerged out of the nation's history of imperial conquest and expansion, with many of the earliest prototypes taking on explicit militarist overtones. With the Meiji restoration of 1868 ending a 250-year period of isolation under the Tokugawa Shogunate, Japan re-entered a world of imperial expansion and rivalry. As a latecomer, Japan had to undertake rapid and intense industrialisation and modernisation, importing new technologies and social practices to radically transform government structures, public education, military organisation and social-cultural practices. But alongside this came Japan's own imperial expansion, beginning with the annexations of Hokkaido (1869) and Okinawa (1879), followed by the acquisition of Taiwan and Korea in the wake of victories in the First Sino-Japanese War (1894–5) and Russo-Japanese War (1904–5), respectively.

Amid these historical events, a wave of translations from other languages entered Japan. Alongside literary, philosophical and scientific materials, translations of Jules Verne's extraordinary voyages, including *Journey to the Centre of the Earth* (1864, trans. 1885) and *20000 Leagues under the Seas* (1870, trans. 1884), and H.G. Wells's scientific romances, Robinsonade adventure stories, utopian fictions and futurist forecasts proved quite popular in Japan (Nagayama *Seishin-Shi* 28–33). By the late nineteenth century, authors of Meiji political novels (*seiji shōsetsu*) began taking an interest in the idea of extrapolating the future, leading to the development of utopian 'future records' (*mirai-ki*) such as Suehiro Tetchō's *Future Record of Meiji Year 23* (*23-nen no mirai-ki*; 1893), which were popular because of their capacity to provide political satire and set off a boom in futuristic extrapolations (Kurita 8). At the same time, adventure novels (*bōken shōsetsu*) incorporated new knowledge about far-off lands and military speculation; for example,

Yano Ryūkei's bestselling *Tales of the Floating Castle* (*Ukishiro monogatari*; 1890) presented a Robinsonade adventure featuring rogue Japanese imperial naval officers exploring and staking territorial claims on unknown lands while developing new technologies and new weaponry to fend off pirates, European imperialists and other dangers. These various texts were loosely grouped under the category of *kagaku shōsetsu* (literally, science novel); a gloss on the term 'scientific romance', it was coined in Ozaki Yukio's introduction to another of Suehiro's *mirai-ki* works, *Plum Blossoms in the Snow* (*Setchūbai*; 1886).

One consequence of the circumstances of Japanese sf's emergence was that it was wedded to a discourse of imperial utopianism, countering while also reproducing the logics of the European imperial presence in Asia. Oshikawa Shunrō's signature work, *Undersea Warship: A Strange Island Adventure* (*Kaitō bōken kitan: kaitei gunkan*; 1900, trans. 2022) is particularly illustrative of these negotiations of Japan's relationship to the world system of inter-imperial rivalries of the period. The first of a series of adventure novels, it tells the story of a man's accidental discovery of the secret development of an advanced submersible warship for the purpose of defending Japan's imperial interests, following its construction, launch and subsequent clashes with pirates and other nations' navies.

The significance of *Undersea Warship* in the history of Japanese sf is difficult to overstate. Despite its arguably questionable literary and technical merits, it lends the challenge of scientific and technological development a noteworthy ideological charge. A constant refrain throughout the novel is the need for Japan to technologically modernise (especially in military terms) in order to oppose imperialist encroachments in East Asia. It endorses Japan's militarisation via a rhetoric of anti-colonialism (or, at least, anti-European colonialism) as an important ideological buttress but remains mute on the subject of Japan's own imperial ambitions, a silence that becomes more striking with the unfolding of Japan's actual imperial expansion marked especially by the Russo-Japanese War of 1904–5. Indeed, the subsequent Russo–Japanese war cemented the reputation of Oshikawa's novel and legitimated its ideas, with its purported anticipation of naval conflicts with the West becoming its primary claim to fame.

Once sf started to formally consolidate as a mass cultural genre in the 1930s in Japan, narratives like *Undersea Warship* became the template, effectively setting the terms for the development of sf, especially at a time when the Japanese Empire renewed its expansion with the 1931 invasion and subsequent annexation of Manchuria. Although Japanese sf had not yet developed dedicated genre-specific publishing venues, certain publications nonetheless came to be associated with the genre. These included literary magazines, such as *New Youth* (*Shinseinen*), and popular science publications, such as *Science Illustrated* (*Kagaku gahō*) and *Children's Science* (*Kodomo no kagaku*). In popular science magazines, military-themed sf featuring nationalistic narratives and advanced war machines by Unno Jūza and Minami Yōichiro, among others, Kigi Takatarō's imperial utopian speculations and Kayama Shigeru's colonial lost world stories shared pages with illustrations depicting future military technologies and articles on the latest colonial adventures, in effect aligning the fictions' sense of wonder with a broader ideology of 'scientific nationalism' (Mizuno 156–9).

It would be easy to dismiss 1930s Japanese sf as mere expressions of jingoism, especially in the case of authors, such as Unno, whom the Japanese military recruited to serve as propagandists with the goal of turning their fiction into vehicles to promote patriotism and the advancement of scientific knowledge. It is thus quite unsurprising that only a scant few examples from this period have been translated into English. However, this critical neglect runs the risk of overlooking the interplay between the sf genre's estranging potential and the ideological constraints of a specific historical conjuncture. Sari Kawana even goes so far as to speculate that, for Unno in particular, public patriotism during wartime served largely as a cover for his interest in promoting science education: he was

> not a genuine believer in nationalism or militarism despite his official persona, but instead someone who sought to usurp these ideologies to make them serve another ideological system, namely, a new Japan-led scientism that would counter the dominance of Western science.
>
> (184)

Hints of such a stance are certainly visible in, for example, Unno's 'Eighteen O'Clock Music Bath' ('Jūhachi-ji no Ongaku-yoku'; 1937, trans. 2021), which presents a post-apocalyptic subterranean totalitarian state in which all citizens must undergo a thirty-minute sonic broadcast every evening. These mind-altering broadcasts are intended to redirect unproductive energies towards productive labour, turning citizens away from such vices as smoking or drinking. But a side effect of this mind-control cultivates a passive stupor, such that a power struggle and collapse of the state takes place unnoticed. Only the head scientist is left to resist an untimely Martian invasion with his android army and to build a utopia out of the ruins.

Similarly, Kigi Takatarō's *The Flag of the Green Rising Sun* (*Midori no nisshoki*; 1938) centres on themes of technocratic utopian imperialism. It recounts a voyage to a secret subterranean utopia – the 'green rising sun' nation – which is represented as a kind of alternate not-quite Japan. Much of the story is devoted to a tour of such wonders as teleconferencing and television shopping, alongside descriptions of the nation's highly regimented and rationalised social system. With no class-based or racial discord, and a perfectly managed economy with no shortages or excesses of production, it is an idealised utopian stand-in for the Japanese puppet state of Manchukuo (in northeast China, from 1932–45) wherein all the technocratic fantasies of its colonial administrators have somehow been realised. Even as Kigi thus expresses a critical stance vis-a-vis the actually existing Japanese empire as insufficiently scientific and incompletely modernised, he is unable to challenge the structural logic of imperialism itself, presenting instead the impossible fantasy of a perfect modernisation and an imperialism without its attendant social consequences. It recalls Istvan Csicsery-Ronay, Jr's suggestion that sf is driven by the desire to imaginatively transform historical imperialism into technocratic, technoscientific empire ('Science' 232).

From *kagaku shōsetsu* to sf

If the tensions between the drives towards utopia and empire structured the development of sf in prewar Japan, after the Second World War they took on a more historical character in the opposition between continuity and rupture. The aftermath of defeat and occupation transformed the US–Japan geopolitical relationship, and with the beginnings of the Cold War, exacerbated by the 1949 Communist victory in the Chinese Civil War followed by the outbreak of the Korean War in 1950, it became necessary to quickly reinvent and rehabilitate the image of Japan, transforming it from the mortal wartime enemy of the US to a Cold War ally and a bulwark against the spread of Communism in Asia.

Of course, things are never so simple, and trans-war continuities nevertheless persist. In Japanese sf, this becomes especially visible in work that traverses the historical divide. Consider, for example, *Atragon* (*Kaitei gunkan*; Honda and Matsubayashi 1963), the adaptation of *Undersea Warship*. Little of the novel's plot remains, replaced by the story of an invasion from a lost undersea civilisation. Only the basic setup – a renegade naval captain constructs a secret super ship that is both submersible and flight-capable – is retained, albeit with the captain a nationalist relic who remains unaware of Japan's surrender and initially refuses to fight invaders since it goes against his personal goal of resurrecting the Japanese Empire.

Given the different historical circumstances surrounding the production of the novel and the film, these changes can be seen to reflect a demand for an adaptation that would not reproduce but instead repudiate the politics of its source. *Atragon* seemingly seeks to exorcise the ghosts of Japan's imperial past in order to valorise postwar politics. However, this gesture – not at all atypical of its time – is undercut by the fact that it is precisely Japan's militarist past and the scientific nationalism of the previous decades, in the form of Jinguji's technical know-how and advanced weaponry, that ends up saving the world. In other words, the film simultaneously denies and recuperates the history of Japanese imperialism.

The political debate that *Atragon* stages between the positions of prewar scientific nationalism and its postwar disavowal is symptomatic of the broader discursive space surrounding discussions of the relationship between history and sf in Japan at the time. This relationship has two facets to it. First, there is the genre's engagement with politically charged questions of history, whether in the form of allegory, counterfactual thought experiment or futuristic extrapolation. Second, there is the history of sf itself in Japan, which proved contentious during this time, especially around questions of definition and origin.

One tendency in existing accounts of the history of Japanese sf is to acknowledge the existence of a few prewar precedents but locate the beginnings of the genre proper during the postwar US occupation. Indeed, one of the earliest histories of Japanese sf, Ishihara Fujio's *Grand Annotated Catalog of Sf Works* (*sf tosho kaisetsu sōmokushiroku*; 1982), which details the ever-growing archive of sf (both foreign and domestic) published in Japan, begins with the 1946 publication of an anthology series of translations from the US pulp *Amazing Stories.* Even when prewar sf is recognised, as in Yokota Jun'ya's *Classical Japanese Sf* (*Nihon sf koten*; 1981), it is distinguished by prefixes like 'classical' (koten), which has the effect of giving the scholarship on these writings an almost archaeological quality of excavating lost treasures, thus implying that they were not quite properly sf (Nagayama *Seishin-Shi* 8).

Perhaps the most well-known proponent of this approach is Tatsumi Takayuki, who describes Abe Kōbō, Yano Tetsu, Komatsu Sakyō and other postwar writers as 'founding fathers' and the first generation of sf authors in Japan (106). He does mention prewar authors like Oshikawa and Unno, but suggests their works are merely precursors to sf proper, which for him only appears with the postwar publications specifically dedicated to sf: 'the origins of Japanese sf as an organized movement are best located in the publications of the first successful fanzine, *Cosmic Dust* (*Uchujin*, 1957–), and the first successful commercial magazine, Hayakawa's *Sf Magazine* (1959–)' (Tatsumi 105).

This approach has the effect of rendering Japanese sf as little more than a derivative of American sf. Moreover, periodisations that draw a stark dividing line between Japan's prewar and postwar periods align with Cold War prerogatives to rehabilitate Japan's image, often downplaying Japan's history of colonial expansion and thus preparing the ground for the disavowal of historical war responsibility. In the context of sf, this in turn also obscures the formative role of the imperial imaginary in Japanese sf.

However, these criticisms aside, the approach has some merit. If, as Gary Westfahl argues, a genre only comes into being when it is defined in contemporary commentary and consolidated into a coherent grouping of texts (8), then it can be argued that this is precisely the process taking place in postwar Japan. Key to this point is a significant shift in terminology. As noted, prewar texts were historically referred to as *kagaku shōsetsu*, but after the war the term was quickly superseded by the

Japanese transliteration of 'science fiction' (saiensu fikushon), which remains the preferred term today, indicating a clear discursive shift taking place. But beyond just terminology, as Nagayama Yasuo has noted, this is also the historical period when all manner of institutional formations that underpin a genre – specialised publications, fan cultures, critical commentaries – consolidated (Nagayama *Jiken-Shi* 50–1).

In this reconfiguration of the genre, Japanese sf explicitly positioned itself in relation to Anglophone, and especially American sf, imbibing and integrating its discourse and debates into its own conversations, albeit asymmetrically. As Tatsumi amply documented, throughout the postwar decades, much of the discussion taking place within the Japanese sf community closely tracked the central issues and terms of debate of American sf. Indeed, at the onset, some of the key topics of discussion concerned the relationship between the two national sf traditions, with Yamano Kōichi criticising what he saw as Japanese sf's imitative quality. The following decades saw debates surrounding the impact of the New Wave and the turn towards 'inner space', the rise of cyberpunk and the subsequent backlash against it, as well as the genre's gender politics, especially in connection with the participation of women in fan activities (Tatsumi 111–3). For the most part, these debates and controversies, not to mention the sf texts that emerged in their midst, remained inaccessible to Anglophone readers. More recently, however, publishers specifically dedicated to translations of Japanese sf, such as the now-defunct Haikasoru imprint of Viz Media and the University of Minnesota Press's *Parallel Futures* series, along with the rise of independent e-book publishing focused on translating Japanese sf, have offered a small glimpse of Japanese sf's range of styles, interests and concerns.

A few texts warrant highlighting for how they seemingly offer commentaries on a range of contemporary concerns. Komatsu Sakyō's *Japan Sinks* (*Nihon chinbotsu*; 1973, trans. 1976) and *Virus: Day of Resurrection* (*Fukkatsu no hi*; 1964, trans. 2012) present different apocalyptic scenarios – the sinking of the Japanese islands, a deadly global pandemic that wipes out most of the Japanese population – that prefigure, respectively, the 2011 Tohoku earthquake and tsunami and the Covid-19 pandemic. Aramaki Yoshio's *The Sacred Era* (*Shinseidai*; 1978, trans. 2017) presents a post-apocalyptic environmentally ravaged world governed by a totalitarian theocracy in a series of surreal, almost painterly tableaus that confuse outer space and inner space as its protagonist journeys from planet to planet in a quasi-religious pilgrimage towards a literal Garden of Earthly Delights. Kawamata Chiaki's *Death Sentences* (*Genshi gari*; 1984, trans. 2012) laments the failure of the revolutionary and utopian politics of the New Wave, with its metafictive depiction of surrealist poems that entrances their readers into drug-like stupors, creating a world-wide crisis when the poems are rediscovered and commodified for the purpose of heightening the cultural capital of a department store. Ōhara Mariko's *Hybrid Child* (*Haiburiddo chairudo*; 1991, trans. 2018) follows the story of an artificial posthuman entity that can sample and mimic any entity they encounter, presenting a being that aligns with Donna J. Haraway's conception of the cyborg that transgresses boundaries of human, machine, animal and gender.

As for more contemporary sf authors, few had more of an impact than Project Itoh (Itō Keikaku), despite his short body of work. It is not just that numerous works inspired by him have appeared since his untimely death from cancer in 2009, but that the term 'post-Project Itoh' has emerged as the term to describe the contemporary conjuncture in Japanese sf. Of particular significance in Itoh's work is the centrality of the zombie to his repeated explorations of posthuman consciousness and systems of organisation. It takes on more sublimated forms in his earlier novels, the military-themed *Genocidal Organ* (*Gyakusatsu kikan*; 2007, trans. 2012) and the satire of a medicalised utopia *Harmony* (*Haamonii*; 2008, trans. 2010), but is much more overt in his posthumously published *Empire of Corpses* (*Shisha no teikoku*; 2012), which depicts an alternate history in which Frankenstein's successful resurrection of a corpse brings about massive social upheavals by enabling the mass production of animated corpses to serve as soldiers for the British empire, as well as a cheap and docile industrial labour force.

This interest places Itoh's fiction in conversation with recent critical work that claims the zombie as the successor to Donna Haraway's cyborg, a more properly posthuman figure appropriate to the contemporary conjuncture (Lauro and Embry 398). Such a shift brings interesting consequences to the study of Japanese sf. After all, the cyborg has so often served as a conceptual apparatus for understanding the cultural politics of contemporary Japan through its use as an analytical device for apprehending techno-orientalism, postwar hybridity and US–Japan relations, as well as the intersections of gender politics and technology. As such, if there is indeed a turn from the cyborg to the zombie in the cultural imaginary, it raises the question of what this might mean for understanding the position of Japanese sf in the global imaginary now.

Animated bodies

Even as the availability of Japanese prose sf remains relatively limited in the Anglophone world, one area where Japanese sf has found greater visibility is in the medium of animation. Unlike translations of literary sf, which are not only few and far between but also often trapped in temporal lag, works of Japanese animation (sf or otherwise) often see simultaneous global release, catering to a now established transnational fan community. The range of styles and subgenres run the gamut, and there are far too many titles that can be named before coming close to a comprehensive account, from space operas like *Space Pirate Captain Harlock* (*Uchū kaizoku kyaputen harrokku*; 1978) and *Legend of Galactic Heroes* (*Ginga eiyū densetsu*; 1988–97), time travel stories like *The Girl Who Leapt Through Time* (*Toki wo kakeru shojo*; Hosoda 2006) or *Steins:gate* (2011), dystopian techno-thrillers like *Psycho-Pass* (2012) and *Mardock Scramble* (2010–2), not to mention countless giant robot series, apocalyptic narratives, so-called *isekai* (other world) fantasies, and so on.

However, this was not always the case. In fact, the global popularisation of Japanese animation is arguably a part of the broader historical process that saw Anglophone sf take greater interest in Japan, made manifest through the techno-orientalising imagery associated with cyberpunk. In the 1970s and early 1980s, the practices surrounding the international export of Japanese animation often involved not just translation, but the wholesale localisation of the material, with character names changed and any traces of references to specific Japanese social and cultural life removed. Such was the case with the English dubs of *Space Battleship Yamato* (*Uchū senkan Yamato*; 1974), which became *Starblazers* (1979), and *Super Dimension Fortress Macross* (*Chōjikū yōsai Makurosu*; 1982), which became the first half of the series *Robotech* (1985). It was not until the international release of Ōtomo Katsuhiro's cyberpunk classic *Akira* (1988) that a shift began to take place, such that the interest in Japanese animation drew precisely from its Japanese origins to the extent that the term 'anime' (from the Japanese shorthand for 'animation') entered use in the English language.

While it was by no means the first work of Japanese animation to see a US theatrical release, the story of *Akira*, centring on biker gangs in a dystopian Tokyo clashing with the Japanese military, apocalyptic cults and psychic children certainly, found an audience. As Christopher Bolton puts it, its opening sequence depicting the detonation of a psychic bomb that destroys Tokyo recalls not only the atomic bombings of Hiroshima and Nagasaki but also served as a signifier of 'a kind of bombshell that set off the anime boom' (296) in North America. *Akira* can also be understood as an instantiation of the Japanese response to American cyberpunk's techno-orientalist construction of an imagined 'Japan'. While typically characterised as misrepresentations of Japan borne out of the anti-Japanese hysteria of the 1980s, many Japanese sf works, especially in animation, embraced and reappropriated these techno-orientalist images. As Ueno Toshiya argues, techno-orientalism serves as an image machine through which 'Western or other people misunderstand and fail to recognize an always illusory Japanese culture, but also is the mechanism through which Japanese misunderstand themselves' (Ueno 228). Cyberpunk anime like *Akira* were the products of such acts of reappropriation, which then found themselves translated back to American audiences.

Another renowned work of Japanese animation that came out of this crisscrossing interchange is Oshii Mamoru's *Ghost in the Shell* (*Kōkaku kidōtai*; 1995) and all its subsequent sequels, remakes and copycats. It tells the story of a female cyborg public security officer and the team she leads as they investigate criminal activities stemming from the increasing use of cybernetics in society, including ghost-hacking, emergent intelligences, and new social phenomena engendered by increasing network connectivity. It is possibly the most studied work of Japanese animation, and much of the scholarship draws on Haraway's cyborg feminism to take up such issues as the interface between gender and artificial bodies and the mass-manufacture and commodification of cyborg women. However, one criticism levelled against much critical writing on cyborgs in Japanese animation (and particularly in *Ghost in the Shell*) is the tendency to focus on representations of the figure of the cyborg, without accounting for how animated bodies are, in a sense, always already cyborgs. Indeed, in the case of Oshii's work, this is especially salient given that the primary obsession that animates his work is the question of animation itself (Ueno 'Kurenai' 114). His interest is not in the cyborg per se, but in the use of the cyborg as a device to meditate on the ontology of the animated body and the spectator's relation to it.

It is here, in this metacommentary on the art of animation, that the broader significance of Japanese animation for sf studies can be located. Although matters of narrative and worldbuilding conventionally inform the classification of texts in the genre, sf anime also bears a potential for staging a metacritical engagement with its own technological materiality, its own science fictionality at a formal level. Animation, in this sense, is more than just another medium for the containment of sf stories. By virtue of its status as itself a media technology, it also stages a technologically charged experience of the condition of modernity that is already enmeshed in science-fictional rhetorics and habits of thought. In this respect, what warrants attention in sf anime is not only the wealth of sf stories and worlds it offers, but also its potential to open up a space to address the challenge issued by Csicsery-Ronay, Jr when he asked what exactly is science fictional, what exactly is cognitively estranged, about sf animation ('What' 35). This would entail approaching sf anime – and Japanese sf, more generally – not merely as an archive of a particular national lineage of sf but, more importantly, as a critical prism that is generative of science-fictional effects in how it constitutes into being different, and potentially cognitively estranging, ways of looking.

Works cited

Aldiss, Brian W. with David Wingrove. *Trillion Year Spree: The History of Science Fiction*. Atheneum, 1986.

Bolton, Christopher. 'From Ground Zero to Degree Zero: Akira from Origin to Oblivion'. *Mechademia* 9.1 (2014): 295–315.

Csicsery-Ronay, Jr, Istvan. 'Science Fiction and Empire'. *Science Fiction Studies* 90 (2003): 231–45.

——. 'What Is Estranged in Science Fiction Animation?'. *Simultaneous Worlds: Global Science Fiction Cinema*. Ed. Jennifer L. Feeley and Sarah Ann Wells. U of Minnesota P, 2015. 29–46.

Fowler, Edward. 'Rendering Words, Traversing Cultures: On the Art and Politics of Translating Modern Japanese Fiction'. *Journal of Japanese Studies* 18.1 (1992): 1–44.

Kawana, Sari. 'Science without Conscience: Unno Juza and Tenko Of Convenience'. *Converting Cultures: Religion, Ideology and Transformations of Modernity*. Ed. Dennis Washburn and A. Kevin Reinhart. Brill, 2007. 183–208.
Kurita, Kyoko. 'Meiji Japan's Y23 Crisis and the Discovery of the Future: Suehiro Tetcho's Nijusan-Nen Mirai-Ki'. *Harvard Journal of Asiatic Studies* 60.1 (2000): 5–43.
LaBare, Joshua. 'The Future: "Wrapped... in That Mysterious Japanese Way"'. *Science Fiction Studies* 80 (2000): 22–48.
Lauro, Sarah Juliet and Karen Embry. 'A Zombie Manifesto: The Nonhuman Condition in the Era of Advanced Capitalism'. *Zombie Theory: A Reader*. Ed. Sarah Juliet Lauro and Karen Embry. U of Minnesota P, 2017. 395–412.
Milner, Andrew. *Locating Science Fiction*. Liverpool UP, 2012.
Mizuno, Hiromi. *Science for the Empire: Scientific Nationalism in Modern Japan*. Stanford UP, 2009.
Morley, David and Kevin Robbins. *Spaces of Identity: Global Media, Electronic Landscapes, and Cultural Boundaries*. Routledge, 1995.
Nagayama, Yasuo. *Nihon sf Jiken-Shi: Nihonteki Sōzōryoku No 70-Nen (A History of Japanese Sf Events: 70 Years of the Japanese Imagination)*. Kawade Shobo Shinsha, 2012.
——. *Nihon sf Seishin-Shi: Bakumatsu/Meiji Kara Sengo Made (The Intellectual History of Japanese Sf: From the Bakumatsu and Meiji Periods to the Postwar)*. Kawade Shobo Shinsha, 2009.
Rieder, John. *Colonialism and the Emergence of Science Fiction*. Wesleyan UP, 2008.
Roh, David S., Betsy Huang and Greta Niu. 'Technologizing Orientalism: An Introduction'. *Techno-Orientalism: Imagining Asia in Speculative Fiction, History, and Media*. Ed. David S. Roh, Betsy Huang and Greta Niu. Rutgers UP, 2015. 1–19.
Shih, Shu-Mei. 'Global Literature and the Technologies of Recognition'. *Proceedings of the Modern Language Association* 119.1 (2004): 16–30.
Sohn, Stephen Hong. 'Introduction: Alien/Asian: Imagining the Racialized Future'. *MELUS* 33.4 (2008): 5–22.
Tatsumi, Takayuki. 'Generations and Controversies: An Overview of Japanese Science Fiction, 1957–1997'. *Science Fiction Studies* 80 (2000): 105–14.
Ueno, Toshiya. 'Japanimation and Techno-Orientalism'. *The Uncanny: Experiments in Cyborg Culture*. Ed. Bruce Grenville. Arsenal Pulp, 2002. 228–31.
——. '*Kurenai No Metalsuits*, "Anime to Wa Nani Ka/What Is Animation"'. Trans. Michael Arnold. *Mechademia* 1.1 (2006): 111–8.
Westfahl, Gary. *Mechanics of Wonder: The Creation of the Idea of Science Fiction*. Liverpool UP, 1999.

14
SCIENCE FICTION FILM, 1895–1950

J.P. Telotte

While the history of sf cinema practically coincides with that of the cinema itself, most genre commentary starts with its spectacular explosion of popularity in the 1950s and tracks through its subsequent development of various themes and concerns that have a particularly cinematic resonance: the reproducible being (robots, androids), the construction of reality (virtual worlds, virtual selves), spectacular threats to our fragile world (alien invasion, an environment on the brink). One of the most famous commentaries on the form, Susan Sontag's 'The Imagination of Disaster', early on staked out this critical perspective, suggesting that cinematic sf was born from those films of alien invasion and threatened apocalypse that dominated the 1950s and capitalised on the visual potential of such spectacles. Claiming such elements as a kind of generic essence, she argued that sf films 'are not about science' but 'disaster' (213). However, sf's earlier history shows that it has been very much about science, along with the technology it produces and the reason that drives both – which sometimes, through humanity's all too common missteps, generate the ruinous consequences she observes. But in sketching a history of sf film, even if only its first half, we should account for those elements that emphasise our potential for conception, construction and projection, as well as those that show the cautionary, even frightening images that flow from this same spring. For this flexibility to speak doubly, both positively and negatively about the work of science and technology, and to align that flexibility with changing cultural needs, may be one of the genre's most telling characteristics.

Rather than simply suggesting that the genre is most concerned with science, then, I want to emphasise how this early period reflects a dynamic, shifting character, as sf cinema began to establish its identity. Sf film could well be understood through the prism of fantasy, a mode that, despite its dreamlike, often unsettling, and even frightening images, remains, at its deepest level, in constant *dialogue* with the real, with the way we operate upon it through our reason, science and technology, and thus with the potentials and pitfalls of these operations (Telotte 10–16). As Rosemary Jackson observes, fantasy constantly 'recombines and inverts the real, [...] it does not escape it' (20). Because of this dialogic stance, the form has proven to be a rather fluid, culturally-bound construct, while also consistently self-conscious, as if intent on interrogating its own reality, including the technology involved in its creation. This point echoes the notion that 'science fiction in the cinema often turns out to be [...] the fictional or fictive science of the cinema itself' (Stewart 159).

 DOI: 10.4324/9781003140269-16

While almost from its origins sf cinema has produced amazing and sometimes disconcerting icons and actions, they are usually not so much 'an inadequate response' (Sontag 224) to specific cultural conditions, but an effort to situate those elements of reason–science–technology within the cultural order and help us gauge how they might both construct and destruct our world. That effort has produced spectacles that are by turns disturbing and affirmative, yet also aware of their curiously double nature – a pattern evident even in sf's first examples, those pre-narrative texts of the 'cinema of attractions' that dominated early film (Gunning 63). Throughout the late 1890s and early 1900s numerous films appear that *point toward* the genre by conjuring astonishing machinery, which, like the cinema, produces entertaining illusions, transformations, impossible shifts in time and place, or enables fantastic travels. For example, *The Sausage Machine* (no director credited 1897), displays a wondrous invention that turns dogs into sausages and sausages back into dogs; *Dr. Skinum* (McCutcheon 1907) depicts a device that changes humans from ugly to beautiful; and *The Lion's Breath* (Davey 1916) offers a machine for transferring minds and personalities. If only with some difficulty recognised as sf today, such works do reflect the genre's spirit. Evoking early Machine Age attitudes toward science and technology, they centre on the amazing properties (and humorous products) of various devices or machines, all trading upon the similarly amazing 'attractions' that comprised the cinema itself.

These largely comic efforts take much of their inspiration from the work of Georges Méliès, typically seen as the father of cinematic sf and best known for his Jules Verne/H.G. Wells adaptation *A Trip to the Moon* (*Le voyage dans la lune*; 1902). Deploying the cinematic apparatus's ability to create a new sense of time and space, Méliès produced amazing appearances and disappearances, animated practically anything, and sent his characters on fantastic journeys and explorations in, for example, *The Impossible Voyage* (*Voyage à travers l'impossible*; 1904), *20,000 Leagues Under the Sea* (*20000 lieues sous les mers*; 1907) and *The Conquest of the Pole* (*À la conquête du pôle*; 1912). While influenced by Verne's *voyages extraordinaires*, he eschewed their emphasis on exposition and explanation, on describing reason and science, in favour of *cinematic* fantasies: exploding Moon-men, a flying train, undersea monsters, interplanetary travel. More than simply spectacles, these efforts demonstrate his contribution to an evolving relationship between sf and cinematic technology. For to create his worlds of wonder, Méliès contributed to a growing arsenal of special effects (substitution effects, models and miniatures, double exposures, primitive matting, filtered photography), illustrating how the development of film technology would inspire both the imagery and techniques of sf. He also established a pattern that continues to inform sf film, as these advances led him not to develop more complex *narratives* but to fashion new and more fantastic *visions*, thereby allowing his audience to experience things impossible in their far less fantastic reality.

Consequently, some historians have downplayed the sf aspect of Méliès's work, arguing that, for example, 'the fantasy powers' of his films displaced 'any real interest in a technological future' (La Valley 146). Lewis Jacobs, emphasising 'the complexity of his tricks, his resourcefulness with mechanical contrivances' (18), echoes this assessment. Yet these views miss Méliès's role in establishing some of sf's key iconography and primary plot concerns, among them rockets, submarines (even flying submarines), automata, aliens, scientists and slightly mad inventors, space travel, monsters both terrestrial and extraterrestrial, and the technologically-driven conquest of various challenges. Thus more recent revaluations have noted how his development of a 'mode of spectatorial address' and emphasis on technological effects 'invite comparisons' to the contemporary digital-effects-heavy sf identified with such figures as Steven Spielberg and George Lucas (Pierson 119). So while Méliès never saw himself as a creator of sf in the manner of H.G. Wells, and while his films offered their various 'attractions' with tongue in cheek, he did sketch out an influential look and manner for early sf cinema. Where his works fell short was in their exaggerated flourishes trumpeting the artifice of his worlds and straining at the science and technology they depict and champion.

The narrative films that immediately followed Méliès's lead would primarily exploit some of the icons and situations he established. Thus, the 1910s and early 1920s saw a number of films offering variations on his fantastic inventions and journeys, as in *The Aerial Submarine* (Booth 1910), *The Pirates of 1920* (Aylott and Coleby 1911) and the more ambitious Danish *A Trip to Mars* (*Himmelskibet*; Holger-Madsen 1917), while others imported sf elements into narratives that drew strongly from the horror, melodramatic and comic forms popular in early cinema. In the horrific vein, for example, we see the kinship of works like the German *Homunculus* (Rippert 1916) and *The Head of Janus* (*Der Januskopf*; Murnau 1920), and the American *Frankenstein* (Dawley 1910), *Dr. Jekyll and Mr. Hyde* (Robertson 1920) and *A Blind Bargain* (Worsley 1922), the first film adaptation of Wells's *The Island of Doctor Moreau* (1896). While science is at the core of these narratives, they also emphasise a kind of *unreason* involved in that scientific work, resulting in monstrous creations and horrific consequences, and producing in the audience a kind of recoil from the scientific.

A more melodramatic inflection appears in *The House of Mystery* (no director credited 1912), *Filibus* (Roncoroni 1915) and the Harry Houdini serial *The Master Mystery* (Grossman and King 1919), which put robots, inventors and criminal scientists at cross purposes with society. Downplaying the actual work of science, they focus instead on solving various mysteries or crimes, either with the aid of or in opposition to the work of science and technology. Tellingly, the same unhinged inventors and amazing inventions prove just as central to many comedies, such as *A Clever Dummy* (Sennett 1917), in which Ben Turpin encounters a robot model of himself; *The Electric House* (Cline and Keaton 1922), wherein Buster Keaton creates a futuristic electrified home, only to see his creations go haywire; *The Crazy Ray* (*Paris qui dort*; Clair 1925), about a device that stops time and freezes all motion; and *A Wild Roomer* (Bowers and Muller 1926), about the creation of a gargantuan machine that frees individuals from labour by performing practically any household task, while also wrecking the house and, like the Turpin and Keaton films, holding technology hostage to laughter. While these narratives focus on the play of reason, the discoveries of science and astonishing pieces of technology, they also stylise or exaggerate those elements, never integrating them into a coherent sf narrative. Rather, with the exception of Keaton, they generally treat their sf elements as 'attractions', as convenient narrative ploys that derive their real 'sense' from the other genres in which they have been granted a liminal status.

However, that liminality helps emphasise the functional nature of their sf elements, making the various man-made monsters, robots, electrified houses and wondrous machines stand out, as if they were the real attractions or reasons for these films. It also helps them point to another order of narrative that stands, as an absence, just outside the world of these films. For example, *A Wild Roomer* quickly visualises this tension when Charlie Bowers constructs his mammoth machine in a tiny apartment, leaving him no room to move around or way to extricate his giant device. It is a telling analogy for the dilemma facing many of these part-sf works that evoke powerful icons or situations, only to find that, in their utility, they threaten to bulk beyond more familiar narrative structures or mundane plot concerns, bursting the seams of their rather conventional containers.

It remained for a series of films, epic in scope, resources and intentions, that appeared in the late silent and early sound period to definitively break with this pattern and insist on a specific identity for the new genre. Films such as *Aelita* (Protazanov 1924), *Metropolis* (Lang 1927), *The Mysterious Island* (Hubbard 1929), *End of the World* (*La fin du monde*; Gance 1930) and *Things to Come* (Menzies 1936) drew on a pre-existing and increasingly popular sf literature, reached out to an international audience and provided plot models for a variety of offspring and imitations. These elaborate films demonstrate the rapid, international flowering of sf, whose various icons, plot devices and themes seem already well understood by filmmakers and audiences.

Aelita is a curious product of the early Soviet film system, directed by a successful pre-First World War filmmaker, Yakov Protazanov, who had originally fled the Communist revolution, and based on the 1923 novel by Alexei Tolstoy, a revolutionary and champion of technological progress. While the film seems at odds with itself, it marshals its generic materials into an ambitious narrative about an engineer, Los, who constructs a rocket, flies it to Mars, there instigates a Soviet-style revolution and becomes the consort of the eponymous Martian queen. This interplanetary extension of the revolutionary spirit, however, proves to be an elaborate daydream, distilled from a combination of Los's ambitions, personal troubles and inability to focus on the everyday work of the revolution. While the dream undermines Tolstoy's revolutionary thrust, it ultimately lends the story a realistic point, suggesting that there is no magical solution – not even technological magic – for our individual and cultural difficulties, and leaving Los committed to the hard work of addressing such problems.

In its retreat from the scientific and technological fantasies of space flight and Martian culture, *Aelita* offers a sober view of the power of that reason–science–technology triad increasingly central to the genre. This view partly results from Protazanov's treatment of the film as unconventional social satire rather than sf. Moreover, he invests the sf imagery with the aura of those early film 'attractions' by framing the Martian world in the stylised manner of Constructivism, which drew on a perceived machine beauty and set a dynamic mix of different materials, divergent lines, and clashing shapes in opposition to the natural. This stylised Mars calls attention not only to its constructed nature, but also to the possibility for (re)constructing human society, to an inherently revolutionary potential. Moreover, this strange imagery lends the film a reflexive dimension, suggesting an alluring dream, constructed from the ill-matching elements of a troubled psyche and consumerist yearnings, that too easily distracts the individual from the realities of communist life. The result is a kind of allegorical commentary on the nature of capitalist cinema that one might read as Protazanov's apologia for that period when he left Russia to direct films in the West.

Easily the most famous work of early sf cinema, *Metropolis* may have been influenced by *Aelita*, which was among 'the most popular films exported to Germany' in this era (Youngblood 60), as it shows similarities in plot and style. However, the German film is more ambitious and polished, and its depiction of a dystopian society was a more recognisable touchstone for post-war social frustrations. Co-scripted by director Fritz Lang and his wife Thea von Harbou and based on her 1925 novel, *Metropolis* depicts a society driven by the powers of science and technology and ruled in a coldly rational manner. While the wealthy live in skyscrapers and enjoy a life of play and leisure, the workers, enslaved to the machines that make the upper world work, inhabit a dreary underground. When they revolt, only the intervention of the Master of Metropolis's son restores some hope. He kills the mad scientist Rotwang, exposes the robot created to mislead the workers, and intercedes with his father in their favour, offering, as a concluding title puts it, a 'heart' – or compassion – to help direct society's 'head and hands'. This formula pointedly addresses the reason–science–technology triad, suggesting both its implicit weakness and a cause – a fundamental imbalance, a lack of human feeling – that in following years would figure into sf's increasingly calamitous visions.

While Lang's formula ill addresses the era's social unrest, the film's iconography was effective and influential, as *Metropolis* conjured two of the most significant images in sf history. The city of Metropolis, characterised by 200-storey skyscrapers, vaulted roadways and aircraft weaving among the giant buildings, reflects some of the era's key visions of urban development, such as the German Bauhaus (which engendered the International Style in architecture), the visionary buildings of Hugh Ferris in America, and Le Corbusier's urban reconceptualisations in France. One reviewer described this impressive, if also disturbing, monumentalist urban vision, wherein humanity itself practically disappears, as 'the chill mechanized world of the future' (Gerstein 187). However, it soon became fundamental to sf's futuristic vision, as the later *Just Imagine* (Butler 1930) and *Things to Come* (1936) illustrate. Just as influential was *Metropolis*'s formulation of arguably the genre's most important icon, the robot, a figure previously developed in Karel Čapek's celebrated play *R.U.R.* (1920). Lang's image of a robotic Maria embodies a duality that attaches to much of technology in this period: on the one hand, an alluring, gleaming image, its seductive power played out in its dance before the city's elite and the easy way it lures the workers into rebellion; on the other, a force of destruction and, striking a note that increasingly figures into robot depictions, a potential human replacement (as Rotwang proclaims, such machines prove 'we have no further use for living workers'). This point would also become the focus of a later German sf effort, *Master of the World* (*Der Herr der Welt*; Piel 1934). In the dual image of technology's attractions and subversions, we might see *Metropolis*' most important legacy to both sf and modern culture.

However, the film's visual style also bears mention since it too recruits the avant-garde to empower its futuristic vision. Lang adopted the expressionist look that had singularly marked post-war German cinema, emphasising unbalanced compositions, irregular spatial arrangements, the play of shadows, oblique and vertical lines, stylised acting and a fascination with reflective surfaces. This look shows especially in depictions of the workers' underworld, where it underscores the precarious nature of their world and the sinister forces that preserve its cultural imbalances. Moreover, in concert with the robot's foregrounding of the powerfully seductive play of images, that expressionist aesthetic subverts our conventional cinematic reality, reflexively challenging audiences to see their own world in a radically different way.

While less challenging stylistically, the American *The Mysterious Island* similarly links a double vision of science and technology with a sense of the period's social unrest. Nominally based on Verne's 1875 novel, it retains much of the Verne spirit, emphasising the technologically driven explorations typical of his work and modelling the sort of fantastic machines – here, twin submarines – that would become the centrepiece of various sf films in following years, including the moon rocket of *Cosmic Voyage* (*Kosmicheskiy reys: Fantasticheskaya novella*; Zhuravlov 1936), the life-restoring apparatus of *Six Hours to Live* (Dieterle 1932), the atomic gold-producing machine of *Gold* (Hartl 1934) and the radium-powered device of *The Invisible Ray* (Hillyer 1935) that both cures blindness and destroys matter. *The Mysterious Island*'s submarines have been developed by reclusive scientist Count Dakkar, who wishes to explore the oceans' mysteries while ruling benevolently over his peaceful island. But the leader of a Soviet-styled revolution on the mainland seizes the submarines, intending to use them to solidify his power and 'rule the world', evoking widespread suspicions of both communism and technology. But Dakkar sinks his submarines and kills himself rather than 'be remembered as one who brought into this world an instrument of death and destruction'.

Yet prior to that abjuring of the fantastic machine, *The Mysterious Island* offers a seductive array of spectacular images and events that for much of the narrative crowds out its warnings against social upheaval. Dakkar discovers an elaborate underwater society, complete with an aquatic version of *Metropolis*'s skyscrapers; his submarines engage in several sea battles; there are fights with a giant octopus and a horned sea serpent; one submarine destroys a fleet of warships; and there are scenes of revolution and counterrevolution, complete with close-ups of the revolutionaries torturing captives. Enabling such fantastic imagery is state-of-the-art technology, as the film was shot in the two-strip Technicolor process, incorporated several expository 'talkie' scenes, demonstrated early underwater photography, and combined elaborate model work with live action. Its narrative of a scientist and his fantastic technology is thus powered by film's own cutting-edge technology, so even as it ends on a cautionary note, its attitude toward science and technology – including film technology – remains ambiguous. Its cautionary conclusion suggests the sort of tunnel vision our technology might foster, as illustrated by Dakkar's isolationism, and the destructive potential that, in the wrong hands, it could unleash, but the film also champions technology's ability to help us penetrate the world's unexplored 'depths', extend our knowledge and – like the cinema – show us things never seen before, and its emphasis on naturalistically-presented images suggests that these fantasies are real possibilities. This double attitude evidences the sort of cultural ambiguity about the work of science and technology that would, throughout the next decade, result in films that often drew the nascent sf cinema into the orbit of horror, such as *Frankenstein* (Whale 1931), *Dr. X* (Curtiz 1932) and *Island of Lost Souls* (Kenton 1933).

Appearing shortly after *Mysterious Island*, the French *End of the World* is far less ambiguous in its attitudes. Its narrative about a comet set to collide with Earth, based on Camille Flammarion's *Omega: Last Days of the World* (*La fin du monde*; 1894), underscores the power of science and technology to detect such calamitous events – to plot their trajectory and predict their results – but it also shows how powerless we are and how ineffective our technology is in dealing with them. In fact, long sequences simply depict the panic that this sobering recognition brings, as reason practically disappears and people descend into acts of desperation and despair, of looting and orgiastic behaviour. When, at the last moment, Earth avoids destruction as the comet deviates from its calculated path, the world's scientists convene, form a new government and promise to 'refashion this world on the basis of a new law' rooted in a thoroughly rational and scientific understanding and dedicated to ideals of 'peace and brotherhood'. This conclusion recalls the sort of balance that *Metropolis* sought to strike and further underscores the political exigencies that crept into many of the era's major sf films, differently inflecting how they portrayed science and technology. The recognition of their inability to avert disaster or solve the seemingly more manageable problems haunting this period also helps explain an upsurge in apocalyptic sf, including *High Treason* (Elvey 1929), *Deluge* (Feist 1933) and *S.O.S. Tidal Wave* (Auer 1939).

Lending an extra level of complexity to *End of the World*'s dissection of scientific attitudes is its framing of much of the action through the mass media, thereby partially critiquing film itself. To depict the various ways people react to this impending calamity (while capitalising on special effects scenes of floods, earthquakes and crumbling human structures), the film emphasises the work of the newspapers, radio and newsreel cameras. Instead of simply reporting and mobilising people to deal with the approaching comet's impact, the media seize on a story that might be more readily embraced, as they portray an international conspiracy, hoping to profit from false rumours of catastrophe by manipulating the stock market and the world's governments. *End of the World* thereby sounds a note of caution about technology and technological attitudes, while pointing up the power of the mass media, including film, and warning against investing too much authority in that mass voice.

A similar combination of apocalyptic destruction and eventual salvation – at the hands of science and technology – structures the most famous British sf effort of this period, *Things to Come*. The first film scripted by H.G. Wells and the most expensive British film to that date, it combines a number of visionary influences to shape its view of where human culture was heading. Reflecting the era's international tensions, much of the narrative presciently details a catastrophic world war that wreaks physical destruction like that seen in *End of the World* and introduces a plague that wipes out much of humanity. However, a significant portion of the film describes how, from the old world's ruins, a new, distinctly futuristic one arises. Following Wells's injunction that this world 'must not seem contemporary' but be 'constructed differently' (Frayling 50), the film gathered various avant-garde influences: the Bauhaus's László Moholy-Nagy designed sets; the surrealist Fernand Léger provided concept sketches and costume ideas; the city planner Le Corbusier helped design the utopian Everytown; the industrial designer Norman Bel Geddes's futuristic airliner inspired the aircraft of the engineers and mechanics who unite in order 'to salvage the world'. The resulting 'great white world', as one character uncritically describes it, visually attests to the forces that these engineers and mechanics wield, as they overcome mankind's most destructive tendencies, refocus humanity's powers on reconstruction, and produce a culture in which the divisions between workers and elite, so central to *Aelita*, *Metropolis* and *The Mysterious Island*, seem to disappear.

Yet even with reason recovered and a society ruled by science and technology firmly established, *Things to Come* evokes an abiding suspicion of these powers and the fragility of humanity's utopian dreams. The monumental design scheme – marked by massive buildings, outsized statuary, multi-storey television screens and a great space gun – produces a sense of awe in both the citizenry and the audience, but it also signifies the *repressive* forces at work, as these monumental elements increasingly make the people feel like 'such little creatures [...] so fragile, so weak', and inspire new unrest. When the people rise up to smash the giant space gun, Everytown's leader deploys the sometimes deadly 'gas of peace' to stop them. While *Things to Come* ends on an image of human aspiration, as the massive gun fires a capsule of astronauts into space, it is amid a climate of resentment and revolt that qualifies the mission and questions the world's technical trajectory.

But *Things to Come* is just one of several films in this vein during the 1930s, all of them emphasising the enormous hopes increasingly attached to the forces of science and technology – and finding their dark reflection in the outsized architecture of Nazi Germany. Both the German and British films of *The Tunnel* (Bernhardt 1933; Elvey 1935) recount the monumental effort to construct a transatlantic tunnel and ring in a new era of international trade and cooperation. Similarly, the multinational *F.P.1 Does not Answer* (*F.P.1 antwortet nicht*; Hartl 1933) describes the building of a mid-ocean airbase to help planes fly from continent to continent and enhance the potential for peace and commerce. Yet these works also suggest that such technology's very *monumental* impact might also diminish the human role, leaving us prey to manipulation, demagoguery and ideological exploitation – a point *Things to Come* makes explicit when a giant television screen becomes the tool for fomenting revolt against the very technological accomplishments it represents.

A similar critique, but offered in a much different tone, marks another significant body of sf films from this era – the animated cartoon. While often overlooked, sf-themed animation, typically in stop-motion form, began appearing in the earliest days of the cinema, producing some of the incredible elements in several Méliès films, the space adventure of a driving couple in *The '?' Motorist* (Booth 1906) and the comic effects of faulty electrical controls in *The Electric Hotel* (*El hotel eléctrico*; de Chomon 1908). Blending the novel effects of animation with such sf subjects as space flight and crazy inventions, these hybrid live-action/animated works built on the appeal of the 'cinema of attractions', usually for comic effect, while setting the stage for an emerging cartoon industry that soon offered a wealth of hand-drawn films exploring similar themes.

From the late 1910s through the 1940s, what might be described as a second-order sf cinema emerged, with major and minor animation studios producing a variety of distinctly sf cartoons.

Most of these efforts cluster around several key concerns: depictions of space flight or fantastic travel, as in Happy Hooligan's *A Trip to the Moon* (La Cava 1917), Felix the Cat's *Astronomeows* (Messmer 1928) and Tom and Jerry's *The Phantom Rocket* (Rufle and Sherman 1933); robots and artificial creatures, typified by *The Mechanical Cow* (Disney 1927), Farmer Al Falfa's *The Iron Man* (Foster 1930) and Superman's battle with *The Mechanical Monsters* (Fleischer 1941); alien encounters, as envisioned in KoKo the Clown's *Trip to Mars* (Fleischer 1924), Oswald the Rabbit's *Sky Larks* (Lance and Nolan 1934), and *Scrappy's Trip to Mars* (Iwerks 1938); and fantastic inventions and inventors, such as Farmer Al Falfa's *Short Circuit* (Terry 1927), *Betty Boop's Crazy Inventions* (Fleischer and Bowsky 1933) and Donald Duck's *The Plastics Inventor* (King 1944). Cartoons would also serve as satiric vehicles, as in the American burlesque of Jules Verne, *20,000 Feats Under the Sea* (Terry 1917) and send-up of the Technocracy movement *Techno-Cracked* (Iwerks 1933), the British take on *Metropolis*, *Whatrotolis* (Noble 1929), and even as propaganda in the case of the Soviet *Interplanetary Revolution* (*Mezhplanetnaya revolyutsiya*; Khodataev and Komissarenko 1924). This body of short films is especially significant because of the way in which it made the sometimes unsettling themes of sf both familiar and comically nonthreatening, thereby opening up new possibilities for appreciating the work of science and technology.

That familiarising effect was also furthered by another popular body of sf films that, in contrast with the genre's earlier epic visions, might almost seem minimalist works – movie serials. Typically produced by smaller studios working with limited budgets, and driven by simple formulas, they deployed the same iconography that the feature films and cartoons described above had developed: robots, rockets, fantastic machines, alien civilizations, even monumental cities. *Buck Rogers* (Beebe and Goodkind 1939) and three *Flash Gordon* serials (Stephani 1936; Beebe and Hill 1938; Beebe and Taylor 1940) further exploited the new science of rocketry and the fascination with possible space travel, already glimpsed in such features as *Aelita*, *Woman in the Moon* (Lang 1929) and *Just Imagine*. Many films emphasised the menace of the robot, seen in an earlier serial like *The Master Mystery*, but given special prominence in *The Phantom Empire* (Brower and Eason 1935), *Mysterious Doctor Satan* (Witney and English 1940) and *The Monster and the Ape* (Bretherton 1945), all of which anticipate a later vogue for this menacing figure. In the immediate post-war period, a host of serials reflected early Cold War fears by introducing the menace of invading aliens, typically aided by weapons of mass destruction. Examples include *The Purple Monster Strikes* (Bennet and Brannon 1945), with its Martian invader wielding an Atomic Ray; *Brick Bradford* (Bennet 1947), wherein the comic book hero battles Moon-men armed with an Interceptor Ray; and *King of the Rocket Men* (Brannon 1949), *Radar Men from the Moon* (Brannon 1952) and *Zombies of the Stratosphere* (Brannon 1952), in all of which a scientist, aided by a rocket belt, combats invaders armed with fantastic weapons. While foregrounding science and technology, these films link them to new sorts of weapons, reflecting widespread cultural anxieties about the Cold War and atomic power, as well as a new international awareness.

Just as significant is the way in which these serials made their impact felt. Their effectiveness lies in their common formula, wherein deadly menaces are revealed and death or destruction seems imminent, yet the protagonists fortuitously escape and eventually, after many such incidents, triumph. It is a machine-like pattern, marked by speed, narrative efficiency and predictability, and its ultimate aim is to grip the audience in its machine-like workings, luring them back to the theatre each week to re-experience those expected thrills and reassuring escapes. If most serials never attain the level of self-consciousness found in many sf features, their systematicity serves a similar function, practically foregrounding their narrative workings and acknowledging ('Don't miss the next thrilling episode …', they repeatedly enjoin) their desire for audience mastery. Moreover, they made this point not sporadically, whenever a new film appeared, but *every week*, for the 12–15 weeks over which the action unreeled. They thereby constantly offered viewers dramatic encounters with the wonders of science and technology – depicted both as a menace and as a potential deliverance from that menace – while working out the conflicted attitudes towards those elements that, in the post-war world, were increasingly bulking into everyday life.

With their repeated stories of rocket flights and interplanetary travel and constant suggestions that something new is 'out there', the serials also helped accustom audiences to the work of the genre while mapping a path for the first post-war sf features, *Destination Moon* (Pichel 1950) and *Rocketship X-M* (Neumann 1950). With its adaptation of Robert A. Heinlein's novel *Rocketship Galileo* (1947), the former, produced by special effects expert and animator George Pal, demonstrated a link to hard-sf literature and added a new level of authenticity thanks to its technical consultant, rocket pioneer Hermann Oberth, and space illustrator Chesley Bonestell's convincing matte paintings. Its documentary-style narrative effectively placed science and technology in a 'starring' role and used those elements to stake out a positive trajectory, as the exploration of space becomes a great adventure. While lacking the technical support (and budget) of *Destination Moon*, *Rocketship X-M* similarly drew much of its impact from its straightforward detailing of the science of space flight. The discovery of a nearly extinct Martian civilisation, destroyed by nuclear conflict, allowed the film to strike an important Cold War political warning, while its concluding note, that the rocket's builders will create another ship to continue the important work of exploration, underscored the necessity for properly – rationally – directing the new powers of science and technology along a positive and peaceful path. Of course, over the next decade the genre would swerve in a rather different direction, proliferating films in another, more threatening vein. Those succeeding narratives of alien invasion, atomic apocalypse and mutant monsters, all suggesting how our technology might control and even destroy us, often demonstrate what has been termed the 'pulp paradox', as filmmakers emphasise the seriousness of the sf vision, yet play up its 'more sensational qualities' with tropes drawn from 'the pulp SF model' (Schauer 7). Coming in the wake of *Destination Moon* and *Rocketship X-M*, this new dualism might be seen as yet another variation on the genre's ability to speak in a nuanced, often changing way about the work of science and technology, and thus as part of the dynamic potential that clearly marks the historical path of early sf cinema.

Works cited

Frayling, Christopher. *Things to Come*. BFI, 1995.

Gerstein, Evelyn. 'Metropolis'. *American Film Criticism*. Ed. Stanley Kauffmann and Bruce Henstell. Liveright, 1972. 186–7.

Gunning, Tom. 'The Cinema of Attraction: Early Film, Its Spectator and the Avant-Garde'. *Wide Angle* 8.3–4 (1986): 63–70.

Jackson, Rosemary. *Fantasy: The Literature of Subversion*. Methuen, 1981.

Jacobs, Lewis. 'Georges Méliès: Artificially Arranged Scenes'. *The Emergence of Film Art*, second edition. Ed. Lewis Jacobs. Norton, 1979. 10–19.

La Valley, Albert J. 'Traditions of Trickery: The Role of Special Effects in the Science Fiction Film'. *Shadows of the Magic Lamp: Fantasy and Science Fiction in Film*. Ed. George E. Slusser and Eric S. Rabkin. Southern Illinois UP, 1985. 141–58.

Pierson, Michele. *Special Effects: Still in Search of Wonder*. Columbia UP, 2002.

Schauer, Bradley. *Escape Velocity: American Science Fiction Film, 1950–1982*. Wesleyan UP, 2017.

Sontag, Susan. 'The Imagination of Disaster'. *Against Interpretation*. Dell, 1966. 212–28.
Stewart, Garrett. 'The "Videology" of Science Fiction'. *Shadows of the Magic Lamp: Fantasy and Science Fiction in Film*. Ed. George E. Slusser and Eric S. Rabkin. Southern Illinois UP, 1985. 159–207.
Telotte, J. P. *The Science Fiction Film*. Cambridge UP, 2001.
Youngblood, Denise J. *Movies for the Masses: Popular Cinema and Soviet Society in the 1920s*. Cambridge UP, 1992.

15
CHINESE SCIENCE FICTION

Wu Yan (translated by Joel Martinsen)

Sf is not native to China, but a cultural response to external environmental changes. In the modern era, scientific and technological developments, capital flows and social transformations affected peoples and cultures around the world. For example, the First Opium War (1839–42) shattered the age-old mentality that the Chinese occupied the centre of the world, and the country was forced to open its doors. Intellectuals, troubled by the lack of adaptability and ideas suited to modernity, turned to culture from abroad, including sf. Edward Bellamy's *Looking Backward: 2000–1887* (1888) was published in 1891 and 1898, on the second occasion as *A Thousand-Year Sleep* (*Bainian yi jiao*). Jules Verne's novels were introduced to China, beginning with *Around the World in Eighty Days* (1872) in 1900. Under the influence of such foreign works, Chinese sf began slowly to appear (Liang).

In 1902, Liang Qichao proposed his theory of fiction renewing the people, and identified sf as one of the categories for the new era. That same year, he launched *New Fiction* (*Xin xiaoshuo*), China's first modern journal devoted to fiction, in which he included his translation of Camille Flammarion's *Omega: The Last Days of the World* (1891) under the 'scientific fiction' heading, but his own futurist novel *The Future of New China* (*Xin Zhongguo weilai ji*; 1902) under 'political fiction'. If Liang was an early proponent of modern Chinese fiction, then Zhou Shuren, who as Lu Xun would become a leader of the May Fourth Movement and a founder of modern Chinese literature, saw a role for scientific fiction. The preface to his 1903 translation of Verne's *From the Earth to the Moon* (1865) declares that humans were the product of biological evolution and would colonise the stars. Sf, he argues, contains theory, beauty and knowledge, and can exercise the mind. Citing Verne, he notes that science and emotion are the warp and weft of superior sf, perhaps the earliest expression of sf theory in China. Liang and Lu opened up two entirely different roads for Chinese sf, one toward a total transformation of Chinese culture, the other toward the study of science.

New original sf came in all flavours in the late Qing Dynasty (1644–1911). The first identified sf work in China is a 35-chapter unfinished novel by Huangjiang Diaosou, *A Tale of the Moon Colony* (*Yueqiu zhimindi xiaoshuo*; 1904), which features a futuristic, high-speed Japanese passenger balloon but is motivated by the corruption of the Qing government. The first complete work is a philosophical novella cum fantastic voyage written in classical Chinese by Donghai Juewo,

 DOI: 10.4324/9781003140269-17

'New Tales of Mr. Braggadocio' ('Xin faluo xiansheng tan') (1905). The author states outright that both science and religion are incapable of resolving the questions of his soul, and in his search for truth the protagonist separates his mind from his body: the former ascends into the sky in the form of pure thought, the latter descends to the centre of the Earth. In traditional Chinese literature, visitors to heaven and the underworld find deities and demons; here, the heavens are occupied by the sun, moon and planets, each home to intelligent creatures and distinctive societies, while the world underground, divided into provinces, is inhabited by ancient immortals. The story overflows with social criticism and ends with the author urging the use of education to save the country. *The New Era* (*Xin jiyuan*; 1908), by Biheguan Zhuren, resembles a traditional novel in language and structure but replaces martial artists with modern fighters equipped with new technology.

Late Qing sf is largely concerned with national salvation, mostly in response to intellectuals' sorrow that China's days as the celestial empire were behind it, and typically demonstrates a poor understanding of Western scientific knowledge. However, it is precisely this primordial imagination that best illuminates the birth of modernity in society and culture (Wang).

During the last decade of the Qing Dynasty and the first two decades of the Republican era (1912–49), Chinese concepts of science underwent a massive transformation. It soon became clear that sf was an unrealistic tool for disseminating scientific knowledge in the cause of national salvation, and the genre parted ways with science popularisation. A feeble government was powerless against the threat, long perceived by intellectuals, of subjugation by the west; the country slowly moved in a semi-colonial direction, at which point the first stirrings of a patriotic democratic movement began to take shape. In 1919, the May Fourth Movement called for the country to absorb 'Mr Science' and 'Mr Democracy', and introduced revolutionary ideas, but during these fierce social and ideological tempests sf went neglected. Writing as Lu Xun, Zhou Shuren published a host of modern fiction that depicted China's feudal society as cannibalistic, but like most intellectuals he abandoned sf. The genre persisted on a small scale in popular fiction journals known as the 'mandarin ducks and butterflies school' and in popular science reading material. The former was regarded as an outpost of decadent, insubstantial romance, bereft of revolutionary feeling, while the latter reduced sf to science education – literature as a tool (Ren).

Despite sf's withdrawal from the literary mainstream during the Republican era, some major individual works did appear. The protagonist of Lao She's *Cat Country* (*Mao cheng ji*; 1932), fed up with corruption on Earth, journeys to Mars, only to find an even more corrupt world of cats, who have no technology to speak of but smoke a narcotic similar to opium. Editor and popular science writer Gu Junzheng's collection *Beneath the North Pole* (*Zai beiji dixia*; 1940) translated Western sf, leaving characters and plots intact but augmenting the stories with a considerable amount of science and technology. This staked out a clear position: sf without science is incomplete, so Gu remedied it in his own fashion.

Enthusiasm for changing the country persisted in the Republican era but was more muted, as people placed less hope in science and China became mired in war. Japan invaded in 1937 and their surrender eight years later was followed by four years of civil war. On the mainland, after the 1949 establishment of the People's Republic, war gave way to peace and construction, and education and publishing began to return to normal. The earliest sf stories of this period are Zhang Ran's 'A Dream Voyage Through the Solar System' ('Mengyou taiyangxi'; 1950) and Xue Dianhui's 'Cosmic Voyage' ('Yuzhou lüxing'; 1951). Each devotes its first half to a fictional story about a space voyage, but then turns into a science essay. The 'mandarin ducks and butterflies' journals had long since disappeared, leaving popular science as the only space open to sf. The genre's value was also recognised by editors working in childhood education, such as Ye Shengtao at Kaiming Press and the team at Juvenile and Children's Publishing House, who developed their own stable of sf authors. Notable authors of this period include Zheng Wenguang, Chi Shuchang, Ye Zhishan, Xiao Jianheng, Wang Guozhong, Tong Enzheng and Liu Xingshi. Zheng, an overseas Chinese returned from Vietnam, was fluent in English and self-taught in Russian; he had studied astronomy and worked at the Chinese Academy of Sciences. His 'Solar Adventure' ('Taiyang tanxian ji'; 1955) describes the sheer magnificence of the universe. Chi had studied in Japan, was fluent in Russian, Japanese and English, and claimed to have fallen in love with sf by copying out Verne stories. His short fiction, including 'Elephants with their Trunks Removed' ('Gediao bizi de daxiang'; 1957), evince a childlike wonder. Ye, Ye Shengtao's son, edited children's science books. His 'Missing Older Brother' ('Shizong de gege'; 1957) describes an accidental freezing that results in an elder brother who is younger than his younger brother. Xiao grew up attending a religious school and majored in radio. His 'The Peculiar Robot Dog' ('Qiyi de jiqi gou'; 1963) is the first Chinese story to mention artificial intelligence. Wang worked as a popular science editor and was involved developing the phenomenally bestselling science series A HUNDRED THOUSAND WHYS (SHIWAN GE WEISHENME; 1961). Many of the stories in his collection *Black Dragon Goes Missing* (*Heilong hao shizong*; 1963) concern future Sino–Russian, Sino–Japanese and Sino–US relationships. Archaeology student Tong found fame with *Fog in the Ancient Gorge* (*Guxia miwu*; 1960), a cultural-political techno-thriller set on a dig among a southwestern ethnic group, and geology student Liu with 'Clouds in the North' ('Beifang de yun'; 1962), in which the ancient art of commanding the forces of nature is realised through modern technology; both also wrote for A HUNDRED THOUSAND WHYS.

Chinese sf flourished in children's literature throughout the 1950s and 1960s, with a 1954 story by Zheng being included in a 1955 national anthology of children's literature. Writing for adults was not so well received. A serialisation in the magazine *China Youth* (*Zhongguo qingnian*) of Zheng's 'A Communist Fantasia' ('Gongchan zhuyi changxiangqu'; 1958) was halted after two instalments, and Huang Yousan's 'Travels in Communist Society' ('Gongchan zhuyi shehui lüxing ji': 1959) had practically no impact at all. Granted, these works were imperfect, but the real problem lay elsewhere: the future of the People's Republic was limited to a single Marxist line, but authors had no way of knowing how it should be written.

While authors of realist literature endured various reforms and criticisms of their work, children's literature provided a safer outlet for flights of imagination. Zheng's 'Builders of Mars' ('Huoxing jianshezhe'; 1957) describes a future of international cooperation to exploit the cosmos; Chi's 'Whimsy of an Eccentric Scientist' ('Kexue guairen de qixiang'; 1963) describes the food chain and metallurgy; Xiao's 'A Soccer Match Held as Scheduled' ('Qiusai ruqi juxing'; 1962) tells of how Martian life pollutes the Earth but brings pleasure to children; Wang's 'The Great Dragon of Bohai Bay' ('Bohai julong'; 1963) tells of an oceanic construction project. Although many such stories feel one-note or simplistic, their intense longing for different futures is palpable.

Soviet sf arrived in China during the 1950s and 1960s, with translations of around a hundred novels and stories, and the genre's name changed from 'science fiction' (kexue xiaoshuo) to the Russian-derived 'science fantasy fiction' (kexue huanxiang xiaoshuo). The addition of 'fantasy' might have signalled greater imaginative freedom but it also came into conflict with Chinese culture, which had long advocated realism over the unrealistic and impractical. Some identified a conflict between fantasy and science, others saw fantasy as the destruction of science. In 1965, the magazine *Knowledge is Power* (*Zhishi jiushi liliang*) published a translation of Soviet writer Anatoly Dneprov's 'Suema' (1958) with the subtitle 'A Robot Story' ('Suema: Yige jiqiren de gushi'), in which an artificial intelligence seeks to further understand the human mind by cutting open the brain of its creator, implying that machines might outdo humans. But was the idea of an artificial intelligence superseding humanity contrary to Marxism? This question prompted the magazine to conduct its own criticism of the story, and a reader even sent a copy to the scholarly *Journal of Dialectics of Nature* (*Ziran bianzhengfa tongxun*) for comment (Qin). The articles criticising the stories concluded that Marx himself had not said that it could not happen (or that it could).

During the Cultural Revolution (1966–76), literary and scientific activity was suppressed, and all parts of the government entered a state of hysterical chaos. Red Guards rebelled, ostensibly to defend Mao Zedong; they attacked intellectuals and those in power and called for taking revolution to the entire world. An uncredited sf poem 'Dedicated to the Brave Warriors of World War Three' ('Xiangei disanci shijie dazhan de yongshimen') circulated widely in autumn 1967. Divided into five parts and running for over 240 lines, it depicts the revisionist Soviet Union eliminated, and China joining forces with the Russian people to restore the revolution and pacify the US, the last major encampment of the exploiting class. The entire poem is delivered as an exclamation before the graves of those killed on American soil in World War III. Another poem 'Believe in the Future' ('Xiangxin weilai'), later identified as the work of Shi Zhi (the pen name of Guo Lusheng), circulated in hand-copied form slightly earlier. It includes the lines,

> As spider webs mercilessly seal off my stovetop
> As smoldering cinders sigh over the sorrows of poverty
> I still stubbornly spread out the hopeless cinders
> And write with finely powdered snow: believe in the future.
> (41)

It was reviled by Jiang Qing, Mao's wife, who was in charge of the arts. She believed it was an attempt to use the future to eliminate the present, that is, to repudiate the Cultural Revolution. Detained, Shi Zhi suffered a mental breakdown, but his poem gave many the courage to live on. There has been no systematic study of the period's sf literature, but these poems, in their radical futurism and masochistic futurism, give a glimpse of its potential.

With the fatal plane crash of Mao's deputy Lin Biao while fleeing to the Soviet Union in 1971, and Mao's own illness preventing him from putting more energy into Red Guard campaigns, China entered a period of stability. The death of Mao, the downfall of the Gang of Four and the end of the Cultural Revolution in 1976, along with Deng's restoration and the proposal of reform strategies, made the future's call palpable once again. Conventional scientific and literary activity resumed and, addressing the 1978 National Science Conference, Guo Moruo, head of the Chinese Academy of Sciences, declared a 'springtime for science' and that 'imagination cannot be monopolised by poets' (Guo). Deng recognised China was one of the world's least economically and technologically developed countries, and therefore proposed opening up the country to keep pace with world development. Classical and pre-revolutionary modern culture, once subject to criticism, were rediscovered, and foreign culture surged into the country. The science and democracy championed by the May Fourth Movement were advanced once again. It was a time for sf to bloom.

The amount of Chinese sf published ballooned, as did the number of authors, from a handful to more than a hundred. From 1976 to 1979, many sf writers active before the Cultural Revolution resumed, producing more mature work, and others were drawn to the genre for the first time. As early as 1961, Ye Yonglie, a contributor to A HUNDRED THOUSAND WHYS, had proposed writing sf, but because of the social and political climate his publisher declined (Ye 'Da *Nanfang*'). His interest had not waned, however, and even before Mao's death his 'Petroprotein' (also translated as 'Strange Cakes'; 'Shiyou danbai'; 1976) appeared in the new magazine *Science for Children*

(*Shaonian kexue*). It was the only sf story officially published during the Cultural Revolution. To forestall any criticism that the fantasy in 'science fantasy fiction' was heretical, it was run as 'scientific fiction' ('science fantasy' would return as a genre label from 1977). Its popular reception prompted Ye to write more sf, including the wildly successful children's novel *Little Smarty Travels to the Future* (*Xiao lingtong manyou weilai*; 1978), which took its young readers on a fantastic voyage through twenty-first century scientific vistas, and became a shared memory for an entire generation.

Ye also contributed to the rise of sf studies in China, devoting an entire chapter of *On Scientific Literature and Art* (*Lun kexue wenyi*; 1980) to it. Along with Takeda Masaya and Hisayuki Hayashi, he helped to trace the history of Chinese sf back beyond Gu in the 1940s to 1904 (Ye 'Qingchao'; Takeda and Hayashi).

Alongside Ye, the most famous authors of the 1970s and 1980s include Zheng, Tong, Song Yichang, Wang Xiaoda and Liu Xingshi. Zheng wrote four novels, two of which, *Flying Toward Sagittarius* (*Fei xiang renma zuo*; 1978) and *Descendants of Mars* (*Zhanshen de houyi*; 1983), yearn for stellar exploration and the future. *The Depths of the Ocean* (*Dayang shenchu*; 1980) turns toward the mysteries of the deep, and *Wondrous Wings* (*Shen yi*; 1982) tells a story about artificial wings. 'Pacific Ocean Man' (*Taipingyang ren*; 1978) marries astronomy and oceanography. Tong's 'Death Ray on Coral Island' ('Shanhudao shang de siguang'; 1978) remade the image of overseas Chinese scientists, a character type authors had shied away from for three decades, fearing that a capitalist mentality could contaminate socialism. Here, though, the scientist firmly believes he is working for the good of science and humanity, as well as for his ancestral homeland and its people. Song's *Depreciation of V* (*V de bianzhi*; 1979) and *After the Catastrophe* (*Huoxia dakai zhihou*; 1982) presented the attitudes and responses of a globalised world to disruptive technology and a threat from outer space. Wang's series of short stories beginning with 'Waves' (also translated as 'The Mysterious Wave'; 'Bo'; 1979) focuses on information technology, while Liu's 'Columbus of the Americas' ('Meizhou lai de Gelunbu'; 1979) tells of how pre-Colombian native Americans reached Europe in dugout canoes.

In the 1970s and 1980s, sf was optimistic and supportive of technological development, but rarely speculated about ensuing social change. There were exceptions. Yan Jiaqi's *Religion, Reason, and Practice: Visits to Three Courts of Law* (*Zongjiao, lixing, Shijian: fang sange shidai guanyu zhenli wenti*; 1978), retitled in 1979 as *A Flight Across the Ages* (*Kuayue shidai de feixing*) explored humanity's criterion for testing truth. Time travel back to 1633 Rome and 1755 Paris, to examine religious and renaissance solutions, is followed by a trip forward to the egalitarian Beijing of 2009, where the Great Hall of the People is no longer barred to the general public but open to all. Serialised in *Guangming Daily* (*Guangming ribao*) from 14 September 1978, it provided support for a movement rejecting dogmatic Marxism. Zheng's short stories, such as 'Star Labour Camp' ('Xingxing ying'; 1980), 'The Mirror Image of Earth' ('Diqiu di jingxiang'; 1980) and 'Club Destiny' ('Mingyun yezonghui'; 1982), shed light on the harm caused by the Cultural Revolution. In journalist Jin Tao's 'Moonlight Island' ('Yueguang dao'; 1980), the protagonist ultimately elects to depart the Earth for outer space when the Cultural Revolution recurs. In 'Dream of a Cosy Home' ('Wenrou zhi xiang de meng'; 1981), Wei Yahua, primarily an author of mainstream fiction, used the protagonist's contretemps with a robot designed according to the three laws of robotics to indicate the harm unchanging political dogma causes to individuals and society. Later, these mild critiques would be used to attack sf for straying from the goals of socialism and, along with a misunderstanding of innovations in the genre, lead to a wider ban on sf.

The 1980s revival of the genre brought considerable media exposure, and traces of sf could be found everywhere from the party newspaper *People's Daily* (*Renmin ribao*) to popular science periodicals that rarely engaged in politics. Politicians, artists, scientists and mainstream novelists joined sf specialists to produce a colourful range of work that transformed the genre. Tong's 'Death Ray on Coral Island' deliberately omitted the scientific basis for the eponymous device, pitting itself against the notion, dating back to Lu Xun, that sf must work in the service of popular science. After his work was lauded at China's inaugural short fiction awards in 1978, Tong remarked that as a major arm of scientific belles-lettres, sf was not easily disposed to the actual dissemination of knowledge; the most it could do was promote a scientific outlook. His opinion gained the swift support of other writers, but it was also interpreted as an attempt to divorce sf from science, thus becoming an empty shell. The subsequent debate over sf's lineage and purpose can be seen as a revolution by writers trying to migrate from popular science into literature.

They did, however, meet with opposition from some scientists and popular science writers. The China Youth League's official organ *China Youth Daily* (*Zhongguo qingnian bao*) launched a column, 'Popular Science Discussions' ('kepu xiaoyi'), whose primary concern was criticising new theories and writers, such as Tong and Ye Yonglie. 'A Strange Fossilized Egg' ('Qiyi de huashi dan'; 1979), a lianhuanhua comic book adaptation of the latter's story about a resurrected dinosaur, 'Miracle on the World's Highest Peak' ('Shijie zuigaofeng shang de qiji'; 1977), was attacked by palaeontologists as an unscientific, anti-science and pseudoscientific contaminant – and since Marxism was regarded as the sole correct science, being labelled a promoter of pseudo-science was tantamount to a death sentence on your political identity.

Beset by criticism, sf fell foul of tightening ideological restrictions. Although not mentioned in Deng's list of works of spiritual pollution, its critics scrambled to get it treated as such, and the government formally instructed the regional scientific publishing houses responsible for the majority of sf to cease publishing it. Other publishers were not so enjoined, but the ban itself was a signal to desist. With no backing, authors simply stopped writing (Ye *Zhulijian chenmo*), publishers and periodicals no longer sought it out, and readers' supportive attitudes shifted. An exam-focused college enrolment system seized the attention of the major readership demographic of primary and secondary school students, compelled by their parents to devote large amounts of time to practicing and forbidden extracurricular reading material. Major outlets launched after 1979 shut down. *Tree of Knowledge* (*Zhihui shu*; 1981–6) and the series SCIENCE LITERATURE IN TRANSLATION (KEXUE WENYI YICONG; 1980–2) were halted due to government pressure and declining readership. *Science Fiction Ocean* (*Kehuan haiyang*; 1981–3), published by the China Ocean Press, which was administered by the State Oceanic Administration, was among those officially barred from publishing sf. *Science Fiction World* (*Kehuan shijie*; 1982) from Popular Science Press (*Kepu chubanshe*) folded. *Science Fiction Translations* (*Kehuan yilin*) aborted before its first issue. The magazine *Science Arts and Letters* (*Kexue wenyi*; 1979–) survived by changing its name to *Strange Tales* (*Qitan*) in 1989, and its staff turned to publishing supplemental educational materials as business remained grim. This state of affairs continued until the early 1990s.

The new decade saw a resurgence of sf in China, with new writers emerging just as ideological controls relaxed. The fundamental direction of reform had not changed since 1980, but in reality progress had faltered and people felt worried about the future. Moreover, readers had been calling for the return of sf since the start of the ban. A 1987 *People's Daily* article discussed why sf had, like Cinderella, disappeared, and argued that untruths about such an important contemporary genre should be eliminated (Tan). In 1991, a struggling *Strange Tales* changed its editor-in-chief and deputy editor and cut back on its eclectic range of departments – which included scientific literature, fairy tales, science essays, reportage – to focus exclusively on sf. Renamed *Science Fiction World* (*Kehuan shijie*) in 1991, it faced a less hostile environment. In 1992, former national leader Deng urged building the economy and ending political argumentation. Despite the opportunities presented by this ideological relaxation, *Science Fiction World* still faced complex problems.

Lacking an established stable of authors, it had to discover and foster new writers, such as Wang Jinkang, Liu Wenyang, Xing He, Yang Ping, Han Song, Ling Chen, Zhao Haihong, He Xi, Yang Peng, Su Xuejun, Liu Weijia and Liu Cixin, all of whom came to prominence in this period. Given the genre's precarious position, it was also important to try to protect it from external interference. This meant moving away from insisting that sf must be serious literature and embracing the possibilities of popular fiction, while at the same time emphasising connections to real-world issues faced by its reader, such as the college entrance exam. A 1997 story about memory transplant technology coincided with an essay question on that year's exam, winning the immediate approval of students and parents and resulting in a spike in subscriptions. That same year the magazine held international sf conventions in Beijing and Chengdu, which five American and Russian astronauts attended, bringing it even more public notice, including a news broadcast on China National Radio (Yang and Yao).

This new generation of writers focused on developing sf as a genre, rather than seeking external recognition by, for example, promoting popular science, even though it had a much more extensive understanding of new science and technology, particularly IT. Wang's 2003 NEW HUMAN tetralogy – *Humanoid* (*Lei ren*), *Cheetah Man* (*Bao ren*), *Cancer Girl* (*Ai ren*) and *Dolphin People* (*Haitun ren*) – explores how biotech might change society, ethics and human bodies. Older than the rest of his cohort, he was a deeper and more thoughtful writer, and his stories won a succession of awards. But younger writers were just as driven. Liu Wenyang's love stories infused AI with feeling; in 'Flicker of Life' ('Shanguang de shengming'; 1994), an AI copy uses its brief lifespan to remedy the shortcomings of its human original. Xing's 'Duel on the Net' ('Juedou zai wangluo'; 1996) and Yang Ping's 'Hacking the MUD' (translated as 'Wizard World'; 'MUD heike shijian'; 1998) pioneered Chinese cyberpunk. Han, the most socially critical of these authors, repeatedly ponders, questions, negates through affirming and explores through negation all of existence. With 'Tombstone of the Universe' ('Yuzhou mubei'; 1991), *Journey Through the West 2066* (*2066 nian zhi xixing manji*; 2000), *Red Ocean* (*Hongse haiyang*; 2004) and 'Regenerated Bricks' ('Zaisheng zhuan'; 2010), he challenged and provoked readers with avant-garde content in unconventional, seemingly incomplete stories. Feminist sf took shape with Hong Ying's *Far Goes the Girl* (*Nüzi you xing*; 1997), Ling's 'Dawn on Mercury' ('Shuixing de liming'; 1998) and Zhao's 'Jocasta' ('Yi'ekasida'; 1999).

This second golden age also saw an influx of foreign works. Arthur C. Clarke, Isaac Asimov, Ray Bradbury and Shinichi Hoshi received systematic translations, alongside fiction by Robert J. Sawyer, Orson Scott Card, David Brin, Philip K. Dick and Kim Stanley Robinson and other Hugo and Nebula winners.

In 1999, Liu Cixin published his first story, 'Whale Song' ('Jing ge'), and he soon succeeded Wang Jinkang as a perennial award winner. In the new millennium, writers born in the 1980s began to appear, including Chen Qiufan, Xia Jia, Bao Shu, Jiang Bo, Fei Dao, Zhang Ran, Xiao Xinghan, Cheng Jingbo, Hao Jingfang and A Que. They were highly educated, well-acquainted with Western sf, Japanese anime, pop music and Hollywood movies, and could read English and Japanese works in the original. An upstart sf subculture took shape through their social events, guiding Chinese sf away from its hermetic developmental mode and into new directions. Subject matter diversified and writing styles grew more sophisticated, but readers had not entirely recovered from the criticism of the 1980s. Complete acceptance of sf did not arrive until the publication of the third volume of Liu's THREE BODY trilogy, *Death's End* (*Sishen yongsheng*; 2010).

Written between 2006 and 2010, the trilogy was unprecedented in size and scope: it begins during the Cultural Revolution with an army group establishing contact with extraterrestrials, and ends with the annihilation of the universe. It successfully combines cosmic history with characters who are memorable and distinct. And it is cosmopolitan from the start: China is part of the world and occupies an important place in it. Previous sf that engaged with international relations either involved a destructive enemy, as in Wang's *Black Dragon Goes Missing* and Tong's *Fog in the Ancient Gorge*, or posited an equality of all nations under the leadership of either Western or Eastern powers. Zheng's 'Builders of Mars' may have placed the weight of responsibility onto Chinese shoulders, but it is clear that the Soviet Union and Eastern Europe occupy the dominant position on the Martian expedition; in *After the Catastrophe*, that position is given to Japan and the United States. The THREE BODY trilogy, which casts the United Nations as world leader and gives the Chinese a decisive role, is brimming with technology, and after its publication, internet entrepreneurs used it as a guide for innovation, distilling its guidance down to an exhortation to 'think in higher dimensions, attack in lower dimensions'.

The first volume, *The Three-Body Problem* (*San ti*; 2007; trans. 2014), is still the only translated work to win the Hugo for best novel, prompting critic Yan Feng to claim Liu had single-handedly elevated Chinese sf to a world-class level. However, Liu was not alone. In the following year, Hao Jingfang won a Hugo for her novelette 'Folding Beijing' ('Beijing zhedie'; 2012; translated 2015), a story critical of social stratification. These successes encouraged Chinese authors, and together they show something of the varied perspectives and breadth of subject matter in contemporary Chinese sf.

Every year sees new authors, magazines, anthologies and, especially, a large number of novels. Wang Jinkang's semi-autobiographical *Ant Life* (*Yi sheng*; 2007) describes the absurdities of the Cultural Revolution, while his TO LIVE trilogy – *Fleeing the Mother Universe* (*Taochu mu yuzhou*; 2014), *Father Sky Mother Earth* (*Tianfu dimu*; 2016) and *Crystal Eggs of the Universe* (*Yuzhou jing luan*; 2019) – appears to address the cosmic questions posed by the THREE BODY trilogy. Han's RAIL trilogy – *Subway* (*Ditie*; 2011), *High-Speed Rail* (*Gaotie*; 2012) and *Tracks* (*Guidao*; 2013) – employs the changes wrought by rail transport that develops at a pace far too rapid for humanity to adapt to as a metaphor for China and the world. His HOSPITAL trilogy – *Hospital* (*Yiyuan*; 2016), *Exorcism* (*Qumo*; 2017) and *Dead Souls* (*Wangling*; 2018) – summons the ghosts of the past through the transformation of AI and medicine. Jiang's trilogy HEART OF THE GALAXY (YINHE ZHI XIN; 2012–6) and an in-progress trilogy starting with *Gate of the Machines* (*Jiqi zhi men*; 2018) explore, respectively, the universe and the development of AI. Chen's cyberpunk *Waste Tide* (*Huangchao*; 2013; trans. 2019) describes current global relationships and China's own internal issues. Bao's *Ruins of Time* (*Shijian zhi xu*; 2013) is a metaphysical meditation on time.

Sf in other media also began to attract public attention. *The Wandering Earth* (*Liulang diqiu*; Gwo 2019), based on Liu's novella, was a smash hit that sent a shockwave through the film industry; both it and its 2023 sequel rank among the top ten all-time box office draws in China. The popular online game *Honor of Kings* (*Wangzhe rongyao*; 2015) develops from an sf set-up. Construction began on sf industrial parks and towns, and Beijing's Shougang complex, the former site of a steel mill, has been approved for redevelopment into an sf industrial park, with an annual investment of more than 50 million yuan in sf start-ups. The administrative region of Lenghu in Qinghai Province has become a destination for sf tourism due to its Mars-like terrain. Since 2017, the state has funded an annual China Science Fiction Convention in the hope that the genre will prove a motivating force for technological development. Well-known awards for Chinese sf include The Galaxy (Yinhe) Award, sponsored by *Science Fiction World*, and the Nebula (Xingyun) Award, created and sponsored by Dong Renwei, Yao Haijun and myself.

In the new millennium, foreign language sf has increasingly appeared in translation, including more systematic publication of older Hugo and Nebula Award-winners, as well as from non-Anglophone countries, especially Japan. Philip K. Dick and contemporary sf film shows how technology has the potential to bring about progress but also to derail society. George Orwell and other dystopian fiction also sells well, and although such works were once seen as critiquing and satirising capitalism, translator Dong Leshan suggests their critique of collectivism could also serve as a warning to all (Dong).

In the *Daodejing*, Laozi treats water as a paragon of creation; it flows as guided by the situation, and always seeks the lowest elevation where it can live in level stillness. It reacts quickly to any environmental perturbance so as to return to its peaceful state. Since ancient times, the Chinese people have set out their lives in the manner of water; the same goes for sf. Its entire course of development can be seen as a series of responses to changes in the external environment, responses that are fundamentally meant to restore peace to human lives and to the universe. So what, then, is the relationship between sf and Chinese culture? If we compare the development of Chinese sf to that of the west, it is only by the turn of the millennium that it finally emerged from incubation and embarked on its own history. But the future is long.

Works cited

Dong Leshan. 'Aowei'er he tade 1984' ('Orwell and his 1984'). George Orwell, *1984*. Liaojing jiaoyu chubanshe, 1998. 1.

Guo Moruo. 'Kexue de chuntian'. ('Springtime for science'). *Kexue de chuntian*. Ed. unnamed. Baihua wenyi chubanshe, 1979. 1–4.

Liang Hua. 'Jin xiandai kehuan xiaoshuo shumu: Wanqing bufen (1891–1911) Zhongdian zuopin shuoming ji chuangzuo mailuo tan' (Description of major works in the catalogue of early modern science fiction, late-Qing (1891–1911) section, and a new exploration of their creation). *Kehuan wenxue lungang*. Ed. Wu Yan. Chongqing chuban jituan Chongqing chubanshe, 2011. 223–36.

Qin Yongnian. '"Suema: yige jiqiren de gushi" xuanyangle shenme guandian?' ('What viewpoint is "Suema: A Robot Story" advocating?'). *Ziran bianzhengfa yanjiu tongxun* 27 (28 April 1966): 44–5.

Ren Dongmei. 'Zhongguo kehuan xiaoshuo dansheng tanyuan: Wanqing zhi Minguo kehuan jianlun' ('Tracing the birth of Chinese science fiction: An overview of late-Qing and Republican science fiction'). *Shanhua* 21 (2015): 120–9.

Shi Zhi (Guo Lusheng). 'Xiangxin weilai' ('Believe in the future'). *Winter Sun: Poems*. Trans. Jonathan Stalling. U of Oklahoma P, 2012. 41.

Takeda Masaya and Hisayuki Hayashi. *Zhongguo kexue huanxiang wenxue shi* (*A History of Chinese Science Fiction*). Trans. Li Zhongmin. Zhejiang renmin chubanshe, 2017.

Tan Kai. 'Hui guniang' weihe yintui?' ('Why is Cinderella hiding?'). *Renmin ribao* (20 June 1987): 8.

Wang, David Der-wei. 'Jia Baoyu zuo qianshuiting: Wanqing kehuan xiaoshuo xin lun' ('Jia Baoyu takes a submarine: A new theory of late-Qing science fiction'. *Xiangxiang Zhongguo de fangfa*. Baihua wenyi chubanshe, 2016. 45–62.

Yang Feng and Yao Haijun. 'Kehuan shijie yu Zhongguo kehuan 30 nian dashiji' ('Timeline of 30 years of science fiction world and Chinese science fiction'). *Kehuan shijie 30 zhounian tebie jinian zhuankan* (2009): 25–32.

Ye Yonglie, 'Da *Nanfang dushibao*: guanyu *Xiao lingtong manyou weilai*' ('In response to *Southern Metropolis Daily*: On *Little Smarty Travels to the Future*'). *Kepu chuangzuo zhaji*. Sichuan renmin chubanshe, 2017. 128–38.

——. 'Qingchao monian de kehuan xiaoshuo' ('Science fiction at the end of the Qing dynasty'). *Guangming ribao* (7 August 1981): 3.
——. *Zhulijian chenmo* (*The Battleship Sinks*), volume 2. *Sichuan renmin chubanshe*, 2017. 145–50.
Yin Bing [Liang Qichao]. 'Lun xiaoshuo yu qunzhi de guanxi' ('On the relationship between fiction and public governance'. *Xin xiaoshuo* 1 (1902): 1–8.
Zhou Shuren [Lu Xun], 'Yuejie lüxing bianyan' ('Preface to *From the Earth to the Moon*'). *Yuejie lüxing*. Zhongguo jiaoyu puji she, 1903. 1–4.

16

ANGLOPHONE PRINT FICTION

The pulps to the New Wave

Patrick B. Sharp

In the 1920s and 1930s, pulp magazines saw an explosion of new work in a genre that was labelled for the first time as 'science fiction'. This period saw sf take on a clear market identity and saw science fictioneers create canons, histories and definitions (Wolfe x, 1–2). In the magazines, debates about the boundaries, meanings and importance of sf raged across editorials, artwork and fan letters, while authors themselves reworked established tropes and charted new ground. These negotiations and battles about sf have raged ever since, with the meaning of sf 'an ongoing process rather than a fixed identity' (Bould and Vint x). As part of this process, myths arose that galvanised many in the sf community and became ways of retelling the past of the genre so as to shape its present and future. The most well-known of these is the myth of a 'Golden Age' that centred around John W. Campbell, Jr's tenure as editor of *Astounding Science Fiction*. It claimed him as an editorial visionary who in the late 1930s and 1940s, along with his most famous authors, turned sf from childish yarns into serious fiction. Another important myth is that of the 1960s 'New Wave', a counterculture-fuelled rebellion against Campbellian social and aesthetic conservatism (Latham 205–6). The heroic figures at the centre of these myths undoubtedly played important roles in the genre's development, but they were hardly the only sources of good sf before 1965. On the contrary, the development of sf from the 1920s to the mid-1960s was a fascinating, ongoing debate, taking place across many publishing venues, about not only the genre but also such issues as the legacies of colonialism, the meaning of race and the importance of sex.

In Britain during the late 1800s and early 1900s, H.G. Wells and his contemporaries generally published their sf in more upscale magazines, such as *The Strand*, *The New Review* and *Pearson's Magazine*, and such US venues, as *Harper's Monthly*. British authors also tended to write novels that – after serialisation in magazines – were published as books. In the US, however, most early twentieth-century sf appeared in pulp magazines, which derived their name from an innovation using cheap paper based on wood pulp to lower production costs. Such relatively inexpensive magazines were designed to appeal to new mass markets and were seen by many as lacking in both literary quality and prestige (Rieder 58–60). The general fiction pulp magazines of Frank Andrew Munsey began publishing sf in the *The Argosy* in the 1890s and *All-Story* in the 1900s, most influentially the serialised BARSOOM Martian adventures of Edgar Rice Burroughs between 1912 and 1919.

 DOI: 10.4324/9781003140269-18

Hugo Gernsback originally published sf in his *Modern Electrics* (1908–13), *The Electrical Experimenter* (1913–20) and *Science and Invention* (1920–8), magazines that were designed to increase the public's scientific literacy and boost his business importing radio parts from Europe (Ashley *Time* 28–35). In the first issue of his new pulp magazine *Amazing Stories* in April 1926, Gernsback published the now-famous editorial 'A New Sort of Magazine' that created the first definition and canon for the genre, giving it a name and market identity (Westfahl 38–9). Gernsback cited scientific literacy as an important goal, but he also asserted that his 'scientifiction' magazine would publish 'the Jules Verne, H. G. Wells, and Edgar Allan Poe type of story – a charming romance intermingled with scientific fact and prophetic vision' (3). To reinforce his canon and drive home *Amazing Stories*' narrow market identity, Gernsback's first issue republished Verne's *Off on a Comet* (1878), Wells's 'The New Accelerator' (1901) and Poe's 'The Facts in the Case of M. Valdemar' (1845), along with two *Science and Invention* stories, G. Peyton Wertenbaker's 'The Man from the Atom' (1923) and George Allen England's 'The Thing from – 'Outside'' (1923), and Austin Hall's novella *The Man Who Saved the Earth* (1919). As Gernsback tried to build his readership in the first year, *Amazing Stories* mostly consisted of reprints from more prestigious magazines. However, as Gernsback created a brand identity for his magazines, sf in the US became marketed based on the genre, whereas in Britain it continued to be marketed based on the individual author (Rieder 85).

Although left out of Gernsback's original definition of sf, Burroughs placed his new BARSOOM novel *The Master Mind of Mars* in *Amazing Stories Annual #1* (1927) and was a major influence on the original stories Gernsback began to publish in the late 1920s (Sharp *Darwinian* 86, 134–7). Another important name left out of Gernsback's canon was Mary Shelley, whose *Frankenstein* (1818) later became recognised as one the most important and influential science-oriented stories of the nineteenth century (Rieder 72–4). Gernsback was certainly not opposed to mad scientist stories: he published dozens of them. However, the Gothic sf tradition that Shelley inspired was more at home in the pages of *Weird Tales*, a competitor magazine that had been publishing sf alongside fantasy, horror and mixed-genre fiction since September 1923. With the arrival of *Amazing* on newsstands, *Weird Tales* editor Farnsworth Wright branded his magazine's kind of sf as the 'weird-scientific', which his advertisements defined as 'tales of the spaces between the worlds, surgical stories, and stories that scan the future with the eye of prophecy' (Sharp *Darwinian* 147). *Weird Tales* reprinted Shelley's *Frankenstein* in 1932, and regularly published original sf by major authors, such as C(atherine) L(ucille) Moore, Edmond Hamilton and Donald Wandrei. Perhaps the best example of the weird-scientific story was Moore's first publication, 'Shambleau', which appeared in the November 1933 issue. It combines fantasy, horror and sf through its tale of the eponymous alien creature who inspired the Medusa myth. When space smuggler Northwest Smith visits a Martian frontier town, Shambleau ensnares him in an erotic trance and feeds on his soul, its alien body shedding its feminine disguise to reveal a mass of wet snakes that both thrill and horrify its victim. This mixture of genres was decidedly different from those appearing in such narrow sf magazines as *Amazing* and *Astounding*, and challenged contemporary understandings of what sf was and could be (Sharp *Darwinian* 158–60).

In the US, over 450 women contributed to pulp sf magazines between 1926 and 1945 as authors, editors, poets, artists and journalists (Yaszek and Sharp xvii). Gernsback and Wright were particularly welcoming to women authors. The first woman to publish in the sf pulps was Clare Winger Harris, who placed 'A Runaway World' in the July 1926 *Weird Tales*. Her second story, 'The Fate of the Poseidonia', was published as a contest winner in the June 1927 *Amazing Stories* and she went on become a regular contributor to the magazine (Sharp *Darwinian* 105–17). Pictures, biographies and editorial comments made clear that authors with androgynous names such as M.F. Rupert and Leslie F. Stone were women, and C.L. Moore followed the common convention of using her initials out of fear of getting fired from her day job, not to hide her gender (Yaszek and Sharp 164). The only woman to masquerade as a man in this period was L(ucile) Taylor Hansen, who had a picture of a man published with 'The City on the Cloud' (1930). In her science essays for Ray Palmer at *Amazing Stories* in the 1940s, Hansen and her editor also used masculine pronouns in her performance as a scientifically informed man to stir up controversies on issues such as race and sex (Yaszek and Sharp 142, 175–89). Hansen's masquerade seems to have been adopted to strengthen her critique of scientific masculinity, to challenge the Eurocentrism of contemporary science using the voice of masculine authority, and to have some fun (Sharp *Darwinian* 170–1).

Gernsback lost control of *Amazing Stories* in 1929 and immediately started up new magazines *Air Wonder Stories* and *Science Wonder Stories*, where he replaced 'scientifiction' with the term 'science fiction' for the first time (Ashley *Time* 66). 1930 saw the competition increase in the market as *Astounding Stories* began publishing under editor Harry Bates, and Gernsback – with his managing editor David Lasser – consolidated his two titles as *Wonder Stories*. Lasser, who had a degree from MIT and was a major rocket enthusiast, cultivated more technologically informed and socially progressive stories than Gernsback had previously published (Sharp *Darwinian* 121–2). At *Amazing Stories* in 1928, Gernsback and his literary editor T. O'Conor Sloane had published sprawling space operas, such as E.E. 'Doc' Smith's *The Skylark of Space* (1928), and race war adventures, such as Philip Francis Nowlan's 'Armageddon – 2419 AD' (1928), the latter of which launched the lead character Anthony 'Buck' Rogers into the popular imagination. In the *Wonder* magazines, Gernsback and Lasser published Stone's feminist space operas, such as 'Women with Wings' (1930) and 'The Conquest of Gola' (1931), Lilith Lorraine's socialist feminist utopia 'Into the 28th Century' (1930), Rupert's feminist battle-of-the-sexes story 'Via the Hewitt Ray' (1930) and Laurence Manning's scientifically detailed space adventure 'The Voyage of the Asteroid' (1932). The quality of the science and the fiction in many stories published by Gernsback and Lasser rivaled anything published during the so-called 'Golden Age' that began in the late 1930s (Ashley *Time* 75; Sharp *Darwinian* 121–2).

Wonder Stories began to go downhill after Lasser departed in 1933. Gernsback sold the magazine and left sf publishing in 1936, with the new owners renaming it *Thrilling Wonder Stories* and switching the editorial policy to focus on action stories instead of technoscientific extrapolation and progressive social experiments (Ashley *Time* 100). The same year Lasser left *Wonder Stories*, F. Orlin Tremaine took over as editor of *Astounding* and began to push what he called 'thought variant' sf alongside the magazine's usual fare. This kind of sf drew more freely from social sciences in trying to produce original stories focused on a speculative idea instead of simple adventure or rigid scientific extrapolation (Westfahl 175). Wandrei's 'Colossus' (1934), for example, was based on the idea by Sir Arthur Eddington that an expanding universe might mean there is life beyond our universe that dwarfs our own. In Wandrei's story, a global war leads a scientist to escape in his faster-than-light ship that leaves our universe and emerges in a larger macro-universe, where he meets a species of giant super-scientists and helps them to explore life in a micro-universe similar to his own. In addition to these kinds of thought variant stories, Tremaine began to publish science articles, mostly written by Campbell. When Campbell took over for the March 1938 issue and renamed the magazine *Astounding Science Fiction*, he continued to publish thought variant stories and science articles (Ashley, *Time* 107–9). Despite his editorial protestations to the contrary, Campbell also continued to promote Gernsbackian ideals for the genre such as scientific extrapolation, prophetic visions of the future and entertaining storytelling (Westfahl 179–81).

So why did Campbell's tenure at *Astounding Science Fiction* become cast as the beginning of a 'Golden Age' for the genre? One reason is generational: many new writers and editors who rose to prominence in the late 1930s and early 1940s had come of age with specialist sf magazines on their newsstands, and therefore had made sf an important part of their personal and professional identities. Campbell and this new generation were true believers in the idea that sf was a special genre for an elect group of intelligent people with the ability to change the world for the better. Campbell was the editor at the highest-profile sf magazine when this generation moved from being fans to producing sf of their own, and therefore became praised as the centre of this generational flowering of talent (Ashley 109; Westfahl 170).

Another reason was that competing sf magazines made major editorial changes around the same time that made *Astounding* seem like the only real home for serious sf. The 1936 decision of *Thrilling Wonder*'s new owners to focus on action was followed by Ray Palmer's ascension to the editorship at *Amazing* in 1938. Sloane had succeeded Gernsback as editor of *Amazing* in 1929, but the retired natural science professor had watched over a steady decline in the magazine's sales for a decade. Where Sloane was perceived to be stodgy and pedantic, Palmer was an energetic fan who sought to bring fun back to the magazine. In 1939, he published gems such as Eando Binder's 'I, Robot', Robert Bloch's 'The Strange Flight of Richard Clayton' and the first two stories from newcomer Isaac Asimov, 'Marooned off Vesta' and 'The Weapon Too Dreadful to Use'. Although he published a lot of quality sf, Palmer's *Amazing* could never be accused of being serious: in the 1940s, he published science articles by Hansen that began to blur the line between science and pseudo-science, he ran fake photos and biographies of authors, and he crafted articles that promoted the Shaver Mystery hoax (Ashley *Time* 170–1; Yaszek and Sharp 264, 275). At *Weird Tales*, Dorothy McIlwraith took over editorial duties from Wright in 1940 and began to publish sf from new authors such as Theodore Sturgeon, Fritz Leiber and Ray Bradbury. However, she preserved the commitment to *Weird Tales* as a multi-genre magazine, and so did not have the focus that Campbell managed at *Astounding* (Yaszek and Sharp 293). Consequently, Campbell stood out as the editor who seemed to care the most that sf be given respect and taken seriously as literature.

Newer sf magazines were sprouting up all the time. The Munsey Corporation began *Famous Fantastic Mysteries* in 1939 with editor Mary Gnaedinger to reprint their back-catalogue of old pulp sf (Yaszek and Sharp 301–2). *Planet Stories* also started in 1939 and branded itself as a purveyor of original space operas written in the old Burroughs-inspired style. In its first few years, it published such rising sf writers as Leigh Brackett, Henry Kuttner and Bradbury. Young editor Frederik Pohl launched *Astonishing Stories* and *Super-Science Stories* in 1940, publishing notable work from authors such as Asimov, Alfred Bester and James Blish before he was fired in 1941. The generation that grew up reading sf magazines was now creating enough content to fill several magazines, so good sf appeared all over the place. In this environment, Campbell tried to distinguish himself by paying well and by pitching the literary quality of his magazine compared to the others.

Campbell once told Leslie F. Stone that women could not write good sf, but his track record indicates that what he really disliked was the feminist sf of the kind Stone had published in Gernsback's magazines that criticised colonisation and scientific masculinity (Sharp *Darwinian* 156). When Moore and her husband Kuttner decided to try to make a living by solely writing sf, they turned first to Campbell to publish their work. Moore left behind the untameable amazon characters she had made popular in *Weird Tales* and centred her stories for Campbell on rational scientific men conquering nature (Sharp *Darwinian* 161–5). Brackett placed her first sf story,

'Martian Quest' (1940), which focuses on men using scientific problem-solving to colonise the new frontier of Mars, with Campbell. Asimov published 'Reason' and 'Liar!' with Campbell in 1941, and over the next few years produced more of his ROBOT stories for *Astounding*, developing his famous laws of robotics as a rational scientific alternative to Shelley's *Frankenstein*. Robert A. Heinlein published almost all of his pre-World War II stories in *Astounding*, including 'Blowups Happen' (1940) and 'Solution Unsatisfactory' (1941), which depict men inventing dangerous nuclear technologies. By promoting stories that centred on the conquest of nature by White scientific men, Campbell participated in the backlash against the socialist and feminist tendencies of 1920s and early 1930s sf.

Campbell was also stolidly racist, something that became increasingly clear in his reactions to the Civil Rights movement (Nevala-Lee 12–13). With very few exceptions, women and non-White characters were either absent or in roles secondary to the White male scientific heroes who marched across the pages of *Astounding* (Bould and Vint 79–80; 151–4). Campbell carefully cultivated his reputation as a myth-skewering gadfly, but he uncritically repeated nineteenth-century myths about race and Eurocentric hierarchies of culture. He stated in letters to authors that Africans had never built a quality civilisation and had basic problems with learning. He asserted that Native Americans could not be enslaved, ignoring the history of the early colonial period in the Americas. He posited that Native Americans died off instead of submitting to slavery, repeating the myth of the 'vanishing Indian'. Though he claimed to be colour-blind in his editorial policies, Campbell rejected the submissions of Samuel R. Delany and indicated to the author that the readers of *Astounding* would not be able to relate to a Black protagonist (Nevala-Lee 360–5). A well-rounded bigot, Campbell laced letters to authors with homophobic slurs and wrote editorials stating that 'homosexuality was a sign of cultural decline' (Nevala-Lee 365). In this way, he ushered in a serious and belligerently conservative vision of sf that centred on the progress of White heterosexual men, a vision that appealed to many adult fans of the genre.

British sf after World War I continued to be characterised by novels, not magazines. However, the optimism of most established British scientific romance novelists was replaced by a deep pessimism in the aftermath of the war. The US continued its rise as an economic superpower, but the war left the UK in deep social and political turmoil that was reflected in its sf (Stableford 150–1). One example of this was H. Rider Haggard's *When the World Shook* (1919), which imagines an ancient being who awakens and sees the devastation in Belgium and decides to destroy human civilisation once again. Arthur Conan Doyle's adventurous Professor Challenger from *The Lost World* (1912) returned in 'When the World Screamed' (1928), and while his new scientific endeavour is successful, he learns (as the title indicates) that the Earth is alive and cries in pain due to 'his deep exploratory drilling' (Bould 103). By the end of the 1920s, the darkness and anxiety of British sf transformed into an urgent concern for the state of the world. The stock market crash of 1929, the rise of European fascism, and the growth of Stalinist oppression in the Soviet Union left many sf authors feeling like the world was disintegrating instead of progressing (Bould 103; Stableford 171–2). Wells retained some of his old optimism in *The Shape of Things to Come* (1933), but civilisation had to be destroyed by a global war and deadly pandemic before enlightened people could build a global scientific utopia in the aftermath.

New British sf writers of the 1920s and 1930s tended to be even more pessimistic. S. Fowler Wright's novel *Deluge* (1927) imagines a global environmental disaster triggered by earthquakes, and the few survivors engage in a vicious struggle to survive. Along the way, Wright 'blames the defects of human nature *on* Civilisation' and embraces a noble kind of 'savagery' to replace it (Stableford 186). Olaf Stapledon's *Last and First Men* (1930) engages in a Wellsian utopian vision of a world state that improves life for everyone, only to collapse due to failing resources in a manner that plunges humanity into darkness for a hundred thousand years. In Stapledon's future, humanity devolves and evolves, with civilisations and daughter species rising and falling over and over again (Bould 103; Stableford 200–1). Many new writers imagined nightmares that were commentaries on the rise of Stalinism and fascism. Aldous Huxley's *Brave New World* (1932) reads like a direct rejection of the old socialist optimism of writers such as Wells with its dystopian global state that engineers children and enforces strict social hierarchies. Joseph O'Neill's *Land Under England* (1935) explores an underground civilisation devoid of free will and dominated by a hive mind (Bould 116). Storm Jameson's *In the Second Year* (1936) envisions a near-future Britain controlled by fascists who closely resemble Hitler and his followers. The novel examines the 'everyday choices, compromises, and inertias' that lead to fascism (Bould 118).

British authors who fancied the more optimistic and adventure-oriented styles of American sf sold their work to the American magazines (Stableford 151–2). Chief among them was John Wyndham, who under a variety of names placed nine stories in Gernsback's *Wonder* magazines between 1931 and 1935. Australian sf was primarily in novel form, but in content was much like American pulp sf of the period. It regularly featured lost races, race wars and utopias that repeated the problematic colonial plots of the nineteenth century. Australian authors also contributed to American pulp magazines: James Morgan Walsh published five stories in *Wonder Stories* in 1931–2, including his novel *Vandals of the Void* (1931); Alan Connell had four stories in *Wonder Stories* in 1935–36; and Desmond W. Hall was an assistant editor at *Astounding*, and wrote or co-wrote at least 15 stories for the magazine under various pseudonyms between 1931 and 1933 (Ikin and McMullen 341–2).

With the dropping of atomic bombs on Hiroshima and Nagasaki in August of 1945, World War II ended with a shock that came straight from the pages of sf magazines. As Campbell noted in his November 1945 editorial 'Atomic Age', in 'the weeks immediately following that first atomic bomb, the science fictioneers were suddenly recognized by their neighbors as not quite such wild-eyed dreamers as they had been thought' (5). This sudden credibility of sf contributed to an explosion of post-WWII sf publishing in upscale 'slick' magazines such as *Life*, *Colliers* and *The New Yorker*. In 1947, South African writer Stuart Cloete published his nuclear frontier story 'The Blast' in the April 12 and 19 issues of *Colliers*, showcasing a formula that would become increasingly common in the 1950s: a White man survives a nuclear attack, and in the aftermath becomes stronger due to his frontier-like struggle to survive against irradiated mutant animals and his encounters with 'savages'. Military officers got into the act by publishing their fictions of what a future atomic war would be like, using their official status to appear like they were spinning serious plans instead engaging in their own brand of sf (Sharp *Savage* 153–61). In the sf pulps, authors such as Judith Merril took a far more critical tone regarding the new destructive potential of the atom. In the June 1948 *Astounding*, her 'That Only a Mother' showed the impact of radiation on the nuclear family through the eyes of a long-suffering mother with a mutated child. Along with authors such as Carol Emshwiller and Alice Eleanor Jones, Merril created housewife heroine stories that engaged in a critique of the Atomic Age through the acceptably conservative lens of domesticity (Yaszek 97–101).

The dawning of the Atomic Age also helped fuel a new market for sf anthologies and novels. Groff Conklin's *The Best of Science Fiction* (1946) gathered stories previously published in the pulps, making them available to a new mass audience. It contained 40 stories, 25 of which were originally from *Astounding*, and began with a section on atomic technologies (Ashley *Time* 197). In Raymond J. Healy and J. Francis McComas's massive *Adventures in Time and Space* (1946), almost every story came from *Astounding*. These new anthologies helped cement the reputation of Campbell and his authors as the creators of a 'Golden Age', with Campbell himself putting together a series of anthologies in the 1950s drawing from work originally published in his magazine. Paperback books, an inexpensive publishing format that emerged in the 1930s, were starting to push pulp magazines out of the marketplace by the 1950s (Ashley *Transformations* 4–5). Some individual authors gathered their pulp stories into paperbacks: Harris collected a dozen of her stories from between 1926 and 1930 in *Away from the Here and Now* (1947), Asimov collected his ROBOT stories from 1940 to 1950 in a slightly modified form as *I, Robot* (1950), and Bradbury revised several post-war stories into *The Martian Chronicles* (1950). After the war, Heinlein turned to writing sf short stories for *The Saturday Evening Post* and young-adult sf novels for Scribner's, including *Rocket Ship Galileo* (1947), *Space Cadet* (1948), *The Rolling Stones* (1952) and *Tunnel in the Sky* (1955). These anthologies, collections and novels reached much wider audiences than the pre-war pulps, in part because they found their way into libraries, enabling many generations to discover this 'Golden Age' for themselves (Wolfe 22).

In 1950, several magazines began to compete with *Astounding* as homes for serious sf. When *The Magazine of Fantasy and Science Fiction* started out, it chose a digest format with cover art and interior layouts that resembled paperback books instead of standard sf magazines (Ashley *Transformations* 20–2). In its second issue (Winter–Spring 1950), it reprinted quality stories from more upscale magazines, such as Ray Bradbury's 'The Exiles' (1949) from *Macleans'*, alongside new work such as Damon Knight's 'Not with a Bang'. In September 1950, the first issue of *Galaxy Science Fiction* appeared with a strong line-up of stories including Richard Matheson's 'Third from the Sun', Katherine MacLean's 'Contagion' and Fritz Leiber's 'Later Than You Think'. Palmer left as editor of *Amazing* at the end of 1949 and began publishing his own magazines, including *Other Worlds* (later changed to *Other Worlds Science Stories*) and *Imagination*. Freed from the oversight of publishing companies, Palmer proclaimed his new magazines would be for adults and often accepted stories that were too radical or unconventional for other sf editors, with Campbell in particular avoiding stories that dealt with topics such as race and sex. Palmer was particularly interested in racism, publishing stories such as Bradbury's 'Way in the Middle of the Air' (1950) and Eric Frank Russell's 'The Witness' (1951) that tackled bigotry and racial intolerance head on (Ashley *Transformations* 9–10).

These new magazines made an immediate impact, and some older magazines continued to reinvent themselves to keep up. In Fall 1950, new editor Jerome Bixby switched *Planet Stories* from a quarterly to bi-monthly magazine and strove to improve the quality of the stories (Ashley *Transformations* 11). In his first year, he published Brackett's 'Black Amazon of Mars' (1951), Poul Anderson's 'Duel on Syrtis' (1951) and Sturgeon's 'The Incubi of Parallel X' (1951), and in his second year, Philip K. Dick's debut story, 'Beyond Lies the Wub' (1952). Samuel Mines took over *Thrilling Wonder* and *Startling Stories* in 1951, and in the August 1952 issue of *Startling* he published Philip José Farmer's Hugo Award-winning first sf story, 'The Lovers'. Although writers such as Stone and Moore had explored the topic of sex with aliens in their fiction from the early 1930s, the conservative culture of sf publishing in the late 1930s and 1940s had rendered the topic off limits. 'The Lovers' is about a romance between a human named Hal and a humanoid alien named Jeannette on a planet called Ozagen. Hal is from a religious dystopia on Earth that is extreme in its repression of all sin, especially sex. The story refers to masturbation and orgasms, and a central plot point comes when Hal unwittingly ruins Jeannette's contraceptive drink: her pregnancy causes her to die and be eaten by her offspring in the natural manner of her species. In his editorial for that issue, Mines renewed the old call to shake up sf and eliminate taboos, using Farmer's story as a model for one direction the genre should develop (Ashley *Transformations*

13–5). With his competitors addressing race and sex, Campbell's *Astounding* looked increasingly stale and unimaginative.

Throughout the 1950s and 1960s, sf magazines continued to serve as small-market launchpads for stories that could be republished or expanded for the larger paperback market. For example, Arthur C. Clarke expanded his 'Guardian Angel' (1950) from *Famous Fantastic Mysteries* into *Childhood's End* (1953), Walter M. Miller, Jr. expanded three short stories from the *Magazine of Fantasy and Science Fiction* into his Hugo Award-winning nuclear apocalypse novel *A Canticle for Leibowitz* (1959), and Farmer expanded 'The Lovers' into a novel of the same name in 1961. A downturn in magazine sales in the US during the mid-1950s caused most sf magazines to go under by the end of the decade, and those that survived had to switch to the smaller digest format. Writers such as Brackett, Moore and Kuttner turned to writing for television and film, and many others shifted to publishing in the slick magazine and paperback markets (Ashley *Transformations* 150). In this environment, anthologies continued to grow in importance: in 1956, Judith Merril began to edit her popular *The Year's Best S-F* series for Dell which republished stories from the surviving magazines such as *Astounding*, *Galaxy* and *The Magazine of Fantasy and Science Fiction* in paperback form. However, as the book marketplace grew in importance, sf magazine editors and genre gatekeepers, such as Campbell, diminished in power and influence.

In Britain, reprint editions of *Astounding* had been published since 1939, and starting in 1949 many of its rivals also published British editions. After a few false starts, the UK-based *New Worlds* began publishing original work on a quarterly basis in 1949 and featured British authors such as Arthur C. Clarke and John Wyndham. In mid-1953, *New Worlds* switched to a monthly publication schedule, and by the late 1950s it was regularly publishing work by rising stars, such as Brian W. Aldiss, John Brunner and J.G. Ballard. Mirroring publishing changes in the US, paperbacks in Britain became an increasingly important market for sf. *New Worlds* folded briefly in 1964 but was then resurrected as a pocket-size paperback with Michael Moorcock as editor, who went on to publish it himself in magazine formats (Ashley *Transformations* 229–36; Luckhurst 144–5). Moorcock's stated goal was to push sf authors to produce better literature and take full advantage of the genre's endless possibilities. *New Worlds* became a home for more experimental work by new writers interested in the inner space of human consciousness and new approaches to sf that later became associated by some with a 'New Wave'. Moorcock heaped special disdain on 'Golden Age' holdovers such as Campbell and Heinlein as he pushed for improvements in the genre. He also encouraged authors to create characters and stories appropriate for the emerging counterculture of the 1960s (Latham 205–7).

In the US, the critical explorations of race and sex that emerged in the sf of the early 1950s carried into the growing rebellion against Campbell and the old conservatives in the 1960s (Luckhurst 160–2). *The Magazine of Fantasy and Science Fiction* was the most progressive of the US magazines that survived into the 1960s (Ashley *Transformations* 215–6). It published feminist icon Joanna Russ's first short stories 'Nor Custom Stale' (1959), 'My Dear Emily' (1962) and 'There is Another Shore, You Know, Upon the Other Side' (1963), and regularly featured work by women such as Carol Emshwiller, Anne McCaffrey and Zenna Henderson. It also published stories by authors later associated with the New Wave, such as Harlan Ellison's 'Paulie Charmed the Sleeping Woman' (1962) and Roger Zelazny's 'A Rose for Ecclesiastes' (1963). The power of paperbacks in the sf market continued to grow in the 1960s with this infusion of new voices. Merril used *The Year's Best S-F* series to promote prominent 'New Wave' writers, such as Ballard, Brunner and Ellison. Ballard helped usher in a new sub-genre with his apocalyptic climate novels *The Drowned World* (1962) and *The Drought* (1964). Ballard also championed redirecting sf writing from outer space to the altered realities and states of consciousness of inner space (Latham 207–9). Dick began his own experiments with identity and reality in his novels *Time Out of Joint* (1959), *The Man in the High Castle* (1962) and *Martian Time-Slip* (1964). Samuel R. Delany, the first African American to publish extensively in the specialised sf market, burst onto the scene with his novels *The Jewels of Aptor* (1962), *Captives of the Flame* (1963) and *City of a Thousand Suns* (1965).

By 1965, sf literature had become thoroughly infiltrated by iconoclastic counterculture sensibilities and was beginning to reflect the rise of social justice and Civil Rights movements. However, mainstream sf publication venues remained the domain of White authors (with the notable exception of Delany). While sex was no longer a forbidden topic, queer sexualities remained unrepresented and second-wave feminism had yet to fully impact the genre. Ecologically oriented sf was taking root, but most of it remained mired in the colonial fantasies of the past or the apocalyptic negativity of the present. The magazines that had dominated the sf marketplace before World War II had dwindled to a few digests. The editorial gatekeeping of the genre shifted to paperback book publishing, which expanded sf to wider audiences and freed authors from some of the constraints that came with dogmatic editors, such as Campbell. Rolling along with the counterculture rebellions of the 1960s, the myth of the 'New Wave' continued to grow despite being disavowed by many of its supposed leading figures. But much more radical rebellions were just around the corner – accompanied by more conservative backlashes – and most of the action was to take place in books, not magazines.

Works cited

Ashley, Mike. *The Time Machines: The Story of the Science-Fiction Pulp Magazines from the Beginning to 1950*. Liverpool UP, 2000.

——. *Transformations: The Story of the Science-Fiction Magazines from 1950 to 1970*. Liverpool UP, 2005.

Bould, Mark. 'Pulp sf and its Others, 1918–39'. *Science Fiction: A Literary History*. Ed. Roger Luckhurst. British Library, 2018. 102–129.

Bould, Mark and Sherryl Vint. *The Routledge Concise History of Science Fiction*. Routledge, 2011.

Campbell Jr., John W. 'Atomic Age'. *Astounding Science Fiction* 36.3 (November 1945): 5–6, 98.

Gernsback, Hugo. 'A New Sort of Magazine'. *Amazing Stories* 1.1 (April 1926): 3.

Ikin, Van and Sean McMullen. 'Australian Science Fiction'. *A Companion to Science Fiction*. Ed. David Seed. Blackwell, 2005. 337–50.

Latham, Rob. 'The New Wave'. *A Companion to Science Fiction*. Ed. David Seed. Blackwell, 2005. 201–16.

Luckhurst, Roger. *Science Fiction*. Polity, 2005.

Nevala-Lee, Alec. *Astounding: John W. Campbell, Isaac Asimov, Robert A. Heinlein, L. Ron Hubbard, and the Golden Age of Science Fiction*. Dey St., 2018.

Page, Michael R. 'Astounding Stories: The Golden Age, 1938–1950'. *The Cambridge History of Science Fiction*. Ed. Gerry Canavan and Eric Carl Link. Cambridge UP, 2019. 149–65.

Rieder, John. *Science Fiction and the Mass Cultural Genre System*. Wesleyan UP, 2017.

Sharp, Patrick B. *Darwinian Feminism and Early Science Fiction: Aliens, Amazons and Women*. U of Wales P, 2018.

——. *Savage Perils: Racial Frontiers and Nuclear Apocalypse in American Culture*. U of Oklahoma P, 2007.

Stableford, Brian. *Scientific Romance in Britain 1890–1950*. St. Martin's, 1985.

Westfahl, Gary. *The Mechanics of Wonder: The Creation of the Idea of Science Fiction*. Liverpool UP, 1998.

Wolfe, Gary K. *Evaporating Genres: Essays on Fantastic Literature*. Wesleyan UP, 2011.

Yaszek, Lisa. 'Unhappy Housewife Heroines, Galactic Suburbia, and Nuclear War: A New History of Midcentury Women's Science Fiction'. *Extrapolation* 41.3 (2003): 97–111.

Yaszek, Lisa and Patrick B. Sharp, eds. *Sisters of Tomorrow: The First Women of Science Fiction*. Wesleyan UP, 2016.

17

ANGLOPHONE SCIENCE FICTION FANDOMS, 1920S–2020S

Robin Anne Reid

'Fandom' is defined as the gathering of individuals with shared interests and/or hobbies. These gatherings originated in the urban areas of industrialised nations beginning in the mid-nineteenth century and were part of a large system of hobby groups and clubs offering alternatives to work which predated sf fandom by over half a century. Anglophone sf fans began organising sf fandom soon after Hugo Gernsback began publishing pulp magazines filled with what he called 'scientifiction' soon after World War I. The first generation of fans wrote letters to the magazines, which were published and thus gave them the opportunity to organise fan clubs in their cities. Fan activities included fan meta, or scholarship, including fan histories and discussion of sf literature and film, as well as creative and transformative works: art, costumes, stories, songs and conventions. Fans shared their work in fan magazines (fanzines and letter 'zines) using the technologies available. Conventions featured sessions, workshops and awards for fan activities (fanac). For the first decades of sf fandom, the meta and histories described a largely White and largely male culture (Knight; Pohl-Weary; Moskowitz; Warner *All*, *Wealth*). From the 1920s to the 1950s, sf magazines dominated. John W. Campbell Jr's time as editor at *Astounding*, which began in 1937, is still often praised as the 'Golden Age' of science fiction (Nicholls and Ashley). The sf of this period, and the fan culture that grew up around it, tended to focus on how technology could solve all problems, including social ones. However, as Peter Nicholls and Mike Ashley note, there is 'no objective measure' (n.p.) that can be used to identify a 'Golden Age', and in recent years the perception of Campbell has changed significantly. Jeanette Ng's 2019 acceptance speech for the John W. Campbell Award for Best New Writer described instances of Campbell's fascism and led to the award being renamed the *Astounding* Award for Best New Writer. Discussions to rename the John W. Campbell Memorial Award for best novel were also under way, but for unrelated reasons it has not been presented since 2019. Thus, as Nicholls and Ashley suggest, it may be more accurate to identify multiple Golden Ages.

Sf fan culture reflects the larger Anglophone culture of the twentieth century, which saw depressions, two world wars, the collapse of the British Empire, the growth of the US into a global colonial power and growing migrations across national borders. Starting in the 1960s, sf fandom grew and diversified, reflecting post-war economic, political and social changes. The second half of the twentieth century saw the growth of a number of progressive movements, including

DOI: 10.4324/9781003140269-19

anti-war, environmental, Civil Rights, feminist and labour movements. In the twenty-first century, movements for the rights of people in Gender, Romantic and Sexual Minorities (GRSM) and people with disabilities developed. Fandom communities engaged in debates about all these issues, whether in the context of discussing sf stories and media or in regard to fan activities and gatherings.

As fandom demographics changed, marginalised groups of fans increasingly challenged oppressive systems within fan cultures. These challenges were met with resistance, including charges that the groups were destroying fandom unity. The underlying assumption that Anglophone sf fandom's past was a golden age of harmony is contradicted by fan histories and memoirs describing political conflicts from the time of the first WorldCon, which was held in New York City in 1939, when the Futurians were barred from attending because of their politics (Jones; Knight; Kyle). The history of fandom is one of ideological and generational conflicts. The recent development of online fan communities has facilitated more activisms, more resistances and better documentation of these conflicts.

From the 1960s to the 1990s, the growth of sf film and television resulted in fandom activities becoming more mainstream, with *Star Trek* (NBC 1966–9) and *Star Wars* (Lucas 1977), both of which were the foundation for elaborate franchises, being key early instances of media sf's success in attracting mass audiences and markets. Just as important were changes in technology, especially the internet. Online communities challenged the tradition of mentoring younger fans through in-person fan clubs and conventions and even led some fans, as Cait Coker notes, to dismiss those who enter fandom online as 'feral' or inauthentic. The boundary between 'authentic' and 'inauthentic' has for decades been gendered, whether through biological rhetoric or hierarchisation of fan activities, both by fandom gatekeepers and by corporate marketing and branding (Scott); the raced boundaries have only recently begun to be acknowledged by White fans.

Harry Potter fandom is considered the first large fandom to originate and grow up on the internet (Burt; Miller). The growing visibility and increasing numbers of fans resulted in corporate practices changing to increase the profit from fan activities (Scott). During the second half of twentieth century, fragmentation of fandom activities along gender lines increased with the default fan defined as male (Coker; Jenkins *Textual*; '2019 Hugo'). During the twenty-first century, fans who are Black, Indigenous and People of Colour (BIPOC) have, in addition to continuing traditions of creative work and community building, challenged structural racism in fandom. The relative lack of critical work on fans of colour indicates structuralist racism within fan studies.

Fans were among the earliest adopters of the internet (Jenkins *Convergence*), from mailing lists and archives to blogging and beyond, with media fandoms especially flourishing on numerous online platforms (Coppa). Fans used Usenet, GeoCities and Yahoo! Groups for numerous fan activities, then moved onto early social networking sites such as LiveJournal and its clones, as well as to large mainstream platforms. Fan communities and forums exist on dedicated websites, on Reddit and Facebook, and younger fans continue to be early adopters of new platforms as they come online, such as Wattpad (from 2006), Tumblr (2007), Instagram (2010), Discord (2015) and TikTok (2016). This growth has resulted in fan communities and productions being more easily accessed by people outside of convention fandom culture and to greater communication between different fandoms, including comics, celebrity, music and anime fandoms as well as sf and media fandoms. Fan movements away from older platforms are often responses to commercialisation or censorship ('Strikethrough'; 'Tumblr NSFW').

LiveJournal (LJ), started in 1991, and was an innovative, open-access programme billed by its college-student founder, Brad Fitzpatrick, as a 'personal diary'. Combining elements of blogs and social networking sites, LJ allowed unprecedented personal customising of journals. The ease of setting up individual and community journals resulted in decentralising, cross-fertilisation and hybridisation of fandoms (Coppa). LJ became the primary platform for transformative and media fandoms, which were dominated by female fans for a decade. However, when LJ was bought out by a Russian company, which moved the servers from California to Russia, resulting in active censorship by Putin's government (Hoffmann), many fans left for the independent Dreamwidth, created by former LJ volunteers who have maintained it as an open-source platform since 2009. The recent sale of Tumblr that resulted in a decision to ban adult content in 2019 has led to a similar exodus (Klink et al.; McCracken et al.).

Women, mostly White, have been sf readers and writers from the beginning (Davin; Larbalestier; Merrick; Yaszek; on BIPOC who read sf and created their own communities outside White sf convention fandom, see Reid 'Wild'). Women fans during the 1920s–50s may not have defined themselves as feminists, but their contributions inspired the women who began creating sf feminism in the 1970s (Merrick). The feminist fanzines *The Witch and the Chameleon* and *Janus*, launched in 1974 and 1975, respectively. The first feminist sf panel, organised by Susan Wood, ran at the 1976 Worldcon. The first feminist sf con, WisCon, debuted in 1977. Other feminist initiatives were the Tiptree (now the Otherwise) Award, founded in 1991, and the Broad Universe organisation founded in 2000. Only recently has postcolonial work started to appear challenging the default assumptions of Anglophone fandom generally, including some of the online transformative work spaces dominated by White women (Pande *Squee*, *Fandom*).

The increasing separation of fan activities along gender lines has been accompanied by ongoing resistance against women's presence and participation in sf, with a recurring accusation that they are 'fake geek girls' (Coker; 'Fake Geek Girl'; Scott). In recent years, preserving and curating print fanzines and documenting fandom history from before the internet is done largely by male fans. Print fanzines are digitised in online collections and archives by fan groups as well as in university special collections, including *The Fanac Fan History Project* (fanac.org), the Mariellen (Ming) Wathne Fanzine Archives Collection (University of Iowa), the S. Gary Hunnewell Collection, 1960– (Marquette University) and the Science Fiction Oral History Organization (sfoha.org). In contrast, female fans create archives and communities for transformative (creative) works (Jenkins *Textual*; Coker). This binary, of course, falls short of the complex variety of gender identifications in fandoms and fails to acknowledge the diversity in fandom activities but, as Scott argues, the taxonomy is necessary because 'it is stringently gendered. How fans participate, and whose participation is valued by media industries and fan scholars alike, is commonly determined by these labels' (4).

Fans created and shared transformative works (fanfiction, fan art, and fan vidding, or creating videos based on clips from source texts) for decades before the internet, but such work has significantly increased and is more accessible due to online archives. The archives range in size and focus from small groups focusing on specific characters or themes to huge multi-fandom collections. Unlike the fanzine and oral history projects, transformative fandom's activities face challenges such as creator disapproval, copyright take-down notices, platforms removing material due to adult themes, and attempted commercialisation of content ('Strikethrough'; 'Fan Lib'). These problems inspired Astolat to propose creating an 'Archive of Our Own' in 2007 (n.p.; cf. 'Archive of Our Own').

Fourteen years later, the Organization for Transformative Works (OTW), a non-profit, oversees a number of projects created and run by volunteers (transformativeworks.org), including a fan fiction archive (*Archive of Our Own* (AO3)), a fan wiki (*Fanlore*), a Tumblr blog (*Fan Hackers*), an open-access online academic journal (*Transformative Works and Cultures*) and Open Doors, which in cooperation with the University of Iowa preserves fan materials. Two projects work to educate fans and the public about copyright and fair use and to advocate for best practices. The Fan Video and Multimedia project focuses on video creation while the Legal Advocacy team supports fans and creates public documents on legal issues.

When the AO3 won the 2019 Hugo for Best Related Work, the resulting celebration was accompanied by a controversy ('Archive of Our Own and the Hugo Awards'; Glyer 'Meaning'). An archiving programme created and supported by the transformative community winning a Hugo was celebrated as an acknowledgement of previously marginalised fans and their fan fiction, which, unlike the original fan fiction, consists of stories based on copyrighted source texts instead of original fiction about fans (Romano). The controversy had two major issues. The first was part of an ongoing debate about what should be considered as a 'Best Related Work'. The conflict is about how online and virtual nominees increasingly compete with non-fiction books about science fiction (Buhlert). The second relates to the World Science Fiction Society (WSFS) Mark Protection Committee (MPC) issuing a clarification that the Hugo was awarded to the Archive as a 'program and a project' not to individual fans, in order to protect the organisation's service marks ('2019 Hugo').

In addition to the Hugo controversy, AO3 has been criticised by anti-racist fans (Lothian and Stanfill). In May 2023, an activist group, EndOTWRacism, began to organise online actions, including calling for more fans to vote in the OTW's 2023 Board Election. In June 2023, a number of volunteers and former volunteers of OTW and AO3 began posting stories of racism and other abuses of volunteers in a variety of online communities, both anonymously and pseudonymously (Synonymous). The existence of systemic racism in sf fandom is not a recent phenomenon. For most of the century that Anglophone sf fandom has existed, White fans assumed that BIPOC readers of sf did not exist (Delux_Vivens; Moskowitz; Reid 'Wild', 'White'). Jewish fans, writers and editors who contributed to early sf publishing and fan communities, especially in New York and California, were subsumed into the default Whiteness of the Anglophone identity (Correspondent; Silver).

The only two Black fans who were well enough known to gain the status of Big Name Fan (BNF) in the early decades of fandom were James Fitzgerald in the 1930s and Carl Joshua Brandon in the 1950s. Fitzgerald led The Sciencers, a New York club that was one of the earliest, if not the first, sf group in the country. Brandon's fame was due to his fan fiction, parodies of literary texts rewritten to satirise fandom activities and conflicts, and to his intervention in a debate about racism and anti-Semitism in fandom, and to the later revelation that 'Carl Joshua Brandon' was a hoax created by a White fan, Terry Carr, working with a few others (carrington 30–67). When White fans began to debate whether 'negros' would be allowed to join the Fantasy Amateur Press Association (FAPA), Brandon sent a letter that was published in the organisation's fanzine saying that he was applying for membership and 'happen[ed] to be just that [a negro], as a few fans know – a *few* because I think it's unimportant, so I don't make an issue of it. But after the discussion in FAPA, I feel it's only fair to mention it' (Carrington 47). The Carl Brandon Society, which started in 1999, was the first organisation created by BIPOC fans and writers. Their goal is to 'increase racial and ethnic diversity in the production of and audience for speculative fiction' (carlbrandon.org/about/) and they administer two annual awards. The Society was inspired by Samuel R. Delany's essay on racism in Anglophone sf, and it was named after Brandon because he did not exist.

The internet embeds systemic racism and both neoliberalism and colour-blind racism contribute to its privatised, profit-driven nature (Nakamura *Cybertypes*, *Digitizing*). Early marketing campaigns were grounded in utopian rhetoric and essentialist ideas of identity, assuming that all 'differences' are visible only on bodies (Chun). BIPOC sf fans and writers refuse to pass as default White men or to allow racist and sexist behaviours to go unchallenged. As a result of their anti-racist work, which has increased during the first two decades of the twenty-first century, sf publishing and fandom is changing (Doctorow; Flood; Harrison; Light; Locke; Low; Minkel and Klink '22A', '22B'; Pande *Squee, Fandom*; 'Race and Fandom'; TWC Editor; 'Vividcon'; White).

Racefail '09, the first major online conflict about racism that involved professional writers and editors as well as fans, took place in January–March 2009, primarily on LiveJournal ('Racefail '09'). Rydra_Wong compiled a list of over 1000 posts in 2009, and although a number of them have since been deleted or closed to public view, many still remain on the original site or in archives ('RaceFail '09/List'). Anti-racist critiques focus on racism in specific texts, in sf publishing and media, in fan communities and fan creations. Fans of colour argue that White privilege, including a range of racist behaviours that institutionalise marginalisation of and discrimination against BIPOC fans, exists in online media fandom in spite of its communal identity as a safe space for (White) women, non-binary and queer fans.

Racefail '09 had some positive effects on sf fandom and publishing, but anti-racist fans still point to ongoing racism more than a decade later (Centrumlumina 'AO3', 'Fandom's'; Jemisin; Hutton 'Let's', 'Thread', 'Over'; Minkel and Klink '22A', '22B'; Wistful Jane). After more White women and more writers of colour began winning Hugo Awards, two groups of conservative writers, the Sad Puppies and the Rabid Puppies, attempted to return the awards and fandom to their imagined politics-free past by organising and promoting voting slates in 2013–16. These efforts were met with voting results of 'No Award' in some categories and, eventually, by changes in the voting process for the Hugos (Benedict; Felapton; Glyer 'Compleat'; 'Puppygate'; Schaub; Waldman). Since 2016, *Fireside Fiction* has published an annual report on 'Antiblack Racism in Speculative Fiction' (White), and in 2020, *Fiyah Magazine* created the first virtual con celebrating BIPOC+ in speculative fiction and featuring the Ignyte Awards.

Fifteen years after Racefail '09, fans of colour continue to identify racisms in fandom. When the OTW used their weekly announcement post to describe fan activism, including fandom support for the Black Lives Matter movement, Zina Hutton and Rukmini Pande were cited with no acknowledgement of their critiques of structural racism in the AO3 ('This Week in Fandom Volume 149' 2020). Hutton and Pande requested that their names be removed because the members and volunteers of OTW and AO3 showed no evidence of having read their work. Their names were removed from the OTW site (but not from the cross-posting at the Reddit AO3), and the organisation posted a response to the criticism, including a list of planned future changes ('Statement'). Anti-racist fans have pointed out that the problems identified during Racefail '09 (racism in source texts; racism in fan communities and productions; White fans' responses to fans of colour) still exist. In addition, additional accusations that originated in Tumblr fan spaces are used to dismiss anti-racist work: either that anti-racist fans are anti-shippers or that they are advocating censorship ('Anti-shipper'; Hutton 'Anti-what'; Klink, et al.; Wistful Jane).

In the 1940s, Anglophone sf fans adopted the motto 'Fans are Slans!', comparing themselves to the evolved humans in A.E. van Vogt's *Slan* (1940), mutants who are superior to but persecuted by the mundane majority around them ('Fans are Slans!'). While this metaphor is no longer widespread, especially among later generations in fandom, white fans' perception that they are the victims, and that the anti-racist fans are the true racists, maps closely to mainstream White people's belief that they are more likely than Black people to be victims of racism. These attitudes worsened during Trump's presidency (Horowitz et al.; 'Whites'). Given the conflicts in sf fandom and in the larger, global context, the question that remains, what futures do we wish to create?

Works cited

'2019 Hugo Awards Clarification'. *The Hugo Awards* (18 December 2019). www.thehugoawards.org/2019/12/2019-hugo-awards-clarification/

'Anti-shipper'. *Fanlore* (n.d.). https://fanlore.org/wiki/Anti-shipper

'Archive of Our Own'. *Fanlore* (n.d.). https://fanlore.org/wiki/Archive_of_Our_Own

'Archive of Our Own and the Hugo Awards'. *Fanlore* (n.d.). https://fanlore.org/wiki/Archive_of_Our_Own_and_The_Hugo_Awards

Astolat. 'An Archive of One's Own'. *Astolat's Live Journal* (17 May 2007). https://astolat.livejournal.com/150556.html

Benedict, R. 'Sorry, Sad Puppies: Science Fiction Has Always Been Political'. *Hornet* (2016). https://hornet.com/stories/sorry-sad-puppies-science-fiction-has-always-been-political/

Buhlert, Cora. 'Some Thoughts on the 2021 Hugo Finalists'. *Cora Buhlert* (16 April 2021). http://corabuhlert.com/2021/04/16/some-thoughts-on-the-2021-hugo-finalists/

Burt, Kayti. 2018, 'How Harry Potter Shaped Modern Internet Fandom'. *Den of Geek* (31 July 2018). www.denofgeek.com/books/how-harry-potter-shaped-modern-internet-fandom/

carrington andré. *Speculative Blackness: The Future of Race in Science Fiction*. U of Minnesota P, 2016.

Centrumlumina. 'AO3 Ship Stats Master Post'. *The Slow Dance of the Infinite Stars* (25 September 2016). https://centrumlumina.tumblr.com/post/150909807989/ao3-ship-stats-

———. 'Fandom's Race Problem'. *The Slow Dance of the Infinite Stars* (13 August 2016). https://centrumlumina.tumblr.com/post/148893785870/fandoms-race-problem-and-the-ao3-ship-stats

Chun, Wendy Hui Kyong. *Control and Freedom: Power and Paranoia in the Age of Fiber Optics*. MIT Press, 2007.

Coker, Cait. 'The Other Digital Divide: Gendering Science Fiction Fan Reading in Print and Online'. *The Edinburgh History Reading: Modern Readers*. Ed. Mary Hammond. Edinburgh UP, 2020. 264–82.

Coppa, Francesca. 'A Brief History of Media Fandom'. *Fan Fiction and Fan Communities in the Age of the Internet*. Ed. Karen Hellekson and Kristina Busse. McFarland, 2006. 41–59.

Correspondent J. 'Small S.F. Publisher Nurtures Jewish Sci-Fi Tradition'. *The Jewish News of Northern California* (1 April 2016). www.jweekly.com/article/full/77238/small-s.f.-publisher-nurtures-jewish-sci-fi-tradition

Davin, Eric Leif. *Partners in Wonder: Women and the Birth of Science Fiction, 1926–1965*. Lexington, 2005.

Delany, Samuel R. 'Racism and Science Fiction'. *Dark Matter: A Century of Speculative Fiction from the African Diaspora*. Ed. Sheree R. Thomas. Warner, 1998. 383–97.

Delux_Vivens. 'Wild Unicorn Herd Check In'. *Deadbrowalking* (11 May 2009). http://deadbrowalking.livejournal.com/357066.html

Doctorow, Cory. 'Report on the Dismal State of Black SF/F Writers in the Short Fiction Markets'. *BoingBoing* (26 July 2016). http://boingboing.net/2016/07/26/report-on-the-dismal-state-of.html

EndOTWRacism. 'Sticky: #Vote to End OTW Racism'. *EndOTWRacism. Dreamwidth* (21 May 2023). https://endotwracism.dreamwidth.org/2713.html

'Fake Geek Girl'. *Fanlore* (n.d.). https://fanlore.org/wiki/Fake_Geek_Girl

'FanLib'. Fanlore (n.d.). https://fanlore.org/wiki/FanLib

'Fans are Slans!'. *Fancyclopedia 3* (n.d.). https://fancyclopedia.org/Fans_are_Slans!

Felapton, Camestros. 'Debarkle'. Camestros Felapton (n.d.). https://camestrosfelapton.wordpress.com/debarkle/

Flood, Alison. 'Black Science Fiction Writers Face "Universal" Racism, Study Finds'. *The Guardian* (9 August 2016). www.theguardian.com/books/2016/aug/09/black-science-fiction-writers-universal-racism-study-finds-fireside-fiction-blackspecfic

Glyer, Mike. 'The Compleat Litter of Puppy Roundup Titles'. *File 770* (2 June 2015). http://file770.com/?page_id=22881

———. 'The Meaning of It All'. File 770 (19 December 2019). http://file770.com/the-meaning-of-it-all/

Harrison, Niall. 'The Next Horizon'. *Strange Horizons* (29 August 2016). http://strangehorizons.com/non-fiction/azimuth/editorials/the-next-horizon/

Hoffmann, Jay. 'Whatever Happened to LiveJournal'. *The History of the Web* (16 October 2017). https://thehistoryoftheweb.com/postscript/whatever-happened-livejournal/

Horowitz, Juliana Menasce, Anna Brown and Kiana Cox. 'Race in America 2019'. *Pew Research Center* (9 April 2019). www.pewresearch.org/social-trends/2019/04/09/race-in-america-2019/

Hutton, Zina. 'Anti-what Exactly?', *Stitch's Media Mix* (11 April 2020). https://stitchmediamix.com/2020/04/11/anti-what-exactly/
———. 'Let's Talk about Racism in the Archive Again', *Stitch's Media Mix* (14 January 2021). https://stitchmediamix.com/2021/01/14/lets-talk-about-racism-in-the-archive-again/
———. 'Over A Year After the OTW/AO3's Statement of Solidarity: Where Are We With That Anti Racism?'. *Stitch's Media Mix* (8 September 2021). https://stitchmediamix.com/2021/09/08/where-are-we-now-ao3-anti-racism/
———. 'Thread Collection: Racefail A Decade Later (1/17/2019)'. *Stitch's Media Mix* (27 December 2020). https://stitchmediamix.com/2020/12/27/thread-collection-racefail-a-decade-later-1-17-2019/
Jemisin, N.K. 2010, 'Why I Think Racefail was the Bestest Thing Evar for SFF'. *N.K. Jemisin* (18 January 2010). https://nkjemisin.com/2010/01/why-i-think-racefail-was-the-bestest-thing-evar-for-sff/
Jenkins, Henry. *Convergence Culture: Where Old and New Media Collide*. New York UP, 2006.
———. *Textual Poachers: Television Fans and Participatory Culture*. Routledge, 1992.
Jones, Tony. 'The History of the World Science Fiction Convention (Worldcon)'. *Starburst Magazine* (17 March 2015). www.starburstmagazine.com/features/history-worldcon
Klink, Flourish, Rukmini Pande, Zina Hutton and Lori Morimoto. 'A Roundtable Discussion about the Cultures of Fandom on Tumblr'. *A Tumblr Book: Platform and Cultures*. Ed. Allison McCracken, Alexander Cho, Louise Stein and Indira Neill Hoch. U of Michigan P, 2020. 167–80.
Knight, Damon. *The Futurians*. John Day, 1977.
Kyle, David. *IMPORTANT! Read This Immediately! A Warning!* (2 July 1939). https://fanac.org/fanzines/Miscellaneous/A_Warning.html
Larbalestier, Justine. *The Battle of the Sexes in Science Fiction*. Wesleyan UP, 2002.
Light, L.E.H. 'The Fireside Fiction Report: A Reader/Critic's Perspective'. *Black Nerd Problems* (n.d.). http://blacknerdproblems.com/the-fireside-fiction-report-a-readercritics-perspective/
Locke, Charley. 'N.K. Jemisin Has a Plan for Diversity in Science Fiction'. *Wired* (18 August 2016). www.wired.com/2016/08/n-k-jemisin-plan-diversity-science-fiction/
Lothian, Alexis and Mel Stanfill. 'An Archive of Whose Own? White Feminism and Racial Justice in Fan Fiction's Digital Infrastructure'. *Transformative Works and Cultures* 36 (2021).
Low, Jason. 'Where Is the Diversity in Publishing? The 2015 Diversity Baseline Survey Results'. *The Open Book* (26 January 2016). http://blog.leeandlow.com/2016/01/26/where-is-the-diversity-in-publishing-the-2015-diversity-baseline-survey-results/
McCracken, Allison, Alexander Cho, Louise Stein and Indira Neill Hoch, eds. *A Tumblr Book: Platform and Cultures*. U of Michigan P, 2020.
Merrick, Helen. *The Secret Feminist Cabal: A Cultural History of Science Fiction Feminisms*. Aqueduct, 2009.
Miller, Laura. 'The New Powers That Be: Harry Potter, the Triumph of Fandom, and the Future of Creativity'. *Slate* (11 September2016). https://slate.com/culture/2016/09/online-harry-potter-fans-transformed-what-it-means-to-love-a-story.html
Minkel, Elizabeth and Flourish Klink. 'Episode 22A: Race and Fandom: Part 1'. *Fansplaining* (18 May 2016). www.fansplaining.com/episodes/22a-race-and-fandom
———. 'Episode 22B: Race and Fandom: Part 2'. *Fansplaining* (19 May 2016). www.fansplaining.com/episodes/22b-race-and-fandom
Moskowitz, Sam. *The Immortal Storm: A History of Science Fiction Fandom*. Hyperion, 1974.
Nakamura, Lisa. *Cybertypes: Race, Ethnicity, and Identity on the Internet*. Routledge, 2002.
———. *Digitizing Race: Visual Cultures of the Internet*. U of Minnesota P, 2007.
Ng, Jeanette. 'John W. Campbell, for Whom this Award was Named, was a Fascist'. *Medium* (18 August 2019.) https://medium.com/@nettlefish/john-w-campbell-for-whom-this-award-was-named-was-a-fascist-f693323d3293
Nicholls, Peter and Mike Ashley. 'Golden Age of SF'. *The Encyclopedia of Science Fiction* (n.d.). www.sf-encyclopedia.com/entry/golden_age_of_sf
Pande, Rukmini. *Fandom, Now in Color: A Collection of Voices*. U of Iowa P, 2020.
———. *Squee from the Margins: Fandom and Race*. U of Iowa P, 2018.
Pohl-Weary, Emily. *Better to Have Loved: The Life of Judith Merril*. Between the Lines, 2002.
'Puppygate'. *Fanlore* (n.d.). https://fanlore.org/wiki/Puppygate
'Race and Fandom'. *Fanlore* (n.d.). https://fanlore.org/wiki/Race_and_Fandom
'Racefail '09'. *Fanlore* (n.d.). https://fanlore.org/wiki/RaceFail_%2709

'RaceFail '09/List of Discussion Posts, Sorted by Author'. *Fanlore* (n.d.). https://fanlore.org/wiki/RaceFail_%2709/List_of_Discussion_Posts,_Sorted_by_Author
Reid, Robin A. 'The White Elephant in the Room: Lois McMaster Bujold's Participation in Racefail '09'. *Short But Concentrated: An Essay Symposium on the Works of Lois McMaster Bujold*. Ed. Una McCormack and Regina Yung Lee. Fifth Storey, 2020. Unpaginated.
———. 'The Wild Unicorn Herd Check-In: Reflexive Racialisation in Online Science Fiction Fandom'. *Black and Brown Planets: The Politics of Race in Science Fiction*. Ed. Isiah Lavender III. UP of Mississippi, 2014. 225–40.
Romano, Aja. 'The Archive Of Our Own Just Won a Hugo'. *Vox* (19 August 2019). www.vox.com/2019/4/11/18292419/archive-of-our-own-wins-hugo-award-best-related-work
Rydra_Wong. 'Racefail '09'. *The Internet is My Prosthetic Brain* (2009). http://rydra-wong.dreamwidth.org/148996.html
Schaub, Michael. 'Women and Writers of Color Win Big at Hugo Awards and The Puppies are Even Sadder'. *Los Angeles Times* (22 August 2016). www.latimes.com/books/jacketcopy/la-ca-jc-hugo-winners-20160822-snap-story.html
Scott, Suzanne. *Fake Geek Girls: Fandom, Gender, and the Convergence Culture Industry*. New York UP, 2019.
Silver, Steven H. 'Jewish Science Fiction and Fantasy'. *Stevenhsilver* (n.d.). www.stevenhsilver.com/jewishsf.html
'Statement from the OTW Board of Directors, Chairs, & Leads'. *Organization for Transformative Works* (24 June 2020). www.transformativeworks.org/statement-from-the-otw-board-of-directors-chairs-leads/
'Strikethrough and Boldthrough'. *Fanlore* (n.d.). https://fanlore.org/wiki/Strikethrough_and_Boldthrough
Synonymous. 'Sticky: That AO3 Callout Post'. *Synonymous. Dreamwidth* (15 June 2023). https://synonymous.dreamwidth.org/1664.html
TWC Editor. 'Pattern Recognition: A Dialogue on Racism in Fan Communities' *Transformative Works and Cultures* 3 (2009): unpaginated. https://journal.transformativeworks.org/index.php/twc/article/view/172/119
'Tumblr NSFW Content Purge'. *Fanlore* (n.d.). https://fanlore.org/wiki/Tumblr_NSFW_Content_Purge
'Vividcon 2009: Some Observations about Race, Gender, and Accessibility'. *Fanlore* (n.d.). https://fanlore.org/wiki/Vividcon_2009:_Some_observations_about_race,_gender,_and_accessibility
Waldman, Katy. 'How Sci-Fi's Hugo Awards Got Their Own Full-Blown Gamergate'. *Slate* (8 April 2015). www.slate.com/blogs/browbeat/2015/04/08/_2015_hugo_awards_how_the_sad_and_rabid_puppies_took_over_the_sci_fi_nominations.html
Warner, Jr, Harry. *All Our Yesterdays: An Informal History of Science Fiction Fandom in the Forties*. Advent, 1969.
———. *Wealth of Fable: An Informal History of Science Fiction Fandom in the 1950s*. SciFi Press, 1992.
White, Brian J. 'Antiblack Racism in Speculative Fiction'. *Fireside Fiction* (26 July 2016). https://medium.com/fireside-fiction-company/blackspecfic-571c00033717#.twe3ig6sq
'Whites Believe They Are Victims of Racism More Often Than Blacks'. *TuftsNow* (23 May 2011). https://now.tufts.edu/2011/05/23/whites-believe-they-are-victims-racism-more-often-blacks
Wistful Jane. 'Mythical Dragons & Wild Unicorns: A Decade Later'. *Wistfuljane* (15 June 2020). https://web.archive.org/web/20200710154012/https://wistfuljane.dreamwidth.org/2020/06/15/a-decade-later.html
Yaszek, Lisa. *Galactic Suburbia: Recovering Women's Science Fiction*. Ohio State UP, 2008.

18
SCIENCE FICTION THEATRE

Christos Callow, Jr.

Theatre – whose literal meaning in Greek is 'a place to see things' – is often described as an art that holds up a mirror to its audience or as a microcosm of society (Lehmann 132). From Aristotle's concept of catharsis to the more contemporary practice of dramatherapy, it is also considered to have therapeutic value. At its best, it possesses a transcendental and a communal character, given its ancient ritualistic origins and its relationship with live audiences. A dialectical and mimetic artform, it shares most of the above elements with prose sf, which can offer similarly cathartic experiences as well as 'cognitive estrangement' (Suvin) – a concept with roots in Bertolt Brecht's alienation effect and which theatre achieves via dramaturgy (Willingham 67) and performance. This chapter will look at sf's place as a theatrical genre, exploring its origins, themes and potential.

The birth of sf in the theatre is generally considered to have occurred in 1921 with the premiere of *R.U.R.,* a Czech play by Karel Čapek that coined the word 'robot'. However, this centenarian genre has not experienced quite the recognition of sf cinema, whose first major production arguably came a few years later with *Metropolis* (Lang 1927). The reasons for the relative absence of criticism and public recognition of sf on stage are several; while an immediate assumption might be simply that cinema can afford to portray sf worlds more efficiently, this neglect is primarily a result of theatre studies and criticism's lack of engagement with sf culture. It is not that sf has not been prominent on the stage but that it has faced resistance to being recognised as sf. Furthermore, identifying as an sf theatre company or playwright in the twentieth century was rare, with noteworthy exceptions including the Science Fiction Theatre Company of Liverpool and the novelist (and playwright) Ray Bradbury, who adapted several of his works for the stage.

As Ralph Willingham's *Science Fiction in the Theatre* (1994), one of the earliest works of academic research on the topic, demonstrates, the majority of twentieth-century sf plays – and mainly those in the English language – were theatrical adaptations. For example, there were several stage versions of Mary Shelley's *Frankenstein* (1818) and Robert Louis Stevenson's *Strange Case of Dr Jekyll and Mr Hyde* (1886) across the nineteenth and twentieth centuries, including musicals, operas and parodies. Thomas Russell Sullivan's 1887 version of Jekyll and Hyde toured for 20 years, and in 1991 David Edgar's adaptation was produced by the Royal Shakespeare Company; recent *Frankenstein* adaptations include Mel Brooks's 2007 musical version of his 1974 film *Young Frankenstein*, which parodied the 1930s Universal film adaptations, and Nick Dear's

DOI: 10.4324/9781003140269-20

2011 production for the UK's National Theatre. Willingham catalogued 328 plays containing sf elements; in 2018 I created the Internet Science Fiction Theatre Database (www.cyborphic.com/database) to catalogue twenty-first century sf plays and theatrical performances, quite a few of which were devised by theatre companies rather than individual playwrights (the database also includes some works labelled 'Afrofuturist Theatre', 'Fantasy Theatre' and 'Horror Theatre').

Twentieth-century sf theatre

In the twentieth century, alongside adaptations, a number of established plays sometimes featured sf elements, although at the time these works were not typically classified as sf, and several sf authors wrote for the theatre too. Čapek's *R.U.R.* is about a scientist, Rossum, who runs a factory that produces humanlike machines, which he aims to distribute internationally. The robots (from the Czech 'robota', meaning 'hard work' or 'serf labour') develop the ability to think for themselves, feel pain and experience emotions, and eventually revolt against humans. The play had its premiere at the National Theatre in Prague in 1921 and quickly became an international success; by 1923 it already had productions in New York (1922) and London (1923) and had been translated into 30 languages; a 25-minute BBC adaptation, broadcast live twice on 11 February 1938, was the first sf play to appear on television, and the BBC broadcast an hour-long adaptation in 1948 (Johnston). Around the same time, George Bernard Shaw wrote *Back to Methuselah (A Metabiological Pentateuch)* (1921), first performed in New York (1922) and by the Birmingham Repertory Theatre in the UK (1923). This several hours-long, high-concept philosophical play attempts to capture a fictional version of the entire human history, starting in the Garden of Eden in 4004 BCE and ending in 31,920 CE when existence without a body is regarded as humanity's ultimate destiny. Other established playwrights who turned to sf include Samuel Beckett and Caryl Churchill. Beckett's *Endgame* (1957) is an absurdist and minimalistic post-apocalyptic tragedy about the human condition, featuring a blind old man in a wheelchair, his servant-like companion and his even older parents who have no legs and live in dustbins. It has been produced numerous times, recently by the theatre companies Complicite in London (2009) and Steppenwolf in Chicago (2010); the BBC produced a feature-length adaptation for the Open University in 1991, it was filmed again as part of the 2001 project *Beckett on Film* and was adapted by György Kurtág as the opera *Fin de partie* (2018). Churchill's dystopian drama *The Skriker* (1994), which blends elements of several genres and styles, such as horror, postmodernism, ecological fiction and fairy tales, is set in a futuristic world full of wicked fairies (such as Skriker) who seduce humans into destroying their own children. She also wrote the near-future *A Number* (2002), exploring the ethics of cloning and the nature of identity.

Most theatremakers who produced such work in the twentieth century would not speak fondly of sf as a theatrical or literary genre. The British playwright Alan Ayckbourn is an exception. He has maintained a consistent interest, as demonstrated in several of his plays, 'in the allegorical properties of science fiction' (Fisher n.p.). He does, however, see certain limitation in producing sf for the stage 'I never call it science fiction because people get a little jumpy about it. Theatre can do domestic sci-fi that doesn't require high technology' (n.p.). Ayckbourn has written three plays featuring androids, *Henceforward...* (1987), *Comic Potential* (1998) and *Surprises* (2012), and a dozen other plays with 'horror/fantastical or sfnal elements' (McGrath 71), such as *Body Language* (1990), *Communicating Doors* (1995), *Virtual Reality* (2000) and *If I Were You* (2006). Ayckbourn's plays include elements of 'time travel, body swapping and ghosts – making him possibly unique amongst major British playwrights in the depth and longevity of his interest in science fiction and fantasy' (McGrath 62). In the tragicomic *Henceforward...*, a lonely composer

Jerome, who has not written anything new for years since his wife and daughter left him, trains a female android, Nan, whose comic and repetitive speech is taken from the women in Jerome's life, to act as his companion in order to convince his former wife that he is living a normal life and so his daughter should occasionally stay at his place; but as things get better, the deception unravels. *Comic Potential* is a romantic sf drama with comic elements featuring androids, called act-oids, which have taken the place of actors.

Another exception is Ken Campbell, who founded the Science Fiction Theatre Company of Liverpool and staged Neil Oram's *The Warp!* in 1979, which premiered at the ICA in London and entered the Guinness Book of Records as the longest play ever performed. The company would do full non-stop 'marathon' performances of all 10 plays in *The Warp!* cycle, with one of the actors being on stage for 22 hours. Like *Back to Methusaleh*, the play covers thousands of years, in this case portraying the protagonist's previous lives. A review in the *International Times* asks of this rare theatrical experience: 'What is it? A church, a cult, a madhouse, a pilgrimage, a cafe with poetry and jazz, a palace of misfits, savants, hermits, flagellants, wizards, witches, and impostors!' (McDevitt n.p.). Such productions bring something unique to sf culture – not just duration, but aspects of the lived experience, of witnessing and participating, that share the ritualistic elements of ancient performances and the communal experience of theatre more broadly.

Perhaps the most established sf novelist who was also a dramaturge was Ray Bradbury, who worked with the Fremont Centre Theatre in South Pasadena, California, which presented several Bradbury productions, including adaptations of *Fahrenheit 451* – his 1953 dystopian novel in which a conflicted fireman whose job is to burn books falls in love with literature instead – and of several of his short stories; he also led the Pandemonium Theatre Company in LA for many years. Bradbury's significance was not merely that he was 'Determined to prove that science fiction deserved a place in the theatre' but that 'for the first time a recognized science fiction writer was challenging the myth that science fiction was unstageable' (Willingham, 54).

The staging of the unstageable is often at the core of the sf theatrical experience – and perhaps explains why one of the main forms of sf that has flourished on stage is the musical. Richard O'Brien's *The Rocky Horror Show*, featuring a transvestite mad scientist from the galaxy of Transylvania, blending elements of sf and horror B-movies, premiered at London's Royal Court Theatre in 1973 and was quickly adapted as *The Rocky Horror Picture Show* (Sharman 1975). Also combining elements of horror and comedy, *Little Shop of Horrors*, with music by Alan Menken and lyrics by Howard Ashman and loosely based on *The Little Shop of Horrors* (Corman 1960), premiered in New York in 1982 and was adapted to film by Frank Oz in 1986 – it featured a mad character from outer space too, in this case a human-eating plant, named Aubrey II by the protagonist, after the woman with whom he was in love. Other productions include Andrew Lloyd Webber and Richard Stilgoe's *Starlight Express* (1984) and, at the turn of the millennium, *We Will Rock You* (2002), based on the Queen songbook and written by Ben Elton, and *Repo! The Genetic Opera* (2002), written by Darren Smith and Terrance Zdunich and adapted to film by Darren Lynn Bousman in 2008. *A Shoggoth on the Roof*, a Lovecraftian parody of the 1964 musical *Fiddler on the Roof* written by an anonymous creator (known as 'He Who [for legal reasons] Must Not Be Named'), was published by the fan organisation H.P. Lovecraft Historical Society in 1979; after many failed attempts, it was finally staged at the Miskatonicon convention in Sweden in 2005.

Beyond some of the more mainstream big-budget musicals, often what makes sf unstageable is a question of budget. But sometimes it is the challenging task of translating well-established cinematic aesthetics for the theatrical stage and in front of a live audience. For this reason, an sf play may, for example, contain the idea of an alien invasion or explore posthuman characters, but be traditional in its theatricality or take on the kind of minimalist aesthetics associated with the Theatre of the Absurd. Other plays might belong primarily to some other genre but contain minor sf elements that are not, in the eyes of many critics or even their creators, enough for these plays to be labelled sf. In the twenty-first century, however, there are more plays and productions unashamed of their genre elements and often innovative both in how they explore sf and in how they explore theatre.

Twenty-first century sf theatre

Sf theatre has flourished in the new millennium, with some very ambitious and notable plays in the early 2010s, such as Anne Washburn's *Mr Burns: a post-electric play* (2012), Jennifer Haley's *The Nether* (2013) and Alistair McDowall's *Pomona* (2014.) In *Mr Burns,* a group of apocalypse survivors recall and perform an episode from *The Simpsons* (Fox 1989–), becoming increasingly distorted with every iteration, including 75 years further into the future. *The Nether* explores ethics and crime in a digital reality where men hide behind avatars to experience perverse fantasies involving avatars of children, while the similarly disturbing *Pomona,* influenced by the tabletop role-playing game *Dungeon & Dragons* and featuring a figure in a Cthulhu mask, tells the story of a woman looking for her lost sister in a mysterious island in the centre of Manchester where she may have been a victim of trafficking. *Mr Burns* and *Pomona* – and also Jordan Harrison's *Marjorie Prime* (2014), which was a Pulitzer Prize finalist in 2015 and adapted to film by Michael Almereyda in 2017 – have had quite an impact, not least in helping to make sf theatre more recognisable for twenty-first century audiences. Of several twenty-first century operas and musicals, *Death and the Powers: A Robot Pageant* is one of the most impressive. Composed by Tod Machover and with libretto by Robert Pinsky, it premiered at the Opera de Monte-Carlo in Monaco in 2010. It was developed at the MIT Media Lab, thanks to the Opera of the Future research group located there. Contemporary theatremakers, more openly geeky in their aesthetics and intertextual references, have been more welcoming of genre labels, with several groups identifying as sf theatre companies and the launch of a number of theatre festivals dedicated to the genre on stage, such as Los Angeles's *Sci-Fest LA* and Chicago's *Paragon Sci-Fi and Fantasy Play Festival* in the US and *Talos: Science Fiction Theatre Festival of London* in the UK.

In the UK, the Royal Court Theatre has produced sf theatre with elements of absurdism, including Thomas Eccleshare's *Instructions for Correct Assembly* (2018). Other playwrights have used the conventions of sf to explore in more depth issues of race in the UK, as in Tajinder Hayer's post-apocalyptic *North Country* (2016). Comic pieces, such as Nessah Muthy's *Sex with Robots and Other Devices* (2018), started as smaller indie productions but received critical acclaim and were published. However, the difficulty of keeping track of fringe productions means there are undoubtedly noteworthy and ambitious examples that one can easily miss, especially if their theatrical life is limited – often due to budget – to a few performances per year. A Twitter thread by the Talos festival attempted to capture productions that took place mainly in the UK online and in-venue during August and September 2021 (@TalosFest). It included sf operas (e.g., for the *Tête à Tête* opera festival), musicals (e.g., an adaptation of *Back to the Future*) and several fringe festival shows (including solo plays) many of which were also presented at the *Edinburgh Fringe* (which has a list of genres, including horror and sf for audiences navigating the packed schedule).

Those artists identifying as sf playwrights/theatremakers, while they do at times produce sf musicals, operas or even anime adaptations, most often work on sf plays with smaller casts and at times in single-location narratives, or in audio drama. In the US, Mac Rogers has written The Honeycomb Trilogy (2012) of sf plays, about giant alien insects taking over the world, and the podcast audio drama *Steal the Stars* (2017), about a Roswell-like crashed alien spaceship. Edward Einhorn has adapted for the stage sf novels that might typically be regarded as unstageable, including in 2008 Kurt Vonnegut Jr's *Cat's Cradle* (1963) and in 2012 Ursula K. Le Guin's *The Lathe of Heaven* (1971), while his play *Alma Baya* – a drama about clones in a pod who know very little about the (presumably now extinct) human race, except what is available in manuals – premiered in 2021 at A.R.T./New York during the Covid-19 pandemic, and was live-streamed and made available online on-demand.

In continental Europe, sf theatre tends to have a more avant-garde aesthetic. For example, in Greece, Vasilis Ziogas's *Medea* (1995) incorporates 'metahumans' in an innovative adaptation of the classical myth blending elements of Greek philosophy, Christian symbolism, astronomy and metaphysics. Andriana Domouzi makes a case for the play's science fictionality, arguing that the metahumans – along with three goddesses, Brimo, Lilith and Hecate – substitute for the typical Euripidean characters, and that all the characters are placed in a 'state of theosis, deification' (n.p.). An even more daring element of this adaptation is the fate of Medea and her sons; rather than being murdered by her, they return to her womb in embryonic states and, pregnant with them once more, she commits suicide. Given that the play consists of metahumans, experiments with time and space, and surreal and grotesque imagery, it comes close to being an example of cosmic horror. *Blood Enemies* (2007) and *Biological Immigrant* (2011), two arguably sf plays by the enigmatic Greek cartoonist known only by his penname Arkas, feature personifications of body organs. He uses an organ transplant analogy to explore the refugee crisis, and address a number of socio-political issues, particularly reflecting on the rise of the neo-Nazi Golden Dawn party. In *Blood Enemies*, for example, the anthropomorphised organ-characters, the Small Intestine and the Colon, find themselves in a 'dystopian' host, a System that is against them, and discuss a coup by other organs against the Brain. Christina Dokou, writing about the play's 'no exit motif', how the playwright traps 'a few individuals inside a closed space' to create drama, notes the novelty of that space being the bodily interior of an alcoholic who has just barely survived a car accident (73). Contemporary Greek theatre has been increasingly genre-friendly, and translated versions of other twenty-first century plays mentioned previously have been staged there as well (Callow).

Elsewhere, in Japan, Oriza Hirata's Seinendan Theater Company has been staging robot theatre shows involving robot and android actors alongside humans, for many years. *I, Worker* (2008) and *Sayonara* (2010) are set in a future where co-existence with robots and androids is common, and existential and philosophical issues around the differences between humans and machines are explored via live performance. In *I, Worker*, the robots are gendered and the male robot is depressed and cannot work, unable to fulfil its primary function and thus the purpose for which it exists. Another noteworthy East Asian example is the Lotus Lee Drama Studio's 2016 adaptation of Liu Cixin's Hugo Award-winning *The Three-Body Problem* (2008), exploring alien first contact during the Cultural Revolution, which premiered in Shanghai and featured 3D mapping, drones, virtual reality and other cutting-edge technology.

Afrofuturist theatre and performance

Afrofuturist performance is often related to sf theatre. A notable practitioner is Andrea Hairston. Theatremaker and professor of theatre, she runs her own company, Chrysalis Theatre, and is a director, actor and musician, as well as a novelist, short-story writer and translator. She describes herself as 'an Afro-Futurist in league with Indigenous-Futurists' adding 'I want to bring the wisdom of recovered ancestors into conversation with the future' ('Novels' n.p.). Her *Lonely*

Stardust, which premiered in 1997, is a key work of Afrofuturist theatre. A diverse and complex play, it features an alien character called Traveler who visits Earth in search of 'impossibility specialists', a term she uses elsewhere to refer to the people 'who improvise a way out of no way' ('What' n.p.). Traveler manages to communicate with different people, to learn their struggles and dreams in an attempt to become more human. More recent plays with Afrofuturist elements include Rachael Young's *Nightclubbing* (2018), Keisha Thompson's *Man on the Moon* (2018), Nuna Livhaber's *I Will Tell You In a Minute* (2019), Inua Ellams's *The Half-God of Rainfall* (2019) and Matilda Ibin's *The Grape That Rolled Under the Fridge* (2019). These shows explore identity in ways that are optimal for live performance; in some cases the main performer and the writer are the same person. Livhaber's play features a successful Black woman who travels back in time from 2039 to inform her younger self that the future is better, that racism and all kinds of bigotry have ceased to exist. Ibini's play is set in a future where the government monitors activities via each citizen's shadow, which contains their entire history; it concerns Seth, whose shadow has been stolen and must be retrieved for her secrets to be protected. A *Guardian* article quotes Thompson as saying

> afrofuturism uses the black experience to create work that is otherworldly, cosmic and surreal. For me, it's about creative freedom. Using political pain and channelling it. Taking the experience of being 'othered' and subverting it into something otherworldly. It's about using the knowledge of our ancestors to battle the erasure that we experience on a daily basis.
>
> (Minamore n.p.)

Conclusion

Sf in theatre has often been approached from other, often distinct but related critical perspectives, including utopian theatre (Sian Adiseshiah), cyborg theatre (Parker-Starbuck) and posthuman theatre (LePage), which tend to be interdisciplinary. Louise LePage's research on posthuman theatre includes studying prose sf as well as producing a website dedicated to exploring the potential of robotic characters in theatre and detailing relevant performances (www.robottheatre.co.uk). In the past decade, there has been a series of articles by theatre critics who have started to embrace the term 'sf' and discuss the genre more enthusiastically. For example, Allison Considine, writing in *American Theatre*, suggests that the prime directive of artists who create sf theatre 'is to stage stories that transcend time and space and venture to other worlds' and to bring 'supernatural and seemingly impossible narratives to the stage' (n.p.). The same magazine also published Mac Rogers inspirational piece 'How to Write Sci-Fi for the Stage, in 7 Easy Steps', the last two of which are 'Don't apologize that it's sci-fi' and 'Don't apologize that it's a play'.

There is no current sense of an established movement or shared tradition, with new theatre artists independently and organically introducing sf themes in their work. However, given the commercial success of big budget sf musicals, it could be argued that sf theatre is (if hitherto unacknowledged) a mainstream genre and thus might begin to sound less like a niche proposition. It seems likely then, that in the coming decades, theatremakers who grew up consuming geek culture will continue to seek and, where it is lacking, create sf for the stage. There have been many recent attempts to produce expensive adaptations of already popular sf and anime on stage, but rather than just replicating the genre on stage it is more interesting to consider what new approaches to sf theatre can offer to theatremakers, audiences, critics and readers.

Works cited

@TalosFest. 'Theatre Shows in August / September 2021 that have Elements of Science Fiction, Dystopian Fic Or Horror! Mainly in the UK (in-venue and online.) With a Couple of Exceptions (e.g. sf workshops.) When in-Venue, I Note the City; Otherwise Write 'Online'. A Thread: 1/13'. *Twitter* (8 August 2021), 12:17p.m. https://twitter.com/TalosFest/status/1424328996372852748

Adiseshiah, Sian. *Utopian Drama: In Search of a Genre*. Bloomsbury, 2022.

Callow, Jr, Christos. 'G(r)eek Theatre: Reflections on Cyborphic & Greek Science Fiction Theatre'. *Vector* (20 June 2022). https://vector-bsfa.com/2022/06/20/greek-theatre-reflections-on-cyborphic-greek-science-fiction-theatre/

Considine, Allison. 'Sci-Fi Theatres Imagine Other Worlds, Often Better Ones'. *American Theatre* (19 November 2015). www.americantheatre.org/2015/11/19/sci-fi-theatres-imagine-other-worlds-often-better-ones/

Dokou, Christina. 'Review of Arkas' Echthroi Ex Aematos'. *World Literature Today* 82.3 (May–June 2008): 73.

Domouzi, Andriana. 'The Metahuman in Modern Greek Theatre: Science Fiction Motifs in Medea by Vasilis Ziogas'. *Performing Greece II: 2nd Annual International Conference on Contemporary Greek Theatre*. Birkbeck College, 3 December 2016.

Fisher, Mark. 'Is that a sci-fi play I spy?' *Herald Scotland* (19 June 1998). www.heraldscotland.com/sport/spl/aberdeen/is-that-a-sci-fi-play-i-spy-1.339293

Hairston, Andrea. 'Novels'. https://andreahairston.com/novels/

——. 'What Art Does: "When the World Wounds" by Kiini Ibura Salaam'. *Los Angeles Review of Books* (25 March 2017). https://lareviewofbooks.org/article/what-art-does-when-the-world-wounds-by-kiini-ibura-salaam/

Johnston, Derek. 'Experimental Moments: *R.U.R.* and the Birth of British Television Science Fiction'. *Science Fiction Film and Television* 2.2 (2009): 251–68.

Lehmann, Hans-Thies. *Postdramatic Theatre*. Trans. Karen Jürs-Munby. Routledge, 2006.

LePage, Louise. *Robot Theatre*. www.robottheatre.co.uk/

McDevitt, Niall. 'Warp Review'. *International Times* (6 November 2014). http://internationaltimes.it/warp-review/

McGrath, Martin. 'Ayckbourn's Artificial People'. *Foundation: The International Review of Science Fiction* 128 (2017): 60–72.

Minamore, Bridget. 'Black to the Future: Afrofuturism Hits the Stage'. *The Guardian* (4 March 2018). www.theguardian.com/stage/2018/may/04/rachael-young-interview-nighclubbing-grace-jones-afrofuturism

Parker-Starbuck, Jennifer. *Cyborg Theatre: Corporeal/Technologica Intersections in Multimedia Performance*. Palgrave Macmillan, 2011.

Rogers, Mac. 'How to Write Sci-Fi for the Stage, in 7 Easy Steps'. *American Theatre* (5 October 2015). www.americantheatre.org/2015/10/05/how-to-write-sci-fi-for-the-stage-in-7-easy-steps/

Suvin, Darko. *Metamorphoses of Science Fiction: On the Poetics and History of a Literary Genre*. Yale UP, 1979.

Willingham, Ralph. *Science Fiction and the Theatre*. Greenwood, 1994.

19
RADIO AND PODCASTS

Karen Hellekson

Today, when radio can be listened to in a car, streamed via satellite or app from anywhere in the world, or played via smartphone or computer, it is hard to remember how transformative the technology was: radio is, after all, instantaneous, real-time voice broadcasting, and in the 1920s, this was thrilling. Early must-listen radio shows had listeners gathering around the radio at the appointed hour. As technology improved and prices dropped, radio receivers appeared in homes, then cars. During the golden age of radio from the 1930s to the mid-1950s, comedy, dramas, educational content, public affairs, quiz shows, religion, soap operas, sports, thrillers – all sorts of radio show content appeared, most of it performed live on air (Hilmes vii–viii). Radio's hallmarks are liveness and therefore time-boundedness, and, as radio entered private spaces like houses and cars, intimacy (Hand). As radio became ubiquitous, distracted listening became common; listeners might catch the latest instalment of a soap opera while ironing, or commuters might listen to music while driving to work (Russo). Radio's golden age revealed the power of mass media, with the technology reaching vast swaths of the population (Sterling; Crisell *Understanding*). Radio permitted nation building by creating a sense of shared community and identity, with the British Broadcasting Company (BBC) in particular serving such a purpose through its remit to educate and inform as well as entertain (Briggs; Crisell *Introductory*, *Understanding*; Noone). Radio also created listener groups, like fans of a particular actor, show, writer or genre.

From the 1930s onwards, interest in radio fell as audio-visual media, like film and television, came to prominence. However, since the early 2000s, the widespread introduction of podcasts – music or talk files made available for internet download – has resulted in a surge of new sound-based artworks. With content as varied as radio, podcasts differ in being time shifted rather than occurring in real time. Podcasts do all the things that radio does – inform, educate and entertain; generate intimacy by penetrating private space; build community and identity – but on the listeners' schedules.

As technologies developed, so did the networks creating and distributing content. Some of today's media empires began as radio companies that expanded into television, perhaps film and now podcasts, with content or properties reiterated across the company's portfolio and accessible via websites or apps. Sf and fantastic texts have long been part of radio, with dramatic readings as well as full-cast audio dramas with music and sound effects. Early radio presented long-form

DOI: 10.4324/9781003140269-21

series as well as short half-hour or hour-long stories, often adaptations, and acted synergistically with other media, notably print and comics.

Podcasts work against the over-professionalisation of commercial radio and, being cheap to record and disseminate, are more democratic. Audioblogs, as they were known before the 2004 coining of 'podcast' (referring to Apple's iPod), were shared by niche early adopters (Hammersley; Berry). Technological advances – RSS feeds in 2000 and iTunes' integration of podcasts in 2015, which mainstreamed them – a made it easy to find, subscribe to and obtain content (Bottomley). Scripted fictional content returned to the contemporary audio drama scene with faux community radio show *Welcome to Night Vale* (2012–), which remains popular, especially with fans of the fantastic. Then true crime podcast *Serial* (2014–22) took the world by storm. Its story of a perhaps wrongly convicted murderer led to national-level interest, reanalysis of the case by intrepid fans, and a stunning 300,000 downloads of season one (Blair). A new audience discovered audio, leading to new demands for content – and to creators deciding to make podcasts of their own (McFarland).

The resulting surge in popularity has led some to advocate that podcasts are a new, relevant way to bring audio back, particularly full-cast audio dramas (McMurtry; Hancock and McMurtry). As one sf writer notes, 'With a script, a decent microphone, actors, and some practice with sound design software, a relative novice can make a riveting, high-quality production' (Puranen). As podcasting matured, it created podcast networks, which release content by multiple makers under a single umbrella, thus providing 'opportunities for exposure, branding, and cross-pollination they could never get if they went it alone' (Caldwell). Podcasting might be the answer to Bertolt Brecht's wish that radio

> be transformed from a distribution apparatus into a communications apparatus. The radio could be the finest possible communications apparatus in public life, a vast system of channels. That is, it could be so, if it understood how to receive as well as to transmit, how to let the listener speak as well as hear, how to bring him into a network instead of isolating him.
>
> (42)

Audio fictional content, whether broadcast or downloaded, generally takes one of two forms. In the first, a written story is simply read aloud, as excitingly as possible, with the voice actor perhaps doing character voices and accents, bringing the text to life via a single performance; occasionally, as in 'enhanced' audiobooks, sound effects and/or music may be added, or even another voice or two, but these performances tend to be spare. In the second, the full-cast audio drama offers full immersion in a storyworld, with voice actors performing characters; sound effects and music imply action, set the scene, direct the listener and provide other information to supplement the dialogue. Elements of sound work together to construct an artwork that listeners interpret using aural cues (Lea; Kingson and Cowgill).

Radio, sound and narrative

Despite dating from the 1920s, radio remains an understudied medium, mostly because popular and critical audiences have privileged media with visual elements. This ocularcentric bias means that sound has mostly been studied in relation to visuals, with media theory focusing on sound's relationship to images rather than on sound, its formal techniques and their impact on or creation of narrative (Hassapopoulou). Early work, some by network producers, laid out tricks of the trade of writing for audio, be it an advertisement or a radio play, including (shockingly sexist) tips on casting for voice contrast and using a 'show, don't tell' approach to providing context and background (Lea; Sieveking; Arnheim). More recent industry and pedagogical guides reflect current technological standards in voice recording and releasing the final product online (Hand and Traynor; Barnard; Collins). These texts lay out modes of sonic expression conventionally used to do things like set a scene's location and ambience, indicate a time shift or simultaneity, or alter focalisation (Bluijs).

Radio uses a variety of expressive techniques, including 'speech, music, sounds and silence which are framed by time, so the experience is ephemeral' (Crook 64). An individual's listening experience is simultaneously shared with an audience, thereby paradoxically conflating individual with community. Other sound-specific dramatic codes that critics have proposed include sound effects (Sieveking) as well as 'noise, fading, cutting, mixing, the (stereophonic) positioning of the signals, electro-acoustic manipulation' and 'original sound (actuality)' (Huwiler 102). These become particularly effective when telling stories. In full-cast audio dramas in particular, formal story elements combine with sound effects, music and the listener's sensorium to generate an ephemeral, time-bound artwork. Directionality combines with sound effects to result in verisimilitude so convincing that listeners often refer to a sense other than sound to express it, saying, 'I could feel it' or 'I could see it'. Some podcasts specifically play with directionality; for example, *Orphan Black: The Next Chapter* (2021–), a podcast sequel to the television show, begins each episode with the words: 'This podcast is a 3-D audio production, so watch out, as sounds may seem to come from beside you or behind you. For the best listening experience, please use headphones'. This body-inflected mode of hearing, which implicates the listener in making meaning and which draws on a phenomenology of perception, has replaced early theoretical notions of audio drama as a 'blind' medium that cast it as working around something presented as a lack (Crisell *Understanding*, 'Better'; Crook; Arnheim; Fryer et al.). As one radio pioneer said in 1934 of the quickness of radio's development, 'It is hard to believe it is only ten years. For the technical advance of "the blind art" during that time has been such as the historian is accustomed to allow several centuries for' (Sieveking 7).

Audio sf utilises auditory codes to fulfil sf's tropes. We can be in a spaceship's huge, empty cargo hold or claustrophobically stuffed in a spacesuit. Voices are altered to sound thrillingly alien. Music cues us emotionally, telling us how to feel. We learn to associate certain sound effects with specific events, like a shimmering sound indicating teleportation. As we listen along, we imaginatively build a storyworld, cued by what we hear. Because sound so strongly evokes the physical world, particularly our intimate, vestibular bodily understanding of space and directionality, it is particularly effective in enabling us to imagine the physical reality of an alien environment. Consequently, audio can seem bigger than film or television, with a soundscape suggesting huge crowds, alien beings, or exotic locales – the kinds of things that are difficult to stage visually, even with CGI. Audio sf cues us to mentally create a fantastical storyworld that cannot be practically rendered, and it does so in a way that feels somatically real.

In the sf examples I mention below, sonic aspects (speech, music, sound, silence) are of course present. In early radio, practical sound effects were performed live. Music might be live; phonograph recordings might be utilised for music or sound effects, particularly those difficult to produce in the moment, like crowd sounds. Stereophonic sound, invented in 1931, was in use by the 1950s, and 'by the late 1960s, […] dominated sound reproduction, and album covers no longer needed to indicate "stereo" or "360 Sound." Consumers simply assumed that they were buying a stereo record' (Borgerson and Schroeder). Today, professional audio setups use individual booths for each voice actor and high-end recording equipment, although as a result of the Covid-19 pandemic, audio dramas began being recorded remotely, with voice actors creating impromptu in-house recording studios. Special effects and music are added in postproduction.

Sf radio in the United States

Early radio starting in the 1930s, now known as old time radio (OTR), has become its own genre. Much OTR is now in the public domain, with downloadable episodes freely available at the Internet Archive and elsewhere, with poor-quality originals sometimes remastered by fans. In early radio, performances were often not recorded, even after recording technology came into wide use, so many primary texts are likely lost forever. Early sf radio shows tended to be serial dramas or anthology shows. Many stories came from other media first, such as comic strips, stories, books or stage plays, and sometimes different forms of media worked together to create what would now call a franchise.

Boys' adventure radio show *Buck Rogers in the 25th Century* (1932–6, 1939, 1940, 1946–7), which was based on novels and comics and aired four times a week, was the first sf serial, followed by *Flash Gordon* (1935–6). Both featured dashing heroes and glamorous science. However, no radio broadcast is as famous as Orson Welles's *War of the Worlds,* based on H.G. Wells's 1898 novel. The hour-long radio play, aired as CBS's *Mercury Theater on the Air*'s Halloween special on 30 October 1938, retains Wells's verisimilitude-creating, site-specific references but relocates the Martian invasion from England to New Jersey. Told in the form of urgent news bulletins interrupting a musical programme, with on-site interviews, first-person accounts and panicked reporters, the radio play channels the energy of the riveting coverage of the previous year's *Hindenburg* disaster. Although the broadcast was preceded by a disclaimer, such were the passion of the performance and the accuracy implied by real place-names that people who tuned in late thought Martians were actually invading New Jersey, causing a real panic (Cantril). The broadcast did not have huge market share, so doubt has been cast on whether the panic was particularly widespread, but it continues to be cited as an example of something that 'offers a self-reflexive meditation on the meanings we make of new media. The broadcast excavates cultural anxieties about new media that have reemerged in the digital era' (Hayes et al. 217).

The 1940s included a few surviving notable radio plays, including Lucille Fletcher's 'The Hitch-Hiker' (1941), a supernatural thriller performed several times by Welles, remade as a 1960 episode of the *The Twilight Zone* (CBS 1959–64) and remade again as part of the BBC's radio adaptation of the series (2002–12). *The Mysterious Traveler*, an anthology programme that included sf, supernatural, fantasy, crime, suspense and mystery, aired on Mutual from 1943 to 1962; its opening credits promised 'another journey into the strange and terrifying'. It was a multimedia franchise, with a magazine and comics books, but only 75 of its 370 episodes survive.

The 1950s included anthology series like NBC's related shows *Dimension X* (1950–1) and *X Minus One* (1955–7), which adapted stories by established sf writers, often from *Astounding* and *Galaxy*; as *X Minus One*'s bombastic opening-credit speech notes

> Countdown for blast-off. X minus five, four, three, two . . . X minus one. Fire! [Dramatic blast-off sound effect.] From the far horizons of the unknown come transcribed tales of new dimensions in time and space. These are stories of the future – adventures in which you'll live in a million could-be years on a thousand maybe worlds. The National Broadcasting Company, in cooperation with Street and Smith, publishers of *Astounding Science Fiction,* presents *X! Minus! One!*

Another anthology series, *Exploring Tomorrow* (1957–8), was hosted by *Astounding*'s editor, John W. Campbell Jr. 'Ticket to the Moon' (1956), an episode of NBC's *Biography in Sound* (1954–8), includes remarks about sf by, among others, Campbell, Isaac Asimov and Ray Bradbury. In 1952, ABC broadcast *Tom Corbett, Space Cadet,* a twice-weekly spin-off of the thrice-weekly television series (CBS/ABC/NBC/Du Mont 1950–5) of the same name, featuring the same actors; *Tom Corbett* was another franchise juggernaut, with books, comic strips, comic books, toys and memorabilia.

The golden age of radio was over by 1960. Networks pivoted to television while broadening their radio offerings over multiple channels as FM gained ground, surging past AM by 1970 (Skretvedt and Sterling). In that year, National Public Radio (NPR) was created to link non-commercial stations, focusing on art and culture, with member stations producing content that NPR distributed.

Mindwebs (1976–84), an anthology series produced by Wisconsin's WHA Radio, comprised staged readings by Michael Hasen of short stories by important contemporary sf genre writers, including Bradbury and Joanna Russ. This sort of hybrid dramatic reading/audio drama (perhaps with sound effects or music), which exists today most notably in the podcast *LeVar Burton Reads* (2017–), performs an important service by making contemporary sf work available to a wider audience.

In 1981, more than 20 years after radio's golden age, NPR aired an audio drama version of *Star Wars* (Lucas 1977), a move perceived as selling out by those who thought NPR too highbrow to embrace a popular franchise. Creator George Lucas, a fan of NPR, sold the rights for $1, Mark Hamill and Anthony Daniels reprised their roles as Luke Skywalker and C-3PO, and the producers were permitted to use music and sound effects from the film. Released as part of anthology series *NPR Playhouse,* it was a hit, with 50,000 phone calls and letters in a week and a jump in audience numbers (John). It put audio back on the map as a mode of cultural engagement. *The Empire Strikes Back* (Kershner 1980) and *Return of the Jedi* (Marquand 1983) adaptations were broadcast in, respectively, 1983 and 1996. Fans especially appreciated inclusion of scenes that did not appear in the films, making the audios a kind of fill-in-the-gap fan fiction with the imprimatur of canonicity. The CD boxsets of all three series are collectibles today, and the STAR WARS franchise continued to release audio-only content, both full-cast audio dramas and dramatised readings, until about 1998 (Petschk).

Sci-Fi Radio (1989–90) aired 26 half-hour or hour-long full-cast audio dramas, adapting stories by such contemporary authors as Ursula K. Le Guin and Philip K. Dick, as well as now-classic works from the 1950s by Tom Godwin and C.L. Moore. *2000X: Tales of the Next Millennia* (2000), an anthology focusing on the theme of the turn of a millennium, was hosted by sf writer Harlan Ellison and included the work of a wide variety of writers, including Octavia E. Butler, Karel Čapek and Jules Verne; famous Hollywood actors participated, such as Robin Williams, who starred in a dramatisation of Ellison's '"Repent, Harlequin!" Said the Ticktockman' (1965).

Sf radio in the United Kingdom

The radio scene in the UK did not follow the competing-network setup adopted by the US. Instead, radio was established in 1922 as a nation-wide public service broadcaster, the BBC, with Britons paying licence fees for their physical equipment to fund programming and infrastructure (Bathgate; Briggs). With its now-famous mandate to 'inform, educate and entertain', the BBC remained a non-commercial monopoly until 1973. It had a reputation, which it retains to an extent, of airing mostly highbrow content, with early radio skewing more to Shakespeare than contemporary literature. Despite moving into other media, including television, film and podcasts, BBC radio never stopped broadcasting audio dramas. BBC Radio 4, an FM station set up in 1967, in particular airs spoken-word content, including drama (most famously *The Archers,* a soap opera that began in 1951 and has now run for over 20,000 episodes). In 1955–6, the BBC dramatised J.R.R. Tolkien's *The Lord of the Rings* (1954–5) in 12 mono episodes; it was not recorded, but the scripts have recently been rediscovered (Tantimedh). In 1968, Radio 4 broadcast Tolkien's *The Hobbit* (1937) in eight mono episodes; in 1981, Radio 4 broadcast its celebrated full-cast version of *The Lord of the Rings* in 26 stereo episodes, starring Ian Holm, Michael Hordern and John Le Mesurier. Like the US audio version of *Star Wars*, which was also broadcast on BBC radio, it was released during a period of relative dearth of good audio dramas that featured stereo, music, sound effects and talented voice actors.

In 1973, Radio 4 broadcast an eight-hour stereo dramatisation of Isaac Asimov's FOUNDATION trilogy (1942–50). As Greg Bear notes, the trilogy 'came free to subscribers [of the Science Fiction Book Club] and introduced a great many readers to science fiction. In time, it was judged the greatest SF trilogy of the age' (Armstrong), suggesting why it was chosen for adaptation. Two humorous full-cast Radio 4 audio dramas that lampoon sf texts and tropes are Douglas Adams's *The Hitchhiker's Guide to the Galaxy* (1978), which later became three albums, plays, a television series, a book series and a film; and Graham Duff's *Nebulous* (2017), a post-apocalyptic workplace comedy starring Mark Gatiss as the titular mad-genius hero and David Warner as his evil archnemesis.

Radio 4 produced the syndicated audio version of TV's classic *Twilight Zone* mentioned above; hosted, in a nod to OTR, by Stacy Keach, son of the famous radio actor of the same name, it featured a host of famous performers, including Lou Diamond Phillips and Mariette Hartley. The BBC has also broadcast audio versions of the work of many popular writers, including a 2009 adaptation of Iain M. Banks's *The State of the Art* (1991), starring Antony Sher; a 2013 version of Neil Gaiman's *Neverwhere* (1996), with an all-star cast including Benedict Cumberbatch, Christopher Lee and Natalie Dormer; a 2009 two-hour dramatisation of Arthur C. Clarke's *Rendezvous with Rama* (1973); and a 2003 full-cast version of Philip Pullman's HIS DARK MATERIALS trilogy (1995–2000). A second audio version of Pullman's young adult fantasy trilogy blends audio storytelling, with Pullman reading the unabridged text, and full-cast audio drama, with actors voicing the characters. This 35-hour audiobook, published by Random House, proved to be the perfect medium for bringing Pullman's storyworld to life.

Several independent outfits are known for their genre audio drama offerings. Big Finish releases both full-cast audio dramas and enhanced audiobooks, including properties in the public domain, such as a 2017 audio drama of H.G. Wells's *The Invisible Man* (1897), starring John Hurt. Since 1999, they have been licensed to produce DOCTOR WHO audio dramas, creating new stories for the classic Doctors, with still-living actors reprising their roles. Big Finish has since added other BBC properties/series, including *Survivors* (1975–77), *Blake's 7* (1978–81) and *Torchwood* (2006–11), and has gained licences for some of the post-2005 DOCTOR WHO actors and companions. Before Big Finish, BBV/Magic Bullet were known for DOCTOR WHO–adjacent content, including *The Time Travellers* (1998–2000), an audio series that cannot legally be called *Doctor Who* but stars Sylvester McCoy and Sophie Aldred, who played the Seventh Doctor and his companion, Ace, as the Professor and Alice.

This chapter has focused mostly on English-language works in the US and UK because they had the earliest national-level uptake of radio as a technology and between them had most radio firsts. In other countries, genre highlights include the 1932 Australian version of Mary Shelley's *Frankenstein* (1818), starring George Edwards, a superstar of his era who could seamlessly transition between multiple characters and voices on the fly, live on air; and in Canada, CBC's *Nightfall* (1980–3) and *Vanishing Point* (1984–91), which both adapted published works for audio, with the same tone as *Twilight Zone.*

Sf podcasts

Despite the relatively short history of podcasts, there are a great number devoted to sf – not just fiction but also state-of-the-field podcasts, review podcasts, interviews and the like. *Wolf 359* (2014–7), which began as a comic series of communication logs with one narrator and evolved into a full-cast audio drama addressing ontological concerns, deliberately styles itself as in the tradition of the golden age of radio shows. *Limetown* (2015–8) is presented by an NPR-esque podcaster piecing together the inexplicable disappearance ten years ago of hundreds of people from a small Tennessee town. Blending sf and horror as the familiar podcast genre slowly turns fantastical, it also spawned a book and television show. Mac Rogers's *The Message* (2015) and *LifeAfter* (2016), produced by GE Podcast Theater, are respectively about first contact and computer-generated versions of deceased loved ones. Each season of *Within the Wires* (2016–), from the makers of *Welcome to Night Vale,* is presented as found footage, including relaxation tapes and self-help seminars, from an alternate universe and requires listeners to piece together clues to help build the narrative storyworld.

These podcasts foreground the audio nature of the text by treating much of the sound we hear as diegetic, featuring found footage and protagonists (and us, the listeners) trying to make meaning of it – the result of podcasters recording ad hoc with a single-microphone setup (Strom). Notable genre podcasts that do not take this approach but instead are full-on audio dramas, with a full cast, music and sound effects, include Rogers's *Steal the Stars* (2017–8), a 'sci-fi noir heist love story' (Zutter), and *The Leviathan Chronicles* (2008–), in the tradition of lost-world sf pulp stories. *The Cipher* (2021–2), a BBC young adult podcast, features an 'imaginative' soundscape (Beaumont) by John Dryden, who is known for his worldbuilding; his other sf audio dramas include a 1997 version of Robert Harris's alternate history *Fatherland* (1992) and a 2000 version of Margaret Atwood's *The Handmaid's Tale* (1985), recorded on location in the US with an American cast and told in the style of a documentary.

Well-regarded sf anthology podcasts, with someone reading stories, include releases from *Clarkesworld Magazine* and *Asimov's Science Fiction*, as well as relevant titles chosen for *LeVar Burton Reads*. Mac Rogers's *Steal the Stars* (2017) was used to seed a new podcast, *Stories from Among the Stars,* by Macmillan Podcasts (2017–). Each season airs a different book, including Liu Cixin's *The Three-Body Problem* (2006) and Arkady Martine's *A Memory Called Empire* (2019), although the podcasts are removed after a time, so only the most recent is available.

Finally, there are a number of paratexts released by franchise owners or showrunners, done as a sort of fan service, or to lure new viewers by dangling fun texts in a different medium. For example, Ronald D. Moore, who produced the *Battlestar Galactica* reboot (2004–9), recorded a podcast about each episode, which included extensive details that provide a window into the production process, and released them as the show aired, thereby providing fans with fun, valuable extra information. The BBC released the podcast *Doctor Who: Redacted* (2022) on BBC Sounds. An audio drama, starring transgender activist Charlie Craggs, about three podcasters making a paranormal conspiracy show entitled *The Blue Box Files,* it is described by the producer as '"very gay, very trans," and sitting "to the left" of the main show' (Hogan). It includes cameos by DOCTOR WHO actors, including Jodi Whittaker as the Doctor, and casts the old franchise in a new light. Three *Welcome to Night Vale* stars do episode breakdowns in an official recap podcast, *Good Morning Night Vale* (2018), showing that a podcast can expand its own franchise by making a podcast. Fan productions have also broken into audio, with podficcing – recording fan-written texts for audio – increasing in popularity (Fanlore Wiki; Riley). Fans also create full-cast audio dramas. STAR TREK fandom in particular has produced in-world audio dramas, including *Outpost* (2009–).

The Mark Time Awards were established in 1996 to recognise achievements in audio sf; since 1999 and 2007 respectively, the Audie and Scribe awards have had specific categories for sf. Audio sf productions have also won BBC Audio Drama Awards (founded 2012), Audio Verse Awards (founded 2013) and Audio Theatre Central (ATC) Seneca Awards (founded 2017).

Conclusion

All paratexts reify the original text by centring it even as they add to its corpus, expanding the text's storyworld in practical, fictive, analytic or anecdotal ways. Audio dramas have long relied on adapting existing works, making the audio drama itself a paratext, but as Gérard Genette remarks,

> the paratext is for us the means by which a text makes a book of itself and proposes itself as such to its readers, and more generally to the public. Rather than with a limit or a sealed frontier, we are dealing in this case with a threshold [...] which offers to anyone and everyone the possibility either of entering or of turning back.
>
> (261)

If at first the audio drama gestures to something else – Asimov's FOUNDATION series, for example – then later it may offer itself as a mode of, in Genette's terms, transition/transaction: the audio drama as an art form becomes the threshold of entry for other texts, to begin weaving paratexts anew. After all, some people undoubtedly came to Asimov novels by way of the audio version. With radio's long history of adaptation and remix, it is no surprise that people accept Genette's offer.

Audio proposes itself as such to the public by presenting, of course, the thing that makes it unique: sound. It implicates us by using our sensorium; its aural, submersive nature tricks us into thinking it is right there – something bigger than television, something that CGI could never get right, but here, in the space of a unique sensorium, absolutely real and believable. We can believe we are in another world.

Works cited

Armstrong, Neil. 'Foundation: The "Unfilmable" Sci-Fi Epic Now on Our Screens'. *BBC* (20 September 2021). www.bbc.com/culture/article/20210920-foundation-the-unfilmable-sci-fi-epic-now-on-our-screens

Arnheim, Rudolf. *Radio*. Trans. Margaret Ludwig and Herbert Read. Faber & Faber, 1936.

Audio Drama Wiki. 'John Dryden'. Audio Drama Wiki. https://audiodrama.fandom.com/wiki/John_Dryden

Barnard, Stephen. *Studying Radio*. Arnold, 2000.

Bathgate, Gordon. *Radio Broadcasting: A History of the Airwaves*. Pen & Sword History, 2021.

Beaumont, Mark. '"The Witcher" Star Anya Chalotra on Cryptic New Podcast Thriller "The Cipher"'. *NME* (3 February 2021). www.nme.com/features/tv-interviews/the-cipher-anya-chalotra-interview-2871650

Berry, Richard. 'Will the iPod Kill the Radio Star? Profiling Podcasting as Radio'. *Convergence* 12.2 (2006): 143–62.

Blair, Elizabeth. 'How the Investigation of Adnan Syed Became a Podcast Phenomenon'. *NPR* (21 September 2022). www.npr.org/2022/09/20/1124141699/serial-adnan-syed

Bluijs, Siebe. 'Earwitnessing: Focalization in Radio Drama'. *Audionarratology: Lessons from Radio Drama*. Ohio State UP, 2021. 82–100.

Borgerson, Janet and Jonathan Schroeder. 'How Stereo Was First Sold to a Skeptical Public'. *Conversation* (12 December 2018). http://theconversation.com/how-stereo-was-first-sold-to-a-skeptical-public-103668

Bottomley, Andrew J. 'Podcasting: A Decade in the Life of a "New" Audio Medium: Introduction'. *Journal of Radio and Audio Media* 22.2 (2015): 164–9.

Briggs, Asa. *The History of Broadcasting in the United Kingdom*. Oxford UP, 1965.

Caldwell, Patrick. 'Podspotting: Where to Start with the Podcast Networks'. *Daily Dot* (26 November 2012). www.dailydot.com/upstream/podspotting-podcast-networks-guide/

Cantril, Hadley. *Invasion from Mars: A Study in the Psychology of Panic*. Princeton UP, 1940.

Cazeaux, Clive. 'Phenomenology and Radio Drama'. *The British Journal of Aesthetics* 45.2 (2005): 157–74.

Collins, Karen. *Studying Sound: A Theory and Practice of Sound Design*. MIT Press, 2020.

Crisell, Andrew. 'Better than Magritte: How Drama on the Radio Became Radio Drama'. *Journal of Radio Studies* 7.2 (2000): 464–73.

——. *An Introductory History of British Broadcasting*, second edition. Routledge, 2005.

——. *Understanding Radio*. Routledge, 1986.

Crook, Tim. *Radio Drama: Theory and Practice*. Routledge, 1999.

Fanlore Wiki. 'Podfic'. *Fanlore* (3 October 2023).

Fryer, Louise, Linda Pring and Jonathan Freeman. 'Audio Drama and the Imagination: The Influence of Sound Effects on Presence in People With and Without Sight'. *Journal of Media Psychology* 25.2 (2013): 65–71.

Genette, Gérard. 'Introduction to the Paratext'. Trans. Marie Maclean. *New Literary History* 22.2 (1991): 261–72.

Hammersley, Ben. 'Audible Revolution'. *The Guardian* (11 February 2004). www.theguardian.com/media/2004/feb/12/broadcasting.digitalmedia

Hancock, Danielle and Leslie McMurtry. '"I Know What a Podcast Is": Post-*Serial* Fiction and Podcast Media Identity'. *Podcasting: New Aural Cultures and Digital Media*. Ed. Dario Llinares, Neil Fox and Richard Berry. Palgrave Macmillan, 2018. 81–105.

Hand, Richard J. 'The Darkest Nightmares Imaginable: Gothic Audio Drama from Radio to the Internet'. *A Companion to American Gothic*. Ed. Charles L. Crow. Wiley-Blackwell, 2014. 463–74.

Hand, Richard J. and Mary Traynor. *The Radio Drama Handbook: Audio Drama in Practice and Context*. Continuum, 2011.

Hassapopoulou, Marina. *Interactive Cinema: The Ambiguous Ethics of Media Participation*. U of Minnesota P, 2024.

Hayes, Joy Elizabeth, Kathleen Battles and Wendy Hilton-Morrow, eds. *'War of the Worlds' to Social Media: Mediated Communication in Times of Crisis*. Peter Lang, 2013.

Hilmes, Michele. *Only Connect: A Cultural History of Broadcasting in the United States*, fourth edition. Wadsworth/Cengage Learning, 2014.

Hogan, Michael. '"Very Gay, Very Trans": The Incredible Doctor Who Spin-off That's Breathing New Life into the Franchise'. *The Guardian* (29 April 2022). www.theguardian.com/tv-and-radio/2022/apr/29/doctor-who-redacted-transgender-podcast

Huwiler, Elke. 'A Narratology of Audio Art: Telling Stories by Sound'. *Audionarratology*. Ed. Jarmila Mildorf and Till Kinzel. De Gruyter, 2016. 99–116.

John, Derek. 'That Time NPR Turned "Star Wars" into a Radio Drama – and It Actually Worked'. *NPR* (18 December 2015). www.npr.org/2015/12/18/460269884/that-time-npr-turned-star-wars-into-a-radio-drama-and-it-actually-worked

Kingson, Walter K. and Rome Cowgill. *Radio Drama Acting and Production: A Handbook*. Rinehart, 1950.

Lea, Gordon. *Radio Drama and How to Write It*. Allen & Unwin, 1926.

McFarland, Kevin. 'Fiction Podcasts Are Trying Too Hard to Be Like *Serial*'. *Wired* (29 October 2015). www.wired.com, www.wired.com/2015/10/fictional-podcasts-serial/

McMurtry, Leslie Grace. '"I'm Not a Real Detective, I Only Play One on Radio": *Serial* as the Future of Audio Drama'. *Journal of Popular Culture* 49. 2 (2016): 306–24.

Noone, Louise. *Radio in the Digital Age: The Evolution of Radio Culture in a New Media Era*. University of Dublin, PhD dissertation, 2013. www.scss.tcd.ie/publications/theses/diss/2013/TCD-SCSS-DISSERTATION-2013-059.pdf

Petschk, Gerald. 'The Comprehensive Guide to Star Wars Audio Dramas'. *CultureSlate* (12 May 2023). www.cultureslate.com/explained/68x8m7iun6et5vf4g03zmhhtsa5jsh

Puranen, Emma Johanna. 'In Space, There's Actually Lots to Hear: Science Fiction Audio Drama'. *SFWA* (28 February 2023). www.sfwa.org/2023/02/28/in-space-theres-actually-lots-to-hear-science-fiction-audio-drama/

Riley, Olivia Johnston. 'Podfic: Queer Structures of Sound'. *Transformative Works and Cultures* 34 (2020): n.p.

Russo, Alexander. *Points on the Dial: Golden Age Radio beyond the Networks*. Duke UP, 2010.

Sieveking, Lance. *The Stuff of Radio*. Cassell, 1934.

Skretvedt, Randy and Christopher H. Sterling. 'Radio: Definition, History, and Facts'. *Encyclopedia Britannica* (18 August 2023). www.britannica.com/topic/radio

Sterling, Christopher H. 'The Golden Age of American Radio'. www.britannica.com/topic/radio/The-Golden-Age-of-American-radio

Strom, Steven. 'Why Tor Books' First Podcast Drama *Steal the Stars* Should Steal Your Attention'. *Ars Technica* (13 August 2017). https://arstechnica.com/gaming/2017/08/steal-the-stars-stakes-its-place-in-the-podcast-drama-resurgence/

Tantimedh, Adi. *'The Lord of the Rings*: J.R.R. Tolkien's Lost BBC Radio Drama Scripts Found'. *Bleeding Cool* (13 March 2022). https://bleedingcool.com/tv/the-lord-of-rings-j-r-r-tolkiens-lost-bbc-radio-drama-scripts-found/

20

COMICS FROM THE 1930S TO THE 1960S

Michael Goodrum

Periodisation is a notoriously difficult endeavour. With comics, as with sf itself, questions relating to definitions, beginnings, continuity and discontinuity can generate more discussion than the comics under consideration. For the purposes of this chapter, 'comics' will be treated as related to, but distinct from, newspaper comic strips; under discussion here are the booklet-style comics conventionally recognised as 'comics' by a modern reader. While that particular form pre-exists the creation of superheroes, it came to prominence nationally (within the US) and internationally with the publication of the first adventures of Superman in *Action Comics* #1 (June 1938). (Here is not the place to rehearse debates about whether certain earlier characters are superheroes.) Comics did not take shape in a vacuum, but emerged in dialogue with newspaper comic strips, pulp fiction, magazines such as *Amazing Stories* (1926–2005), films and the work of such authors as H.G. Wells, Jules Verne and Mary Shelley. The comics under consideration in this chapter also emerged in the context of particular social tumults and debates around the construction and place of race, gender and sexuality in American culture. It is not possible to consider all these elements in detail, but it is important to acknowledge them as mutually constitutive factors in the development of sf comics (and sf more generally).

Since Superman is so central to the beginnings of the comics form and the superhero genre, it is only fitting to begin with him. A significant debt to sf is obvious in his alien origins: he was dispatched as an infant to Earth by his parents in a rocket from the dying planet of Krypton. Created by Jerry Siegel and Joe Shuster, two poor, young, Jewish men, it is easy to read their creation of such a character as a response to the violence directed against Jewish communities in Germany at the time, and equally as arising from the challenges of the Great Depression. The utopian impulse of imagining a figure coming to build a better world, to act as a 'champion of the oppressed' in an embodiment of the more radical rhetoric of the New Deal, is evident in the work of these two young men. There is an 'intrinsic connection between utopian dreams and the dark conditions that inspire writers' (Edwards 72) that we must bear in mind throughout this chapter, and in the 1930s sf 'increasingly used its speculative mode to examine fascism' (92), resulting in a shift from utopian dreaming to dystopian nightmares. Superman, and indeed all superheroes, function as floating signifiers, with much of their meaning fashioned in reception, so it is all-but impossible to arrive at 'the meaning' of a particular character. What can be seen is that Superman

 DOI: 10.4324/9781003140269-22

did very good business, sparking a rush of competitors, including Batman, created in 1939 by Bob Kane and Bill Finger. When a mugger kills his wealthy parents in front of him, the young Bruce Wayne commits himself to dedicated physical and mental study and, being in possession of an inherited fortune, eventually transforms himself into Batman – a master scientist, detective and martial artist. Superman and Batman consciously represent different approaches to sf, so it is vital to remember that these characters developed in relation to each other (as well as to the wider contexts of genre and contemporary events).

In relation to the growth of the genre, it is important to consider not only who was creating it but also who was reading it. Brian W. Aldiss describes the 'active fandom', which was key to the development of early sf, as 'lads who read every word of the magazine with pious 'fervour' and 'formed themselves into leagues and groups, issued their own amateur magazines or "fanzines", and were generally a very vocal section of the readership' (208). Relatively dismissive of these fans, he goes on to argue that while 'many writers and editors later rose from their ranks [...] several promising writers have been spoiled by seeking popularity exclusively from the fans who – like any other group of enthusiasts – want more of what they have already been enjoying' (208). Comics fandom developed in similar ways and spaces to sf fandom, although comics rarely carried letters pages of their own until the 1950s, in the case of EC, or the 1960s, in the case of DC and Marvel (Goodrum; Hanley). However, the debates featured in these letters pages are far from characterised by simplistic demands for 'more of the same'. By the 1950s, fans were able to articulate the value of both individual stories within comics and the worth of comics as a form in the US in the context of McCarthyism and debates around race, Civil Rights, gender and sexuality, and the place of the family (Whitted). These processes were, in part, driven by the construction of the comics themselves: Qiana Whitted describes how EC tried to foster a 'dynamic set of reading practices that the company worked to cultivate among consumers' (21), offering narratives and images that engaged with contemporary issues but, crucially, sought to engage their readers with them, too.

Aldiss's use of 'lads' implies a gendered dimension of fandom that was certainly not the case for comics. Bradford Wright provides estimates by the Market Research Company of America that in November 1945:

> 70 million Americans – roughly half of the US population – read comic books. The report found that the comic book audience comprised approximately 95% of all boys and 91% of all girls between the ages of six and eleven, 87% of boys and 81% of girls between twelve and seventeen, 41% of men and 28% of women aged eighteen to thirty and 16% of men and 12% of women over thirty.
>
> (57)

Audience numbers and demographics of this magnitude drove diversification of the industry, which stimulated further growth as 'average monthly circulation [increased] from 17 million in 1940 to nearly 70 million by 1953' (155). Such massive visibility, in combination with some of the genres and causes comics took up, made them a magnet for criticism from conservative cultural guardians.

Superheroes clearly borrowed from sf: Superman's alien origins, Batman's scientific endeavours, the serum that transforms young Steve Rogers into Captain America, Wonder Woman's advanced Amazonian science. However, comics did not just borrow; they also offered their own takes on the genre. Newspaper strips like *Buck Rogers* (1929–67) and *Flash Gordon* (1934–2003) are typically seen as the first stirrings of recognisably sf comics (Benton). In an approach that will come to be very familiar with comics, *Flash Gordon* began as an imitation of the successful *Buck Rogers*, which was in part itself an imitation of the traveller to the future narrative in the style of Edward Bellamy's *Looking Backward: 2000–1887* (1888), William Morris's *News from Nowhere* (1890) and H.G. Wells's *When the Sleeper Wakes* (1899) as filtered through Philip Francis Nowlan's novella 'Armageddon – 2419 AD' published in *Amazing Stories* in 1928. However, it was as part of the drive toward generic diversification in the late 1940s and early 1950s that sf comics reached their highest prominence. The popularity of superhero titles in the late 1930s and during the Second World War meant there was little demand for generic experimentation, but as that popularity ebbed publishers and creative teams began to look to other genres. Romance, crime, war, Western, funny animal, teen humour and horror series all began to appear from the late 1940s and the early 1950s. One of the prime agents in this shift was Bill Gaines, editor of EC Comics, and the team of writers and artists around him. He was influenced by the plot twist endings of O. Henry, and 'the suspense and science-fiction pulps of the period' (Whitted 16), with EC going on to build up relations with some major sf writers of the time, such as Ray Bradbury. Comics began borrowing from sf writers to make sf comics, while also making some startlingly original interventions of their own.

Sf comics, as distinct from newspaper strips, are identifiable from as early as *Planet Comics* (1940–53), a sister magazine to the *Planet Stories* pulp (1939–55), but 1950 marks the true arrival of sf comics. EC launched both *Weird Science* (1950–53) and *Weird Fantasy* (1950–53) in May 1950, followed by DC's *Strange Adventures* (1950–73) in August/September and *Mystery in Space* (1951–66) in April/May 1951, and Atlas (the publisher that evolved into Marvel) produced a series of sf titles throughout the decade. 1950 also witnessed the release of such seminal sf films as *Rocketship X-M* (Neumann 1950) and *Destination Moon* (Pichel 1950) – *Strange Adventures*' first issue contained an adaption of the latter – and the pre-production for *The Day the Earth Stood Still* (Wise 1951) and *The Thing from Another World* (Nyby 1951). There was also a rash of UFO sightings following the interest in Kenneth Arnold's 1947 experience in Mineral, Washington, which led to the coining of the term 'flying saucer' (Bader 74). By 1952, George Adamski and Desmond Leslie published the first UFO contact stories, with Adamski's account of alien visitors significantly shaping subsequent ones (Bader 76). The climate was clearly conducive to sf, and as always comics publishers were prepared to leap aboard any passing bandwagon in their pursuit of potential revenue.

The need for revenue was particularly evident after the 1954 Senate subcommittee hearings on juvenile delinquency and the subsequent introduction of the Comics Code, which severely limited what could be represented in comics. The situation was made even more difficult for comics publishers as American News Company, which distributed and vended a significant percentage of the industry's titles, was subject to anti-trust investigations from 1952. As the company foundered, the distributor in the best position to pick up the slack was Independent News, but they were owned by DC so other publishers either had to come to terms with them, often by limiting the number of comics they would publish, or risk going out of business altogether. After 1954, the situation worsened as comic books became a toxic commodity, subject to national political censure and grassroots campaigns by parent–teacher groups and moral guardians like the National Office for Decent Literature (Nyberg; Hajdu). Comics therefore underwent a similar fate to many of the new prose sf magazines: significant difficulties in securing distribution and retail outlets following the collapse of ANC. There were also international problems, with campaigns against American comics in, particularly, Britain and France (Barker; Jobs). Britain mounted its own sf comic as a response. Frank Hampson's *Dan Dare, Pilot of the Future* ran for the first 17 years (12 of them on the cover) of *The Eagle* (1950–69), an anthology comic created by Marcus Morris, a Church of

England vicar, in an attempt to provide British children with 'suitable' alternatives – 'suitability' being defined by Morris and the parents, teachers and cultural guardians who rallied to the campaign against the American invaders (Chapman).

1950s sf comics are often either overshadowed by the controversies around crime and horror comics or positioned as a precursor to the renaissance of superhero comics. Both are understandable positions: crime and horror series undoubtedly enjoyed greater notoriety, with EC horror comics in particular being championed over the decades by Stephen King and others. The superheroes that began to return to popularity after DC's reintroduction of the Flash in 1956 owed a clear debt to sf. When Marvel debuted *The Fantastic Four* (1961–96), the template for the sf-based superhero with which the company is now so closely associated was established. Space travel, nuclear science, mutation, advanced military science – Marvel superheroes of the 1960s explored the effects of applied science and the Cold War, drawing on established sf themes to do so. To pass over the sf comics so quickly, though, overlooks some significant work.

EC was a minor player under Max Gaines, but when he died in 1947, his son William Gaines inherited and began to overhaul the business. In 1950, the 'New Trend' line introduced by Gaines and Al Feldstein included the comics for which the publisher is still known – *Haunt of Fear* (1950–4), *The Vault of Horror* (1950–5), *Tales From The Crypt* (1950–5), *Crime Suspenstories* (1950–5), *Shock Suspenstories* (1952–5) and *Two-Fisted Tales* (1950–5), along with the sf titles *Weird Science* and *Weird Fantasy*. EC's sf comics talked up rather than down to their readers, often using the comic form to take aim at contemporary moral debates. While EC looms large in the cultural consciousness, Bradford Wright makes its contemporary position clear: 'with only nine titles and a weak distribution network, EC was a relatively small publisher' (149) that enjoyed outsized success and notoriety. These kinds of stories, perhaps, come the closest of the comics so far under consideration to fulfil the idea of sf as opening 'new horizons and giv[ing] a fresh and objective point of view on the world and culture' (Clareson xiii) – except, inevitably, for objectivity, a goal beyond the realms of all subjects.

In EC's most famous sf 'preachie', 'Judgment Day!' (1953), by writer Al Feldstein and artist Joe Orlando, readers are given a fresh perspective on contemporary American culture through the experience of Tarlton, an astronaut who travels to Cybrinia, a planet peopled by robots, to see whether they meet the requirements set out by their original creators (from Earth) to join the Great Galactic Republic. There, Tarlton discovers that the robots have constructed systems of institutionalised racism between blue and orange robots based on the colour of their 'sheathings' and the education and environment inhabited by the blue robots. As Tarlton notes, 'the Educator is the parents and the relatives and the environment and the school all rolled into one', to which his orange robot guide responds by saying that 'you are lecturing me as though all this were my fault, Tarlton! This existed long before I was made! What can I do about it? I'm only one robot!'. EC's obligatory twist ending has Tarlton remove his helmet, revealing that he is Black, meaning that the reader, regardless of their own identity, has been aligned with a marginalised and oppressed minority. Such narratives and images function as good sf – at least as far as Clareson's definition goes.

Not all of EC's preachies were sf, and not all its sf comics were as successful as 'Judgment Day!' (on its shortcomings, see Whitted 19–20; Goodrum and Smith 139). It is also worth remembering that, in the 1950s, not all sf comics were exclusively sf – often, sf and horror blurred. As Andrew Tudor observes, 'the belief that science is dangerous is as central to the horror movie as is a belief in the malevolent inclinations of ghosts, ghouls, vampires, and zombies' (133). The reasons for such a blurring are relatively obvious: the atomic bombings of Hiroshima and Nagasaki; heightened nuclear hopes and fears in the context of the hydrogen bomb (first tested by the US in 1952); and the revelation of medical experimentation in Nazi concentration camps. Many narratives with sf themes therefore appeared in horror comics, just as films such as *Them!* (Douglas 1954), *Tarantula!* (Arnold 1955) and *The Incredible Shrinking Man* (Arnold 1957) blurred generic boundaries.

Blur is, in fact, an opportune word for considering subsequent developments in sf comics. It is 1956 and Barry Allen is a forensic chemist, working late on a case in a police laboratory. Unexpectedly, the lab is hit by lightning and Barry is soaked with vials of chemicals and knocked out. When he wakes, he has heightened speed and reflexes – and names himself The Flash (a similar character of the same name had appeared in various series from 1940–51). Here we see a fusion of superhero narratives (the scientific 'accident' origin story becomes crucial in the 1960s), sf (many 1960s superheroes are scientists) and body horror (Barry Allen's transformation is not monstrous, but several 1960s superhero transformations foreground horror more explicitly). Therefore, the origin of Barry Allen's Flash in issue four of *Showcase* (1956–70) is often posited in fan chronology as the beginning of the 'Silver Age' of comics. Debates about the merits or otherwise of periodisation exceed the scope of this chapter, but it is worth noting the significance of this for the stories that follow (as well as the way such nomenclature looks back to that which went before, establishing both continuity and discontinuity in approaches to superhero comics).

The 1961 arrival of the Fantastic Four shapes much of the modern understanding of superhero sf. Their success prompted the rest of the characters who filled out the basics of that understanding: Spider-Man, Hulk and Iron Man. Key to many Marvel characters is exposure to nuclear radiation of some kind (Iron Man is an exception but makes up for that absence with his work in applied science developing weapons for the US government – as well as enhanced armoured flying exoskeletons for himself.) Spider-Man, the X-Men, Hulk and The Thing from the Fantastic Four dramatise anxieties about the transformative effects of exposure to radiation, with Hulk updating the Victorian Gothic science of Robert Louis Stevenson's *Strange Case of Dr Jekyll and Mr Hyde* (1886) for the nuclear age. Many of the Marvel superheroes are also scientists working on things that blur the boundaries of sf and science fact. Reed Richards/Mr Fantastic, for example, is part of the team that seeks to achieve space travel while also politicising it: Sue Storm pleads with the reluctant Ben Grimm that they have to push ahead with their space mission 'unless we want the commies to beat us to it!' Furthermore, Matt Yockey persuasively argues that 'as another product of white corporate America, *The Fantastic Four* uncritically duplicates the silently racist ideology of the space program' (66), offering in the process 'a conservative vision of the present that resonates with an imagined glorious past as it suggests a paradisiacal technological future' (67). Despite the narrative and thematic innovation in these comics, it is worth pointing out, as Yockey does, how they continue to buy into a glorious vision of the US in a way alien to publishers such as EC in the 1950s.

This is not to say that Marvel and DC did not take steps to diversify the content of their comics in the 1960s. As with EC before them, some elements worked better than others and not all of it stands up well to hindsight – but, crucially, reader scrutiny was encouraged as a tactic for reflecting on both comics and the context of their creation and reception. This allowed comics to act as a space for dialogue between diverse groups – rather than talking to their readers, comics began more routinely talking with them. Increasing representation of ambiguity and contemporary issues also meant that 'old ideas of an "American" identity based on White men split to reveal the inconsistencies that underpinned them' (Goodrum 110), positioning comics as part of larger discussions about the nature of American national identity (on superheroes and nationality, see Dittmer). These discussions tied American comics into Cold War narratives of the US; sometimes they sought to reinforce those narratives, as with the early adventures of Tony Stark/Iron Man in Vietnam, and sometimes there were attempts to contest or deepen ideas about the nature and role of the US (Genter; Costello). The X-Men in particular have been seen as a metaphor for Civil Rights, but as Richard Reynolds notes, they are best seen as a 'parable of the alienation of any minority' (79) rather than as a direct reference to any one group (although see Baron; Doran; Fawaz; Loadenthal; Ratto; Shyminsky).

The Avengers #33 (1965) is indicative of how comics sought to incorporate more diverse groups. When Hank Pym needs to hire a research assistant, Tony Stark recommends Dr Bill Foster, a Black American working at Stark Industries. Before he can take up that position, however, Foster is attacked by the Sons of the Serpent, a Ku Klux Klan-style organisation intent on expelling 'foreigners'. The Avengers break up the group and the Supreme Serpent turns out to be General Chang, a Vietnamese general seeking to harness divisions in the US to guarantee a communist victory in the Cold War. Such attempts to diversify comics framed racism as bad, but ultimately as something to be dealt with because of the Cold War threat it posed. A more radical break with this practice came in 1966 with the introduction of the Black Panther and the Afrofuturist country he rules, Wakanda (Posada; Nama; Whaley). Wakanda is one of the more fully realised sf environments in the Marvel universe, offering a vision of an African nation that had been able to follow its own path of development and make best use of its own natural resources in the process. While this was and has been largely well-received, DC's equivalent venture, Vathlo Island, has met with far more resistance. In attempting to diversify the (up to that point in the comics) entirely White planet of Krypton, E. Nelson Bridwell introduced Vathlo Island, which he identified as 'home of highly developed Black race'. In effect, and with the apparent best of intentions, Bridwell instituted a separate but equal approach to Kryptonian racial politics.

Other sf comics came and went in the 1960s. For instance, Charlton's *Space Adventures*, which had ended in 1956, returned with a second series that ran from 1958 until 1964, then for a third series from 1968 to 1969. Dell's *Space Man* had its first eight issues between 1962 and 1964, with #9 and #10 appearing in 1972, and their *The Outer Limits* ran for 18 issues between 1964 and 1969 (although the last two issues were reprints of #1 and #2). Based on the television series of the same name, the frequency of publication picked up in 1967, with #10–16 all published that year – perhaps as a response to growing interest in sf after the 1966 debut of another television show, *Star Trek* (NBC 1966–9), (which spawned its own comic by Gold Key in 1967 that ran, for 61 issues, until 1978, when they lost the licence to Marvel. As always, the fortunes of comics fluctuated in connection with their contexts of creation and reception.

The period under consideration here witnessed the beginning of sf comics, their spectacular growth, and the penetration of sf concepts into other genres, such as superheroes. Some still command attention today, especially those published by EC in the 1950s, and the Marvel sf superheroes who first came to prominence in the 1960s now dominate global box offices.

Works cited

Aldiss, Brian W. with David Wingrove. *Trillion Year Spree: The History of Science Fiction*. Gollancz, 1986.

Bader, Christopher. 'The UFO Contact Movement from the 1950s to the Present'. *Studies in Popular Culture* 17.2 (1995): 73–90.

Barker, Martin. *A Haunt of Fears: The Strange History of the British Horror Comics Campaign*. UP of Mississippi, 1992.

Baron, Lawrence. '*X-Men* as J-Men: The Jewish Subtext of a Comic Book Movie'. *Shofar* 22.1 (2003): 44–52.

Benton, Mike. *The Comic Book in America: An Illustrated History*. Taylor Publishing, 1993.

Bridwell, Nelson E. and Sal Amendola, 'Map of Krypton's "Old World" Hemisphere' and 'Map of Krypton's "New World" Hemisphere'. *Superman* #239 (July 1971). unpaginated.

Chapman, James. 'Onward, Christian Spacemen: *Dan Dare, Pilot of the Future* as British Cultural History'. *Visual Culture in Britain* 9.1 (2008): 55–79.
Clareson, Thomas D. 'Prefatory Comments'. *Science Fiction: Contemporary Mythology – The SFWA-SFRA Anthology*. Ed. Patricia Warrick, Martin Harry Greenberg and Joseph Olander. Harper & Row, 1978. xi–xv.
Costello, Matthew J. *Secret Identity Crisis: Comic Books and the Unmasking of Cold War America*. Continuum, 2009.
Dittmer, Jason. *Captain America and the Nationalist Superhero: Metaphors, Narratives, and Geopolitics*. Temple UP, 2012.
Doran, Fionnuala. 'Alone amidst X-men: Rogue, Sexuality, and Mental Illness'. *Journal of Graphic Novels & Comics* 11.4 (2020): 425–37.
Edwards, Caroline. 'Utopian Prospects, 1900–49'. *Science Fiction: A Literary History*. Ed. Roger Luckhurst. The British Library, 2017: 72–101.
Fawaz, Ramzi. *The New Mutants: Superheroes and the Radical Imagination of American Comics*. New York UP, 2016.
Feldstein, Al and Joe Orlando. 'Judgment Day!'. *Weird Fantasy* #18 (March/April 1953): unpaginated.
Genter, Robert. '"With Great Power Comes Great Responsibility": Cold War Culture and the Birth of Marvel Comics'. *Journal of Popular Culture* 40.6 (2007): 953–78.
Goodrum, Michael. *Superheroes and American Self Image: From War to Watergate*. Routledge, 2016.
Goodrum, Michael and Philip Smith. *Printing Terror: American Horror Comics as Cold War Commentary and Critique*. Manchester UP, 2021.
Hajdu, David. *The Ten-Cent Plague: The Great Comic Book Scare and How it Changed America*. Picador, 2009.
Hanley, Tim. 'The Evolution of Female Readership: Letter Columns in Superhero Comics'. *Gender and the Superhero Narrative*. Ed. Michael Goodrum, Tara Prescott and Philip Smith. UP of Mississippi, 2018. 221–50.
Jobs, Richard I. 'Tarzan under Attack: Youth, Comics, and Cultural Reconstruction in Postwar France'. *French Historical Studies* 26.4 (2003): 687–725.
Lee, Stan and Jack Kirby. *The Fantastic Four* #1. Marvel Comics, 1961.
Loadenthal, Michael. 'Professor Xavier is a Gay Traitor! An Antiassimilationist Framework for Interpreting Ideology, Power, and Statecraft'. *Journal of Feminist Scholarship* 6 (2018): 13–46.
Nama, Adilifu. *Super Black: American Pop Culture and Black Superheroes*. U of Texas P, 2011.
Nyberg, Amy Kiste. *Seal of Approval: The History of the Comics Code*. UP of Mississippi, 1998.
Posada, Tim. 'Afrofuturism, Power, and Marvel Comics' Black Panther'. *Journal of Popular Culture* 52.3 (2019): 625–44.
Ratto, Casey M. 'Not Superhero Accessible: The Temporal Stickiness of Disability in Superhero Comics'. *Disability Studies Quarterly* 37.2 (2017). https://dsq-sds.org/article/view/5396/4649>
Reynolds, Richard. *Superheroes: A Modern Mythology*. UP of Mississippi, 1992.
Shyminsky, Neil. 'Mutant Readers, Reading Mutants: Appropriation, Assimilation, and the X-Men'. *International Journal of Comic Art* 8.2 (2006): 387–405.
Tudor, Andrew. *Monsters and Mad Scientists: A Cultural History of the Horror Movie*. Blackwell, 1989.
Whaley, Deborah Elizabeth. *Black Women in Sequence: Re-inking Comics, Graphic Novels, and Anime*. U of Washington P, 2015.
Whitted, Qiana. *EC Comics: Race, Shock, & Social Protest*. Rutgers UP, 2019.
Wright, Bradford W. *Comic Book Nation: The Transformation of Youth Culture in America*. Johns Hopkins UP, 2003.
Yockey, Matt. 'This Island Manhattan: New York City and the Space Race in *The Fantastic Four*'. *Iowa Journal of Cultural Studies* 6 (2005): 58–79.

21

SCIENCE FICTION FILM AND TELEVISION

The 1950s to the 1970s

Lincoln Geraghty

Introduction: Disaster, death and despair

A period that spawned some of the most memorable film and television from across the globe, the three decades between 1950 and 1980 are the crucible of sf media. Giving us the bug-eyed monster movies of the 1950s, the more cerebral stories of space exploration and alien encounters in the 1960s and technophobic warnings of the future in the 1970s, the production of screen sf was at its height and most influential. While the blockbuster took over as the mainstream alternative to the genre in the late 1970s, with George Lucas's *Star Wars* (1977) laying a course for the mega sf franchises of today, the 30 years of sf on both big and little screens were not just about setting up what was to come at the end of the twentieth century. Those three decades were characterised by important trends and ideas that resonated with contemporary audiences and speculated on issues that were increasingly important on national and international stages. Sf film and television from the 1950s to 1970s depicted disasters both human and extra-terrestrial, debated death as a result of nuclear war and described the despair of what a technological future might bring.

Disaster in the 1950s

The figure of the alien was a predominantly cinematic character in the 1950s. A mainstay of the B movie sf–horror film hybrid, it challenged existing definitions of normality. In many films, the threatening alien actually focused fears and anxiety about developments *within* society, represented by the pod people in *Invasion of the Body Snatchers* (Siegel 1956), while others presented the alien as a persecuted figure oppressed by intolerance. Films such as *The Thing from Another World* (Nyby 1951), *War of the Worlds* (Haskin 1953), *Invaders from Mars* (Menzies 1953), *It Came from Outer Space* (Arnold 1953) and *This Island Earth* (Newman 1955) presented the world in the grip of disaster – disasters 'that jeopardized the future of the race; they were not national, nor even international, but planetary' (Biskind 102). The first big budget Hollywood studio sf movie of the decade, *Forbidden Planet* (Wilcox 1956), used the familiar extra-terrestrial motif to interrogate the human impulse for death and destruction. Its story illustrated the precarious position humanity held 'on the cusp of destruction or development – a position of obvious relevance during the Cold War tensions of the year' (Grant 175).

DOI: 10.4324/9781003140269-23

In the 1950s, science and scientists were represented in the popular media as saviours; after all, it was nuclear power that brought an end to the war with Japan. Although the disastrous effects of the bomb in Hiroshima and Nagasaki were seen by the whole world, the potentials for atomic power to improve people's lives were made very apparent in the American media. Nuclear power symbolised America's dominance and, even though it had many dangerous consequences, responsible use could bring about a potential utopia: 'The Manhattan Project may have been a secret, and Hiroshima a shock, but Americans of 1945 were prepared in a general way for news of atomic breakthroughs that would transform their lives' (Boyer 109). Inevitably, sf films picked up on these contradictory themes and began to question America's faith in the atom and its willingness to ignore the dangers of harnessing nuclear power.

The first sf film to really caution against nuclear weapons and critique the US Cold War with the USSR was *The Day the Earth Stood Still* (Wise 1951). Inspired – like *Earth vs. the Flying Saucers* (Sears 1956) and many others – by the American fascination with UFOs, it is seen by some as promoting a positive message. As the alien Klaatu's closing words to the world state, 'Humanity is now free to discover its true self with respect to the powers and forces that run through the cosmos' (Lucanio 45). However, the film can also be seen as fascistic, or at least authoritarian, suggesting that 'what the Earth needs is to be policed by aliens to control mankind's worst instincts and save the Universe from destruction' (Humphries 57). In either case, it warned of potential disaster through the misuse of nuclear power.

The dangers of nuclear power also appeared in films that depicted mutants and monsters created by the leaking or exploding of radioactive elements: Joyce A. Evans describes this as the 'radiation-produced monster' genre (93). Popular examples include *The Beast from 20,000 Fathoms* (Lourié 1953), *Them!* (Douglas 1954) and the Americanised version of Japan's *Godzilla, King of the Monsters!* (Honda and Morse 1956). For Jerome F. Shapiro, these films were inspired and energised by real life events in the South Pacific as the superpowers upped their commitment to developing and testing hydrogen bombs during the mid-1950s (112). The various mutated beasts created as a result of science gone wrong 'typically seem drawn to our modern cities, where they proceed to carry out nature's revenge on a reckless, environmentally heedless human culture' (Telotte 98). Labelled by Susan Sontag as films that depict the 'Imagination of Disaster', they are 'concerned with the aesthetics of destruction, with the peculiar beauties to be found in wreaking havoc, making a mess' (41). However, the scientists that cause these monstrous mutations rarely escape. They are usually disfigured or destroyed by their creation and therefore punished for their misdeeds in trying to overcome nature.

An interesting counterpoint to such films produced in the US, Japanese sf films in the late 1950s emphasised the devastating effects of nuclear power, as well as its potentials for human advancement. *Godzilla* (*Gojira*; Honda 1954) offered warnings of mutation brought about by nuclear radiation, with *Rodan* (*Sora no daikaijû Radon*; Honda 1956) also suggesting nuclear testing created the monstrous threat of a giant pterosaur. These two films started the *kaiju* cycle that saw giant monsters wreak havoc on cities across the globe. However, they were also part of a wider tendency in Japanese film and television referred to as *tokosatsu* (literally, special effects), which influenced global popular culture well beyond the 1950s. *Tokosatsu* relied heavily on practical effects to create a sense of drama and threat that was equally represented in the monster, alien or human protagonist. *The Mysterians* (*Chikyû Bôeigun*; Honda 1957) saw alien invaders defeated by superior fire power and in *Battle in Outer Space* (*Uchû daisensô*; Honda 1960) atomic weapons help to save humanity from alien enslavement. Despite being a victim of atomic power Japanese audiences developed a more complex relationship with nuclear themes as seen in the popularity of the *Astro Boy* (*Testuwan-Atomu*) manga (1952–68), live-action series (1959–60) and (the first of several) anime series (1963–66) of stories about a robotic boy superhero. Using futuristic technology to save, rather than destroy, people and the planet, ASTRO BOY (aka MIGHTY ATOM) was the first transmedia franchise and its eponymous hero the first major merchandisable character.

According to J.P. Telotte, film looked different to its televisual competition through the increasing use of 'Technicolor, Cinemascope [*sic*], and 3D technologies' (95). As a result, I would add, the threat of the alien was intensified on the big screen during the 1950s and television's contribution to the genre was largely postponed until the beginning of the 1960s. What the small screen did offer initially were cinema-like serials, such as *Captain Video and his Video Rangers* (DuMont 1949–55), *Rocky Jones, Space Ranger* (Roland Reed 1954), *Space Patrol* (ABC 1950–5) and *Tom Corbett, Space Cadet* (CBS/ABC/NBC/DuMont 1950–5). While lacking in adult story-telling and complex character development, these series showed that television was a suitable medium through which the alien, usually men with face paint, and the human, albeit idealised visualisations of the human male, could be shown in a futuristic setting. As Rick Worland points out, these series were considered to be 'aimed at children' yet the fact that they appeared on television showed just how much the medium was affected by 'a repressive political climate that obstructed presentation of any ideas outside the commonplace' (104).

Television as an icon of technological progress was a powerful symbol and is part of the reason for sf's huge popularity in the 1950s: 'With such fantastic devices right in their living rooms, Americans were ready to believe anything was possible through science and technology' (Lucanio and Coville 1). Seeing outer space on the screen only fuelled the nation's passion and drive to win the Space Race. Patrick Lucanio and Gary Coville stress that we should not discount this period as simply childish hokum. Indeed, *Tales of Tomorrow* (ABC 1951–3) is considered to be the first adult orientated anthology series, the antecedent of *Science Fiction Theatre* (Ziv 1955–7) and *The Twilight Zone* (CBS 1959–64), and is representative of the shift in television production to more mature programming. The development of anthology series such as *The Twilight Zone* and *The Outer Limits* (ABC 1963–5), with their more critical take on the political and ideological struggle between the US and the USSR, signalled an attempt on behalf of writers such as Rod Serling and Leslie Stevens to comment on the very conservativism that had pushed the Cold War into the suburbs and had driven the television networks to produce uncritical and problematic representations of the US's race to dominate outer space.

Television began to supersede film as the dominant form of mass media in the late 1950s and early 1960s while sf remained popular. It was trying to attract a different kind of audience – perceived as a more adult audience – therefore film had to change in order to cope with the declining box office receipts. David Marc and Robert J. Thompson record that 'By 1960 TV use had soared to some five daily hours per household', and as a result other forms of media, such as radio and the cinema, 'had to redefine themselves to fit the new communications regime' (76). In the 1960s, both film and television became sites of more sophisticated sf that not only questioned the ideologies of earlier texts but offered more nuanced interrogations of nuclear disaster.

Death in the 1960s

Following the plethora of bug-eyed alien and nuclear mutation films of the 1950s, sf in the 1960s turned away from its B movie roots and started to focus on the more geopolitical aspects of nuclear proliferation. While depictions of disaster were core to 1950s sf, films of the 1960s focused on the inevitable outcome of nuclear war: global death. While *On the Beach* (Kramer 1959), *Fail Safe* (Lumet 1964) and others continued to use the threat and fatal consequences of nuclear war as a backdrop to their stories, 'a small trend in satirical sf films' (Brosnan 139) also emerged, including

Dr. Strangelove, Or How I Learned to Stop Worrying and Love the Bomb (Kubrick 1964) and *Barbarella* (Vadim 1968). However, sf was in a state of flux as it struggled to attract audiences tired of alien invasion narratives and more impressed with the colourful action adventure serials now appearing on television. Like most genres, sf was experiencing the changes and uncertainties brought about by the industrial shake-up in Hollywood, starting in the mid-1960s and stretching to the mid-1970s.

Part of this New Hollywood, *2001: A Space Odyssey* (Kubrick 1968) is an example of the 'new art' cycle of sf, 'marked by the simultaneous display of the creative energies and sensibilities associated with the counter-cultural movements of the 1960s/1970s and the industry's efforts to engage with a new and younger audience' (Cornea 82). Similarly, Kubrick's *Dr. Strangelove* was one of the many films to highlight overreliance on technology and criticise the need for nuclear weapons. The Cuban Missile Crisis (1962) not only renewed fears of the bomb first brought to attention in the mutant monster movies of the 1950s but also reminded people of the fine line between life and death during the Cold War. Sf tapped into this nascent fear of nuclear holocaust by continuing to depict scientists and engineers as Faustian figures, corrupted by technology and an ever-present God complex. The eponymous Strangelove, played by Peter Sellers, is deformed, his mechanical hand evidence of his physical corruption and transformation brought about by an insane devotion to scientific experimentation.

Kubrick wanted to show the absolute absurdity of the Cold War and the superpowers' policy of Mutually Assured Destruction (MAD). For David Seed, the film's 'treatment of fears of extinction and mutation exemplify how black humour feigns to deprioritise subjects presumed to carry weight' (147) and thus the ultimate fear of nuclear destruction is reduced to absurdity through the inaction of principal characters and the coincidental events that bring about an American B-52 bomber dropping its nuclear payload on Russia. Yet, also, 'the realism of the settings and the machinery, particularly the interior of the B52, gives an added impact to the horrifying absurdity of the action and characters' (Brosnan 157). Likewise, the juxtaposition of images of nuclear mushroom clouds with a wartime Vera Lynn song at the end of the film disturbs the audience's perception of reality (Baxter 168). Should we be celebrating the use of nuclear weapons? Can they ensure the 'right' side will win? Will humanity survive the fall out?

Such questions are perhaps answered by *Planet of the Apes* (Schaffner 1968). Based on Pierre Boulle's *La Planète des singes* (1963), the film sees astronaut George Taylor, played by Charlton Heston, crash land on a planet he believes to be alien. Injured and unable to talk, he is captured by a civilisation of apes who can walk, talk and use guns. The apes deem humans to be vermin-like savages and kill them for sport. Taylor's discovery at the end of the film is one of sf's, indeed cinema's, most shocking twists. On a secluded beach Taylor and Nova find the remains of the Statue of Liberty buried in the sand, thus confirming that he did not crash land on an alien world but in fact travelled thousands of years into the future and landed back on a post-apocalyptic Earth; humans had destroyed themselves with their nuclear weapons and the apes evolved to become the dominant species. The message of this film is clearly death is inevitable, and humanity will bring about their own demise.

The success of series like *The Twilight Zone* and *The Outer Limits* in the late 1950s and early 1960s showed that audiences and networks were just as keen to experiment with thought provoking stories on the small screen. Television sf matured as programming changed narrative emphasis from ray guns and rocket ships to political allegory and moral lessons in *The Twilight Zone*. Space in the schedules for sf did grow, thereby giving writers and producers such as Serling, Stevens and Gene Roddenberry opportunities to push the boundaries. Such intelligent genre programming reached its 1960s' zenith with *Star Trek* (NBC 1966–9) but its contemporaries should not be dismissed just because they did not garner the same level of critical and cultural attention. In fact, without the success and influence of people like Irwin Allen, producer of *Voyage to the Bottom of the Sea* (ABC 1964–8) and *Lost in Space* (CBS 1965–8), and of camp series like *The Man from U.N.C.L.E.* (NBC 1964–8), there may never have been an audience for *Star Trek* in the first place.

Political and social issues were coming to the fore on television, inspired by news reporting that dramatised 'the various social revolutions of the decade – the Civil Rights movement, black radicalism, women's liberation, youth unrest, opposition to the Vietnam War, and so on' (Alvey 17). Television sf was able to address a countercultural audience through the displacement of the contemporary onto the future settings of alien planets and spaceships, tackling divisive topics without attracting too much attention from censors and network bosses. The rise and popularity of colour television literally exposed the nation to its own inherent racial discrimination as few non-White faces appeared on screen, and networks had begun to broadcast shows that better reflected the nation's social, racial and ethnic diversity. In the competition for key audience, they could not ignore the significant growth in minority groups who represented new potential markets for advertisers.

Sf series offered networks a chance to experiment, gambling with the bigger budgets needed for special effects and large sets – and for colour – to attract new audiences. *Star Trek* and other series in this period were clearly products of these cultural and industrial contexts. Big social issues were discussed, and while sf film and television in the 1960s largely focused on self-destruction and death, they still offered hope. The subsequent decade offered audiences little else than dystopia and despair.

Despair in the 1970s

In 1978, Joan F. Dean examined the state of the sf film and the commercial failure of many productions between the release of *2001: A Space Odyssey* and *Star Wars*. According to her, this failure was due to their focus on the conflicts arising from America's escalating social and political problems and the continued resentment of military involvement in Vietnam. These issues were often reflected in dystopian visions of the future in films such as *Beneath the Planet of the Apes* (Post 1970), *THX-1138* (Lucas 1971), *Silent Running* (Trumbull 1972), *Soylent Green* (Fleischer 1973), *Westworld* (Crichton 1973), *Zardoz* (Boorman 1973), *Rollerball* (Jewison 1975), *A Boy and His Dog* (Jones 1975) and *Logan's Run* (Anderson 1976). Furthermore, she argues that, because of these concerns, there was a corresponding lack of interest in the perennial favourite icon of American sf: the alien. This situation was particularly ironic given that the period was framed by *2001* and *Alien* (Scott 1979). Those films that Dean allows did deal with the possibilities of extraterrestrial life, including *The Andromeda Strain* (Wise 1971), *Slaughterhouse-Five* (Hill 1972), *The Rocky Horror Picture Show* (Sharman 1975) and *The Man Who Fell to Earth* (Roeg 1976), displayed a 'developing neo-isolationism' and did little to broaden the genre's comprehension of anything beyond America's domestic and foreign interests (36). One can agree that 'The unknown and subliminal messages of the 60's sf became overt, aided by increasingly monumental displays of special effects' (Anderson 11), but those overt messages were unceasingly downbeat, with films such as *No Blade of Grass* (Wilde 1970), *The Omega Man* (Sagal 1971), *Soylent Green*, *Silent Running* and *Logan's Run* showing Earth on the brink of ecological disaster. This eternal precipice, this overarching sense of impending doom, was envisaged so regularly and with such aplomb that it is hard to imagine that 1970s sf cinema could and would give way to the more upbeat sf blockbusters of George Lucas and Steven Spielberg.

Reeling from Watergate and the OPEC crisis, defeated in Vietnam and battered by stagflation, the US was going through significant social and political changes, and they were broadcast day after day by the nation's media. President Jimmy Carter went so far as to say that America was suffering from a 'crisis of confidence'. A 'nation in existential despair', the events of the decade served to 'deflate' and 'mock' the hopes and dreams of America's White middle classes who, seeing themselves as survivors, developed a siege mentality (Graebner 158–9). This is evident in the Hollywood films of the period, which William Graebner describes as reflecting the inner turmoil middle America was experiencing. Irwin Allen's disaster movies, such as *The Poseidon Adventure* (Neame 1972) and *The Towering Inferno* (Guillermin 1974), along with George A. Romero's original DEAD trilogy (1968–85), showed Americans going through the motions of living without really appreciating life. People in these films were merely surviving, trying to live without pain, trauma or dying.

Often causes of angst and despair were rooted in technology, specifically how an over reliance on it would cause more problems than solve. Indeed, *The Stepford Wives* (Forbes 1974) and *Demon Seed* (Cammell 1977) followed the genre's traditional slant on technology, cautioning against the development of cybertechnology and supercomputers to help improve human society. In the former, replacing the women of Stepford with beautiful android copies poses a threat to female independence and notions of individuality; in the latter, the hybrid offspring of a supercomputer and a human serves as a warning that we may one day become obsolete, replaced by the technologies we created to serve us. However, both these films use technology as a device to critique patriarchy. For example, *The Stepford Wives* is 'a feminist allegory that stems from the ideological and political concerns of feminists' such as Betty Friedan and Pat Mainardi (Silver 109). It draws attention to the insidious nature of the very same things that the Women's Liberation Movement fought against in the late 1960s and early 1970s: namely sexism and inequality in the workplace and the ideologies of female beautification, domesticity and the nuclear family.

If film's representations of the technological body reflected 'our increasingly troubled sense of identity by exploring how we might be enhanced, reconfigured, and ultimately even replaced by the product of our science' (Telotte 103), television offered audiences glimpses of how notions of the corporeal were changing. With humans being literally rebuilt with cybernetic implants in *The Six Million Dollar Man* (ABC 1974–8) and *The Bionic Woman* (ABC 1976–8), there was clearly a concern about the limitations and fragility of the human body. This anxiety can most clearly be seen in the aftermath of the Vietnam War where the most harrowing aspects of the conflict, such as physical injury and psychological trauma, affected thousands of veterans on their immediate return and for many years afterwards. Soldiers who fought and civilians who watched it unfold on television felt deeply traumatised in confronting their own mortality for the first time – and in conceding that America's self-image was not invincible. According to Fred Turner, Vietnam, more than any other war, 'had demonstrated that the body politic could be dismembered' (80). To recover from the loss in South East Asia, notions of the national hero had to be rebuilt, like many of the returning GIs who had lost limbs and other body parts; therefore, it is not hard to see why these biotechnology series proved so popular.

Star Wars, subtitled *A New Hope*, cost only $11 million to make. It 'began as a summer movie, ran continuously into 1978, and was re-released in 1979', and took 'over $190 million in U.S. rentals and about $250 million worldwide, on total ticket sales of over $500 million' (Thompson and Bordwell 522). The sf blockbuster reignited audiences' imaginations. Despair was banished or forgotten as people were drawn into the heroic rebellion against the Empire. The film (and ensuing franchise) has always had close links with contemporary American politics. Right wing Cold War politics were indelibly etched onto the characters and back-story that of STAR WARS universe when, in 1983, 'Senator Edward Kennedy on the floor of the Senate' described President Ronald Reagan's televised speech asking for support for increased defence spending so as to fund the Strategic Defense Initiative as 'misleading Red Scare tactics and reckless *Star Wars* schemes' (Krämer 46). Suddenly, heroic rebels versus the evil Empire became reconfigured as the US against the Soviet Union.

The sf films of the early 1970 were unable to imagine the possibility of redemption, viewing humanity as simply doomed. Thus, while they have been seen as radical, they were also profoundly nihilistic, proposing no alternative to the decadent order of things. In contrast, *Star Wars* was an attempt to imagine an alternative and establish a sense of hope. James Chapman acknowledges the impact that American film such as *Star Wars*, and television series such as *Battlestar Galactica* (ABC 1978–80) and *Buck Rogers in the 25th Century* (NBC 1979–81), both broadcast in the UK on ITV, had on attempts to modernise the look of British television sf, especially *Doctor Who* (BBC 1963–89), whose producer Graham Williams nonetheless had to comply with the BBC's tight budgetary requirements (123). However, the 1970s were a boom time for the genre in the UK and many of the best productions made their way back across the Atlantic and created a solid fanbase of American viewers, including *Doomwatch* (BBC 1970–2), *UFO* (ITV 1970–1), *Space: 1999* (ITV 1975–7), *Survivors* (BBC 1975–7) and *Blake's 7* (BBC 1978–81). Both the BBC and ITV were keen to cash in on the new sf craze. *Blake's 7* was created by the BBC in an effort to hold its own 'in a post-*Star Wars* era' (Bould 221) while ITV, in addition to funding its own productions, began scheduling imported big-budget US series in a bid to break *Doctor Who*'s stranglehold on Saturday evening audiences.

Conclusion

Having undergone remarkable transformations during the preceding decades, by the end of the 1970s, film and television sf had consolidated its position as a popular genre capable of tackling difficult and divisive issues affecting the real world. More often than not, it depicted the future as a dystopian nightmare that contemporary society may find hard to avoid if immediate changes were not put into effect. Yet it was also able to offer spectacular, big budget adventures that entertained audiences and confirmed it as one of Hollywood's most reliable genres. Although film seemed more concerned with warning than wonder, television series offered an alternative outlet for more traditional forms of action adventure and space opera that had typified the genre through the fifties and sixties. Many of the themes and tropes that emerged in the cinema of the seventies, however, would resurface in later cycles and as a result the genre would go from strength to strength as studios and networks realised the money-making potential of the sf blockbuster through the 1980s and into the new millennium.

Work cited

Alvey, Mark. '"Too Many Kids and Old Ladies": Quality Demographics and 1960s U.S. Television'. *Television: The Critical View*. Ed. Horace Newcomb. Oxford UP, 2007. 15–36.

Anderson, Craig W. *Science Fiction Film of the Seventies*. McFarland, 1985.

Baxter, John. *Hollywood in the Sixties*. Tantivy, 1972.

Biskind, Peter. *Seeing is Believing: How Hollywood Taught Us to Stop Worrying and Love the Fifties*. Bloomsbury, 2000.

Bould, Mark. 'Science Fiction Television in the United Kingdom'. *The Essential Science Fiction Television Reader*. Ed. J.P. Telotte. UP of Kentucky, 2008. 209–30.

Boyer, Paul. *By the Bomb's Early Light: American Thought and Culture at the Dawn of the Atomic Age*. U of North Carolina P, 1994.
Brosnan, John. *Future Tense: The Cinema of Science Fiction*. MacDonald and Jane's, 1978.
Chapman, James. *Inside the TARDIS: The Worlds of Doctor Who*. I.B. Tauris, 2006.
Cornea, Christine. *Science Fiction Cinema: Between Fantasy and Reality*. Edinburgh UP, 2007.
Dean, Joan F. 'Between *2001* and *Star Wars*'. *Journal of Popular Film and Television* 7.1 (1978): 32–41.
Evans, Joyce A. *Celluloid Mushroom Clouds: Hollywood and the Atomic Bomb*. Westview, 1998.
Graebner, William. 'America's *Poseidon Adventure*: A Nation in Existential Despair'. *America in the Seventies*. Ed. Beth Bailey and David Farber. UP of Kansas, 2004. 157–80.
Grant, Barry Keith 'Movies and the Crack of Doom'. *American Cinema of the 1950s: Themes and Variations*. Ed. Murray Pomerance. Rutgers UP, 2005.155–76.
Humphries, Reynold. *The American Horror Film: An Introduction*. Edinburgh UP, 2002.
Krämer, Peter. '*Star Wars*'. *The Movies as History: Visions of the Twentieth Century*. Ed. David W. Ellwood. Sutton, 2000. 44–53.
Lucanio, Patrick and Gary Colville. *American Science Fiction Television Series of the 1950s: Episode Guides and Casts and Credits for Twenty Shows*. McFarland, 1998.
Lucanio, Patrick. *Them or Us: Archetypal Interpretations of Fifties Alien Invasion Films*. Indiana UP, 1987.
Marc, David and Robert J. Thompson. *Television in the Antenna Age: A Concise History*. Blackwell, 2005.
Seed, David. *American Science Fiction and the Cold War: Literature and Film*. Edinburgh UP, 1999.
Shapiro, Jerome F. *Atomic Bomb Cinema: The Apocalyptic Imagination on Film*. Routledge, 2002.
Silver, Anna Krugovoy. 'The Cyborg Mystique: *The Stepford Wives* and Second Wave Feminism'. *Arizona Quarterly* 58.1 (2002): 109–26.
Sontag, Susan. 'The Imagination of Disaster'. *Liquid Metal: The Science Fiction Film Reader*. Ed. Sean Redmond. Wallflower, 2004. 40–7.
Telotte, J.P. *Science Fiction Film*. Cambridge UP, 2001.
Thompson, Kristin and David Bordwell. *Film History: An Introduction*, second edition. McGraw Hill, 2003.
Turner, Fred. *Echoes of Combat: The Vietnam War in American Memory*. Anchor, 1996.
Worland, Rick. 'Sign-Posts up Ahead: *The Twilight Zone*, *The Outer Limits*, and TV Political Fantasy 1959–1965'. *Science Fiction Studies* 68 (1996): 103–22.

22

VIDEO, INSTALLATION ART AND SHORT SCIENCE FICTION FILM

Dan Byrne-Smith

Installation, video and short film have become prominent forms in the globalised spaces of contemporary art. They allow for a reimagining of spatial and temporal encounters with art. 'Installation' describes an artwork that creates a space which can be physically entered by an audience. It is often associated with immersion or experiential encounters, and sometimes has a theatrical dimension. It can be understood in relation to an awareness of the embodied presence of an audience rather than just visual perception, and it differs from the more general immersive properties of an exhibition in that it is a singular entity, rather than a collection of independent works gathered together for the purposes of display. However, this distinction can be difficult to maintain, as the context of presentation depends so much on the conditions associated with installation. Moving image work, once bound to film projectors and small monitors, has become increasing integrated into spaces of installation, particularly through the migration of images onto large surfaces through the development of video projectors. Becoming ubiquitous by the end of the twentieth century, video projectors are now a default technology for presenting moving image work.

Nevertheless, during the period in which the video projector became a popular tool for artists, it was an expensive device that was capable of unfamiliar and miraculous visual encounters. The haunting life-sized images of performers as projections, triggered by motion sensors in Gary Hill's *Tall Ships* (1992) appeared to address individual audience members. The moving faces projected onto the heads of hand-made dolls in Tony Oursler's work from the 1990s, such as those in the series *(Telling) Visions* (1994), seemed to give an uncanny life to inanimate objects. These were encounters of a phantasmagoric nature, startling engagements with an unfamiliar technology. Susan Hiller's *An Entertainment* (1990) established a familiar kind of installation that uses video projection in a dramatic form, helping to define a set of conditions for working that are still commonplace. Designed for a large room with four equal sized walls and taking material originally shot on Super 8 film, the video installation made use of four video projectors to show different footage on each of the walls and was accompanied by a soundtrack played on speakers mounted in the space. It established the video installation as an environment in which viewers must change their position to experience the work from different perspectives. *An Entertainment* used this spatial and technological approach to create an unsettling space of estrangement, showing footage of Punch and Judy puppet shows as a creepy performance of violence. Hiller's installation is still

DOI: 10.4324/9781003140269-24

effective, still performing the original act of estrangement but now looks entirely familiar as a method. What once felt like a bold statement in the use of a medium is now just another possible method for an artist to make work.

Installation emerged out of a range of historical precedents in Western art. In the 1930s, Kurt Schwitters built the *Merzbau*, an environmental work that took up eight rooms of a house in Hannover, and prominent among the precursors that emerged in the second half of the twentieth century were Environments and Happenings, both methods associated with artist Allan Kaprow, who in turn had been influenced by John Cage. These forms reflected a desire not to represent but rather to employ materials and other elements directly, a reflection of an urge to integrate art with the everyday. With this also came the integration of artwork and audience. Experiments by Kaprow and others in the early 1960s led to what can now be recognised as installation works in the 1970s, often characterised by positions of critique or opposition. At times, this was aimed at the authority of the very institutions in which the work was made.

The 1980s saw an increasing interest in immersion, a tendency fully realised by the 1990s. More recently, installations have frequently been seen as opportunities for visitors to share their own images, particularly since the rise of social media platforms. Often leaning towards conceptual, technological and experiential novelty, installation can offer speculative encounters, exploring the potential of the new and generating a sense of cognitive estrangement. Yet there has also been a noticeable tendency for installation, video and short film to develop deeper entanglements with sf in terms of content, themes and narratives. These relations are indicative of a much broader presence of sf in contemporary art that has become more obvious since the beginning of the twenty-first century. Sf is increasingly being adopted by artists as a tool to make sense of a broad range of ideas, anxieties, hopes and demands. It feeds into contemporary art and the discourses around it and, it seems, has been recognised as a range of formal and conceptual investigations, not only reflecting but also shaping the cultural spaces in which they operate.

The emerging relationships developing between contemporary art, theoretical discourse and sf have complex historical lineages, too extensive to comprehensively map in this chapter. However, there are moments of particular significance that can be foregrounded in relation to the spatial investigations common to the overlaps between installation, video and artists' film. The *This is Tomorrow* exhibition, held at London's Whitechapel Gallery in 1956, is one such moment. Twelve collaborative groups worked together to create an environment as a totality, rather than an accumulation of individual artworks. Modernity, pop culture and the excitement of experiencing a lived futurity were articulated, in part, in terms of mainstream sf imagery. In particular, the Independent Group were drawn to sf, albeit characterised by pop imagery, bringing it to prominence as part of a world of advertising, magazines, comics and Hollywood film. Yet the whole endeavour was characterised by a sense of the speculative, in terms of technology, social forms and methods of working together in the production of art as a social form. The exhibition was seen by J.G. Ballard, shortly before he had his first work published in *New Worlds* magazine, and it had a profound influence on how the young writer imagined lived reality as part of an unfolding future.

In the late 1960s and early 1970s, the American artist Robert Smithson turned towards recent sf writing, in particular Brian W. Aldiss and Ballard, to help formulate new kinds of spatial and temporal interventions. The theme of time travel echoed throughout his work. Smithson developed the term 'Non-Site' as a substitute for conventional ideas of medium, a sense in which space or place become indistinguishable from metaphor. He brought materials into the gallery space – stone, slate, earth, sand – to arrange and contain. They were often accompanied by images, maps and a sense of a broader practice beyond discrete sculptural objects, reflecting a sense of a world and temporality outside of the gallery. He is probably best known for *Spiral Jetty* (1970), a 1,500 foot long coil of earth and rock built on the edge of the Great Salt Lake in Utah, documented and presented as a 32-minute film. The term used to describe his outdoor interventions was earthworks, taken from the title of Aldiss's *Earthworks* (1965), although the more general term land art would come to be used to describe work by many artists made outside of galleries or urban settings. Years later, Ballard wrote about Smithson, leading to correspondences with Tacita Dean, an artist with an interest in Smithson and Ballard, known for her dedication to working with 35 mm film.

Smithson's entanglements with sf were revisited by Mike Nelson in the installation *Triple Bluff Canyon* (2004) at Modern Art Oxford. The centrepiece of the exhibition was a recreation of Smithson's *Partially Buried Woodshed* (1970), an abandoned structure found on the Kent State Campus in Ohio that Smithson covered with earth to the point at which it began to collapse. Nelson's version was covered in sand, as if the desert of a future apocalyptic landscape had swallowed it. The contextual framing of the installation spelt out the science fictional recreation of Smithson's famous work and listed the thematic presence of authors who had influenced Nelson's installation, including William S. Burroughs, the Strugatsky brothers and Stanisław Lem, while the accompanying publication included 'The Enigma of Isidore Ducasse', a short story by Aldiss commissioned for the exhibition. *The Coral Reef* (1999), first presented at Matt's Gallery in London, established Nelson's interest in creating immersive installations that suggest elements of narrative. Nelson intended the work to refer to Burroughs's *Naked Lunch* (1959) and sought to trap visitors in a space that also referred to Lem's *A Perfect Vacuum* (1971), a collection of reviews of non-existent books.

Korean American artist Nam June Paik offers a different historical tangent in the emergence of relationships between installation and sf. He demonstrated an obsessive fascination with technology, which he saw as the necessary characteristic of art as it moved towards futurity. From the 1960s onwards, he felt that art should be experienced as a system rather than an object. Technology belonged in his installations not because it was a novelty but because it was already ubiquitous in the world. In 1974, he used the term 'electronic superhighway' to describe how it might be possible to imagine networks of images and information; the term became the title for a 1995 work, a 51-channel video installation in which a huge bank of monitors is overlaid with a neon map of the United States. On 1 January 1984, he used satellite transmission to broadcast a work composed of live events in New York and Paris, which could be viewed in The Netherlands, West Germany and South Korea. Paik's work often had the sense of being science fictional. His artworks were imagined as cybernated, that is, as a process controlled by computing, and for him, the lived experience of audiences was already cybernated. Paik's *M200/ Video Wall* (1991) demonstrated his belief in the cathode ray tube as the cultural technology of the future. Throughout the 1990s, both Paik and Japanese artist Tatsuo Miyajima enjoyed international success in popularising large-scale installation as a form that immersed audiences in technologically saturated environments. Miyajima's installations, such as *Running Time* (1998), an installation in a large dark space filled with 85 autonomous miniature vehicles, each mounted with a blinking LED display, were mesmerising interpretations of a science fictional modernity reimagined as a vertiginous experience.

Alongside these formal and technical developments, the 1990s also saw the emergence of theoretical and thematic entanglements with sf. For the touring exhibition *Posthuman* (1992–3), curator Jeffrey Deitch brought together artists, including Mike Kelly, Charles Ray, Paul McCarthy, Janine Antoni, Robert Gober, Yasumasa Morimura, Karen Kilimnik and Kiki Smith, who documented a transition to an irrational, neurotic and increasingly technological futurity that challenged traditional constructions of embodied subjectivity. *Posthuman* remains significant, not only because of its prescience in identifying themes that would return but also because it acted as a kind of science fictional argument. Deitch framed the selection of theme and artists with a call for art to shape emergent futures rooted in the present. As an exhibition, *Posthuman* is a form of critical sf, rather than an example of contemporary art referencing sf. It operated as a set of creative explorations of technology, modernity and futurity, framed within current conditions. Comprised of practices that had emerged in the 1980s, it also corresponded to the growing conflation of science-fictional ideas with the critical theory that was being read by artists, particularly Jean Baudrillard and Donna J. Haraway. Both explored different ways in which contemporary lived experience and notions of subjectivity were increasingly understandable in relation to aspects of sf.

Some artists in the 1990s were drawn to very particular references. Graham Gussin's video *Beyond the Infinite* (1994) looped moments from *2001: A Space Odyssey* (Kubrick 1968). While Gussin drew on the seriousness, conceptual strangeness and ambiguity of *2001*, Brian Griffiths's sculptural installations from the mid-1990s, comprised of cardboard spaceship consoles, playfully evoked generic tropes, conjuring an affectionate pastiche of low budget television shows remembered from childhood. While Griffiths and Gussin exemplify different tonal and formal approaches, they share a somewhat nostalgic approach to sf as something from the past, looked back on with fond memories. However, others went further than allusion, turning their practice into forward-looking worlds of speculative narrative. From the early 1990s, Mariko Mori embraced futuristic strangeness in an ongoing process of worldbuilding that folded layers of traditional Japanese myths, beliefs and rituals into a configuration that moves between spirituality and technology. *Dream Temple* (1997–9) epitomised the trajectory of her work during this period. A recreation of a structure in the Horyuji monastery dating back to 739 CE, it appears transparent, an ethereal vision of impossible futurity rooted in enduring traditions. The installations and sculptures that Lee Bul has produced since the late 1990s have also incorporated sf as part of her construction of an elaborate personalised universe, which is turned outwards to face and challenge patriarchal authority and oppression. *Cyborg W1-W4* (1998) consists of four stylised figures cast in silicone and suspended from a metal structure, each with one leg, one arm and no head. Tight fitting armour and costumes give the impression that these exaggerated female forms could be warriors of some kind from an sf manga, yet they also look back to European art history, from classical sculpture to the striding figure of Umberto Boccioni's *Unique Forms of Continuity in Space* (1913).

The growth of sf installations since the 1990s has also been characterised by an interest in narrative. Rather than presenting linear or conventional approaches, artworks offer oblique forms of narrative suggestion or play. Staged by the organisation Artangel, *H.G.* (1995) was an ambitious installation created by Hans Peter Kuhn and Robert Wilson in the Clink Street Vaults, a former medieval prison in London. It led audiences through a sprawling environment years before the fashion for immersive theatre experiences emerged, loosely taking narrative cues from H.G. Wells's *The Time Machine* (1895). The work was imbued with a sense of drama, making use of sculptural elements and props in an evocative space, foreshadowing things to come. By the twenty-first century, it had become commonplace to find installations that could exploit scale and location both to create an impact and to engage with a large number of visitors. *TH. 2058* (2008), an installation by Dominique Gonzalez-Foerster, is an effective example of this. Staged in the huge Turbine Hall of London's Tate Modern, it immersed a mass audience in an sf narrative setting. The installation's title does a lot of work to make clear that this is a work of sf, performing two operations very directly: it points to the low-budget sf dystopia *THX 1138* (Lucas 1971), and to the future date of 2058. A huge printed text in the space confirms it is set 50 years in the future, when the Turbine Hall has become a shelter, as well as a storage facility for artworks, protecting both people and sculptures from a constant rain that has uncanny mutative properties. The space is filled with rows of metal beds, evoking bomb shelters, refugee camps and detention centres. Upon each bed is placed a single sf novel, building a library of works. Projected scenes from experimental film works and sf films are projected on a huge screen, reiterating the sense of a compiled list of sources staged as an experiential encounter.

Kara Uzelman's *The Cavorist Projects* (2009) installation, at Sommer and Kohl Gallery in Berlin, is on a much more intimate scale. It presents itself as documentary proof of the work of a group known as the Cavorists, who according to the narrative built on the achievements of Cavor, the inventor from Wells's *The First Men in the Moon* (1901). In the novel, Cavor develops a method for negating the effects of gravity. The Cavorists spent much of the twentieth century attempting to replicate his success, until it was finally proved impossible. In this archival excavation of a fictional history, prints, reel-to-reel tape, a video interview shown on a small monitor and sculptural objects resembling preposterous scientific apparatuses all coexist in a small space. Each element acts as a piece of an oblique narrative, as evidence in the construction of a playful fiction presented as historical actuality, which blurs the actual influence of Wells with a speculative influence of one of his characters.

Narrative is more prevalent in Suzanne Treister's *Hexen 2039* (2006–7). It is framed as the work of (the fictional) Rosalind Brodsky, who makes delusional claims to be a time traveller, and spins out an elaborate conspiracy theory that brings together Hollywood cinema, British and US armed forces, intelligence agencies, witchcraft and occultism in an intricate network of affinities and correspondences. The work is composed of different elements – pencil drawings based on photographs, a pseudo-documentary video, and a series of ink drawings that manage to be simultaneously cursive and diagrammatic. The paranoid conspiracies that Treister conjures evoke a breakdown of boundaries between science and superstition in a web of espionage and post-Cold War neurosis. What results is a strange form of speculative estrangement that feels like an immersive encounter in a work of sf.

Oblique approaches to narrative have also characterised short film works by artists. Two highly influential films, not defined by a contemporary art context, continue to inform many artists. *La Jetée* (Marker 1962) is a short sf film composed almost entirely from still images, accompanied by a narrative voiceover, that plays on its own use of medium, opening up a rich territory of memory and speculation. *Space is the Place* (Coney 1974), a formative example of what would come to be known as Afrofuturism, is an sf film built around the mission of jazz musician Sun Ra to bring African Americans out of their oppressive present and into a new world of political power and agency. Its fragmentary, non-linear and low-budget nature, intercutting narrative with musical performance, demonstrates possibilities for how artists might use story in their own film works. The influence of both films can be seen in the self-reflexive, experimental video essay *The Last Angel of History* (1996), written by Edward George and directed by John Akomfrah, both members of the Black Audio Film Collective. It situates documentary elements – including interviews with Octavia E. Butler, Sun Ra, George Clinton, Lee 'Scratch' Perry and Samuel R. Delany, among others – within an sf narrative framework to explore the relationships between displacement, pan-African culture, music, sf and technology. Like *La Jetée*, it makes use of the premise of a time travelling protagonist, exploring the past to find a way to unlock a possible future.

Ben Rivers's *Slow Action* (2010) uses conventions of documentary and ethnographic film within the narrative framework of a future world of rising sea levels and isolated ecosystems. Rivers commissioned a script from sf writer Mark von Schlegell, which was unread by Rivers until he had shot the 16 mm film footage at four locations: Lanzarote, the Japanese island Gunkanjima, Tuvalu, and the county of Somerset in the UK, where Rivers was born. The script narrates the development of each location, in terms of geology and ecology. While Rivers is interested in what seem to be inevitable and catastrophic forms of collapse, he is also concerned with elements of the medium in which he works, such as employing sound effects taken from an earlier age of sf cinema. He also makes use of production limitations, filming on rough, grainy stock with a wind-up Bolex camera that allows a maximum shot-length of 30 seconds.

Artists have been drawn to the pseudo-ethnographic or anthropological potential of sf as a tool for defamiliarisation and estrangement. Paweł Althamer's *Common Task* (2009), comprising video and installation, presents a group of travellers from Bródno, the artist's Warsaw neighbourhood, dressed in shiny gold outfits meant to resemble space suits. His intention is to stage a new perspective, to allow these explorers to see the world as if they were travellers from another world. These travellers explore their own neighbourhood but move beyond to Brasilia, Brussels and Oxford, as well as to Mali to meet members of the Dogon people. Shezad Dawood's *Piercing Brightness* (2013) is a 77-minute film in which a spaceship lands outside Preston, in northern England, with the goal of establishing contact with the 'Glorious 100', who came to Earth long ago to observe the development of humans. Many of those with whom the aliens make contact have forgotten their mission and now consider Earth their home. Dawood uses this premise to address hierarchies of class, race and religion, with echoes of *Space is the Place*.

Some contemporary works explicitly look to notions of who a future might be for, such as Palestinian artist Larissa Sansour's video *In the Future, They Ate From the Finest Porcelain* (2015). It uses narrative in addressing the politics of archaeology and the idea that myths of the past can generate future hopes of nationhood. Sophia al-Maria's video *Beast Type Song* (2019) draws upon Etel Adnan's complex, formally experimental poem *The Arab Apocalypse* (1980–9), which explores post-colonial experience in relation to a deep sense of history. The poem informs al-Maria's concern with speech and the speechless, colonial legacies, subjectivity and identity in an oblique sf narrative that alludes to a cosmic solar war to create a resonance with the politics of the present. Al-Maria demonstrates how some artists are using sf, not necessarily in terms of elements that immediately look like sf but as a method. In contrast, Hetain Patel's video works rely on overt sf tropes, drawn particularly from sf action cinema and superhero narratives. *Don't Look at the Finger* (2017) stages an Afrofuturist ritual, prefiguring the elaborate designs of film *Black Panther* (Coogler 2018) with a nod to the martial arts combat of *The Matrix* (Wachowski sisters 1999). *Trinity* (2021) sees Patel take on a more conventional narrative approach, presenting a story of a young British Indian woman discovering she has inherited special abilities. It culminates in a sequence, part dance, part combat, in which martial arts and sign language are combined. Patel has reconfigured popular sf and fantastic cinematic experience for subjects who would generally not be represented.

The Boat People (2020) by Tuan Andrew Nguyen, an artist born in Saigon and raised in the US, was shot on 16 mm film and transferred to video for editing and display. It presents a loose narrative set at some point in the future. A group of children arrive in the region that had been known as Bataan in the Philippines. Led by a young girl, they travel to collect stories and objects from the world they never knew. The children are striking in their appearance: one wears an ornamented motorbike helmet, another a pink plastic colander as part of their head gear, with wire attached to a glass jar lid acting as a lens. This bricolage of junk, implying strange and indeterminate possible functions, acts as shorthand for post-apocalyptic sf tropes. Accompanied by a rhythmic soundtrack by the band Gamelan Salukat, the children emerge from the sea and begin to carve objects from wood. They then burn these objects and enter into dialogue with the animated head of a statue as they seek the stories of their ancestors, whoever they might be. With a title that evokes the Vietnamese refugee crisis, *The Boat People* explores reconfigured narratives of identity, history and futurity. It enters the territory of fable, the spiritual and the supernatural, emphasising the ways in which this is a form of sf not strictly defined by Western expectations. An ambitious production, with a cast, crew, soundtrack musicians and technicians, *The Boat People* demonstrates the potential for contemporary art to offer complex and ambitious forms of story-telling free from the specific commercial pressures of mainstream film or television. Institutions and structures that enable the funding of film as artworks, particularly with the intention of being to be displayed in gallery contexts, continue to be a rich and valuable ecosystem for sf works.

For many artists, the distinction between film/video work and the staging of an encounter as an installation is no longer particularly significant. Rather, the realisation of moving image work often entails the creation of some kind of environment for it to be experience in. For example, Sejin Kim's video installation *2048* (2019) makes use of three large walls of screens built from commercial digital signage displays to tell a speculative narrative on the future of Antartica after the expiration of the treaty that protects the continent from exploitation of its material resources. Gerard Byrne's *1984 and Beyond* (2005–7) is presented on three monitors. Playing on documentary and re-enactment, it is based on a 1963 panel discussion from *Playboy* in which famous sf writers, including Arthur C. Clarke and Ray Bradbury, were assembled and asked to speculate on various aspects of life in the year 1984. Byrne's video installation uses actors shot on location in modernist buildings. They pontificate and deliver predictions, such as a permanent base on the moon by 1980. The script is divided into 12 scenes, spread in non-sequential order across three monitors. The audience listen with headphones, sitting in chairs set out in front of each monitor, making this an intimate work in which history and speculative futurity are unpacked and reconfigured in a gallery space.

Some recent examples of installation art resonate with Nam June Paik's fascination with technology as a form of futurity. Haroon Mirza creates installations, video works and performances that enact oblique modes of sf. This acknowledged interest drives and informs his work, which covers a broad set of investigations, including scientific knowledge, colonialism, ritual, belief and narrative. His work can be visceral, immersing audiences in experiences that are as much physical as they are cognitive modes of estrangement. He considers electricity to be his medium, while sf is used as a tool to speculate and attempt to make sense of global modernity. The installation */\/\/\ /\/\/\ (Aquarius)* (2017) uses four channels of video and 12 channels of audio, along with LED lights, water and an echo-free chamber to create an immersive encounter that references both constellations and astrological sign – an age of Aquarius alongside AI, science coexisting with shamanism. Andrew Luk and Samuel Swope collaborated on *Ready/Set/Fulfill* (2021) at de Sarthe Gallery in Hong Kong. In the installation, visitors observe the video feeds of drone cameras being flown through an elaborate series of environments. These spaces reference the imagined architecture of an encroaching future, in which drones traverse a hive-like space, echoing Paik's refusal to differentiate technology from nature. Slime Engine, an artist collective based in Shanghai, explore technological futurity through an interest in online and offline networks. Slime Engine were already considering methods of communicating with audiences from a distance before the Covid-19 pandemic made the remote presentation of art a practical necessity. Since 2017, they have been working on manipulating and expanding a sense of virtual space as a new participatory environment in a work titled *Oceans* (2019–), a new kind of physical installation as a vast VR experience. They create interactive situations reminiscent of games, drawing on cinematic influences and futuristic tropes. The interactive situations and the virtual environments that Slime Engine create offer glimpses of a future world, with fictional institutions dealing with new realities of politics and pandemics. *Headlines* (2020) is an online work that parodies media platforms, fusing what is with what might be.

Sf has the power to explore social, political, psychic and cognitive dynamics. It can be a critical tool, offering spaces of challenge and possibility. Tai Shani's hybrid practice of installation, video, performance and text brings sf into a realm composed of experiential and obliquely narrative encounters. They are shaped by theoretical and historically explorations of feminism and myth, generating an idiosyncratic and politicised field of aesthetics. Shani's ongoing project *Dark Continent*, also known as *D.C. Productions*, began in 2016 and is imagined by the artist as a *gesamtkuntswerk*, a total work of art, which is not a singular form but composed of multiple iterations. The work references authors including Christine de Pizan, Marge Piercy, Joanna Russ and Octavia E. Butler in generating sensory and speculative modes that resist models of patriarchal hierarchy. Shani combines multiple forms of practice within a whole, a process that generates a world of speculative outcomes. Her practice points to formal, technical and critical possibilities for how art can continue to build relationships with sf. In particular, Shani's practice demonstrates ways in which video, installation, performance and speculative fictions can be a part of the creation of spaces for an inclusive and transformative politics. This sf potential points beyond art's tendency to respond to the challenges of technological modernity and towards a future for contemporary art as a speculative form in its own right.

23

ANGLOPHONE PRINT FICTION

The New Wave to the new millennium

Rebecca McWilliams Ojala Ballard

For histories of literary fiction, describing one period stretching from the 1960s to the end of the twentieth century, covering the emergence and evolution of postmodernism before the rise of the twenty-first century's new post-postmodern, is relatively standard. However, most histories of Anglophone sf divide this 40 year span into two distinct periods: the first, the New Wave, stretches from the early 1960s into the 1970s, at which point (the story often goes) the literary vision of the previous decade attenuates; the second, cyberpunk, begins in the 1980s and is influential throughout the 1990s. This two-part historical schema reinforces the importance of both avant-garde movements to mid-to-late twentieth century sf, but implies they are best approached separately. While taking seriously their differences and the ways that each helped shape roughly 20 years of print sf production and reception, this chapter offers a more unified history of late-twentieth century prose sf. It traces the common threads across both halves of this period *and* attends to the important work that emerged in the gaps surrounding this two-movement version of sf history (such as the late 1970s to the early 1980s and the latter half of the 1990s, after cyberpunk's influence had begun to wane).

From the New Wave to the new millennium, three (often overlapping) issues dominated the field of sf. First, the genre's ability to claim literary prestige and market share. This was inflected by shifts in the publishing industry: both the New Wave and cyberpunk were in many ways 'crises of legitimation' (Landon 149), which played out in debates about literary substance and style and in widespread concerns about market impacts on creative production in relation to the post-WWII shift from magazine to paperback publication that consolidated from the 1970s onward. Second, sf's alignment with radical and liberatory rather than conservative politics, a contentious development often expressed as a move from optimistic to pessimistic perspectives. Third, the genre's engagement with technology – whether sf was to be 'hard', 'soft' or some cyborg synthesis of the two. This chapter pays particular attention to the ways in which the New Wave and cyberpunk movements, as well as works contemporaneous to but not directly associated with the latter, responded to these issues. The varied expressions of and responses to these concerns give shape to a coherent narrative in which post-Golden Age developments were defined and defended by way of describing sf's ever-closer relationship to *reality*. The increasing 'science-fictionality' of contemporaneous life was often linked directly to the shapes that sf itself took, especially in relation

DOI: 10.4324/9781003140269-25

to prestige, politics and technoculture: in other words, as the world became more science fictional, sf adapted to represent it.

These themes take on additional significance for our understanding of the period because sf's formalisation as an academic area of study – which took place between the New Wave and cyberpunk – relied on positions being staked out about them. The establishment of sf studies is largely a product of the 1970s, beginning with the founding of the Science Fiction Research Association in 1970 and of a number of academic journals (the *SFRA Review*, formerly the *SFRA Newsletter*, in 1971; *Foundation* in 1972; *Science Fiction Studies* in 1973) and cemented by the publication of several significant critical books near the decade's end, including Samuel R. Delany's *The Jewel-Hinged Jaw* (1977) and Darko Suvin's *Metamorphoses of Science Fiction* (1979). Although this chapter focuses on the history of sf *literature*, it is helpful to consider sf studies as a fulcrum between the New Wave and cyberpunk – one in which questions of prestige, political significance and technological engagement were articulated in ways that spoke back to these movements and beyond.

The New Wave

The New Wave was 'a turning point in the genre's development and history' (Link and Canavan 8). It is most often dated to 1964, when author Michael Moorcock took over editorship of *New Worlds*, a mainstay of British sf since the 1950s. Under Moorcock's leadership, which would last until 1971, the magazine launched a sea change in sf, defining the genre's present and future in direct opposition to its Golden Age predecessors.

This transformation was championed and extended by anthologists, who were becoming more important as magazines' influence waned and the paperback book market became increasingly central to sf publishing. American–Canadian writer turned anthologist Judith Merril, an outspoken fan of British New Wave sf, sought to bring the movement to American audiences with her anthology *England Swings SF* (1968), which collected stories by such New Wave luminaries as Brian W. Aldiss, J.G. Ballard, Thomas M. Disch, Pamela Zoline and Moorcock himself, and earned the description 'disturbingly mod' in a *Publishers Weekly* review. Meanwhile, Harlan Ellison launched the New Wave in the US with his anthologies *Dangerous Visions* (1967) and *Again, Dangerous Visions* (1972). These featured exclusively original stories by a diverse group: Golden Age stars such as Poul Anderson, Isaac Asimov, Lester Del Rey and Theodore Sturgeon, some of whom would take on equally central roles in the new movement, alongside established and emerging New Wave writers, such as Disch, John Brunner, Samuel R. Delany, Philip K. Dick, Carol Emshwiller, Philip José Farmer, Ursula K. Le Guin, Larry Niven, Joanna Russ, James Tiptree, Jr, Gene Wolfe and Roger Zelazny. (This heterogeneity reflected the distinct sensibilities of the American New Wave, which was less of a radical break than an evolution of pre-existing experimental tendencies from the previous decade's sf.) Beyond these anthologies, the New Wave saw a more general shift away from magazines (*New Worlds*' dominance in the 1960s aside); as Beth S. Luey argues, 'Perhaps the most important story in post-war American commercial publishing was the growth of the paperback', as paperback books became 'not a technological innovation but a marketing and selling revolution' (42–3). In the specific context of sf, the 'paperback revolution' accounted for a massive part of the New Wave's growing market share – and was an important element in the New Wave's literary self-fashioning, as the genre addressed the newly expanded readership that the paperback explosion helped produce.

Debates over terminology and categorisation – such as whether the 'New Wave' was properly limited to the smaller original group of British writers or could be said to include stylistically and thematically similar American authors, many of whom rejected the designation – are common in discussions of the New Wave. Regardless of label, however, Anglophone sf in the 1960s and 1970s was dominated by writers and editors dedicated to bold, self-aware experiments in which they rejected previous genre norms and expectations along three axes: stylistic prowess; radical and countercultural ideology; and an expansion of the proper terrain of the speculative beyond technology into other aspects of human experience.

Style and substance

The most immediately evident difference between the New Wave and its predecessors was a commitment to the experimental style in vogue in contemporaneous literary fiction. As Asimov wrote, because in *Dangerous Visions* 'The accent moved very heavily toward style' he asked to write the foreword rather than contribute fiction: 'I felt that any story I wrote [...] would be too sober, too respectable, and, to put it bluntly, too darned *square*' (xxvi, xxvii). This 'growth in literariness', in which sf writers nodded to modernist experimentation while taking up postmodernism's self-conscious fragmentation, surrealism and irony, was enabled by larger shifts in the genre publishing world that 'largely liberated the writer from editorial control' (Sutherland 174, 173). Indeed, Ellison described *Dangerous Visions* as necessary precisely because magazine editors would not accept this kind of writing. Shifts in style were thus tied to shifts in publishing and, in turn, in readership: the 'economic change' as the paperback market expanded 'was mirrored by a generational shift which brought a different kind of reader and writer to sf' (Merrick 106), one invested more in literary qualities than in either fandom or science and technology. For example, as R.E. Fulton argues, Donald A. Wollheim – founder of the Futurians, pioneering figure in the field of original and mass market sf anthologies, and influential editor first at Ace Books (which, along with the newly established Ballantine, shaped the expanding audience for sf's paperback market in the 1960s) and then at DAW Books, which he founded in 1971 as the first sf/fantasy mass market publishing house – 'discovered in the paperback book the potential to elevate a genre formerly marked as lowbrow, and to encourage innovation and experimentation within that genre' (350).

On the page, then, this expansion in readership through the paperback revolution meant a new interest in experimental literary techniques. Farmer's 'Riders of the Purple Wage' (1967), published in *Dangerous Visions*, reads as both an homage to the densely associative and experiential modernist style of James Joyce's *Ulysses* (1920) and *Finnegans Wake* (1939) – 'Dunghill and cock's egg: up rises the cockatrice and gives first crow, two more to come, in the flushrush of blood of dawn of I-am-the-erection-and-the-strife' (37) – and as a contribution to emergent modes of postmodern pastiche refracting the media-saturated society of late capitalism. Meanwhile, Zoline's 'The Heat Death of the Universe' (1967), first published in *New Worlds* and reprinted in Merril's *England Swings SF*, proceeds not as a coherent narrative but as a disjunctive set of 54 narrative fragments. Linguistic experiments and difficult, nonlinear patterns of prose increasingly became part of sf, as in Delany's *Dhalgren* (1975), a nearly 900-page text characterised by circular structures, surrealist scenes and fragmented consciousness.

This integration into sf of 'the literary techniques and standards of the mainstream' was part of a shift in which it became 'extremely important to invigorate its prose style, to create a new kind of SF that would be taken seriously as literature' (Landon 150, 152). Literary techniques and postmodern style thus took on new centrality in New Wave-era sf. Conversely, with the rise of postmodernism, sf tropes and themes began to enter the literary mainstream, with major writers such as Thomas Pynchon, whose 'Entropy' (1960) was reprinted in *New Worlds* in 1969, and Kurt Vonnegut, Jr, whose 'The Big Space Fuck' (1972) appeared in *Again, Dangerous Visions*, rendering the formal boundaries between literary fiction and sf increasingly porous. The New Wave's experimental style thus became one way to distinguish itself from its predecessors, laying claim to greater artistic depth and literary prestige.

Politics and ideologies

Style was only one of the ways in which sf remade itself in the 1960s and 1970s. The New Wave also announced itself via shifts in subject matter, increasingly aligning with countercultural, radical and progressive political sensibilities, concerns and movements as it 'began to peel open the ideological myths of supreme scientific competence and galactic manifest destiny' (Broderick 52). A 'new freedom with sex and politics' (Sutherland 174) meant that sexually explicit content became more and more the norm. When, for example, Ballard published 'Why I Want to Fuck Ronald Reagan' (1968) as a pamphlet in the UK, the pseudoscientific story became the subject of an obscenity trial; it was subsequently included in *The Atrocity Exhibition* (1970), the first American edition of which was actually destroyed by its own publisher. This particularly dramatic example indicates the New Wave's interest in countercultural signalling, from explicit sexual content to representations of drugs, especially psychedelics. It also helps to position it as in conversation with literary fiction, especially the Beats (Moorcock, Ballard and Merril all championed William S. Burroughs, whose novels from the 1950s and early 1960s can be seen as progenitors in experimental style and shocking content). Beyond the 'addition of sex, violence, and strong language', however, the New Wave more substantively evinced a 'newly contentious politics' (Harris-Fain 34); 'reflect[ing] the cultural turbulence and controversy of the 1960s' (Landon 150), New Wave sf adopted 'a more liberal, and sometimes radical position' (Sutherland 184) on major issues of the day including gay rights, feminism, environmentalism and Cold War-era geopolitics.

Many New Wave fictions set personal interactions against larger political backdrops speaking to gender and sexuality. For example, Delany's 'Aye, and Gomorrah' (1967), a futuristic tale of a space age society published in *Dangerous Visions*, juxtaposes open same-sex attraction with a taboo fetish among 'frelks' for the androgynous 'Spacers' neutered to protect them from radiation encountered during routine astronautical work. Like much of Delany's oeuvre, it uses sf 'to confound prejudice and illuminate otherness' (Broderick 59). Le Guin's *The Left Hand of Darkness* (1969) traces a relationship between an 'ambisexual' from the planet Gethen and a male human ambassador from Earth who finds his assumptions about sex, gender, attraction and intimacy upended by his companion's androgyny and fluidity. These queer and feminist strands of sf became increasingly radical in step with political movements in the 1970s, with more militant works including Joanna Russ's multiverse parable *The Female Man* (1975) and Marge Piercy's critical utopian novel *Woman on the Edge of Time* (1976). James Tiptree, Jr, who wrote under a male pseudonym until her identity as Alice Sheldon was revealed in 1977, drew particular scrutiny in her treatment of sexual politics. A similar pattern characterised New Wave engagement with environmentalism: early interest in the 1960s led to relatively more committed activist positions in the 1970s.

The Vietnam War also became a subject of increasing interest in the US, refracted allegorically through sf scenarios and addressed directly in critical conversations. Works such as Le Guin's 'The Word for World is Forest' (1972) from *Again, Dangerous Visions* and Joe Haldeman's space opera *The Forever War* (1974) presented powerful opposition to the war, addressing neo-imperialism, ecological and social destruction and the devastating effects on veterans. Vietnam also became a Golden Age/New Wave shibboleth in spring 1968, when *Galaxy Science Fiction* magazine ran two full-page facing ads, one supporting and one opposing the US presence in Vietnam: while the former was signed by 'a roll call of champions of super-science and supermen, of manly and military virtue', signatories of the latter included 'almost the entire vanguard' (Franklin 342) of the New Wave. This shift toward activist literary and paraliterary work, an expression of a larger 'master narrative fatigue' (Mancus 338), helped the New Wave define itself as progressive, sceptical, and radical, not only attentive to but indeed participating in the movements and issues of its time.

Technology and beyond

The countercultural politics of the New Wave dovetailed with its relative suspicion of narratives of progress, technological and otherwise. While 'a strong cautionary streak' (expressed in dystopian and apocalyptic narratives) was certainly part of the genre's repertoire, previous eras of sf, particularly in the US magazine tradition, had largely tended toward optimistic perspectives, and the 'growing pessimism about humanity's present and future that permeated the New Wave scandalized many in the field' (Harris-Fain 34). New Wave pessimism manifested not only in dystopian narratives but also in a broader interest in exploring 'novums' (Suvin) that had to do less with technological developments than with diverse forms of social change. The New Wave's 'attitude toward science and technology' was linked, then, to 'its growing concern with the "soft" sciences of psychology, sociology, and anthropology' (Landon 150). Le Guin's *The Left Hand of Darkness,* the plot of which has less to do with technology than human sexuality, culture, philosophy and religion, exemplifies this dynamic. Even sf offering the 'traditional' fare of extrapolated technological change foregrounded social, political, cultural and psychological considerations. For example, Philip K. Dick's near-future dystopia *A Scanner Darkly* (1977) investigates mental health, drug use and social disposability as much as, if not more than, the speculative policing and surveillance technology its undercover protagonist uses.

Indeed, particularly in Britain, the New Wave's shift away from a focus on technology was even more revolutionary: Moorcock's position was that 'the speculative notion need not be applied just to alien cultures, spacetravel, etc., but might also be used to explore internal concerns, such as madness or loneliness, or to describe transitory experiences, such as drug-taking or listening to music' (Priest 199). As the world became more science fictional, the New Wave began to consider every element of consciousness and culture available for speculative treatment.

In short, then, as the New Wave differentiated itself from earlier sf, its stylistic, political and thematic experiments stretched the genre's parameters, allowing it to define itself as an independent aesthetic movement and as a response to a rapidly changing world. As Jean Baudrillard would write, 'SF of this sort is no longer an elsewhere, it is an everywhere' (312).

Cyberpunk and its contemporaries

In the early 1980s, a new avant-garde emerged that shared the New Wave's affinity for 'oppositional rhetoric' (Landon 159). Cyberpunk quickly developed a remarkably coherent thematic and aesthetic identity. Preoccupied with virtuality, cybernetics and technological advances, its studied aesthetic oversaturation mirrored the information overload of contemporary technoculture. It featured hackers, coders and data pirates, depicted grim dystopian futures, and (per its name) borrowed punk's joyfully grimy and disruptive aesthetics while, also like punk, thumbing its nose at the neoliberal policies and re-emergent conservative culture of the Reagan and Thatcher era. Some have argued that early cyberpunk superstars such as William Gibson and Bruce Sterling were *too* successful in formalising its conventions and parameters, producing such a dominant and unified account that it had no room to evolve and quickly petered out. By the 1990s, although cyberpunk aesthetics were increasingly popular in film and video games, its influence on prose fiction had waned, with Neal Stephenson's *Snow Crash* (1992) perhaps less a sincere contribution to cyberpunk than a parody of its tropes.

The tight parameters – formal, thematic, historical – that made cyberpunk so immediately, explosively recognisable also make it a challenging periodising marker. Unlike the New Wave, which (despite contemporaneous protestations) is now read as broadly characterising two decades of sf cultural production, cyberpunk was always an uneasy container for the 1980s and 1990s. (As early as 1986, Michael Swanwick's 'The User's Guide to the Postmoderns' drew a provocative binary between the 'cyberpunk' and the 'humanist' sf of the moment.) This chapter therefore situates cyberpunk as *one* major manifestation of a broad science fictional preoccupation with the emergent concepts of biopolitics and biopower through the 1980s and 1990s – a preoccupation evident not only in cyberpunk and its closest relatives (particularly steampunk and biopunk), but also in other subgenres, such as the new space opera, and a range of dystopian and utopian projects. A shared sense that biopolitics were rendering the world ever more science fictional motivated the stylistically and thematically varied sf movements of the period. After all, despite its lasting influence (particularly on film and video game aesthetics), cyberpunk was relatively limited historically, with its literary heyday lasting at best a scant decade from the mid-1980s to the mid-1990s. Attending instead to the broader range of 1980s and 1990s sf engaging neoliberalism and biopolitics reveals alignments not only between cyberpunk and the New Wave, but also between cyberpunk and its contemporaries.

Punk and other aesthetics of postmodernity

Of all of the sf movements of the 1980s and 1990s, cyberpunk was the most deliberate in its projection of a new aesthetic. 'New', of course, does not mean without precedent; cyberpunk owed, and acknowledged, a major stylistic debt to the New Wave (Tiptree and Ballard in particular), as well as to other genre traditions such as noir. In the preface to *Mirrorshades: The Cyberpunk Anthology* (1986), Sterling identified aesthetic affinities between New Wave and cyberpunk – 'Many of the cyberpunks write a quite accomplished and graceful prose; they are in love with style' (x) – while insisting that the latter's most important stylistic influence was punk rather than high modernism: 'like the punks of '77, they prize their garage-band esthetic' (x). The result, Sterling argued, was 'sensory overload that submerges the reader in the literary equivalent of the hard-rock "wall of sound"' (xv). Take, for instance, the famous first sentence of Gibson's *Neuromancer* (1984), the exemplar of cyberpunk style: 'The sky above the port was the color of television, tuned to a dead channel' (9). Like this opening, the novel continuously both references and replicates its world's media ecology, paralleling 'the information overload of electronic culture with a sensory overload of embedded images' (Landon 163–4).

Like the New Wave, cyberpunk leveraged this avant-garde aesthetic not only for identity and notoriety but also for cultural capital, which was especially resonant for sf readers concerned with what the trends toward corporatisation and the rise of the conglomerates would mean for the genre (Brouillette 190–2). Cyberpunk's self-conscious allegiance to punk rather than to an elite aesthetics was, in fact, a roundabout way of claiming prestige: the genre's emergence dovetailed with the heyday of literary theory in Anglophone universities, and postmodernism – the hot ticket item of 1980s theory – seized on cyberpunk, anointing it as 'the supreme *literary* expression if not of postmodernism, then of late capitalism itself' (Jameson 417, n1). Cyberpunk's avowed distaste for high modernist aesthetics, then, was paradoxically part of its elite intellectual position. Whereas the New Wave sought to position itself as serious literature, cyberpunk found an identity in conversation with serious literary theory.

On the other side of the ostensible cyberpunk/humanist divide, less self-consciously avant-garde works also invested in style and form. As the trend away from magazines and toward books continued, sf authors emphasised their relationships to non-genre literature – in part, arguably, because of widespread concerns about prestige and artistic integrity that were linked to the rise of conglomeration and 'the changing science-fiction publishing industry' (Brouillette 192). Dan Simmons's space opera epic *Hyperion* (1989), for example, takes up Chaucer's *Canterbury Tales* as a major intertext through extensive allusion. Meanwhile, Margaret Atwood's feminist dystopia *The Handmaid's Tale* (1985), a critically acclaimed and academically canonised novel following the life of a woman after a fundamentalist Christian coup transforms the US into an oppressive patriarchal hellscape, was published with a literary press (McClelland and Stewart) rather than a genre press or imprint, despite engaging classically dystopian tropes and themes. This period also saw the emergence of Kim Stanley Robinson, who remains one of the foremost utopian thinkers, from his debut novel *The Wild Shore* (1984), the first novel in his Three Californias trilogy (1984–90), through the instantly canonical Hugo-, Locus- and Nebula-winning Mars trilogy (1992–6) and on into the twenty-first century. Despite Robinson's alignment with the 'humanists', his work shares cyberpunk's preoccupation with literary theory; his alignments with Marxism in particular are explicitly informed by Fredric Jameson, the supervisor of his PhD thesis on Philip K. Dick.

This commitment to elite aesthetics and experimentation, and its underlying relationship to literary prestige, thus highlights affinities not only between the New Wave and cyberpunk movements, but also between cyberpunk and the myriad other subgenres active during the 1980s and 1990s. Here, Delany provides an important case study in the artificiality of these ostensible boundary lines: an important figure in the New Wave (although he rejects the label) and a stylistic influence on cyberpunk, he published several of his most important works between the two movements, including *Triton* (1976) and the first volumes of the Return to Nevèrÿon series (1979–85). Offering frequent epigraphs from and allusions to structuralist and poststructuralist theory, and self-consciously framed by appendices that situate the novels in relation to a fictional ancient manuscript, Return to Nevèrÿon shows the extent to which the concerns with style, prestige, theory and 'seriousness' that had characterised the New Wave's self-definitions continued to drive literary production across later decades.

Speculative biopolitics and leftist critique

The post-New Wave period saw the emergence of neoliberal economic policies and conservative cultural norms, crystallised in the US and UK by Reagan and Thatcher. A great deal of sf during this period took aim at these political realities from the left, casting a critical eye on global corporate capitalism and its new technologies. Indeed, the political emphasis of sf during this period – whether from the cyberpunks or the humanists – was on the workings of biopower and biopolitics, concepts proposed by Michel Foucault in the 1970s to describe the ways in which modern states adopted forms of surveillance and control at the level of the population via the management of bodies.

Cyberpunk's interest in neoliberal biopolitics is integral to its dystopian techno-pessimism. Frequently focusing on characters enmeshed in global systems of control (both states and, increasingly, militarised corporations), cyberpunk fiction such as Gibson's Sprawl trilogy (1984–8), Pat

Cadigan's *Synners* (1991) and Stephenson's *Snow Crash* model complex transnational networks of interaction and influence extending far beyond the individual while focusing on struggles over technologised forms of population-level management and control. In the cyberpunk imaginary, the attenuated neoliberal state is succeeded by global corporations seeking technologically enabled biopolitical management – a pessimistic political position rooted in contemporaneous leftist critique, and, as Sarah Brouillette argues, magnified by authors' and fans' concerns about the shifting structure of corporate consolidation among paperback publishers.

Even beyond cyberpunk, concerns with militarised biopolitical management characterise many of the major works and movements of the 1980s and 1990s, such as feminist sf, including Atwood's *The Handmaid's Tale*, Octavia E. Butler's *Kindred* (1979) – an Afrofuturist time-travel story examining the intimate systems of intersectional oppression wrought against Black women – Nicola Griffith's *Ammonite* (1992) and Nancy Kress's *Beggars in Spain* (1992). In space opera, another incredibly popular subgenre whose stars included Lois McMaster Bujold, Dan Simmons and Vernon Vinge, Orson Scott Card's *Ender's Game* (1985) reveals the enmeshment of biopolitical control with militarisation and techno-entertainment. Finally, the emergent subgenre of biopunk, with notable authors including Greg Bear and Michael Crichton, was preoccupied with the relationship between biotechnology and social control. Butler's LILITH'S BROOD trilogy (1987–9), a particularly field-defining example of biopunk, follows the emergence of human–alien hybrids after a 'gene trading' species called the Oankali arrive on a post-apocalyptic Earth, and offers provocative, unsettling insights onto community formation, coercion and genetic determinism. Biopolitics also infused the utopian texts of the period, such as Le Guin's lengthy post-apocalyptic anthropological tour de force *Always Coming Home* (1985), which treats an imaginary future society in relation to its biopolitical and ecological self-management and population control, and Kim Stanley Robinson's THREE CALIFORNIAS and MARS trilogies, which probe in sometimes uncomfortable detail the management of life and death in variously utopian states.

Across and after the years most commonly associated with cyberpunk, then, diverse authors and movements underscored sf's alignment with systemic political critiques, expressed both as dystopian cautionary tales and utopian possibilities. Cyberpunk may have been the genre of late-capitalism/postmodernity, but the political and especially the biopolitical concerns of the neoliberal moment of the 1980s and 1990s shaped the commitments – in particular, the leftist commitments – of a much broader range of sf in the period.

Technocultural transformations

Whereas the New Wave sought to create space between sf and technology, cyberpunk took up technoculture as the most important feature of contemporary life. At the same time, 1980s and 1990s sf distinguished between, as Sterling put it his *Mirrorshades* preface, 'the giant steam-snorting wonders of the past' and new technology – 'pervasive, utterly intimate' – that 'sticks to the skin, responds to the touch' (xiii). Rather than regarding technology as a shibboleth dividing 'hard' cyberpunk from its 'soft' sf contemporaries, the emergent interest in biopolitics and embodiment can be seen as an affinity between cyberpunks focused on virtuality and technology and contemporaneous sf investigating other aspects of embodiment.

Neuromancer, for instance, offers the canonically cyberpunk take on technology, featuring artificial intelligence, an immersive virtual reality space called (influentially) the matrix, and the computerised preservation of uploaded consciousness. Similarly embodied technocultural imaginaries, though, are also evident in works that do not claim primary affinity with cyberpunk. For example, Delany's *Stars in My Pocket Like Grains of Sand* (1984) is primarily a queer and interspecies take on space opera, but it carefully embeds both its key interpersonal relationship – between diplomat Marq Dyeth and formerly enslaved refugee Rat Korga – *and* its larger interstellar imaginaries in profoundly embodied forms of technological access. Rat's narrative arc begins with a destructive 'anxiety termination' neurological procedure, carried out by profiteering entities that promise social relief while harvesting compliant labour, and continues through the discovery of sophisticated rings that give him new cognitive powers, while Marq's personal and political arcs proceed through an intergalactic information technology called the Web. In Butler's PARABLE series (1993–8) immersive virtual reality videos called 'Dreamasks' exist alongside less canonically cyberpunk forms of embodied technology, such as pharmaceuticals that produce a disability called hyperempathy, which causes the protagonist to feel whatever pain or pleasure she observes others experiencing, and biometrically coded shock collars used by slavers to keep prisoners compliant. As technology became ever more intimately embodied, sf's engagement with it shifted from explicitly 'hard' tropes to more diverse manifestations, both within and beyond cyberpunk.

Across the 1980s and 1990s, then, sf engaged in literary practices speaking to issues of academic prestige and canonisation, tackled the dystopian prospects of neoliberal biopower, and used new technological concerns to probe the borders between 'hard' and 'soft' sf. When 'distinctions between the imaginary and the real [were] blurred by science and technology', sf writers carved out new space for a 'soft agenda SF' capable of grappling with a world whose realities were as science fictional as sf itself (Landon 176).

Conclusion

Although the period from the 1960s to 2000 saw a number of disparate movements in Anglophone print sf, three consistent concerns motivated both the broad sweep of the New Wave and the varied subgenres contemporaneous with cyberpunk: prestige and legitimisation, often framed in terms of literary style and value, against a backdrop of shifting publishing infrastructures; sf's privileged relationship to (especially leftist) political critique; and the role of technology within sf. Indeed, the same concerns guided the emergence of sf studies as an academic field, both reflecting and shaping the history of the genre. These three concerns cut in two historical directions. On the one hand, they were aimed at distinguishing new movements from those that had come before. On the other, they were directed at the present and future, seeking to position sf as uniquely able to speak to the growing science fictionality of the late twentieth century world. If, as Donna J. Haraway wrote in 'A Cyborg Manifesto', 'The boundary between science fiction and social reality is an optical illusion' (149), then sf from the New Wave to the new millennium continuously reinvented itself so as to make that illusion visible.

Works cited

Asimov, Isaac. 'Foreword'. *Dangerous Visions*. Ed. Harlan Ellison. Orion, 2002. xxii–xxviii.

Baudrillard, Jean. 'Simulacra and Science Fiction'. Trans. Arthur B. Evans. *Science Fiction Studies* 55 (1991): 309–13.

Broderick, Damien. 'New Wave and Backlash: 1960–1980'. *The Cambridge Companion to Science Fiction*. Ed. Edward James and Farah Mendlesohn. Cambridge UP, 2003. 48–63.

Brouillette, Sarah. 'Corporate Publishing and Canonization: *Neuromancer* and Science-Fiction Publishing in the 1970s and Early 1980s'. *Book History* 5.1 (2002): 187–208.

Farmer, Philip José. 'Riders of the Purple Wage'. *Dangerous Visions*. Ed. Harlan Ellison. Orion, 2002. 37–113.

Franklin, H. Bruce. 'The Vietnam War as American Science Fiction and Fantasy'. *Science Fiction Studies* 52 (1990): 341–59.

Fulton, R.E. 'Donald A. Wollheim's Authoritative Universe: Editors, Readers, and the Construction of the Science Fiction Paperback, 1926–1969'. *Book History* 19 (2016): 349–83.
Gibson, William. *Neuromancer*. Ace, 1984.
Haraway, Donna J. 'A Cyborg Manifesto: Science, Technology, and Socialist-Feminism in the Late Twentieth Century'. *Simians, Cyborgs and Women: The Reinvention of Nature*. Routledge, 1991. 149–81.
Harris-Fain, Darren. 'Dangerous Visions: New Wave and Post-New Wave Science Fiction'. *The Cambridge History of Science Fiction*. Ed. Gerry Canavan and Eric Carl Link. Cambridge UP, 2018. 31–43.
Jameson, Fredric. *Postmodernism, Or, The Cultural Logic of Late Capitalism*. Duke UP, 1991.
Landon, Brooks. *Science Fiction after 1900: From the Steam Man to the Stars*. Routledge, 2002.
Link, Eric Carl and Gerry Canavan. 'On Not Defining Science Fiction: An Introduction'. *The Cambridge History of Science Fiction*. Ed. Gerry Canavan and Eric Carl Link. Cambridge UP, 2018. 1–9.
Luey, Beth. 'The Organization of the Book Publishing Industry'. *A History of the Book in America, Volume 5. The Enduring Book: Print Culture in Postwar America*. Ed. David Paul Nord, Joan Shelley Rubin and Michael Schudson. U of North Carolina P, 2015. 29–54.
Mancus, Shannon Davies. 'New Wave Science Fiction and the Counterculture'. *The Cambridge History of Science Fiction*. Ed. Gerry Canavan and Eric Carl Link. Cambridge UP, 2018. 338–52.
Merrick, Helen. 'Fiction, 1964–1979'. *The Routledge Companion to Science Fiction*. Ed. Mark Bould, Andrew M. Butler, Adam Roberts and Sherryl Vint. Routledge, 2009. 102–11.
Priest, Christopher. 'British Science Fiction'. *Science Fiction: A Critical Guide*. Ed. Patrick Parrinder. Routledge, 1979. 187–202.
Sterling, Bruce. 'Preface'. *Mirrorshades: The Cyberpunk Anthology*. Ed. Bruce Sterling. Ace, 1986. ix–xvi.
Sutherland, J.A. 'American Science Fiction since 1960'. *Science Fiction: A Critical Guide*. Ed. Patrick Parrinder. Routledge, 1979. 162–86.
Suvin, Darko. *Metamorphoses of Science Fiction: On the History and Poetics of a Literary Genre*. Yale UP, 1979.

24

COMICS SINCE THE LATE 1960S

Martin Lund

It is not possible to neatly sum up what sf comics have looked like since the late 1960s, not least because it is impossible to say, in an uncontroversial way, what a comic even is. While many of us can say that we know a comic almost instinctively when we see one, it is not actually that easy to make that call, and it never has been. Although perhaps not the best barometer of how general discourses go, the world of academic comics scholarship is a good illustration of this problem. There are plenty of attempts to define the medium (or genre, or art form), and many of them overlap, but there are also some that categorically exclude one or more criteria that another definition considers essential. In short, while comics studies scholars all say we study comics, what we mean by 'comics' is not necessarily the same thing. For simplicity's sake, this chapter follows Noah Berlatsky's broad definition of comics as 'those things which are accepted as comics' (n.p.).

Even with such inclusivity, the problem of scope remains. What should be included? Anglophone overviews of comics genres, types or forms tend to be Americo-centric or at least focused on the Anglophone comics world, without discussing this narrow purview or what is missed by applying it. Particularly common is the use of the 'Ages' schema of comics history: in a framing that seems to suggest diminishing value over time, the 'Golden Age' (usually dated from 1938 to the mid-1950s), followed by the 'Silver Age' (usually ca.1956–ca.1970), followed by the 'Bronze' or 'Modern Age'. Originating in certain forms of comics fandom, this schema poses a significant problem. In most formulations, any given 'Age' is outlined according to a particular understanding of what unites so-called 'superhero' comics of the period and is always limited to US comics – implicitly or explicitly, the 'Ages' naturalise US superhero comics as the primary shape of comics. While any discussion about sf comics must include US superheroes, it should not be limited to them. Superhero comics are not the only sf comics, nor are they ever only, 'purely' sf – not in the US and certainly not in the wider world of comics.

There are few, if any, comics cultures that have not seen works published in the past six decades that fit any given definition of sf. Some are mentioned more often than others. Japanese sf manga such as Katsuhiro Otomo's *Akira* (1982–90) or Masamune Shirow's *Ghost in the Shell* (1989–91) tend to be well-known among audiences outside Japan and are often even considered 'canonical'. But John Lent shows, for example, that comics that can be labelled sf were among the most

DOI: 10.4324/9781003140269-26

popular in Hong Kong in the 1960s (51) and have remained popular since, and he also discusses sf comics from Taiwan (107), Indonesia (148), Malaysia (163), Singapore (209), Thailand (209) and Sri Lanka (312). As these limited examples make clear, sf comics are a global matter. While language barriers and space limitations mean many of these comics and comics cultures cannot be addressed in this chapter, they must be mentioned to lay bare its limitations. Primarily focusing on US sf comics and texts that have been influential on that field of cultural production and consumption, its restricted perspective offers just one possible way into a topic too vast to capture in overview.

As noted, superheroes tend to be considered as prime examples of what sf comics are or can be. In the vein most associated with Marvel and DC, they certainly often include sf: Superman (first introduced in 1938) is probably the most famous of a whole host of aliens with special powers; super-geniuses like the Batman (1939) and Iron Man (1963) use high-tech suits and gadgets to achieve their ends; the Fantastic Four (1961) got their superhuman powers from 'cosmic rays', the Hulk (1962) from 'gamma rays', Spider-Man (1962) from a radioactive spider, the Atom (1961) from harnessing 'white dwarf star matter', and the Flash (1956) from being struck by lightning and doused in chemicals; meanwhile, the Guardians of the Galaxy (1969) and the Green Lantern Corps (1959) police the far reaches of space, even if their conflicts often end up making Earth the centre of the universe. Science and technology, then, play important roles in constituting the worlds of superheroes, sometimes as a source of amazement and sometimes as a source of danger. But if 'science was in earlier comics usually presented as a motor of progress and the promise of a glorious future, this has changed with the generally more critical perspective of recent decades' (Jüngst 259–60), starting around 1968.

Like any comics, those featuring superheroes are products of history and tap into cultural and political concerns of their day. Many long-standing DC and Marvel characters have origins and missions couched in sf tropes and conventions. As the years have gone by, and the languages and concerns of sf have changed, so have the ways these characters are framed. For example, many of Marvel's 1960s stories and characters were preoccupied with atomic power and the Cold War (Costello), including Spider-Man, but in *Ultimate Spider-Man* (2001–11), which tapped into more pressing concerns to reimagine the character for the twenty-first century, he was instead bitten by a genetically modified spider. After the fall of the Iron Curtain, superheroes have found new enemies and fears to fight, in recent decades generally serving in the shadow of the so-called War on Terror.

Similarly, while superheroes of this kind had arrived from or travelled into space for decades before the 1970s, in many ways that decade and the one following marked an increase scope of the generic formation's galactic imagination. For example, writer Chris Claremont brought in space opera themes through intergalactic war stories with arcs that ran across years, drawing on influences including *Star Wars* (Lucas 1977) and *Alien* (Scott 1979). Earth-connected superheroes have repeatedly been engaged in alien wars, such as Marvel's Kree–Skrull war (1971–2) and DC's Rann–Thanagar war (2005). DC and Marvel also increasingly offered explorations of multiple and parallel realities in titles such as DC's *Crisis on Infinite Earths* (1985–6) and Marvel's Squadron Supreme stories, particularly in the 1985 limited series with scripts by Mark Gruenwald and the J. Michael Straczynski-scripted early-2000s run, which also leaned heavily into alien infiltration tropes. Many of these stories frame the Earth readers know as special and superior to any imaginable alternative.

Jeffrey A. Brown argues that in superhero comics, 'specific plots are almost irrelevant, what the superheroes repeatedly enact for readers is a symbolic policing of the borders between key cultural concepts: good and evil, right and wrong, us and them' (78). Indeed, a largely reactionary framing is common in such comics: so-called superheroes use their powers, knowledge, wealth and technology to defend the status quo, implying that advocating for alternative social, economic, gender or racial formations is a form of evil. This framing often includes villains who embody some form of critique of the world as it is. During the Cold War, enemies were often self-identified communists or coded as such. Increasingly since the 1970s, anti-imperialist, environmentalist and anti-racist critiques have instead been increasingly subject to vilification.

While the X-Men's first foe, Magneto (introduced in 1963), was initially coded primarily as a communist, he has become increasingly coded as a revolutionary protector of mutants, whose violent response to anti-mutant persecution marks him as beyond the pale. As a sometime villain and sometime anti-hero, shifts in his characterisation mark a particularly clear negotiation of what is to be considered acceptable political behaviour. But by no means is Magneto alone. In a 1977 Aquaman story in *Adventure Comics* #452, for example, Black Manta took off his helmet for the first time since his creation a decade before; at which moment, the moniker Black Manta became coded as a racialised name, as the writer and artist made him a Black man. He speaks of wanting to find a place where he and 'his people' can live in peace, but this desire is rendered suspect when he reveals he is willing to commit infanticide to achieve it.

More often than not, the politics of superheroism are implicit, naturalised. This is rarely clearer than when a conservative outlet or pundit criticises how these comics are 'politicised' by taking a clear liberal or progressive stance. As noted above, superhero comics have always been political, but more often than not adopt a conservative or reactionary stance. The vast majority of DC and Marvel superheroes were ardent Cold Warriors, for example. Superhero comics have catered to and continue to cater to the male gaze through a preponderance of female-coded characters with impossible physiques, in tight and skimpy outfits, posing in 'broke-back' positions (i.e., positions designed to show as much of the female anatomy as possible in a single image, even though a living woman would have to break her back to achieve it). As already suggested, superhero comics have also historically reproduced structural racism, opposed structural anti-racist change, and have defended White supremacist social and racial formations. Many continue to do so.

One famous and perhaps overexplicit example of how often superhero comics can reinforce reigning political moods and currents, is December 2001's so-called 'Black Issue' of *Amazing Spider-Man* (vol. 2, #36), which offered a superheroic response to the 9/11 terrorist attacks. It praised first responders in melodramatic and unrealistic ways, spoke of 'infinite justice' – the original code name for the so-called War on Terror. It framed the attacks as acts of war, and as unmotivated and impossible to understand, even though the attackers announced their reason. And it spoke of a united US, ignoring, like the government and much of the news media, that racial profiling and Islamophobic and other hate crimes had spiked since the attacks. However, the attacks were not outside history and not everybody felt equally part of this supposedly newly-*United* States. Even the possibly illegal US invasion of Afghanistan on false pretences seems to have been accepted and supported in the comic's bombastic threat: 'You wanted to send us a message [...] Look for your reply in the thunder'.

None of this is to say that the superhero as generic formation and generic character type is inherently conservative or reactionary. It is likely that concerns about marketability, and a drive to ensure that the story engine does not stop, play into the recurring reproduction of social hegemonies. It is also likely that the historical and continuing dominance of White Male writers and executives help keep a White racial frame and male gaze firmly in place. None of this prevents superhero works that challenge these very structures from being produced. In 1993, for example, African American comics creators Dwayne McDuffie, Denys Cowan, Michael Davis and Derek T. Dingle founded Milestone Comics in an attempt to redress the underrepresentation of minority characters in US superhero comics. Recent years have undoubtedly seen an increase in diversity in the transmedial rosters of Marvel and DC, but it remains to see whether it lasts or is merely a marketing issue. Other creators work outside the established centres of the superhero business. Kwanza Osajyefo, Tim Smith 3 and Jamal Igle's *Black* (2016) and its spin-offs, published by newcomer Black Mask Studios, tells the story of a world in which a fraction of Black people have the potential to exhibit superpowers and how White people have been trying for centuries to keep all Black people down. Aside from commenting on current events – protagonist Kareem Jenkins discovers his powers after being shot by a cop who had racially profiled him and two friends – *Black* addresses centuries of anti-Black racism in the US and elsewhere, but also responds to the continuing lack of Black representation in mass market superhero comics and to the difficulties of being a Black creator or creator of colour in a field dominated by White people.

While superheroes are generally regarded as primarily a US phenomenon, some non-US publishers have met with a certain amount of success. *The 99* (2007–14), spearheaded by Naif Al-Mutawa and published by Kuwait-based Teshkeel Comics, centred Islamic culture and attempted to tell a superhero narrative that presented Muslim role models and to counter Islamophobic stereotyping. And since 2015, YouNeek Studios has been offering African-inspired superhero stories under the guidance of Nigerian-born Roye Okupe, who felt that there was a notable lack of African and African-inspired representation in the genre and set out to redress the balance and empower African creatives and storytelling.

Although superheroes have always been subject to revision and parody, superhero comics-makers' gaze has turned more and more inward since the 1980s. It is almost impossible to read a broad discussion of US comics that does not put particular emphasis on Frank Miller's cyberpunk-ish *The Dark Knight Returns* (1986) or Alan Moore and Dave Gibbons's *Watchmen* (1986–7). Both mused on the limits and politics of the comics superhero figure, albeit from different vantage points. In telling the story of a retired Batman returning to active duty in a Gotham ravaged by mutants, Miller embraced the authoritarian tendencies displayed by many superhero figures and made an argument about society's ills and needs in Reaganite terms. To critique concerns like those Miller elevated, Moore and Gibbons took the murder of a government-sponsored superhero as the point of departure for a story that grew to global and cataclysmic proportions.

Lost in the veneration of these comics is an array of other comics that had as much, or perhaps an even larger impact, by working on the tropes of the genre, such as Kevin Eastman and Peter Laird's *Teenage Mutant Ninja Turtles* (1984–2014). In the first issue (May 1984), four baby turtles and a rat are covered in radioactive ooze that falls into the sewers. They mutate and the rat, which had belonged to a murdered martial arts master, trains the turtles to exact revenge. Initially intended as a one-shot that parodied Frank Miller's ninja-heavy *Daredevil* (1979–83) and *Ronin* (1983–4), Marvel's teenager-focused *New Mutants* (1982–), and Dave Sim's talking animal epic *Cerberus* (1977–2004), the comic was a hit, slowly blossoming into a multimedia franchise of comic books, television shows, movies and mountains of merchandise, with sf themes becoming increasingly common. It also inspired a glut of small-press black-and-white comics that wreaked havoc on the comics store industry and collector's culture, and although the child-oriented version of the franchise had a clear environmentalist framing, it has had a severe negative environmental impact in at least two ways: first, many fans got pet turtles and lost interest in them, leading to high numbers of non-native terrapins finding their way into and disrupting local ecosystems, with particularly disastrous consequences in the UK; second, the franchise's popularity led to massive sales of plastic toys, many of which relatively soon came to rest with other non-biodegradables in landfill sites and the Great Pacific Garbage Patch. If the 'Black Issue' shows how comics are not divorced from the world around them, the Ninja Turtles are a good illustration of how the world is not immune to the effects of comic books.

The Teenage Mutant Ninja Turtles did not invent marketing and merchandising synergy, nor were they the first or most efficient marketing machines in the realm of sf comics. Almost as soon as Superman had proved attractive to readers, his visage and symbol was put on all manner of consumer product. And while the Ninja Turtles cartoon was largely produced to bring children's attention to the toy line, this also had precedents. Two years earlier, in 1982, toy company Hasbro had launched a reimagined version of its older G.I. Joe action figure. The original version, introduced in 1963, had been a fairly simple, larger and realistic military-themed toy; the new, smaller version, was tag-lined 'A Real American Hero' and largely left mimeticism behind. In this new version, G.I. Joe was the codename for a team of military specialists who lived in a world of high-tech machinery, laser weapons and, in the form of the main antagonist Cobra Command, scientific terrorism. Following the above-discussed pattern common to superhero comics and showing again how deeply Cold War concerns about infiltration and totalitarianism run, Cobra Commander's radical evil sprung from disillusionment with the federal government and a personal desire for revenge. Channelling his anger into a pyramid scheme, he managed to turn the formerly 'nice little town' of Springfield into a totalitarian front for Cobra, from which he could wage his war for global dominion, with the eponymous team opposing him at every turn. These stories were told in a licensed comic book produced in 1982–92 by Marvel (and in an animated television show that ran between 1983–6). The comic book served to sell and popularise Hasbro's toys and was itself the first comic book advertised on television. Two years later, in 1984, Hasbro and Marvel duplicated their success with the launch of the Transformers toy line and accompanying comic book about two factions of robots from the planet Cybertron who bring their civil war to Earth and hide in plain sight as various everyday machines, such as cars, aeroplanes and construction machinery. Although both franchises have switched publishers over the years, and the emphasis on explicitly tying into and marketing toy-lines may have decreased a little, both G.I. Joe and Transformers continue to deliver sf narratives to comic book, television and movie audiences.

In the US market, perhaps the two most common comics formats are the stapled, floppy comic book, usually 20-some pages in length and telling a single instalment in a longer narrative, and longer-form bound books, whether telling a longer, self-contained story or collecting a number of shorter comics stories. The latter type of collection ranges from trade paperbacks with story arcs from serialised comics to Will Eisner's *Life on Another Planet* (1983), for example, which collects a story originally titled 'Signal from Space' serialised between 1978–80 in the reprint vehicle *Spirit Magazine*. With deep roots in the Cold War context, *Life* presented a pessimistic thought experiment about the psychological, social and geopolitical consequences of humanity encountering proof of extraterrestrial life.

However, no overview of sf comics can omit anthology comics. One of the best-known examples is the French *Métal Hurlant*, co-founded in 1974 by comics artists Jean Giraud (aka Moebius) and Philippe Druillet along with Jean-Pierre Dionnet and Bernard Farkas. Collecting sf and other kinds of stories, it initially ran until 1987 and was revived in 1998–2004. *Métal Hurlant* spun off into or inspired the Anglophone *Heavy Metal* (1977–), the German *Schwermetall* (1980–99) and Swedish *Pulserande Metall* (1984) and *Tung Metall* (1986–90), among others. *Métal Hurlant* and its spin-offs and imitators were influential and introduced readers in their markets to sf comics they otherwise would likely not have encountered. Some serials initially published in the anthology were later collected in album form and have gone on to garner much popularity. Since around the turn of the century, the publisher behind *Métal Hurlant* also publishes longer-form, mostly sf, comics, in French under the name Les Humanoïdes Associés and in the US as Humanoids.

Another highly influential anthology comic is the British *2000 AD* (1977–). Primarily sf, its most well-known offering is the Judge Dredd franchise, which premiered in the second issue. A law enforcement officer in the dystopian Mega City-One, Dredd is judge, jury and executioner rolled into one. The series is known for its satirical edge and thanks to its success has spun off into its own comic book, two movies and other transmedial properties.

On the opposite end of the spectrum, so to speak, are albums and other long-form comics that run over the middle-to-longer term. Pierre Christin and Jean-Claude Mézières's *Valérian et Laureline* (1967–2010) is a prominent example. Originally serialised and ultimately collected in twenty-one albums, this space opera revolves around 'spatio-temporal agents' Valérian and Laureline as they travel through space and time to guard a utopian world from temporal dangers. Alejandro Jodorowsky and Moebius's *Incal* (1980–8) was serialised in *Métal Hurlant* and followed by several sequels and spin-offs by Jodorowsky and other artists, published between 1988–2014. The first story establishes a dystopian setting and focuses on private detective John DiFool's adventures with a mystical artifact sought after by several factions in the galactic empire he inhabits. Mexican American brothers Jaime, Gilbert and Mario Hernandez's *Love & Rockets* (1982–) has told a sprawling story mixing elements from romantic melodrama to interplanetary travel in more than 30 volumes. In an interview, Gilbert Hernandez notes that the use of Latino identity in his work 'was about humanizing Latinos. A *conscious* effort to humanize Latinos' (González 72).

The uses of science in sf comics is not one-to-one representation of science 'as it is', but 'ways of *thinking about* science' (Jüngst 259): 'telling stories and creating "as-if"-scenarios, are ways of dealing with these phenomena' (Locke qtd in Jüngst 259). Along the same lines, visions of the future – utopian, dystopian or otherwise – are not really about the future, but the present. They can vary greatly, as can the temporal distance between imaginer and the imagined, as can the uses to which they are put. In the 1980s, for example, French SF *bandes dessinées* tended to look to the immediate future and to do so with a more pessimistic perspective (Miller 38). For example, Serbian-born French cartoonist Enki Bilal's NIKOPOL trilogy (1980–92) was set in 2023, when Alcide Nikopol returns to Earth after three decades in an orbital prison to find France under totalitarian dictatorship and Egyptian gods roaming the planet. Teaming up with Horus, and allowing the god to inhabit his body, Nikopol sets out to oppose the powers that be. Bilal considers the stories as being less about sf than about 'power and its potential to make life unbearable for the individual' (qtd in Miller 38).

Other dystopian sf comics also offer critiques of power, but in more clearly delineated ways. For example, Kelly Sue DeConnick and Valentine De Landro's *Bitch Planet* (2014–) presents an intersectional feminist critique. Set in a dystopian future, a literally patriarchal society run by 'the Fathers', where non-compliant women are sent to an off-world prison for such crimes as cutting their hair and being ill-tempered, and for such 'aesthetic offenses' as '"wanton obesity" or refusing to conform to various beauty standards' (Oleszczuk 227), *Bitch Planet* turns things that are considered to be outside contemporary gender norms into crimes. In doing so, the series takes the readers' world and makes it strange in order to critique the absurdity of what is otherwise too easily normalised and naturalised; as Anna Oleszczuk notes, 'The creators of this series intentionally use it to engage in the discussions of privilege, power, as well as hypersexualization and archetypes of women in science fiction' (227).

Many of the comics discussed above, can be described with Reynaldo Anderson's critical framing, as 'project[ing] the utopian tendencies of the Eurocentric Enlightenment phenomenon into the future, extending white psychological spaces, political influences, and economic control' (171). Increasingly, Black US comics creators have challenged this Eurocentrism and the White racial frame that has dominated Western comics' engagement with sf and its speculative offshoots. Writing about contemporary Black women comics writers and artists, Deborah Elizabeth Whaley highlights Afrofuturist comics as one major attribute of their works. She defines Afrofuturism as 'an articulation of science-fiction narratives of dystopia and utopia with postmodern interpretations of blackness' (25). The creators about whom she writes 'reach beyond the present and the past to create futuristic settings that demonstrate the potential of depicting what is yet to come' (170). Among her examples is Ashley Wood's *Millennia War* (2006–9), a story about a war between humans and elves based on 'a history of colonialism and cultural misunderstanding' (171).

Afrofuturist, Africanfuturist and Black speculative comics are becoming increasingly common on the US market, as are comics that challenge established patterns of thought and structures of power. While part of this output comes from long-established comics publishers, much more likely owes to the emergence in the past decade of several new actors that promote more critical imaginings. For example, Black Mask Studios – founded in 2012 to publish *Occupy Comics* in the wake of the protest movement for which the comic was named – remains an outlet for titles that critique the present and envision a different future trajectory, often but not exclusively in sf terms; in addition to publishing Osajyefo, Smith 3 and Igle's *Black*, it also offers titles such as Matteo Pizzolo and Amancay Nahuelpan's *Young Terorrists* (2015), about a group of youths who take on a corporate plutocracy in the near future. Rosarium Publishing, founded in 2013, is described on its website as 'a fledgling publisher specializing in speculative fiction, comics, and a touch of crime fiction – all with a multicultural flair'. It includes Afrofuturism, sf and speculative fiction in its sprawling catalogue of comics and other writing. Vault Comics, a publisher specialising in sf, fantasy and horror since 2016, tells visitors to its website that working in these genres 'requires confronting the new, the bizarre, the unimagined' and that 'creators can break the established order, dissolve conceptions of social identity, and give voices to the silenced. They can ask hard questions, and if they are brave, venture bold answers'. And in mid-2021, artist and comics scholar John Jennings launched the Megascope imprint at publishing house Abrams. While not exclusively Afrofuturist, but rather 'dedicated to showcasing speculative works by and about people of color', it is poised to produce sf and other genre works that upset long-standing Whiteness-centring frames.

There are no set rules about what an sf comic can contain or the form it should take; to claim otherwise is to impose an unnecessary limit to understanding what sf comics are or can be. Although sf comics often speak in terms that go beyond the world as most readers encounter it, they have since the late 1960s been firmly rooted in that world. They have spoken about it, spoken to it, spoken in defence of and in protest against it. It is impossible to know for certain what the future will hold, where the limits of scientific and technological accomplishments lie, and what is out there in the vastness of space. Every comic discussed above, and innumerable others from across the planet, have seen an opportunity in those gaps to imagine and speculate for readers' enjoyment and edification – to comfort or to unsettle. Sometimes these comics police the limits of the sayable and believable in a world where capitalism, patriarchy and Whiteness not only rule the present, but can seem destined to extend their rule to the ends of time and space. Sometimes they challenge those structures, and tell readers that something else is possible, that the future is unwritten and that we can all help author it.

Works cited

Anderson, Reynaldo. 'Critical Afrofuturism: A Case Study in Visual Rhetoric, Sequential Art, and Postapocalyptic Identity'. *The Blacker the Ink: Constructions of Black Identity in Comics and Sequential Art*. Ed. Frances K. Gateward and John Jennings. Rutgers UP, 2015. 171–92.

Berlatsky, Noah. 'If You Don't Know, I Can't Tell You'. *Hooded Utilitarian* blog (21 March 2010). < www.hoodedutilitarian.com/2010/03/if-you-dont-know-i-cant-tell-you/>

Brown, Jeffrey A. 'Supermoms? Maternity and the Monstrous-Feminine in Superhero Comics'. *Journal of Graphic Novels and Comics* 2.1 (2011): 77–87.

Costello, Matthew J. *Secret Identity Crisis: Comic Books and the Unmasking of Cold War America.* Continuum, 2009.

González, Christopher. 'Three Decades with Gilbert and Jaime Hernandez: An Odyssey by Interview'. *Graphic Borders: Latino Comic Books Past, Present, and Future.* Ed. Frederick Luis Aldama and Christopher González. U of Texas P, 2016. 64–80.

Jüngst, Heike Elisabeth. 'Science Comics'. *Handbook of Comics and Graphic Narratives.* Ed. Sebastian Domsch, Dan Hassler-Forest and Dirk Vanderbeke. De Gruyter, 2021. 247–64.

Lent, John A. *Asian Comics.* UP of Mississippi, 2015.

Miller, Ann. *Reading Bande Dessinee: Critical Approaches to French-Language Comic Strip.* Intellect, 2008.

Oleszczuk, Anna. 'Gender'. *Handbook of Comics and Graphic Narratives.* Ed. Sebastian Domsch, Dan Hassler-Forest and Dirk Vanderbeke. De Gruyter, 2021. 219–30.

Whaley, Deborah Elizabeth. *Black Women in Sequence: Re-Inking Comics, Graphic Novels, and Anime.* U of Washington P, 2016.

25

TRANSMEDIA AND FRANCHISE SCIENCE FICTION

Dan Hassler-Forest

To misquote Fredric Jameson's famous quip about capitalism, it is easier to imagine the end of the world than the end of STAR WARS. We live in an age where media franchises appear to have established a presence that feels frighteningly permanent. In the twenty-first century, transmedia franchising has indeed become so ubiquitous that it sometimes seems to occupy the entire horizon of our cultural landscape. From STAR WARS and the MARVEL CINEMATIC UNIVERSE to HARRY POTTER'S WIZARDING WORLD and the Godzilla MONSTERVERSE, high-profile sf franchises are much more than extended film series: they stretch across media into a multitude of licensed storytelling extensions, merchandising commodities, and experiential spaces like theme parks.

But this global proliferation of corporate-owned Intellectual Property (IP) is not just a case of particular properties growing popular to the point of cultural saturation. The explosive growth of media franchising has been the result of political and economic shifts that dramatically increased corporations' power within the media landscape. From the late 1970s onward, the implementation of neoliberal policies ushered in an age of corporate deregulation and conglomeration. At the same time, these interlocking transformations were sped up by the rapid growth of digital technology from the 1980s onwards. This process radically reshaped media production and distribution, while digital media convergence eroded longstanding barriers between media platforms.

This chapter reflects on both aspects of this historic shift in sf history: it describes on the one hand how transmedia sf franchises are organised as complex networks of media texts, while on the other contextualising this shift from the perspective of changes at the level of political economy. The phenomenal success of *Star Wars* (Lucas 1977) developed over the years not only into a basic template for sf franchising across media, but it also stood at the dawn of a new era in which a wide variety of transmedia expansions has come to revolve around every major form of IP. Since it has been so central to the development of media franchising over the past 50 years, STAR WARS will inevitably loom large in this discussion – especially since its absorption by the Walt Disney Company illustrates the simultaneous processes of media diversification and corporate monopolisation. But this overview will also draw on a wide range of other examples, from *The Matrix* (Wachowski sisters 1999) to *The LEGO™ Movie* (Lord and Miller 2014), to flesh out this brief history of transmedia and franchise sf.

DOI: 10.4324/9781003140269-27

The *Star Wars* event: Transmedia storytelling takes flight

'A long time ago, in a galaxy far, far away…' The fairy-tale phrase that precedes a deafening blast of horns is by now a ritualistic entry point into a deeply familiar sf universe. When it first appeared on cinema screens in 1977, the words paved the way for a semi-mythical space opera that nostalgically revived the serialised sf of the 1930s and 1940s. Two generations after its momentous premiere, this nostalgia has turned in on itself: aging fans are reminded of the wonder they felt watching *Star Wars* as a child, eagerly introducing their offspring to what has by now become a prime example of transgenerational entertainment.

As *Star Wars* swiftly developed into the pop-cultural phenomenon of its era, the film's cultural impact was marked above all by its merchandising footprint. The astonishing success of the film's action figures, T-shirts, lunch boxes and bedspreads taught Hollywood studio executives a valuable lesson: whereas licensed merchandising had previously provided ancillary profits, the wildly popular commodities showed that these derivative products, if properly handled, could be developed into a long-term source of profits (Booth 188). And while the growing variety of licensed toys kept a youthful audience engaged with the film's storyworld, a multitude of other media extended the storyworld in different directions.

Writer-director George Lucas proved himself shrewdly aware of how sf fans were already skilled at navigating media networks, obsessively exploring connections between different platforms and formats. Anticipating that a high-risk endeavour like *Star Wars* would depend heavily on the interest and support of organised sf fandom, the film's novelisation (ghost-written by Alan Dean Foster) was published a good six months ahead of the film's release. Quickly selling out its first printing, the book sold over 3.5 million copies in the first few months after its appearance (Van Parys 75). Without deviating substantially from the screenplay it was adapted from, Foster's novelisation deftly illustrated how strongly *Star Wars* depended on the productive connections between media from the very start.

This interrelation took a further turn even before the film's unprecedented success. Nervous about his troubled production's financial prospects, Lucas commissioned Foster to write a sequel that could be used as the basis for a more low-budget sequel in case the film failed financially. The resulting book *Splinter of the Mind's Eye* (1978) followed the further adventures of the characters who had already been contracted for possible sequels. To facilitate a lower production budget, its story was set on a fog-shrouded planet and featured far fewer action set pieces. This sequel was the first original plot to follow the movie's storyline – but its narrative was abandoned in favour of a much more ambitious sequel once the first film's record-breaking success became clear (Freeman 66).

While Foster's sequel novel offers a compelling imaginary detour from the developing franchise's overall plotting, it also opened the door to a rapidly proliferating industry of novels, games, comics and cartoons that would become known as the Expanded Universe (EU). The EU would give fans regular doses of officially licensed STAR WARS content, thereby both expanding the mythology surrounding the films and maintaining a stable presence within fandom in the gaps between new film releases. So even though there were certainly periods in which the STAR WARS franchise had only a limited presence in popular culture, Lucasfilm was still able to maintain an ongoing fanbase through the continued production of EU expansions in other media.

The combination of these developments made the STAR WARS franchise one of the most striking examples of *transmedia storytelling*, a term popularised by Henry Jenkins to indicate the structural integration of multiple media platforms to develop a single, more or less coherent storyworld (97–8). In its 'ideal' form, transmedia storytelling distributes narrative elements across media in ways that play to each individual medium's strength, 'so that a story might be introduced in a film, expanded through TV, novels and comics; its world might be explored through game play or experienced as an amusement park attraction' (97–8).

As the STAR WARS franchise developed, this kind of transmedia cross-fertilisation did indeed start to emerge. But it is important to note that this happened incrementally and provisionally rather than as a coordinated effort to integrate multiple media into a single storyworld. As the *Splinter of the Mind's Eye* example attests, transmedia storytelling forms are shaped first and foremost by the specific limitations and opportunities posed by specific media-industrial conditions. The STAR WARS novels that followed Foster's non-canonical sequel, for instance, initially had very little oversight in terms of narrative consistency, just as the proliferating STAR WARS comic books freely experimented with the franchise's main characters without much eye for planning or consistency (Guynes 145).

It is also important therefore to distinguish between transmedia storytelling as an ideal on the one hand, and the forms it tends to take in cultural and industrial practice on the other. For while Jenkins's oft-cited definition gave media scholars a provocative starting point, it also clearly exaggerated the degree of organised and consistent cross-platform development of fictional storyworlds. In order to employ the term 'transmedia' meaningfully, we must first attend to the hierarchical structures that we inevitably encounter both within existing transmedia multitexts, and in the industries and audiences that engage with them. We might therefore more accurately typify Jenkins's original description as *integrated* transmedia, dispersing a storyworld evenly across a variety of media platforms that offer different entrance points to the narrative (Eder 75).

But as the STAR WARS example shows, a far more common variation is the *supplementation* model, in which one primary media text (often referred to as the 'mothership') is expanded via a range of 'satellite texts' (Eder 76). Most commonly, the mothership is a costly, labour intensive and high-profile mass media production, such as a feature film, television series or AAA video game, while the satellites are less expensive secondary texts that function simultaneously as world-building expansions and as possible entrance points. For most of its long history, the STAR WARS franchise has also followed this logic, with the saga films operating as the mothership, and the many spin-offs and expansions supplementing its story in a variety of ways. Historicising these distinctions allows us to foreground the inherent connections between transmedia as a narrative form – *transmedia storytelling* – and the political economy in which it circulates – *transmedia franchising*.

The political economy of transmedia franchising

To understand how transmedia sf franchises came to dominate the culture industry, we first need to consider how the political economy of media production changed in the neoliberal era. In response to the global economic crisis of the 1970s, Western governments in the 1980s embraced an aggressive programme of corporate deregulation, facilitating businesses to access labour and resources much more freely in wave after wave of 'flexible accumulation' (Harvey 147). Firmly embracing a radical conception of free market ideology, the Reagan administration unleashed forces that would irrevocably alter the global media landscape. The transformation that occurred in this period can be summed up by three key terms: *globalisation*, *deregulation* and *market concentration* (Holt 10).

These policies led to a series of mergers made possible by the abandonment of most forms of effective antitrust legislation within the US media industry: a first wave around the year 1985, a second in 1989–90 and a third in 1994–5, 'as the last remaining regulations separating film studios and broadcast networks fell away, cross-ownership rules were dismantled, and the door was open for the deregulated telecommunications industry to join the global media conglomerates' (Holt 18). Effectively reversing most of the policies designed to limit media monopolies, this onslaught of mergers and acquisitions yielded a political economy that was ideal for the transmedia franchising of sf properties.

The historic second-wave merger of publishing giant Time Inc. and the already-diversified entertainment conglomerate Warner Communications, Inc. was paradigm-shifting in this regard. The newly formed media corporation united a tremendous variety of production and distribution infrastructure with an enormous stable of IP and contracted talent. Mere weeks after the historic merger was announced, its unprecedented power was vividly illustrated by the cultural phenomenon of *Batman* (Burton 1989). As a blockbuster production designed to capitalise on Time-Warner's synergistic potential, the film popularised a character and storyworld that were part of the corporation's existing holdings, recruited the Warner-contracted pop icon Prince for the soundtrack, surrounded the film with transmedia satellites and spin-offs, and made strategic use of every available media platform and distribution channel to amplify the film's impact (Pearson and Uricchio 183).

The Time-Warner conglomerate instantly became the new example that other businesses quickly learned to emulate, as the already blockbuster-focused 'New Hollywood' further increased its focus on big-budget sf spectacles that lent themselves to Star Wars-type transmedia licensing (Holt 122). The resulting wave of Batman franchising in the 1990s typified this emergent corporate strategy, as 'the balance of franchise discourse shifted toward describing the ongoing production of content across a range of genres and industrial contexts' (Johnson 55). In this period, the word 'franchising' soon took on a distinct cultural significance as 'a new way of thinking about networks of collaborative content production constituted across multiple industrial sites' (6). Transmedia franchising is therefore in most cases a more appropriate term than transmedia storytelling, as it relates directly to the many decentralised, episodic and non-narrative modes of production that tend to typify media franchises in the IP age (31).

The structural tension between storytelling and franchising is best illustrated by *The Matrix* – one of the most frequently cited examples of transmedia storytelling. Arriving after all three major waves of corporate consolidation had been completed, the film played to Time-Warner's key strengths: saturation marketing was pushed through all available media channels, a bestselling soundtrack CD featured a collection of contracted metal and alt-rock bands, a ground-breaking website capitalised on Time-Warner's recent merger with internet service provider AOL, and the film's high-concept sf plot and innovative digital effects perfectly matched the reigning focus on spectacular entertainment that translated easily to other media platforms.

Following the film's financial success, Time-Warner developed more ambitious plans for the budding franchise. Not one, but two film sequels went into production simultaneously, while the Wachowski sisters also involved themselves creatively with the development of elaborate transmedia expansions. The videogame *Enter the Matrix* (2003), for instance, included a full hour of live-action footage featuring actors from the films, while the promotional texts tirelessly emphasised that the game constituted an integral part of the story presented in the films. By the same token, the DVD *The Animatrix* (2003) collected an anthology of animated shorts, which also had been overseen by the Wachowskis to fill important narrative gaps in the films. For media theorists eager to identify blossoming forms of transmedia storytelling, *The Matrix* therefore became a gratifying case study (Jenkins 98–102).

But even this rare kind of 'entertainment super system' remains most illuminating for what it tells us about the emergent media-industrial logic of the franchising age (Johnson 31). For while these transmedia extensions involved an unusually high degree of narrative coordination, they could not have been produced outside a very specific industrial organisation of horizontally and vertically integrated media conglomerates. In other words, franchises like *The Matrix* 'do not dictate, but rather are *dictated by* the contexts of the contemporary creative industries' (Archer 22).

Transmedia franchising comes of age: Marvel superheroes in the age of Disney

After the interlocking forces of globalisation, deregulation and market concentration reshaped the media industries in the 1980s and 1990s, the twenty-first century has seen a further consolidation of these developments. The rise of social media websites like Facebook, YouTube and Instagram pushed the generalised presence of media monopolies to unprecedented new heights. As the internet's early potential as a global commons was rapidly eclipsed by privately owned and commercially oriented corporations, a *convergence culture industry* emerged that skilfully integrated audience participation within its hegemonic power structure (Scott 12).

While sf fans had previously been seen as a pesky niche group, the convergence culture industry has fostered a much more dynamic relationship with them. Two key elements contributed to this more participatory engagement: first, the tremendous growth in cultural status and visibility that sf accrued post-*Star Wars* as a mass cultural genre (Rieder 54–7); and second, the cultural mainstreaming of fandom, which has led participatory culture to foster new forms of audience exploitation described as 'Consumption 2.0' (Stanfill 84). This new dynamic between media industries and sf fan cultures caters on the one hand to fandom's taste formations, while on the other demanding that fans constantly play the long game of anticipating, consuming, praising and promoting the franchises they worship in seemingly endless iterations.

Having added both STAR WARS and Marvel Studios to its growing collection of media franchises, the Walt Disney Company has by now long eclipsed every other company as the epitome of deregulated media conglomerisation – including Time-Warner, which would become WarnerMedia before being rebranded once more as Warner Bros. Discovery following another big wave of mergers and acquisitions. As a company that has consistently sought to integrate its multiple forms of IP into a single unified brand experience, Disney was uniquely positioned to become the dominant media conglomerate in a media landscape ruled by branded transmedia worldbuilding (Wasko 156–7). Following the operative logic of its own theme parks, Disney now marks its various primary media franchises as individually branded domains that still fit comfortably under a unifying corporate umbrella.

The MARVEL CINEMATIC UNIVERSE (MCU) is a case in point. This Disney-owned media franchise currently stands as the most financially successful film series in entertainment history. But it paradoxically also expresses how the convergence culture industry has changed from 'a state in which the film itself functioned as the primary revenue-generating product in the industry to it being just one part of an extensive multi-media tapestry' (McSweeney 4). For no matter how much money the many MCU films might make at the box office, those numbers are negligible compared to the enduring value the Marvel brand represents for an IP-driven conglomerate. In this sense, the ongoing production of films is mainly necessary to sustain the relevance and longevity of branded characters that can be licensed, reproduced and consumed in seemingly limitless ways.

As a media franchise, the MCU began with the release of *Iron Man* (Favreau 2008). Having spent the previous decade strategically reinvigorating public interest in superheroes by licensing some of its characters to movie studios, Marvel founded its own studio to develop 'a cohesive narrative in which the characters and events portrayed reside within the same diegetic world'

(McSweeney 14). Where previous sf film franchises had followed the dominant industrial logic of following a hit film with a number of sequels until public interest waned, Marvel Studios hoped to develop a complexly tiered narrative universe that mimicked their interlinked comic book universe (Wright 218). Thus, *Iron Man* was not followed directly by *Iron Man 2* (Favreau 2010) but first by *The Incredible Hulk* (Leterrier 2009), with post-credits 'stings' in both films that established connections between the individual films.

As the franchise gained momentum and popularity, connections between individual films became more elaborate, while occasional cross-over 'event films' like *The Avengers* (Whedon 2012) brought together major characters who also had their own ongoing film series. Shortly after Marvel Studios' 2009 acquisition by The Walt Disney Company, the MCU's ongoing film series was expanded as a franchise in other media as well: television series such as *Agents of S.H.I.E.L.D.* (2013–20) and *Agent Carter* (2015–6) were broadcast on the Disney-owned ABC network, while a collaboration with streaming platform Netflix yielded an additional set of superhero-driven limited series from 2015 to 2018.

This partnership introduced new audiences to the MCU franchise, in part by the combination of adult-oriented themes, explicit violence, and a stronger focus on race and gender (McSweeney 224–6), but it was abandoned once Disney unveiled its competing streaming service Disney+. Besides offering access to its archive of animated films alongside its other properties and brands, the new service promised to expand them further with exclusive serialised expansions. Unlike the earlier TV series, which were peripheral in most ways to the 'mothership' constituted by the feature films, the Disney+ series were designed from the start to be a much more integral part of the ongoing MCU narrative.

This higher degree of narrative integration across media platforms indicates a stronger commitment to transmedia storytelling. But as with *Star Wars*, *Batman* and *The Matrix* before it, the MCU's newfound commitment to integrated transmedia storytelling is again best understood in political-economic terms. Placing a greater emphasis on the importance of franchise expansions that are exclusively available on Disney's streaming channel drives Marvel fans to become paying subscribers, thereby strengthening the corporation's hold over the convergence culture industry. While this certainly allows for new storytelling opportunities, Disney's ongoing expansion surely owes more to media power than it does to narrative complexity or innovation (Archer 41).

While shows such as *WandaVision* (2020), *Falcon and the Winter Soldier* (2021) and *Loki* (2021) do take the MCU in some new directions, their ongoing development of Marvel's fictional universe remains fatally constrained by what Gerry Canavan has described as *franchise time*: since every new iteration in the franchise must be set in a recognisable 'now', every new development, no matter how impactful, will fade into the background as every new instalment resets itself, 'just in time for the start of the next show, forever' (n.p.). As successful as the MCU has been as a transmedia franchise, its internal organisation therefore continues to be determined primarily by the Disney media conglomerate's commercial imperatives.

Disney's competition: DC, *Star Trek* and the Lego-verse

As Disney's Thanos-like acquisition of studios and franchises cemented its twenty-first century media dominance, competing conglomerates played variations of Disney's franchising game. From the post-*Star Wars* series of Superman films (1978–87) to the Dark Knight trilogy (2005–12), DC characters had largely dominated the superhero genre. But while Time-Warner has ownership of many of the most enduringly popular superhero icons, the studio was still developing them according to an older franchising logic: twenty-first-century reboots were produced by default as standalone films, like *Batman Begins* (Nolan 2005) and *Superman Returns* (Singer 2006), ideally to be followed by one or more sequels.

But as Disney's many acquisitions established a new paradigm for transmedia franchising, competing studios like Time-Warner, Paramount and Universal scrambled to develop their own narrative universes, or *transmedia worldbuilding*. While similar in some ways to the film series of the early blockbuster era, transmedia *worldbuilding* emphasises a different logic that has come to typify the convergence culture industry:

1. Transmedia worldbuilding takes place *across* media.
2. Transmedia worldbuilding involves *audience participation*.
3. Transmedia worldbuilding is a process that *defers narrative closure*. (Hassler-Forest 5)

Popular entertainment franchises in the 2010s mostly adopted this logic, focusing their film production output increasingly on 'worlds' and 'universes' that translate easily to other media, that foster participatory engagement with fan cultures, and that perpetually hold out the promise of further expansion.

But for Time-Warner, the road to a robust and commercially viable transmedia superhero franchise turned out to be more challenging than expected. Initial attempts to jump-start a DC Extended Universe (DCEU) floundered, as the first two films *Man of Steel* (Snyder 2013) and *Batman v Superman: Dawn of Justice* (Snyder 2016) failed to meet expectations, and the rushed crossover team-up *Justice League* (Snyder 2017) sank at the box office. Largely abandoning the use of a single 'house style' that has defined the most successful transmedia franchises, subsequent DCEU films explored a variety of styles and registers, all of which existed in a cultural realm that remained separate from DC's Arrowverse: the collection of interlinked superhero series broadcast on young-adult-oriented television channel The CW, and further supplemented by web series on Time-Warner's digital platform CW Seed.

Along similar lines, the Star Trek franchise has been revived in the twenty-first century, again in ways that foreground changing industrial practices. In 2009, the perennial fan favourite and sf classic was rebooted as a Star Wars-like space opera that cast young actors as the original crew of the starship *Enterprise*. The action-oriented blockbuster followed the logic of the *legacy film*, as it introduced a new generation to a beloved franchise by creating a sense of continuity with what came before (Golding 70) – in this case, by having original series icon Leonard Nimoy appear alongside the newer incarnation of his beloved character. This provides both a sense of continuity with the franchise's history and a renewed sense of relevance, as the new team takes the familiar mythology in new directions. The 2009 franchise reboot deviated in such substantial ways from the series' existing chronology that the film and its ongoing sequels are now commonly referred to by fans as the 'Kelvin timeline', thereby indicating a separate continuity within the franchise's governing logic.

While the films gave Paramount a foothold within the increasingly competitive and franchise-oriented media landscape, the industry's transition to streaming would yield another series of franchise reboots in the following decade. As part of Paramount's plan to launch its proprietary subscription-based streaming channel CBS All Access (later re-named Paramount+), *Star Trek: Discovery* (2017–24) was developed as the new service's flagship property – with distribution outside the US handled by production partner Netflix. While this series mapped out yet another origin story for the early days of the Federation, a second series titled *Star Trek: Picard* (2020–3) was developed simultaneously to focus on one of the franchise's most beloved characters in his older years. While *Discovery* constituted an attempt to rejuvenate the narrative formula of the STAR TREK television with fresh faces and situations, *Picard* was largely defined by the nostalgic return of a multitude of familiar actors.

These proliferating styles and storytelling logics illustrate an expansive multiplicity that resides at the core of these projects: the simultaneous co-existence of multiple variations that makes up 'the generational engine at the heart of any successful transmedia franchise' (Rehak 64). As these franchises accumulate meanings over the years in sometimes wildly different incarnations, the dominant logic of the convergence culture industry has increasingly embraced these differences rather than attempt to iron them out into a single canonical storyworld or house style. This sensibility expresses an attitude that acknowledges the audience as a participatory presence, while simultaneously limiting this participation to a position that remains 'inherently consumptive' (Stanfill 96).

The best example of this proliferation of difference is surely *The LEGO™ Movie* and the transmedia franchise it spawned. Since the 1990s, the LEGO toy brand has licensed a variety of prominent media franchises, such as STAR WARS and HARRY POTTER, to sell a tremendous range of branded sets that reproduce characters, locations and props from transmedia storyworlds (Geraghty 24). The popularity of these sets led LEGO to produce a variety of licensed spin-off productions, including a line of bestselling video games, an ongoing series of parodic recreations of famous movie scenes for the LEGO website, and television series featuring LEGO versions of franchised characters. Through this strong association with some of the biggest transmedia sf franchises, LEGO thereby became a meta-franchise that incorporated licensed IP in a playful and participatory manner.

Franchise entry *The LEGO™ Batman Movie* (McKay 2017) perfectly illustrates both the inherent multiplicity of transmedia franchises and their basic dependence on corporate interests grounded in licensable IP. Rather than embracing a singular conception of the main character and his storyworld, the film constantly reminds the viewer of his many competing incarnations amassed over the years, including clear references to the 1960s television series, the critically pummelled Joel Schumacher films and the more recent DARK KNIGHT trilogy. The film's own Batman, voiced by Will Arnett, is not so much a new version of the caped crusader as a self-conscious composite character, playing off the audience's familiarity with the brand's history while adding new elements to the shared cultural archive.

Ultimately, the film and its overarching franchise represent the cultural and industrial logic of the convergence culture industry in the age of corporate IP: participatory and playful in the way they erode boundaries between media, while engaging viewers through an explicit acknowledgment of their cultural knowledge as media fans. But at the same time, their primary task is to keep reproducing only those kinds of content that can be profitably licensed across a variety of media platforms. As creative as these franchises therefore might be in incorporating fan culture's unruly energies, this creativity also remains fatally limited by the industrial constraints imposed by franchise time.

Works cited

Archer, Neil. *Twenty-First-Century Hollywood: Rebooting the System*. Wallflower, 2019.

Booth, Paul. 'Disney's Princess Leia'. *Disney's Star Wars: Forces of Production, Promotion, and Reception*. Ed. William Proctor and William McCullough. Iowa UP, 2019. 179–91.

Canavan, Gerry. 'The Limits of Black Panther's Afrofuturism'. *Frieze* (27 February 2018). www.frieze.com/article/limits-black-panthers-afrofuturism

Eder, Jens. 'Transmediality and the Politics of Adaptation: Concepts, Forms, and Strategies'. *The Politics of Adaptation: Media Convergence and Ideology*. Ed. Dan Hassler-Forest and Pascal Nicklas. Palgrave Macmillan, 2015. 66–81.

Freeman, Matthew. 'From Sequel to Quasi-Novelization: *Splinter of the Mind's Eye* and the 1970s Culture of Transmedia'. *Star Wars and the History of Transmedia Storytelling*. Ed. Sean Guynes and Dan Hassler-Forest. Amsterdam UP, 2018. 61–72.
Geraghty, Lincoln. 'In a "Justice" League of Their Own: Transmedia Storytelling and Paratextual Reinvention in LEGO's DC Super Heroes'. *Cultural Studies of LEGO: More Than Just Bricks*. Ed. Rebecca C. Hains and Sharon R. Mazzarella. Palgrave Macmillan, 2019. 23–46.
Golding, Dan. *Star Wars after Lucas: A Critical Guide to the Future of the Galaxy*. U of Minnesota P, 2019.
Guynes, Sean. 'Publishing the New Jedi Order: Media Industries Collaboration and the Franchise Novel'. *Star Wars and the History of Transmedia Storytelling*. Ed. Sean Guynes and Dan Hassler-Forest. Amsterdam UP, 2018. 143–54.
Harvey, David. *The Condition of Postmodernity: An Enquiry into the Origins of Cultural Change*. Blackwell, 1990.
Hassler-Forest, Dan. *Science Fiction, Fantasy, and Politics: Transmedia World-building Beyond Capitalism*. Rowman & Littlefield, 2016.
Holt, Jennifer. *Empires of Entertainment: Media Industries and the Politics of Deregulation, 1980–1996*. Rutgers UP, 2011.
Jenkins, Henry. *Convergence Culture: Where Old and New Media Collide*. New York UP, 2006.
Johnson, Derek. *Media Franchising: Creative License and Collaboration in the Culture Industries*. New York UP, 2013.
McSweeney, Terence. *Avengers Assembled: Critical Perspectives on the Marvel Cinematic Universe*. Wallflower, 2018.
Pearson, Roberta and William Uricchio. 'I'm Not Fooled by That Cheap Disguise'. *The Many Lives of the Batman: Critical Approaches to a Superhero and his Media*. Routledge, 1991. 182–213.
Rehak, Bob. *More Than Meets the Eye: Special Effects and the Fantastic Transmedia Franchise*. New York UP, 2018.
Rieder, John. *Science Fiction and the Mass Cultural Genre System*. Wesleyan UP, 2017.
Scott, Suzanne. *Fake Geek Girls: Fandom, Gender, and the Convergence Culture Industry*. New York UP, 2019.
Stanfill, Mel. *Exploiting Fandom: How the Media Industry Seeks to Manipulate Fans*. Iowa UP, 2019.
Van Parys, Thomas. 'Another Canon, Another Time'. *Star Wars and the History of Transmedia Storytelling*. Ed. Sean Guynes and Dan Hassler-Forest. Amsterdam UP, 2018. 73–86.
Wasko, Janet. *Understanding Disney: The Manufacture of Fantasy*. Polity, 2001.
Wright, Bradford W. *Comic Book Nation: The Transformation of Youth Culture in America*. The Johns Hopkins UP, 2001.

26

SCIENCE FICTION FILM AND TELEVISION

The 1980s and 1990s

Sharon Sharp

In an era often defined by excess, media sf enjoyed its own expansion in the last two decades of the 20th century. Sf film and television were more stylised, serialised, immersive, commercially successful, culturally visible and globally consumed than ever before. Indeed, many of the elements often cited as signs of the prominence of contemporary media sf – the central place of sf in the production and distribution of global media industries, innovative storytelling from independent and global voices, immersive worldbuilding, blockbuster franchises – originated in the 1980s and 1990s. This chapter traces how the industrial, cultural and technological changes of the period enhanced sf film and TV's capacity for cultural commentary on concerns of the present, focusing on the thematic preoccupations with technoscience, time travel, alien encounters, dystopias and post-apocalyptic futures.

An expanded universe: Industries, technologies and aesthetics

Key industrial and technological transformations contributed to shifts in aesthetics that provided more serialised, immersive and engaging environments in much media sf. The accelerating convergence of global media conglomerates in the 1980s that established complex vertical and horizontal business relationships, synergies and an expansive global marketplace also established Hollywood as the dominant producer of media sf. In film, sf blockbusters began to dominate the studio release slates after the success of *Star Wars* (Lucas 1977) and *Close Encounters of the Third Kind* (Spielberg 1977) as conglomerates focused on producing big-budget effects-driven films aimed to be profitable in domestic, international and ancillary markets. Economics, as well as innovations in special effects technologies and filmmakers interested in expressing ideas visually, produced a blockbuster style that is 'overflowing with kinetic action, taking place within a minutely detailed, intricately composed mise-en-scène, comprising an all-encompassing, expandable environment' (Turnock 109). Special effects technologies tied to the blockbuster enabled 'a sense of immersion and bodily engagement' and enhanced sf worldbuilding (3). Although less prolific, global cinemas and a flourishing American independent film industry used imaginative strategies to overcome their uneven access to resources and provided compelling alternatives to the Hollywood dominant. Globally distributed US midlevel and low budget films persisted as well, providing a mix of sf forms and aesthetics.

 DOI: 10.4324/9781003140269-28

Starting in the 1980s, when the classic network era dominated by three networks was replaced by the multichannel era, television shifted from a limited selection of least objectionable programming to an abundance of niche-oriented programming. Facing economic competition from cable, satellite and other media in the multichannel era, television became more stylised as new digital tools became available (Caldwell). While some shows retained a conventional style, many series moved style from the background to the foreground of storytelling. Higher production values, cinema style editing, cinematography and effects, as well as the importation of such sf film directors as Steven Spielberg (*Amazing Stories*, NBC 1985–77) and David Lynch (*Twin Peaks*, ABC 1990–1), enabled sf television to standout in a newly competitive and cluttered television landscape (Johnson-Smith). By the 1990s, in order to narrowcast to a now economically viable and participatory niche audience in the ever-expanding, fragmented and convergent multichannel universe, many sf television narratives moved away from conventional episodic and anthology narratives structures to seriality and narrative complexity. As in other genres, such sf series feature cumulative narratives that 'redefine the boundary between episodic and serial forms, with a heightened degree of self-consciousness in storytelling mechanics, and [demand] intensified viewer engagement focused on both diegetic pleasures and formal awareness' (Mittell 53). Not all sf television produced during this time was narratively complex or 'televisual' in Caldwell's sense, and aesthetically stylistic sf television was circulated alongside evergreen conventional episodic sf television reruns from previous eras of US and British production, which found audiences in domestic and global syndication. US-based global cable network Sci Fi, launched in 1992, devoted to a broadly conceived sf to appeal to a niche audience, was also a key site for engagement with conventional sf television as its programming largely consisted of sf television reruns and sf films intermixed with limited original programming. The imaginary worlds created in television and film were expanded further through transmedia storytelling across other media texts in this period, particularly during the 1990s with the rise of the Internet and digital fan cultures.

Technoscience

Space opera's fascination with technology and space travel made it a key site for commenting on the technological advances in computers, warfare, media and medicine that were altering daily life in new ways. The popular, technology-laden space adventures of the original STAR WARS trilogy, completed by *The Empire Strikes Back* (Kershner 1980) and *Return of the Jedi* (Marquand 1983), and the prequel trilogy, beginning with *Episode 1: The Phantom Menace* (Lucas 1999), influentially visualised the space opera's iconic gadgets, futuristic weaponry, spaceships and space stations, often battered and lived-in. STAR TREK's techno-utopia offered a more optimistic view of technology as an agent of progress and social change, with effortless space travel and futuristic hardware across the interconnected narratives of ten films between 1979–2002, and three television series *Star Trek: The Next Star Generation* (syndicated 1987–94), *Star Trek: Deep Space Nine* (syndicated 1993–9) and *Star Trek: Voyager* (UPN 1995–2001). *Babylon* 5 (PTEN/TNT 1994–8) juxtaposed an everyday futuristic technology with a sublime vision of interstellar exploration enabled by the advanced technology of spaceships, space stations and alien jump gates in a complex narrative and mise-en-scène (Johnson-Smith 236). The trope of space exploration enabled by advanced alien stargate and wormhole technologies was also part of the spectacle offered in the globally syndicated *StarGate SG-1* (Showtime 1997–2002) and *Farscape* (Sci Fi 1999–2004).

A cycle of narratives in media sf self-reflexively took up the influence of television in the new context of global media abundance and consolidation. In its lurid depiction of flesh penetrated by technology, the sf horror film *Videodrome* (Cronenberg 1983) ambivalently explores television as a means of social control. *La mort en direct/Death Watch* (Tavernier 1980), based on D.G. Compton's *The Continuous Katherine Mortenhoe* (1973), takes a critical look at reality television exploitation, portraying the cynical production of a docusoap facilitated by a cameraman who has had cameras implanted in his eyes in order to secretly record the final days of a dying woman. *The Prize of Peril* (*Le Prix du Danger*; Boisset 1983), about television contestants who pit their survival skills against each other in a fight to the death for cash prizes, as in the later Stephen King adaptation *The Running Man* (Glaser 1987), offers another biting critique of reality television. Lizzie Borden's experimental intersectional feminist near-future *Born in Flames* (1983) uses television news media combined with radio and verité documentary to critique how media shape racism and sexism. Early cyberpunk media sf critiqued television's commercial support and pervasive influence. Television is omnipresent in *Tetsuo: The Iron Man* (Tsukamoto 1989), a black-and-white Japanese experimental cyberpunk film that foregrounds anxieties about dehumanising technologies through affecting images of twisted metal fused with human flesh and an industrial music score. US television's first attempt to depict cyberpunk culture, *Max Headroom* (ABC 1987–8), developed from the UK teleplay *Max Headroom: 20 Minutes into the Future* (Channel 4 1985), critiques the commercial support of television and foregrounds its incursion of privacy in a dystopian future defined by class disparity, powerful corporations and violence, and in which ever-present TVs can never be switched off and track their viewers' every move and purchase. In a comic vein, *Mystery Science Theater 3000* (KTMA-TV 1988–9; Comedy Central 1989–91; Sci Fi 1997–9) uses the sf mad scientist trope and the intentionally microbudget look and feel of cable-access television sets to lampoon film and television conventions, often using cheesy sf media, while modelling ironic reading strategies.

Tron (Lisberger 1982) was one of the first films to innovate the representation of virtual reality using computer-generated effects and by the 1990s, after the proliferation of the Internet and home computers, sf films increasingly addressed the implications of video games and virtual reality technology. *Strange Days* (Bigelow 1995), set in a near-future dystopian Los Angeles, imagines an advanced technology that records subjective human experiences that can then be played back and vicariously enjoyed by others. A cyberpunk noir sf film, it offers a feminist critique of voyeurism, police brutality and the capitalist and racial hierarchies embedded in media. Numerous other films explore the blurring of boundaries between the virtual and the real. The labyrinthine narrative of cult Italian cyberpunk comedy noir *Nirvana* (Salvatores 1997), about a videogame programmer who discovers the protagonist of his game has acquired consciousness, creatively intertwines the varied perspectives of digital and human characters. In the visually striking tech-noir *Dark City* (Proyas 1998), a dying race of alien energy beings with a collective consciousness inhabit human bodies to explore individual consciousness and create a simulacral city based on their hosts' memories. Reality and artifice blur in sf body-horror *eXistenZ* (Cronenberg 1999), which focalises the consequences of the technologisation of the body through a virtual reality game powered by players' nervous systems. The decade ended with the influential *The Matrix* (Wachowskai sisters 1999) about a dystopian future of ecological crisis initiated by a techno-apocalypse; humans live in a simulated reality created by sentient machines while their bodies function as batteries. The animation aesthetic of the film's special effects, which popularised the 'bullet time' visual effect technique, was widely imitated and further developed in a transmedia franchise with sequels, animated shorts and videogames extending the film's narrative into the twenty-first century.

Created beings – figures that that cross the boundaries between the human and the artificial – featured prominently in media sf exploring human-technology relations. Blockbuster action films typically depicted cyborgs as masculine hardbodies. The first two TERMINATOR films, *The*

Terminator (Cameron 1984) and *Terminator 2: Judgment Day* (Cameron 1991), combine action sequences, cutting edge special effects and time-travelling killer cyborgs to present technophobic anxieties. Set in near-future deindustrialised Detroit, *Robocop* (Verhoeven 1987) satirises capitalism and its demands for flexible labour through its violent depiction of a deceased police officer who becomes an unwilling armoured cyborg designed by a callous corporation intent on privatising the police for profit. On television, cyborgs often literalise anxieties about the impact of technologies on human embodiment: in *Doctor Who* (BBC 1963–89), the monstrous Daleks and Cybermen repeatedly dramatise fears of cyborg embodiment; across several story arcs, the hivelike Borg, introduced in *Star Trek: The Next Generation*, represent technology as something beyond human control and allegorise fears of assimilation and the loss of individuality in the face of technological advances (Calvert 20, 46). However, STAR TREK also developed synthetic beings and cyborgs in a more utopian mode, tracing the optimistic potential of human-technology interfaces through *The Next Generation* android Data's quest to become more human and the gradual incorporation of *Star Trek: Voyager*'s female Borg, Seven of Nine, into the eponymous spaceship's crew.

Artificially created and modified beings were also used to explore questions about developments in genetic engineering and medicine. Critically acclaimed *Blade Runner* (Scott 1982), adapted from Philip K. Dick's *Do Androids Dream of Electric Sheep?* (1968) and set in the polluted overpopulated Los Angeles of 2019, portrays a bounty killer who hunts genetically engineered replicants. The replicants, exploited for labour and virtually indistinguishable from humans, allegorise the disappearing boundaries between the human and artificial enabled by advances in science. The experimental Soviet space opera *Humanoid Woman* (*Per Aspera ad Astra*; Viktorov 1981) explores cloning and ecological themes, while *Star Trek: The Wrath of Kahn* (Meyer 1982) expresses anxieties about the dangers of genetic engineering in a story about genetically modified soldiers from a previous century's eugenics wars. Similar ideas resurface in *Star Trek: Deep Space Nine*, in a narrative about the Founders, an antagonist alien species who engineer the Jem'Hadar, an alien race of brutal and obedient soldiers. The franchise blockbusters *Jurassic Park* (Spielberg 1993) and *Jurassic Park: The Lost World* (Spielberg 1997), adapted from Michael Crichton's 1990 and 1995 novels, imagine dinosaurs created through advanced biotechnology for human amusement. The films used cutting-edge computer-generated imagery (CGI) and action sequences to explore scientific hubris and the ethics of recreating life from the past. *Gattaca* (Niccol 1997) meditates on the social consequences of genetic engineering in a retrofuture world of social stratification in which genetically modified Valids, free from defects, are social elites and unmodified Invalids are socially marginalised. Set in a near-future New York City, the horror sf *Mimic* (del Toro 1997), based on Donald A. Wollheim 1942 short story, warns about scientific manipulation of nature in a story about a genetically engineered insect species that evolves to take on human form – and to prey on humans.

Time travels

A cycle of blockbusters focalised on male characters explored the conundrums of time travel enabled by scientific inventions and futuristic technologies. In Robert Zemeckis's commercially successful *Back to the Future* (1985), *Back to the Future Part II* (1989) and *Back to the Future Part III* (1990), a teenage boy time travels in a DeLorean modified by an eccentric scientist to change the past so as to influence the present (and avert a dystopian future). The trilogy centres on nostalgia and the humorous contrasts between the past, present and future. *Bill and Ted's Excellent Adventure* (Herek 1989) plays out a fantasy of interacting with famous historical figures, who the teenage heroes kidnap, courtesy of a phonebooth time machine, to ensure a utopian future inspired by the titular characters; sequels followed in 1991 and 2020. The dystopian *Twelve Monkeys* (Gilliam 1995), an adaptation of *La Jetée* (Marker 1962), uses time travel to dramatise environmental catastrophe in the aftermath of a global pandemic as a man is sent back to avert the spread of the deadly virus. The experimental Afrofuturist *The Last Angel of History* (Akomfrah 1996), about the journey of a time-travelling data thief to collect and visualise artifacts of the history of the Diaspora and Black contributions to technoscience and culture, notably uses a complicated database structure. Independent film *The Sticky Fingers of Time* (Brougher 1997) reorients time travel to explore queer desires and histories by focusing on the encounters of two women writers who, because of an H-bomb inflicted mutation, are 'time freaks', able to move between the 1950s and the 1990s.

Television from the period often featured time travel stunt episodes to inject aesthetic novelty into the worldbuilding of ongoing series by revisiting different moments in the past. Several episodes of British working-class space opera sitcom *Red Dwarf* (BBC 1988–99) satirised sf time travel conventions, while STAR TREK often visited Holodeck simulations of the historical past. Voyages to the past also provided opportunities to revisit the franchise's own canon and immense interconnected storyworld; for example, *Deep Space Nine*'s 'Trials and Tribble-ations' (1996) photo-realistically engages with the original series' 'The Trouble with Tribbles' (1967). Time travel served as an ongoing narrative premise to visit the past in several series, including the conventionally episodic *Voyagers!* (NBC 1982–3) and the British sf sitcom *Goodnight Sweetheart* (BBC 1993–9). *Quantum Leap* (NBC 1989–93) was the most notable series to consistently engage with time travel, using cinematic recreations of the past to attract viewers intellectually and to elevate the series above its competitors. It used an out-of-control scientific experiment as a mechanism for the White male protagonist to 'leap' into other lives located in the past, 'striving to put right what once went wrong', and offer lessons about race, gender and social disempowerment to the audience while nostalgically referencing the past.

Alien encounters

A diverse body of media sf engaged with the trope of alien encounters, and the 1980s began with films largely representing aliens in a sympathetic light. *E.T.: The Extra-terrestrial* (Spielberg 1982), with its coming-of-age narrative and beloved childlike alien, served as a counterpoint to previous depictions of malevolent aliens. Similar encounters provided enriching experiences for humans in *Cocoon* (Howard 1985), in which elderly residents of a retirement community are rejuvenated by aliens in **batteries not included* (Robbins 1987), in which flying saucers save tenement residents from gentrification, and in *Contact* (Zemeckis 1997), adapted from Carl Sagan's 1986 novel, where the potential to connect with an alien life force inspires human cooperation. James Cameron's big-budget flop *The Abyss* (1989) used ground-breaking CGI to depict benevolent contact with bioluminescent non-terrestrial Intelligences and to explore human interconnectedness with nature. On TV, benign aliens satirised traditional gender and family norms in the continuing tradition of fantastic family three-camera sitcoms, such as *Mork and Mindy* (ABC 1978–82), *Alf* (NBC 1986–90) and *3rd Rock from the Sun* (NBC 1996–2001).

Released just after *E.T.*, and in stark contrast to such benevolent aliens, *The Thing* (Carpenter 1982), adapted from John W. Campbell, Jr's 'Who Goes There?' (1938), follows a team of male Antarctic researchers as they encounter a shapeshifting parasitic alien, and fuses a pessimistic view of extra-terrestrial contact with practical body horror effects. Initially a commercial and critical failure, it later gained cult status and portended the tendency of 1990s sf films to depict aliens as foes, as in the jingoistic *Independence Day* (Emmerich 1996), which imagines predatory aliens defeated by patriotism, cooperation and American technological prowess. Other alien invasion narratives critiqued the US military industrial complex. In *Mars Attacks!* (Burton 1996), a stylised parody of traditional alien invasion movies based on the 1962 trading cards of the same name, the cartoonish aliens are defeated by socially marginalised characters rather than by scientists or the military. The hyperbolic satire of *Starship Troopers* (Verhoeven 1997), adapted from Robert A. Heinlein's 1959 novel, links militarism to fascism and racism through its representation of military trainees who gleefully destroy alien invaders. In contrast, *Men in Black* (Sonnenfeld 1997), an interracial buddy cop sf comedy adapted from Lowell Cunningham's comic book (1990–1), features members of a paramilitary organisation which protects Earth from hostile aliens and manages extra-terrestrial refugees, promotes a message of peaceful coexistence between species.

Television series featuring predatory alien invasions began with the *V* (1984–5) miniseries and its sequels, which offered socio-political commentary in a narrative about the small band of resistors who battle the 'visitors'. Clearly designed to parallel World War II-era Nazis, the visitors arrive seeking to deplete the Earth of natural resources and turn the globe in to a fascist dystopia by manipulating the population through mind control and using the media to foster paranoia and social prejudice. Similar territory is explored less successfully in the low-budget *War of the Worlds* (syndicated 1988–90), loosely adapted from H.G. Wells's 1898 novel as a sequel to Byron Haskins's 1953 film, and in the British *The Tripods* (BBC 1984–5), which imagined a post-apocalyptic dystopia in a pre-industrial countryside stalked by alien tripods – based on John Christopher's 1967–8 YA trilogy. The most influential example of alien invasion is the critically acclaimed and eminently televisual *The X-Files* (Fox 1993–2018), which links alien invasion to distrust of government and corporate authority through its chronicling of the investigations of FBI agents Fox Mulder and Dana Scully. Its complex narrative is structured by the integration of a seasons-long continuous narrative arc about the government's ongoing elaborate plot to cover up the presence of aliens on Earth and standalone 'ghoul-of-the week' episodes about the investigation of various paranormal phenomena, including myriad aliens (Sconce 107). *Dark Skies* (NBC 1996–7) shared a similar premise but was cancelled after a single season. Following the global success of *The X-Files,* British television featured two invasion series: the ecologically-focused *The Uninvited* (ITV 1997), in which aliens drawn to the Earth's climate changed atmosphere attempt to destroy humanity in order inhabit the planet, and the international coproduction *Invasion: Earth* (BBC/Sci-Fi 1998), focused on the Earth caught in a war between alien species.

Throughout the 1980s and 1990s, aliens continued to serve as allegories for alterity in media sf. The sf buddy cop film *Alien Nation* (Baker 1988) and its televisual adaptation (Fox 1988–90) treat racial conflict through the story of genetically modified alien slaves who crash land on Earth and attempt to assimilate in Los Angeles as 'newcomers', in a reference to cultural anxieties about white displacement by immigrants. In *Enemy Mine* (Petersen 1985), based on Barry B. Longyear's 1979 novella, racial reconciliation and the importance of cultural understanding are metaphorically treated in a story about two stranded space fighter pilots, a white human man and a humanoid-reptilian alien coded as Black, who must overcome species-based animus and work together to survive on a hostile planet. John Sayles's independent film *The Brother from Another Planet* (1984) depicts the alien main character as a Black man rather than as a metaphorical alien and explores the cultural politics of Black identity and issues of disenfranchisement by framing the story around his experience of contact with humanity in Harlem. Set in New York City's new wave subculture, the cult independent *Liquid Sky* (Tsukerman 1983) uses a striking new wave aesthetic and one of the first computer-generated scores to explore queer female sexuality in a narrative about space aliens who embody and steal opiates from the alienated sexual encounters of an androgynous lesbian. Less imaginatively, female sexuality is represented as alluring and deadly to men in the form of hyper-sexualised female fatale aliens in *Lifeforce* (Hooper 1985) and *Species* (Donaldson 1995) and its three sequels. Space operas foreground alien encounters in their worldbuilding, as in *Star Trek*'s inclusive multispecies future governed by a United Federation of Planets. Alien alterity in *Star Wars* often falls into racist stereotypes, as in the Black Caribbean patois and bumbling antics of *The Phantom Menace*'s Jar-Jar Binks, but the epic space opera *Babylon 5* uses its complex narrative to depict detailed alien worlds and multi-layered alien characters so as to argue in favour of unity 'despite surface differences of race, religion, nation, and class' (Vint 261).

In the US, a number of films engaged with the fallout from Reagan/Bush economic policies, and critiques of the corporation and consumer capitalism play a key role in alien encounters from the era. In the *Alien* franchise, *Aliens* (Cameron 1986) critiques corporate greed, depicting the Weyland Yutani Corporation's desire to harness aliens as weapons for profit at the expense of human life, including the working-class crew, the colonists and humans on Earth. *Alien 3* (Fincher 1992) extends the critique by setting the action on a Weyland Yutani prison planet, and *Alien Resurrection* (Jeunet 1997) by focusing on the exploitation of aliens as weapons through the alien-hybrid clone of series protagonist Ellen Ripley. Independent sf punk comedy *Repo Man* (Cox 1984) lambasts consumer culture through its story of a young man resisting mainstream consumer culture while working for a car repossession company trailing a Chevy Malibu with dead aliens in the trunk through a bleak deindustrialised Los Angeles. The buddy cop movie *The Hidden* (Sholder 1987) features an evil alien parasite which inhabits human bodies and represents the insatiable consumerism of the Reagan era, while *Critters* (Harvey 1986) and its three sequels critique consumerism, corporate greed and carnism in the form of hungry extra-terrestrials who devour animal flesh without concern for the consequences. *They Live* (Carpenter 1988) reimagines the alien invasion trope to skewer the social consequences of Reaganomics by encouraging viewers to see the world from the perspective of the marginalised. Its resonant imagery – special sunglasses unveil the subliminal ideological messages infesting billboards, books, magazines, money and television, and reveal social elites to be skinless humanoid aliens – continues to be remediated across popular culture.

Dystopias and post-apocalyptic futures

While dystopian and post-apocalyptic futures did not find a sustained home on television, instead acting as counterpoints to the premise of ongoing series in standalone episodes and story arcs, films of the period could not resist their allure. A cycle of films centred on dystopian totalitarian societies. Notably, *1984* (Radford 1984), adapted from George Orwell's 1949 novel, bleakly recreated totalitarian Oceania with a desaturated colour palette and mise-en-scène references to Nazi Germany. *Brazil* (Gilliam 1985), a darkly comic Orwellian sf art film also set in a bureaucratic police state, satirises consumer culture with striking surrealistic visuals and complex storytelling. *The Sleepwalker* (*La Sonámbula*; Spiner 1998), set in a post-apocalyptic near-future Argentina, features mind control and memory erasure by a totalitarian government that parallels the recent past of Argentinian politics.

Dystopian and post-apocalyptic futures often centre on ecological themes. Dystopian comedy *Kin-dza-dza!* (Danevila 1986), about two men transported to the ecologically devastated alien planet Plyuk, in the galaxy Kin-dza-dza, satirises late Soviet society. *The Handmaid's Tale* (Schlondorff 1990), adapted from Margaret Atwood's 1986 novel, centres women's experiences and reproductive politics in its depiction of a repressive near-future religious totalitarian regime in which environmental destruction has led to human sterility. Nuclear anxieties are taken up in the Argentinian *Nuclear Shelter* (*Arbrigo Nuclear*; Pires 1981), in which humans live underground in a radiation-poisoned, totalitarian dystopia. *The Last Battle* (*Le Dernier Combat*; Besson 1983), a black-and-white film without dialogue, shot using the rubble of derelict areas of 1980s Paris, critiques nuclear warfare and unchecked technological progress. More obliquely, nuclear themes are referenced in the New Zealand art film *The Quiet Earth* (Murphy 1985), which follows three survivors of 'the effect', an apocalypse caused by an international scientific project to create a global energy grid. Australia's Mad Max trilogy – *Mad Max* (Miller 1979), *Mad Max 2: Road Warrior* (Miller 1981), *Mad Max Beyond Thunderdome* (Miller and Ogilvie 1985) – imagine a violent post-apocalyptic future where survivors compete for scarce petroleum in a wasteland landscape. *Escape from New York* (Carpenter 1981) satirises American politics in a narrative set against the backdrop of a potential nuclear conflict in 1997; its vision of ruined urban landscapes and institutional breakdown was transplanted to Los Angeles in the less successful sequel, *Escape from LA* (Carpenter 1996). The depictions of lawlessness, ragged punk denizens, resource scarcity and industrial and ecological wastelands in the Mad Max and Escape films were hugely influential on future post-apocalyptic worldbuilding, as in the Italian cycle of post-apocalyptic films, including *1990: The Bronx Warriors* (*1990: I guerrieri del Bronx*; Castellari 1982), *The New Barbarians* (*I nuovi barbari*; Castellari 1983), *Endgame* (*Bronx lotta finale*; D'Amato 1983) and *Rats: Night of the Terror* (*Rats: notte di terrore*; Mattei 1984). In contrast, Marc Caro and Jean-Pierre Jeunet visualised dystopia as an idiosyncratic, intricate retrofuture referencing French history and culture in their dark sf comedy *Delicatessen* (1991), an allegory of the German occupation of France and excessive human appetites, and their tale of mad science, *City of Lost Children* (*La cite des enfants perdus*; 1995).

Into the 21st century

In several ways, the worldbuilding of sf film and television from the 1980s and 1990s continued its expansionist tendencies into the new millennium. The valuable back catalogue from the period populates many of the new streaming outlets and the transmedia extensions of the era's franchises continue to engage fans and generate revenue streams across the media landscape. Much of sf film and television from the period also lives on through sequels, reboots and remakes, demonstrating both their continuing importance to the media industries' bottom line and the enduring cultural resonance of their compelling visions and ideas.

Works cited

Caldwell, John T. *Televisuality: Style, Crisis, and Authority in American Television.* Rutgers UP, 1995.
Calvert, Bronwen. *Being Bionic: The World of TV Cyborgs.* I.B. Tauris, 2017.
Johnson-Smith, Jan. *American Science Fiction TV: Star Trek, Stargate and Beyond.* I.B. Tauris, 2005.
Mittell, Jason. *Complex TV: The Poetics of Contemporary Television Storytelling.* New York UP, 2015.
Sconce, Jeffrey. 'What If? Charting Television's New Boundaries'. *Television after TV: Essays on a Medium in Transition.* Ed. Lynn Spigel and Jan Olsson. Duke UP, 2004. 93–112.
Turnock, Julie A. *Plastic Reality: Special Effects, Technology, and the Emergence of 1970s Blockbuster Aesthetics.* Columbia UP, 2015.
Vint, Sherryl. '*Babylon 5:* Our First, Best Hope for Mature Science Fiction'. *The Essential Science Fiction Television Reader.* Ed. J.P. Telotte. UP of Kentucky, 2008. 247–65.

27
SOUTH KOREAN SCIENCE FICTION

Sunyoung Park

Until very recently, quite a few observers have been lamenting the marginality of sf in contemporary South Korean culture (Sellar 154; D Kim 312). With growing interest in the genre's history, however, we are gradually learning that the minor role of sf in the country is less a textual actuality than an effect of the local mechanisms of cultural validation, in which the speculative and often cosmopolitan genre has long been eclipsed and excluded by the hegemonic ethnonational and realist critical paradigms.

A historical study of sf in Korea reveals the genre's formative relationship with political factors that are often downplayed in the studies of sf in the West – not just colonialism but also state censorship and democratisation. Sf was first introduced to Korea at the turn of the twentieth century in the context of the national enlightenment movement, but unlike in imperial Japan or semi-colonial China, the genre failed to take root in colonial Korea (1910–45), where the lack of science education, along with an intense ambivalence toward imperial technoscientific modernity, hindered its development. Following Korea's independence from Japan in 1945 and its national division in 1948, sf soon became an integral part of mass culture in both Koreas. In the North, the genre enjoyed a steady progression from the 1950s on, much as it had in other Communist countries, but it lapsed after the consolidation of Kim Ilsung's personality cult through the *Juch'e* (self-reliance) doctrine in the late 1960s (Berthelier 375, 379; Zur 327–8). Meanwhile, in the South too sf came to prosper across media in the 1960s under the influence of US and Japanese popular culture. The genre, however, declined in creativity during the authoritarian developmentalist era of the 1970s and 1980s, when writers, filmmakers and artists kept their distance from what was mainly perceived as a state-sponsored developmentalist youth culture (S. Park, 'Between'). Sf began to flourish again in South Korea only after the 1987 political democratisation, coinciding with the advent of cyberpunk and the beginning of the digital era. Since then, it has continued to grow across the media including literature, comics, film, TV, webtoons, theatre, music, arts and videogames.

Benoit Berthelier, Sunyoung Park and Dafna Zur offer detailed historical accounts of sf in the two Koreas, so this chapter focuses on introducing three prominent movements that have exercised a particular influence on the practice of sf in contemporary South Korea. These movements are not to be understood as organised formations but as something closer to Raymond Williams's unorganised, diffusive 'tendencies' (117–9). Taken together, they illustrate the critical vocation

 DOI: 10.4324/9781003140269-29

of speculative fiction in the country and provide a key for reading many recent productions such as Bong Joon Ho's sf films, which are, to a substantive extent, outgrowths of their local cultural matrix despite their cosmopolitan appearances.

Protest sf

A distinctive vein of protest sf made its appearance in South Korea in the early 1970s. It could also be retrospectively called *minjung* sf. The label *minjung* (common people) is shorthand for South Korea's democratisation movement of the 1970s and 1980s. Deployed by democratic activists in their struggles against military dictatorship, the term gave a name to the then converging forces of civil protestors from various walks of life, which then acquired a cohesive agency that was able to shape Korean history (N. Lee 5). Culture played a major role in the *minjung* movement, and it was often writers and artists who gave voice to counterhegemonic forces and to their alternative visions of the nation's present and past.

Sf did not gain much cultural recognition during these decades. *Minjung* counterculture typically found its preferred aesthetics in social and historical realism and, because of its irrealistic aesthetic, sf has been commonly regarded as antithetical to it. In fact, however, one of the genre's most consequent transformations took place during the democratisation era. If sf in the 1960s had largely espoused a techno-utopian outlook and sought to promote technoscientific knowledge, the small number of writers and artists who engaged with it in the 1970s and the 1980s appropriated its tropes and worldbuilding imaginations to critique the ills of top-down militarist industrialisation. As Darko Suvin, Fredric Jameson and others have demonstrated, sf has often lent itself to the formulation of analogical social critiques, wherein a story's utopian or dystopian contents act as a term of comparison with the status quo. In addition, in a period of intense state censorship, the genre could serve as a discreet outlet for dissident voices, since its young adult character and speculative imagination helped writers and artists evade the censors' scrutiny.

Among the most interesting examples of *minjung* or protest sf are Cho Sehŭi's *The Dwarf* (*Nanjangi ka ssoaoilin chagŭn kong*; 1978, trans. 2006), a slipstream labour fiction published as a serial novel between 1975 and 1978, and Bok Geoil's *In Search of an Epitaph: Kyŏngsŏng, Shōwa 62* (*Pimyŏng ŭl ch'ajasŏ: Kyŏngsŏng, Shōwa 62*; 1987), an alternate history published on the cusp of the country's political democratisation. While not strictly sf, *The Dwarf* uses a worldbuilding imagination to project increasingly bipolarised South Korean society as a dystopian planet, where its working-class masses live in a 'City of Machines' as the de facto prisoners within its walls of polluted air (120–2). In its surreal, fragmented proletarian bildungsroman, the protagonists, a dwarf and his three children, undergo a series of class-consciousness awakening experiences through which they also increasingly come to feel 'like aliens' in their own world and constantly dream or talk of leaving it 'to the moon' (63) or 'a space travel'(218–9). Through this novel, South Koreans first became acquainted with the equation of the proletarian, the disabled and the alien, which has since become familiar through zombie films. The use of sf tropes and narrative conventions for a metaphorical social critique was explored in a fuller scale in Bok's *Epitaph*, which drew its inspiration from Philip K. Dick's *The Man in the High Castle* (1962) to portray a fictional Seoul under Japan's continued colonial rule. Its protagonist, an ordinary middle-class Korean man, embarks on an unexpected search for his forgotten ethnic and linguistic identity through his accidental encounters with banned books. His growing anticolonial consciousness is interwoven, in Bok's parallel universe, with roundabout critical representations of the South Korean government, police violence and the protest movement, all in sf camouflage (S. Park 'Reciprocal'). Both of these examples are marked by the *minjung* historical consciousness, which opposes grassroot Koreans to the government that serves the interests of foreign and domestic capitalists and their political allies.

In terms of its legacy in Korean popular culture, protest sf has had a clearly discernible influence on contemporary film. Exemplary are Bong Joon-ho's sf films *The Host* (*Koemul*; 2006), *Snowpiercer* (2013) and *Okja* (2017), whose computer-generated spectacles unfold a class-based environmentalist narrative against Western, particularly American, industrial and military authorities and their Korean collaborators (Lee and Manicastri 212–3; Yu 47). Also illustrative of the trend are a number of indigenised zombie narratives, such as Yeon Sangho's *Train to Busan* (*Busanhaeng*; 2016), its animation prequel *Seoul Station* (*Seoulyŏk*; 2016) and its sequel *Train to Busan Presents: Peninsula* (*Busanhaeng 2: Pando*; 2020), as well as Kino Mangosteen's six-episode omnibus film *The Neighbor Zombie* (*Iutchip chombi*; Hong Young-guen, Ryu Hoon, Jang Yun-jeong and Oh Young-doo 2010), in which zombies represent less alien monsters than innocent citizens victimised by a corporate capital and persecuted by a tyrannical government and its military force. We may also include here Jo Sung-hee's underdog space opera *Space Sweepers* (*Sŭngniho*; 2020), in which a squad of misfits, who are 'overworked, mad, and struggling with debt' (Baker-Whitelaw n.p.), save the Earth by fighting against an American tycoon space coloniser.

No specific affiliation brings these works together; rather, they share an ethos of putting sf to the service of social critique. There is much diversity among these cultural products – after all, the *minjung* movement itself was at once class-based and ethnonational, and it could be both nationalist and internationalist in its promotion of anticolonial third-world alliances. Its cultural legacies in sf are thus multifaceted, encompassing allegories of class struggle, populist nationalist alternate histories, and planetary or intergalactic sagas about a cosmopolitan community of the working poor. Protest sf inaugurated the critical use of sf in the 1970s, and to these days much South Korean sf can be seen as either belonging to or influenced by it.

Post-IMF sf

The 1997 Asian financial crisis caused national bankruptcy in South Korea, which was followed by radical economic restructuring that inflicted tremendous economic and psychological damages upon ordinary Koreans. The ensuing social turmoil became known locally as the 'IMF crisis' as South Koreans blamed the International Monetary Fund for demanding draconian measures that included the deregulation of the labour market. In its cultural reverberations, the crisis triggered an epochal shift, as South Koreans *en masse* became disillusioned and started questioning the value of ideas such as globalisation, social progress and democracy.

In the years following the crisis, local production of sf increased and diversified partly thanks to the government's IT development policy of Cyber Korea 21 (1999–2002). Aside from the flourishing of sf literature, this period saw a new boom in sf filmmaking. The early new millennium years yielded big-budget special-effect movies, such as Min Byeong-cheon's neo-noir *Natural City* (*Naech'urŏl sit'i*; 2003) and Kim Munsaeng's cyberpunk animation *Sky Blue* (*Wŏndŏp'ul teijŭ*; 2004). Also notable was Chi Minho's indie short *Squadron Vignette* (*P'yŏndae tanp'yŏn*; 2003), a work of military space sf featuring homemade CGI effects. Many such films attempted to emulate and indigenise Western and Japanese examples, often displaying a technophilia that celebrated the advances of hyper-wired South Korea.

Drawing a contrast with such genre-conforming productions, a new trend of scrappier sf also emerged around 2003. It consisted of novels and films that in various ways fictionally encoded the bitterness of the post-IMF era. While its socially critical use of sf was inspired by protest sf, it lacked any positive hint of a utopian promise; frequently apocalyptic, it included absurdist humour in its dystopian narratives.

A prime representative of this post-IMF crisis trend would be the oeuvre of writer Park Mingyu. Pak's well-known *Legend of the World's Superheroes* (*Chigu yŏngung chŏnsŏl*; 2003), a surrealist superhero novel, features a Korean boy who joins the Justice League out of his admiration for Superman, only to be turned into 'Bananaman' in crass reference to his racial identity. In a world dominated by Superman, Batman and Wonder Woman, who represent respectively US political, economic and cultural hegemony, Bananaman endures a failing career of subalternity and humiliation. In a surrealist breach of the superhero genre, the narrative includes a metafictional chapter in which cartoonists at DC comics dismissively discuss the character of Bananaman. The chapter is open to interpretation, but it arguably adds yet another layer to the Bananaman's debasement and his unfulfilled dream of belonging in the league of his heroes.

Park's 'Roadkill' ('Lodŭ k'il'; 2011, trans. 2019) depicts a near future world in which surplus labourers are banished from the corporatised mega-state of 'Asia'. Described as 'trash', or those 'who are no longer even the members of th[e] proletariat' (310), these people are confined to squalid slums and seek thrill in death by playing Russian roulette. The protagonist, a slum resident, takes the risk of crossing the border into Asia in the hope of improving the lot of himself, his girlfriend and their newborn baby. Like others before them, however, they fail to complete the crossing and are run over by an ultra-speed train. A pair of robot border guards named Maksi and Mao rescue the baby, but they are promptly punished for their illegal act of charity. Mao is rebooted, and the more stubborn Maksi is switched off. The sf and fantasy stories in Park's collection *Castera* (*K'asŭt'era*; 2005) teem with electronic, virtual and phantom animals, whose sub- and post-human existences amplify the desperation of the human condition as experienced by the precariat.

Post-IMF sf is also well established in cinema, especially among B-movie cult films. Jang Joonhwan's *Save the Green Planet!* (*Chigu rŭl chik'yŏra!*; 2003), a black comedy sf horror thriller, adds a surreal absurdist twist to the familiar theme of class struggle (Workman 260). Its protagonist, a seemingly deranged former factory worker, kidnaps and brutally tortures a corporate CEO he suspects of being an alien invader. Throughout the film, the protagonist's madness seems to be due to the tragic death of his parents, the victims of a mega-corporation. In an ironic turn of events, however, the CEO actually is an alien prince who is rescued by his own species and eventually orders the destruction of the earth. In a similar vein, Lee Eung-il's *The Uninvited* (*Pulch'ŏnggaek*; 2010) offers a parody of financial capitalism (S. Park 'Decolonizing' 56). In this indie sf film, three young and unemployed slacker male roommates are suddenly lifted into space inside their own shabby apartment. Their kidnapper is a Konglish-speaking alien, a shadowy figure who proclaims himself as the 'would-be master of the universe' and the Pointman of the Galactic Federation's 'Bank of Life' The alien proposes 'a contract' to his 'surplus human' abductees and tries to force them to sell years of their 'wasteful' life to a rich American businessman in exchange for galactic credit points, whose accumulation could be converted back to a longer lifespan. Rejecting this apparently senseless deal, the trio find themselves in a life-and-death struggle with the alien. The movie ends with two of them waking up back on the Earth, but the third is missing. Both films are outrageous in their B-movie visuality and sensibility. They exemplify the implicit and yet constitutive argument of much post-IMF production. Their self-deprecating humour undermines at once capitalism and the capitalist-generated genre of sf, in a move that projects the futility of sf's typically grand reflections on humanity and its future.

Post-IMF sf may be seen as a cultural response to 'capitalist realism', a neoliberal epistemological outlook in which no alternative exists to the established capitalist world order (Fisher 2).

After the financial crisis, this seeming 'end of history' came to be experienced as a cruel trap in South Korea, and it awakened citizens to the realities of being a developing economy increasingly integrated into the global financial system. Post-IMF sf is the culture of a new age in which utopian visions of social progress have become scarce, and many of its authors have escaped to speculative genres to imagine an alterity in fictional spaces. The influence of post-IMF sf can be felt in younger writers' works, such as Bae Myung-hoon's 'Smart D' ('Smart D'; 2006), in which a struggling sf novelist is forced to renounce the use of the letter D out of legal troubles with a multinational tech corporation, and Lim Taewoon's 'Storm Between My Teeth' ('Ippal e kkin tolgae param'; 2008, trans. 2019), which mixes absurdism with social activism and whose hero is an alien warrior disguised as a young and Black illegal immigrant trying to fit into Korean society.

Feminist and queer sf

Gender-conscious sf writers have been active in South Korea for at least three decades. Feminist social and cultural movements started gaining independence from the *minjung* movement around the time of democratisation in 1987, and gay and lesbian activism also emerged in the early 1990s. The two movements have been distinct for most of their existence, but they have been increasingly collaborating in recent years for causes such as gender equality and the fight against sexual violence. Intriguingly, young women's culture had a boost in South Korea in the 1980s through the explosion of girls' comics, which frequently thrived on queer representations of gender and sexuality. It was in this cultural field that women's sf storytelling first emerged in works such as Sin Ilsuk's alien-invasion military sf *Born in 1999* (*1999-nyŏnsaeng*; 1989) and Kang Kyŏngok's space opera *In the Starlight* (*Pyŏlbit soke*; 1986–90), both of which featured a psychic girl superhero.

Feminist and queer sf found early literary expression in the fictional as well as critical work of pseudonymous author Djuna, whose real identity is unknown to this day as they tightly protect their privacy by communicating exclusively online. Djuna's first short story collection, *The Butterfly War* (*Nabi chŏnjaeng*; 1997), makes ample use of posthuman tropes such as the cyborg, the gynoid and the zombie in an attempt to thwart gender binarism and other normative gender expectations. In 'Pentagon' ('P'ent'agon'), for example, a brain-dead Vietnamese woman is given a Korean male gangster's brain through a surgical transplant. Her consequent identity crisis turns the story into an exploration of queer hybridity all the while questioning the fixity of racial and gender boundaries. In other stories, human bodies evolve into animal forms and vice versa, rendering any anthropocentric gender ideals rather pointless. Thus, 'The Big Dark Eye' ('Kŭ k'ŭgo kŏmŭn nun'; 1995) is a tale of queer girlhood in which a shape-shifting alien caterpillar transforms into a humanoid girl and, in her new form, develops an affective tie to an androgynous female alien space captain. In 'The Bloody Battle of Broccoli Plain' ('Brok'oli p'yŏngwŏn ŭi hyŏlt'u'; 2008, trans. 2019), a group of North Korean children headed by a girl take refuge on an alien planet after they have been banished from the Earth. Through the generations, their descendants evolve into a species of green animals that resemble sheep and are called 'broccoli', in an absurdist touch that celebrates mutability and hybridisation. At the heart of Djuna's carnivalesque, multiethnic, multilingual, multispecies and gender-fluid universe are radical provocations of the heteronormative, illiberal and conformist South Korean society.

The works of writers such as Charlotte Perkins Gilman, Ursula K. Le Guin and Joanna Russ were translated into Korean between the late 1980s and the mid-1990s. They encouraged writers of later generations to take to sf for its generic efficacy in subverting gender, sexual and bodily norms. For example, in 'How Alike Are We' ('Ŏlmana talmannŭn'ga'; 2017, trans. 2019), Kim Bo-young casts an alienated eye on misogynistic language and behaviour by having a gender-blind

AI system investigate the conflicts that arise between the male and female members of the crew in a spaceship.

In addition to gender and sexual orientation, issues of disability have also recently become prominent in South Korean sf. Jeong Soyeon's 'Cosmic Go' ('Ujuryu'; 2009, trans. 2019) features a disabled woman scientist who accomplishes her dream of going to space in the face of patriarchal, racist and ableist prejudices. In *Customers* (*Kŏsŭt'ŏmŏ*; 2017), Yi Chongsan creates a genetically engineered future world in which disabled people and those who 'customise' their body at will struggle against the hatred of conservative hegemonic forces. Similarly, Kim Ch'oyŏp's 'Those Who Chose Exile' ('Sullejadŭl ŭn oe toraoji annŭn'ga'; 2019) presents two contesting utopias for the disabled: the curative techno-utopia where genetic engineering creates perfect humans, and a separatist egalitarian 'village' where body-based discriminations are non-existent. All villagers take a pilgrimage to the outside world as a coming-of-age ritual, and some do not return home because they choose to join the underclass of people who were born without access to engineering.

Feminist and queer sf is currently one of the most exciting literary developments in South Korea, a movement in which we can encounter radical voices along with innovative speculative imaginations. Partly as a response to misogyny and homophobia in South Korean society, women and sexual minority writers have in effect struck an alliance that has symbolically occupied the fictional space. The popularity of this trend accounts for the robust representation of women and sexual minorities in the country's Science Fiction Writers Union, which is an advocacy group as much as it is a cultural organisation. By contrast, queer and feminist themes are rarely found in sf film due to the ongoing patriarchal hegemony of the country's film industry. Better days may be coming, however. Shin Su-won's sf horror mystery *Glass Garden* (*Yuri chŏngwŏn;* 2017), for example, has as its protagonist a young disabled woman scientist who pursues her research on a plant substitute for blood. Also *SF 8*, a television series aired in 2020, includes Yoon-Jung Lee's 'Joan's Galaxy', a short film about a romance between two young women of different economic and biological castes in an eco-dystopian world. We may perhaps hope to see more sf storytelling by women filmmakers in the near future.

Conclusion

This chapter has focused on three outstanding movements in contemporary South Korea sf: *minjung* protest sf, post-IMF sf, and feminist and queer sf. Together, they demonstrate the distinctive patterns of the local critical practice of sf and the significant contributions that sf has made to the past and ongoing democratisation of South Korean society and culture. Long regarded as a lowly, irrelevant and even 'foreign' genre, sf has grown mainly in the subcultural margins of the country's strong countercultural tradition, which developed in reaction to the government's Cold War politicisation of national culture through its propagandistic mobilisation and its forced depoliticisation. Sf shares the critical vigour of the mainstream counterculture but has also pushed aesthetic boundaries to broaden its expressive capacity as well as its thematic range.

Necessarily selective, this chapter has left out a plethora of important writers whose work can be understood through various combinations of these critical approaches. For example, Kim Changgyu merits mention for his persistent speculation on techno-utopian possibilities in stories such as 'Brain Tree' ('Noesu'; 2015) and *Samsara* (2017), both of which probe the question of human existence after the Singularity. Also noteworthy are Park Seonghwan's Buddhism-infused sf stories, including 'Readymade Boddhisattva' ('Redimeidŭ posal'; 2004, trans. 2019), a tale of a spiritually enlightened robot, that was effectively adapted by Kim Jee-Woon as 'The Heavenly Creature', part of the anthology film *Doomsday Book* (*Illyu myŏlmang pogosŏ*; Kim and Yim

Pil-sung, 2012). Finally, environmental sf, whose local origin dates back at least to the publication of Sin Kihwal's comic satire *Here Come Nuclear Bugs* (*Haekch'ung i nat'anatta*; 1985–9) during the rise of environmental civil activism, is a currently a fastest-growing trend, as is well illustrated by Bong's films.

Today, sf is enjoying a peak of popularity in South Korea. Given the annually increasing volume of submissions to sf contests and the continuing stream of new sf films and dramas, the boom shows little sign of fading. Part of the momentum no doubt comes from the country's hi-tech culture that has permeated ever deeper into everyday life in recent decades, demanding cultural representations of its wonders and risks. If 'thinking means venturing beyond' (Bloch *Principle* 4), however, part of the driving force of the South Korean speculative imagination might be what Ernst Bloch elsewhere calls the 'spirit of utopia', soaring against every reification of the status quo.

Works cited

Baker-Whitelaw, Gavia. 'Netflix's "Space Sweepers" is the First Good Blockbuster of 2021'. *Daily Dot* (14 February 2021). www.dailydot.com/upstream/movies/netflix-space-sweepers-review

Berthelier, Benoit. 'Encountering the Alien: Alterity and Innovation in North Korean Science Fiction Since 1945'. *Science and Literature in North and South Korea*. Ed. Christopher Hanscom and Dafna. Special issue of *The Journal of Korean Studies* 23.2 (2018): 369–96.

Bloch, Ernst. *The Principle of Hope*, volume one. Trans. Neville Plaice, Stephen Plaice and Paul Knight. MIT Press, 1986.

———. *The Spirit of Utopia*. Trans. Anthony A. Nassar. Stanford UP, 2000.

Cho, Sehŭi. *The Dwarf*. Trans. Bruce and Ju-Chan Fulton. U of Hawaii P, 2006.

Fisher, Mark. *Capitalist Realism: Is There No Alternative?* Zero, 2009.

Kim, Dong-Won. 'Science Fiction in South and North Korea: Reading Science and Technology as Fantasized in Cultures'. *East Asian Science, Technology and Society: An International Journal* 12 (2018): 309–26.

Lee, Fred and Steven Manicastri. 'Not All are Aboard: Decolonizing Exodus in Joon-ho Bong's *Snowpiercer*'. *New Political Science* 40.2 (2018): 211–26.

Lee, Namhee. *The Making of Minjung: Democracy and the Politics of Representation in South Korea*. Cornell UP, 2007.

Park, Min-gyu. 'Roadkill'. Trans. Esther Song and Gord Sellar. *Readymade Boddhisattva: The Kaya Anthology of South Korean Science Fiction*. Ed. Sunyoung Park and Sang Joon Park. Kaya, 2019. 295–323.

Park, Sunyoung. 'Between Science and Politics: Science Fiction as a Critical Discourse in South Korea, 1960s–1990s'. Science and Literature in North and South Korea. Ed. Christopher Hanscom and Dafna. Special issue of *The Journal of Korean Studies* 23.2 (2018): 347–67.

———. 'Decolonizing Future: Postcolonial Science Fiction in South Korea'. *Routledge Handbook of Modern Korean Literature*. Ed. Yoon Sun Yang. Routledge, 2020. 56–67.

———. 'Reciprocal Assets: Science Fiction and Democratization in 1980s South Korea'. *Revisiting Minjung: New Perspectives on the Cultural History of 1980s South Korea*. Ed. Sunyoung Park. U of Michigan P, 2019. 247–73.

Sellar, Gord. 'Another Undiscovered Country: Culture, Reception, and the Adoption of the Science Fiction Genre in South Korea'. *Acta Koreana* 14.1 (2011): 153–74.

Williams, Raymond. *Marxism and Literature*. Oxford UP, 1977.

Workman, Travis. 'Parodies of Realism at the Margins of Science Fiction: Sin Sang-ok's *Pulgasari* and Jang Jun-hwan's *Save the Green Planet*'. *Simultaneous Worlds: Global Science Fiction Cinema*. Ed. Jennifer Feeley and Sarah Wells. U of Minnesota P, 2015. 257–71

Yu, Sang-Keun. 'Necropolitical Metamorphoses: Bong Joon-ho's *The Host* and *Parasite*'. *Science Fiction Film and Television* 14.1 (2021): 45–69.

Zur, Dafna. 'Let's Go to the Moon: Science Fiction in the North Korean Children's Magazine *Adong Munhak*, 1956–1965'. *The Journal of Asian Studies* 73.2 (2014): 1–25.

28
TWENTY-FIRST CENTURY FILM

Barry Keith Grant

Since the millennium, sf has dominated blockbuster film production, especially in the US. Many sf films, especially those produced in Hollywood, have continued to rely on kinetic action and visual spectacle to explore sf premises, a trend that was launched in the late 1970s with *Star Wars* (Lucas 1977), *Close Encounters* (Spielberg 1977) and *Superman* (Donner 1978). As with other genres, the majority of these films have endorsed dominant ideological values, often centred around the valorisation of the nuclear family. However, some sf films, often produced outside of Hollywood, have sought to provide a more progressive vision or at least a more balanced representation in terms of gender and race. On the one hand, for example, there have been numerous space operas featuring typical male action heroes, such as *Pitch Black* (Twohy 2000), *Mission to Mars* (De Palma 2000) and the appositely named *Space Cowboys* (Eastwood 2000), and, on the other, films set in space that question conventional thinking, whether about gender, as with the international co-production *High Life* (Denis 2018), or anthropocentrism more broadly, as in *Aniara* (Kagerman and Lilja 2018), or even the very notion of what an sf film is, as with *The Wild Blue Yonder* (Herzog 2005).

But whatever an individual film's politics and representational strategy might be, sf cinema since the millennium has been decidedly technophobic and pessimistic in vision. With the notable exception of *Interstellar* (Nolan 2014), there is no equivalent to the ultimately optimistic view of an earlier sf film like *Things to Come* (1936), only dystopian visions of social collapse, technology out of control and ironically oppressive utopias such as those in *Minority Report* (Spielberg 2002), *The Purge* (DeMonaco 2013) or *Equals* (Doremus 2015). Utopian visions like the one in *Don't Worry Darling* (Wilde 2022) are merely illusory. The genre's profound technophobic vision is encapsulated by films such as *The Belko Experiment* (McLean 2016) and *The Cabin in the Woods* (Goddard 2012), both of which imagine scenarios in which people are unknowingly placed in life-threatening situations and surveilled by technological panopticons, with their courses of action technologically manipulated.

In retrospect, two sf films released on the cusp of the millennium accurately anticipated this dark view of the future. Both *Strange Days* (Bigelow 1995) and *The Matrix* (Wachowski sisters 1999) – the former set, tellingly, on New Year's Eve, 1999, and the latter released that year – were technophobic warnings about the seductive potential of digital technology, an attitude reiterated

DOI: 10.4324/9781003140269-30

in the latter's sequels, *The Matrix Reloaded* (Wachowski sisters 2003), *The Matrix Revolutions* (Wachowskis 2003) and *The Matrix Resurrections* (Wachowski 2021). The same technology has rapidly become central to everyday life in the new millennium. In Steven Spielberg's 2018 adaptation of Ernest Kline's *Ready Player One* (2011), the quality of real life is so poor, with squalid living spaces literally stacked one upon another, that people obsessively flee to virtual reality, and in *Tron Legacy* (Kosinski 2010) an evil digital entity threatens to break out into the real world. *Edge of Tomorrow* (Liman 2014) tellingly features a repetitive narrative structure itself reflective of the videogame experience, while in *Sky Captain and the World of Tomorrow* (Conran 2004), one of the first films to combine live actors with computer-generated backgrounds, the performance of the late Laurence Olivier was constructed entirely out of digitally sampled bits of the actor's earlier performances. Such a possibility was considered sf in *S1m0ne* (Niccol 2002), released just two years earlier, in which a digitally constructed movie starlet is mistaken for an actual person. Fears of such technological displacement of the human is expressed most directly in movies about androids and robots, such as *A.I.: Artificial Intelligence* (Spielberg 2001), *I, Robot* (Proyas 2004) and *Ex Machina* (Garland 2014), and those about clones, including *Moon* (Jones 2009) and *Oblivion* (Kosinski 2013). The fact that most of these technophobic warnings rely heavily on computer generated imagery (CGI) is an irony that has not gone unnoticed.

The remake of *The Stepford Wives* (Oz 2004) and *Blade Runner 2049* (Villeneuve 2017), both of which involve androids, are indicative of the trend toward greater representational inclusivity found in many of the period's sequels or new instalments of established series. *Star Trek* continued its exploratory mission with *Star Trek: Nemesis* (Baird 2002), the last of the 'Next Generation' series, and the rebooted *Star Trek* (Abrams 2009) and its sequels *Star Trek into Darkness* (Abrams 2013) and *Star Trek Beyond* (Lin 2016), although the series has been mostly an all-boys affair. It was essentially business as usual, too, for the stalwart *Godzilla*, the beast appearing in five Japanese films and three from the US (Guillermo del Toro also offered a tribute to the *kaiju eiga* with *Pacific Rim* (2013)). Yet while the behemoth was crowned *Godzilla: King of the Monsters* (Docherty 2019), the film's narrative features two female protagonists. Similarly, the Men in Black franchise continued with *Men in Black II* (Sonnenfeld 2002), *Men in Black 3* (Sonnenfeld 2012) and *Men in Black: International* (Gray 2019), the last presenting a Black woman in black; and Australian filmmaker George Miller added a fourth instalment to his *Mad Max* series, *Mad Max: Fury Road* (2015), with the focus shifting from a metaphorically castrated Max to a female warrior who rebels against the local leader and sets out to rescue his multiple wives from their patriarchal oppression (her origin story is told in *Furiosa: A Mad Max Saga* (Miller 2024)). Much of the film's non-stop action was shot without CGI effects, relying instead on numerous stunt performers, including the Cirque de Soleil troupe. Similarly, the four films adapted from Suzanne Collins's Hunger Games trilogy (2008–10) – *The Hunger Games* (Ross 2012), *The Hunger Games: Catching Fire* (Lawrence 2013), *The Hunger Games: Mockingjay Part I* (Lawrence 2014), *The Hunger Games: Mockingjay Part 2* (Lawrence 2015) – feature a feisty female action hero, Katniss Everdeen. And, of course, the original series of nine Star Wars films concluded its prequel trilogy, begun in 1999 with *Episode I – The Phantom Menace*, with *Episode II – Attack of the Clones* (2002) and *Episode III – Revenge of the Sith* (2005), all three directed by George Lucas, and then continued with a sequel trilogy, *Episode VII – The Force Awakens* (Abrams 2015), *Episode VIII – The Last Jedi* (Johnson 2017) and *Episode IX – The Rise of Skywalker* (Abrams 2019), as well as two related films, *Rogue One: A Star Wars Story* (Edwards 2016) and *Solo: A Star Wars Story* (Howard 2018). The post-Lucas films often feature a strong female who is a key figure in the Resistance (following on Carrie Fisher's Princess Leia becoming an icon of female empowerment).

The period also saw remakes of several classic sf movies, thematically updated with varying degree of success, among them *Rollerball* (McTiernan 2002), *Solaris* (Soderbergh 2002), *The Time Machine* (Wells 2002), *The Manchurian Candidate* (Demme 2005), *The War of the Worlds* (Spielberg 2005), *The Day the Earth Stood Still* (Derrickson 2008) and *Total Recall* (Wiseman 2012). In *The Invasion* (2007), the fourth adaptation of Jack Finney's classic 1955 novel *The Body Snatchers*, protagonist Miles Bennell is changed from a patriarchal male to a professional woman who describes herself as a 'postmodern feminist'. In 2005, between making the LORD OF THE RINGS (2001–03) and THE HOBBIT (2012–14) trilogies, New Zealand filmmaker Peter Jackson remade *King Kong* (Cooper and Schoedsack 1933), which he has cited as his favourite movie. Counterpointing its sentimentality regarding simians, *Planet of the Apes* (Schaffner 1968) was reimagined by Tim Burton in 2001, providing a twist ending different from both the original and the novel, and was followed by a reboot series of four films to date: *Rise of the Planet of the Apes* (Wyatt 2011), *Dawn of the Planet of the Apes* (Reeves 2014), *War for the Planet of the Apes* (Reeves 2017) and *Kingdom of the Planet of the Apes* (Ball 2024), the first three all starring motion capture actor Andy Serkis (who also portrayed Jackson's Kong and Gollum), revealing astonishing advances in special effects and makeup. The APES films carry the connotations of racial commentary established in the original but reverse their dramatic terms so that it is the other primates rather than the humans who are the victims.

Since 2000, the genre's most pronounced development has been the overwhelming popularity of the superhero cycle, many but not all of these characters taken from the pages of comic books. The many superhero films range from the silly (*Superbabies: Baby Geniuses 2* (Clark 2004)) to the serious (*Upgrade* (Whannell 2017)). *Brightburn* (Yarovesky 2019) is a deliberately dark retelling of the Superman origin story with a maladjusted version of Kal-El, its obvious generic awareness signalling the film's, and the audience's, familiarity with superhero conventions. This surfeit of superhero movies in such a relatively brief period and their box-office domination reveals how urgent audiences in the twenty-first century have felt our collective problems to be. Films featuring children with superpowers especially, such as *Beyond the Black Rainbow* (Cosmatos 2010), *Chronicle* (Trank 2012) and *Midnight Special* (Nichols 2016), along with *Battle Royale* (Fukasaku 2000), the HUNGER GAMES and MAZE RUNNER films – *The Maze Runner* (Ball 2014), *The Scorch Trials* (Ball 2015), *The Death Cure* (Ball 2018) – express specifically the feelings of victimisation and injustice on the part of contemporary youth. Together, the superhero films suggest that our fears are now so deeply entrenched that only a superhuman effort could resolve them – the same feelings of despair and disempowerment that contributed to the surprise victory of Donald Trump in the 2016 US presidential election.

Undoubtedly, the most successful superhero movies belong to the MARVEL CINEMATIC UNIVERSE (MCU), a transmedia enterprise of intersecting properties across film, television, online content, comic books and other media. The box-office success of *Spider-Man* (2002), *Spider-Man 2* (2004) and *Spider-Man 3* (2007), all three directed by Sam Raimi and starring Tobey Maguire, brought comic book adaptations into the mainstream. The first MCU film was *Iron Man* (Favreau 2008), followed by 39 films and sequels (by mid-2026) featuring the Hulk, Captain America, Thor, The Avengers, Guardians of the Galaxy and others, while other Marvel properties – multiple X-Men movies, and associated Wolverine and Deadpool movies; a pair of Spider-Man movies starring Andrew Garfield, and associated Venom, Morbius and Madame Web movies; and a trilogy of Spider-Man animations, beginning with *Spider-Man: Into the Spider-Verse* (Persichetti, Ramsey and Rothman 2018) – continue to appear outside the MCU. Not to be outdone, rival DC comics responded with its own EXTENDED UNIVERSE (DCEU) of 15 films by the end of 2023. Batman, the only major superhero without any superpowers, has yet to appear in his own DCEU film, although he featured in Christopher Nolan's DARK KNIGHT trilogy – *Batman Begins* (2005), *The Dark Knight* (2008) and *The Dark Knight Rises* (2012) – and in several animated feature films released since 2000. While most of these superheroes are, as per tradition, White males, two of the most popular of these films were DC's *Wonder Woman* (Jenkins 2017), in which the Amazonian warrior princess helps end World War I, and Marvel's *Black Panther* (Coogler 2018), with its Black hero T'Challa, king of Wakanda. Both films broke numerous box-office records and were embraced by audiences in large part because they offered alternatives to the typically White male superhero.

These numerous movie superheroes have been counterbalanced by hordes of zombies, often of the flesh-devouring type, the millennium's preferred monstrous metaphor for contemporary alienation. George Romero, who launched the contemporary fascination with zombies with *Night of the Living Dead* (1968) and its two sequels, continued to explore the subgenre with *Land of the Dead* (2005), *Diary of the Dead* (2007) and *Survival of the Dead* (2009), concluding one of the most remarkable film series ever produced. In the UK, *The Girl with All the Gifts* (McCarthy 2016) presented the apocalypse as the result of a fungal infection that has left the world full of dormant cannibalistic creatures that awaken at the smell of blood, human or otherwise. It focuses on a small enclave of survivors who keep a group of infected children imprisoned and carefully guarded. The scientist experiments on them in a desperate attempt to find a cure as time runs out, while the teacher instructs them in the hope of giving them some humanity; the conflict between them, with the military in the middle, invokes the dramatic conflicts of Romero's *Day of the Dead* (remade in 2008), the conclusion of the director's initial zombie trilogy, but with female characters.

In American cinema, zombies have been so common since the millennium, as in *Resident Evil* (Anderson 2002) and its five sequels and reboot, based on the survival horror video games of the same name, that the country has become a *Zombieland* (Fleischer 2009). The characters in Jim Jarmusch's *The Dead Don't Die* (2019) have clearly seen some of them because they become aware that they are in one. A viral outbreak that turns people into raging zombies also spreads across the UK, bringing social collapse, in *28 Days Later* (Boyle 2002) and its sequel, *28 Weeks Later* (Fresnadillo 2007), in which the virus spreads to Europe. Zombies infest Ireland in *The Cured* (Freyne 2017) and the continent in the French *They Came Back* (*Les Revenants*; Campillo 2004) and the Spanish *[Rec]* (Balagueró and Plaza 2007, remade in the US as *Quarantine* (Dowdle 2008)). Korea is ground zero for the zombie outbreak in *Train to Busan* (*Busanhaeng*; Yeon 2016) and *Peninsula* (*Busanhaeng 2: Bando*; Yeon 2020), Cuba in *Juan of the Dead* (*Juan de los Muertos*; Brugués 2011) and Canada in *Pontypool* (McDonald 2008), *Fido* (Currie 2006) and *Blood Quantum* (Barnaby 2019). The latter, directed by Quebec-based Listuguj Mi'kmaq film-maker Jeff Barnaby, offers a strong statement about colonialism and its legacy as civilisation is wiped out, except for the Mi'kmaq people on the fictional Red Crow Reserve, who are immune. The reason for the zombie plague remains vague, although one of the Mi'kmaq men explains: 'The earth is like an animal; it lives, it breathes', adding that now it is sick because of all that White men have done to it. In *Blood Quantum*'s bloody climax, hordes of indistinguishable, zombiefied Whites invade the safe haven of the reservation and consume the Indigenous peoples there.

The zombie film tends to blend horror tropes with sf premises, although numerous other plagues have befallen the world in millennial sf. In the international co-production *Blindness* (Meirelles 2008), a generic city is hit by a contagious affliction of sightlessness, in *V for Vendetta* (McTeigue 2005) the St. Mary's Virus has swept through Europe, and in *Children of Men* (Cuarón 2006) global infertility has brought civilisation to the brink of extinction. The entirely plausible *Contagion* (Soderbergh 2011) depicts a pandemic caused by a new viral mutation that within months kills one-twelfth of the world's population. Periodic rhythmic montages emphasise the interconnecting global mobility of humanity today. As in the disaster films of the late 1970s, some characters live and others die irrespective of their morality or the star status of the actors portraying them – everyone is susceptible. *Contagion* also taps into widespread doubt about the effectiveness of government intervention in disaster scenarios, a doubt that has only grown with each passing year and new emergency, showing conflicting and uncoordinated responses at the federal and state levels – a scenario that subsequently played out in the 2020 Covid-19 pandemic (when *Contagion* became one of the most popular films on Netflix).

I Am Legend (Lawrence 2007), the fourth film adaptation of Richard Matheson's 1954 novel of the same name, provides a post-9/11 take on the author's story of a world destroyed by a plague, the unforeseen result of a supposed cure for cancer, that has either killed everyone or turned them into vampires, and of the efforts of the sole remaining man, now African American, to survive. Virologist Robert Neville tellingly refers to New York City as 'ground zero' of the zombie virus, and the vampires, like nightmarish incarnations of terrorists, are relentless in their destruction of Western civilisation. In the final scene, which has no counterpart in either Matheson's novel or the earlier film versions (all of which end with Neville's death and the ascendency of the mutated humans), the woman and child to whom Neville gives the cure he has discovered and for whom he has sacrificed himself find the survivors' enclave that the woman claims God had revealed to her in a vision. In a concluding voiceover, she explains that Neville became legendary for finding the cure – whereas in the novel Neville ironically has become legendary as the last human to die in the now dominant society of mutants. Setting box-office records upon its release and one of the year's top grossing films, *I Am Legend* provided a relatively comforting vision of the apocalypse, with its reassuring message that, although Black lives matter, they would sacrifice themselves in the national interest and that, moreover, God is on our side.

Apocalypticism suffuses post-millennial sf cinema. In *Melancholia* (von Trier 2011), the world meets its end by colliding with a rogue planet, and in *The Book of Eli* (Hughes brothers 2010) it is a nuclear apocalypse. *The Day* (Aarniokoski 2011), in which a handful of people try to survive widespread cannibalism in a post-apocalyptic world, does not even bother to provide a reason for the calamity, while the apocalypse is a mere detail in the epic narrative of *Cloud Atlas* (Wachowski sisters and Tykwer 2012). *The Road* (Hillcoat 2009), based on the Pulitzer Prize-winning 2006 novel by Cormac McCarthy, is set in the near future after an unexplained global environmental disaster ('There were signs', an old man reminisces). In addition to the conventional apocalyptic images of eroding highways and crumbling industrial parks, greenery was digitally removed from exterior shots. The narrative follows an unnamed father and his young son as they travel on foot through a dying world of pervasive, constantly falling grey ash, the man protecting the boy from scavengers and cannibals. After the pair reach the sea and the man dies, the son – in a jarringly optimistic ending that is nevertheless consistent with the novel – is taken under the protection of a family that suddenly appears. Even as the planet is dying, the traditional nuclear family, complete with two children and a dog, somehow survives.

A similarly upbeat ending is provided in *WALL-E* (Stanton 2008), a computer-animated feature produced by Pixar Animation Studios that was nominated for six Academy Awards, winning Best Animated Feature, and one of the top-grossing films of 2008. There have been numerous animated sf features since 2000 addressing family audiences (e.g., *Jimmy Neutron: Boy Genius* (Davis 2001), *Monsters vs. Aliens* (Letterman and Vernon 2009)) as well as adults (e.g., *Final Fantasy: The Spirits Within* (Sakaguchi and Sakakibara 2001), *A Scanner Darkly* (Linklater 2006)), with many, as in Japan, focusing on superheroes and technological fears. *WALL-E*, one of the most commercially successful, follows the eponymous robot (short for Waste Allocation Load Lifter – Earth Class), an automated waste collector, centuries in the future, when the Earth has been ruined by garbage and pollution and the megacorporation Buy n Large (BnL) has evacuated the population in fully automated galactic cruise ships. WALL-E teams up with the indolent humans, grown fat and torpid after centuries in their untroubled environment, to defeat BnL and reclaim the Earth. The machines communicate with body language and robotic sounds resembling human vocal intonations designed by Ben Burtt, whose credits include several of the STAR WARS films and Spielberg's *E.T.: The Extra-Terrestrial* (1982), making them far more sympathetic (even if they abide by traditional notions of gender) than the wasteful humans. The final shot zooms away to reveal vegetation beginning to grow in various places and a closing credits sequence shows humans and robots working together to rebuild civilisation.

Anxieties over environmental pollution and global warming, as might be expected given the accelerating rate of climactic disasters since the millennium, inform numerous other sf movies, including *The Day after Tomorrow* (Emmerich 2004), in which the planet plunges into a new ice age, and *2012* (Emmerich 2009), in which solar flares cause the collapse of the Earth's crust. Solar flares also cause the immolation of most of humanity in *Knowing* (Proyas 2009). *The Happening* (Shyamalan 2008) shows plant life around the world rebelling against environmental abuse by releasing deadly toxins into the air that cause people to commit suicide in gruesome ways. In *The Mist* (Darabont 2007), adapted from Stephen King's 1980 novella, the environment is completely obscured by a preternaturally thick fog that contains a host of monstrous and deadly creatures. Joon-ho Bong's *The Host* (*Gwoemul*; 2006), one of the most commercially successful South Korean films ever made, imagines a deadly and destructive mutant amphibian caused by the US military presence in Korea when an American army pathologist orders a hesitant Korean assistant to dump hundreds of bottles of formaldehyde into the Han River. Later, with US military assistance, the colluding Korean government deploys 'Agent Yellow' (an allusion to the toxin Agent Orange, widely used by the US during the Vietnam War) in a failed attempt to kill the monster, and in the final scene government officials in Washington explain away the recent 'Korean Virus Crisis' as merely 'misinformation'.

Several films about alien contact also tilted toward the apocalyptic. Aliens are wholly other and remorselessly destructive in *Cloverfield* (Reeves 2008), with its rampaging monster in the process of levelling New York City, and in *Life* (Espinosa 2017), where the joyful discovery of life on Mars quickly turns to death – not just for the crew of the ship that discovers it but also, it would seem, for the entire world as an apparently intelligent being that consumes other living things is accidentally brought back to Earth. *Color Out of Space* (Stanley 2019), an adaptation of H.P. Lovecraft's 1927 story, is faithful to the author's conception of an incomprehensible, ancient alien lifeform that infects and distorts DNA. A similar premise informs *Annihilation* (Garland 2018), based on the first volume of Jeff VanderMeer's SOUTHERN REACH trilogy (2014). The film features an all-female crew assigned to penetrate the 'shimmer' but adds an ending different from the novel in which the genetic changes brought about by the extraterrestrial lifeform are destroyed in a chain reaction. The heptapods of *Arrival* (Villeneuve 2016), based on Ted Chiang's 'Story of Your Life' (1998), have no apparent malevolent intentions, although their very presence precipitates a global crisis, but both the British *Attack the Block* (Cornish 2011) and the American *Battle: Los Angeles* (Liebesman 2011) envision alien invasions as requiring massive and organised armed resistance. Spielberg's *War of the Worlds* reimagines Wells's classic invasion narrative within the context of 9/11 and the 'war on terror'. Now set in New York City, its biggest departure from Wells's novel and the 1953 adaptation is the premise that the Martian machines have been buried under the Earth for aeons, like terrorist sleeper cells waiting activation. The alien invasion is already *a fait accompli* in *Battlefield Earth* (Christian 2000) and *Captive State* (Wyatt 2019), the latter a Trump-era look at humans collaborating in their own oppression in a fascist state imposed by alien rulers known as 'legislators'.

Less apocalyptic in scale but no less dire are the inevitable threats to the nuclear family, also the emphasis of films about environmental catastrophe. Even as aliens are wreaking mass destruction around the globe, the focus is on the family in *A Quiet Place* (Krasinski 2018) and *Bird Box* (Bier 2018), as it is in *War of the Worlds*, *The Day after Tomorrow* and *2012*. In *Dark Skies* (Stewart 2013), an average American family is targeted by 'the Grays', aliens who have been lurking undetected on Earth for some time, experimenting with people for reasons unknown – a situation expressing a sense of helplessness in the face of forces beyond human ken, like 'the Plan' in *The Adjustment Bureau* (Nolfi 2011), based on Philip K. Dick's 'Adjustment Team' (1954). In *Dark Skies*, the family suffers from the Grays's tormenting whims as if they were living with poltergeists in a haunted house, beginning, tellingly, when the husband and father is laid off and economic pressures start to mount. Trying to protect themselves from the Grays, the family board up their house, evoking both Romero's *Night of the Living Dead* and the images of foreclosed homes that were broadcast regularly on television news when the country was deep in recession during the Bush administration. As aliens invade Earth in M. Night Shyamalan's *Signs* (2002), the film focuses on a former Episcopalian priest who has lost his faith in God and left the Church after his wife died in an accident. He barricades his rural family home and two children against the invading aliens, ultimately defeating them, his faith as a result restored because there is clearly more in his philosophy than he had dreamt of. In the coda, the former priest is seen donning his clerical collar once again, the film thus restoring the father on multiple levels simultaneously.

Opposed to such fearful and deadly aliens are the noble savages of James Cameron's *Avatar* (2009). Despite its enormous budget of over $300 million, its explicitly pro-ecology (and anti-militarist) message struck a chord with appreciative audiences: it broke numerous box-office records on its way to becoming the highest-grossing film of all time ($2.9 billion), earning nine Academy Award nominations and winning three of them (*Avatar: The Way of Water* (Cameron 2022), the first of the belated sequels, took $2.3 billion). The plot is set in 2154, when humanity has moved into space in its continuing search for natural resources, including an especially prized mineral from Pandora, a world with an atmosphere poisonous to humans but inhabited by an Indigenous species of blue-skinned humanoids, the Na'vi, who live there in harmony with nature. To win the hearts and minds of the Na'vi, a rapacious mining company utilises Na'vi–human hybrids (avatars) operated by genetically matched humans for purposes of subversion; but in his avatar form, Jake Sully, a paraplegic former soldier, comes to embrace the Na'vi ways, including its pantheistic reverence of nature, and lead them in their fight against the human despoilers. In the end, having defeated the Terran imperialists, Sully is able to stay in his avatar identity permanently. Despite the film's feel-good liberalism and derivative plot, borrowed from such sf novels as Ursula K. Le Guin's 'The Word for World is Forest' (1972), it nonetheless succeeds in immersing the spectator into the complexly realised world of Pandora, largely through Cameron's own pioneering 3-D techniques that enable the moving camera to give physical depth to the planet's elaborate ecology and state-of-the-art motion capture techniques that provide the Na'vi with a complete range of facial expressions equalling that of the live-action actors. *Avatar: The Way of Water* shows the same impressive motion capture techniques, but the plot is merely a pastiche of action movie tropes and motifs from Cameron's previous movies, including even a sinking ship that recalls *Titanic* (1997), as bereft of ideas as the Earth apparently is of resources.

District 9 (Blomkamp 2009) employs the same 'going native' fantasy as *Avatar*, but for a different purpose. Inspired by events that transpired in apartheid-era South Africa, including the designation in 1967 of District Six, a residential part of Cape Town, as a 'Whites only' area, and the resultant forced relocation of thousands of people, *District 9* confronts issues of racism and segregation by playing on the double meaning of the world 'alien'. A surprise box-office hit, it is one of the few sf films ever to be nominated for an Academy Award for Best Picture. In the film's alternate timeframe, in 1982 a massive alien spacecraft came to Earth filled with sick and starving aliens, a collection of intergalactic boat people who were confined to District 9, a government camp established just outside the city. Now the government is forcing them to relocate, and the Afrikaner functionary in charge is accidentally exposed to a strange fluid that affects his genetic makeup, causing him to begin to mutate into one of the crustacean-like aliens. As the film builds towards its dramatic climax, it drops the racial metaphor in favour of action-film thrills, with plenty of graphic CGI effects as both humans and aliens are blown to bits in battles between the private military company overseeing the relocation program, the aliens and a gang of Nigerian gunrunners. These sustained action sequences within the film's political parable are a particularly vivid instance of the tension between spectacle and speculation that informs post-millennial sf films. Still, despite the pyrotechnics, *District 9* is effective in eliciting the spectator's sympathy for the aliens, impressively designed by Peter Jackson's WETA Workshop, and also for the initially racist official who, ironically, becomes more sympathetic as he grows less human. (Director Neill Blomkamp employs the same approach of building audience sympathy for his victimised android exploited by corrupt humans in *Chappie* (2015).)

Questions of post-colonial exploitation are also addressed in the Mexican–American *Sleep Dealer* (Rivera 2008) and the German *Transfer* (Lucacevic 2010). *Sleep Dealer* depicts a near future in which the global digital network allows for the remote exploitation of virtual labour and memory sharing, as a result destroying local communities even as actual national borders have become more entrenched. A wall now separates the United States from Mexico, as in Gareth Edwards's *Monsters* (2010), and instead of attempting illegal immigration, Mexican laborers teleoperate robotic drones in the US from south of the border, exploited until they burn out from the process. Tellingly, the technology requires the workers to wear eyepieces and a face plate that metaphorically obscures their vision and silences their voices. *Transfer* imagines a future in which virile, young Africans put their consciousness on hold and allow their bodies to be appropriated for use by rich, aging Europeans – a similar premise to that of Jordan Peele's breakout horror film, *Get Out* (2017) – foregrounding racial as well as class difference.

Snowpiercer (Bong 2013) allegorises class tensions as a train moving through an apocalyptic landscape with the privileged elite up front and the disenfranchised masses huddled in squalor in the back cars. The Spanish *The Platform* (*El Hoyo*; Gaztelu-Urrutia 2019) similarly envisions oppression metaphorically, in vertical rather than horizontal space, as a prison with multiple levels in which social position changes periodically and randomly depending on which level one finds oneself. While sf movies often show futuristic oppressive social structures being overthrown, as in *Snowpiercer*, these regimes are typically depicted as evil for opposing capitalism and bourgeois individualism and are simply replaced by the values of dominant ideology, as in, for example, the American *Elysium* (Blomkamp 2013). But whether individual films are revolutionary in vision or merely in plot, post-millennial sf cinema reveals a marked tension between spectacle and speculation that articulates our collective awareness of the increasingly pressing social and technological challenges facing the world even while feeling compelled to entertain.

29
TWENTY-FIRST CENTURY TELEVISION

Sherryl Vint

In the twenty-first century, television has expanded far beyond its traditional purview, becoming one of the most vibrant sites of contemporary cultural production. The radical changes in how people imagine and consume television have been driven by technological developments that have reshaped the political economy of the medium, creating new methods of distribution, which have in turn multiplied the number of content providers: streaming platforms such as Netflix and Hulu joined traditional and niche networks, which in turn launched such streaming platforms as Peacock TV (NBC) and CBS All Access (which became Paramount+ in 2021), while a range of companies, such as Facebook, Amazon and Direct TV, began to create original content.

Currently, though, we are beginning to see signs of truncation after the period of 'peak television': the scramble for subscribers has given way to a renewed emphasis on corporate profitability. The proliferation of streaming services is being reversed, as corporate consolidations seek to aggregate their IP under a single brand, often pulling beloved series from the available catalogue so that they may be sold for syndication elsewhere, and in some cases even refusing to air already-completed work, as is the case for the final season of *Snowpiercer* (TNT 2020–3). Platforms once supported by subscription alone, such as Netflix, have introduced new tiers of pricing and a return (for some) to traditional advertisement-funded distribution. As I write, we are in the middle of a combined Screen Writers Guild and Screen Actors Guild strike, in response to a streaming distribution political economy that offers actors no shared revenue in profits, and fuelled by fears of the capacity of new AI tools to replace labour in the industry.

These changes result in twenty-first century sf television looking very different to that of previous decades for three main reasons. First, the range of distributors often frees the content of television from the rigid episode lengths and narrative forms required to succeed on broadcast-scheduled, episodic television (Lotz). This enables new kinds of stories to be told, often without concessions to advertisers' fear of provocative content, and for stories to be told more complexly when viewers might binge or repeatedly watch privileged content (Mittel). Second, while some of these new services are available only to domestic audiences, many aggregate content obtained from multiple producers and distribute it transnationally (with Netflix taking the lead in this regard). Finally, the distinction between film and television has blurred, because people interchangeably watch either on the same – if also on multiple types of – devices, from large-screen

DOI: 10.4324/9781003140269-31

televisions that seek to mimic the theatrical experience in homes to smartphone screens tinier than the smallest boxset television. Binge-watching means that serialised narrative is often tightly integrated in a way more akin to film than to the traditional beats of episodic television. In this context, distinctions between series and miniseries also erode, as many series are planned with definitive endpoints measured in seasons instead of episodes. Thus, changes in technology and political economy enable changes in aesthetics and narrative form.

These industry shifts apply to all of twenty-first century television, but sf television plays a particular role in this story. During the 1990s, sf series such as *Babylon 5* (PTEN/TNT 1993–8) pioneered the narrative arc storytelling that has become paradigmatic of television overall (Creeber). The startling success of sf-inflected *Lost* (ABC 2004–10), the exemplar of puzzle narrative, pushed television overall toward complex narratives and fragmented temporalities as a dominant aesthetics (Newman and Levine). The committed practices of fan viewing, also strongly associated with sf, provide new ventures with the expectation of a ready-made audience, and thus sf series have often been anchors for the launch of new streaming service, such as *Star Trek Discovery* (2017–) on CBS All Access, the Marvel Cinematic Universe and Star Wars series on Disney+, the miniseries *Brave New World* (2020) on Peacock and the post-apocalyptic adventure series *See* (2019–22) on AppleTV+.

The overwhelming number of sf television series produced today, widely distributed across platforms and countries, means that it is impossible to discuss them all. Therefore, this chapter will categorise the overall thematic trends in sf television over the past two decades and highlight series that are particularly noteworthy for innovations that shaped subsequent television. It will emphasise live-action television, although numerous animated series exist, the most notable of which are *Rick & Morty* (Cartoon Network 2013–) and *Steven Universe* (Cartoon Network 2013–9); both link sf with comedy, situating themselves somewhere between satire of and homage to the genre, a trend evident in such live-action series as *Eureka* (Syfy 2006–12), *Chuck* (NBC 2007–13), *Better Off Ted* (ABC 2009–10), *The Orville* (Fox/Hulu 2017–), *Resident Alien* (Syfy 2021–) and *Mrs. Davis* (Peacock 2023). This chapter will also not discuss series that are part of wider transmedia franchises (there is a chapter on franchise sf elsewhere in this volume), other than to note that multiple such titles exist, reflecting an overall trend in recent television toward building out shared diegetic worlds.

Realities, conspiracies, catastrophes

In the early twenty-first century, US sf television was dominated by series that worked through the trauma of 9/11, including *Threshold* (CBS 2005–6), about a government agency prepared to face all contingencies, including alien invasion. In this and similar series, repeated motifs of confused identity and personal loss recur. *The 4400* (USA Network 2004–7) and *The Event* (NBC 2010–11) concern returned missing people who may or may not be who they claim to be; their mysteries point toward conspiracies led by the powerful. In *The Crossing* (ABC 2018) the returned are migrants from a dystopian future. *Lost*'s narrative is anchored by a missing plane, evoking 9/11, while *Manifest* (NBC/Netflix 2018–23) has passengers from its missing plane return, out of temporal synchronicity with the rest of the world. Several series about memory deepen this sense that political reality unfolds strangely, like a fiction that might be shaped – manipulated – by forces of either good or evil, including early series such as *The Dead Zone* (USA Network 2002–7), about a man who awakens from a coma with psychic powers, and *Dollhouse* (Fox 2009–10), about people turned into programmable commodities by the elite. In *FlashForward* (ABC 2009) everyone on Earth momentarily blacks out to awaken with a brief glimpse of the perhaps-inevitable future, while in *Stitchers* (Freeform 2015–7) a secret government technology allows an agent to be 'stitched' into the memories of the recently deceased to retrieve data. Most recently, *The Last Days of Ptolemy Grey* (Apple 2022), adapted from Walter Mosley's 2010 novel, invents a technology that enables Alzheimer's patients briefly to recover their memories as a way intergenerationally to explore the trauma of Black experience in a White supremacist America. In these series, time, memory, reality and virtuality enter into unstable relationships with one another, speaking to anxiety about a future that no longer seems destined to secure American hegemony and to a context of online, mediated life in which reality itself seems increasingly open to editing and revision. The Korean series *Circle* (*Sseokeul*; tvN 2017), about alien technology that can turn memory into digital recordings, addresses similar concerns.

Such series are joined by another trend toward narratives that use an aesthetic technique that might be described as anachronistic retrofuturism. *Tales from the Loop* (Amazon 2020) and *Hello Tomorrow!* (Apple 2023) have ambiguous temporal settings, evoking both the future and the past as they are out-of-step with the quotidian present, and yet convey a sense of futurity through retrofuturist aesthetics. By conveying a sense of the gap between the prosperous future once projected by the Space Age and the banal actual present of austerity, they seem to suggest that the only way one can imagine a 'good' future is by returning to the past, as if to undo the twenty-first century to try again. A similar sensibility is conveyed by the German series *Dark* (Netflix 2017–20), a narrative about conspiracy and family entanglements that involves time travel, a nuclear power plant and an ominous sense of threat emanating from the future. Tonally very different, the American series *Night Sky* (Amazon 2022), about a retired couple who discover a portal to another planet in their back garden, is similarly nostalgic for a past when the future seemed brighter.

Much recent sf television blurs sf and realist settings, especially several new anthology series, the most celebrated of which, *Black Mirror* (Channel 4/Netflix 2011–), evokes screens in its title as the reflective surfaces in which we see ourselves and our world, while its move from the UK's Channel 4 to Netflix in its third season demonstrates the increasingly transnational audience for television. Frequently focusing on social media technologies, if expresses a sensibility that reality itself now feels like sf. Several episodes of its most recent sixth season, released after a four-year hiatus, evoke the television itself as the dystopian screen, featuring a diegetic corporation, Streamberry, that is all but indistinguishable from Netflix. The fact that the algorithmic turn in what content is made drives the narrative of these episodes is further evidence that shifts in the television landscape overall show up first within sf. Other new anthology series include *Electric Dreams* (Channel 4 2018), inspired by Philip K. Dick's fiction, a relaunched *Amazing Stories* (Apple 2020) and a renewed *The Twilight Zone* (CBS All Access 2019–20), notably helmed by Jordan Peele, who follows Rod Serling in using the affordances of sf to address political issues, in this case centrally racism.

The thematic interest in rewriting memory, even reality itself, infuses numerous series about time travel, including *Odyssey 5* (Space/Showtime 2002–3), the rebooted *Doctor Who* (BBC 2005–) – who finally, in 2017, regenerated as a woman – *Journeyman* (NBC 2007), *Charlie Jade* (Space 2005), *Life on Mars* (BBC 2006–7; US remake NBC 2008–9; Spanish remake *La chica de ayer* Antena 3 2009; Russian remake *Obratnaya storona Luny* Channel One 2012–8; South Korean remake *La-i-peu on Ma-seu* OCN 2018), *Terra Nova* (Fox 2011), *Alcatraz* (Fox 2012), *Continuum* (Showcase 2012–5), *Timeless* (NBC 2016–8), *Time After Time* (ABC/AXN 2017), *Travelers* (Showcase 2018) and *Russian Doll* (Netflix 2019–2021). There are also many Korean time-travel series, most in some way connecting present-day Korea with the Joseon era and thus speaking to the ongoing resentment of Japanese imperialism. The sheer number of these series suggests a widespread sense that, in the twenty-first century, history itself has somehow gone off course and needs to be corrected: some evoke ecological themes, such as *Terra Nova,* which is about colonising Earth's own Cretaceous past where resources are still plentiful. The Canadian series *Continuum* is notably for its critique of the coming 'corporate congress'; in its second season it allowed fans to have input into the storyline through an online poll, which asked them to take sides in a diegetic battle about resisting or capitulating to this future. Among the most significant of such narratives are those seeking to come to terms with the 'afterlife of slavery' (Hartman 6), that is, the ongoing systemic racism that continues to disadvantage and shorten the lives of African Americans. Adapted from novels by Colson Whitehead and Octavia E. Butler, respectively, *The Underground Railroad* (Amazon 2021) and *Kindred* (FX on Hulu 2022) use estranging aesthetics to convey the ongoing effects of slavery in the structures of American life.

Similar concerns with the inadequacies of the status quo shape a range of series that include alternative worlds, inviting viewers to reflect critically on what shapes contingent political outcomes, including *Fringe* (Fox 2008–13), which deliberately echoed *The X-Files* (Fox 1993–2002, revived for two further seasons in 2016 and 2018), *The Man in the High Castle* (Amazon 2015–9), based on Philip K. Dick's 1962 novel, *Counterpart* (Starz 2017–9), *Maniac* (Netflix 2018), based on the Norwegian series of the same name (TV2 2015), *The I-Land* (Netflix 2019) and the British *Noughts + Crosses* (BBC 2020 -), based on Malorie Blackman's YA novel series. *Counterpart* notably evokes divisions between first and second worlds via a Cold War cultural imaginary, documenting through the differences between its two realities (and the doubles of each character within them) how political ideologies shape economics, social structures and personalities. While *Noughts + Crosses*' narrative is rather conventional – a Romeo and Juliet love story across racial and class difference – its premise of a world in which Africa colonised Europe shines in its production design and costuming. Its alternative world built on Afrocentric philosophy, politics and aesthetics shows how thoroughly Western imaginaries are formed by colonial logics.

These alternative-world series are very often dystopian, as in *High Castle*'s critique of fascism, and dystopian or post-apocalyptic settings are central to twenty-first century sf television. Recurring motifs include environmental disaster, critique of authoritarianism, and social fragmentation in the wake of disruptive events (chiefly wars or pandemics). Virus narratives were quite common before the Covid-19 pandemic; in its wake, there were adaptations of Emily St. John Mandel's 2014 novel *Station Eleven* (HBO Max 2021) and Brian K. Vaughan's 2002–8 comic *Y: The Last Man* (FX on Hulu 2021). Viral apocalypse series include *Jeremiah* (Showtime 2002–4), about a future build by adolescents after all adults die of infection, a premiss repeated in more recent series, including *Between* (City 2015–6), *The Society* (Netflix 2019), the Danish *The Rain* (Netflix 2018–20) and *The Ark* (Syfy 2023), about a colonisation mission in which an accident wipes out the officers and technical crew. This focus on youth rebuilding a ruined world is also widespread in contemporary YA sf, embodying the burden of a generation now inheriting earlier failures to resolve the environmental and economic crises produced by modernity. Other viral apocalypse series include the UK reboot of the 1970s series *Survivors* (BBC 2008–10), *12 Monkeys* (Syfy 2015–8) and *The Last of Us* (HBO 2023–), adapted from a popular videogame. In *Jericho* (CBS 2006–8), *The 100* (The CW 2014–20) and the German *Tribes of Europa* (Netflix 2021) war ends the world, but intergenerational conflict over leadership shapes these series as well.

But the world ends in many ways and for many reasons in recent sf television. *Snowpiercer* and the Brazilian *3%* (Netflix 2016–) stress climate change and class conflict; *Revolution* (NBC 2012–4) lays the blame on corporations and the end of access to electricity; perhaps strangest of all, *Wayward Pines* (Fox 2015–16) is about a small town sinister in its excessive wholesomeness, which turns out to be an outpost in the far-future attempting to reboot the human species after years of cryonic storage. The Indian *Leila* (Netflix 2019) and the Australian *The Commons* (Stan 2019–20) combine environmental crisis with infertility in stories about reproductive politics, which are also central to the resurgent misogyny explored in *The Handmaid's Tale* (Hulu 2017–). Sometimes the end of the world is imminent or unexplained: in *Under the Dome* (CBS 2013–4), based on Stephen King's 2009 novel, a town is cut off from the world outside, while in the near-future British detective series *Hard Sun* (BBC 2018) a looming solar disaster will soon destroy life on Earth. *Silo* (Apple 2023–), adapted from Hugh Howey's novels, features a future humanity confined to underground silos on a poisoned Earth, while *The Peripheral* (Amazon 2022), adapted from William Gibson's novel, explores the various contemporary trends leading to a polycrisis disaster that Gibson calls 'the jackpot', after which a kleptocracy rules a population-depleted future.

Among the most compelling – and disturbing – of these series about the looming end of life as we know it is the British *Years and Years* (BBC 2019), which follows the fates of a Manchester family from 2019–34, during which time the UK elects a right-wing populist who accelerates the move toward an authoritarian state, enacts racist immigration policy and accelerates climate catastrophe. Similarly ambitious is the miniseries *Extrapolations* (Apple 2023), a set of loosely connected episodes that chart the consequences of rising temperatures and sea levels from 2037 through to 2070. Its concluding episode shows the CEO of the corporation most responsible for delaying an adequate response to the climate crisis (so as to ensure continuing profitability) being convicted for 'crimes against the planet' once political hegemony finally turns toward ecological priorities.

More-than-human protagonists in near-futures

Several series that focus on humans with enhanced abilities develop critiques of the politics of marginalisation and oppression, including *Heroes* (NBC 2006–10), *Agents of S.H.I.E.L.D.* (ABC 2013–20), *The Gifted* (Fox 2017–9), the British *Misfits* (E4 2009–13), *The Tomorrow People* (The CW 2013–4), remaking the British series (ITV 1973–9, 1992–5), *Almost Human* (Fox 2013–4) and *The Boys* (Amazon 2019–21), based on Garth Ennis and Darick Robertson's comic (2006–12). While *The Gifted* and *Misfits* show how those with morphological differences can be persecuted by a fearful mainstream, others locate the danger in the power fantasy of special abilities itself. *The Boys* takes the tropes of the superhero genre to task for their celebration of violence, toxic masculinity and homophobia, and centres on the pathology of Homelander, a dangerous and openly fascist version of Superman created by corporate genetic engineering. *Legion* (FX 2017–9) similarly suggests that with great power comes disastrous entitlement. Connected to the world of X-Men comics, but different in tone, it focuses on David Haller who, diagnosed as schizophrenic and mistreated due to his psychic powers, becomes monstrous when he recognises the full extent of his ability to manipulate reality and especially other people. Structured by an associative logic and surrealistic dream imagery, the series is an aesthetic and narrative triumph.

Raising Dion (Netflix 2019–), based on Dennis Liu's 2015 comic and short film, explores these issues dialectically in its story of an African American single mother who navigates the difficulties of responsibly raising a child with powers. The Australian *Cleverman* (ABC 2016–7) shows the struggles of another kind of hominid living within a settler culture that disdains them and appropriates their land. These nonhuman characters live by different values and have powers associated with indigenous cosmologies. Focusing on gender difference, the British *The Power* (Amazon 2023–), adapted from Naomi Alderman's 2016 novel, explores the consequences of a world in which a mutation gives women the capacity to electrocute people at will, ensuring that they can no longer be physically intimidated and controlled by men, but also raising questions as to whether a simple power reversal enables a better politics.

Multiple other kinds of stories are told of those with enhanced abilities: often individuals with powers struggle against corporate forces who seek to control and exploit them, such as *The Invisible Man* (Sci-Fi 2000–2), *Dark Angel* (Fox 2000–2), the *Bionic Woman* (NBC 2007) reboot, *Second Chance* (Fox 2015–6) and *The Umbrella Academy* (Netflix 2019–). Although its protagonists lack superhuman abilities, *Orphan Black* (Space 2013–7), about clones manufactured by a corporation, is noteworthy in this context as another model of how commodified biology can be a vector of dehumanisation. In other series, the powerful more willingly use their skills to serve government agencies, often the same agencies that engineered them in the first place, including *Jake 2.0* (UPN 2003), *Intelligence* (CBS 2014) and *Limitless* (CBS 2015–6). *No Ordinary Family* (ABC 2010–1) fuses domestic dramedy with an entire family who gains superpowers by accident, while series such as *Helix* (Syfy 2014–5) and the French *Ad Vitam* (Arte 2018) explore technologies designed to extend the lifespan of their elite consumers. Fusing similar bioengineering experiments with a thriller plot, the German *Biohackers* (Netflix 2020–1) is one among several recent sf series that demonstrate the increasing difficulty of drawing a line between sf and non-sf television because of how technology is changing daily life.

Century City (CBS 2004–5), *Person of Interest* (CBS 2011–6), *Mr. Robot* (USA Network 2015–9), *APB* (Fox 2016–7), *Wisdom of the Crowd* (CBS 2017–8), *Reverie* (NBC 2018), *Next* (Fox 2020) and the Brazilian *Omniscient* (Netflix 2020) project novel technologies, but only into a very-near future. All concern IT and often surveillance systems and predictive algorithms, imagining technologies and the worlds they will create almost as if they are start-up funding pitches. The most science-fictional among them, *Person of Interest*, imagines the emergence of an AGI (artificial general intelligence), but its plotlines have more to do with government and policing than with sentient machines. Similarly, *Mr. Robot* has an sf sensibility, especially in its conspiracy plot about an elite cabal, but the series responds thematically to the 2007–8 financial crash and its depictions of hacking are famed for their real-world precision. *Next*'s story of an AI with sinister plans addresses concerns about surveillance, algorithms and the manipulated worldview that can be a consequence of algorithm-driven media bubbles. In reality, AI is able to follow us anywhere through our smartphones and our GPS-enabled automobiles, to turn our smart homes into prisons, and to destroy reputations through manufactured social media posts. Yet *Next* obscures, rather than illuminates, this reality by attributing agency for destructive media to the AI itself rather than to humans who code and profit from 'surveillance capitalism' (Zuboff). While in earlier generations dangerous AI tended to emerge from military projects, such as THE TERMINATOR's Skynet, which makes a television appearance in *Terminator: The Sarah Connor Chronicles* (Fox 2008–9), in this century the AI has intimate access to our homes and lives via the Internet of Things. This total surveillance shapes the police miniseries *Class of '09* (FX on Hulu 2023), which touches on sf in its story of the FBI's invention of an algorithm designed to eliminate the racist bias of American policing; the Black protagonist, who champions this system, must eventually destroy it when it turns too rigidly against any human deviance from the system's rigid standards of patriotic behaviour.

Several near-world-technology series focus on the next stage of dating apps, one of the ways that twenty-first century sf television speaks equally to genre fans and to larger audiences experiencing how technology is remaking social life. *Soulmates* (AMC 2020), the French *Osmosis* (Netflix 2019) and the British *The One* (Netflix 2021), based on John Marr's 2016 novel, are all premised on the idea of finding the perfect match through ever-more-precise software that harvests data not only from your answers to profiling quizzes but also by scanning your biology and brainwaves. Yet in each, the focus is on how human sociality exceeds and vexes such analytics, showing that love is more complicated than coding. *Soulmates* is an anthology series: each episode tells a new match story, and a few address queer or polyamorous possibilities that show how algorithms are coded to reproduce the normative, not to enable the new. In the British *The Feed* (Virgin/Amazon 2019) software designed to allow partners to share thoughts becomes a tool of sinister governance, while *Upload*'s (Amazon 2020–) depiction of a company offering class-differentiated, virtual afterlife services suggests that no realm of human experience is immune from colonisation by profit-oriented media technology. The thriller miniseries *DEVS* (FX on Hulu 2020) takes the hubris of Silicon Valley culture to task in its story about the development of a quantum computer in a project aimed at hacking temporality, and thus reality itself.

Alongside these stories of technologically-modified humans are several of artificial entities created to serve as exploitable labour. This has been the story of robots since Karel Čapek coined the word in *R.U.R.* (1920), but these new series often speak to the conflation of robots and racialised migrant labour in the contemporary context (Rhee; Atenesoski and Vora). The Swedish *Real Humans* (*Äkta människor*; Sveriges Television 2012–14) was remade in the UK as *Humans* (Channel 4 2015–18) and in China (Tencent/iQiyi 2021), and similar topics are addressed by the Russian *Better Than Us* (*Luchshe, chem lyudi*; C1R/ Start 2018–9). These series speak equally to anxieties about expected job loss due to automation and to the way economic distress is directed by right-wing Western politicians toward anti-immigration and racist rhetoric. *Raised by Wolves* (HBO Max 2020–2) tries to go a step further in its depiction of robots programmed to raise the next and better generation of humans after cataclysmic religious wars. Undoubtedly the most important series in this category, however, is *Westworld* (HBO 2016–22), which redirects its source film's anxiety about humanity losing control over robots to tell the story from the robots' point of view. The imperialist fantasy design of Westworld – and related theme parks such as Raj World and Samurai World – opens a space for telling stories about the racialised imaginary that shapes our view of robots as free labour and about the psychological damage that results from repeated trauma.

Related issues of exploited labour and ongoing neoliberal austerity as key engines of the present-as-dystopia are explored in the Korean *Squid Game* (Netflix 2021–) and in *Severance* (Apple 2022–). The former is presented as a survival competition game show in which contestants in deep financial hardship risk their lives in a deadly series of challenges for the chance to win several million dollars. Speaking powerfully of a widespread sense of political and economic disenfranchisement, it rapidly became the most widely watched series in Netflix's history, securing a global audience as well as several Emmy and Golden Globe nominations. Reminiscent of such sf films as *Punishment Park* (Watkins 1971) and *The Running Man* (Glaser 1987), *Squid Game* is aesthetically closer to the former and easily mistaken for a real game show due to the way it illuminates existing class disparities and financial desperation in its characters' backstories. Notably, these earlier films put convicted (however unjustly) criminals in the position of competing in lethal games, while those on *Squid Game* are guilty only of being poor. *Severance* is a strange workplace drama premised on the idea that one can undergo a procedure to sever one's full personality from one's work persona, illustrating the total separation of full personhood from labour-power fantasised by neoliberal capital.

Invasions, empires, the new space age

Although much twenty-first century sf television focuses on the near-future and the extension of existing technologies, several influential series reimagine such Golden Age themes as space travel, interplanetary civilisations and alien invasion. The last was dominant in the US in the early 2000s, another way of working through a new sense of vulnerability that dominated public life in the wake of 9/11. Series such as *Invasion* (ABC 2005–6), a title reused for an Apple series (2021–), *Surface* (NBC 2005–6), *V* (ABC 2009–11), a reboot of NBC's 1983–5 series, and especially *Falling Skies* (TNT 2011–5) show America under threat from alien invaders, some of whom pass as human. *Falling Skies* puts a Revolutionary War historian at the centre of its narrative of resistance, jingoistically rewriting settler colonial Americans as beleaguered defenders of their native lands. Other series depict more complex politics and the difficulty of negotiating community among divergent cultures, including *Defiance* (Syfy 2013–5), *Star-Crossed* (The CW 2014), *Colony* (USA Network 2016–8), and *Roswell New Mexico* (The CW 2019–22); the last, an updated version of *Roswell* (The WB/UPN 1999–2002), maps the prejudice experienced with its displaced, teenaged space aliens onto the racism experienced by Latinx people in New Mexico. Love interest Liz is reimagined as Latinx, and her father, an undocumented immigrant, faces consequences if outed as an 'illegal alien' similar to those feared by the extraterrestrials. Such interrogation of colonial politics is also evident in two adaptations of H.G. Wells's *The War of the Worlds* (1898), a British production (BBC 2019) and a French/UK/US coproduction (Canal+ 2019–), and, most surprisingly, in *Outer Range* (Amazon 2022–), about a Wyoming rancher fighting to protect his land from property developers, complicated by a mysterious portal to another realm that proves to be his place of origin. As interest in space travel has returned, so has interest in alien visitors to Earth, including *Project Blue Book* (History 2019–20), based on the US government's investigations of UFO phenomena, and *Debris* (NBC 2021), about newly discovered crashed artefacts.

The widespread interest in colonising Mars, fuelled as much by private corporations such as SpaceX as by NASA, prompted numerous series about space travel, including *Mars* (National Geographic 2016–8), which mixes documentary and narrative segments. Many of these series are set in space but are workplace dramas, anticipating a coming future in which interplanetary travel could be just another job: *Defying Gravity* (ABC/CTV 2009), *The First* (Channel 4/Hulu 2018), *Another Life* (Netflix 2019–21) and *Away* (Netflix 2020). Some are closer to sf conventions, such as *Ascension* (CBC/Syfy 2014), whose crew believe they are on a centuries-long mission to colonise a new world but really are part of a simulation. *Salvation* (CBS 2017–8) is about planning a colonising mission mandated by the approach of an asteroid that will destroy human life on Earth, while *Nightflyers* (Syfy 2018) and *Origin* (YouTube Premium 2018) are both about crews facing an enigmatic onboard menace. Perhaps one of the most surprising series in this vein is the reimagined *Lost in Space* (Netflix 2018–), a mature treatment of the original series' (CBS 1965–8) plot of a family who crash-land on an alien planet. *Moonhaven* (AMC+ 2022) features a pastoral colony on the moon, established with a duty to pioneer a better way of life and then export it back to a diminished Earth, who fear giving up their privilege by restoring contact with those left below. Many of the workplace series put women in charge of the missions and *Lost in Space* similarly renews space age tropes with more complex treatment of gender, ethnic diversity and other social issues. *Away* in particular strives to make sure that its storylines include people of multiple genders, orientations, nationalities and embodied abilities – a sign of the changing culture of television overall and of the fact that these series expect audiences that extend beyond sf fandom.

For All Mankind (Apple 2019–), created by Ronald D. Moore, combines several of these tropes to create a novel sf series set in an alternative past, thus rewriting the original space race itself. The opening premise sees the Soviets achieving the first manned moon landing, prompting the US to direct its space programme towards the active colonisation of Mars and to enrol women into astronaut training, aiming to put the first *woman* on the Moon and thus beat the Russians at something.

This difference allows the series organically to include a more diverse cast and to explore how the space race might have unfolded otherwise had a wider range of people been empowered to make decisions. The second and third seasons each jump ahead a decade, with humans now living on Mars, and the series has a planned ending that would bring its timeline in sync with the present day. *For All Mankind* thus draws on twenty-first century fantasies of moon colonisation and resource extraction in space, while also critically revisiting the ideologies and exclusions that shaped the historical space race of the 1960s through 1980s.

Moore is better known for his earlier reboot of *Battlestar Galactica* (Sci-Fi 2003–9), which spun-off the prequel *Caprica* (Syfy 2009). It is no exaggeration to say that the reboot series transformed what was possible for sf television in the twenty-first century. Eschewing the optimism of STAR TREK, it reinvented ABC's campy 1978–9 series as a grim story of warfare, displacement, ethnic difference and political strife. In March 2009, it was the focus of a panel discussion at the UN about human rights, terrorism and more – a first for sf television – and in its wake space opera became available as a site for political storytelling as never before. While superficial military adventures series, such as *Stargate SG-1* (Showtime/Sci-Fi 1997–2007) and its spinoffs *Stargate Atlantis* (Syfy 2004–9) and *Stargate Universe* (Syfy 2009–11), were popular in the early 2000s, they have not prompted sustained critical attention. *Dark Matter* (Space/Syfy 2015–7) and *Killjoys* (Space/CTV Sci Fi Channel 2015–9) combine military adventure with political revolution, while *Krypton* (Syfy 2018–9) renews Superman mythology by focusing on Kal-El's grandfather and the political struggles that doomed the planet. One of the strangest of these series, *Extant* (CBS 2014–5), features a spacewoman mysteriously impregnated while in space, who is also mother to a manufactured AI child. Undoubtedly the most important space opera after *BSG*, however, is *The Expanse* (Syfy/Amazon 2015–22), saved from cancellation before its narrative was complete by a move to Amazon Prime Video; it follows the political and economic struggles among Earth, Mars and the outer colonies of the solar system in the aftermath of a first contact experience. *Foundation* (Apple 2021–), adapted from Isaac Asimov's book series (1951–93), intriguingly rewrites its political premise: Asimov suggests that the importance of the Foundation lies in its capacity to preserve human knowledge in the dark period after the coming fall of the Empire; the television series depicts the Foundation, repressed by the Empire, as the home of counterhegemonic knowledges and cultures seeking to hasten the fall and to create something better in its wake.

The utopian, the strange, the visionary

Recent sf television is thus a rich and diverse site of cultural production, with some titles defying the categorisations of this chapter and thus providing some of the most exciting and inventive uses of sf on television. These include strange allegorical works, such as *The Prisoner* (AMC 2009), a remake of the British series (ATV 1967–8), the British conspiracy series *Utopia* (Channel 4 2013–4; US remake Amazon 2020), the surrealist *Falling Water* (USA Network 2016–8) and *Undone* (Amazon 2019), which uses its animated mise-en-scène to depict how lived experience makes and remakes reality. Celebrated series such as *Sense8* (Netflix 2015–8) and *The OA* (Netflix 2016–8), both of which were made possible by Netflix's willingness to experiment with narrative form, catalysed devoted fan communities fascinated by their blend of affective appeal and community-centred worldbuilding. *Sense8*, about a worldwide group of people connected by their dreams, is noted for its inclusion of trans and other queer characters well before this became a practice in mainstream television. *The OA* is similarly about a group of strangers connected across multiple realities who come together against oppressive forces bent on their destruction. Both series capture and convey an intense desire for connection and purpose in a world dominated by informational networks but lacking true intimacy and solidarity. Not quite sf, *Dispatches from Elsewhere* (AMC 2020) draws on the same sensibilities; based on a real-world viral marketing experiment that became something else, it offers a glimpse of the utopian possibility that manifests in speculative aesthetics.

Watchmen (HBO 2019) and *Lovecraft Country* (HBO 2020), based on Matt Ruff's 2016 novel, are examples of recent sf television that speak urgently to the political crisis of the twenty-first century by reinhabiting sf tropes of an earlier era. *Watchmen* is not an adaptation of Alan Moore's comic (1986–7) but an extension of its narrative world articulated through antiracist critique. It tells a new story and offers new ways to think about the meanings speculative aesthetics can mobilise, but also demonstrates, through its intersections with the earlier narrative, the racial biases endemic to much of earlier sf storytelling. *Lovecraft Country*, as its name implies, does parallel work in revisiting H.P. Lovecraft's overtly racist imaginary, rewriting its tropes to embody the violence and horror of White supremacist history and to lay the foundation for a new kind of imaginary centred on the experiences of BIPOC communities. While both series focus on African American experience, they are intersectional and extend their analyses to America's global imperialism, reflecting on the Korean War and the culture of the war on terror as much as they engage with US histories of Jim Crow, lynching, White supremacist race riots and redlining. Importantly, both focus on the capacities of oppressed people to thrive despite oppression, to shape their own futures as they refuse to be victimised by these histories.

As this brief overview reveals, in the twenty-first century sf television has become a central site of cultural production, in parallel with the increasing importance of the medium itself. The affordances of sf to tell stories that allegorise political and social struggle have been central to the most celebrated series of the past two decades, which are often the most popular ones as well. While there is a diversity of political viewpoints in twenty-first century sf television, those that critique racist histories of violence, exploitative economic structures and heteronormativity, and that allegorise political conflict, have been influential in shaping future directions for the genre. The best and most beloved of these series demonstrates the desire for solidarity and community across diversity and embody the utopian possibilities of the better worlds we might yet inhabit as we continue to imagine different worlds and to manifest them through the serial narrative form that is television in the twenty-first century.

Works cited

Atanasoski, Neda and Kalindi Vora. *Surrogate Humanity: Race, Robots, and the Politics of Technological Futures*. Duke UP, 2019.

Creeber, Glen. *Serial Television: Big Drama on the Small Screen*. BFI, 2005.

Hartman, Saidiya. *Lose Your Mother: A Journey along the Atlantic Slave Route*. Farrar, Straus, and Giroux, 2007.

Lotz, Amanda. *The Television Will Be Revolutionized*, second edition. New York UP, 2014.

Mittel, Jason. *Complex TV: The Poetics of Contemporary Television Storytelling*. New York UP, 2015.

Newman, Michael Z. and Elaine Levine. *Legitimating Television: Media Convergence and Cultural Status*. Routledge, 2012.

Rhee, Jennifer. *The Robotic Imaginary: The Human and the Price of Dehumanized Labor*. U of Minnesota P, 2018.

Zuboff, Shoshana. *The Age of Surveillance Capitalism: The Fight for a Human Future at the Frontier of Power*. Public Affairs, 2019.

30

ANGLOPHONE PRINT FICTION

The new millennium

John Rieder

For a few decades in the first half of the twentieth century, print sf published in niche market, genre-specialising magazines comprised sf's economic and artistic core. As the role of such magazines gradually gave way to paperback publishing in the mid-century, film and TV production of sf grew more important as well. The event that would push print sf to the periphery of the sf economy was the success of *Star Wars* (Lucas 1977), not primarily because of the impressive moneymaking of the film itself, but more decisively because of the business model under which the sf narrative became a form of publicity for marketing a wide array of related products including games, toys, clothing and spin-off narratives (on the growth of franchises, see Rabitsch and Fuchs). Thereafter, the enormous capital investment attracted by sf film and gaming put print narrative in a different position. By the twenty-first century, the franchises radiating from *Star Wars* (Lucas 1977) and *Star Trek* (1966–), along with the MARVEL CINEMATIC UNIVERSE (2008–), determined a field of cultural production within which print sf could be subordinated to them – as for instance in the hundreds of novels elaborating the STAR WARS and STAR TREK universes – or present itself, whether willingly or not, as an alternative to the cultural hegemony of the franchises. Yet although print may no longer be the dominant medium of sf in terms of capital investment and economic consumption, it remains the medium hosting the greatest diversity and largest sheer volume of narrative production. In its role as alternative to the franchises, print sf carries on formal and imaginative traditions rooted in but often significantly divergent from the practices of sf that prevailed in the niche market era and were developed and challenged in the rest of the twentieth century. The mapping of twenty-first-century Anglophone print sf offered here makes no claim to encompass its diverse and voluminous totality, but instead highlights the trends that seem most significant in light of their continuity or discontinuity with the genre's earlier history.

The repetitiveness and interconnectedness of the franchises' products confirms and intensifies one of the most fundamental features of mass cultural narrative genres, the *seriality* which results from their dependence upon and encouragement of habitual consumption, the very *raison d'etre* of most narrative publication within the domain of mass-cultural production (Rieder 54–7). According to John Frow (80), genre practices – whether fictional, historical, scientific, political or philosophical – both presuppose and continually reconstruct worlds based on the protocols of truth, authority and plausibility specific to them. The seriality of mass cultural fiction raises

DOI: 10.4324/9781003140269-32

intertextual worldbuilding to an altogether different level of visibility than in most other genres, as theorists of the science fictional 'megatext' (Broderick; Attebery and Hollinger) and students of modern epic fantasy and fantasy franchises have well recognized (Wolf). As a consequence, although speculation about scientific possibility and the social impact of technological innovation remain prominent features of much sf, when sf consciously positions itself as an alternative to Hollywood hegemony it often finds its main point of departure in critical response to the ideologies implicit within the imaginary worlds of the franchises. Thus, while extrapolation and speculation remain integral to the genre, they increasingly share that space with practices of resisting and recoding dominant versions of the true, the just and the possible. This leads on the whole toward more politically ambitious agendas and tends to strengthen the appeal of the genre to those sympathetic with movements for social justice. By the same logic this sort of sf is increasingly practiced and consumed by those who feel historically excluded from or marginalised by the dominant culture.

None of this is new to twenty-first century sf. The responsiveness of sf to the Civil Rights, anti-war, environmental and women's and gay liberation movements of the 1950s, 1960s and 1970s set its professional subculture at odds with itself and interwove those ideological disputes with the stylistic and formal challenges to pulp era sf now called the New Wave. However, the steady trend toward becoming less White, less male and more politically ambitious is certainly one of the important features of sf over the last two decades. Within the contemporary landscape of rhetorical and ideological options, the franchise sf emanating from corporate Hollywood can on the whole be characterised as supportive of a liberal status quo trying to figure out how to accommodate itself to the legal reforms demanded by campaigns for social justice and the infrastructural transformations necessary to deal with climate change. There is, of course, some sf that aligns itself with the American right's wholesale resistance to Civil Rights, feminist, LGBTQ and environmental reforms. But the far more significant trend in twenty-first century sf is toward fiction that contests the apparent naturalness and inevitability of status quo dispensations of power, wealth and dignity. The estrangement of the status quo practiced in this sort of sf is not so much cognitive, or based in scientific rationality (à la Suvin), as it is critical and epistemological, based on the different ways of knowing the world that open up when the status quo's perspective is challenged by the experience of historically oppressed subjects and peoples.

A few landmark anthologies have played a crucial role in providing a venue and constructing a genealogy for an sf attuned to these perspectives and the history behind them. The first, one of the most significant sf publications of the twenty-first century, is *Dark Matter: A Century of Speculative Fiction from the African Diaspora* (2000), edited by Sheree R. Thomas. Thomas sets out, as she says in her introduction, 'to correct the perception that black writers are recent to the field' of speculative fiction, and to 'encourage more talented writers to enter the genre' (xi). The anthology accordingly offers fiction by W.E.B. Dubois, Charles W. Chesnutt and George S. Schuyler from the early twentieth century alongside classics by Samuel R. Delany and Octavia E. Butler and a generous sampling of recently emerging artists of the diaspora including Nalo Hopkinson, Nisi Shawl and Tananarive Due. In her introduction, Thomas recruits Ralph Ellison's *Invisible Man* (1952) and Douglas Turner Ward's *Day of Absence* (1965) into the genealogy of what would quickly come to be called Afrofuturism. Thomas's editorial intervention might be compared to Hugo Gernsback's retrospective identification of science fiction as 'the Edgar Allan Poe, Jules Verne, H.G. Wells type of story' in the first issue of *Amazing Stories.* In contrast to his entrepreneurial motives, Thomas elaborates a politically and ethically motivated agenda: to redirect scholarship so as to construct a broader and more inclusive history of the genre, and to open up the field to a generation of Black writers, many of them women (she acknowledges the large body of work on Delany and Butler, but asserts that 'both sf and mainstream scholarship have overlooked or ignored the contribution of less well known black artists' (xi)).

Similar anthologies have followed in *Dark Matter*'s wake, introducing new artists to the field and retrospectively widening its history. Nalo Hopkinson and Uppinder Mehan's *So Long Been Dreaming: Postcolonial Science Fiction & Fantasy* (2004) curates a collection of 'postcolonial science fiction short stories written exclusively by people of colour' (Hopkinson 8) in order to call into question the 'binaries of native/alien, technologist/pastoralist, colonizer/colonized' by 'radically shift[ing] the perspective of the narrator from the supposed rightful heir of contemporary technologically advanced cultures to those of us whose cultures have had their technology destroyed and stunted' (Mehan 270). As Hopkinson puts it, the editors' project was to present 'stories that take the meme of colonizing the natives and, from the experience of the colonizee, critique it, pervert it, fuck with it, with irony, with anger, with humour, and also, with love and respect for the genre of science fiction' (9).

Sharing these goals while also echoing Thomas's project of constructing an sf counter-tradition, Grace L. Dillon's *Walking the Clouds: An Anthology of Indigenous Science Fiction* (2012) constructs what she calls Indigenous Futurisms. Her introduction explains how the five sections of the anthology organise an international range of Indigenous speculative/science fiction bringing Native epistemological and storytelling practices ('Native Slipstream', 'Indigenous Science and Sustainability') to bear on colonial history ('Contact', 'Native Apocalypse') in order to enact a robust Indigenous resistance and 'survivance' that she calls 'Biskaabiiyang, "Returning to Ourselves"'. Dillon offers one of the most explicit and clear challenges to the dominance of Western scientific rationality over setting the criterion for 'cognitive' participation in sf by clearly setting forth the claims of 'Indigenous scientific literacies' to 'constitute a science despite their lack of resemblance to taxonomic western systems of thought' (7). She argues that 'writers of Indigenous futurisms sometimes intentionally experiment with, sometimes intentionally dislodge, sometimes merely accompany, but invariably *change* the perimeters of sf' (3). Certainly Dillon's editorial selection sets out to change the perimeters of the genre, including not just recognised sf practitioners such as William Saunders and Andrea Hairston but also literary figures not usually associated with the genre, such as Gerald Vizenor and Leslie Marmon Silko.

One more anthology that both indicates and initiates important trends within the practice of sf is *Octavia's Brood: Science Fiction Stories from Social Justice Movements* (2015). Its editors, adrienne maree brown and Walidah Imarisha, deliberately place their anthology in the tradition of Afrofuturism through the title's play on Octavia E. Butler's great trilogy LILITH'S BROOD (1987–9) and by including a foreword by Sheree R. Thomas. However, instead of directing themselves to Black writers' contributions to the history of sf, they declare that the purpose of the volume is to support and encourage activism for social justice. The fiction collected in the anthology grows out of their 'collective science-fiction/visionary fiction workshops' which are 'designed to encourage collective ideation' about social justice issues (brown 281). They identify the genre of this workshop-generated fiction, some of it produced by writers with little or no professional experience or previous sf credentials, as 'visionary fiction', a genre which 'encompasses all of the fantastic, with the arc always bending toward social justice' (Imarisha 4). But according to Imarisha, this commitment to social justice allies itself easily, if not inevitably, with the protocols of sf per se: 'All organizing is science fiction. Organizers and activists dedicate their lives to creating and envisioning another world [...] so what better venue for organizers to explore their work than science fiction stories' (3). Like these other anthologies, then, *Octavia's Brood* sets out not just to alter the demographics and redirect the thematics of sf but also to redefine its identity.

This is not to say that White males are no longer a significant part of the sf subculture or no longer comprise some of its most important artists (e.g., William Gibson, M. John Harrison, China Miéville, Kim Stanley Robinson and Jeff VanderMeer, all of whom will be mentioned again). But consider the 2019 winners of sf's most prestigious annual awards, the Nebulas: for the novel, Sarah Pinsker's *A Song For A New Day*; novella, Amal El-Mohtar and Max Gladstone's *This Is How You Lose the Time War*; novelette, Cat Rambo's *Carpe Glitter*; and short story, A.T. Greenblatt's 'Give the Family My Love'. All four are authored or co-authored by women (18 of the 27 nominees were women), and all four feature female protagonists. Far from this indicating some sort of uniformity, however, the formal variety as well as the critical ambition of current sf is evident in the four works. Both Greenblatt and Pinsker use well-worn sf devices to explore strongly topical material: 'Give the Family My Love' is an alien contact story with a strong environmental theme; *A Song For A New Day* takes place in a dystopian near future hyperbolising the monopolistic practices of Apple and Amazon, against which its two main characters struggle in different ways that explore the options of rebellion against the system versus acting within it but against its worst tendencies. *Carpe Glitter*, in contrast, exemplifies what has been called the evaporating boundaries between sf and some of its generic neighbours, combining a very clever ghost story with fantasy and steampunk material that involves the protagonist's struggle with her devious and probably murderous mother over control of a Nazi-made automaton that turns out to have been at least partially her father. *This Is How You Lose the Time War*, the most resonant of the four in terms of contemporary political and ideological controversies, is a love story between two female time warriors named Red and Blue. Red works for the Agency, Blue for the Garden, in a war ranging over the whole of history – or rather over thousands of alternative histories – for a future dominated by one or the other of two social possibilities: a techno-utopia of disembodied information and prosthetic immortality, or an eco-utopia of genetic mastery over death and disease. In a stylistic *tour de force*, El-Mohtar and Gladstone weave together the dizzying inventiveness of the lovers' modes of epistolary communication (letters encrypted, in order to avoid surveillance by their superiors, in the growth lines of a tree, on a fish swallowed by a seal, and a dozen other improbable vehicles), the wit and passion of the letters themselves, and dense allusions to literary and sf tradition. Designating the main characters Red and Blue no doubt intentionally evokes America's intransigent partisan politics, but not for the purpose of equating Agency and Garden with Republicans and Democrats. Instead, the plot makes the ironic suggestion that 'losing' the time war means escaping its antagonists' refusal of mutual recognition.

The Afrofuturist, Indigenous Futurist and postcolonial expansion of sf is as clearly evident in lists of recent award nominees and winners and in the attention such writers now gain in sf criticism and scholarship. Along with those already mentioned, the most highly honoured Black writers are Nnedi Okorafor (who identifies herself as an Africanfuturist, emphasising her Nigerian roots rather than claiming an African American identity) and N.K. Jemisin, whose BROKEN EARTH trilogy (2015–7) received the unprecedented recognition of winning three consecutive Hugo Awards (not to mention a 2017 Nebula). Indigenous Futurist Rebecca Roanhorse, of mixed Pueblo and Afro-American descent, has become a regular on Nebula nominee lists, and her short story 'Welcome to Your Authentic Indian Experience' (2017) won a Nebula and a Hugo. But more to the point, attention to race and the legacies of colonialism among writers of all sorts is a far more explicit element of both artistic and critical sf practices in the twenty-first century than it was formerly. This more widespread critical focus upon colonial history and racism does not challenge so much as it joins with and reinforces more longstanding concerns with gender critique and environmentalism, and of course all of these topics are still, as they always have been, interwoven in sf with speculation about the social impact of technological change. Some examples of twenty-first century treatments of one of sf's oldest motifs, the plot of invasion, can illustrate the way the genre has been changing and staying the same.

Thoughtful contemporary versions of the invasion plot necessarily find themselves in dialogue with sf tradition, on the one hand, and contemporary franchise and blockbuster sf, on the other. The foundational classic, H.G. Wells's *The War of the Worlds* (1898), opens by presenting its Martian invasion as a metaphor for British imperialism. As with European imperialism of the later nineteenth century, the keynotes of his imaginary invasion are the Martians' technological superiority and the ruthless unconcern for native life with which they pursue their project of resource extraction. In blockbuster film, resource extraction tends to fade into the background or disappear, while an anaesthetised version of warfare as a Manichean struggle between good and evil takes centre stage. One way to respond to the cartoon violence and easy morality of the franchises is to restore something about the human suffering and racialised social conflicts attendant upon colonial resource extraction to the space opera setting, something accomplished quite well in S.A. Corey's very popular series *The Expanse* (beginning with *Leviathan Wakes* (2011) and currently consisting of nine volumes and nine spin-off short stories and novellas). Another is to turn directly back to colonial history itself, as Nisi Shawl does in her steampunk alternate history *Everfair* (2016). Yet another is to undermine the entire fantasy of extraterrestrial colonisation by attending realistically to problems of scientific plausibility, both concerning interstellar travel and the likelihood of finding a liveable environment for human beings on another planet, as Kim Stanley Robinson does in *Aurora* (2015).

A second classic sf version of invasion, one perhaps more resonant than Wells's with the contemporary geopolitical and biopolitical situation, is John W. Campbell, Jr's 'Who Goes There?' (1938). In contrast to *The War of the Worlds* (but not in contradiction of colonial history), it compares the alien presence to an accidentally introduced disease rather than a military campaign. The danger it presents is not conquest but contagion. This contagion takes the form, not of deadly infection, but of biological assimilation, so that the biological plot can be read as a kind of allegory of the cultural impact of European hegemony and colonial mimicry on native peoples. Rather than an imperialist takeover and violent subjugation of the native population, the threat in Campbell's Golden Age thriller is that of a complete erasure of the species accomplished by the invaders turning themselves into exact copies of the natives. The logic of imperialism is replaced by that of settler colonialism, then, and given the centrality of native invisibility to settler colonialism, it is not surprising that Campbell, unlike Wells, provides no hint of any metaphorical correspondence between the isolated scientific station where his story takes place and any actual political entity.

One consistent feature of Afrofuturist and Africanfuturist versions of the invasion plot is to restore the political charge missing in Campbell by imagining an invasion more attuned to the dynamics of assimilation and erasure than to the straightforward slaughter practiced by Wells's Martians. Even the blockbuster film *Avatar* (Cameron 2009) wraps its very old-fashioned fantasy of becoming native and marrying the native princess in the package of an environmentally sensitive critique of rapine resource extraction. Dispensing altogether with that kind of nostalgic fantasy, Nisi Shawl sets her short story 'Deep End' (first published in *So Long Been Dreaming*) aboard a prison ship engaged in an interstellar colonisation project accomplished through biological assimilation and erasure. Upon arrival at their destination, the prisoners' consciousnesses are to be implanted into artificial bodies carrying the DNA of the ruling class of the colonisers' home planet, so that the children born on the new planet will be the rulers' biological descendants. In Tade Thompson's Wormwood trilogy (2016–9), an enormous, inscrutable, fungus-like entity called Wormwood establishes the basis of a biotechnological colonisation of earth that aims, like Campbell's alien or the pod people of *Invasion of the Body Snatchers* (Siegel 1956), to take over the bodies of earthlings with transplanted alien consciousnesses. Wormwood's incursion tellingly originates in London but establishes its ultimate centre of operations in Nigeria. And like Octavia E. Butler in LILITH'S BROOD, Thompson grants powerful ambivalence to the invasion plot by attributing quasi-miraculous healing powers to Wormwood.

Rather than the subversion of native body–mind identity in these recent narratives, some others depict the invasion as a transformation of the land itself. Andrea Hairston's *Mindscape* (2006) imagines a remapping of the Earth's surface by the mysterious extraterrestrial entity known as the Barrier, cutting it into three zones with severely limited contact with one another. The purpose behind the Barrier's invasion remains entirely mysterious to the human population, although the conditions it imposes do challenge them to redefine themselves in relation to one another and to their lost pasts and possible futures. The alien in Nnedi Okorafor's *Lagoon* (2014) purges Lagos lagoon of pollution, empowers its sea creatures to resist the degradation of their waters by oilmen and fishermen alike, and proceeds to catalyse a wholesale satirical exposure of corruption and an upheaval of social and political norms in the city itself. The inscrutability of an environmentally transformative alien invasion becomes the central concern of one of the most critically celebrated recent invasion narratives, Jeff VanderMeer's SOUTHERN REACH trilogy (2014). Like Shawl and Thompson, VanderMeer features the replacement of humans by body doubles, and like Thompson and Okorafor, his alien presence has purgative and healing effects as well as bizarre and deadly ones. While the strong connection to political history in the other invasion stories just mentioned is absent, the SOUTHERN REACH trilogy does join *Lagoon* in forging an imaginative alliance between the sf invasion narrative and environmentalist concerns about species extinction and climate change.

The SOUTHERN REACH trilogy is one of the most remarkable examples of what is probably early twenty-first century sf's most widely recognised emergent subgenre, climate fiction or cli-fi, a category not restricted to sf but overlapping with it to a great extent. It is not surprising that recognition of the reality and long-term effects of anthropogenic climate change, as in the widespread adoption of the term Anthropocene to designate the era of its measurable impact on the geological record, should have inspired writers of all sorts to try to address the formidable threats it poses to the contemporary status quo. Amitav Ghosh reasonably complains, however, that too much cli-fi consists of global disaster scenarios set in the future, while the Anthropocene is 'precisely not an imagined "other" world apart from ours; nor is it located in another "time" or another "dimension"' (72–3). Nonetheless, Ghosh also argues that sf is far better suited than conventional realism to confronting the topic because, unlike conventional realism, it presupposes disruption of everyday reality rather than depending upon it as a basis. An excellent example of sf that confronts the topic of climate change without turning its future scenario into a mere spectacle of disaster is Kim Stanley Robinson's *New York 2140* (2017). Robinson sets his novel in another time, a future drastically affected by rising ocean levels, but emphatically not in an imaginary place, since his depiction of a twenty-second century Manhattan adapting itself to the altered conditions is meticulously realistic in its geographic and historical details. Most important, Robinson's novel is about collective action successfully confronting the challenges both of the climate disaster and of a political crisis clearly modelled on the global financial meltdown of 2008. That emphasis on collective action antithetically opposes itself to scenarios of individual survival in a postapocalyptic wasteland, a treatment of the topic perhaps most skilfully accomplished in Cormac McCarthy's grim *The Road* (2006). Colson Whitehead's zombie plague novel *Zone One* (2011) finds a kind of mean between Robinson's revolutionary politics and McCarthy's individualism. Colson's everyman protagonist is involved in a collective effort to restore some sort of pre-apocalyptic normalcy after having survived a period of individual kill-or-be-killed struggles with the walking dead. That this effort ultimately fails seems less the point than the way the novel's running stream of deadpan humour targets the pre-apocalyptic world's comfortable illusions of invulnerability and the subjection of its lifestyles to inconsequential consumer desires. If the looming, ever more evident disaster of climate change forces upon us the question of what the end of the world may look like, the best recent sf asks us instead not to confuse the end of the world with the end of the status quo.

Another topic of growing importance in twenty-first century sf, one at least as pervasive as climate change and its attendant apocalypticism, is posthumanism. Some sf explorations of posthumanism proceed from the foundations laid by cyberpunk explorations of artificial intelligence and various forms of bodily transformation, as in the space-operatic noir future of M. John Harrison's KEFAHUCHI TRACT trilogy (2002–12). The fantasy of uploaded consciousness escaping the limits of the human body, explored with gusto and humour in Charles Stross's 'Rogue Farm' (2003) and *Accelerando* (2005), remains strong; while an antithetical approach to problems of body–mind identity informs Karen Joy Fowler's exploration of the moral and legal ramifications of anthropocentrism posed by animal rights in *We Are All Completely Beside Ourselves* (2013). Some notable explorations of online identities and digital commerce join Fowler's novel in bringing the topic squarely into the realm of the familial, such as Alexander Weinstein's poignant 'Children of the New World' (2016) or Ted Chiang's rigorously conceived *The Life Cycle of Software Objects* (2010), both of which explore the difficult emotional, economic and legal issues connecting artificial intelligence and legal personhood. Yet others concern themselves with the transformative effects of online media on the formation of communities, perhaps the best example being William Gibson's *Pattern Recognition* (2003).

No piece of fiction pulls together all of the things discussed so far better than N.K. Jemisin's BROKEN EARTH trilogy. The way Jemisin's far-future narrative explores issues of race, gender and ecology can accurately be called Afrofuturist, feminist, queer, posthumanist, environmentalist and apocalyptic. The central characters are members of a racialised group, known politely as Orogenes and impolitely as Rogga, whose social situation clearly evokes comparison with both the history and the present status of Blacks in America. The Orogenes' ability to interact with the planet's tectonic energies is both necessary in order to assure the stability of the status quo and threatening because of its destructive potential. They are scapegoated and persecuted in the society at large, while their special talents are exploited in a system of sequestration and forced breeding. The narrative begins with an enormously destructive act of rebellion by the most powerful of the Orogenes. This act is initially presented as the end of the world, but it turns out over the course of the three volumes that it is intended to be, and actually is, only an attempt to end the status quo. Alongside this complex metaphor of racism the novel develops a striking set of gender dynamics. One of its main features is the forced breeding system that couples Alabaster, the instigator of the end of the world, with Syenite, the female protagonist (also known at different stages of her life as Damaya and Essun). The coupling violates Alabaster's same-sex preference and takes no account at all of Syenite's desires, but nonetheless ends up in a lasting friendship based on resistance to the oppressive system rather than on sexual attraction. The other main feature of the novel's treatment of gender is its reversal of traditional Western patriarchal patterns of association with earth and sky. There are no stargazers in this world and no sky gods. Instead, the mythology – which turns out to be no mere fiction – has to do with Father Earth, also known as Evil Earth. Rather than a nurturing goddess, the land has been transformed into an angry father who needs to be calmed and placated rather than fertilised and respected. That transformation is not just a metaphor, however, but rather the result of a failed attempt to harness the planet's geothermal and tectonic energies so as to enable its endless, unrestricted consumption to humankind, making obvious the relevance of its upside-down estrangement of contemporary conventions to the current regime of fossil fuel extraction and consumption. The story's dialogue with sf tradition goes all the way back to Mary Shelley's *Frankenstein* (1818), then, and the posthuman turn of the twenty-first century is called into the trilogy's mix via the posthuman products of the failed experiment, the Orogenes themselves and the mysterious, immortal, chthonic Stone Eaters.

A final word about genre in the BROKEN EARTH trilogy can draw this chapter to its close. Although published as a trilogy, it is really one very long novel, following in this respect a form made dominant in epic fantasy by J.R.R. Tolkien's *Lord of the Rings* (1954–5) and exemplified more recently by the 5,000-plus pages (so far) of George R.R. Martin's A SONG OF ICE AND FIRE (1996–). Orogenic power itself seems initially like a fantasy invention but turns out to be science fictional. Yet in the process of this cognitive transition it is revealed to be 'magic'. Thus the *Broken Earth*'s odd straddling of the fantasy and sf border might invite comparison to the work of China Miéville, the main figure in the emergence of the early twenty-first century sf movement called the New Weird. Certainly, the worldbuilding in Miéville's BAS-LAG trilogy (2000–4) better resembles and prefigures Jemisin's, both in its intellectual seriousness and in its inclusion of quasi-magical energies, than either Tolkien's or Martin's does. Both Jemisin's and Miéville's works confirm that the commercial and artistic importance of immersive long-form worldbuilding and the porous boundary with fantasy are among the most salient and influential trends in early twenty-first century sf.

Works cited

Attebery, Brian and Veronica Hollinger, eds. *Parabolas of Science Fiction*. Wesleyan UP, 2013.

Broderick, Damien. *Reading by Starlight: Postmodern Science Fiction*. Routledge, 1995.

brown, adrienne maree. 'Outro'. *Octavia's Brood: Science Fiction Stories from Social Justice Movements*. Ed. adrienne maree brown and Walidah Imarisha. AK Press, 2015. 279–81.

Dillon, Grace L. 'Introduction'. *Walking the Clouds: An Anthology of Indigenous Science Fiction*. Ed. Grace L. Dillon. U of Arizona P, 2012. 1–12.

Frow, John, *Genre*, second edition. Routledge, 2015.

Gernsback, Hugo. 'A New Kind of Magazine'. *Amazing Stories* 1.1 (April 1926): 3.

Ghosh, Amitav. *The Great Derangement: Climate Change and the Unthinkable*. U of Chicago P, 2016.

Hopkinson, Nalo. 'Introduction'. *So Long Been Dreaming: Postcolonial Science Fiction & Fantasy*. Ed. Nalo Hopkinson and Uppinder Mehan. Arsenal Pulp Press, 2004. 7–9.

Imarisha, Walidah. 'Introduction'. *Octavia's Brood: Science Fiction Stories from Social Justice Movements*. Ed. adrienne maree brown and Walidah Imarisha. AK Press, 2015. 3–5.

Mehan, Uppinder. 'Final Thoughts'. *So Long Been Dreaming: Postcolonial Science Fiction & Fantasy*. Ed. Nalo Hopkinson and Uppinder Mehan. Arsenal Pulp Press, 2004. 269–71.

Rabitsch, Stefan and Michael Fuchs. 'The Birth of the Science Fiction Franchises'. *The Cambridge History of Science Fiction*. Ed. Gerry Canavan and Eric Carl Link. Cambridge UP, 2019. 481–501.

Rieder, John. *Science Fiction and The Mass Cultural Genre System*. Wesleyan UP, 2017.

Suvin, Darko. *Metamorphoses of Science Fiction: On the History and Poetics of a Literary Genre*. Yale UP, 1979.

Thomas, Sheree R. 'Introduction: Looking for the Invisible'. *Dark Matter: A Century of Speculative Fiction from the African Diaspora*. Ed. Sheree R. Thomas. Warner, 2000. ix–xiv.

Wolf, Mark J. P. *Building Imaginary Worlds: The Theory and History of Subcreation*. Routledge, 2012.

31
DIASPORIC LATINX FUTURISMS

Taryne Jade Taylor

Defining Latinx Futurisms

In the 1990s, when Afrofuturism was first defined, it was specific to African Americans, that is, the African diaspora in the US whose ancestors were enslaved peoples and whose racial identity category is directly connected to the legacy of chattel slavery. In sf studies, Afrofuturism was often presented as an alternative or response to a White-dominated genre that, as a whole, historically excluded Black people and other peoples of colour from its imagined futures. However, Afrofuturism has always been more than that. It is a movement that contests those visions and imagines futures that transcend White, Western hegemonic thinking, and has expanded to become an intersectional movement encompassing a wide variety of Blackness and connectedness to the African diaspora. This is particularly true of Afrofuturisms created on the African content – now often distinguishing itself as Africanfuturism – and by diasporic populations outside of the US. Similarly, when Catherine S. Ramírez coined the related term 'Chicanafuturism' in 2004, it was centred in the US context, focusing on the speculative productions of Chicanas (Mexican-Americans). In 2014, I defined the emerging field of Latinx Futurisms as 'when artists use speculative or science fiction in a variety of art mediums from literature to hip-hop as a method of decolonization' ('Singular' 103); in 2015, Cathryn Merla-Watson and B.V. Olguín described Latinx Futurisms as

> Latin@futurist cultural producers harness[ing] the most visionary aspects and radical potential of sci-fi and the speculative arts to generate productive disorientation about the nature of our reality, to re-see our present and past, to meditate on the world and the universe, and to pressure our collective event horizons beyond which lies no set course.
>
> (144)

Just as popular interest in Afrofuturisms exploded with *Black Panther* (Coogler 2018), enthusiasm for Latinx Futurisms is developing worldwide. Sf fans are already engaging with mainstream sf in Latinx Futurist ways, asserting, for example, that Grogu (Baby Yoda) of the *Mandalorian* (Disney+ 2019–) is Latinx. *Black Panther – Wakanda Forever* (Coogler 2022) reimagines the popular Marvel anti-hero Namor as the ruler not of Atlantis but of the Mesoamerican underwater

DOI: 10.4324/9781003140269-33

kingdom, Talocan. He is revealed as Kulkulkan, the Feathered Serpent, and is played by Tenoch Huerta, a Mexican actor of Indigenous descent. Throughout the diaspora and across Latin America fans have embraced this new Namor. For example, even prior to the film's release, US-based Chicano artist Qetza designed several visual art iterations of Tenoch as Namor, and artist Tomer Linaje painted a Latinx Futurist mural of him in downtown Mexico City.

Latinxs are not a homogenous group, but Latin America and her diaspora have long been mistakenly presented as monolithic, particularly in the US but throughout the Global North. In the broader US imaginary, Mexicans and Mexico are synonymous with the entire Latin American region. Donald Trump's infamous statement from his first official Presidential campaign speech in 2015 expressed an extreme version of this viewpoint, conflating all migrants from Latin America (especially Central America) with Mexican migrants. Furthermore, he stereotyped Latin American immigrants to the US as drug dealers, criminals and rapists. This homogenisation and vilification of Latin Americans is not new. As Juan Gonzales explains, following the post-election crises in the Dominican Republic (themselves a result of the US Occupation), the US facilitated a mass exodus of Dominicans. By the 1990s, Dominican Americans were the second largest Latinx group in New York City, but this was largely unnoticed by White New Yorkers as the Dominicans immigrants settled into historically Black and Puerto Rican neighbourhoods; thus, most White people in the city assumed they were Puerto Rican or Black. That changed on 4 July 1992, when Dominican immigrants rioted in Washington Heights (partially in response to the LA riots two months earlier). This drew public attention to them, and new coverage and other media began casting Dominican immigrants as violent and unsavoury. Thus, stereotyping and the inability to recognise diversity colour the view of the Latinx diaspora and Latin America more broadly in the US.

This tendency to erase the rich diversity of the diaspora and Latin America echoes the anti-Indigenous and anti-Black sentiments instilled in Latin Americans by the European colonisers. This is particularly troubling for the role it plays in reinforcing internal colonisation and racism. Latin America and her diaspora are made up of a variety of races – and indeed, many of Latinx American descent are of mixed race or mestizaje. This is further overdetermined where the anti-Indigenous and anti-Black racism of Latin America is overlayed with the particular brand of racism and genocidal history of the US and Canada. The Latinx diaspora in these countries thus have a unique experience of double oppression that creates a common experience even in the face of an extreme diversity of backgrounds (national origin, race, class, language and so on). Thus, although this chapter focuses on the iteration of Latinx Futurisms built out of the unique diasporic experience in the US and Canada, it nonetheless insists on the plural form because the diaspora, like Latin America as a whole, encompasses such a diverse range of cultures and experiences. For similar reasons, this chapter uses 'Latinx'. The term 'Hispanic', created and imposed by the US state, emphasises the Spanish heritage of many of the diaspora, linguistically erasing those of Indigenous and African descent and those who speak languages other than Spanish. 'Latino' is a masculine term and Latino/a is rooted in binary gender thinking, whereas Latinx is an inclusive pan-ethnic identity category that includes US residents who identify with their Latin American and Caribbean heritage (Allatson 140). Recently, some have argued for Latine, suggesting it sounds better, but the 'x' ending is a nod to Indigenous Mesoamerican languages. Latinx is an attempt at decolonization and radical inclusivity, and Latinx Futurisms are a political and aesthetic mode encompassing a diverse range of cultural production from an equally diverse diaspora

Diasporic Latinx Futurisms, in which the themes of alienation and homogenisation are central, grapple with the psychological and material realities of being Latinx in the diaspora through science fictional thinking. As with all futurisms from the margins of the Global North, Latinx

Futurisms works across a range of genres, not just sf. Through the incorporation of Indigenous Science, they ask us to question the way Western science pervades our understanding of sf. They decolonise our imaginations through worldbuilding that places the diaspora at the centre of sf, contesting the narrative of Latinxs as 'other'. Like Afrofuturisms and Indigenous Futurisms, Latinx Futurisms are an aesthetic, a philosophy and a movement that contests the dominant narrative of Anglo-European speculative fiction. In Latinx Futurist fiction, writers such as Daniel José Older, Silvia Moreno-Garcia, David Bowles, Zoraida Córdova, Rudy Ch. Garcia, Sabrina Vourvoulias and Malka Older explode traditional boundaries of nationality and genre.

Four tenets of Latinx futurisms

Latinx Futurist works (1) bear witness to the erased past and present, particularly colonisation and racism; (2) expose and reject Anglo stereotypes about Latinxs; (3) redefine Latinidades (while rejecting the Anglo role in Latinx identity construction); and (4) unify Latinx cultures (Taylor 'Latinxs' 34). All four tenets are tied to theories of Latinidades, a plural term coined by Frances R. Aparicio and Susana Chavez-Silverman to highlight the complexity of Latinx identity.

One of many reasons it is important to recognise diversity is that many Latinxs are of mixed race. Across the Americas there has been and continues to be an erasure and denigration of Black and Indigenous heritage and peoples. One infamous example is the concept of mestizaje as developed by twentieth century Mexican philosopher José Vasconcelos. Operating under the racist notion that European equals better, his *The Cosmic Race* (*La raza cósmica*; 1925) imagines a future where the Indigenous element of the racial mixing is bred out by the European element, thus creating an 'ideal' Mexican identity and a future Mexico without Indigenous peoples (his eugenicist thinking completely overlooks the fact that many Mexicans also have African ancestry). Thus, the theories around Latinidades are themselves grounded in science fictional thinking, whether the utopian impulse towards unification and community building we see in Aparicio and Chavez-Silverman and in the work of Gloria Anzaldúa or, on the other extreme, Vasconcelos's dystopian eugenicism.

In her foundational essay on Chicanafuturism, Catherine S. Ramírez focuses on sf art that works to dismantle the stereotype of Chicanas not being technologically advanced, She also counters the false assumption that Latinxs do not create or engage in sf, as do several recent scholarly and creative anthologies (Merla-Watson and B.V. Olguín; Hernández et.al; Goodwin *Latin@* and *Latinx*). Centring Latinxs in the discussion of sf and in the futures we imagine significantly disrupts stereotypes about Latinx scientific literacy and what we consider science and sf.

Latinx writers have long pointed out the science fictional nature of being Latinx in the diaspora. As Ernest Hogan explains, 'Chicano is a science fiction state of being. We exist between cultures, and our existence creates new cultures: rasquache mashups of what we experience across borders and in barrios all over the planet' ('Chicanonautica' 131). Susana Ramírez argues that 'the recurrent themes of alienation, misrecognition, and estrangement felt by many communities of color in the United States' (58) make all Chicanx texts sf. Joy Sanchez-Taylor describes this as 'double-estrangement', combining Darko Suvin's theory of cognitive estrangement with W.E.B. DuBois's theory of double consciousness, to explain that in addition to 'presenting the unfamiliar as familiar to estrange their readers', sf authors of colour 'frequently include critiques of science fiction by altering established science fiction tropes' (7). Indeed, much Latinx sf plays with this idea of alienation, especially since border-crossers are legally labelled as 'resident' or 'illegal' aliens – a form of linguistic othering if ever there was one. As Matthew David Goodwin shows, Latinx sf creators are reclaiming the alien (*Latinx*).

Laura Molina's Latinx Futurist autobiographical painting, *Amor Alien* (2004), tackles the theme of alienation by asking, who is the real alien here? In the foreground, Molina portrays herself as the stereotypical green alien, sitting on the lap of White astronaut Naked Dave. The background shows a planet that is not Earth, so the alien is certainly not Molina. Naked Dave represents first contact with the coloniser, making it clear that it is the colonisers who are the aliens who do not belong.

Pablo Brescia's 'Code 51' (2014) also engages with the notion of alienation. Mexican American sheriff Steve Torres suffers from asthma which makes 'him feel like he belonged to another species' (13). His White partner Wilson tells him, 'you're a fuckin' Mexican living on our land. You don't belong here understand?' (14), making it clear that his sense of alienation is not only due to his asthma, but also being Mexican American. Brescia critiques Wilson's White supremacy, as exemplified by his assumption that he can just claim Susan Navajo as his (unwilling) love interest and take her away. When aliens arrive, we learn that they are in fact the ancestors of the Navajo and all people of colour. They have come to purify the diseased land and unify people of colour, transforming Susan and Steve into gilled aliens. Underwater Steve breathes better; he belongs.

Both Molina's and Brescia's work exemplify the four tenets of Latinx Futurisms. By questioning the construction of Chicanxs as 'aliens', Molina bears witness to the racist inheritance of colonisation – in which White Anglo US citizens forget they too were once immigrants to the Americas, not to mention their ignorance about the way the border moved on many Mexican American families in the US Southwest (tenet 1). Placing Naked Dave in the role of the 'alien' rejects the Anglo narrative of belonging, highlighting White America's immigrant history, while at the same time critiquing the settler colonialist mentality behind conquering territory (tenet 2). Furthermore, *Amor Alien* reaffirms the erased Indigenous heritage of many members of the Latinx diaspora. Not only is the alien represented as indigenous to the planet while Naked Dave is not, but the painting also mirrors Mexican artist Jesus Helguera's painting *Amor Indio* (1946). Helguera's paintings take pride in Mexico's Indigenous history, particularly Aztec cosmology. Molina's painting encourages the Latinx diaspora to reject the sense of alienation forced upon us by dominant Anglo culture, while also providing us a common point of connection – our outsider status, the sense of being perceived as alien as a way to unify diverse Latinx experiences (tenets 3 and 4). As Molina explains: 'I portrayed myself as a green-skinned, indigenous resident of the fictional red planet Dave is visiting. The joke is that he's the alien' (Ramirez-Dhoore 25).

Similarly, in Brescia's story, Wilson's White supremacist sense of ownership and superiority over both Mexican Americans and Native Americans demonstrates that he has inherited the racist thinking of the colonisers (tenet 1). All of the characters of colour reject his sense of superiority and refuse to be placed in subordinate roles (tenet 2). By revealing the characters of colour belong to a superior alien race, Brescia insists on redefining the Latinx diaspora as more powerful and more advanced than Anglo society, directly opposing the deleterious stereotypes about Latinxs in the US (tenet 3). The story ends with the characters of colour unifying against their oppressor and finding freedom (tenet 4).

Tenet 1 is also evident in David Bowles's *Smoking Mirror* (2015) and Daniel José Older's SHADOWSHAPER CYPHER series (2015–20). In *Smoking Mirror*, the Garza twins discover a hidden family history – that they are naguals, shapeshifters descended from the Aztec gods. Throughout the novel, we see how the continuing legacy of colonisation – in the form of White supremacy and forced Christianity – have concealed the truth of their heritage. In Older's series, racism and misogyny collide to hide the protagonist Sierra's inheritance as a shadowshaper, a spirit worker who calls on the ancestors to fight against White supremacy. Shadowshaping is drawn from, or in Older's description (Taylor 'Daniel' 1) an analogue for, Santería – itself a syncretisation of Yoruba traditions that African slaves to the Americas were forced to renounce and practice in secret. In Carlos Hernandez's 'The Assimilated Cuban's Guide to Quantum Santería' (2016), following a visit from his recently deceased mother, protagonist Salvador and his father begin practicing Santería. His father had been a practitioner before but stopped because Anglo-Catholic indoctrination cast Santería as witchcraft. By recovering this lost tradition, they aim to decolonise themselves.

All of these stories expose and reject Anglo stereotypes about Latinxs and redefine Latinidades. They directly address racism and anti-Latinx sentiments, pushing back against White characters who draw on US stereotypes about Latinxs as a homogenous group. In *Smoking Mirror*, the Garza twins have to fight against the idea they are not Mexican enough because their father is a professor and they have light complexions. Sierra, the Afro-Puerto Rican protagonist of the SHADOWSHAPER CYPHER series, has to deal with teachers' and cops' stereotypes about her; even her Black, non-Latinx friends ignorantly call her 'Spanish'. *Smoking Mirror* reaffirms the often-erased Indigenous heritage of Latinxs, while the SHADOWSHAPER CYPHER series and 'The Assimilated Cuban's Guide' recentre the importance of African heritage.

Most importantly, these works demonstrate the importance of unifying Latinx cultures without effacing diversity. In the SHADOWSHAPER CYPHER series, Sierra's friends demonstrate a mix of Latinx identities. Older emphasises both the specificity of Sierra's Puerto Rican culture and the possibility of Latinx unity through the rest of her friends: Robbie is Haitian American, Tee is Martinican American and Izzy is Jamaican American. All three friends represent Latinx identities that are often excluded. As Afro-Latinxs, these characters have similar experiences of racism. As people with Caribbean heritage, they have cultural similarities that create points of connection, but Older never effaces the important differences between their cultures, or other facets of their identities, such as gender, sexuality or class.

Indigenous science and Traditional Knowledge in Latinx Futurisms

As the above descriptions might suggest, not all Latinx Futurist work is sf as it has been historically defined. The way we think about Latinx Futurisms and sf more broadly must be expanded past the Western models of science and progress. As Grace L. Dillon's work on Indigenous Futurisms ('Indigenous Scientific', 'Indigenous Futurisms') and Bodhi Chattopadhyay's work on Kalpavigyan demonstrates, Anglo 'Western' notions of science are limiting, erasing other forms of knowing accepted by Global South cultures. Many Latinx Futurists draw on Indigenous science, such as Maya and Taíno creation stories, as well as Santería, Candomblé and Brujería. In so doing, they reject the privileging of White Latinidad so often idealised in the diaspora and Latin America, and by the dominant cultures in Global North nations with large Latinx populations. Latinx Futurists call for the reclamation and celebration of pre-colonised identities, recognising that the othered subjectivity represents the path to a better future.

Drawing on Indigenous cosmologies as a way of imagining the future is particularly prevalent in Mesofuturisms – works of speculative fiction where the worldbuilding is inspired by Mesoamerican storytelling, typically Aztec or Maya. This can be seen in Ernest Hogan's *Smoking Mirror Blues* (2018), Rosaura Sánchez and Beatrice Pita's *Lunar Braceros 2125–2148* (2019) and Silvia Moreno-Garcia's *Signal to Noise* (2016). Alex Rivera's Latinx Futurist cyberpunk film *Sleep Dealer* (2008) is also Mesofuturist: it draws upon Indigenous science and centres Mesoamerican values to open a pathway that rejects the Global North's White supremacism. Although the protagonist, Memo, embraces the alleged opportunities provided by the cyberpunk dystopia, he is actively presented as learning to value the Indigenous science shared by his father. In early scene, they look out over their milpa together. A several thousand-year-old Maya technology for growing beans, corn and squash together, milpa, also known as tres hermanas, is, according to *Sleep Dealer*, 'just as elegant as the internet and other hi-tech innovation'. Frustrated by the neo-imperialist exploitation of the capitalist Global North that has reduced his family to abject poverty, forcing them to pay for water to irrigate their farm, Memo initially turns away from and devalues Indigenous science. In order to survive and support his family, he embraces Western science in the form of the exploitative TruNode technology and cyberbracero labour. However, as he becomes enmeshed in this dystopian technology, the value of Indigenous science becomes clear, not only to him, but to the other characters, and the film ends with him planting milpa in the city.

A scene in which Memo interacts with an older, blind cyberbraceros, juxtaposes Indigenous science with Western technology. The cyberbraceros uses the technology of storytelling to warn Memo about the pitfalls of this technology. He values this storytelling, which is done not as transactional but to build community, unlike Luz, who betrays his trust by exploiting his story for financial gain. However, Memo's story serves to begin the decolonisation process for Luz and former US drone-pilot Rudy, both of whom are disconnected from their Indigenous heritage.

Latinx and Mesofuturist works that engage with Indigenous science and cosmologies enact 'remembering to remember' (cajete) and 're-remembering' (Wall Kimmerer). These ideas resonate because of the legacies of colonisation, imperialism and neo-Imperialism in Latin America and the diaspora, which resulted in the genocide and forced assimilation of Indigenous Peoples and the erasure, discrediting and suppression of Indigenous science. Indigeneity itself was treated as something to be conquered or hidden, especially for those whose mestizaje allowed them to 'pass'. Rivera celebrates Indigeneity and rejects the idea that only Western science and cosmology has value by 'remembering to remember' milpa and centring it in his cyberpunk future as a contrast to the deleterious cyberbracero technology. This is an important form of decolonisation for the diaspora, particularly in the US, which has to deal with not only the inheritance of racist values from Latin America's colonisation but also the racist and eugenicist views held by the dominant culture.

This is particularly clear in the philosophical history of Latin America and the diaspora. Many mestisx thinkers have reimagined Vasconcelos's dehumanising work to reject anti-Indigenous view of mestisaje. Feminist theorist Gloria Anzaldúa draws upon Mesoamerican cosmologies as well as Santería to imagine the new mestiza who, as part of the process of decolonisation, fully embraces her Indigenous and Black heritage. In the future Anzaldúa imagines, the cosmologies suppressed by colonisation and imperialism are drawn upon to reaffirm wholeness.

One of the more radical moves Mesofuturists and Latinx Futurists can make is to champion and celebrate Indigenous and Black heritage through Indigenous science so as to decolonise our psyches. Silvia Moreno-Garcia's *Gods of Jade and Shadow* (2020) draws on Maya cosmologies to take the protagonist and readers on a journey of feminist decolonisation. Protagonist Casiopea Tun discovers her family's connection to the Maya god Hun-Kamé. Although the Maya gods are not saviours, she is able to use her experience to escape the patriarchal grasp of her grandfather and cousin and to begin her own feminist journey. The Mesofuturist threads are clear in the engagement with Maya cosmology, but the feminist decolonisation is more subtle than Memo's internal decolonisation in *Sleep Dealer*.

This turns towards embracing Indigenous science in speculative fiction is significant for the Latinx diaspora. For far too long English-language sf has been rooted in the cosmologies of the Global North and, as a result, people of colour are often not imagined in the future. This lack of presencing also extends to the fan community. Latinx Futurists are upending that narrative, making space not only for Latinx speculative fiction but also for futures that centre Latinxs and reject stereotypical presentations of Latinidades. Through their Latinx Futurist works, they assert that we do belong – not just to speculative fiction communities, but also in the future, in the secondary worlds of fantasy novels and in any blueprints for immediate political change.

This presencing is demonstrated in the work of Mesofuturist artist Qetza (Jorge Garza), whose *GalAztec* series presents STAR WARS characters in the style of Aztec gods. Debora Kuetzpal Vasquez's Mesofuturist painting series *Citlali: Cortando Nopales y Hechando Tortillas En Outer Space* (2015) presents, a superhero named after the Aztec princess Citlali (who is also believed to be the basis for La Llorona). In these paintings we see a future where Chicana identity and cultural tradition coexist with space travel and technology.

However, it is not only Mesoamerican Indigenous science Latinx Futurists centre in their work. Edgardo Miranda-Rodriguez's graphic novel *La Borinqueña* (2016) turns to Taíno cosmology as a method of decolonisation and imagining a Latinx future. His protagonist Marisol, is a Nuyorican college student, who goes to Puerto Rico to study the caves. There, she meets the Taíno goddess, Atabex, who shows him several important scenes from Puerto Rican history, including Indigenous resistance to Spaniards, the Grito de Lares uprising and even the Pulse Nightclub shooting, to demonstrate how Puerto Ricans have suffered and why Marisol must become the champion of Boriken. Then, the gods imbue her with powers and she becomes a superhero. Through these stories of remembering to remember Taíno cosmology, *La Borinqueña* bears witness to the erased past and present, particularly the trauma caused by colonisation and racism, and questions the devaluing of Indigenous science and Indigeneity. It emphasises Marisol's Taíno ancestry and her Afro-Latinx heritage. Marisol proudly refers to herself as 'negra' and reminds readers how much Puerto Rican (and Latinx culture more broadly) is rooted in African ancestry. Marisol references bomba, a traditional music and dance with African roots, and sancocho, a traditional stew with African origins. By valorising both heritages Miranda-Rodriguez rejects the Western privileging of White, Anglo Latinxs and imagines a future where Blackness and Indigeneity are celebrated.

The novel also addresses the diversity of Latinidades. Marisol, as a Nuyorican, is not seen as Puerto Rican until after she demonstrates her cultural knowledge. Atabex also affirms Marisol's heritage noting 'I am the ancient spirit of your deep past' (Miranda-Rodriguez n.p.). Here, Miranda-Rodriguez comments on a struggle the Latinx diaspora faces: honouring cultural heritage, avoiding stereotypes and/or persecution for being a minority while, at the same time, being perceived as too 'Americanised'. Dominant US and Canadian cultures devalue and stereotype Latinx cultures, commodifying Latinx cultures at the same time they encourage assimilation, while Latinxs are often judged for not being 'Latinx enough' both from within and without their own cultures. In representing and rejecting this conflict, *La Borinqueña* exposes and rejects stereotypes about Latinxs.

Miranda-Rodriguez imagines a future where simplistic understanding of Latinidades, nationality and belonging are erased – a future of inclusion where the diaspora can embrace the multitude of Latinidades. Indeed, Marisol's best friend is Chinese Dominican. Like Older's SHADOWSHAPER CYPHER series, *La Borinqueña*'s presents the multiplicity of Latinidades while showcasing Latinx unity. Older's Latinx protagonists call on the spirits of the ancestors to protect their community from White supremacy and capitalism, just as Miranda-Rodriguez's Latinx protagonist draws on the powers bestowed by the Taino gods. Therefore, a work does not need to be sf in order to be Latinx Futurist, but instead it must engage in science fictional reconfigurations of such diverse but unified futures.

Moreover, a work need not be speculative fiction to be Latinx Futurist. The music video 'If I Was President' (2021) by Chicanx band Las Cafeteras, featuring Sa-Roc, QVLN, Mega Ran and Boog Brown is an excellent example of a realist Latinx Futurist text that engages science fictional thinking. It imagines a future where Latinxs and Black Americans are united in imagining and advocating for a better future.

The 2021 remix is based on Las Cafeteras's original 2017 song of the same name. Through the lyrics, Las Cafeteras calls out Donald Trump, and America more broadly, for institutional racism and corruption, particularly for systemic injustice: police killings of Black men; flawed immigration policies; and lack of affordable healthcare, educational opportunities, a living wage and clean water. The song asserts that a Latinx president would work to rectify institutional racism and corruption by being president 'pa' toda la gente' (for all the people) so they can 'ride to their future/Not their past' and begin healing intergenerational trauma. The music video is aspirational, imparting hope for a better future and presenting a unified Latinx community in the face of oppression. Las Cafeteras asks us to acknowledge the past and present and to bear witness to and fight against corruption, reminding us of the survivance and power of the Latinx community.

The January 2021 remix offers a powerful continued vision of hope, following the 2020 presidential election. Las Cafeteras and the Center for Cultural Power, which supported the remix, detail its Latinx Futurist nature: '5 artists, 4 cities and 3 swing states come together to elevate a Collective Vision of America that represents Black, Indigenous, Working People of Color who changed the direction of the country'. Just as Older's SHADOWSHAPER CYPHER series imagines a unified community of colour, Las Cafeteras and their collaborators demonstrate a real-world collaboration between Black and Brown artists. The collective future vision they imagine first requires acknowledging the history of trauma and current inequality. In Sa-Roc's words

> If this was truly the land of the free and the brave
> Instead of stolen ground built by the hand of a slave
> And if the justice system worked on behalf of the people
> Then maybe my leadership could create the future we crave.

'If I Were President' imagines dismantling the prison-industrial complex by shutting down private prisons and ICE, taxing the 1% to end 'new age plantations', and defunding the police. In addition, the future imagined offers reparations, universal healthcare, free college, antiracist education, automatic voter registration, equitable redistribution of the wealth and granting Native nations sovereignty. As QVLN sings, in this future there will be 'No more war, no more fear, it's time to thrive, change is near'. Thus, this music video imagines a future where Latinx, Black and Indigenous peoples have collaboratively upended institutional racism and can finally thrive.

This imagined future is based on all four tenets of Latinx futurisms. The song (1) bears witness to the erased past and present of Latinx, Black and Indigenous peoples and highlights the way that past and the present are defined by the legacies of colonisation and White supremacy; (2) exposes and rejects Anglo stereotypes by showcasing strong, intelligent people of colour; (3) redefines Latinidades by subtly nodding to New York's Black and Latinx communities' collaborative creation of hip hop; and (4) promotes unity, not only for the Latinx diaspora, but all historically marginalised groups in the US.

Conclusion

Latinx Futurisms existed far before scholars began defining them. It is my hope that highlighting the work done in Latinx Futurisms will inspire the creation of more Latinx Futurist art, just as Grace L. Dillon's scholactivism has done for Indigenous Futurisms. Studying futurisms from the Global South and the margins of the Global North is itself a form of presencing – of insisting we belong in visions of the future and as architects of those futures.

Latinx Futurists place Latinx protagonists at the centre of the future, confront histories of racism and colonisation, and imagine worlds where internal and external decolonisation is possible. Latinx Futurisms show that community unity can and will build a better future for the diaspora. These are the futures that I, as a member of the Latinx diaspora, want to see. Futures where I am present, and where my ancestors and history are honoured. Futures where intergenerational trauma can be healed and oppressed cultures, which represent integral parts of our identities, are re-remembered and celebrated.

Works cited

Aparicio, Frances R. and Susana Chávez-Silverman, ed. *Tropicalations: Transcultural Representations of Latindad*. UP of New England, 1997.

Allatson, Paul. *Key Terms in Latino/a Cultural and Literary Studies*. Blackwell, 2007.

Anzaldúa, Gloria. *Borderlands/La Frontera: The New Mestiza*. Aunt Lute, 2007.

Brescia, Pablo. 'Code 51'. *Latin@ Rising: An Anthology of Latin@ Science Fiction and Fantasy*. Ed. David Matthew Goodwin. Wings Press, 2017. 11–15.

Cajete, Gregory. *Native Science: Natural Laws of Interdependence*. Clear Light, 2016.

Chattopadhyay, Bodhisattva. 'Kalpavigyan and Imperial Technoscience: Three Nodes of an Argument'. *Journal of Fantastic in the Arts* 28.1 (2018): 102–22.

Dillon, Grace L. 'Indigenous Scientific Literacies in Nalo Hopkinson's Ceremonial Worlds'. *Journal of Fantastic in the Arts* 18.1 (2007): 23–41.

——. 'Indigenous Futurisms, Bimaashi Biidaas Mose, Flying and Walking towards You'. *Extrapolation* 57.1–2 (2016): 1–6.

Gonzalez, Juan. *Harvest of Empire: A History of Latinos in America*. Penguin, 2011.

Goodwin, David Matthew. *Latin@ Rising: An Anthology of Latin@ Science Fiction and Fantasy*. Wings Press, 2017.

——. *The Latinx Files: Race, Migration, and Space Aliens*. Rutgers UP, 2021.

Hernández, Robb Tyler Stallings and Joanna Szupinska-Myers, ed. *Mundos Alternos: Art and Science Fiction in the Americas*. U of California Riverside P, 2017.

Hogan, Ernest. 'Chicanonautica Manifesto'. *Aztlan: A Journal of Chicano Studies* 40 (2015): 131–34.

Merla-Watson, Cathryn Josefina and B.V. Olguín, eds. *Altermundos: Latin@ Speculative Literature, Film, and Popular Culture*. U of California Los Angeles P, 2017.

——. '¡Latinx Futurisms Ahora! Recovering, Remapping, and Recentering the Chican@ and Latin@ Speculative Arts'. *Aztlan: A Journal of Chicano Studies* 40 (2015): 135–46.

Miranda-Rodriguez, Edgardo. *La Borinqueña #1*. Somos Arte, 2016.

Ramírez, Catherine S. 'Deus ex Machina: Tradition Technology, and the Chicanafuturist Art of Marion C. Martinez'. *Aztlan: A Journal of Chicano Studies* 29 (2004): 55–92.

Ramirez-Dhoore, Dora. 'The Cyberborderland: Surfing the Web for Xicanidad'. *Chicana/Latina Studies* 5.1 (2005): 10–47.

Ramírez, Susana. 'Recovering Gloria Anzaldúa's Sci-Fi Roots: Nepantler@ Visions in the Unpublished and Published Speculative Precursors to *Borderlands*'. *Altermundos: Latin@ Speculative Literature, Film, and Popular Culture*. Ed. Cathryn Josefina Merla-Watson and B.V. Olguín. U of California Los Angeles P, 2017. 55–71.

Sanchez-Taylor, Joy. *Diverse Futures: Science Fiction and Authors of Color*. Ohio State UP, 2021.

Taylor, Taryne Jade. 'Daniel José Older on the *Shadowshaper Cypher* Series: Part I'. *Label Me Latina/o* 11 (2021): 1–7.

——. 'Latinxs Unidos: Futurism and Latinidad in United States Latinx Hip-Hop'. *Extrapolation* 61.1–2 (2020): 29–52.

——. 'A Singular Dislocation: An Interview with Junot Díaz'. *Paradoxa* 26 (2014): 97–109.

Vasconcelos, José. *La raza cosmica/The Cosmic Race*. Trans. Didier T. Jaén. John Hopkins UP, 1997.

Wall Kimmerer, Robin. *Braiding Sweet Grass: Indigenous Wisdom, Scientific Knowledge and the Teachings of Plants*. Milkweed, 2013.

PART II

Science fiction praxis

32

ADVERTISING, PROTOTYPING AND SILICON VALLEY CULTURE

Jordan S. Carroll

Scientific and technical speculations now pervade commercial culture. Corporations sell audiences on futuristic utopias of luxury and leisure. Technologists entice investors by projecting worlds where their inventions are so popular they have become commonplace. Silicon Valley visionaries ply the public with cyberpunk fantasies and post-Singularity mythologies. Just like sf authors, these institutional actors seek to narrativise the future, to render it visible, exciting and desirable. In the process, they often draw upon the formal techniques and familiar tropes of the genre to make claims about real world scenarios. To keep up with these developments, sf studies has expanded its focus beyond fictional narratives to include examples of what Brooks Landon calls 'science fiction thinking' in other fields such as advertising, prototyping and Silicon Valley culture (4–10).

Even as capitalists and technologists have appropriated sf, the genre has turned its gaze back to critique these opportunistic discourses. Sf and speculative design have challenged the hubris of copywriters, prototype-builders and tech billionaires who subordinate politics to their narrow technical or professional goals. Sf reopens the conversation about what our future should look like while reminding audiences that there are limits to the wealthy and the influential's powers of prediction.

Advertising

Advertising has always been central to sf, which emerged as a genre when pulp magazines such as Hugo Gernsback's *Amazing Stories* solicited stories that would appeal to an advertiser-friendly target audience of readers anxious to ascend to the middle class (Rieder 44–54). Serialised narratives with predictable themes ensured that pulp readers would come back month after month to read sf stories alongside advertisements for self-improvement products such as correspondence courses in radio, electrical work and career-building skills (52). Gernsback and other editors in the field cultivated sf fans as dependable customers for their advertising partners.

At the same time, advertising has always been speculative: advertisements predict what would happen if the customer bought the product on display, even as they promise to fulfil wishes that seem impossible under the present social order. Glimpsing an advertisement for salt, Walter Benjamin saw an 'image of the everyday in Utopia' (174), while Ernst Bloch suggested that advertising 'makes magic out of the commodity, even out of the most incidental commodity, a magic

DOI: 10.4324/9781003140269-35

in which each and every thing will be solved if only we buy it' (*Principle* 344). Advertising not only appeals to the buyer's aspirations and desires – it also offers a window into an imaginative world where all conflicts and contradictions appear to have been resolved. Nevertheless, these wish-dreams seem to disappear once the customer has made the purchase: as Bloch warns, all too often technological utopias are 'made banal through fulfillment' ('Something's' 2). Although we can read a utopian residue, a hint of a better world, in advertisements, we should remember that even these subversive moments function as a 'fantasy bribe' to keep us invested in the capitalist system (Jameson 144).

This is perhaps clearest in the science fictional attractions offered by the mid-century automotive industry. Car manufacturers caught the public's attention by drawing inspirations from pulp magazine illustrations and futuristic concept cars, adorning their vehicles with enormous tailfins that evoked the sf dream of the flying car (Woodham 374–5). Advertisers for domestic appliances also tapped into fantasies about technological progress. Laura Scott Holliday traces the 'domestic futurism' found in the 'Kitchen of Tomorrow' narratives that proliferated in the two decades following World War II (80). Magazine advertisements and touring exhibits showed homemakers a future where women would be freed from cooking, dishwashing and other forms of reproductive labour through new push-button devices. But even as domestic futurism looked forward to a moment when women were emancipated from drudgery, it reinscribed conservative gender relations: the housewives of the future could use their newfound free time to beautify themselves for their husbands (82–3). Davin Heckman explores another domestic futurist narrative – the smart home. Advertisers and futurists promoting automated home environments promise the 'Perfect Day', a vision of everyday life where all ethical problems have been solved through technical solutions (15). Behind this suburban façade, however, lurks a sinister dream of technological control in which autonomous computers take command of all household tasks, eliminating all the inefficiencies associated with human interference (74–84).

Other space age advertisements promised escape from the private sphere entirely. Lynn Spigel details how postwar advertisers for television sets recast consumer electronics as rocket ships that could transport viewers from their living rooms (69–70, 84). Sf also helped promote real-life exploration of outer space. As Megan Prelinger demonstrates, speculative advertising drew liberally from pulp sf imagery to consolidate public support and recruit personnel for NASA during the years following the launch of Sputnik-1.

Since then, sf has become ubiquitous in advertising. For example, Apple's famous '1984' Macintosh advertisement cast its rivalry with IBM as a revolt against a dystopian government enforcing totalitarian conformity on its citizens (Heckman 72). Sf has also come to pervade marketing in more subtle ways. Norah Campbell argues that advertising borrows from sf conceits to promote the 'technological gaze' ('Technological' 3). Advertisements for companies such as Toyota and Nike take viewers onto fantastic voyages where they shrink down to the subatomic level or travel faster than the speed of light. Along the way, spectators become habituated to posthuman ways of seeing. Nike's *Eye D* advertisement (2004), for example, offers a kind of augmented reality display in which we see a runner's performance data flash onto the screen. Advertisements such as this condition spectators to see humans as informational machines (Campbell 'Technological' 10), and often they literalise this metaphor by presenting us with images of cyborg and robot bodies (Campbell 'Future'). Similarly, advertisements for investment banking firms model what Josh Pearson calls 'corporate vision', a 'posthuman perspective' that takes in complex arrays of images from across the globe and extrapolates from them to predict the future (18–9). Speculative finance sells itself as omniscient through speculative fictions. Sf frequently calls these kinds of marketing claims into question but, as Lee Konstantinou suggests, sf and advertising have often promoted competing fantasies of ever-greater consumer affluence and economic growth (252–4).

H.G. Wells's *When the Sleeper Wakes* (1899) is one of the earliest sf treatments of advertising in literature, forecasting a dystopia so busy with advertisements that even the sky is filled with kites or balloons carrying them aloft. Frederik Pohl and Cyril M. Kornbluth's *The Space Merchants* (1953) sets the tone for later sf critiques of advertising by depicting a world in which rival firms reengineer society itself to produce new consumer demands for their clients' products. Corporate anthropologists interfere with consumer folkways to create viral campaigns for their clients while companies insert addictive chemicals into consumables that engender craving for other product lines. One firm – Fowler Schocken Associates – controls all the advertising business in India in a 'spherical trust' called 'Indiastries' (3), and throughout the novel the company seeks to become the sole advertiser on a soon-to-be-colonised Venus. Thanks to the rapaciousness of advertising, rampant consumerism has depleted the world's resources to the point where conservationism is now seen as a subversive doctrine analogous to Communism and corporations have begun to turn from an ecologically depleted Earth to other planets to exploit for profit.

Advertising's apparent ubiquity takes on a theological dimension in Philip K. Dick's *Ubik* (1969), where a god-like being interrupts the narrative with plugs for Ubik, an all-purpose commodity. James Tiptree, Jr. underscores the insidious nature of marketing in 'The Girl Who Was Plugged In' (1973). After all advertisements have been banned by the 'Huckster Act', corporations rely on lab-grown celebrity influencers controlled by remote operators to promote their goods through covert endorsement campaigns and product placement on holographic television programs.

Later sf narratives depict advertising as equally intrusive. William Gibson's *Neuromancer* (1984) and *Pattern Recognition* (2003) are filled with references to brand names, as if advertising jargon has colonised language itself. The protagonist of the dystopian *Brazil* (Gilliam 1985) drives down a road where every inch of landscape has been blocked by continuous rows of billboards, while *Blade Runner* (Scott 1982) and *Blade Runner 2049* (Villeneuve 2017) feature animated advertisements that threaten to eclipse the skyline. *Minority Report* (Spielberg 2002) goes one step further, depicting personalised advertisements that follow the potential customer around on different displays wherever they go. There is often something absurd or hyperbolic about these futuristic advertisements. Paul Verhoeven plays with inserting satirical advertisements into his sf films: *RoboCop* (1987) mocks the excesses of conspicuous consumption with advertisements for products such as a luxury vehicle – the 6000 SUX – proudly engineered to obtain a low mileage of 8.2 miles per gallon, while *Starship Troopers* (1997) punctuates its violent storyline with over-the-top propaganda for the film's military dictatorship. The cyberpunk comedy *Max Headroom: 20 Minutes Into the Future* (Channel 4 1985) centres on a superfast television spot – the blipvert – that overloads the viewer's brain with subliminal messages until it is liable to explode. As Scott Bukatman observes, these often-funny images of invasive advertising point to a more anxious suspicion that our very subjectivity is being reformatted to suit the needs of consumer capitalism (69). What could be scarier than the neural implants in M.T. Anderson's *Feed* (2002), networked devices that fill the user's senses with targeted advertisements based on preference data scraped from their minds?

Prototyping

Whereas advertising typically drums up interest in existing products, prototyping tests out products that are not yet available. A prototype is an approximate version of the final product that allows designers and developers to experiment with design ideas, investigate alternatives, uncover hidden problems and attract people to their projects. While every prototype tells a speculative narrative about what might be produced in the future, sf itself can just as easily be understood as prototypical. Artist and technologist Julian Bleecker argues that sf 'creates prototypes of other worlds' (7), allowing creators to explore possibilities in a low-cost manner. The conceptual distinction between prototyping and sf seems to blur.

Sf and prototyping prove to be intimately linked in practice, as well. David A. Kirby argues that sf cinema builds audience support for new or emerging technologies through what he calls 'diegetic prototypes' (18), representations of inventions at work in the world of the film. These 'pre-product placements' (196) allow the filmmakers and scientists to elicit demand for new technology while allaying the public's anxieties by establishing the prototype's 'necessity', 'normalcy' and 'viability' (194); when they succeed, they allow audiences to see that innovative technologies are safe, feasible and compatible with their everyday lives. While much of sf dedicates itself to presenting the strange and unfamiliar, diegetic prototypes often strive to make novelty seem mundane.

Design fiction, 'a mix of science fact, design and science fiction' (Bleecker 6), produces prototypes unconstrained by the limits of technical feasibility or commercial viability in order to provoke critical conversations, expand our utopian imaginations and, according to sf author Bruce Sterling, 'suspend disbelief about change' (Bosch n.p.). Others follow Bleecker in reconceptualising the broader field of sf as part of the prototyping process. For example, Intel futurist Brian David Johnson explores sf prototypes, which he defines as 'a short story, movie or comic based on science fact for the purpose of exploring the implications, effects and ramifications of that science or technology' (3). Although design fiction and sf prototyping sometimes serve purely speculative or critical purposes, these practices have been adopted by organisations more interested in practical results, including the final delivery of products intended to solve real-world problems.

Anthony Dunne and Fiona Raby suggest there is value in generating prototypes with no intention of using them to create a new model for mass production. They propose 'speculative design' as an alternative form of prototyping practice that allows designers to explore futures falling outside of the realms of plausibility, possibility or preferability, including scenarios that call into question the techno-optimism Dunne and Raby find in many design fictions (100). By producing bizarre, fanciful or dystopian objects, speculative design allows us to see that the present is more 'malleable' (6) than we previously realised. Indeed, while design fiction and sf prototyping tend to emphasise the prototype's functionality, speculative design often asks the user or spectator to imagine the world the object implies, including the cultural assumptions and social relations it entails (92). Insofar as speculative design acts as a diagnostic tool, it does so because its proposed design objects express larger structural problems without pretending to resolve them through a technological quick fix.

Colin Milburn also undermines the idea that there is a straightforward relationship between sf and technology. Scientists have often poached from sf texts to invent new technologies, but while science reporting makes this seem like a one-to-one transposition of the invention from fiction into reality – 'Yesterday it was science fiction; today it is science fact' – Milburn argues that scientists are more like fans in participatory cultures that sample, mod and remix their favourite media to make something new ('Modifiable' 561). In 'blueprint mods', innovators seek to implement designs from sf narratives, abstracting and adapting the original source material to make it work (566). When scientists produce 'supplementary mods', they create prototypes that are the next best thing to the sf device, reproducing some of its effects without functioning in the same way (567–8). Prototype developers turn out to be sf creators in their own right.

Japanese robotics represents perhaps one of the most sustained interchanges between sf media and commercial prototyping. Yuji Sone shows that anime and manga franchises such as Astro Boy (1951–) and Mobile Suit Gundam (1979–) play a prominent role in the Japanese social imaginary governing how roboticists and the broader public approach humanoid robots such as Honda's ASIMO prototype. Research and development groups such as the Humanoid Robotics Project now integrate anime and manga directly into the design process: after abandoning plans to model the robot design on Astro Boy, they hired Yutaka Izubuchi, an artist who worked on the anime series *Patlabor* (1988–9), to create a look for their industrial robots that would help them win acceptance from consumers (Šabanović 353). Jennifer Robertson observes that Japanese roboticists sometimes import normative assumptions from anime and manga, casting robots in stereotyped gendered roles and enrolling them as family members in traditional kinship relations (129–36). Once again sf prototyping navigates the tensions between producing inventions with potentially world-changing implications while also reassuring conservative audiences that scientific and technological innovations will not disrupt the status quo.

Silicon Valley culture

Although prototyping may sometimes promise business as usual, disruption is the prevailing ideology for tech companies in the Silicon Valley. With every product launch and initial public offering, tech companies sell us an sf novum, the innovation that will radically change everything. Sf thinking is therefore baked into the political economy of Silicon Valley. Tech startups sustain themselves through 'hype' (Rajan 111), a speculative discourse that makes statements about the technoscientific future in order to generate 'the conditions of possibility' (267) that would allow that same future to be realised. When investors buy into the hype about a proposed product, they make it possible that the wild speculations promoted by a company might turn out to have been true all along (132–3). As Steve Wozniak suggests, 'We are the people who make fantasies real. We do take old science fiction, things we see in movies, and we do try to make them real and we succeed sometimes' (Hasan n.p.).

Silicon Valley spins out sf stories for venture capitalists as well as the press, but they are not just cynical ploys for funding or public relations purposes. Many computer programmers really believe the hype. Sf culture has been central to the computing field from its earliest beginnings (Milburn *Respawn* 25–30). Mark Pesce's provocatively subtitled 'Magic Mirror: The Novel as a Software Development Platform' shows that sf influences only intensified after the advent of personal computing. Cyberpunk novels such as John Brunner's *The Shockwave Rider* (1975) and Vernor Vinge's *True Names* (1981) served as key texts for the early hacker community, but it was Gibson's work that really galvanised the coders of the 1980s. *Neuromancer* popularised the term 'cyberspace', first introduced in Gibson's 'Burning Chrome' (1982), providing a shared vocabulary and a cultural imaginary for what would soon come to be known as virtual reality. While Gibson's cyberspace often seemed abstract and elusive – the province of a technological avant-garde – the videogame aesthetic of the Metaverse in Neal Stephenson's *Snow Crash* (1992) caught the attention of programmers at a later moment in the software industry's development when computer networks were increasingly commercialised spaces designed to be user-friendly (Kelly 71–6).

Cyberpunk provided Silicon Valley not only with a storehouse of ideas for software design but also with an ethos for computer programmers to emulate. Richard Barbrook and Andy Cameron argue that the anarchic hacker heroes of cyberpunk novels seemed to embody an ideology of individual liberty and self-reliance that appealed to free market capitalists in computing culture. Although most critics read cyberpunk narratives as *critiques* of capitalism, many programmers read into them the message that government regulations and bureaucratic organisations stifle innovation, which can only emerge when technical geniuses are allowed the unconstrained freedom to 'move fast and break things', as Facebook's CEO would put it.

For these technolibertarians, anything that hinders technological change is an obstacle to be dismantled – including matter itself. N. Katherine Hayles suggests that cyberpunk novels such as *Neuromancer* reinforced a sense that the computer programmer was a disembodied subject detached from material concerns and dealing with pure information (36). The coder's reflexive contempt for the body – a useful attitude for enduring punishingly long sessions in front of the computer – persists within the industry, expressed through fads such as Soylent, a meal-replacement shake named after the liquified human bodies in *Soylent Green* (Fleischer 1973). Sf recasts programmers as an ascetic elite capable of ignoring the pleasures of mere appearances in order to explore their underlying structures. Although Stephenson's Metaverse adopts the visual metaphors common to Graphical User Interfaces, the novel maintains a reverence for hackers such as Hiro Protagonist who still knows how to see past the slippery mediations of the GUI to read the code itself (Kelly 70). Programmers tend to generalise from expertise within this domain to claim a deeper understanding of the rest of the world. When they are not approaching politics as an engineering problem or treating the body as a machine, tech gurus like to indulge in the sf fantasy that all of reality is a simulation running on a computer of unbelievable power. Learning to code makes them masters of metaphysics.

Moreover, sf fan practices also help tech workers form the skills and capacities that they need to concentrate on their work for long periods of time. Time-consuming hobbies and repetitive activities, which reward a great deal of close attention, allow geeks to habituate themselves to the time crunches that often come with coding for a demanding employer. Indeed, both sf readers and computer programmers report losing themselves in timeless moments of heightened absorption that the sf community calls the sense of wonder and the tech field calls the flow state (Carroll 'Geek'). Geeks therefore often find themselves desynchronised from normative timelines: they work nights as well as days, they engage in putatively child-like behaviours well into adulthood, they may postpone or avoid heterosexual reproduction, and they may seem slow to react to stimuli outside of their favourite interests. This condition often leaves many geeks feeling like robots, androids or artificial intelligences who do not move at the same speed or follow the same developmental patterns as everyone else (Carroll 'Lifecycle' 210–11).

Unsurprisingly, then, many Silicon Valley tech entrepreneurs proudly describe themselves as sf fans. Jeff Bezos, Sergey Brin, Bill Gates, Elon Musk, Peter Thiel, Steve Wozniak and Mark Zuckerberg all engaged deeply in sf culture at different moments in their careers. We see this clearly in Silicon Valley's push to privatise space travel. When Amazon founder Bezos began acquiring land for Blue Origin, his private aerospace manufacturer and spaceflight company, he purchased it under the name Zefram, LLC, named after Zefram Cochrane, the inventor of the warp drive in STAR TREK (Davenport 20). After Bezos tapped Stephenson to imagine alternative methods for launching a ship into space, the novelist described himself as 'like Spock on the deck of the *Enterprise*', holding forth at great length on the science involved in their endeavour (Stephenson n.p.). Even before Bezos attempted spaceflight in real life, he appeared as an alien in *Star Trek Beyond* (Lin 2016).

Bezos is unusual for embracing an sf franchise founded on a socialist vision of the future. Peter Diamandis, the tech entrepreneur who founded the XPRIZE Foundation to promote private spaceflight, cites as his primary inspiration Robert A. Heinlein's 'The Man Who Sold the Moon' (1950), which follows the dealings of a businessman as he finances and launches a corporate lunar expedition (Christensen). One of his schemes involves tricking a cola corporation into thinking that their competitor is going to transform the surface of the moon into an enormous billboard advertisement for their rival product line. Musk, another major player in the billionaire space race, often namedrops Heinlein's *The Moon is a Harsh Mistress* (1966) (Vance 33), which chronicles the Moon's war of independence from Earth and the founding of a lunar society based on libertarian principles. The anti-democratic impulse to avoid mass politics by seceding from the state – best expressed in Ayn Rand's *Atlas Shrugged* (1957) – motivates other movements circulating within Silicon Valley culture, including seasteading, survivalism and the alt-right. Quinn Slobodian draws a parallel between such right-wing secessionist movements and Stephenson's cyberpunk futures, where national sovereignty has fractured into privately controlled zones (96–7). Zuckerberg's Metaverse virtual reality program begins to look like an attempt to start a corporate-run digital polity that may someday escape the restrictions of territorial governments (Slobodian 203–23).

Still others in Silicon Valley think that these political struggles will soon be rendered moot by the Singularity, a term coined by Vinge to describe the rapid acceleration of technological progress beyond human comprehension. Ray Kurzweil, a technologist who works for Google, predicts that computing power will continue to grow exponentially until a superhuman artificial intelligence emerges around the year 2045. At that point, the artificial intelligence will obtain god-like powers and confer immortality upon humankind. Philosopher Nick Bostrom, on the other hand, warns that superintelligent machines could pose an existential risk to life on this planet. Some philanthropists in Silicon Valley – calling themselves 'effective altruists' – devote their resources to funding research into preventing the outbreak of hostile artificial intelligences and other sf doomsday scenarios because, following a utilitarian calculus, they believe that the good that would come from averting a planet-killing event outweighs the good that might be done helping, for example, the houseless population in San Francisco (Srinivasan).

Martin Paul Eve and Joe Street argue that the Silicon Valley novel follows the tradition of sf and, especially, the literary dystopia (82). However, whereas most dystopian fiction allows readers to see the present from a distanced perspective by representing it in an exaggerated future, the Silicon Valley novel functions more like a Menippean satire, typified by Swift's *Gulliver's Travels* (1726), which estranges present-day trends by displacing them onto an exotic locale (92–3). As in Gulliver's visit to the island of Laputa, Silicon Valley novels take us into a dystopian enclave – the Silicon Valley workplace – characterised by both advanced technology and social dysfunction. In Dave Eggers's *The Circle* (2013), the classic example of this genre, a company not unlike Google and Facebook abolishes secrecy by bringing its employees and the rest of society under total surveillance through ubiquitous cameras and wearable tracking devices. Protagonist Mae Holland rises through the company ranks when she agrees to wear a camera with a social media feed throughout the day, but, as the novel suggests, she eventually sacrifices all semblance of intimacy or individuality for public acclaim. Alissa Nutting's *Made for Love* (2017) provides an interesting counterpoint. It follows the narrative of a woman who is fleeing her husband, a billionaire tech CEO, who has implanted a microchip in her head to record her thoughts. Although he receives a daily download of her experiences, she remains opaque to him. Nutting finds hope in the idea that the sheer perversity of our desires will prevent tech companies from ever predicting our future actions based on data about our past behaviours with anything like perfect precision.

However, most film and television narratives treat the failure of technological solutionism in a tragic rather than a comic mode. The anthology series *Black Mirror* (Channel 4/Netflix 2017–)

has become almost a cliché for describing the dreadful unintended consequences of digital apps and gadgets. In *Ex Machina* (Garland 2014), Nathan Bateman, the CEO of a search engine company, draws upon user data to create artificial intelligences, which he installs in feminised robotic bodies. Bateman abuses the robots, forcing them to fulfil his sexual fantasies and confining them to an underground bunker where they spend much of their time performing domestic labour for him. The film comments upon how tech companies have moved towards a business model centred on capturing data about emotions (Vint 82). The new artificial intelligences are no longer cold, calculating machines: they are feminine helpmates like Siri, who dedicate themselves to anticipating their users' desires. These artificial intelligences reflect the prejudices of a predominantly white, male population of programmers: they have been encoded with a host of gendered and racialised assumptions, including the notion that women are naturally ingratiating (82–4). Thus, Bateman designs his submissive robotic servant Kyoko to appear as Asian, reflecting the racist underpinnings of Techno-Orientalism (Nishime 34–5). Alex Garland's subsequent miniseries *Devs* (Hulu 2020) continues to explore how Silicon Valley's God complex prevents it from seeing the limits of its worldview.

Many of the commercial futurists explored in this chapter attempt to make a claim on the future. Advertisers try to convince us that their products will answer our unfulfilled utopian longings, prototype makers promise to solve our problems with smart new technologies, and Silicon Valley culture insists that its programmers' technical expertise gives them the right to remake our lives. Although all these groups have cited speculative fiction as an inspiration, critical forms of sf have often challenged their designs on the future. At the same time, the gap between the hype and the finished product only reveals the inability of our present social system to fulfil its promises. Commercial futurism's fundamental inadequacies must be understood not as a cause for cynicism but instead as an incitement to more radical utopian imaginings.

Works cited

Barbrook, Richard and Andy Cameron. 'The Californian Ideology'. *Mute* 1.3 (1 September 1995). www.metamute.org/editorial/articles/californian-ideology

Benjamin, Walter. *The Arcades Project*. Trans. Howard Eiland and Kevin McLaughlin. The Belknap Press of Harvard UP, 1999.

Bleecker, Julian. *Design Fiction: A Short Essay on Design, Science, Fact and Fiction*. Near Future Laboratory, 2009. http://drbfw5wfjlxon.cloudfront.net/writing/DesignFiction_WebEdition.pdf

Bloch, Ernst. *The Principle of Hope*, volume one. Trans. Neville Plaice, Stephen Plaice and Paul Knight. MIT Press, 1986.

——. 'Something's Missing: A Discussion Between Ernst Bloch and Theodor W. Adorno on the Contradictions of Utopian Longing'. *The Utopian Function of Art and Literature*. Trans. Jack Zipes and Frank Mecklenburg. MIT Press, 1988. 1–17.

Bosch, Torie. 'Sci-Fi Writer Bruce Sterling Explains the Intriguing New Concept of Design Fiction'. *Slate* (2 March 2012). https://slate.com/technology/2012/03/bruce-sterling-on-design-fictions.html

Bukatman, Scott. *Terminal Identity: The Virtual Subject in Postmodern Science Fiction*, Duke UP, 1993.

Campbell, Norah. 'Future Sex: Cyborg Bodies and the Politics of Meaning'. *Advertising & Society Review* 11.1 (2010).

——. 'The Technological Gaze in Advertising'. *Irish Marketing Review* 9.1-2 (2007): 3–18.

Carroll, Jordan. 'Geek Temporalities and the Spirit of Capital'. *Post45* 3 (2019). https://post45.org/2019/08/geek-temporalities-and-the-spirit-of-capital/

——. 'The Lifecycle of Software Engineers: Geek Temporalities and Digital Labor'. *Practices of Speculation: Modeling, Embodiment, Figuration*. Ed. Jeanne Cortiel, Christine Hanke and Colin Milburn. Transcript, 2020. 209–20.

Christensen, Bill. 'Heinlein Prize Trust to Honor X Prize Founder, Peter Diamandis'. *Space.com* (27 June 2006). www.space.com/2542-heinlein-prize-trust-honor-prize-founder-peter-diamandis.html
Davenport, Christian. *The Space Barons: Elon Musk, Jeff Bezos, and the Quest to Colonize the Cosmos*. Public Affairs, 2018.
Dunne, Anthony and Fiona Raby. *Speculative Everything: Design, Fiction, and Social Dreaming*. MIT Press, 2013.
Eve, Martin Paul and Joe Street. 'The Silicon Valley Novel'. *Literature & History* 27.1 (2018): 81–97.
Hasan, Zaki. 'Interview: Steve Wozniak on Sci-Fi, Comic Books, and How Star Trek Shaped the Future'. *Zaki's Corner* (19 April 2017). www.zakiscorner.com/2017/04/interview-steve-wozniak-on-sci-fi-comic.html
Hayles, N. Katherine *How We Became Posthuman: Virtual Bodies in Cybernetics, Literature, and Informatics*. U of Chicago P, 1999.
Heckman, Davin. *A Small World: Smart Houses and the Dream of the Perfect Day*. Duke UP, 2008.
Holliday, Laura Scott. 'Kitchen Technologies: Promises and Alibis, 1944–1966'. *Camera Obscura* 47 (2001): 78–131.
Jameson, Fredric, 'Reification and Utopia in Mass Culture'. *Social Text* 1 (1979): 130–48.
Johnson, Brian David. *Science Fiction Prototyping: Designing the Future with Science Fiction*. Morgan & Claypool, 2011.
Kelly, Nicholas M. '"Words Like Magic": Metaphor, Meaning, and the GUI in Stephenson's *Snow Crash*'. *Science Fiction Studies* 134 (2018): 69–90.
Kirby, David A. *Lab Coats in Hollywood: Science, Scientists, and Cinema*. MIT Press, 2011.
Konstantinou, Lee. 'Better Living Through Chemisty: Fiction and Consumerism in the Cold War'. *The Cambridge History of Science Fiction*. Ed. Gerry Canavan and Eric Carl Link. Cambridge UP, 2019. 247–64.
Landon, Brooks. *Science Fiction after 1900: From the Steam Man to the Stars*. Routledge, 2002.
Milburn, Colin. 'Modifiable Futures: Science Fiction at the Bench'. *Isis* 101.3 (2010): 560–9.
——. *Respawn: Gamers, Hackers, and Technogenic Life*. Duke UP, 2018.
Nishime, LeiLani. 'Whitewashing Yellow Futures in *Ex Machina*, *Cloud Atlas*, and *Advantageous*: Gender, Labor, and Technology in Sci-fi Film'. *Journal of Asian-American Studies* 20.1 (2017): 29–49.
Pearson, Josh. 'Seeing the Present, Grasping the Future: Articulating a "Financial Vision" in Capitalist Realism'. *Paradoxa* 27 (2015): 1–28.
Pesce, Mark. 'The Novel as Software Development Platform'. *Media in Transition* conference at MIT, 1999. https://web.mit.edu/comm-forum/legacy/papers/pesce.html
Pohl, Frederik and C.M. Kornbluth. *The Space Merchants*. Ballantine, 1953.
Prelinger, Megan. *Another Science Fiction: Advertising the Space Race 1957–1962*. Blast, 2010.
Rajan, Kaushik Sunder. *Biocapital: The Constitution of Postgenomic Life*. Duke UP, 2006.
Rieder, John. *Science Fiction and the Mass Cultural Genre System*. Wesleyan UP, 2017.
Robertson, Jennifer. *Robo Sapiens Japanicus: Robots, Gender, Family, and the Japanese Nation*. U of California P, 2018.
Šabanović, Selma. 'Inventing Japan's 'Robotics Culture': The Repeated Assembly of Science, Technology, and Culture in Social Robotics'. *Social Studies of Science* 44.3 (2014): 342–67.
Slobodian, Quinn. *Crack-Up Capitalism: Market Radicals and the Dream of a World without Democracy*. Metropolitan, 2023.
Sone, Yuji. *Japanese Robot Culture: Performance, Imagination, and Modernity*. Palgrave Macmillan, 2017.
Spigel, Lynn. *Welcome to the Dreamhouse: Popular Media and Postwar Suburbs*. Duke UP, 2001.
Srinivasan, Amia. 'Stopping the Robot Apocalypse'. *London Review of Books* 37.18 (24 September 2015). www.lrb.co.uk/the-paper/v37/n18/amia-srinivasan/stop-the-robot-apocalypse
Stephenson, Neal. 'Neal Stephenson Responds with Wit and Humor'. *Slashdot* (20 October 2004). https://slashdot.org/story/04/10/20/1518217/neal-stephenson-responds-with-wit-and-humor
Vance, Ashlee. *Elon Musk: Tesla, SpaceX, and the Quest for a Fantastic Future*. Ecco, 2017.
Vint, Sherryl. *Science Fiction*. MIT Press, 2021.
Woodham, Jonathan M. 'Advertising and Design'. *The Oxford Handbook of Science Fiction*. Ed. Rob Latham. Oxford UP, 2014. 364–82.

33
ALTERNATE HISTORY

Glyn Morgan

Alternate history is sometimes overlooked within sf scholarship, perhaps because it often contains none of the (quasi-)scientific markers associated with the genre such as scientists or engineers or new technologies. Indeed, the *novum* of alternate history, as Darko Suvin might identify it, is not in the present or future as it is in other sf, but in the past. This chapter demonstrates the extent to which alternate history is enmeshed with sf *and* the manner in which it has its own genre identity within a wider field of speculative fiction, as well as presenting a case for its increasing importance and relevance.

Like romance or crime, alternate history is easily hybridised with the more amorphous genre of sf but can also stand apart from it. Associated with sf because both explore the vital speculative question 'what if?', alternate history has its own conventions around that question, as do horror and fantasy. It also has its own literary genealogy, distinct from that of sf or fantasy, although just as contentious and debatable. The longest view begins with the Roman writer Livy who, in the ninth book of his history of Rome *Ab Urbe Condita* (circa 25 BCE), speculates about what might have occurred had Alexander the Great encountered the Roman Empire by attempting to conquer the West. This seems to be the earliest surviving expression of what historian E.H. Carr railed against in 1961 as the '"might-have-been" school of thought – or rather emotion': 'one can always play a parlour game with the might-have-beens of history. But they have nothing to do with determinism […]. Nor have they anything to do with history' (96–7).

Not all historians agree with Carr's rejection of historical hypotheticals. Indeed, classicist Mary Beard notes that Livy's digression 'is one of the few cases in which he looks beneath the surface of the narrative, to underlying social and structural factors, from the organisation of Roman command to Rome's resources of manpower' (161). It is unconvincing to suggest that this is the first piece of alternate history *fiction*, but it does represent a tool or technique (or, as Carr would have it, a game) historians have continued to employ. Isaac D'Israeli wrote the first of these published in English, 'Of a History of Events Which Have Not Happened' (1824), and an important early collection, J.C. Squire's *If It Had Happened Otherwise* (1931), includes essays by Hillaire Belloc, G.K. Chesterton and Winston Churchill. More recent volumes of such essays include Niall Ferguson's *Virtual Histories* (1997), Robert Cowley's *What If?* (1999) and *More What If?* (2001), and Andrew Roberts's *What Might Have Been* (2004). Many contributors to such volumes, such as Ferguson, utilise the form to rebut deterministic models of history.

 DOI: 10.4324/9781003140269-36

Despite Ferguson's attempts to put clear water between historiographic works and sf because 'of course, Hollywood and sf are not academically respectable' (3), the core intellectual premise of such speculations are not dissimilar to their fictional counterparts. However, they do also clearly attempt something different, with their more singular focus on historical causality and relative uninterest in such concerns of narrative fiction as character development and plot structure. Thus, to distinguish them, historiographic essays are referred to as 'counterfactuals' rather than alternate histories.

Other scholars have proposed their own foundational texts for alternate history as a literary form. Adam Roberts suggests Samuel Gott's *Nova Solyma, the Ideal City: or Jerusalem Regained* (1648), while Catherine Gallagher begins her history of counterfactual thought with Gottfied Wilhelm von Leibniz's *Theodicée* (1710). A more general consensus identifies Louis-Napoléon Geoffroy-Château's *Napoléon et la conquête du monde* (1836), in which Napoleon's invasion of Russia is a success, his armies then conquer England and the entire Earth becomes a single French Empire; the ensuing golden age of peace allows for numerous technological and civic innovations and improvements. It is the first novel-length alternate history to expand upon its initial supposition (what if Bonaparte had taken a different route) to spin out a cascade of changes which result in a radically altered alternate world. It is the first work in a French literary tradition of *Uchronie* (Uchronia) – a term taken from Charles Renouvier's novel *Uchronie* (1876) to describe a temporal equivalent of utopian literature – and a strong reminder that writing alternate history is, like writing history itself, never not a political act: Geoffroy-Château was so passionate a supporter of Bonaparte that he adopted 'Napoléon' into his own name, and *la conquête du monde* could be considered a form of Napoleon fanfiction.

It was not until the publication of Murray Leinster's 'Sidewise in Time' (1934) in the pulp magazine *Astounding* that alternate history made full contact with genre sf. The story features multiple alternate histories existing parallel to the narrator's dimension: a natural cataclysm causes the boundaries between them to break, first causing the sun to temporarily vastly increase in temperature, then animals to divide asexually in the manner of an amoeba, and then rivers to run uphill. Finally, sections of the world exchange places with their counterparts in other dimensions: a global Roman Empire's fort replaces St. Louis; patches of Kentucky are replaced with an American Confederacy which won the Battle of Gettysburg and a driver who enters their territory is promptly arrested for displaying the flag of the United States on his car. Vikings raid the Eastern Seaboard. Forests spring up where plains once stood. Leinster does not do much to flesh out or explain the alternate histories of the other dimensions, and indeed it is strange that in the 1935 in which the story is set the Vikings are still sailing longboats, the Romans still wear leather skirts and use short swords, and the Confederates still have grey uniforms. Nonetheless the mere potential of these alternate realities planted a seed for the genre.

Since then, alternate histories have been a feature of sf, adding consequential twists or some semblance of scientific credibility (through an association with the physicists Hugh Everett and Bryce De Witt's 'Many Worlds' interpretation of quantum mechanics) to time travel narratives. Indeed, Leinster's story is so foundational that its name was chosen for The Sidewise Awards for Alternate History, established in 1995. Held slightly apart from sf, with its own history and awards, alternate history also seems much more comfortably able to cross into other genres. Or, perhaps, its associations with sf are perceived as being sufficiently weak by those outside sf that it is more willingly embraced than other sf story types. One could easily imagine sf fan Michael Chabon writing a conventional sf narrative to sit alongside his alternate history of Yiddish Alaska, *The Yiddish Policeman's Union* (2007), but few would harbour similar ideas about fellow Pulitzer Prize-winner Philip Roth, despite his bestselling tale of a fascist takeover of the US, *The Plot Against*

America (2004), and his less well remembered short story '"I Always Wanted You to Admire My Fasting": or, Looking at Kafka' (1975). Nor was anyone realistically waiting for *Friends* (NBC 1994–2004) to feature an alien invasion, despite an alternate history of the coffeehouse group taking up the double episode 'The One That Could Have Been, parts 1 & 2' (2000).

The prevalence of alternate history moments in long-running non-sf television series – including *Frasier* ('Sliding Frasiers' (NBC 2001), a reference to *Sliding Doors* (Howitt 1998)), *The Fresh Prince of Bel-Air* ('The Alma Matter' (NBC 1993)), *Scrubs* ('My Butterfly' (NBC 2004) and others), *The O.C.* ('The Chrismukk-huh? (Fox 2006)), *NCIS* ('Life Before His Eyes' (CBS 2012)), *Bones* ('The End in the Beginning' (Fox 2009)) and *many* others – has its own lineage which likely owes something to the prominence of *It's a Wonderful Life* (Capra 1946) on American holiday schedules (which itself descends from the ideas of fate's branching paths in another seasonal classic, Charles Dickens's *A Christmas Carol* (1843)). The recurrence of this special episode format suggests their popularity with audiences, while also giving writers a chance to flip the status quo without significant consequences. However, these moments also speak to something more fundamental in the popularity of the alternate history story: the backwards-facing novum capable of embracing not only grand geo-political questions of Napoleons and Civil Wars, but also the quieter introspective moments of daydream, regret or self-analysis. This historical 'what if?' can be legitimately used to ask, what would have happened if I had caught that train, or applied for that job, or never been born?

Including such smaller-scale personal stories under the banner of alternate history admits the time loop plot as a specific sub-genre. Perhaps best known from *Groundhog Day* (Ramis 1993), the idea of a character re-living portions of their life (or, in some cases, their entire life) over and over, enacting events in such a way that they trigger differing consequences, is clearly a form of alternate history, but because of the personal nature of the changes it is often overlooked in surveys of the genre. Many serialised narratives, both sf and non-sf, have used some form of this narrative structure, including Yasutaka Tsutsui's *The Girl Who Leapt Through Time* (1965), Hiroshi Sakurazaka's *All You Need is Kill* (2004; adapted as *Edge of Tomorrow* (Liman 2014)), Kate Atkinson's *Life After Life* (2013), *About Time* (Curtis 2013), Claire North's *The First Fifteen Lives of Harry August* (2014), *Russian Doll* (Netflix 2019–22), *Palm Springs* (Barbakow 2020) and Luis Antonio's short videogame *Twelve Minutes* (2021). Indeed, many videogames could be read as alternate histories of themselves anyway: every time a player replays a level, they run an alternate time loop against the pre-scripted programming of the game, triggering different responses and marginally different results.

The moments of fracture within timelines, where the path departs from the one not taken, are known by various names. Some scholarship uses the term 'Jonbar Hinge', a dated and unnecessarily obtuse reference to Jack Williamson 'The Legion of Time' (1938), which features a split between two possible realities caused by character John Barr. If this term was ever a useful shorthand, its moment has surely passed. Alternate history's fan community has an identity and sub-cultures independent of the mainstream sf community, with their own message boards and wikis expanding on alternate histories from other works or creating and critiquing scenarios of their own. Among these forums, the most common term in use is POD for 'point of divergence' (or, sometimes, 'departure') and is thus perhaps the preferable formulation for scholarship to employ.

Such fan communities create a striking quantity of alternate maps, flags and other visual paraphernalia to accompany counterfactual thought experiments. This preoccupation with territory and nationhood is also seen in the genre more widely. By far the most common location for a point of divergence in an alternate history is in the middle of a battle or war. This tallies with a particular (normally gendered) view of history in which certain battles are seen as key turning points in the narrative of civilisation, and certainly the chaos of battle offers ample opportunities for an enterprising mind to manipulate the variables and conditions to achieve a different result. Indeed, there is a connection between alternate history and recreational wargames stretching back to at least 1780, when German entomologist Johann Christian Ludwig Hellwig developed his *Kriegspiel* (literally, 'war game') by expanding the principles of chess to encompass features such as artillery, forts and terrain spanning over a thousand squares. Tabletop war games have since allowed professional soldiers and amateurs alike to recreate and 'replay' conflicts, both historical and fantastical in nature, to achieve different results. The idea that a small change might be all that is needed to alter the course of the battle, and thus the war, and thus history, is also much older than the modern fiction and captured in proverb at least as early as the seventeenth century: 'For want of a nail, the shoe is lost; for want of a shoe, the horse is lost; for want of a horse, the rider is lost' (Dent 1420). Reformulated countless time over the centuries, its most explicit use in alternate history is Robert Sobel's *For Want of a Nail: If Burgoyne Had Won at Saratoga* (1973), which presents itself as a work of historical nonfiction written in a world where the American Revolution was unsuccessful.

The most common war to receive an alternate history treatment is the Second World War (although in the US it may just be held in second place by the American Civil War). Given that it is so frequently mythologised as a war between good and evil, it offers an easily acceptable narrative cache for writers to lean into, or to work against. It also helps that the war is heavily documented and still saturates Anglo-American culture through the education system and through a glut of historiography and historical novels and films, since most alternate histories are at their most effective if the reader/viewer knows enough of the real history to appreciate the changes. Second World War alternate histories explore many scenarios, ranging from global to local or even individual repercussions. However, by far the most popular grouping coalesces around the question 'what if the Nazis had won?', also known as the 'Hitler Wins' scenario, which varies wildly in quality, tone, politics and form (Rosenfeld). Curiously, not all 'Hitler Wins' narratives are necessarily alternate history, or at least were not when first published: a body of work predating Germany's surrender in 1945 presents dystopian futures, including Katharine Burdekin's *Swastika Night* (1937) and Douglas Brown and Christopher Serpell's *Loss of Eden* (1940). While later alternate histories may share elements of their grim visions, these writers were not engaging with historical records and memory, but with their lived presents and possible futures. While they intend to warn what might come to pass, many alternate history writers intend to warn of what could yet be repeated.

Anglophone alternate histories concerned with the Second World War can very easily be read as conservative and celebratory, their depiction of fascist dystopias justifying our own history as the best possible option. Some, however, can also be read as critiques of their contemporary moment, including Roth's *The Plot Against America.* Not actually a 'Hitler Wins' narrative, it charts an alternate course for the US, taking cues from the political atmosphere of the 1930s and 1940s. In interviews about the novel, Roth made clear that the imaginative construction of an alternate history provided him a new set of tools with which to analyse a particular moment in American history and the national psyche: 'in the 30's there were many seeds for [fascism] happening [in America], but it didn't' (n.p.). The novel features a fictionalised version of the author as a child, an unhappy witness to the 1940 presidential campaign of famed aviator Charles Lindbergh as an isolationist candidate (the real Lindbergh was a spokesperson for the America First Committee). Ultimately, policies of neutrality become policies of tacit support for German expansion in Europe, and fascist and anti-semitic politics become progressively evident in the Lindbergh presidency. Despite the supposedly anti-war stance of this alternate US Government, many journalists and scholars wrote about the novel at the time as being an obvious allegory of post-9/11 America, particularly on issues of domestic policy. As one journalist noted, 'References to George W. Bush's America are impossible to miss' (Brownstein n.p.), with the novel's twentieth-century anti-semitism translating to twenty-first century Islamophobia and paranoia about the new 'Axis of Evil', and with George W. Bush resembling Lindbergh, especially in his willingness to don a US Air Force flight jacket for his infamous 2005 post-invasion of Iraq 'Mission Accomplished' speech. (See also Jo Walton's SMALL CHANGE trilogy (2006–8) of detective novels, adopts similar critiques of post-2001 British politics through its setting in a Britain which made peace with Nazi Germany after Dunkirk.) *The Plot Against America* received renewed attention a decade later, with the presidency of Donald Trump having demonstrated the fragility of American Democracy and its susceptibility to conservative populism. New editions were published, new articles written and in 2020 an HBO miniseries adaptation aired. That the novel can be seen as successful commentary on these three different periods demonstrates that just as sf about the future is not actually about the future, so too alternate history is not only about history but about the time in which it is being written and continues to be relevant as a result.

The point of divergence in Roth's novel (Lindburgh's electioneering) is contemporaneous with the novel's setting, but that need not always be the case. Building on sub-divisions in alternate history texts proposed by William Joseph Collins, Karen Hellekson posits the following variants:

> (1) The nexus story, which includes time-travel–time-policing stories and battle stories; (2) The true alternate history, which may include alternate histories that posit different physical laws; and (3) the parallel worlds story. Nexus stories occur at the moment of the break. The true alternate history occurs after the break, sometimes a long time after. And the parallel world story implies that there was no break – that all events that could have occurred did occur.
>
> (5)

So *The Plot Against America* is a nexus story, while Philip K. Dick's alternate history of Nazis in America, *The Man in the High Castle* (1962), is a true alternate history because it is set in an alternate 1962 decades after the Nazis and the Japanese Empire win the war. Philip José Farmer's 'Sail On! Sail On!' (1952) is also then a true alternate history because, although Columbus sets sail on schedule in 1492, the story results in him sailing off the edge of the world (the point of divergence being somewhere at the foundation of the universe when an Aristotelian model of physics, rather than our own, became reality). Frederik Pohl's *The Coming of the Quantum Cats* (1986) is a classic parallel world story in which alternate Earths wage war on one another, as is *Sliders* (Fox/Sci Fi 1995–2000), in which a group of lost travellers 'slide' between alternate Earths trying to get back to their original homes. The *STAR TREK* mirror universe, with its evil goatee-sporting Spock and fascistic Earth Empire, is a parallel world storyline, but the episode 'The City on the Edge of Forever' (1967), written by Harlan Ellison and D.C. Fontana, flirts with being a nexus story as Captain Kirk saves the life of a woman who goes on to prevent America's entry into the Second World War, thus unintentionally securing Nazi supremacy.

The minutiae of categorisation, neatly slotting different narratives into different boxes, is less interesting than the implications of the narratives themselves, but it does demonstrate the flexibility of the genre and its various permutations. Worth considering alongside these classifications are those narratives which we now have a tendency to read as alternate history after their moment in history has passed: *Swastika Night* has been mentioned but a case could be made to admit

George Orwell's *Nineteen Eighty-four* (1949) and Arthur C. Clarke's *2001: A Space Odyssey* (1968). If we are to examine such texts through the prism of alternate history, then the term 'palaeofutures' or 'alternate futures' seems appropriate. We can also consider conspiracy theory fiction, which suggests a shadow history of which we are unaware but which does not derail our existing known historical narrative. These 'secret histories' include the Vatican's conspiracy to obscure the bloodline descended from Jesus and Mary Magdalene in Dan Brown's *The Da Vinci Code* (2003) and the conflict between postal delivery companies in Thomas Pynchon's *The Crying of Lot 49* (1965).

Consideration should be given, too, to the question of what is being made alternate. Many of the narratives conventionally categorised as alternate history fall within a Western sphere of influence, deviating as they do from Western conceptions of history. No doubt other forms exist in world literatures, *alternate* alternate histories, perhaps, which broaden our thinking. By considering narratives both fictional and historical from outside Western hegemony, we can challenge our thinking about genre. Afrofuturism, for example, necessarily engages with Black history, both real and mythologized, and as Kodwo Eshun writes of countermemory:

> By creating temporal complications and anachronistic episodes that disturb the linear time of progress, these futurisms adjust the temporal logics that condemned Black subjects to prehistory. Chronopolitically speaking, these revisionist historicities may be understood as a series of powerful competing futures that infiltrate the present at different rates.
>
> (297)

One topic which an alternate history narrative cannot help but engage with, however fleetingly, is the nature of history itself. As texts which problematise and manipulate historical narratives, alternate histories are inevitable disruptors of historiography. No matter how conservative the intentions of the author, the very existence of a narrative which proposes that history could have been conducted in another fashion decentralises historiographic accounts by calling into question our existing history, not only in the way events unfolded but also, often, in the people upon whom the historical narrative focuses.

The central historiographic debate with which alternate history inevitably engages is that of great men versus structural forces. Structuring history around key biographies is not a modern phenomenon: Plutarch's *Parallel Lives* (second century CE) lays the foundation (at least in European literature), but the clearest and most powerful articulation comes in the nineteenth century from Scottish historian, essayist and racist Thomas Carlyle, who stated 'The history of the world is but the biography of great men' (17). In alternate history terms, changes in the biographies of such men would cause radical changes in major historical events. For example, in Kingsley Amis's *The Alteration* (1976), Henry VIII never becomes king because his elder brother Arthur produces an heir before his untimely death, blocking Henry from the line of succession. Consequently, the Reformation does not occur, and England remains a Catholic nation in the 1970s setting of the novel. The 'great men' need not be the celebrities of history, however, as demonstrated by Sophia McDougall's ROMANITAS trilogy (2005–11), which alters the fate of the Roman Emperor Pertinax, a figure likely unfamiliar to anyone without a classical education. By thwarting an assassination plot, McDougall's Pertinax lives 11 years longer than in reality and introduces reforms that stabilise the Roman Empire and enable it to continue intact into the twenty-first. Well-known or not, the greatness of the 'great men' the genre presents as shapers of history is sometimes questionable, but invariably they are men. The model, combined with the similarly rooted penchant for military history, preselects figures such as generals, kings and emperors, and while alternate histories do circulate around Elizabeth I, Victoria and others, female figures are in the minority, let alone people of colour.

Conversely, structuralist views have more in common with Marxist historiography and present a view of history in which individuals may affect the nuance of events, but the broadest brush strokes are determined by large and complex systems of political, social, economic and cultural factors set into motion long before they manifest in specific events. In Stephen Fry's *Making History* (1996), for example, Hitler's birth is prevented by time travellers, but it does not prevent the rise of authoritarian rule in Germany or the systematic extermination of Jews and other groups. Fry, taking his lead from Daniel Goldhagen's *Hitler's Willing Executioners* (1996), recognises that resentment about the First World War, the economic crisis of the Great Depression and rampant antisemitism, as well as the rise of fascism elsewhere in Europe, were not reliant on Hitler's birth.

However, not all alternate history fits easily into these two approaches. In Kim Stanley Robinson's *The Years of Rice and Salt* (2002), the bubonic plague in medieval Europe is even more deadly than in reality, resulting in the effective collapse of society and removing the European kingdoms from the world stage before intercontinental colonialism. Rather than focus on specific individuals from history, the centuries-long narrative asserts a reassessment about whose histories are privileged in historiography, and about the presumptions of superiority associated with European history and the imperial project. Similarly, Mary Robinette Kowal's LADY ASTRONAUT series (2018–) posits a more inclusive NASA, with female and minority astronauts flying missions far earlier than in reality. Kowal's point of divergence is Thomas Dewey beating Harry S. Truman to the presidency in 1948, but the largest changes are triggered by a meteorite which smashes into Chesapeake Bay and obliterates most of the Eastern Seaboard. This allows Kowal to sidestep many of the specific debates of historiographic detail in order to focus on the gender politics of spaceflight and an alternate space age in detail, more isolated from real history.

Alternate history's capacity to engage meaningfully in historiographic debate feels more relevant now than ever, and is reflected in recent trends for high-profile television series, including such adaptations as *The Man in the High Castle* (Amazon Prime 2015–9), *The Plot Against America* (HBO 2020) and Stephen King's JFK 2016 assassination novel *11.22.63* (Hulu 2016). Other original narratives include alternate space race drama *For All Mankind* (Apple TV+ 2019–), in which the Soviet Union lands on the moon first, and the Polish series *1983* (Netflix 2018), where the iron curtain remains intact and Poland is still a communist nation in 2003. The comic book superhero genre's long-standing interest in the narrative potential of alternate histories are now transferring to mainstream cinema and television. *Watchmen* (HBO 2019), cross-series events such as the 'Flashpoint' storyline in *The Flash* (The CW 2014–23), the tangled continuity of twentieth Century Fox's X-MEN films (2000–20), the SPIDER-VERSE trilogy (2018–) and the introduction of the multiverse as a key plot point in the MARVEL CINEMATIC UNIVERSE's Phase Four onwards, including the animated series *What If...?* (Disney+ 2021–), all demonstrate an increased appetite for this sort of plot. They all exist against the backdrop of a heavily editorialised 'culture war', in which history is a significant battlefield, whether over the toppling of slaveowner statues in British port towns, the presence of the Confederate flag in American iconography or the constructedness of history (which conventional education and popular historiography has rarely acknowledged beyond the aphorisms that it is 'written by the victor').

The moment seems both ripe and vital for radical alternate history that captures this moment of reassessment to interrogate national heritages. Bernadine Evaristo's *Blonde Roots* (2008), set in a world with different geography, may stretch the credibility of what some are willing to label alternate history, but its powerful narrative of Black slavers trading White bodies across the middle passage to African colonies in the Americas cannot be denied. Colson Whitehead's *Underground Railroad* (2016; television adaptation Amazon Prime 2021) imagines the eponymous network as a literal infrastructure of trains, tunnels, stations, and all, running beneath the slaveholding US. More interested in effect than cause, these books lack a clear point of divergence and are perhaps more akin to historical fantasies, but they use the tools of alternate history to engage with and dismantle our own historical timelines, casting the institutions of slavery and colonialism in new lights in an attempt to distil new meaning from the horror.

Similarly, Nisi Shawl's *Everfair* (2016), a more conventionally structured alternate history, posits the creation of an independent African nation in the nineteenth century when the Fabian society buy large tracts of Congolese land from King Leopold of Belgium, instead of investing the money in the foundation of a university (the London School of Economics). The colony becomes a refuge for victims of colonial abuses of power in Central-Western Africa, and a disruptor of European colonial power in the region. Shawl was inspired to write it, and the short story upon which it expands, by 'the author of *King Leopold's Ghost*, Adam Hochschild, and [...] the brave women and men who stood against the tyrant' (383). Alternate history allows Shawl to reclaim the narrative of Hochschild's historical work and offer tribute to resistors, while demonstrating that, liberated from sabotage by colonial powers, African nations were just as capable of flourishing into modernity. *Everfair*, with its airships and mechanised prosthetics, is also a strong example of an alternate history, which crosses into steampunk. Beginning as an alternate history subgenre, steampunk has branched out into wider aesthetic-based narratives removed from requiring historical reference points. It extends Victoriana by imagining vast expansions of steam-based technology rather than them being usurped by electricity and oil. Because of its historical roots, steampunk has an unfortunate tendency to glorify the colonial era, although some writers work to actively counter this. *Everfair* is a rare example of steampunk set in Africa with African protagonists, and as such it is also an important intervention in that related-but-separate sub-genre.

Another recent example of the radical potential of alternate history is Analee Newitz's *The Future of Another Timeline* (2019), which combines with a time travel plot to make explicit the sense that historiography is a battle of ideas and ideologies. The novel features competing groups of time travellers who move into the past to alter the timeline in accordance with their beliefs. The protagonists, a group known amongst themselves as the 'daughters of Harriet', take their inspiration from Harriet Tubman, who in their timeline became the first female US Senator (women having received the vote, alongside men of colour, in the fifteenth amendment). They travel through time to improve society for women and LGBTQ+ communities in the present, placing them in direct opposition to a group of incel-like anti-choice men who model themselves on nineteenth century moralist and anti-abortion campaigner Anthony Comstock. The novel demonstrates that social change is not unidirectional, and that even when victories are won battles must continue to be fought not just for the expansion but also the maintenance of rights. This is evoked most poignantly in the repeated refrain 'I remember abortion being legal in the United States' (time travellers retain their memories of alternate versions of their present when they return from the past). Newitz's novel is the latest in a line of feminist sf interested in the shaping of time and history that includes such powerful antecedents as Joanna Russ's *The Female Man* (1975) and Marge Piercy's *Woman on the Edge of Time* (1976), each demonstrating that the control of history is a way of controlling the present and the future.

Alternate history is now more popular and mainstream than ever. This comes at a time in which Western societies are revisiting the mistakes and missed opportunities of the past, whether in the fights for justice on the grounds of race, gender or sexuality, or in confronting such challenges as climate change and wealth inequality. Alternate history offers a powerful set of tools to storytellers, political thinkers and others, which can be employed to help us come to terms with the past, rethink our present and change the future.

Works cited

Beard, Mary. *SPQR: A History of Ancient Rome*.Profile, 2015.

Brownstein, Gabriel. 'Fight or Flight'. *The Village Voice* (21 September 2004). www.villagevoice.com/arts/fight-or-flight-7139189

Carlyle, Thomas. *On Heroes, Hero-Worship and the Heroic in History*. Adelaide UP, 2010.

Carr, E.H. *What is History?* Penguin, 1961.

Dent, Susie, ed. *Brewer's Dictionary of Phrase & Fable*. 9th edition. Chambers, 2013.

Eshun, Kodwo. 'Further Considerations on Afrofuturism'. *The New Centennial Review* 3.2 (2003): 287–302.

Ferguson, Niall. 'Virtual History: Towards a "Chaotic" Theory of the Past'. *Virtual Histories: Alternatives and Counterfactuals*. Ed. Niall Ferguson. Picador, 1997. 1–90.

Gallagher, Catherine. *Telling It Like It Wasn't: The Counterfactual Imagination in History and Fiction*. U of Chicago P, 2018.

Hellekson, Karen. *The Alternate History: Refiguring Historical Time*. Kent State UP, 2001.

Roberts, Adam. 'Napoleon as Dynamite: Geoffroy's *Napoléon Apocryphe* and Science Fiction as Alternate History'. *Sideways in Time: Critical Essays on Alternate History Fiction*. Ed. Glyn Morgan and C. Palmer-Patel. Liverpool UP, 2019. 31–45.

Rosenfeld, Gavriel D. *The World Hitler Never Made: Alternate History and the Memory of Nazism*. Cambridge UP, 2005.

Roth, Philip. 'The Story behind "The Plot Against America"'. *New York Times* (19 September 2004). www.nytimes.com/2004/09/19/books/review/19ROTHL.html

Shawl, Nisi. *Everfair*. Tor, 2016.

34
ANIMAL STUDIES

Anna Maria Grzybowska

Human–nonhuman relations are of a turbulent kind: harmonious, caring, affectionate at times; at others, violent, exploitative, vicious. Sometimes nonhuman presence is acknowledged, occasionally even cherished. Sometimes, quite the opposite. Until the nonhuman turn that coincided with the turn of the millennium (Grusin), other animals' lives have been largely overlooked even within academia, unless considered in terms of their usefulness to the human species, in both material and abstract terms. This was not, however, an unfortunate oversight, nor an innocent carelessness. In fact, the repression of nonhuman subjectivity is one of the processes foundational to the expansion of human civilisation and the formation of human identity. With its quixotic human–animal binary, anthropocentric humanism's failure to acknowledge nonhuman animals is, paradoxically, 'as great as their presence in our daily lives' (DeMello 5), and Animal Studies (AS), a field that emerged in the late twentieth century, addresses this lacuna by bringing nonhumans into the foreground. Nonetheless, AS is more than a study of 'the animal' per se; as Margo DeMello argues, it enquiries into the complexity of animal – both human and nonhuman – interactions, particularly nonhuman animals' embedment in human sociocultural realities. To parse the intricacies of interspecies relationships, AS scholars engage with the academic output of various disciplines, including biology, cognitive ethology, environmental studies, psychology, sociology, history and philosophy, as well as cultural and literary studies. The primary aim of this interdisciplinary approach is to thoroughly understand nonhuman entanglements within human systems of meanings and, considering the role of speculation in human engagement with other animals, the interface between AS and sf is a source of invaluable insight. In essence, as Joan Gordon suggests, 'animal studies often feels quite "science-fictional"' itself ('Animal' 332).

To understand the nature of human speculations on nonhumans, it is necessary to briefly revisit the history of their role within human civilisation. Nonhumans' presence has been systematically pushed into the background, if not virtually erased from most human narratives of the world. Yet (animal) history encompasses all kinds of species entangled in the networks of interdependence, woven by each encounter, within each environment. Roughly ten thousand years ago, domestication revolutionised both human and nonhuman animal lives. Usually considered an improvement in the quality of human life, domestication was a violent mechanism of confining nonhumans and denying their freedom of self-determination, exploration and bond formation and the fulfilment

DOI: 10.4324/9781003140269-37

of their other physical and psychological needs. Since then, animal enslavement has not only contributed to a great acceleration of civilisational development but also given impetus to various forms of oppression, profoundly shaping the logic of capitalism, with the animal body being 'the surface on which capitalist modernity first perfected many of its characteristic techniques of alienation and rationalised violence' (McCorry and Miller 4). With time, the institutionalisation of exploitation sublimated into the animal-industrial complex, which encompasses the meat, dairy and egg industries, as well as the use of animals for research, clothing and labour, and human interest in nonhumans for entertainment purposes, including the pet industry. Likewise, the majority of other animals have been embroiled in, or affected by, human worlds indirectly: they have, for instance, suffered the consequences of wars, colonialisms and general anthropogenic ecological destruction. Ultimately, all animals share the past, the present and – as sf can sometimes help us envision – a future.

Simultaneously, though in arbitrary proportions, 'the question of the animal' has percolated within philosophical thought, from Aristotle through René Descartes to Donna J. Haraway. Reflecting the tumult of interspecies co-existence, perception of 'the animal' is intrinsically conflicted, shaped and reshaped to either justify human's oppressive treatment of other animals or acknowledge their autonomy. In accordance with the logic of domestication, nonhuman animals have often been considered inferior to humans, supposedly lacking in reason, according to Aristotle, and feelings, according to Descartes, an argument that paved the way to the widespread abuse of animals' lives, habitats and dignity. Against this background rose the violent political fiction of the human, promulgated by anthropocentric humanism and its apotheosis of the human expression of consciousness (Weitzenfeld and Joy). Nonetheless, while human entitlement to other animals' lives is still the dominant attitude, alternative ways of thinking have been on the rise. In response to the fixation on nonhuman's cognitive abilities, Jeremy Bentham famously stated, steering the course for the contemporary animal advocacy movement, 'the question is not, Can they *reason* nor, Can they *talk*? but, Can they *suffer*?' (Bentham 236). Drawing on Bentham's ideas, Peter Singer's *Animal Liberation* (1975), one of the foundational texts for AS, popularised the term 'speciesism'; along with it came other conceptualisations of 'the animal' within human culture, including Jacques Derrida's 'carnophallogocentrism', Carol J. Adams's 'absent referent' and Melanie Joy's 'carnism', all of which aim to expose humans' non-reflective and fallacious view of other animals. A similar objective guides posthumanist questioning of human subjectivity, in for example Cary Wolfe's *Animal Rites* (2003), Donna J. Haraway's *When Species Meet* (2008) and Rosi Braidotti's *The Posthuman* (2013). Moreover, alongside AS in the twenty-first century developed the discipline of Critical Animal Studies (CAS), 'an academic field of study dedicated to the abolition of animal exploitation, oppression, and domination' (DeMello 5). Unlike AS, which does not state the ethical treatment of animals as its primary goal, CAS actively challenges the structures of speciesism through its engaged scholarship and opposes the 'theoretical vivisection' performed by AS, namely, the overshadowing of the nonhuman's harrowing experience within the human civilisation by 'jargon-filled, elitist theories' and 'elaborate wordplay' insensitive to living beings (Nocella II et al. xxiv). In light of this insight, it is crucial to acknowledge that theorising animals comes with responsibility for beings who could never oppose, debunk or respond in any other way to claims made about/for/with them. Respectful engagement with animals requires deep and consistent self-reflection and, equally important, awareness of their experiences in the human world, for the representation of the animal is not – and never was – apolitical.

One of the spaces for such self-reflection are speculative texts in general, and sf in particular. With the abundance of texts devoted to the exploration of various subjectivities, sf plays a pivotal role in challenging human ontology. In this respect, the genre deeply interlaces with posthumanism, harnessing imagination for revamping, reshaping and essentially revising the human, not only through technological enhancement but also through blurring the boundary between the human and the whole ecosystem of beings. According to Wolfe, the posthumanist project involves recontextualising granted modes of human experience 'in terms of the entire sensorium of other living beings and their own autopoietic ways of "bringing forth a world"' (xxv); with this objective in mind, combining the theoretical apparatuses of posthumanism and AS with sf has a lot to offer. These 'autopoietic ways', however, are beyond human comprehension and thus they constitute an 'inevitable paradox of animal studies' (Gordon 'Animal' 338). For even if their impact on the world (including its human component) should not be underestimated, they are too alien and too sophisticated to be dissected – despite the literal subjection of other animals to this treatment – and our nature too inescapably human to pursue such a fundamentally anthropocentric endeavour without reinforcing speciesist hierarchies. Decentralising human perception is, nonetheless, crucial for building multi- and inter-species communities or for 'staying with the trouble' and 'living-with and dying-with each other potently' on a damaged Earth, in which sf plays a crucial role as 'a method of tracing, of following a thread in the dark' (Haraway *Staying* 2–3).

Particularly interesting in this regard are sf narratives that explore other animals' perspectives. As Steven Shaviro notes, 'Fictions and fabulations can provide us with a sort of feed forward [...] of those mental processes that are not available to introspection' (16). This 'feed forward' is conceivable through sf's 'emotional and situational' method, which situates itself beyond mere rational cognition, 'connecting how and what we know to *how we feel*, and to *how we might act*: to *what is it like*?' (15 italics in the original). In other words, sf engages in 'discognition', that is, 'something that disrupts cognition, exceeds the limits of cognition, but also subtends cognition' (10–11), an exploration of sentience. When inviting its audience to *become* more than human, the sf narrative contributes to disrupting, exceeding and subtending the granted modes of human experience. Significantly, Gilles Deleuze and Félix Guattari employed 'becoming' as 'a verb with a consistency all its own' (Deleuze and Guattari 239), for their theory of 'becoming-animal' concerned with deterritorialising identity, described by Sarah Dillon as 'a shift from a logic of being to a logic of becoming' (146). To further represent the liminality of human/animal interface, Gordon introduces the term 'amborg', which encompasses 'becoming' and 'suggests in "ambi" an organism that can be both human and animal, an ambiguous organism; an organism about which we feel ambivalent; and perhaps an ambitious organism, spanning nature and culture; a new way of organizing the world, an amborganization' ('Gazing' 191). Certain aspects of this amborganisation can be explored through temporary speculative 'becoming-animal' in sf narratives, which express our longing for understanding other animals and ourselves through them, epitomising the ineluctable interdependence. For example, this exploration of subjectivity can take the form of a role reversal, as in Carol Emshwiller's *The Mount* (2002) and Don LePan's *Animals* (2010), or of morphing into the animal, as in Emshwiller's *Carmen Dog* (1988) and Kathleen Ann Goonan's *Queen City Jazz* (1994). Yet representing animals in fiction often involves a certain degree of anthropomorphisation, which may either emerge as 'a form of narcissistic projection that erases boundaries of difference' (Weil 19) or foster understanding of the other animals' condition and experience. To strengthen the latter effect, Kari Weil suggests a 'critical anthropomorphism', grounded in awareness of our limitations in understanding others' experiences. Thus, while we may never learn 'What is it like to be a bat?' (Nagel), nor what are bat's 'autopoietic ways of "bringing forth a world"' (Wolfe xxv), we can – and, for the sake of reframing multispecies coexistence, *should* – explore less pointed propositions, such as 'What it *could be like* to be a bat' and engage critically with our responses, with speculation as our ally in relating to the animal other.

When considering speculations on amborganisation, sf video games deserve particular attention as a medium offering not only a vicarious experience of but also an immersion in imaginative nonhuman perspectives. While other animals or animal-like creatures often serve as part of the landscape, a mere background for the action proper, sf games have a long history of breaking this barrier and exploring nonhuman subjectivity, including titles such as *Aliens Versus Predator* (Rebellion/Fox 1999), which allows the player to direct both monsters. Moreover, sf and games both encapsulate the speculative essence; as Cameron Kunzelman argues, 'games can provide platforms for us to take actions in speculative contexts as well as create actions that allow us to do moment-by-moment speculations', prompting us to 'gain experience outside of the regular conditions of our lives' (53). Games' 'mechanics of speculation' (4), as defined by Kunzelman, allows the player to immerse in the otherwise inaccessible experience of other animals: to efficiently function within the interactive speculative reality, one is required to temporarily unlearn the rules of the human world and adhere to those governing the world of the virtual nonhuman. One may, for instance, explore 'what it could be like' for other animals to live in the remnants of human civilisation and fight for survival, as in *Tokyo Jungle* (Sony 2013), or to be a fox looking for her abducted cub in a world ravaged by the human-induced ecological collapse, as in *Endling: Extinction is Forever* (Herobeat/HandyGames 2022).

Essentially, games' technological mediation creates a potentially constructive space for decentring the human perspective, spurring the process of amborganisation. In video games, this process occurs on two elemental levels: performative and interactive. Consider *Stray* (BlueTwelve/Annapurna 2022), a game that follows the story of an unfortunate cat who falls down a hole leading to a forgotten underground city inhabited by humanoid robots. Separated from her cat-friends who stayed above the ground, the eponymous stray needs to find her way around and out of the sunken city, navigating a dystopian cyberpunk world with the help of a buzzing insectoid robot, a carrier for the consciousness of a long-gone human scientist who once lived there. In this arrangement, the player *performs* the cat, enacting pre-programmed actions and their consequences, both following and building her story. The cat herself is a silent character (unless one makes her meow loudly) with an array of behavioural options that mimic typical feline mannerisms; for instance, the player can choose to knock objects off shelves or scratch various surfaces using their cat-avatar's paws. Confronted with the strangeness of the posthuman city, the cat's behavioural familiarity is the main anchoring point, joining the player together with the cat in a quest to explore the unknown. Nonetheless, the player is simultaneously looking *as* the cat and *at* the cat, *interacting* with her at all times: despite the merger of the player's and cat's individuality in the fictional world, there is always a certain distance, a certain voyeurism involved. Ultimately, the player 'becomes-animal' by performing the other animal and interacting with them, never being but always becoming, a process infused with speculation.

Along with *Stray*'s cat who invites us to decentre our perception for a brief moment, there is another famous cat who profoundly sparked a change in human understanding of other animals. In *The Animal Therefore I Am* (2008), Derrida recognises *being seen* by his companion, '*truly a little cat*' (6 italics original), and acknowledges her unique point of view, her absolute alterity. The significance of this encounter lies in its humbling quality of stepping off the human pedestal and meeting – and being met by – the other species without feeling threatened by their otherness. With its long-established tradition of alien encounters, sf is perhaps the most suitable of the genres to work through the challenge of meeting the Other, which, considering the limitations of 'becoming-animal', offers even more in terms of understanding interspecies communities. Sf narratives often do not confine themselves to mere passive encounters with the Other but open our imaginations to the possibility of actively establishing contact and of interspecies communication. In *When*

Species Meet, Haraway accuses Derrida's writing of 'failing a simple obligation of companion species', namely, being *curious* about the Other and inquiring further how to respond to them in return: 'Incurious', she writes, 'he missed a possible invitation, a possible introduction to other-worlding' (20). Unlike Derrida, sf authors have accepted this invitation time after time, thoroughly exploring more-than-human interactions. For example, Adam Roberts's *Bête* (2014) opens with a dialogue between a cow and the farmer who is about to kill her, and Cordwainer Smith's 'On the Gem Planet' (1965) includes a telepathic interview with an immortal horse longing for death.

Sf is a prolific ground for (re)imagining human interactions with other animals otherwise inaccessible to first-hand experience, yet still deeply entangled within and dependent upon human societies. For instance, a number of narratives engage with marine animals, including Frank Schätzing's *The Swarm* (2004) and Nnedi Okorafor's *Lagoon* (2014), both of which explore a merger of alien and nonhuman sentience in opposition to human species. Similarly, Ray Nayler's *The Mountain in the Sea* (2022) invites the reader to a curious exploration of a human–octopus encounter. In the near future, marine biologist Dr Ha Nguyen joins a team consisting of a security agent, Altansetseg, and the world's first android, Evrim, to research the octopi of the Con Dao Archipelago. Gradually, they discover that their cephalopod subjects demonstrate greater intelligence than any other known nonhuman species, as indicated by the octopi's own elaborate system of symbolic communication. Ha, a devoted scientist who is also deeply concerned for the octopi's welfare, strives to establish meaningful communication without violating their integrity as beings. Nonetheless, the human–octopi relationship is not an idyllic one. Ha hypothesises that the high intelligence of octopi has evolved through adapting and readapting to the violence humans inflict on the oceans; as Evrim contemplates: 'These are the heroes of the sea. And who are we? We are their *nemesis*. We are the enemy' (154). Unsurprisingly, while at the core of Ha's motivation lies curiosity, the octopi do not share her enthusiasm: their initial message, as decoded by the researchers, is '*Get out of my house*' (180). Guarding the barely researched vastness of the ocean, the octopi epitomise the other animal responding to human presence, more specifically, to decades of flagrant violation of marine ecosystems, 'scraping the oceans of protein for centuries' (60). If, as Stacy Alaimo notes, 'many figurations of marine species as alien or the seas as outer space are fantasies induced by *environmental guilt* or [...] a wish for a timespace before the Anthropocene' (159 *my emphasis*), *The Mountain in the Sea*'s cephalopods compel the reader to face that guilt by facing the gaze of the octopus, and outwardly reject the human, setting boundaries for co-existence: '*Octopus habilis* watches us, watching them. Studies us, studying them. *Octopus habilis*? Or *Octopus sapiens*?' (Nayler 438). Yet '*Octopus sapiens*' is still uncannily human, tailored to soothe the human need for familiarity, or to meet – often faulty – criteria for 'intelligence'. This tendency has its roots in the long history of not acknowledging other ways of being in the world and not accepting that which cannot be elucidated. While attempts to imagine animals entering human systems of communication may be futile – as Ludwig Wittgenstein famously claimed, 'If a lion could speak, we could not understand him' (223) – the novel's main premise is not to represent the human–octopi communication per se, but rather to encourage curiosity, to explore the possibility of acknowledging other worlds parallel to our own and, essentially, to fulfil the 'simple obligation of companion species'. In the end, the octopi of Con Dao and humans do not establish a meaningful exchange of symbols but they do seem to achieve something far more valuable: mutual recognition. After the last encounter Ha has with one of the octopi, Evrim asks 'What did it show you?'; Ha responds, 'Myself [...] It showed me myself. It knew me. And I knew it. She knew me. And I knew her' (437). And with this knowledge the characters continue to pursue their research, to *respond* to *being seen*.

However, sf's exploration of animal entanglements transcends localised exchanges of subjectivities. The genre's worldbuilding affordances facilitate reflection upon nonhumans' role in human societies. Questions of other animals' placement in speculations are crucial to unpacking relationality under capitalism, serving as a litmus paper for our extrapolative capabilities. If the estimated number of species oscillates around 8.7 billion, which ones (do not) figure in those visions? If our relationships with other animals take various forms, which ones (do not) get represented? If nonhumans play such a crucial role in our daily existence, what does it mean that we (do not) include them in visions of the future? Since throughout history other animals have been rendered merely 'selectively visible' (Ortiz-Robles 9), these questions concern the quality of our interactions with reality, particularly our awareness of what 'living-with and dying-with' actually entails within the reality of the animal-industrial complex; for humans are animals, too.

Development of the complex itself is inextricably linked with technological advancement, and the two reinforce each other. Sherryl Vint directly connects this process to the origins of sf: 'Animals are an important but often invisible presence in the very constitution of scientific knowledge and thus also central to the conditions informing the emergence of the industrialized, scientifically oriented Western society that gave birth to sf' (182). Strikingly, there is a negative correlation between the progress of industrialisation and the recognition of other animals' role in the society, especially the violation of their psychological and bodily integrity. For instance, Timothy Pachirat explored this 'politics of sight' in the context of industrialised slaughter. As he noticed, despite the prevalence of mutilated animal bodies, 'the contemporary slaughterhouse is "a place that is no-place," physically hidden from sight by walls' (3) or 'a zone of confinement' (4). This, in turn, detaches us from violence that underlies the operating of our civilisation, with 'distance and concealment as mechanisms of power in modern society' (3). That being said, other animals' presence in sf which, more or less, imagines the trajectory of further civilisational development, proves to be particularly significant: it can be a reversal of the dominant 'politics of sight' promulgated by the technological advancement, a renegotiation of the dynamics between animals and technology. For example, speculative narratives have the potential to breach the slaughterhouse's 'zone of confinement', as in Agustina Bazterrica's *Tender Is the Flesh* (2017), which follows the story of an abattoir worker who manages the supply and distribution of the 'special meat', that is, the processed human flesh that became a delicacy after a virus rendered other animals inedible.

One of the most significant sf texts in this regard is the food industry satire *Okja* (Bong 2017). The eponymous Okja is a super-pig bred in a peculiar experiment. Claiming that they are attempting to solve the looming global food-shortage, the Mirando Corporation announces a contest for raising the best specimen of the newly-discovered super-pig, a non-GMO and environmental-friendly potential livestock species. Twenty-six super-piglets are placed with local farmers around the world, who are expected to breed them for ten years in harmony with the sustainable, traditional practices of their cultures. After the designated time, a delegation from Mirando visits the super-pigs and chooses the one that will clinch the title of 'the best pig' and be brought back to the US as a display for the launch of their meat products. Raised in the mountains of South Korea by a poor elderly man and Mija, his young granddaughter, Okja is announced the winner and reclaimed by the Mirando; in exchange, her caretakers are awarded a gold figurine of a pig. Mia, however, refuses to let Okja go and embarks on a rescue journey to New York City, but she is not the only would-be saviour. Okja is also followed by the Animal Liberation Front, which aims to expose the horrific breeding practices of the corporation, as well as its duplicity in manipulating consumers (the super-pigs were genetically engineered by Mirando). Eventually, traumatised Okja is transferred to the slaughterhouse and seconds before she can be killed, Mija rescues her by buying her back with the figurine. Mija's success is, nonetheless, bitter-sweet: as the reunited friends leave the slaughterhouse side by side, they pass by thousands of super-pigs cramped behind an electrified fence, awaiting their death.

With its representation of the animal intended for slaughter, *Okja*, too, counters the dominant 'politics of sight', inviting a reflection upon interspecies relationships in the context of capitalist exploitation. Although Mija emanates innocence proper to a child and cares for Okja regardless of her 'animal status', their relational dynamic is defined by capital: Okja is not saved, but bought, and thus remains property. While the story has many layers, it is its science-fictional component that drives the narrative; namely, the fact that Okja is a product of science. This positions the film within a long tradition of sf narratives engaging with uplifted – genetically or otherwise 'enhanced' – animals, such as H.G. Wells's *The Island of Doctor Moreau* (1896), Olaf Stapledon's *Sirius* (1944), Pierre Boulle's *Planet of the Apes* (*La Planète des singes*; 1963), David Brin's UPLIFT series (1980–98), Lawrence M. Schoen's BARSK series (2015–8) and Jeff VanderMeers's *Borne* (2017). While 'uplift' is usually associated with granting other animals a wide range of cognitive abilities proper to humans (particularly speech), *Okja*'s super-pigs' only major cognitive alteration seems to have been making them capable partners in emotional exchanges with humans. Still, as an alteration in itself, the super-pigs' and other animals' imaginative modifications raise questions of human responsibility for the ethical boundaries between (imaginative) technological development and its influence on nonhumans.

All of the above explorations, from becoming to responding and further, are in conversation with one another, clashing, diffusing and merging. Spurred by internal tension, the human–nonhuman interface is constantly in flux, reflecting the complexity of co-existence and living with others whose subjectivity will never be fully comprehended. However, settling into this uncertainty and deepening our understanding, and thus building more harmonious interspecies communities, is certainly within our ability. Through imagining more-than-human worlds, sf can support us in developing these competencies, for 'it allows us to be amborgs, both to gaze at the other and to gaze through the eyes of the other' (Gordon 'Gazing' 192).

Works cited

Alaimo, Stacy. 'The Anthropocene at Sea: Temporality, Paradox, Compression'. *The Routledge Companion to the Environmental Humanities*. Ed. Ursula K. Heise, Jon Christensen and Michelle Niemann. Routledge, 2017. 153–61.

Bentham, Jeremy. *An Introduction to the Principles of Morals and Legislation*. W. Pickering, 1823.

Deleuze, Gilles and Félix Guattari. *A Thousand Plateaus: Capitalism and Schizophrenia*. Trans. Brian Massumi. U of Minnesota P, 1987.

DeMello, Margo. *Animals and Society*, second edition. Columbia UP, 2021.

Derrida, Jacques. *The Animal That Therefore I Am*. Ed. Marie-Louise Mallet. Trans. David Wills. Fordham UP, 2008.

Dillon, Sarah. '"It's a Question of Words, Therefore": Becoming-Animal in Michel Faber's *Under the Skin*'. *Science Fiction Studies* 113 (2011): 134–54.

Gordon, Joan. 'Animal Studies'. *The Routledge Companion to Science Fiction*. Ed. Mark Bould, Andrew M. Butler, Adam Roberts and Sherryl Vint. Routledge, 2009. 331–40.

——. 'Gazing across the Abyss: The Amborg Gaze in Sheri S. Tepper's *Six Moon Dance*'. *Science Fiction Studies* 105 (2008): 189–206.

Grusin, Richard A., ed. *The Nonhuman Turn*. U of Minnesota P, 2015.

Haraway, Donna J. *Staying with the Trouble: Making Kin in the Chthulucene*. Duke UP, 2016.

——. *When Species Meet*. U of Minnesota P, 2008.

Kunzelman, Cameron. *The World Is Born from Zero: Understanding Speculation and Video Games*. De Gruyter Oldenbourg, 2022.

McCorry, Seán and John Miller. 'Introduction: Meat Critique'. *Literature and Meat Since 1900*. Ed. Seán McCorry and John Miller. Palgrave. 2019. 1–17.
Nagel, Thomas. 'What Is It Like to Be a Bat?'. *The Philosophical Review* 83.4 (1974): 435–50.
Nayler, Ray. *The Mountain in the Sea*. Weidenfeld & Nicolson, 2022.
Nocella II, Anthony J., John Sorenson and Atsuko Matsuoka. 'Introduction: The Emergence of Critical Animal Studies: The Rise of Intersectional Animal Liberation'. *Defining Critical Animal Studies*. Ed. Anthony J. Nocella II, John Sorenson, Kim Socha and Atsuko Matsuoka. Peter Lang, 2014. xix–xxxvi.
Ortiz-Robles, Mario. *Literature and Animal Studies*. Routledge, 2016.
Pachirat, Timothy. *Every Twelve Seconds: Industrialized Slaughter and the Politics of Sight*. Yale UP, 2011.
Shaviro, Steven. *Discognition*. Repeater, 2016.
Vint, Sherryl. *Animal Alterity: Science Fiction and the Question of the Animal*. Liverpool UP, 2010.
Weil, Kari. *Thinking Animals: Why Animal Studies Now?* Columbia UP, 2012.
Weitzenfeld, Adam and Melanie Joy. 'An Overview of Anthropocentrism, Humanism, and Speciesism in Critical Animal Theory'. *Defining Critical Animal Studies*. Ed. Anthony J. Nocella II, John Sorenson, Kim Socha and Atsuko Matsuoka. Peter Lang, 2014. 3–27.
Wittgenstein, Ludwig. *Philosophical Investigations*. Macmillan, 1953.
Wolfe, Cary. *What Is Posthumanism?*. U of Minnesota P, 2010.

35
BIOPOLITICS

Sherryl Vint

Biopolitical theory refers to a set of concepts about the nature of power and governance which Michel Foucault began to explore in his work on how power and knowledge were entangled in a new modern mode of governance that emerged in Europe from the late seventeenth century. He first articulated these ideas through the concept of 'biopower', a technique of governance that focuses on the biological bodies of the populace through individualising techniques of discipline that cultivate distinct modes of subjectivity and through collectivising operations of power that sort valued life from life deemed disposable. Such measures are rationalised as being necessary for the 'health' of the overall body politic. The most notable philosophers to build upon Foucault are Giorgio Agamben, who suggests that sorting of life into 'proper' and 'improper' expressions of the human is the foundation of the entire Western philosophical and political tradition, and Roberto Esposito, who articulates a paradigm of immunitary power by which he seeks to transform the Agamben's thanatopolitical thought into a communitarian, affirmative biopolitics. Other thinkers, most prominently Sylvia Wynter, Achille Mbembe and Jasbir Puar, draw attention to the intersections of biopolitical power with European colonial projects, pointing to the violence of racism as key to understanding how biopolitics operates to segregate and differentially nurture people conceptualised through biologically essentialist frameworks.

Biopolitical theory seeks first to describe – and thus make visible and available for critique – the ways biological life and political power are entangled in modernity. This chapter focuses on the overlaps between these core thinkers' work and sf motifs. Rather than attempt to engage with the full range of debates in biopolitical theory or outline significant areas of disagreement and divergent among biopolitical theorists, this chapter suggests ways that biopolitical theory informs sf representations and indicates how the estrangements of sf can provide a distinct vantage point through which to respond to the operations of biopower. It emphasises intersections between biopolitical theory and sf as a site of popular theorising, including: reflections on the nature of being human and what it might mean to be post- or non-human; the possibilities for agency, ethics and community for a species reimagined outside of Western modernity; and the impact of science and technology, particularly related to surveillance and bodily augmentation. The biopolitical theorists discussed below share a sense that, by mapping the reality of how governance of the body permeates modern society, we can find ways to resist or shift or elude such power, thereby insisting

DOI: 10.4324/9781003140269-38

on another ethics of the human and its communities. In this way, biopolitics as a descriptive theory, like the critical tradition of sf, is invested in the emergence of counterhegemonic knowledges and ways of living.

Just as biopolitical techniques have become dominant in governance, so sf has become more ubiquitous in Western modernity. Unsurprisingly, then, there are many sites of convergence between biopolitical theory and sf, including surveillance technologies controlling access to public space, medical devices monitoring and perhaps policing one's habits and health, fusions of our social lives with media apps that alter the realties we inhabit, and the integration of automation and AI into workplaces and homes. The impact of Darwinian theory that H.G. Wells interrogates as a concern with devolution in *The Time Machine* (1895) and *The Island of Doctor Moreau* (1896) embodies the degree to which the biopolitical life of the human species was central to state concerns with productivity, competitiveness and narratives of progress. More recently, the proliferation of sf concerned with women's bodies and the future of reproduction – from tales of authoritarian control of fertility, such as Meg Ellison's Road to Nowhere trilogy (2014–9) and Bina Shah's *Before She Sleeps* (2018), to those of technological control of women's bodies, such as Hilary Jordan's *When She Awoke* (2011) and Christina Dalcher's *Vox* (2018) – reflect how controversies over access to reproductive choice, especially to abortion, have become key political issues of our day.

In the wake of the US Supreme Court's *Dobbs* decision (2022) that overruled the earlier *Roe v. Wade* (1973), which had interpreted abortion access as a constitutionally protected matter of bodily autonomy, such narratives will undoubtedly flourish. They can be understood as products of a biopolitical framework in which governance of biological matters, such as birth- and death-rates, is central to state power, and of a context in which social reproduction is complexly bound up with ethno-nationalist politics panicked about demographic shifts in Western states (Vint). The preoccupations and effects of biopolitics always extend beyond the body it takes as its object of governance. It is concerned not just with controlling and shaping bodies but also the knowledges and institutions that secure the political order, which differentially values distinct ways of being human. This somewhat abstract nexus of power and knowledge became starkly legible during the Covid-19 pandemic, evident in much higher rates of infection and mortality in communities of colour and in the balancing of personal health with economic need that mandated blue collar 'essential' workers endured greater risk of exposure than white collar employees in the knowledge economy. Biopolitical theory charts how such techniques of governance came to be 'common sense' and offers tools to contest or replace this order.

Foucault and the order of biopolitical governance

The first hints of Foucault's biopolitical theory are evident in *The Order of Things* (1966; English trans. 1970) when he asks, what are the consequences for modern knowledge systems when humanity takes itself as both the agent and the object of enquiry? Tracing the origins of the 'human sciences' (biology, linguistics, economics), he detects a shift in the culture of knowledge that differentiates antiquity from modernity; from this, he theorises the entanglement of power relations, the possibilities for knowledge production and the creation of specific ways of being human. One consequences of this shift is that 'life itself' becomes a concept studied separately from its specific instantiation in living organisms. What emerges when 'man' constitutes himself as an object of knowledge, Foucault argues, is the dark or shadow side of unthought, the unconscious, that which is 'exterior to him and indispensable to him' (*Order* 326). When we make ourselves the central object of knowledge, we cut ourselves off from the rest of the material world; yet human existence remains dependent upon, indeed is continuous with, this 'exteriority'. There is thus a constitutive blindness to humanity taking itself as both subject and object of knowledge.

At the end of *The Order of Things*, Foucault suggests that a renewal of philosophy is possible if we would cease to take ourselves as the starting point of all knowledge: humanity emerged from a certain 'arrangement of knowledge' (157) and should the framework and assumptions change, something else would emerge. He developed this insight across several volumes concerned with moments of epistemic shift related to how bodies are disciplined into specific styles of being. This operation of power/knowledge on subjectivity and embodiment opened up his enquiry to questions of how and why governance begins to focus on the biological life of the population, on the management of life at the level of conduct and on ensuring certain metrics (longevity, productivity, reproduction) are met. Embodiment in this context connotes not just the simple fact of having a body but also the larger political framework by which certain kinds of bodies and bodily practices are normalised or criminalised via the dominant culture, a perspective which has played a major role in the development of queer theory and disability studies.

Foucault's interest in biopolitics emerged in relation to medicine, and the field of biomedicine often takes Foucault as its starting point. Nikolas Rose fuses Foucauldian concepts with social theory to study biotechnology and medicine, especially changing regimes for managing life through genetics, synthetic biology and pharmacotherapy. One result of this fusing is a shift away from sovereignty expressed through the power to 'make die or let live' (Foucault *Society* 240), as in executions, and toward strategies to 'make live and let die' (241), that is, toward policies and institutions that foster life in particular configurations and toward distinct ends, while withdrawing resources and support elsewhere. Foucault's later work exploring modes of state governance in greater detail was presented in his Collège de France lecture series from 1975–84, which were only posthumously translated and published in 2004–17, delaying Anglophone scholarship's engagement with this aspect of his thought.

Foucault's earliest work elaborating these concepts focused on methods by which the state disciplined or normalised bodies, often through medical discourses, and he investigated sexual and gender norms as a particular site through which the state seeks to regulate conduct, but the living body always exceeds and disrupts set categorisations. This work aligns with and has been influential on queer theory, which sees queerness not merely as a sexual preference but as a mode of living and being that refuses bourgeois family values and the domestic reproduction of labour power that Marxist feminism also critiques (Federici; Ferguson; Hennessy). Foucault's theorisation of how knowledge systems, the institutions built from them and hegemonic power systems intersect to authorise or prohibit certain ways of living finds concrete expression in multiple works of queer sf that challenge heteronormative orthodoxy. For example, Melissa Scott's *Shadow Man* (1995), written in dialogue with contemporary nonbinary activism, explores what happens when humans from Earth – rigidly attached to a binary gender system, albeit one that allows for heterosexuality and homosexuality – encounter a colony that has been isolated for generations. The rate of intersex births is higher on the colony world, a side effect of a drug used to facilitate interstellar transit, and, in this context, the colonists developed a social order that recognises five genders and nine sexual orientations. A political thriller plot, in which challenging sexual dogma is viewed as a threat to established power structures, reveals the degree to which sex/gender identity is always bound up with state power and the degree of violence that can emerge in the name of defending an abstract concept of appropriate human life.

The management of life at the level of the biological also gives rise to what Foucault terms 'modern racism' by which the citizenry of a state comes to understand themselves in terms of ethnic homogeneity. Thus conflicts become matters of protecting the 'health' of the state by repelling or conquering the invader, who is often deemed insufficiently human: wars are fought in the name of defending or preserving an abstract 'humanity', resulting in a *bio*politics dedicated to the protection of life frequently being expressed via *thanato*political methods, that is, by killing or '*disallow*[*ing*] to the point of death' (*History* 138) that life which does not align with the ethnoracial human ideal: 'entire populations are mobilized for the purpose of wholesale slaughter in the name of life necessity: massacres have become vital' (137). It is this strain of Foucault's thought – focused on discourses articulating not only a boundary between humans and other organisms, but also one within humanity that divides 'real' from 'sub' human exemplars – that Agamben centres as he theorises the biological segregation of life from its multifarious embodiment as the core of modern political thought.

Agamben and biopolitical fractures of modernity

While Foucault examines regimes through which modernity produces specific bodies and subjectivities, Agamben's interest lies more firmly in the life and death aspects of governance. *Homo Sacer* (1995; trans. 1998) argues that, from their very beginning, Western political systems rely on a biopolitical distinction between humans recognised as citizens/subjects existing within the scope of state protection (*bios*) and those who are excluded from this political definition of the human, existing merely as bare life (*zoe*), exposed to violence without legal cover. Agamben emphasises the degree to which we understand human community primarily as a juridical concept, not as a species identity. Just as the sovereign is above or outside the law, a constitutive exception to the law's function, the *homo sacer* (the scapegoat or sacrificial figure) is below the law, included in the polity solely by its exclusion from the category of the human, an outside figure against whom violence is not a crime. Such constitutive exceptions, Agamben warns, mean that the liberal state is founded not on the protection of life, as its biopolitical rhetoric would proclaim, but instead on a disavowed lethal violence. Thus, the liberal polity can never fully include all humans because Western philosophy relies on a metaphysics that ontologically splits people into 'real' and 'sub' human categories, *bios* and *zoe*. For Agamben, biopolitical power is always power *over* life.

The Nazi concentration camp exemplifies his theory of biopolitical governance, but his focus on European experience overlooks the degree to which colonialism is a more pervasive expression of biopolitical segregation. For Agamben, the camp is central because it demonstrates that the state can at any time withdraw or suspend the protections supposedly offered under frameworks of human rights. Thus, despite discourse about the body politic and the populace as a unified people, Western political systems function as if 'what we call "people" were in reality not a unitary subject but a dialectical oscillation between two opposite poles': the 'whole political body' exists always in tension with 'the subset of the people as a fragmentary multiplicity of needy and excluded bodies [...] of the wretched, the oppressed, and the defeated' (*Homo* 177). This split is rooted in the human/animal boundary that sets human life apart from other kinds of being, a framework explored in *The Open* (2002; trans. 2004), which provides a critique of what he will later call the 'shipwreck' (*Use* xxi) of Heideggerian metaphysics of subjectivity that requires the human to recognise itself as separate from other life. He calls this philosophical tradition the 'anthropological machine' (*Open* 33) and strives to articulate a philosophy premised on stopping its operation so that people might begin to understand themselves in ways that do not rely on repressing the 'animal' elements of their embodiment, thereby disrupting the conditions out of which a biopolitics based on the *bios*/*zoe* distinction might emerge. In his later work, synthesised in *The Use of Bodies* (2014; trans. 2016), he offers the term 'natural life' (263) to describe this possibility for living outside the structures of biopolitical modernity: bare life is what remains, abjected, after the anthropological machine, 'presupposing the not-truly-human' (45), produces and separates 'the human' from it on the basis of some special capacity; natural life is our capacity for organic living, should such segregations never have been conceived at all.

Agamben is useful for exploring sf that foregrounds other kinds of subjectivities and challenges the distinction between human and other life. Although he is not specifically interested in animal subjectivity, his emphasis on the human/animal boundary as the foundation of the racialised segregation of humanity into valued and neglected sites of vitality illuminates sf that disrupts or rewrites the divisions between humans and other species. Understanding how the category of 'the animal' functions as a technique for making ethical distinctions in modernity helps us see how environmental exploitation is entangled with colonial racial categorisations. It also provides insights into the extractive politics of a warming planet through which a better life for those in privileged areas comes at the expense of conditions for thriving in 'zones of expulsion' – water and land transformed into lifeless wastelands by extractive industries – and spaces deadened by climate change; in all such places, the possibility for life, human and otherwise, has been enervated, 'an expulsion of bits of life itself from the biosphere' (Sassen 2).

Sf often explores terrain similar to Agamben's critique of the Western 'human' as a technology that enables colonial and environmental violence, depicts other models for being human in ways that privilege 'natural life' over *bios*, and explores how the 'anthropological machine' is imbricated in colonial projects of racialised worldmaking. For example, N.K. Jemisin's BROKEN EARTH trilogy (2015–7) shows how power over people with specific kinds of embodied capacities (orogenes, who can shape geology) are bound up with ethical discourses that essentialise embodied appearance (racialised ways of attributing qualities to peoples based on bodily morphology or skin or hair colour). The power the orogenes possess to manage violent seismic disruptions makes their skills essential to the stable functioning of the social order, yet political power has unfolded in such a way that they are ostracised and violently controlled by the dominant state. Throughout the trilogy, Jemisin shows the anthropological machine in action: while the racial categorisations of her fiction do not map directly to the ones we have inherited through modernity, they function similarly, essentialising bodily features/capacities into ontologised classifications so that some people (the Sanze) operate under the sign of *bios* while the orogenes are relegated to the bare life of *zoe*. By connecting structures of racial discrimination to matters of resource monopolisation, Jemisin starkly reveals how biopolitics distributes vitality unevenly in the service of economic ends.

Esposito and the autoimmune disorder

Building on Agamben's contention that the division of valued from disposable life epitomises biopolitical governance in modernity, Esposito investigates how the mechanisms proclaimed to foster life seem inevitably to turn to thanatopolitical projects of eliminating 'improper' life. *Immunitas* (2002; trans. 2011) and *Bios* (2004; trans. 2008) restructures biopolitical thought through the figuration of immunity, focusing on its political meaning before it came into medical use to connotate resistance to infection. He characterises the modern state as suffering from an 'immunity disorder' by which 'the protection of life' turns into 'its potential negation' (*Bios* 116). To reorient our understanding of biopolitical techniques, he moves away from understanding the immune system as being designed to protect life by negating what threatens it, and towards a model by which immunity is best served by regular exposure to otherness. Contra earlier metaphors of medical immunology, which envisioned preserving health by eradicating all 'foreign' pathogens, recent immunobiological work suggests that the immune system is better understood as a permeable membrane that remains healthy through interaction with difference (Fishel). Esposito's affirmative biopolitics, then, seeks to disrupt the autoimmune disease of thanapolitical modernity, which is characterised by an 'excess of immunitization' (*Bios* 9).

The opposite of excess immune response is community, an ideal Esposito links to the political origins of the concept of immunity as an exemption from the *munus*, that is, from the mutual entanglements that foster community. *Munus* originally referred to 'an office – a task, obligation, duty (also in the sense of a gift to be repaid)', while its opposite, *immunis*, 'refers to someone who performs no office [...] Disencumbered, exonerated, exempted [...] from the *pensum* of paying tribute or performing services for others' (*Immunitas* 5). The exaggerated biopolitical hygiene of modernity, then, stands in the way of more communal political forms. Esposito shares Agamben's view that the biopolitical state functions through dehumanisation and expulsion, but where Agamben sees this as the only form the biopolitical can take, Esposito suggests the *munus* offers other possibilities: 'If *communitas* binds its members together in a mutual commitment, *immunitas* exonerates them from this burden. Community refers to something general; immunity, on the contrary, points to the privileged particularity of a condition exempted from the common obligation' (*Philosophy* 175). In *Third Person* (2007; trans. 2012) and *Persons and Things* (2014; trans. 2015), Esposito is interested in a different metaphysics of subjectivity that does not rely on liberal notions of 'rights' that must be recognised and granted by the state, a recognition that 'applies only to the upper part, which is rational or spiritual in nature, exercising its dominion over the remaining area' (*Third* 11). He wants a biopolitics that values life at the level of the vital body, and he begins to articulate this through metaphysics of the impersonal or the 'third' person, a category that lies between the I/you, subject/object binary that defines Western thought. The Western concept of the person rests on an 'assumed superiority of the personal over the impersonal: only a life that can provide the credentials of personhood can be considered sacred or qualitatively significant' (*Third* 2). Similar to Agamben's interest in 'natural life' before or outside of the *bios/zoe* distinction, Esposito's third person offers a way of framing identity that does not rely on the abjection and expulsion of qualities of being human as a living, embodied organism.

Ruthanna Emrys's *A Half-Built Garden* (2022) offers a vision of the messiness and promise of a more inclusive polity that demonstrates how we might envision such an affirmative biopolitics more concretely. This first-contact novel depicts the barriers that must be overcome for a divided humanity to develop diplomacy with an alien species who have come to save us from ourselves. The aliens believe humanity is doomed if it stays on Earth, due to the irreversible effects of climate change, and are so convinced of their assessment that they plan to use force if people refuse to leave. Human protagonist Judy, a member of 'Watershed' coalition governing structures, who has dedicated her life to restoring ecological balance, refuses to give up on the possibility of planetary life. She lives according to the precepts of the Dandelion Manifesto of 2043, which describes how humanity once recognised nature as the '*first power*' but was misled into believing that '*spirit*', '*law*' or '*money*' gave humanity a greater power to escape nature: only with wisdom does humanity return once more to acknowledging nature as the '*fifth power*' that must work in tandem with humanity's techne: '*Power is ours, but not ours alone, and we can create harmony with the world*' (1). The alien culture – a fusion of two species with distinct morphologies who have learned how to create cooperative society – is matriarchal. It prioritises discourse over displays of strength and values those (of any gender) who are mothers as diplomats most likely to develop solutions that enable a viable future for all.

Judy's family consists of her wife and their child, and another couple and their offspring: all co-parent the children, and sexual relationships are not the only ties that create family. Their practice of dispute resolution within the family finds an analogue in larger structures of participatory democracy that shape the Watershed, modelling the entanglements between embodied ways of living, domestic arrangements, vectors of biopolitical governance and the plasticity of human 'nature'. Judy and her family represent one way of being human among others: remnants of nation-state governance also persist, alongside corporation-based enclaves premised on metrics of productivity. As Emrys charts the various negotiations and misunderstandings, the novel repeatedly emphasises the connection between embodied experiences and impulses with political forms and possibilities: both humans and aliens must learn to respect their diverse bodily proclivities as core to questions of governance, and to cultivate ways of shaping their 'nature' towards greater community within heterogeneous ways of being people and with greater mutuality between such subjects and the rest of the living world. The result is a provisional, 'half-built' better future, which embodies Esposito's embrace of *munus* as the scaffold from which to develop an affirmative biopolitics.

Biopolitical elision, decolonial critique

Scholars working in decolonial frameworks have critiqued and supplemented biopolitical classifications to more fully account for the ways in which colonialism and its racist underpinnings shaped Western ideas of the human and Western political frameworks for inclusion and exclusion. Achille Mbembe's 'necropolitics' places greater emphasis on those the state chooses to 'let die', suggesting that such spaces of neglect are more crucial for understanding how such a politics of governing life produces concrete results (Gerry Canavan theorises this idea as 'necrofuturism' in sf). For Mbembe, it is not the concentration camp but the colony that, as the original and permanent site of necropower, defines the modern state: that is, the fostering of life in the colonial centre is only made possible by the genocidal suppression of life in the colonies. Colonial methods of governance took the form of an 'expulsion of humanity altogether' (169) for designated subjects. The aim was not to foster the lives of slaves, nor simply to let them die; rather, they were valuable 'kept alive but in a *state of injury*' (170) as a source of free labour-power without civic rights. Mbembe foregrounds the relation of dominance inherent to biopolitical techniques, arguing that biopolitics is always therefore an imperial formation. He reminds us that the sovereign power to 'make die' (Foucault *Society* 240), which Foucault suggested was less central with the rise of the bureaucratic state, remained the principal technique in the colonies.

Sylvia Wynter focuses on the ways that biopolitics produces the Western idea of the human, revising Foucault's work to address the centrality of racialisation as a nexus of knowledge/power/institutionalised-truth. She argues that a narrow, ethnocentric, patriarchal and White version of the human, which she calls Western bourgeois man or 'ethnoclass Man' (261), 'overrepresents itself as if it were the human itself' (260). Contra Foucault's emphasis on the epistemic break constituted by new formations of knowledge, Wynter emphasises what is preserved: in this case a structure of Otherness, first oriented to those who do not embrace Christian doctrine and thus are infidels, outside the community, and later attached to those deemed 'dysselected' (267) by evolution as inferior, not-quite human species. Western modernity invents itself as the only 'genre' of the human and simultaneously invents 'the indigenous peoples of the Americas as well as the transported enslaved Black Africans as the physical reference of the projected irrational/subrational Human Other to its civic-humanist, rational self-conception' (281–2). Where Agamben and Esposito attempt to dismantle Western philosophy in order to remake it, Wynter looks outside it, suggesting that in the lifeways of those deemed the 'irrational/

subrational Human Other' we find living alternatives to shortcomings of the human produced by the anthropological machine.

Jasbir Puar focuses on ongoing sites of colonial oppression, particularly Palestine. She argues that biopolitical power produces three outcomes, not merely life or death, but also debility as a state of bodily injury and social exclusion produced by economic and political structures. Debility is 'a product – not a by-product, but a deliberate product – of exploitative labor conditions, racist incarceration and policing practices, militarization, and other modes of community disenfranchisement' (65). This biopolitical strategy, which she names 'the right to maim', operates at the intersection of biopolitics and racial capitalism, 'a source of value extraction from populations that would otherwise be disposable' (xviii). By incorporating sites of colonial exclusion and oppression into the framework of biopolitical theorising, Puar shows that biopolitical power over life operates differently than it seems to if we theorise only from within European experience. She also highlights ways that biopolitical power can navigate the contradictions of continuing to operate in genocidal colonial modes while rhetorically conceding to liberal 'human rights' frameworks that posit a universal human subject. By subjecting colonised bodies to endemic conditions of debilitation, rather than to the direct use of lethal force, the biopolitical state can simultaneously extract value from such bodies, expose them to premature death through neglect and maintain a pretence that its operations are in the service of protecting life.

These decolonial corrections to biopolitical theory insist on the centrality of the afterlives of slavery (Hartman) to the ongoing operations of biopolitics today. Similar concerns are reflected in such sf as Rivers Solomon's *An Unkindness of Ghosts* (2017) and Tochi Onyebuchi's *Goliath* (2022). The former depicts a generational starship stratified by deck and thus reflecting how structural racism shapes labour markets from the period of slavery through to today. Solomon's richly imagined cultures for each deck depict different allocations of resources, living space and kinds of work among peoples who are sorted by skin colour, recapitulating the history of colonial labour exploitation. Each deck develops different dialects, knowledge systems and modes of comportment, reflecting the entanglements of state power and human subjectivity that lie at the heart of biopolitical thought. The neuro-atypical and queer protagonist also points to an other 'genre' of the human who experiences and interprets the world outside hegemonic frameworks, a source of hope in this otherwise grim future. Onyebuchi depicts a future American northeast, long abandoned by the mostly White people of economic privilege who avoided the ravages of climate change by migrating to orbital colonies. Despite state abandonment, the protagonists of colour who remain in the neighbourhood find ways to persist and build something better. Yet the improvements they make come to be seen as valuable by those above who long for an Earth-based lifestyle, and some settlers begin to return and initiate a process of gentrification, which the protagonists both resist and critique. One notes, for example, that the municipality, having failed to provide water supplies for years, turns them back on for settlers. The settlers' investment in protecting their property leads to an increased police presence, which culminates in a police shooting of a young Black man. The novel thus embodies the politics of debilitation.

Biopolitical governance shapes modernity and its uneven distribution of opportunities to thrive or decline, issues ever more urgent on a planet where climate change and wars over resources have made many regions inhospitable for continued life. The multiple crises over human migration, and the racist panics about borders they fuel, are but one manifestation of how Western governance, because of its foundation in a split between valued and disposable life, must be annulled. Sf can help us imagine what comes next.

Works cited

Agamben, Giorgio. *Homo Sacer: Sovereign Power and Bare Life*. Trans. Daniel Heller-Roazen. Stanford UP, 1998.
——. *The Open: Man and Animal*. Trans. Kevin Attell. Stanford UP, 2004.
——. *The Use of Bodies*. Trans. Adam Kotsko. Stanford UP, 2016.
Canavan, Gerry. '"If the Engine Ever Stops, We'd All Die": *Snowpiercer* and Necrofuturism'. *Paradoxa* 26 (2014): 1–26.
Emrys, Ruthanna. *A Half-Built Garden*. Tor, 2022.
Esposito, Roberto. *Immunitas: The Proection and Negation of Life*. Trans. Zakiya Hanafi. Polity, 2011.
——. *Bios: Biopolitics and Philosophy*. Trans. Timothy Campbell. U of Minnesota P, 2008.
——. *A Philosophy for Europe: From the Outside*. Trans. Zakiya Hanafi. Polity, 2018.
——. *Third Person: Politics of Life and the Philosophy of the Impersonal*. Trans. Zakiya Hanafi. Polity, 2012.
Federici, Silvia. *Caliban and the Witch: Women, the Body, and Primitive Accumulation*. Autonomedia, 2004.
Ferguson, Roderick. *Aberrations in Black: Toward a Queer of Color Critique*. U of Minnesota P, 2004.
Fishel, Stefanie R. *The Microbial State: Global Thriving and the Body Politic*. U of Minnesota P, 2017.
Foucault, Michel. *A History of Sexuality: An Introduction*, volume 1. Trans. Robert Hurley. Random House, 1990.
——. *Society Must Be Defended: Lectures at the Collège de France, 1974–1976*. Trans. David Macey. Ed. Mauro Bertani and Alessandro Fontana. Picador, 2003.
——. *The Order of Things: An Archaeology of the Human Sciences*. Vintage, 1994.
Hartman, Saidiya. *Scenes of Subjection: Terror, Slavery and Self-Making in the Nineteenth Century*. Oxford UP, 1997.
Hennessy, Rosemary. *Profit and Pleasure: Sexual Identities in Late Capitalism*. Routledge, 2000.
Mbembe, Achille. *Necropolitics*. Trans. Steven Corcoran. Duke UP, 2019.
Puar, Jasbir. *The Right to Maim: Debility, Capacity, Disability*. Duke UP, 2017.
Rose, Nikolas. *The Politics of Life Itself: Biomedicine, Power and Subjectivity in the Twenty-First Century*. Princeton UP, 2009.
Sassen, Saskia. *Expulsions: Brutality and Complexity in the Global Economy*. Harvard UP, 2014.
Vint, Sherryl. *Biopolitical Futures in Twenty-First Century Speculative Fiction*. Cambridge UP, 2021.
Wynter, Sylvia. 'Unsettling the Coloniality of Being/Power/Truth/Freedom: Towards the Human, After Man, Its Overrepresentation – An Argument'. *CR: The New Centennial Review* 3.3 (2003): 257–337.

36
CLIMATE CRISIS AND ENVIRONMENTAL HUMANITIES

Melody Jue

You wake up one morning and notice a couple of texts from your friends about watching a movie later. Maybe they suggest the dystopian desert of *Mad Max: Fury Road* (Miller 2015), the flooded spectacle of *Waterworld* (Reynolds 1995) or the icescapes of *Snowpiercer* (Bong 2014). Hollywood loves an environmental disaster, spectacularly thrown on screen. But as you move on to check the news, maybe your stomach drops as you read about the latest superstorm, the record drought, the increasing acidification of the ocean. Or perhaps the view out your morning window is eerily red from the latest wildfire, making the entire day feel like sunset. You wonder if the air will be breathable today, and how much the experience of weather is part of a worsening climate pattern. Sitting with a pang of anxiety (Ray), you are not sure if you want to watch that sf movie anymore. You wonder if you are living it.

Among my students, the experience and anticipation of the climate crisis is a common entry point for thinking about sf and the environmental humanities. Although sf is often thought of as something that could happen in the future, the effects of climate change are *now* and have been long in motion. As human societies continue to pour carbon dioxide emissions into the air, setting records year after year, there is the sense that the material of Hollywood disaster movies is becoming closer to our present reality. The genre of climate fiction (or 'cli-fi') is sometimes categorised under the genre of 'speculative fiction' to emphasise this connection to the near future, in contrast to the broad umbrella of sf, which includes themes like intergalactic space exploration or alien contact. Although cli-fi was coined in 2007, many climate fictions predate the term. From the melted ice caps of J.G. Ballard's *The Drowned World* (1962) and the polluted air of John Brunner's *The Sheep Look Up* (1972) to the fiery landscapes of Octavia E. Butler's *Parable of the Sower* (1993), sf has a long history of inhabiting moments of climate disaster (Canavan and Robinson; Kaplan).

Yet cli-fi does not just *represent* climate change – the ways that climate change is described in reports and media often draw upon the vocabulary of sf itself. For example, calling the climate crisis a 'new normal' echoes Darko Suvin's argument that sf involves confronting 'a new set of norms' ('Poetics' 384). Bill McKibben suggests calling this changed, less comfortable world 'Eaarth', to emphasise how humans have altered the climate so dramatically that it might as well be an alien planet. Others argue that climate change marks the onset of a new geologic epoch called the 'Anthropocene' shaped by the agency of humans and marked by evidence in the

DOI: 10.4324/9781003140269-39

strata, such as traces of radiation from nuclear tests (Chakrabarty; Crutzen). Some point out how Anthropocene discourse, intended to draw attention to a rupture between the past climate and the present, characterised as science-fictional, also appropriates or obscures Indigenous ideas (Todd) and presumes a masculine subject ('the age of man') that passes as universal (Alaimo). Others use such variant terms as Capitalocene, Plantationocene or Chthulucene, the alternative prefixes emphasising different agents of causation (Haraway).

However, collapsing climate change and sf presents its own crisis, since one of the defining characteristics of the genre is the necessary distancing effect of estrangement. Consider how science fictions anticipate something yet to be realised or introduce a fictional world that is noticeably, even disturbingly, different from our own. Although science fictions can be set at any point in time (past or future), what makes them distinctive is their ability to produce a sense of estrangement (what Bertolt Brecht called *Verfremdungseffekt*). Istvan Csicsery-Ronay, Jr hones in on the distancing effect of estrangement, describing sf as 'characterized by two linked forms of hesitation, a pair of gaps' (3): the space between an imaginary future and its actualisation, and the ethical and social implications of a possible change. So if the context of reading matters – if sf is structurally dependent on a gap between the real world of the reader and the imaginary world of the fiction – what happens when the distance between these collapses, as it does with climate fiction? Does climate fiction become a variety of realistic fiction – and, in doing so, change how we think about literary realism (Ghosh)?

Although this question remains unresolved, the variable contexts of reading remind us that sf is not always a property of books, but also lives in discourse, distributed across various media and conversations. We encounter forms of science-fictional and speculative thinking when news headlines forecast new patterns of drought and historically severe wildfires. We participate in speculative thinking when we explore the National Ocean and Atmospheric Administration's 'Sea Level Rise Viewer', which features an interactive map for visualising the effects of up to six feet of sea level rises. Governments, businesses and militaries generate science-fictional writing when they write reports ('grey literature') that anticipate the effects of climate change in ten, fifty or a hundred years on international relations, economic stability, security and conflict (Thomas). Conversely, literary sf sometimes *pretends to be* grey literature: a mayday, a report, a transcript. A good example of this 'found document' genre is Margaret Atwood's two-page story, 'Time Capsule Found on a Dead Planet' (2009), addressed to an alien visitor to Earth, now devoid of life due to the capitalist obsession with profit rather than planetary care – a harrowing fable that presages the ecological collapse in her MaddAddam trilogy (2003–13).

Ecological sf also proliferates across media forms, including video games and augmented reality, involving players directly in the navigation and exploration of climate-changed worlds and science-fictional ecologies. Eschewing a strict division between artificial and natural, Alenda Y. Chang's *Playing Nature: Ecology in Video Games* (2019) shows how ecology and environmental science offer useful ways to understand game worlds such as 'Altered State', where players can explore the possible implications of climate change for California, or the 32-week alternate reality game (ARG) *World Without Oil*, whose slogan 'play it before you live it' urges people to contemplate a world after peak oil. Yet even as we contemplate ecological isues and learn from these games, they contribute to carbon emissions through the high consumption of electricity for gameplay and streaming (Maxwell and Miller). The material conditions of video gaming depend on all kinds of ecological elements that enable smooth functioning, including energy cost, rare earth metals and undersea fibre-optic cables (Yusoff; Starosielski). Critical games like *Phone Story* draw attention to these ecological costs, showing how our technology consumption depends on Chinese sweatshop labour and generates e-waste, topics dramatised in Chen Qiufan's cyberpunk

Waste Tide (*Huangchao*; 2013; trans. 2019). Gulfs of inequality exist between those who consume technology and those who produce it, those who enjoy higher levels of security and those who bear the full force of climate disasters in their many forms.

Awareness of the uneven effects of climate change has shaped many humanities conversations about environmentalism and what it means. One common criticism of American environmentalism is when it advocates for the protection of nature by separating it from the sphere of human culture. For example, the creation and conservation of national parks depended on the forced eviction of Indigenous Native Americans from those very parks – one example of how defining 'nature' as an untouched landscape without people has had violent effects and requires a deeper examination of histories of settler colonialism (Spence). Such themes are deftly taken up in Rebecca Roanhorse's short story about virtual environments, 'Welcome to Your Authentic Indian Experience™' (2017), where the most 'authentic' Indian experience turns out to be total dispossession. However, the word 'environmentalism' can still mean many other things beyond protecting a separate, pristine nature: advocating for clean water, arguing against the use of agricultural toxins like DDT (Carson) or protesting the harmful effects of oil drilling and hydraulic fracturing, such as at Standing Rock, connected to conversations around Indigenous futurism (Dillon; Estes).

When the focus of environmental activism shifts to include multiple forms of inequality and harm that affect specific populations, such work is often described as 'environmental justice' (EJ). Robert Bullard defines EJ as the principle that, 'all people and communities are entitled to equal protection of environmental and public health laws and regulations' (495). David Naguib Pellow adds that EJ involves imagining 'a transformative vision of what an environmentally and socially just and sustainable future might look like, at the local, regional, national, and global scales' (4). Thus, Pellow shows how speculative thinking and the imagination of possible futures is key to the EJ movement – and its extension in 'climate justice' (CJ), a key matter of concern in the United Nations Conference of the Parties (COP) meetings that attempt to negotiate international action on climate change. CJ in particular has been a focal point of youth activism, perhaps most visibly with Greta Thunberg and her weekly 'Skolstrejk för klimatet'/'School strike for climate' (Thunberg), as well as *Juliana vs. United States*, a lawsuit alleging that the government's actions that contribute to climate change are violating the rights of future generations to life, liberty and property.

Indeed, a number of scholars, activists and journalists see the crisis of climate change as an opportunity to imagine and redesign more socially just futures. Naomi Klein argues that climate change should be 'everything change', an opportunity to reduce inequality, strengthen democracy and rebuild economies. *After Oil* (2016), collaboratively written by the Petrocutures Research Group, highlights the importance of envisioning what it would be like to live in a post-oil future, while adrienne maree brown's *Emergent Strategy: Shaping Change, Changing Worlds* (2017) takes inspiration from Octavia E. Butler's sf to encourage the active imagination of more socially just and equitable futures. What seems of utmost importance across these many activist texts is the utopian imagination, or 'ecotopian' imagination, inspired by Ernst Callenbach's *Ecotopia* (1975) and later taken up by projects like Matthew Schneider-Mayerson and Brent Ryan Bellamy's *The Ecotopian Lexicon* (2016). As Fredric Jameson, commenting on Kim Stanley Robinson's MARS trilogy (1992–6), wrote 'What is Utopian becomes, then, not the commitment to a specific machinery or blueprint, but rather the commitment to imagining possible Utopias as such, in their greatest variety of forms' (*Archaeologies* 217); that is, not the 'representation of radical alternatives' but 'the imperative to imagine them' (416).

The more you read about climate fiction, the more you will encounter the following wish: if only we could write better (or more effective) climate fiction, then people would take climate change more seriously, and this would catalyse the movement. In this way, climate fictions tend to exhibit a directional politics (the desire to achieve specific political aims). This is not a bad goal in itself, but when climate fiction is connected to the desire to influence or legislate collective human behaviour, it ceases to exist on the same plane as other open-ended fictions: it now circulates as a biopolitical mechanism, closer to the genre of public policy. Yet consider Suvin's observation that, in sf 'The aliens – utopians, monsters, or simply differing strangers – are a mirror to man just as the differing country is a mirror for his world. But the mirror is not only a reflecting one, it is also a transforming one, virgin womb and alchemical dynamo: the mirror is a crucible' (*Metamorphoses* 17). There are many ways of holding a mirror up to the world, and ecological science fictions that (at first glance) are not directly about the climate can also be powerful and transformative mirrors, playing with unfamiliar configurations of species, gender, sexual orientation, reproduction, symbiosis and parasitism, labour, class and more.

Sf studies calls the effort to vibrantly describe the ecological and social character of a possible future or place 'worldbuilding'. It is the hinge that connects climate fiction with a longer history of ecological sf, involving the exploration of extra-terrestrial planets, alien ecologies and other life forms – as well as their entanglements with resource extraction, anthropocentrism and settler-colonialism. Worldbuilding, which involves imagining, designing and creating a unique sense of environment and culture, is especially useful to describe the detailed texture of Kim Stanley Robinson's THREE CALIFORNIAS trilogy (1984–90), the cyberpunk border and water crisis of *Sleep Dealer* (Rivera 2008) and the spectacular lifeforms of *Avatar* (Cameron 2010) – novels and films in which it would be reductive to pin down a *single* novum amidst the *multiple* ecological details. Indeed, Carl D. Malmgren has even argued that 'the generic distinctiveness of SF lies not in its story but in its world' (259). In place of worldbuilding, scholars sometimes use the variation 'worlding', where changing the noun 'world' into a verb describes the work of bringing a world into being. Although the term 'worlding' was introduced in Martin Heidegger's *Being and Time* (1927), it has since been conceptually elaborated in post-colonial contexts. Gayatri Chakravorty Spivak cautioned against the 'worlding of a world on a supposedly uninscribed territory', where the imperialist project 'had to assume that the earth that it territorialised was in fact previously uninscribed' (*Post-Colonial* 1). This is a helpful caution for the study of sf, given the colonialist tendencies of the genre to explore new worlds, often without consideration of who already lives on these worlds. For example, Octavia E. Butler calls the obligation to repay a world's original inhabitants 'paying the rent' in 'Bloodchild' (1995), in which she imagines human refugees on an alien planet establishing a tenuous compromise with the indigenous T'lic, a centipede-like species that requires mammalian hosts for its young.

Ecological sf can be useful for thinking about questions of planetary scale (Heise *Sense*). A famous example is Stanisław Lem's *Solaris* (1962), which imagines a sentient ocean planet that thwarts all attempts at scientific measurement and understanding. As one scientist remarks, 'Our instruments had intercepted minute random fragments of a prodigious and everlasting monologue unfolding in the depths of this colossal brain, which was inevitably beyond our understanding' (22). Taking a different sentient planet as her subject, Ursula K. Le Guin's 'Vaster than Empires and More Slow' (1971) imagines a plant-planet, World 4470, encountered by a misfit group of space explorers. Satirising tales of space heroism, it dramatises intense interpersonal conflicts between the crew, who do not realise they are walking on a single organism. The story foreshadows this realisation: 'Subdued by the incredible silence, the three surveyors set up their instruments and collected their samples, three viruses twitching minutely on the hide of an unmoving giant' (192). When World 4470 finally senses the humans, it radiates a strong sense of fear, prompting one crewmember to comment: 'To a forest [...] we might appear as forest fires. Hurricanes. Dangers. What moves quickly is dangerous, to a plant. The rootless would be alien, terrible' (209). What does cognition look like from the point of view of a planet? In engaging with this question, Le Guin is in conversation with philosophical concepts like the Nöosphere and Gaia Theory, which were heavily influenced by science of the biosphere and cybernetics (Clarke; Lovelock; Vernadsky).

It is important to remember that what literary scholars have written about the environment has often been in conversation with the history of the natural sciences. For example, the German naturalist Ernst Haeckel coined the term 'ecology' in 1866 as a way of describing the relations of the organism and environment, inclusive of inorganic elements and relationships to other organisms (Egerton 222). However, at the time Haeckel was writing, most scientific interest focused on species identification and taxonomy (natural history). It was not until 1935 that Arthur Tansley coined the term 'ecosystem', which later guided studies on lakes – specifically, how lakes and their biota interacted through the exchange of energy (Golley). Subsequent experiments tracing the food chain and flow of elements (like nitrogen) through whole systems were fundamental to distinguishing a new science of ecology from a previous focus on species and classification.

Worlding also takes place through the imagination of alien ecologies in fiction about space travel and the exploration of other planets. Olaf Stapledon's *Starmaker* (1937) imagines a disembodied, roving observer who takes a celestial tour across different worlds with strange life forms. In contrast, in Naomi Mitchison's *Memoirs of a Spacewoman* (1962) embodiment is key: the explorer Mary finds herself radically changed through every moment of successful communication, which requires inhabiting points of view as strange as the radial symmetry of a starfish – an example of what Natasha Myers calls meta-morphism (opposed to anthropomorphism or personification) or moving one's body to detune human habits. Such questions about alien species and communication also saturate Ted Chiang's 'Story of your Life' (2002), adapted as *Arrival* (Villeneuve 2017), where the radial-symmetry of the alien Heptapods turns out to be important in decoding their complex writing system.

Other speculative fictions explore the significance of embodiment and the environment in relation to cognition and language. Ursula K. Le Guin's light-hearted "The Author of Acacia Seeds" and Other Extracts from the *Journal of the Association of Theolinguistics*' (1988) imagines how the subterranean environment of ants might affect the way that they use metaphors in writing, such as 'up' and 'down'. Similarly, Vilém Flusser's fable *Vampyroteuthis Infernalis* (1987) explores how human thought may have evolved differently had it occurred in the conditions of the oceanic abyss. Flusser speculatively imagines how the vampire squid may have used different kinds of media (ink clouds, skin paintings) to communicate in a liquid environment, hostile to inscriptions (marks on a page). In *Wild Blue Media: Thinking Through Seawater* (2020), I suggest that we think of the ocean as a science-fictional environment – not because it has alien-like creatures, but because it can helpfully produce a sense of estrangement from terrestrial metaphors that anchor many of the ways we speak.

Other science fictions imagine alien ecologies that involve non-heteronormative gender relations and forms of reproduction. Becky Chambers's WAYFARER series (2015–21) explores queer family configurations amongst a spacefaring crew, while Ursula K. Le Guin's *The Left Hand of Darkness* (1969) imagines a wintry planet where everyone is of a neutral gender until a certain time each month, and then becomes temporarily male or female, depending on their inclinations, desires and situation. One might think that this alternative to fixed notions of gender would lead to a more utopian society; however, in Le Guin's fiction, gender neutrality does not result in a less hierarchical society, only a different distribution of power – and even that distribution looks different in different locations. Octavia E. Butler explores similar questions about gender and hierarchy in her LILITH'S BROOD trilogy (1987–9), which introduces the Oankali, a race of inquisitive aliens that 'gene trades' with new species as they move throughout the galaxy. The Oankali have male and female sexes, as well as a third sex – the Ooloi – which 'mediates' in two senses: it mediates sexual contact and pleasure between male and female partners, and also the mixing of genetic material from male and female partners to produce offspring with desirable traits. All the while, Butler develops an astounding degree of ecological worldbuilding through her nuanced descriptions of an organic spaceship, a multi-species assemblage of the Oankali's many botanical, animal and other partners, as well as imagining the remediation of a post-nuclear apocalypse Earth.

Indeed, much ecological sf confronts the spectre of extinction (Heise *Imagining*; Kolbert), such as H.G. Wells's 'The Star' (1897), Philip K. Dick's *Do Androids Dream of Electric Sheep?* (1968) and Atwood's MaddAddam trilogy. N.K. Jemisin's Broken Earth trilogy (2015–7) conjures a geological imaginary in which the aspiration for natural resources and power has led to a deep rift between Father Earth and humanity that materialises in climate-shifting natural disasters. It also contains social fracturings, including a deeply-engrained prejudice against people who are capable of 'orogeny'. This ability to sense, deflect and control geologic energy enables 'orogenes' to quell earthquakes – or, if they lose control, to cause them. The first volume, *The Fifth Season* (2015), begins: 'Let's start with the end of the world, why don't we?' (1). This immediately challenges narratives that talk about climate change as if cultural extinctions had not happened before, such as Alan Weisman's *The World Without Us* (2007) and David Wallace-Wells's apocalyptic *The Uninhabitable Earth* (2019). As Jemisin goes on to say, 'When we say "the world has ended," it's usually a lie, because the planet is just fine' (1). Although the trilogy is not set in a world physically continuous with our own, its close attention to resource extraction, geology and climate disaster makes it a powerful allegory of the Anthropocene.

Allegories are a compelling form for any attempt to understand totalities, including the global climate system. Elizabeth Deloughrey argues that allegories are particularly useful for thinking about scale, where a story functions as a small-scale model of the world: 'As a mode, allegory can be utilized to comment effectively on the ways in which colonialism has ruptured cultural and ecological relations to the past' or, less ideally, to 'naturalize colonial discourses that depict non-European cultures as outside of time' (9). Sometimes stories offer clear hints that they should be read as allegories, while at other times, the act of interpretation frames something as an allegory, in a process called allegoresis (Jameson *Political*). For example, when I asked Ted Chiang about his short story 'Exhalation' (2008), he said he saw it as an allegory of the heat death of the universe, not climate change – that is, of something inevitable, rather than of a political situation that could be addressed through cooperation. Yet there are elements of the story that evoke climate change through the imagination of air. It depicts an enclosed world full of mechanical beings that, in a steampunk fashion, use air as a source of energy. The pressure differential between their atmosphere and the tanks of air they fill from an underground reserve is a substitute for electricity, powering everything, from their own bodies to clocks and other machinery. The discovery that all of their exhalations are contributing to a 'fatal equilibrium' (50), in which atmospheric pressure will equal that of their underground reserve, is also the discovery of their own mortality, the day when they will no longer be able to function. It is no great stretch to compare the exhalations of this story to our own societal exhalations of carbon dioxide, and the underground 'reservoir' (50) of air to the oil reserves upon which we currently depend on.

Other sf more directly engages with the imagination of oil and energy (LeMenager; Petrocultures Research Group). Such novels could be called 'petro-fictions', a term coined by Amitav Ghosh in 1992 to describe the role of oil in literary imaginations. Nnedi Okorafor's Africanfuturist novel

Lagoon (2014) imagines a fantastical situation where shape-shifting aliens land off the coast of Nigeria, precipitating a variety of changes that enable Nigeria to abandon its reliance on oil extraction and shift towards new forms of energy and alien-assisted technology. In Frank Herbert's *Dune* (1965), the 'spice', mined on the desert planet Arrakis, is the substance that enables interstellar travel. The resource wars to control its extraction and distribution are close parallels to the oil wars waged in the Middle East for oil. At the same time, Herbert, inspired by visiting the dunes of the Oregon coast that were encroaching inland, closely engages with the science of ecology and planetology, with the scientist Kynes noting that 'The highest function of ecology is the understanding of consequences' (346).

The subject of terraforming is one place where ecological sf circles back to coincide with climate fiction. Some view climate change as accidental terraforming, through changing the gas composition of the atmosphere, the acidity of the oceans and temperature of the Earth. Yet by imagining the terraforming of other planets, might we learn something about the changes taking place on our own? Kim Stanley Robinson's MARS trilogy explores not only the physical processes of terraforming, but also the ethics of colonisation, possibilities of political organisation, and the relationship between Mars and Earth. Ken Liu's 'Dispatches from the Cradle: The Hermit – Forty-Eight Hours in the Sea of Massachusetts' (2016) cautions that no matter how much Earth changes, the decision about whether or not to terraform may belong to the few and powerful, even if the hot Earth has given rise to new ecologies like fantastical heat-adapted coral reefs. Holly Jean Buck's *After Geoengineering: Climate Tragedy, Repair, and Restoration* (2019) argues that we need to start thinking about what the future might look like if human societies decide to reverse-terraform (geoengineer) the Earth's climate back to a more comfortable range. It combines discussions of policy with short, speculative vignettes that imagine what it could be like to live on Earth after effective climate mitigation – vignettes about emplacement in a world that are also a call to participate in the utopian project of imagining possible ecologies that centre meaningful work, multispecies thriving and socially just futures.

Works cited

Alaimo, Stacy. *Exposed: Environmental Politics and Pleasures in Posthuman Times*. U of Minnesota P, 2016.

brown, adrienne maree. *Emergent Strategy: Shaping Change, Changing Worlds*. AK Press, 2017.

Bullard, Robert. 'Environmental Justice: It's More Than Waste Facility Siting'. *Social Science Quarterly* 77.3 (1996): 493–9.

Canavan, Gerry and Kim Stanley Robinson, eds. *Green Planets: Ecology and Science Fiction*. Wesleyan UP, 2014.

Carson, Rachel. *Silent Spring*. Houghton Mifflin, 1962.

Chakrabarty, Dipesh. 'The Climate of History'. *Critical Inquiry* 35 (2009): 197–222.

Chang, Alenda Y. *Playing Nature: Ecology in Video Games*. U of Minnesota Press, 2019.

Chiang, Ted. 'Exhalation'. *Exhalation: Stories*. Knopf, 2019. 37–57.

Clarke, Bruce. *Gaian Systems: Lynn Margulis, Neocybernetics, and the End of the Anthropocene*. U of Minnesota P, 2020.

Crutzen, Paul. 'Geology of Mankind'. *Nature* 415.3 (2002): 3.

Csicery-Ronay, Jr, Istvan. *The Seven Beauties of Science Fiction*. Wesleyan UP, 2008.

Deloughrey, Elizabeth. *Allegories of the Anthropocene*. Duke UP, 2020.

Dillon, Grace L., ed. *Walking the Clouds: An Anthology of Indigenous Science Fiction*. U of Arizona P, 2012.

Egerton, Frank N. 'History of Ecological Sciences, Part 47: Ernst Haeckel's Ecology'. *Bulletin: Ecological Society of America* 94.3 (2013) https://doi.org/10.1890/0012-9623-94.3.222

Estes, Nick. *Our History is the Future: Standing Rock versus the Dakota Access Pipeline, and the Long Tradition of Indigenous Resistance*. Verso, 2019.

Ghosh, Amitav. *The Great Derangement: Climate Change and the Unthinkable*. U of Chicago P, 2017.

Golley, Frank Benjamin. *A History of the Ecosystem Concept in Ecology*. Yale UP, 1993.
Haraway, Donna J. 'Anthropocene, Capitalocene, Plantationocene, Chthulucene: Making Kin'. *Environmental Humanities* 6 (2015): 159–65.
Heise, Ursula K. *Imagining Extinction: The Cultural Meanings of Endangered Species*. U of Chicago P, 2016.
——. *Sense of Place, Sense of Planet: The Environmental Imagination of the Global*. Oxford UP, 2008.
Herbert, Frank. *Dune*. Ace, 2005.
Jameson, Fredric. *Archaeologies of the Future: The Desire Called Utopia and Other Science Fictions*. Verso, 2004.
——. *The Political Unconscious: Narrative as a Socially Symbolic Act*. Cornell UP, 1981.
Jemisin, N.K. *The Fifth Season*. Orbit, 2015.
Jue, Melody. *Wild Blue Media: Thinking Through Seawater*. Duke UP, 2020.
Kaplan, Ann E. *Climate Trauma: Foreseeing the Future in Dystopian Film and Fiction*. Rutgers UP, 2015.
Klein, Naomi. *This Changes Everything: Capitalism vs. the Climate*. Allen Lane, 2014.
Kolbert, Elizabeth. *The Sixth Extinction: An Unnatural History*. Henry Holt, 2014.
Le Guin, Ursula K. 'Vaster than Empires and More Slow'. *The Wind's Twelve Quarters: Stories*. Harper Collins, 1975. 181–218.
Lem, Stanislaw. *Solaris*. Mariner, 2002.
LeMenager, Stephanie. *Living Oil: Petroleum Culture in the American Century*. Oxford UP, 2014.
Lovelock, James. *Gaia: A New Look at Life on Earth*. Oxford UP, 1979.
Malmgren, Carl D. 'Towards a Definition of Science Fantasy'. *Science Fiction Studies* 46 (1988): 259–81.
Maxwell, Richard and Toby Miller. *Greening the Media*. Oxford UP, 2012.
McKibben, Bill. *Eaarth: Making a Life on a Tough New Planet*. Henry Holt, 2010.
Myers, Natasha. 'Growing the Planthropocene'. *For the Wild* podcast, episode 204 (October 2020). https://forthewild.world/listen/dr-natasha-myers-on-growing-the-planthroposcene-204
Pellow, David Naguib. *What is Critical Environmental Justice?* Polity, 2018.
Petrocultures Research Group. *After Oil*. West Virginia UP, 2016.
Ray, Sarah Jaquette. *A Field Guide to Climate Anxiety*. U of California Press, 2018.
Schneider-Mayerson, Matthew and Brent Ryan Bellamy, eds. *An Ecotopian Lexicon*. U of Minnesota P, 2016.
Spence, Mark David. *Dispossessing Wilderness: Indian Removal and the Making of National Parks*. Oxford UP, 2000.
Spivak, Gayatri Chakravorty. *The Post-Colonial Critic: Interviews, Strategies, Dialogues*. Ed. Sarah Harasym. Routledge, 1990.
Starosielski, Nicole. *The Undersea Network*. Duke UP, 2015.
Suvin, Darko. *Metamorphoses of Science Fiction: On the Poetics and History of a Literary Genre*. Ed. Gerry Canavan. Peter Lang, 2016.
——. 'On the Poetics of the Sf Genre'. *College English* 34.3 (1972): 372–82.
Szeman, Imre. *On Petrocultures*. West Virginia UP, 2019.
Thomas, Lindsay. *Training for Catastrophe: Fictions of National Security after 9/11*. U of Minnesota, 2021.
Thunberg, Greta. *No One is Too Small to Make a Difference*. Penguin, 2019.
Todd, Zoe. 'Indigenizing the Anthropocene'. *Art in the Anthropocene: Encounters Among Aesthetics, Politics, Environment and Epistemology*. Ed. Heather Davis and Etienne Turpin. Open Humanities Press, 2015. 241–54.
Vernadsky, Vladimir I. *The Biosphere*. Trans. M.A.S. McMenamin and D.B. Langmuir. Copernicus, 1998.
Yusoff, Kathryn. *A Billion Black Anthropocenes or None*. U of Minnesota P, 2018.

37

CRITICAL ETHNIC STUDIES

Christopher T. Fan

American sf has certainly earned its stereotype as predominantly White (not to mention male, cisgender and heterosexual). It is even possible that American sf writers are a more homogenous group than the one that produced English-language fiction between 1950 and 2018, which we now know was 95 percent White (So). That said, we slip into service of the stereotype when we allow it to overshadow the presence and influence of writers of colour, who have flocked to the genre over the past 30 years. The stereotype also indirectly contributes to a longstanding elitist interest in maintaining the sf's 'low' status, thus erasing twice the writers and constituencies that its condemnation believes itself to be defending. In the US, sf's marquee authors now include Black authors such as N.K. Jemisin, Nalo Hopkinson and Nnedi Okorafor; Latinx authors such as Malka Older and Arturo Ernesto Romo; Asian American authors such as Ted Chiang and Ken Liu; and Indigenous authors such as Cherie Dimaline and Louise Erdrich. This landscape differs enough from the stereotype that it has provoked White supremacist activism (Wallace).

Scholarly interest in these writers has tracked this uptick. However, a trend that is often called the 'genre turn' – in which the conventions of 'genre fiction', *especially* sf, are incorporated into works of literary fiction – generates difficulties for the literary historian (Rosen). Accounts of the genre turn have often had the effect of foreshortening minority literary histories. Daniel Hartley attributes this tendency to an 'epic' scope: 'A mind attuned to the shifts between modes of production or the transitions between stages within a single mode of production [...] is sketched out on so vast a scale as to lose all sight of the more immediate formal and political configurations in which literary works arise' (194). An example of this would be Mark McGurl's influential and convincing account of how post-war US fiction was shaped by the research university, whose focus on generating expertise brought into alignment 'technomodernism' (a reframed postmodernism) and 'high cultural pluralism' (knowledge production about social difference). The common origin of these two genres means that 'what [Philip] Roth knows about the Jewish experience, and [Toni] Morrison knows about the African American experience, writers like [Richard] Powers, [Don] DeLillo, and [Thomas] Pynchon know about the second law of thermodynamics' (62–3). While it would be reasonable to argue that equating Jewishness and Blackness with scientific expertise is unnecessarily flattening, this chapter argues that such an equation in fact accords with *Asian American* literary history. The particularity of minority, even 'ethnic', literary histories give 'epic' accounts a dialectical depth.

DOI: 10.4324/9781003140269-40

This chapter sets out to establish a methodological relation between sf and ethnic studies as a way of historicising the increasing presence of the ethnic in sf production and criticism, and offers a case study of how the material determinants of Asian racial form over the last half century have shaped Asian American sf and the vocabulary of so-called 'techno-orientalism'.

Mediating late capitalism

Since the late 1980s, literary historians have paid closer attention to global patterns of literary production and consumption. One might attribute this to factors like the rise of postcolonial theory, the 'transnational turn' in American and ethnic studies, the influx into academia of faculty and students hailing from immigrant families, and the translation of capital's global exigencies into the idiom of 'multiculturalism'. Until recently, sf has served as a shadow archive for these developments, an open secret among scholars of the proliferating complexities of global capitalism and its cultural forms. The genre's paradoxically central yet subordinate status in the intellectual discourses of this period was perhaps most strikingly emblematised in 1991 by the first footnote in Fredric Jameson's *Postmodernism, or, The Cultural Logic of Late Capitalism*: 'This is the place to regret the absence from this book of a chapter on cyberpunk, henceforth, for many of us, the supreme *literary* expression if not of Postmodernism, then of late capitalism itself' (419 n1). Sf has registered the structures of feeling emerging from proliferating ethnic differences, lending the genre a critical realist capacity that offers glimpses of late capitalist totality.

Istvan Csicsery-Ronay, Jr points out that 'The dominant sf nations are precisely those that attempted to expand beyond their national borders in imperialist projects: Britain, France, Germany, Soviet Russia, Japan, and the US' (231). Sf's ideological location at the centre of the imperialist imagination makes it a natural object for the field of ethnic studies, which has interrogated the conditions of global capitalism since its origins in the Third-Worldist student movements of the late 1960s. In the words of John D. Márquez and Junaid Rana, the inaugural editors of the journal *Critical Ethnic Studies*, the field's central line of enquiry could be summed up thus 'How do histories of colonialism and conquest, racial chattel slavery, and White supremacist patriarchies and heteronormativities affect, inspire, and unsettle both scholarship and activism in the present?' (5). Where sf was once quite guilty of celebrating many of these histories, it is now as likely to critique them.

Of late, ethnic studies' methodologies have converged upon 'racial capitalism', a term coined by Cedric J. Robinson, who argued that capitalism grew out of feudalism's racist soil and sought to forge a rapprochement between class and race reductionism. Apocalyptic, post-apocalyptic and zombie sf have been especially attractive to ethnic studies scholars because they provided writers and critics with vocabularies for describing racial capitalism. Taking the 2008 financial crisis as a key inflection point in these genres, Camilla Fojas argues that

> white protagonists cede the representational territories of the global South. This is the story for those that experience crisis as episodic, emerging only along with global economic trends. It is not the story for those for whom every day is a crisis, those who exist in the persistent crises of racial capitalism: dispossession, economic oppression, imperialism, and small and large forms of violence that accrue to genocide.
>
> (17)

Films such as *Children of Men* (Cuarón 2006), *Sleep Dealer* (Rivera 2008), *District 9* (Blomkamp 2009), *World War Z* (Forster 2013) and *Train to Busan* (*Busanhaeng*; Yeon 2016), television shows such as *The Walking Dead* (AMC 2010–22) and novels such as Emily St. John Mandel's *Station Eleven* (2014) and Chang-rae Lee's *On Such a Full Sea* (2014) make concerted efforts to elevate the aesthetic prestige of sf, and do so by leveraging racial tropes, which generate reality effects that allegorise contemporary social conflict.

As preeminent symbols of crisis, racial tropes also possess what Mark Jerng calls cognitive 'affordances' (16). He argues that race is used in a broad array of genres to expedite the process of 'worldmaking'. Sf has a special status, he argues, because it 'orients readers to the material ways in which the world is organized, how situations and landscapes are composed, and how objects are arranged' (15) and thus has 'played a significant and overlooked role in teaching readers how to form racial meanings' (18). For Ramón Saldivar, younger generations of writers of colour have demonstrated shared formal tendencies in how they adopt metafictional techniques, emphasise social and historical realism, and mix genres. These writers are especially attracted to conventions of sf, and indeed most of the writers Saldivar cites have written sf, including Percival Everett, Dexter Palmer, Sesshu Foster, Larissa Lai, Salvador Plascencia, Junot Díaz, Michelle Serros and Yxta Maya Murray (3). The motor of these formal innovations is a desire to imaginatively bridge the historical distance between the political contexts in which these writers came of age and the 'heroic era of the struggle for Civil Rights' (5), whose racial vocabularies continue to define the relationship between the ethnic writer and their fiction. Contemporary ethnic American sf, in other words, offers '*formal* stand-ins for the concrete *content* of justice' (12).

For other critics aligned with ethnic studies, sf and the speculative mode of imagination and cognition are compelling precisely because they hint at the possibility of imagining beyond liberal juridical frameworks for subjectivity and social organisation. Of late, Octavia E. Butler has drawn the lion's share of attention in this kind of work. For scholars and activists like Aimee Bahng, adrienne maree brown and Christine M. Frazier, Butler's fiction offers salutary alternatives to the 'prevailing disciplinary and theoretical frameworks for comprehending black feminist subjectivity and its integral relationship to world/land/territory/earth ethics' (Frazier 40).

Relatedly, Bahng's take on the speculative mode itself is part of a broader reconsideration among ethnic studies scholars of speculative modes of cognition, imagination and futurity. The Foucauldian critique of Enlightenment rationality behind such approaches informs science and technology studies scholars who rethink categories like race and the human in relation to transformative scientific developments in the fields of biology and genetics. Regarding Asian American and orientalist aesthetics, Rachel Lee argues that

> we cannot begin to understand [Asian American literature's] focus on form, aesthetics, affect, theme, autonomy (and all those other things supposedly lending the field coherence outside of 'biology') without understanding the cultural anxieties around being biological in an era that is reconceptualizing the body in informational, molecular, and posthuman terms. (20)

In her reading of Kazuo Ishiguro's *Never Let Me Go* (2005), for instance, orientalist social imaginaries, while not explicitly depicted, wend their way into the novel's social hierarchy, in which 'normals' breed clones – or, as Lee dubs them, 'minoritized bioavailable subject[s]' (59) – for the purpose of organ farming, which resonates with the postsocialist availability of Chinese labour.

To adapt an argument by Csicsery-Ronay, Jr, the presence of the ethnic in sf makes us 'sensitive to [sf's] function as a mediator between national literary traditions and that chimerical beast, global technoculture' (231). For literary historians, the difficulty, again, is returning those traditions to a broader, 'epic' account without blurring them out altogether – indeed, this could be understood as a restatement of ethnic studies' mission.

Case study: Asian American sf

As Min Hyoung Song notes, 1991 was an 'annus mirabilis' (8) in Asian American literary history because of the huge uptick in publication and awards that year: an uptick that has apparently continued unabated (8). More than two decades would pass, however, before scholars noted that 1991 was significant for another reason: it was the year that Ted Chiang became the first Asian American to win a major sf award, a Nebula for 'Tower of Babylon' (1990). This recognition would appear to be belated, given what was by then a long-established discourse of 'techno-orientalism', which, beginning in the late 1980s, grew out of the work of scholars like Jameson, Toshiya Ueno, David Morley and Kevin Robins. As a category that responded to the proliferation of orientalist tropes in sf and mainly US-based racial forms structured by US–Japan economic rivalry, techno-orientalism would have seemed an obvious focus for the interests and commitments of Asian American studies.

Since Chiang's (first) major award, Asian American writers have published in sf magazines and imprints with increasing frequency, and authors whose work is more aligned with the institutions of literary fiction have, per the genre turn, increasingly embraced sf conventions. This period has seen the emergence of such writers as Aliette de Bodard, Vikram Chandra, Mike Chen, John Chu, Amitav Ghosh, S. Huang, Gish Jen, Maggie Shen King, Alice Sola Kim, Chang-rae Lee, Yoon Ha Lee, Eugene Lim, Thea Lim, Ken Liu, Ling Ma, Jamil Nasir, Ruth Ozeki, Vandana Singh, Nghi Vo, Xuan Juliana Wang, Karen Tei Yamashita, Isabel Yap, Charles Yu and E. Lily Yu. Young adult sf has also seen significant growth during this period, as seen in the success of Julie Kagawa, Kazu Kibuishi, Malinda Lo, Marjorie Liu, Cindy Pon and Gene Luen Yang, among others. Many of these writers are included with other Asian American women writers in Ellen Oh and Elsie Chapman's anthology *A Thousand Beginnings and Endings* (2018).

To put this boom into perspective, prior to the 1990s there were extremely few Asian American sf writers. Most published only one or two pieces of short fiction; very few generated a body of work, and even fewer published novels. Al T. Miyadi's 'It Came upon a Midnight Clear' (1950), published in the Japanese American Citizen League's *Pacific Citizen* newspaper, was perhaps the first piece of sf short fiction published by an Asian American but it seems to have been his only work of fiction. Laurence Yep's *Sweetwater* (1973) was perhaps the first sf novel by an Asian American, and although he would go on to produce a large body of work, he would only produce one more sf novel: *Shadow Lord: A Star Trek Novel* (1985). In 1979, the actor George Takei published a one-off sf novel, *Mirror Friend, Mirror Foe*, co-written with Robert Asprin. In the 1970s and 1980s, Glenn Chang, Brenda W. Clough, S.P. Somtow and William F. Wu launched prolific careers, but it would still be years until other Asian American sf and fantasy writers would join them in significant numbers.

As Song argues, 1991 was a watershed year because it was around that time that the children of Asian immigrants who came to the US after 1965 began to publish. When the 1965 Hart–Celler Immigration and Nationality Act went into effect in 1968, it transformed Asian America almost overnight. Prior to this, 'Asian America' did not yet exist as a political identity. It consisted overwhelmingly of only three groups (Japanese, Chinese, Filipinx) and its population was small in numbers, just under a million. By 1980, the population had grown to about 3.5 million, and its national origins had multiplied. Today, Asian America consists predominantly of post-1965 arrivals and is the fastest growing ethnic group in the US. According to Census data from 2017–9, over

70 percent of Asian American adults were born outside the US (Budiman and Ruiz). America's emergence as a destination for many Asian immigrants – especially involuntary immigrants like the Southeast Asian refugee communities that arrived in the US after 1975 – was determined by the entanglements of US empire: the legacy of colonialism in the Philippines, war on the Korean peninsula and in Southeast Asia, and the Cold War direction of industrial policy in South Korea, Japan and Taiwan. These geopolitical dynamics generated push factors that complemented pull factors in the US related to demands for scientific and technical (STEM) labour and the refurbishing of the US's Cold War persona as a country based on racial equality rather than racial dictatorship (R.G. Lee). Consequently, Asian Americans have become the most 'occupationally concentrated' ethnic group in the US, entering STEM professions at three times the rate of the general population (Min and Jang 845, 848). The stereotype of the Asian maths and science nerd has its origins in the Cold War and in the economic global restructuring of the 1970s in which East Asian rapid industrialisation furnished a spatial fix for a falling rate of corporate profit (Ong et al.).

The intrafamilial emotional landscapes shaped by the transnational mobility of STEM talent are most directly depicted in Charles Yu's fiction – especially his short story collections *Third Class Superhero* (2006) and *Sorry, Please, Thank You* (2012), and his first novel, *How to Live Safely in a Science Fictional Universe* (2010). Thea Lim's *An Ocean of Minutes* (2018) remediates the visa and professional skill mechanisms, as well as their class divisions, for a time travel narrative that allegorises immigration. Karen Tei Yamashita's novels *Through the Arc of the Rainforest* (1990) and *Tropic of Orange* (1997) take stock of a longer history of Asian global migration and conceptualise Asian subjectivity as a privileged standpoint for what Jameson calls 'cognitive mapping' (Ling). Recent works like Ruth Ozeki's *A Tale for the Time Being* (2013) and Ling Ma's *Severance* (2018) situate post-1965 Asian racial form against the backdrop of late capitalist economic stagnation, and demonstrate how the transnational mobility of Asian technical talent challenges the coherence and relevance of identities like 'Asian American'.

In Asian American sf, the strong influence of occupational concentration – especially as felt by those Asian Americans who have become writers of fiction and sf – is registered in an aesthetic dynamic that could be characterised as a 'two cultures' conflict between the arts and sciences, in which one becomes an antagonist or limit to the other (Fan 'Melancholy'). This appears to be the case even in work that does not include racially marked characters, such as Ted Chiang's 'Understand' (1991) and 'Story of Your Life' (1998) and Charles Yu's *How to Live Safely*. This tendency, which emerges in literary form both literally and figuratively, is the result of a dynamic between stereotypes and what Song calls the 'racial expectations' (74, 76) that weigh upon Asian American writers through private factors as well as institutional and structural ones. The preeminent 'expectation' of occupational concentration might be a species of neoliberal model minoritisation, in which assimilation is a function of economic integration (rather than political behaviour), but its force is generated by its post-1965 specificity.

Asian Americanist scholarship on sf by Asian Americans has mostly taken the form of journal article and book chapter studies of single texts. The only systematic account of sf by Asian American writers remains Betsy Huang's chapter, 'Reorientations: On Asian American Science Fiction', in her *Contesting Genres in Contemporary Asian American Fiction* (2010). Other accounts generally take up a critique of Stephen Hong Sohn outlined in his 'Alien/Asian' special issue of *MELUS* as 'the re-articulation and re-emergence of the yellow peril' (10), which derives from Morley and Robins's critique of 'techno-orientalism'. The landmark critical anthology that Huang edited with David S. Roh and Greta Niu, *Techno-Orientalism: Imagining Asia in Speculative Fiction, History, and Media* (2015), approaches this problematic from the perspective of Asian American studies.

The main challenge facing a systematic account of Asian American sf is a tautology anchored in an essentialism, in which Asian American-ness is tautologically extracted from an archive of texts produced by Asian American authors who are defined as Asian American based on unstated assumptions about biological or cultural essence. Since the 1990s, the theorisation of Asian American identity has generally proceeded through Michael Omi and Howard Winant's framework of 'racial formation', in which racial categories are 'inhabited, transformed, and destroyed' by struggles between the state and social movements (55). For good reason, this approach has continued the deferral of a pan-ethnic theorisation of Asian American identity, which has always been grounded in a self-conscious strategic essentialism that brackets various forms of difference (e.g., national origin, class, and especially the antagonisms of intra-Asian histories) in pursuit of a political bloc. From the very beginning of the Asian American movement in the late 1960s, these contradictions have both hampered and invigorated Asian American social, cultural and intellectual formations.

Any possible Asian American literary history would require a set of empirical factors that cuts across these contradictions. Providing just this cohering set of factors are occupational concentration and the broader phenomenon of economic model minoritisation, which, as Jennifer Lee and Min Zhou have demonstrated, have applied even to poor and refugee Asian immigrant groups who do not transfer their class status through the 'hyper-selection' of professional trajectories. While Asian Americans are by no means 'crazy rich Asians' that sublimate difference through the general equivalent of the money-form, they are also no longer easily reducible to the subhuman coolie that had grounded Asian racial form until the mid-twentieth century. Since 1965, the common denominator of Asian American identity, despite the Asian American political and intellectual class's important rhetorical insistence otherwise, has been economic upward mobility and professional specificity. The challenges facing a truly syncretic Asian American literary history are intensified in the case of Asian American sf, which is a preeminent articulation of Asian 'hyper-selection'. This historical project, to be sure, overlaps but is no longer homologous with a political identity that has as its destination a 'civil rights project' whose vision of enfranchisement refortifies 'the state as the guarantor of rights' (Lowe 23). Asian American literature can no longer be the metonymic 'textual coalition' that Sau-ling Wong (3–17) was able to assert in the early 1990s. Rather, such a project demands a more forceful articulation of the interpenetration of class and racial formation: a project that would be incoherent if it was narrowly limited to the spaces of the US nation state and its empire, not to mention politically self-defeating.

The diminishing returns of Asian American political identity are thus one key reason why critical interest in Asian American sf has primarily sought to establish transnational connections. Another key reason is China's rise, which is not so much an object of direct representation in Asian American sf as a condition that has complicated the economic and transnational dimensions of Asian American racial forms. In other words, Asian America – understood not as a racial meaning or identity, but as a set of material relations with racial forms of appearance – has undergone profound structural transformations in the post-1965 period, mainly pertaining to economic integration, such that Asian American identity itself has become vulnerable to characterisation as an apotheosis of neoliberal hegemony (Lye).

As the predominant material basis for Asian racial forms of appearance, China's rise has altered the formal vocabulary of techno-orientalism insofar as it has displaced Japan's economic and technological threat to the West (Fan 'Techno-Orientalism'). Morley and Robins coined the term 'techno-Orientalism' in *Spaces of Identity* (1995), in which they sought to describe a response to the shifting economic and geopolitical relationship between the US and Japan. As Japan's postwar, US-dictated economic miracle began to manifest in the daily lives of Americans (in the form of personal electronics and especially automobiles), a distinct cultural logic coalesced. 'If the future is technological', Morley and Robins wrote, 'and if technology has become "Japanised," then the syllogism would suggest that the future is now Japanese too. The postmodern era will be the Pacific era. Japan is the future, and it is a future that seems to be transcending and displacing Western modernity' (168). *Blade Runner* (Scott 1982) and William Gibson's *Neuromancer* (1984) were, for Morley and Robins, the paradigmatic works of techno-orientalist aesthetics.

Despite such highly visible and psychologically significant inroads into the US economy and culture, the US–Japan relationship never deepened into the kind of irrevocable economic interdependency that now exists between the US and China. Since Deng Xiaoping initiated the 'reform and opening' period in 1978, China's economy has expanded at world-historical rates. In more recent decades, its economic expansion has underwritten its expanding geopolitical influence. Meanwhile, the political and economic antagonism between the US and China has been a consequence of China's continued growth and long-term US economic stagnation. The 'China threat' arrived just as Japan entered its so-called 'Lost Decade' of economic stagnation in the 1990s. Techno-orientalism could thus be said to have lost its referent. In Toni Hays's reading, recent revivals of Japan-inflected techno-orientalist aesthetics – such as Disney's *Big Hero 6* (Hall and Williams 2014), which routes that aesthetic through the cityscape of 'San Fransokyo' and the main character Hiro Yamada's mixed-race, Japanese and white background – in fact nostalgically exchange the China threat for the bygone, aestheticised threat of Japan panic. Techno-orientalist forms in the twenty-first century are now more likely to be China-inflected, and more likely to take deindustrialisation as their referent (e.g., *Big Hero 6*'s employment apocalypse portended by Hiro's 'microbots', in which large-scale construction projects can be completed by a single person) rather than the glitzy hand-held technologies of Japan's economic miracle.

Techno-orientalism's genre shifts are observable in Mike Daisey's monologue *The Agony and the Ecstasy of Steve Jobs* (2012), in which he recounts a trip to Shenzhen to visit the factories where his Apple products are assembled, as well as in such video games as *Cyberpunk 2077* (2020). Generally, China-inflected techno-orientalism shifts attention away from cyberpunk's high-tech objects to more overtly political themes like authoritarianism, economic predominance and geopolitical rivalry and, as in, respectively, Maureen F. McHugh's *China Mountain Zhang* (1995), Gary Shteyngart's *Super Sad True Love Story* (2010) and *Arrival* (Villenueve 2016). These shifts are not generally seen in work by Asian American sf writers, who tend not to employ techno-orientalist tropes (although there are exceptions, including *Robot Stories* (Pak 2003), *Advantageous* (Phang 2015) and Yu's *How to Life Safely*).

Conclusion

As this brief case study hopefully demonstrates, Asian American writers and critics have turned to sf under conditions highly particular to the post-1965 period. For Asian American writers, sf has become an aesthetic solution to the contradictions introduced by 'hyper-selectivity' to class and racial 'expectations' pertaining to Asian American identity. Asian Americanist critics' belated attention to sf was due, on the one hand, to a political reluctance to transnationalise Asian American studies, and, on the other, to the fact that Japan never became an immediate threat. In a way, China's rise has forced Asian Americanist critics to contend with transnationalism. In addition to intensifying the anxieties behind these nationally delimited hesitations, historicising Asian American sf demands a wholesale reimagination of what Asian America is in an era when the strategy behind the political identity's strategic essentialism has weakened.

The contradictions underlying Asian America are thus the same ones underlying an 'epic' scope of literary history, which also struggles to reconcile the particular with the general. While we should certainly encourage aspirations to totality, the durability of such projects depends on how successfully and adequately they account for the 'immediate formal and political configurations in which literary works arise' (Hartley 194). The point of placing the 'epic scope' in tension with particular histories that challenge its coherence is to hold focus on the uneven development of modernity and to resist the fetishisation of capital's uniform existence. If the street finds its own uses for things, as Gibson would say, then critical ethnic studies is preeminent among those uses precisely for its relevance to such a project.

Works cited

Bahng, Aimee. *Migrant Futures: Decolonizing Speculation in Financial Times*. Duke UP, 2018.

brown, adrienne maree and Walidah Imarisha. *Octavia's Brood: Science Fiction Stories from Social Justice Movements*. AK Press, 2015.

Budiman, Abby and Neil G. Ruiz. 'Key Facts about Asian Americans, a Diverse and Growing Population'. *Pew Research Center* (29 April 2021). pewresearch.org/fact-tank/2021/04/29/key-facts-about-asian-americans/

Csicsery-Ronay, Jr., Istvan. 'Science Fiction and Empire'. *Science Fiction Studies* 90 (2003): 231–45.

Fan, Christopher T. 'Melancholy Transcendence: Ted Chiang and Asian American Postracial Form'. *Post45* (11 May 2014). post45.org/2014/11/melancholy-transcendence-ted-chiang-and-asian-american-postracial-form

——. 'Techno-Orientalism with Chinese Characteristics: Maureen F. McHugh's *China Mountain Zhang*'. *Journal of Transnational American Studies* 6.1 (2015). https://escholarship.org/uc/item/8n70b1b6

Fojas, Camilla. *Zombies, Migrants, and Queers Race and Crisis Capitalism in Pop Culture*. U of Illinois P, 2017.

Frazier, Chelsea M. 'Troubling Ecology: Wangechi Mutu, Octavia Butler, and Black Feminist Interventions in Environmentalism'. *Critical Ethnic Studies* 2.1 (2016): 40–72.

Hartley, Daniel. *The Politics of Style: Towards a Marxist Poetics*. Brill, 2017.

Hays, Toni. *Open Concept: Land and Home in Asian/America*. Dissertation in progress. UC Irvine.

Huang, Betsy. *Contesting Genres in Contemporary Asian American Fiction*. Palgrave Macmillan, 2010.

Jameson, Fredric. *Postmodernism, or, the Cultural Logic of Late Capitalism*. Duke UP, 1989.

Jerng, Mark. *Racial Worldmaking: The Power of Popular Fiction*. Fordham UP, 2017.

Lee, Jennifer and Min Zhou. *The Asian American Achievement Paradox*. Russel Sage Foundation, 2015.

Lee, Rachel C. *The Exquisite Corpse of Asian America: Biopolitics, Biosociality, and Posthuman Ecologies*. New York UP, 2014.

Lee, Robert G. 'The Cold War Origins of the Model Minority'. *Asian American Studies Now*. Ed. Jean Yu-Wen Shen Wu and Thomas Chen. Rutgers UP, 2010. 256–71.

Ling, Jinqi. *Across Meridians: History and Figuration in Karen Tei Yamashita's Transnational Novels*. Stanford UP, 2012.

Lowe, Lisa. *Immigrant Acts: On Asian American Cultural Politics*. Duke UP, 1996.

Lye, Colleen. 'Racial Form'. *Representations* 104 (2008): 92–101.

McGurl, Mark. *The Program Era: Postwar Fiction and the Rise of Creative Writing*. Harvard UP, 2009.

Márquez, John D. and Junaid Rana. 'On Our Genesis and Future'. *Critical Ethnic Studies* 1.1 (2015): 1–8.

Min, Pyong Gap and Sou Hyun Jang. 'The Concentration of Asian Americans in STEM and Health-Care Occupations: An Intergenerational Comparison'. *Ethnic and Racial Studies* 38.6 (2015): 841–59.

Morley, David and Kevin Robins. *Spaces of Identity: Global Media, Electronic Landscapes and Cultural Boundaries*. Routledge, 1995.

Omi, Michael and Howard Winant. *Racial Formation in the United States*, second edition. Routledge, 1994.

Ong, Paul, Edna Bonacich and Lucie Cheng, eds. *The New Asian Immigration in Los Angeles and Global Restructuring*. Temple UP, 1994.

Robinson, Cedric. *Black Marxism: The Making of the Black Radical Tradition*, U of North Carolina P, 2000.

Rosen, Jeremy. 'Literary Fiction and the Genres of Genre Fiction'. *Post45* (7 August 2018). post45.org/2018/08/literary-fiction-and-the-genres-of-genre-fiction
Saldivar, Ramón. 'The Second Elevation of the Novel: Race, Form, and the Postrace Aesthetic in Contemporary Narrative'. *Narrative* 21.1 (2013): 1–18.
So, Richard Jean. *Redlining Culture: A Data History of Racial Inequality and Postwar Fiction*. Columbia UP, 2020.
Sohn, Stephen Hong. 'Introduction: Alien/Asian: Imagining the Racialized Future'. *MELUS* 33.4 (2008): 5–22.
Song, Min Hyoung. *The Children of 1965: On Writing, and Not Writing, as an Asian American*. Duke UP, 2013.
Wallace, Amy. 'Who Won Science Fiction's Hugo Awards, and Why It Matters'. *Wired* (23 August 2015). wired.com/2015/08/won-science-fictions-hugo-awards-matters
Wong, Sau-ling. *Reading Asian American Literature: From Necessity to Extravagance*. Princeton UP, 1993.

38
DIGITAL CULTURES

Elizabeth Callaway

In twenty-first century America, omnipresent smartphones, laptops and Wi-Fi demonstrate that digital culture is all around us. Many of the typical activities that comprise culture (e.g., art, literature, film, critique, conversation, entertainment) are carried out using digital devices at some point in their production or consumption cycle. One has only to think about how much connection between human beings, whether one-to-one (messaging), one-to-many (news articles) or many-to-many (social media) happens via digital devices to see the ubiquity of digital culture. Unless we plan otherwise, our days are permeated with texting, surfing, scrolling, swiping, clicking and sharing on our digital devices. We consume entertainment content, email friends, slack colleagues, take photos, shop, get directions, listen to music, learn new skills, book vacations and self-diagnose our maladies using digital devices. In every one of these activities the infrastructure and affordances of digital technologies affect social relations, communication, information, art, the environment and identity. The influence of digital technologies on culture is transformative, and rarely neutral. Sf has long thought through the implications of technological changes, and the digital revolution is no exception. This chapter examines the ways that sf imagines the digital cultures that emerge with and through digital technologies, focusing on texts that are invested in imagining the consequences that follow from the *design* (rather than the mere existence) of digital technologies.

Theorising digital cultures

Early in the history of the internet, scholars, technologists and sf authors, influenced by the work of Marshall McLuhan, enthusiastically predicted the liberating effects this new digital technology would have on culture. In what Richard Barbrook and Andy Cameron called 'The California Ideology', the internet was hailed as a space where anyone could speak and be heard, which would usher in a new era of personal freedom of speech and expression. As Henry Jenkins points out, many also believed that creative work would no longer be guarded by elite gatekeepers like publishing houses, but art and literature would be produced and distributed by any soul who felt the inclination to create (18). In this new world, information and currency would flow globally from person to person unimpeded, as states, boundaries and governments lost their meaning (Castells xviii). Even death, it seemed, would eventually lose its power as computers enabled the possibility of uploading human consciousnesses into a digital afterlife (Hayles 1). In the early days of digital

DOI: 10.4324/9781003140269-41

culture, writers and technologists were interested in how the mere existence of digital technologies would drastically change society, politics and religion.

Soon this initial outpouring of enthusiasm was replaced by interest in the way that digital technologies are designed, owned, managed and used. Instead of describing the internet as a virtual agora that would inherently democratise communication and society more broadly, scholars began to dig into the details of search engine algorithms, the business models of social media companies, the choices offered in the user interface of massive online games, the collection of user data, and other structural features of various spaces on the internet. For example, an array of recent work focuses on the ways that decisions made in the design of software increase racial inequality. Lisa Nakamura's early work on cybertypes, with their double-layered construction out of code and culture (3), proved foundational for later insights about algorithmic digital racism. Safiya Noble sheds light on the racism built into Google's search algorithm; her most memorable example is the deluge of pornography and racist content that she encounters when typing 'black girls' into her search bar (3). Ruha Benjamin notes a similar instance of algorithmic racism in a machine learning algorithm designed to judge a beauty contest that ended up penalising dark skin. An investigation of the AI's methods revealed the racism implicit in its training set of millions of online photos, a racism that is almost certainly present in many more scenarios. Benjamin notes,

> Employers resort to credit scores to decide whether to hire someone, companies use algorithms to tailor online advertisements to prospective customers, judges employ automated risk assessment tools to make sentencing and parole decisions, and public health officials apply digital surveillance techniques to decide which city blocks to focus medical resources.
>
> (64)

These analyses focus not just on the mere existence of statistically predictive AI but on the ways it is designed and deployed.

While algorithmic racism is one of the most troubling manifestations of the way digital technologies intermingle with digital cultures, there are many other areas open for investigation. Scholars are noting a trend of decreased attention spans and a reduced capacity for deep work (Alter; Newport; Zomorodi) that they chalk up not just to the existence of smartphone apps but the 'thousand people on the other side of the screen whose job it is to break down the self-regulation you have' (Tristan Harris qtd in Alter 3). Adam Alter takes the position that 'Tech isn't morally good or bad until it's wielded by the corporations that fashion it for mass consumption' (8), then focuses in on the particulars of this fashioning in order to interrogate what deliberate design is doing to attention. John Cheney-Lippold examines the way corporations track, package and use our innumerable internet activities. Some scholars concentrate on the conditions for the proliferation of disinformation on social media (Benkler et al.; Bennett), while some activists examine the role of social media feeds and recommendation algorithms in the polarisation of American politics (Orlowski; Harris and Raskin). In one study on YouTube's recommendation algorithm, a group of researchers showed that across 2 million recommendations, viewers moved from watching moderate to extremist videos (Ribeiro et al.). It might not be immediately apparent why the YouTube recommendation system would serially recommend content that is a little more extreme than what a user has just watched. For many of the people doing work in the above areas, the problem is the underlying business model of earning money from selling ads. In what has been called the 'attention economy', tech companies sell advertising spots and so earn money for the time users spend on their app. Companies are therefore incentivised to keep users on their platform. The machine learning algorithms used by tech companies to choose recommendations based on previous watch history have landed on a successful strategy; showing outraging or progressively more extreme content is a remarkably effective tactic for keeping users engaged (Harris and Raskin).

Digital culture is not just about the design and business choices made in constructing spaces where people engage; it is also made up of narratives about technology (Bollmer 20). These narratives are particularly important in shaping how we see digital technology and cultures, as they give us a means of understanding chaotic and complex assemblages with many actors. Moreover, narratives about technology both reflect digital cultures and, in turn, influence the development of those cultures. Sf is especially salient in this regard as it has long been recognised to both comment on and influence technological developments. One particularly pertinent example is William Gibson's early cyberpunk depiction of what he termed 'cyberspace' that influenced the parameters of actual online spaces for many years (Bollmer 104). The narratives examined in this chapter highlight aspects of digital cultures of which we may not already be aware, extrapolate consequences of the business models of digital technologies, and elaborate worlds in which these digital cultures are fully imagined. What ties these works together is their interest in the details of design and deployment of digital technologies and their effect on digital cultures.

Turning into data

An important aspect of any digital technology is the economic model behind it. For many social media, search and streaming companies, this is the attention economy, which relies on substantial data surveillance of users in an effort to model and manipulate their actions – to keep them engaged and to show them targeted ads. This collection of massive amounts of user data is one major way contemporary sf explores the current economic model. In the following examples, the human subject is conceptualised as essentially a large aggregate of data. This manifests in a variety of ways, including uploaded human consciousnesses, intense digital surveillance systems and predictive mathematical modelling of human behaviour.

Recent stories that feature the conversion of consciousnesses into computer code constitute the most extreme example of how sf can approach the datafication of human existence. Darryl Smith's 'The Pretended' (2000), for example, interrogates typical ideas of the uploaded consciousness as a way to live forever, unbounded by human flesh. Instead, the digital replication of human beings is presented as a new mode of control and racialised power. 'The Pretended' takes place after a White supremacist society has completed a genocide of all Black Americans. Set on a train full of robots due to be destroyed, it becomes clear that these robots were designed to replicate the Black people that were murdered and are even imbued with their personalities and bits of memories: the digital consciousnesses of real Black people. One of these human/robot hybrids explains the process: 'Jes take thinkin outa real black people brains, put it into computers, rase the memory a bit, make our talk the way they think it should sound, and piss the whole kit'n'kaboodle into robots' (362). These Black robots were created in an ever-failing endeavour to pretend that Black people were not ever human. Predictably, these robotic reconstructions turn out to exhibit personhood and thus have to be eliminated for inconveniently reminding those in power that Black people are and always have been fully human. In this case the capacity for uploading a human consciousness into a computer is not inherently liberating but in fact another mechanism used to control Black bodies and minds. In this vein, several *Black Mirror* (Channel 4/Netflix 2011–) episodes explore how uploaded consciousnesses could be used for forced labour ('White Christmas' (2014)), endow the ability for perpetual imprisonment and never-ending torture ('Black Museum' (2017)) and allow for sociopaths to use digital humans as their personal playthings ('USS Calister' (2017)). Neal Stephenson's *Fall: or, Dodge in Hell* (2019) also focuses on the idea of the uploaded consciousness, this time of a tech billionaire. While it does present the conversion of a brain into computer code as granting an immortal afterlife, at the heart of the story are questions of ownership, control, rights and differing creative visions for the digital afterlife.

Transforming consciousness into bits and bytes is only one trope through which current sf explores the ways that our endlessly tracked digital interactions turn human life into data. Other works examine the quantification of every aspect of modern existence, including digitisation of information about bodies and actions, AI targeted manipulation of human behaviour and the conceptualisation of human beings as programmable. Ted Chiang's 'Understand' (1991) explores the ever-expanding role of data in culture that only ever figuratively turns humans into computers. Through an experimental treatment with 'hormone K', an average man, Leon Greco, becomes superintelligent, able to foresee the future of stocks, hack into any government database, carry out one-man heists, and manipulate human behaviour by reading micro-facial expressions and sensing pheromones. Data permeates Greco's daily life in familiar ways. He is a patient in a hospital where they create and collect massive amounts of data about his health, brain and body. The results of brain scans, blood tests and psychiatric questionnaires all go into electronic files his doctors use to make decisions about his care. These are then collected and combined with data from other patients in massive medical databases, which Greco later exploits for his own purposes – stealing a fourth hormone K treatment. Even in its initial, rather quotidian, presentation of data collection 'Understand' hints at a conception of people as merely walking aggregates of data. Greco says of his doctors' stance toward him, 'I'm just a source of PET scan images and an occasional vial of cerebrospinal fluid' (38). As the story progresses, it points to more of the data generated by everyday life: license plate numbers, DMV records, surveillance footage, encrypted files, databases, CIA records and reports. All these bits of digital detritus left in the wake of twenty-first century life together create a sense of a world awash in data. Or a world that is, in all the important ways, essentially data.

Chiang poses more speculative and intriguing questions about digital cultures when Greco himself becomes a processor of big data. 'Understand' presents a view of human beings as comprised of a set of machine-like processes that can be entirely understood and manipulated if a supremely intelligent being could only process every single piece of data about each person. As Greco becomes more and more intelligent, gestures, pheromones, tone, eye movements and the 'electric field' generated by muscle tension all become raw data for him to process, find patterns in and manipulate. When he masters these techniques, he equates them with mind control abilities.

In his collection, processing and forecasting of data, Greco himself becomes a type of machine intelligence. He begins to talk like a stereotypical AI. When he learns of Reynolds, the other human with extreme intelligence, he says 'I begin extrapolating his likely progress, and will incorporate new information as I acquire it' (60). He speaks of 'adjusting the programming of his [own] mind' (55), and conceptualises his thinking as mathematical equations: 'I see myself thinking, and I see the equations that describe my thinking, and I see myself comprehending the equations, and I see how the equations describe their being comprehended' (54).

Greco's extrapolating, predicting, tweaking and adjusting is described as fundamentally pattern recognition, something that computers are often. He seems at times like a machine learning algorithm: 'With my near-total recall, and my ability to correlate, I can assess a situation immediately, and choose the best course of action for my purposes; I'm never indecisive' (39). He even argues that he will need to hybridise with computers in order to keep growing and processing data as a human/computer cyborg.

In the end, this computerised vision of a human allows for Greco's great breakthroughs in science and art and for his immense vulnerability. Only when the story gets readers to buy into this version of humanity, where we are just a series of inputs to our sensory system and biofeedback loops of blood pressure and pheromones, can we then believe that a single word or sentence (or a string of memory perceptions) could destroy a human being, like the command rm* removes all files from a directory. In his final moment, before Reynolds wipes Greco's personality with a single 'self-destruct command' (69), the reader is taken to the extreme of this humans-as-data vision where Greco anticipates that Reynolds can erase people and reprogramme their brains to be someone else, such as 'savants, having focused intentions and restricted self-metaprogrammers' (69). This kind of destruct code on something as complex as a human being would normally be laughable, but in the world of the story, where human beings have first been turned into data and later grown into computers, it makes perfect sense. Readers are primed by the story's data-filled worldview to accept the possibility of this chilling, final destruct command. 'Understand' thus prompts a critical turn towards thinking about our own digital cultures. It suggests that the conversion of ourselves and our lives into data does provide unprecedented possibilities for analysis and prediction but also that it simultaneously simplifies our conceptions of a human being into something that is more easily controlled.

Evie Shockley's 'separation anxiety' (2000) also focuses on the excessive data collection of contemporary US digital cultures, but emphasises its racialised dimension. In the future, Black Americans live together in blocked off areas of the country dedicated entirely to Black life and cultures, called 'African American Cultural Conservation Units' or as the main character, Peaches, calls it, 'the ghetto'. These separate states within America were a solution for the challenges to Black survival within the US. Hate crimes, murders, massacres, and the pernicious 'slowly starving of our bodies and minds' (52) made it unsafe for Black Americans to live with White Americans. However, these physically safe Units are not self-determining but controlled by the same White hegemonic society that incited their creation. The purpose of the Unit in which Peaches lives is Black cultural *preservation* (as opposed to thriving), which manifests itself as an imposed stagnancy. Peaches is a dancer who is expected to learn traditional forms of Black American dance and travel to perform it for people in White cities without ever actually meeting them. She is not allowed to see anything except hotel rooms and concert halls, and is discouraged from creative innovation. Peaches bristles at this managed and confined existence, and at the vast amount of data collection people in 'the ghetto' have to endure, especially when a new directive requires residents to dispose of trash related to sexual activity and sexual health in its own bin. This is proposed as a means of filling a gap in the archive of human history; when this collection of detritus-as-data is questioned, the typical response is 'we owe it to our grandchildren and their grandchildren to preserve a record of what african american culture was like in the twenty-second century. remember the middle passage era! they always added. 'unknowable' history' (58). This fervid data collection is also reminiscent of real-world racialised data practices: crime prediction software based on the hyper-policing of Black neighbourhoods and the use of zip codes as a proxy for race in targeted ads and political campaigns (Benjamin 35, 82), and the profiling that allows predatory lenders to target communities of colour (Burd-Sharps and Rasch 6). Shockley's 'separation anxiety' reminds us that data-surveillance, like surveillance in general, is experienced unevenly across races and is one of the mechanisms through which structural racism operates. The story also suggests that a new technology is not necessarily an impetus towards cultural transformation. Depending on the design, purpose and ownership of the instrument, it can just as easily bring about enforced cultural stagnation.

Radicalisation and disinformation

While 'The Pretended', 'Understand' and 'separation anxiety' focus on the ways that power and control operate through data collection, other works focus on how this datafication is used to create simplified and manipulable versions of ourselves. If 'Understand' proposes a mechanistic vision of humanity in order to create a believable kill switch for personality, then E. Lily Yu's 'Darkout' (2016) and Stephenson's *Fall* examine how current economic models and recommendation algorithms use outrage, fear and anger to simplify human thinking so as to make users more predictable and addicted to digital devices. They investigate the way the attention economy radicalises individuals and contributes to the widespread and enduring belief in misinformation that we see in digital cultures around the world. 'Darkout' follows Brandon, an unhappy young White man, over one evening spent obsessing about his ex-girlfriend and watching ubiquitous social media screens with his racist and sexist older friend, Mark. During the evening they switch between watching a football game and live feeds from people's mandated home and street cameras, which comprise an entertainment system crossing the state surveillance of George Orwell's *Nineteen Eighty-four* (1949) with today's social media platforms. While every minute of every life is available for live viewing, people only start getting paid for ad spots if they can attract an audience. As it slowly becomes clear that Brandon is on a path toward White supremacist and misogynistic ideologies, the story imagines the role of social media as a force pushing people toward such viewpoints.

'Darkout' couples this social media/surveillance with a YouTube-like recommendation algorithm that, based on the characters' watch histories, promotes content likely to grab their attention and keep them glued to the screen in order to increase advertising revenue. Apart from a few cute animal videos, these recommendations consist entirely of violent or sexual content, much of it racialised: 'CATFIGHT BETWEEN OFFICER, BLACK WOMAN IN FIVE INCH HEELS', 'SEXY BROWN SUGAR MMM' and '$$$WANK TOKYO NEIGHBORHOOD ON FIRE' (197). When Mark says of Black people, 'They're violent people. Not like us' (190), the connection between this racist opinion and the algorithm – which never recommends he watch live feeds of Black families eating dinner or of Black parents helping their kids brush their teeth – is clear.

Beyond radicalising personal belief, this story also presents a picture of how digital technologies and the cultures they promulgate reinforce structural racism. The way the algorithms are designed and deployed in this story widens structural inequality. Not only does the recommendation algorithm promote harmful content but the deployment of the technology results in disproportionate monitoring of non-White people and the poor (Brandon remembers cameras were put into the poorest neighbourhoods first). And as Ruha Benjamin points out, extra monitoring can result in a higher number of legal infractions being caught and cited, leading to the rationalisation that these communities need even *more* monitoring (82). 'Darkout' presents not only a picture of the obvious mental health consequences of constant access to the lives of other people, but the extremism that users are pushed toward in the attention economy.

Fall shares similar concerns with the effects of the way social media is designed, managed and manipulated. One plot point revolves around an elaborate hoax: what is really a denial-of-service attack, in which Moab, Utah residents cannot get online or use any communication device except a single satellite phone, is reported through social media posts as a terrorist nuclear attack. Fuelled by a careful initial deployment of doctored videos, the hoax later takes on a life of its own with a large section of the population refusing to believe any evidence that suggests Moab was never bombed. This fictional hoax proposes a more general problem digital culture has with disinformation, especially dramatic and divisive disinformation that captures user attention. Ironically, the Moab hoax was initially designed as a means of proving to humanity the complete unreliability of the internet (or 'the miasma', as Stephenson's protagonist likes to call it). But it escapes its perpetrator's control, gains a life of its own and cannot be recalled or undone – thus becoming a rather more emphatic argument about the power of internet disinformation.

Fall extrapolates the consequences of having an information ecosystem dominated by misinformation, disinformation and outrage. Twenty years after the Moab event, the US is essentially divided into two countries. 'Blue' America consists of large cities connected by a functioning and protected highway system, while 'Ameristan', a chaotic set of religious city-states and warlords, exists interstitially between these infrastructural veins. Blue America and Ameristan operate on entirely different information ecosystems. The rich and educated have figured out how to function in an information environment rife with bot-generated content, rampant with conspiracy theories and teeming with revisionist history. They use personal editors, whose job it is to vet and manage the information that makes it into their 'edit streams', or the reliable news, entertainment and content rich citizens see. While this information hygiene works well for the set of characters who attend Princeton and are traveling through Ameristan during their summer vacation, the complete separation of the media they consume and that of the people they meet on their travels indicates a complete separation of realities as well. Those who cannot afford such editors subsist on 'an intoxicating mélange of homemade pharmaceuticals and hallucinatory memes' (221). Their edit streams are flooded with conspiracy theories and content that is an 'algorithmically generated mishmash of images, sounds [...] no sense at all. Just whatever *worked,* you know, in the sense of getting the viewer to watch a little more' (222). Like the characters in 'Darkout', the Ameristans have been radicalised by being fed information that is both incorrect and harmful, as demonstrated by their strafing of bridges and their unassailable belief in conspiracies. An America divided, where two factions do not share a social reality, information bubbles do not overlap and belief is not based on evidence, is a powerful vision of where the attention economy leads. Particularly telling is that the rich find individual solutions to this information problem while collective regulation of the corporations profiting from division, conspiracy and outrage is never addressed.

Conclusion

The recent sf narratives surveyed here imagine digital cultures in ways that are aligned with the turn in scholarship toward examining the funding, design and use of digital technologies. In their imagination of racialised data surveillances, exploited uploaded consciousnesses, predictive behaviour manipulation, radicalising recommendations and divided populaces, these texts ask who benefits from a technology and who pays – and in what ways. They imagine how cultures are influenced by digital innovations and how those cultures affect digital technologies. In the end, they present us with worlds where the ubiquity of data collection combined with the volume of computer-facilitated human interactions lead to a conceptualisation of human beings as informational patterns and collections of data. This restriction of what constitutes a person then fits neatly into the schemas that use predictive modelling to manipulate human behaviour, whether that behaviour modification is as simple as keeping attention on a screen or as complex as suppressing cultural change or rewriting a personality.

Works Cited

Alter, Adam. *Irresistible: The Rise of Addictive Technology and the Business of Keeping us Hooked*. Penguin, 2018.
Barbrook, Richard and Andy Cameron. 'The Californian Ideology'. *Science as Culture* 6.1 (1996): 44–72.
Benjamin, Ruha. *Race after Technology: Abolitionist Tools for the New Jim Code*. Polity, 2019.
Benkler, Yochai, Robert Faris and Hall Roberts. *Network Propaganda: Manipulation, Disinformation, and Radicalization in American Politics*. Oxford UP, 2018.
Bennett, Lance W., ed. *The Disinformation Age*. Cambridge UP, 2020.
Bollmer, Grant David. *Theorizing Digital Cultures*. Sage, 2018.
Burd-Sharps, Sarah, and Rebecca Rasch. Impact of the US Housing Crisis on the Racial Wealth Gap Across Generations. *Social Sciences Research Council* (June 2015). www.aclu.org/files/field_document/discrimlend_final.pdf
Castells, Manuel. *The Rise of the Network Society*, second edition, Wiley-Blackwell, 2009.
Cheney-Lippold, John. *We Are Data: Algorithms and the Making of Our Digital Selves*. New York UP, 2018.
Chiang, Ted. 'Understand'. *Stories of Your Life and Others*. Vintage, 2016. 29–70.
Harris, Tristan and Aza Raskin. *Down the Rabbit Hole by Design* 4. www.humanetech.com/podcast/4-down-the-rabbit-hole-by-design
Hayles, N. Katherine *How We Became Posthuman: Virtual Bodies in Cybernetics, Literature, and Informatics*. U of Chicago P, 2008.
Jenkins, Henry. *Convergence Culture: Where Old and New Media Collide*, revised edition. New York UP, 2008.
Nakamura, Lisa. *Cybertypes: Race, Ethnicity, and Identity on the Internet*. Routledge, 2002.
Newport, Cal. *Deep Work*. Platkus, 2016.
Noble, Safiya Umoja. *Algorithms of Oppression: How Search Engines Reinforce Racism*. New York UP, 2018.
Orlowski, Jeff. *The Social Dilemma*. Netflix, 2020.
Ribeiro, Manoel Horta, Raphael Ottoni, Robert West and Virgilio A.F. Almeida. 'Auditing Radicalization Pathways on YouTube'. *Proceedings of the 2020 Conference on Fairness, Accountability, and Transparency*. Association for Computing Machinery, 2020. 131–41.
Shockley, Evie. 'separation anxiety'. *Dark Matter: A Century of Speculative Fiction from the African Diaspora*. Ed. Sheree R. Thomas. Warner, 2001. 51–68.
Smith, Darryl A. 'The Pretended'. *Dark Matter: A Century of Speculative Fiction from the African Diaspora*. Ed. Sheree R. Thomas. Warner, 2000. 356–71.
Stephenson, Neal. *Fall; or, Dodge in Hell*. HarperCollins, 2019.
Yu, Lily E. 'Darkout'. *Cyber World: Tales of Humanity's Tomorrow*. Ed. Jason Heller and Joshua Viola. Hex, 2016. 184–201.
Zomorodi, Manoush. *Bored and Brilliant: How Spacing Out Can Unlock Your Most Productive and Creative Self*. St. Martin's, 2017.

39
DISABILITY STUDIES

Josefine Wälivaara

With its depictions of future worlds and alternative societies, and its explorations of the limits and possibilities of the human (and non-human) body and mind, sf provides plenty of opportunities to question the normative ideas and taken-for-granted truths of present-day society. Much has been done by scholars, writers, filmmakers and fans to critically examine sexist, racist and homophobic depictions in sf, to reveal the ways in which the genre has reinforced biases and discriminatory power relations, and to demonstrate how such ideas and attitudes are culturally, socially and historically constructed. Until recently, however, few have critically examined and questioned how sf narratives depict power relations of disability/ability or ableism. Disability is often unquestioningly represented as an undisputed fact of individual bodies and minds, rather than as a sociocultural phenomenon in need of critical scrutiny. Sf can showcase that the present-day biases and normative notions of disability are ideas that can be challenged, and that the future can offer other possibilities, while disability studies can further our understanding of individual sf texts and genre conventions.

This chapter conceptualises disability 'not as an individual defect but as the product of social injustice' (Siebers 3). Such an approach does not seek cures or the elimination of disability but is instead devoted to studying the 'social meanings, symbols, and stigmas attached to disability identity and ask[ing] how they relate to enforced systems of exclusion and oppression [so as to attack] the widespread belief that having an able body and mind determines whether one is a quality human being' (Siebers 3–4). This involves not only issues concerning disability and impairment but also the wider social system of power around disability and ability that, like gender or class, addresses both marginalised and privileged groups (Schalk 'Resisting' 137).

Disability and sf

Questions about disability have for a long time been the domain of moral and medical discourses, in which disability was conceptualised as either a divine punishment for sinful behaviours or a pathological defect. The moral discourse has been prominent throughout history, but the medical perspective originates from the mid-nineteenth century and eventually became hegemonic in societal views on disability (Goodley 7–8). From these perspectives, disability is solely considered an individual concern, a personal tragedy that requires rehabilitation, treatment and cures (Goodley 6).

DOI: 10.4324/9781003140269-42

Disability studies, a critical reaction to the dominance of these moral and medical models, instead understands disability as a socio-cultural phenomenon as well as personal, psychological and corporeal (Goodley 6, 1). It emerges from two main perspectives, both with roots in academic and activist circles. The social model of disability, developed in the 1980s in the UK, adopted the divide between *impairment,* which is located in the individual's body or mind, and *disability,* which describes limitations upon or loss of equal participation in society because of social and physical barriers (Oliver *Social Work*, 'Social'; Goodley 9–11). A minority model, developed in North America and influenced in part by civil right movements of the 1960s and 1970s, considers people with disabilities a minority group and thus a Civil Rights concern. By theorising disability as a social construction, disability studies moved focus from the individual to social and environmental barriers as the causes of disability. Rather than advocating for the individual to adapt to society, like the moral and medical models, disability studies instead contends that social changes are required to incorporate a wider spectrum of bodies and minds. The problem of disability, then, is not located in the individual but in society, including preconceptions about people with non-normative bodies and/or minds. Since then, disability studies has developed as an interdisciplinary field, with different branches of theory and practice from across numerous academic disciplines.

In its early stages, disability studies was the domain of the social and political sciences, but by the end of the 1990s it was also becoming more common in the humanities, in for example cultural studies and literary theory (Davis 508–9). Among other things, disability scholars from the humanities, influenced by postcolonial, queer and feminist theories, investigated disability across culture, media and literature as a cultural construction (Goodley 18). David T. Mitchell and Sharon L. Snyder suggest that studies of images of disability in the humanities developed from an initial focus on theorising negative images of disabilities (such as stereotypes in film and literature), critiquing inaccurate portrayals of disability, and investigating representations in their historical contexts, to uncovering authors and filmmakers with disabilities and reclaiming representations that had been seen as stigmatised (15–45). Their seminal research into disability as a 'narrative prosthesis' explores the cultural abundance of disability and its symbolic or metaphorical uses.

A more recent development, referred to as critical disability studies, extensively incorporates the intersection of disability with other vectors of power, including gender, class, sexuality, race and ethnicity (Goodley 191). It includes perspectives such as crip theory and studies in ableism, which both focus on questioning normativity, centring not only upon disability but also on normative ableism. Critical disability studies could also be seen as a methodology for 'studying power, privilege, and oppression of bodily and mental norms' informed by disability (Schalk 'Critical' n.p.).

Critical engagement with disability in the study of genre texts is also quite recent. In a 2012 special issue of the *Journal of Literary & Cultural Disability Studies* dedicated to the topic, editor Ria Cheyne ('Introduction' 117) notes how limited disability perspectives on popular genres, including crime fiction, romance and sf, were. Realist fiction was the main focus for the study of disability (Ellis 58; Schalk *Bodyminds* 21), and those scholars who did discuss genre fiction were reluctant 'to discuss popular genre texts *as* popular genre texts – to engage fully with the genre context' (Cheyne 'Introduction' 118). Hence, her call to deal specifically with genre, so as to broaden the understanding of disability representation and advance the understanding of specific texts and forms (117).

Despite increasing critical interest in sf scholarship engaged with gender, sexuality, race, ethnicity and postcolonialism, few scholars worked with disability perspectives prior to the 2010s

(Cheyne 'Introduction' 118; Allan 'Introduction' 2). There were some notable exceptions (Cheu; Kanar; Melzer; Moody; Stemp; Weinstock), but pivotal to the emergence of the field was Kathryn Allan's edited collection *Disability in Science Fiction: Representations of Technology as Cure* (2013), the first comprehensive work devoted to disability and sf. (Other notable publications at this juncture include Allan 'Disability'; Cheyne 'She'; and a chapter on sf cinema in Ellis.) The subsequent increase and interest in disability perspectives on sf is evident in special issues of *Journal of Science Fiction* in 2019 and *Journal of Literary & Cultural Disability Studies* in 2020, as well as Sami Schalk's *Bodyminds Reimagined: (Dis)ability, Race, and Gender in Black Women's Speculative Fiction* (2018) and the chapter on sf in Cheyne's *Disability, Literature, Genre: Representation and Affect in Contemporary Fiction* (2019). Over the course of the decade, this research has expanded from sf literature and film to include television, games and comic books.

Why a disability perspective on sf?

People with disabilities have throughout history been subjected to various types of oppression, such as discrimination, hate, violence, pity, objectification, social exclusion and limited access to different parts of society, including education, and uneven distribution of economic resources; moreover, disability is recurrently connected to debates about what constitutes quality of life, including questions about assisted suicide, eugenics and reproductive technologies (Goodley 2). The negative views and discourses that underscore such oppressions are often (re)produced in representations of people with disabilities. According to Rosemarie Garland-Thomson, the dominating narratives of disability across culture are oppressive, disempowering and prejudicial. Seldom is disability portrayed as an integral part of life or as part of the wide spectrum of what it is to be human. Instead, it is presented as a tragic flaw in individuals, when it should in fact be understood as one of the most universal experiences: we all eventually become disabled if we grow old enough (Garland-Thomson 1567–8). These types of representations perpetuate a medical model of disability, in which disability is seen as nothing else than a tragic loss for an individual who needs diagnosis, rehabilitation, cure and normalisation. These stories circulating in culture shape our society, relationships, our views of ourselves and others, and how we view disability (Garland-Thomson 1567; Cheyne 'Introduction' 117). It is thus vital to critically engage with such narratives.

Mainstream culture and literature have often been criticised for thier lack of depictions of marginalised groups. In contrast, however, images of disability appear widely throughout history, although paradoxically this frequency has often been overlooked (Mitchell and Snyder 52; Longmore 131–2). A similar paradox can be found in sf. Ever since its inception, sf has not only included but been quite preoccupied with depicting disabled bodies and minds. Allan contends that 'SF has long explored deviant and disabled bodies: from Mary Shelley's Frankenstein's monster to James Cameron's wheelchair-bound hero, Jake Sully [...] in *Avatar* (2009), SF is inhabited by people (and aliens) whose embodiments are situated along the entire spectrum of ability' ('Introduction' 2). Despite this abundance, disability has been rendered peripheral and the presence of disabled bodies and minds obscured in many of the critical approaches to sf. Schalk argues that the lack of scholarly investment and recognition of disability in sf is part of the erasure of disability in speculative media ('Resisting').

Allan argues that critical engagement with representations of disability in sf narratives are important not least in order to 'condemn the repeated instances of the erasure, "curing," prosthetization, and negative marginalization of people with disabilities' in the genre – a critical endeavour that sf scholars must undertake as they have with racist, sexist, classist or homophobic representations (Allan 'Disability' 1.1). These motives for studying disability in sf are important, but it remains imperative not only to condemn negative imagery. Scholars must also explore and understand the place disability takes in sf, how it can be conceptualised specifically within generic conventions, and how perspectives on disability and ability can contribute to interpreting individual texts and the genre as a whole.

As Allan and Cheyne note, the groundwork is currently being laid to bring disability studies and sf together (393). While there are several ways in which disability can be read in sf and numerous issues within sf that could benefit from a disability perspective, this chapter focuses on two interrelated issues. First, by applying a critique of the medical model to sf narratives about the future, it demonstrates ways in which sf narratives perpetuate this view of disability. Second, by considering not only the presence but also the absence of disability, it establishes the imperative to consider non-realist elements when analysing disability in sf.

Conceptualising the future: Medical and technological cures

The medical model is closely intertwined with discourses of the future and often (re)produced in cultural representations. Johnson Cheu, for example, argues that '[p]opular media is already pushing society toward a Utopian model of bodily perfection and cure' (198). Future discourse is often framed in terms of a linear process: from the past, into the present and towards the future. As I have argued elsewhere, this linear process is infused with discourses of progress, development and betterment, and the future is presented as a site in which present-day issues potentially can be solved and our world improved as it leaves its shortcomings in the past (Wälivaara 'Marginalized'). Depending on when a story is created, different issues, such as racism, sexism or homophobia, can be framed as regrettable remnants of the past, while the future holds the promise of a more developed society. Sf, of course, deals with such promises as well as their failures.

For some, this unfortunately means the risk of not having a future at all. From the perspective of the medical model, any improved progressive future society is a society where disability no longer exists. This 'disability-free future' is taken for granted as the valued and 'good' future, the future everyone should strive for, while failing to recognise that there is value to be found in futures that include people with disabilities (Kafer 3). In her exploration of the use of the disabled body in imagined futures, Alison Kafer shows this connection between the way disability is understood and its relationship to the future:

> If disability is conceptualized as a terrible unending tragedy, then any future that includes disability can only be a future to avoid. A better future, in other words, is one that excludes disability and disabled bodies; indeed, it is the very *absence* of disability that signals this better future. The *presence* of disability, then, signals something else: a future that bears too many traces of the ills of the present to be desirable.
>
> (2)

One recurring way in which the medical model becomes apparent is found in variations of the cure narrative, one of the most prevalent types of disability narrative. The issue is not to argue for or against medical interventions or cures, but to question the hegemonic discourse of the medical model in order to counteract its view of disability. Cure narratives perform cultural work in spreading beliefs about disability and quality of life, and thus devalue different bodies and minds. In his historical overview of disability representation in cinema, Martin F. Norden points to what he calls 'Cure or kill', a recurring narrative in which the character with a disability is either cured and thus reintegrated into society or killed (107). Reflecting the medical model, such stories imply that having a disability is a tragic fate worse than death, and if the individual cannot be cured, they are better off dead.

Cure narratives are frequent in sf. Norden points to the return of such stories in genre films of the 1970–80s, with the original STAR WARS trilogy (1977–83) as a one of the prime examples (Norden 292–5). Instead of the miraculous interventions common throughout film history, these films introduced technological cures. Allan contends that 'more often than not, whenever there is disability in a SF narrative, there is the parallel trope of "cure"', a trope that runs through the history of the genre in a variety of forms, including utopian sf that imagines the end of disability and dystopian sf that depicts failed cures or societies in which only some can afford cures ('Introduction' 8–9). Cheu argues that the medical cure is a recurring theme in sf cinema (199), and Jane Stemp likewise suggests that writers of sf, even those who otherwise seem eager to challenge notions of progress, seem unwilling to abandon the idea of a medicalised future of cures. While these cure narratives are problematic in themselves, as they often adhere to a solely medical understanding of disability, suggesting that disability is only tragic and in need of curing or elimination, they also serve as a device for the eradication of disability in narratives, or at least, for the 'ambiguity of existence' of disabled bodies and minds (Wälivaara 'Marginalized' 229).

Reading the absence

Technological or medical interventions can serve to eradicate explicit representations of disability from fictional worlds (Cheyne 'Freaks' 41; Cheu 198–9). Therefore, it is important also to read the absence, and the social meanings of this absence, in visions of the future. The absence (or presence) of disability reveals, as Allan argues, the text's implicit assumptions about 'the ideal future human' ('Disability' 3.4). If the absence signals a better future, as suggested by Kafer, then how does this absence relate to the systems of exclusion or oppression, as asked by Tobin Siebers?

Schalk contends that when sf deals with issues of oppression and privilege, it typically does so either through a future setting in which these issues have already been resolved, which often leads to an erasure of all difference, or by relocating difference onto non-humans, such as aliens or robots (*Bodyminds* 86). Such allegorical figures – a quite specific trait of speculative or fantastic fiction – often obscure the presence of disability, as they are more commonly read in terms of gendered, sexual, racial or national difference and thus might appear to not be dealing with disability at all. For example, disability scholar Michael Bérubé describes his surprise upon realising that sf narratives, which he 'never considered to be "about" disability', were indeed filled with 'blind Daredevils, mutant supercrips, and posthuman cyborgs', leading to suggests that the genre 'is as obsessed with disability as it is with space travel and alien contact' ('Disability' 568).

Disability studies commonly critiques metaphoric uses of disability rather than depictions based on the lived experiences or the political and social dimensions of disability (Mitchell and Snyder 48; Schalk *Bodyminds* 39–45). But applying a disability perspective to speculative fiction, where the texts often rely on worldbuilding that differs from our own, requires us to consider and take seriously those depictions of disability that per definition cannot be based on lived experiences, such as cyborgs, aliens and mutants in order 'to engage fully with the genre context' (Cheyne 'Introduction' 118; cf. Wälivaara 'Blind'; Schalk 'Reevaluating' and *Bodyminds* 26–8).

If disability is considered a social and cultural construction, then it can take on different meanings and guises in sf's non-realist cultures and societies. It is thus important to read disability not only in terms of our own society, but also in relation to the premises of the fictional text itself and the genre's conventions.

Indeed, the most frequent way in which disability is 'deployed' (Bérubé *Secret* 2) in sf is not through realistic representations of characters with disabilities or through depictions of 'realist disabilities' recognisable from our world (Schalk *Bodyminds* 118). There are unquestionably sf characters who quite easily read as representations of disabilities, such as Charles Xavier in *X-Men* (1963–), Davros in DOCTOR WHO (1963–), Captain Pike in STAR TREK (1966–) and Jerome Morrow in *Gattaca* (Niccol 1997). However, the genre particularly engages with representations that, at a first glance, do not seem to deal with disability because they lack the more explicit, culturally recognisable, realistic traits that dominate more conventional representations of disability. Instead, sf invites multiple deployments of disability: the many unruly human and non-human bodies and minds infused with technology or prosthesis, or with different abilities, or living in alternative societies or temporalities. For example, Schalk shows how speculative fiction's portrayals of realist disabilities on 'nonrealist bodyminds' and in fantastic worlds, and portrayals of 'nonrealist disabilities' that do not exist in current reality, serve to defamiliarise disability – and thus can encourage readers to question taken-for-granted understanding of categories, their boundaries and their meanings (*Bodyminds* 118).

Therefore, the absence of explicitly (realist) disabled bodies and minds does not always mean that disability as a system of power and oppression is omitted. For sf scholars, reading this relocation of difference from a disability perspective can make visible how certain generic conventions (non-realist elements, characters and worlds) relate to systems of power and oppression in terms of disability/ability. As Cheu argues, even though disability as a medical construction seems to be eradicated in such films as *Gattaca*, *Blade Runner* (Scott 1982) and *The Matrix* (Wachowski sisters 1999), it remains a dominating social construction.

Conclusion

While it is important to critically engage with those more explicit, realist representations of disability in sf, it is equally important to theorise and make visible the ways in which the genre narratively deploys disability as a system of power and injustice. This means that a disability studies, or critical disability studies, approach is useful for analysing not only explicit representations of disability, but also the wider social system of power associated with normative notions of disability/ability, bodies, and minds – even in those narratives where disability seems absent. It is also important to remember that disability does not stand alone but intersects with other categories and representations of identity, such as gender, sexuality, race, ethnicity and class.

Allan and Cheyne's contention that disability is a central concern of the sf genre, across time and in all its forms (389–90), is borne out by the growing field of research that deals with sf and disability. But there is paramount work to be done to adapt and incorporate disability theories with non-realist explorations of disability, and make visible the ways in which disability is, explicitly and inexplicitly, deployed and represented in sf. This extends beyond physical disabilities to include questions of neurodiversity and able-mindedness.

Sf is often framed in terms of its potential for social critique and commentary. This capacity can be used to challenge normative conceptions about disability as a solely individual concern in need of curing or elimination, and instead provide alternatives to those many disability-free futures, alternatives in which the presence of people with disabilities are of value.

Acknowledgments

This chapter has been written within a project headed by Lotta Vikström: 'Ageing with disabilities in past, present and future societies: Risks and loads from disabilities and later life outcomes'. It has received funding from the Wallenberg Foundation (Stiftelsen Marcus och Amalia Wallenbergs Minnesfond, MAW 2019.0003).

Works cited

Allan, Kathryn, ed. *Disability in Science Fiction: Representations of Technology as Cure*. Palgrave Macmillan, 2013.

——. 'Disability in Science Fiction.' *SF 101: A Guide to Teaching and Studying Science Fiction*. Ed. Ritch Calvin, Doug Davis, Karen Hellekson and Craig Jacobsen. Science Fiction Research Association, 2014. Kindle.

——. 'Introduction'. *Disability in Science Fiction: Representations of Technology as Cure*. Ed. Kathryn Allan. Palgrave Macmillan, 2013. 1–15.

Allan, Kathryn and Ria Cheyne. 'Science Fiction, Disability, Disability Studies: A Conversation'. *Journal of Literary & Cultural Disability Studies* 14.4 (2020): 387–401.

Bérubé, Michael. 'Disability and Narrative'. *PMLA* 120.2 (2005): 568–76.

——. *The Secret Life of Stories: From Don Quixote to Harry Potter. How Understanding Intellectual Disability Transforms the Way We Read*. New York UP, 2016.

Cheu, Johnson. 'De-gene-erates, Replicants and Other Aliens: (Re)defining Disability in Futuristic Film'. *Disability/Postmodernity: Embodying Disability Theory*. Ed. Tom Shakespeare and Mairian Corker. Continuum, 2002. 198–212.

Cheyne, Ria. *Disability, Literature, Genre: Representation and Affect in Contemporary Fiction*. Liverpool UP, 2019.

——. 'Freaks and Extraordinary Bodies: Disability as Generic Marker in John Varley's "Tango Charlie and Foxtrot Romeo"'. *Disability in Science Fiction: Representations of Technology as Cure*. Ed. Kathryn Allan. Palgrave Macmillan, 2013. 35–46.

——. 'Introduction: Popular Genres and Disability Representation'. *Journal of Literary & Cultural Disability Studies* 6.2 (2012): 117–23.

——. '"She was born a thing": Disability, the Cyborg and the Posthuman in Anne McCaffrey's *The Ship Who Sang*'. *Journal of Modern Literature* 36.3 (2013): 138–56.

Davis, Lennard J. 'Crips Strike Back: The Rise of Disability Studies'. *American Literary History* 11.3 (1999): 500–12.

Ellis, Katie. *Disability and Popular Culture: Focusing Passion, Creating Community and Expressing Defiance*. Ashgate, 2015.

Garland-Thomson, Rosemarie. 'Feminist Disability Studies'. *Signs: Journal of Women in Culture and Society* 30.2 (2005): 1557–87.

Goodley, Dan. *Disability Studies: An Interdisciplinary Introduction*, second edition. Sage, 2017.

Kafer, Alison. *Feminist, Queer, Crip*. Indiana UP, 2013.

Kanar, Hanley E. 'No Ramps in Space: The Inability to Envision Accessibility in *Star Trek: Deep Space Nine*'. *Fantasy Girls: Gender in the New Universe of Science Fiction and Fantasy Television*. Ed. Elyce Rae Helford. Rowman & Littlefield, 2000. 245–64.

Longmore, Paul K. 'Screening Stereotypes: Images of Disabled People in Television and Motion Pictures'. *Why I Burned My Book and Other Essays on Disability*. Temple UP, 2003. 131–46.

Melzer, Patricia. '"And How Many Souls Do You Have?": Technologies of Perverse Desire and Queer Sex in Science Fiction Erotica'. *Queer Universes: Sexualities in Science Fiction*. Ed. Wendy Gay Pearson, Veronica Hollinger and Joan Gordon. Liverpool UP, 2008. 161–79.

Mitchell, David T. and Sharon L. Snyder. *Narrative Prosthesis: Disability and the Dependencies of Discourse*. U of Michigan P, 2000.

Moody, Nickianne. 'Untapped Potential: The Representation of Disability/Special Ability in the Cyberpunk Workforce'. *Convergence* 3.3 (1997): 90–105.

Norden, Martin F. *The Cinema of Isolation: A History of Physical Disability in the Movies*. Rutgers UP, 1994.
——. 'The Social Model of Disability: Thirty Years On'. *Disability & Society* 28.7 (2013): 1024–6.
Oliver, Mike. *Social Work with Disabled People*. Macmillan, 1983.
Schalk, Sami. *Bodyminds Reimagined: (Dis)ability, Race, and Gender in Black Women's Speculative Fiction*. Duke UP, 2018.
——. 'Critical Disability Studies as Methodology' *Lateral* 6.1 (2017). https://csalateral.org/issue/6-1/forum-alt-humanities-critical-disability-studies-methodology-schalk/.
——. 'Reevaluating the Supercrip'. *Journal of Literary & Cultural Disability Studies* 10.1 (2016): 71–86.
——. 'Resisting Erasure: Reading (Dis)Ability and Race in Speculative Media'. *The Routledge Companion to Disability and Media*. Ed. Katie Ellis, Gerard Goggin, Beth Haller and Rosemary Curtis. Routledge, 2019. 137–46.
Siebers, Tobin. *Disability Theory*. U of Michigan P, 2008.
Stemp, Jane. 'Devices and Desires: Science Fiction, Fantasy and Disability in Literature for Young People'. *Disability Studies Quarterly* 24.1 (2004). https://dsq-sds.org/ index.php/dsq/article/view/850/1025
Wälivaara, Josefine. 'Blind Warriors, Supercrips, and Techno-Marvels: Challenging Depictions of Disability in *Star Wars*'. *The Journal of Popular Culture* 51.4 (2018): 1036–56.
——. 'Marginalized Bodies of Imagined Futurescapes: Ableism and Heteronormativity in Science Fiction'. *Culture Unbound. Journal of Current Cultural Research* 10.2 (2018): 226–45.
Weinstock, Jeffrey A. 'Freaks in Space: "Extraterrestrialism" and "Deep-Space Multiculturalism"'. *Freakery: Cultural Spectacles of the Extraordinary Body*. Ed. Rosemarie Garland-Thomson. New York UP, 1996. 327–37.

40
DIY SCIENCE FICTION

Jonathan Alexander

Fan communities have actively participated in the circulation and development of a wide variety of speculative narratives, practically since the inception of the genre in its contemporary form a century ago. In the mid-twentieth century, fanzines were an important part of sharing information and ideas, as well as allowing would-be writers to try their hand at crafting stories, some of whom would later become best-selling sf authors. Mike Ashley's five-volume history of sf magazines since the late nineteenth century (2000–22) notes how many of them began as fan projects, both print and online, and maintains that the story of such zines will continue, with some fans aiming for professionalisation and more formal publication and others writing and creating for the sheer enjoyment of doing so.

Fanfiction has long been understood as an important way in which readers interact with commercially produced narratives, filling in desired storylines and recreating characters' identities. More ambitious fans of specific sf texts and of the genre more generally also produced other kinds of content, including homemade movies of varying length, such as John Cosentino's 16 mm STAR TREK fan film, *Paragon's Paragon* (1974). The advent of widely accessible, increasingly affordable and easy-to-use digital technologies at the end of the twentieth century further propelled fan culture and those fans who were interested in making and disseminating their own content or riffing off commercial narratives.

This chapter provides an overview of and attempts to theorise the value of such DIY sf production. Given the scope of such efforts, it can only touch on a few remarkable examples and identify a couple of salient trends. Other scholars, such as Henry Jenkins in *Textual Poachers: Television Fans & Participatory Culture* (1992), have explored the importance specifically of fan fiction for sf fandom, so this chapter will instead concentrate primarily on homemade video and film, especially as it combines cosplay, set design and other aspects of fan material culture in increasingly complex forms of sf storytelling. Such DIY video storytelling represents one of the most ambitious – and in some cases controversial – forms of fan engagement, contributing to an ever-expanding 'participatory culture'. It also demonstrates the growing tension between fan desires to create and disseminate their own content and corporate ownership of intellectual property (IP), which sometimes leads to corporate attempts to control fan production. However, other kinds of

DOI: 10.4324/9781003140269-43

DIY sf production, not beholden to existing IP, stretch the possibilities of sf and speculative storytelling beyond what is currently considered marketable.

Theorising DIY sf

In many ways, Henry Jenkins has been at the forefront of analysing both why and how fans adopt and adapt various pop culture stories in general and sf stories in particular for their own uses. Early in his career, he focused on fan literacy practices in fanfiction, calling fans' use of popular culture characters and narratives for their own purposes a form of 'textual poaching'. In *Convergence Culture* (2006) and *Spreadable Media* (2013), he turned his attention to how contemporary culture in the developed West is increasingly *transmediated*, with content spanning multiple media, platforms and communication channels, as well as *participatory*, with content providers sometimes asking for consumer input. Today's media ecologies thus promote a 'participatory culture' in which individuals and communities are encouraged to be not just consumers but 'prosumers' engaged in sharing content and, in more sophisticated instances, creating their own remixed content through fan fiction and video production, resulting in sometimes powerful forms of personal and collective creative expression. Jenkins no longer characterises such fan use as 'poaching'; it is now more explicitly called 'participatory', and he uses the term 'spreadable media' to suggest how media content production, dissemination and consumption all occur across many different platforms and venues.

Jenkins is not just interested in the forms that such media prosumption assume but also the 'value' of their content – with 'value' being the word *Spreadable Media* uses to describe the intense investment that some people make into popular narrative. He has strongly argued, for instance, that the copyrighted characters and narratives of the HARRY POTTER franchise should be open to manipulation and recasting through fan media, if only because those stories constitute not just an attractive narrative for younger generations but an important kind of *mythologising*, a common set of stories shared by millions in the absence of other binding or shareable narratives, such as religious belief. The same is true for STAR TREK fandom, some of which is self-consciously based on promulgating the spirit and ethos of the Federation, an interstellar alliance committed to better living through technology, peaceful co-existence, multicultural tolerance and acceptance of diversity. The ability, then, to mix and remix such narratives performs an important role in attempting to make sense of a complex, contradictory and sometimes dangerous world.

John Rieder reiterates the ideological value of popular narrative and fan engagement with it, explaining that his interest in a popular genre such as sf stems in large part from his concern 'with the kind of critical and anti-hegemonic power SF narratives often exercise. This critical power does not depend on SF's formal grammar, but rather on the way some narratives appropriate and recode the genre's resources' (12). For example, despite its faults, STAR TREK's Federation, and fan adoption and adaption of it, signals a desire for a different kind of world, one based less on competition for resources and more on cooperation, collectivity and mutual understanding. That said, Rieder acknowledges that the culture industry is a large, interlocking set of producers, businesses, marketers, consumers and prosumers designed to generate monetisable attention, and that 'The mass cultural genre system plays a key role in organizing the production, distribution, and reception of storytelling within the milieu of mass culture' (34). He notes how 'the management of narrative in mass culture includes [...] the way it negotiates the tension between the commercial status quo and class-based fantasies of liberation from that social order' (42). At stake in such a tension is often fan adoption and creative use of corporately owned IP, which has prompted a range of responses, from legal action to the production of approved guidelines for DIY fan work and even, in some cases, more cooperative contact with fans to meet their needs and interests.

Other scholars are far more utopian in their outlook, considering DIY sf production within larger contexts of political activity. Jenkins in particular understands the value of such work as contributing to desires for increased democratised participation. He argues that DIY culture 'was associated with the counterculture going back to the beatniks of the 1950s. These impulses helped to define the early internet culture – the culture of amateurs, hackers, and home brew' (*Participatory* 18) – a move that historicises DIY production within a larger arc of questioning the status quo and offering alternative visions for worldbuilding. Most recently, in *Popular Culture and the Civic Imagination*, he has begun documenting numerous efforts throughout the world to mobilise popular narrative, especially sf, through DIY efforts to imagine better, more equitable and more sustainable futures. In their introduction, he and his co-editors note that 'Many changemakers maintain a passionate relationship with popular culture, using that cultural vocabulary to broker relations across different political groups' (8). More grandly, such work manifests

> the desire to expand and diversify the contents of the imagination as a means of resisting and ultimately overturning any systems of power that curtail or criminalize the rights of all people to imagine and work toward a world that allows them to thrive in happiness, security, and humanity.
>
> (21)

On one hand, these scholar-activists acknowledge that 'civic engagements with popular culture involve complex negotiations between oppositional world views with fraught relationships with commercial institutions' (7); on the other, they point to DIY cosplay that mobilises sf imagery for real-world political ends, such as the adoption of the handmaid's uniform from *The Handmaid's Tale* (Hulu 2017–) in a variety of global protests about women's rights. To further study and support such DIY efforts, Jenkins and his team conduct workshops in the Los Angeles area and, at times, globally (www.civicimaginationproject.org; Peters-Lazaro and Shresthova).

Fan production from groups traditionally understood as marginalised is particularly important in pushing the boundaries of speculative narrative, not only to be more inclusive but to re-centre sf storytelling in the lives of Black, queer, Indigenous and other groups and experiences. As andré m. carrington argues, fanfiction from people of colour often 'reconfigures the relationship between race, nation, and genre conventions' (29) and, more specifically, 'elaborates on fantasies and realities in which Blackness is already an integral part and always will be' of sf narratives and the human story in general (237). Looking more closely at DIY video production, Alexis Lothian sees the rise of vidding in fanworks as a significant contribution to pushing critically the ways in which marginalised groups find and disseminate representations that they have not readily seen in the mainstream media. The next section considers some of this work and its complex engagement with IP issues.

DIY fan films

Perhaps the most significant form of DIY sf production occurs when fans take existing sf narratives and create their own storylines (through fan fiction) or videos (sometimes as full-length homemade movies) – a practice that has grown so much in popularity and is so readily facilitated by contemporary digital technologies that Adrienne Russel, Mizuko Ito, Todd Richmond and Marc Tuters proclaim that 'Social networking technologies [...] have given consumers the power to transform brands' (63). How such transformation emerges is the subject of some controversy and central to the story of how corporate IP holders and fans interact.

Sometimes such 'films' consist of recasting primarily, if not exclusively, pre-existing footage, often readily available for manipulation on the web. Lothian argues that 'Through the processes of juxtaposition, repetition, and audiovisual suturing by which they make meaning within their subcultural community, vids have the capacity not only to comment on science fiction cultures but also to reinscribe, reimagine, and queer media histories and temporalities' (220). Such 'vidding' is 'retelling by re-editing' (223), and she cites the example of Flummery's 2005 'Walking on the Ground', which 'uses fan video's queer methods to explore anxieties surrounding the future of media' (223). It remixes numerous pre-existing clips from a wide range of sf and speculative media about the history of transportation, while also foregrounding the evolution of video editing software, creating a 'meta-vid', while gesturing to some of the anxieties about fast-paced, rapid technological change that characterise the experience of many in the contemporary world. At the same time, Lothian argues for a somewhat *queered* understanding of this work – queered in the sense of troubling normal relations of official content production and passive audience consumption:

> Through labors of piracy, file-sharing, and informal education to teach the technical skills that make video remix possible, popular media becomes a shared archive, its images as cathected to personal lives as family photographs. The processes involved in vidding – both for the creator and for the watcher – are as important as the narratives they create.
>
> (227)

Some fan films are fairly simple, staging or recreating various fight scenes from action and adventure films with sf themes. Two early famous digital creations are 2008's 'Batman vs. Predator' (www.youtube.com/watch?v=vACtvTsvcyg) and 2010's 'Batman vs. Predator vs. Aliens' (www.youtube.com/watch?v=cKxL2GnGFrw), which obviously mix different narrative arcs and characters from different IP holders. A more ambitious film in the same vein is 2012's 'The Punisher: Dirty Laundry' (www.youtube.com/watch?v=bWpK0wsnitc), which features Thomas Jane, reprising his lead role from *The Punisher* (Hensleigh 2004). Created by Adi Shankar, showrunner for the animated *Castlevania* (Netflix 2017–21), it has its own narrative, not just fight scenes, even if it adheres to the original character's ethos. Shankar, like many DIY content creators, has embraced YouTube as the platform for disseminating original and fan-based videos, and he runs what he calls the 'Bootleg Universe' (www.youtube.com/channel/UCNgSkSyLpwJckPsCcpDc2Ow) to distribute his content. The popularity of such films is extraordinary. Shankar's 'Mighty Morphin' Power Rangers Bootleg Film By Joseph Kahn', released in 2015, already has over 25 million views.

Even before such films were made, some DIY filmmakers were experimenting with gaming software, using the graphics of video and computer games to create what has come to be called Machinima. One of the earliest short films made with computer game software is 1996's 'Diary of a Camper' (www.youtube.com/watch?v=mq4Ks4Z_NGY), based on the first-person shooter *Quake* (id/GT 1996). Made by a group called United Ranger Films, it is unsurprisingly composed almost entirely of a fight scene, but it nonetheless helped open up to other DIY content creators the power of gaming software platforms. Starting in 2003, Burnie Burns and his production company, Rooster Teeth, released 'Red vs. Blue', based on the sf game *Halo: Combat Evolved* (Bungie/Microsoft 2001). Ostensibly about a civil war, the series' first 'season' (www.youtube.com/watch?v=XnsRdaZTMas) was so popular that it has now run to 18 seasons and well over 300 episodes; it can be seen on YouTube and, periodically, on streaming services such as Netflix. The series eventually became fully animated, leaving behind its Machinima roots, but it nonetheless attests to the power of Machinima in providing DIY creators an opportunity to make and disseminate content that others want to see.

Other fan films are even more ambitious in embracing live action content creation. Suzanne Collins's Hunger Games trilogy (2008–10) spawned a great deal of fan engagement, with numerous fan fictions and fan media productions, including some full-length films. Many of these films are set in the 'arena' of the hunger games, which is unsurprising given that any wooded area will suffice as a set. One popular fan film set in the Hunger Games universe is 2014's 'Weeping Willow' (www.youtube.com/watch?v=o-xwmNDuGgI). Set in the arena, the 20-minute film has already garnered nearly four million views, its popularity likely resting on its relatively high production values and poignant plot: 'When Willow is picked for the 52nd Hunger Games, her brother Tristan chooses to volunteer so she does not have to face the games alone. As they struggle through the arena, Willow must come to terms with the fact that only one of them can make it home'.

Like many DIY fan works, these homemade films often seek to extend, sometimes even complicate, the original storyworld. In fact, such remixes and uses of existing media platforms for fan interests are not just about displaying technical ability or love of certain franchises. Such work often showcases fans' *cultural and political* investments as well. For example, the Hunger Games fan film, 'Rising Hope' (www.youtube.com/watch?v=Dn9-EyaKjM8), is set in the arena but features characters who rely on their Christian faith to help them survive the horrors of battling to the death. These fans' introduction of religion into the Hunger Games narrative allows them to explore issues and content of interest to them but absent from the original story. Such fan work is an important extension of some of the earliest fan fiction, particularly that based on Star Trek, which imagined characters such as Kirk and Spock in romantic and sexual situations. Indeed, the introduction of queer content into fan fiction and fan media has been one significant way in which fans have developed storylines and narrative arcs that mass media corporations and IP owners have often been reluctant to introduce. The same is likely true for religious issues, identities and communities, which are sparsely represented in commercial sf narratives.

Religious and queer interests are hardly the only ones remixed into existing narrative content. While 'Subcultural science fiction media fandom is often assumed to be predominantly occupied by white people' (Lothian 232), many fans remix sf narratives 'to show how [sf] reproduces the erasures of the United States' racial past and present' (237) and those of the White supremacist West in general. Skawennati, a Mohawk artist living and working in Montréal, uses Machinima to explore possible Indigenous futures. From 2007–14, the nine episodes of *TimeTraveller*™ (www.youtube.com/user/TimeTravellerTM) 'offer[ed] a postcolonial rereading of the history of the Indigenous peoples of Turtle Island'. A young Mohawk, Hunter, uses virtual reality to explore important turning points in the history and experiences of his people, including episodes in pre-Columbian America and the 1990 Kanehsatà:ke Resistance, a land dispute between Mohawks and the descendants of colonial settlers in Quebec. The series also imagines the possible future of the Mohawk people in 2121. As a whole, *TimeTraveller*™ constitutes a significant use of Machinima to open up perspectives within sf narrative from Indigenous standpoints, contributing to the ways in which DIY production mobilises sf tropes to counter hegemonic narratives centring White or European experiences by recentring the views and values of traditionally marginalised peoples.

DIY *Trek*

Some of the most intense DIY fan work has focused on STAR TREK. Homemade films range in length, production quality and narrative complexity, and some even feature professional actors, including actors from the official franchises and other sf media. Some of the more popular DIY films include *Star Trek: Of Gods and Men* (2007–8), a three-part miniseries featuring some actors from the original NBC series (1966–9); *Star Trek: Renegades* (2015), originally conceived as the pilot for a fan-based web series; and *Star Trek: Horizon* (2016), which was funded in part by a Kickstarter campaign, a popular way for DIY filmmakers to raise money for increasingly sophisticated projects. DIY creators also work on multiple homemade series, often released on the web through platforms such as YouTube. These include *Star Trek: Hidden Frontier* (2000–7), consisting of fifty episodes; *Star Trek Continues* (2013–7) and *Star Trek: New Voyages* (2004–16), both attempts to 'complete' the original crew's five-year mission; and *Star Trek: Intrepid* (2007–18), a fan production based in Scotland (for one of the most up-to-date archives of such work, see https://en.wikipedia.org/wiki/Star_Trek_fan_productions). Fan production is so widespread that Atlanta's annual Treklanta convention presents the Bjo Awards to honour the best fan-made films and series (named after Bjo Trimble, a founding member of STAR TREK fandom).

Such fan production is not without controversy, and some of the above-mentioned work prompted legal proceedings from Paramount and CBS, intent on squelching use of their STAR TREK IP. Perhaps the most famous case concerns *Axanar*, which was to be a fan-made full-length feature of extraordinary quality. Based on a confrontation between the Federation and the Klingon Empire only glancingly mentioned in the episode 'Whom Gods Destroy' (1969), the film was previewed in 2014's 'Prelude to Axanar' (www.youtube.com/watch?v=1W1_8IV8uhA), a documentary-style short featuring interviews with major characters from the battle, some of them played by actors who had appeared in official STAR TREK (Gary Graham) or other sf series (Richard Hatch from *Battlestar Galactica* (ABC 1978–9)). 'Prelude' reveals the filmmakers' great care, attention to detail and high production values. However, when production began on *Axanar*, CBS and Paramount filed copyright infringement charges against them, effectively halting production. The lawsuit was eventually settled when CBS released new guidelines for the production of STAR TREK fan films, that dictated fan work must be strictly non-commercial. Other limitations include the following:

1. The fan production must be less than 15 minutes for a single self-contained story, or no more than 2 segments, episodes or parts, not to exceed 30 minutes total, with no additional seasons, episodes, parts, sequels or remakes.
2. The title of the fan production or any parts cannot include the name '*Star Trek*'. However, the title must contain a subtitle with the phrase: 'A *STAR TREK* FAN PRODUCTION' in plain typeface. The fan production cannot use the term 'official' in either its title or subtitle or in any marketing, promotions or social media for the fan production. (www.startrek.com/fan-films)

Many fans expressed extreme dissatisfaction with such guidelines, suggesting that they radically limit fans' creativity and ability to produce high-quality, original, feature-length work or narratives with substantial story arcs. More critically, while this move on the part of the official media industry to create such guidelines might be a way to manage IP infringement, it is also a way to mobilise fan work as a form of free advertising for corporate IP holders.

However, corporate/fan engagements are not necessarily hostile. While even a DIY booster such as Jenkins acknowledges that the 'fan community must negotiate from a position of relative powerlessness and must rely solely on its collective moral authority, while the corporations, for the moment, act as if they had the force of law on their side' ('Quentin' 232), not all IP owners are 'stingy' with fans. Joshua Green and Jenkins note that some 'companies are reappraising the value of fan engagement and participation – in some cases, openly collaborating with fans and in others, allowing fans some free space to repurpose their content toward their own ends. Yet each also suggests potential conflicts since fan and corporate interests are never perfectly aligned' (219). Derek Johnson offers a fascinating example of corporate interest in harnessing DIY sf work, describing how

> enfranchisement of the audience as collaborative industrial labor occurred in summer 2007 when NCT-Universal's Sci-Fi Network sought to sustain viewers' interest in *Battlestar Galactica* in the off-season through the 'BSG VideoMaker Toolkit'. This kit contained a collection of establishing shots, visual effects, sound effects, and stock cutaway images, inviting fans to combine these professional materials with their own original footage to generate new *Battlestar* content. The resulting four-minute episodes could then be uploaded for public viewing on the official Sci-Fi website, with the promise that a few lucky contributors would see their work aired on television during the upcoming season. In aggregate, hundreds of these videos helped animate and refresh the series' online content offerings despite the production hiatus in television.
>
> (211–2)

The site no longer seems to be active, but you can still find fan commentary about the effort, which was frequently called 'interesting', even as fans noted that it seemed a commercial effort by Universal to promote not only their shows but also a suite of media making tools.

Original DIY sf

The production and dissemination of fully original DIY sf content is perhaps less well developed than fan content production, but many sf aficionados actively develop their own original content – again, of highly varying quality and skill level. Many of these are short films designed to catch the interest of major production companies or others in the industry who might want to take a chance on an unknown or amateur filmmaker. Periodic 'roundups' of such work appear on the web, such as '13 of the Best Sci-Fi Short Films' (www.filmcrux.com/blog/sci-fi-short-films), which features homemade shorts of startling quality, testifying to the significant advances in DIY video production technologies. In fact, some of them, such as Erik Wernquist's 'Wanderers' (2014), seem to exist primarily as demonstrations of technical and special effects skills, containing almost no narrative. *Uncanny*'s 'The Short List: The Ten Best Science Fiction & Fantasy Shorts on the Web' (https://uncannymagazine.com/article/short-list-ten-best-science-fiction-fantasy-shorts-web/) shows how interested sf short filmmakers are in mixing genres. For example, Til Nowak's 2011 'The Centrifuge Brain Project' (www.icr-science.org/) combines sf with the 'fake documentary' as 'Dr. Nick Laslowicz discusses the experiments he's been undertaking [...] on the effects of centrifugal force on brain development that required the building of outlandishly complex medical devices that just so happen to make incredible amusement park rides'. This genre-mixing speaks powerfully to the ways in which many fans experience rapid technological change and scientific development as interpenetrating their day-to-day lives, making reality itself seem like sf.

The international reach of such work should not be underestimated, and many DIY sf films are in languages other than English. For example, the Serbian Sava Zivkovic's 2021 sf-horror short

'Irradiation' (www.shortoftheweek.com/2021/08/19/irradiation/) is in Russian but could have been written by J.G. Ballard or Jan VanderMeer. Its plot is slight – an explorer in an irradiated zone starts to have strange visions – but the effects are impressive, creating a moody atmosphere of speculative dread.

Many of these shorts are also entered into film festivals across the globe, reaching audiences before they are put on the web for more widespread viewing. The video sharing platform Vimeo is a major repository of such work, but YouTube has hosted, and through its periodic video-making workshops, helped filmmakers produce 'YouTube Originals', including such web series as 2018's ten-episode sf-horror 'Origin' (www.youtube.com/playlist?list=PLmosFzxUfkqUcZ-IsKJ7ZjJPQpiJvvu24), which 'follows a group of passengers lost in space – each of them desperate to escape their past'. The interest in creating such work, with increasingly high production values, has spawned a number of sites that guide would-be filmmakers through some of the technical details of developing their content. *Create Sf* (https://createscifi.com/), for instance, is run by Anthony Ferraro, who 'want[s] to help you make your sci-fi film or series, complete with funky star ships, bizarre planets, alien races and of course a space creature, with limited resources'. *Homemade Sci-Fi* (www.homemadescifi.com/) gives content creators the chance to connect with one another and preview a variety of indie filmmaking efforts; it is even slightly activist in orientation, arguing that 'The most innovative sci-fi movies aren't from Hollywood, but from the exploding indie/DIY sci-fi film movement'. Part of that innovation might actually lie in the willingness of fans to explore content, including issues of race and sexuality, that have only recently been approached in earnest by some mainstream shows and franchises.

While Jenkins and others express a utopian sensibility with regard to DIY sf production, others remain sceptical, specifically about the liberalising efficacy of such work. For example, Dan Hassler-Forest notes that, while the 'creative and self-organizing world of fan culture does indeed resonate with [Hardt and Negri's] description of the multitude's political mobilization' that seems to at least gesture toward anti-hegemonic desires and sensibilities, much fan production is nonetheless marked by 'hyperconsumerism and [a] general lack of radical political activity', adding that

> visiting a fan convention or watching a documentary [...] one is struck by the overwhelming reproduction of an intense market logic, with fans desperately attempting to achieve the kind of fame and fortune associated with celebrity culture, competing fiercely in one of the many cosplay shows, or else embracing consumerism to the fullest by paying extortionate fees for celebrity photos and autographs, and by the never-ending quest to seek out the most valuable collectables and 'limited collector's editions'.
>
> (41–2)

As in the examples above, much fan work seems more invested in demonstrating technical prowess than in progressive storytelling. Furthermore, so much DIY fan work 'still requires significant technology and communications infrastructure' so that, no matter how participatory 'participatory culture' might seem, many people are often excluded because they are on 'the other side of the digital divide' and do not 'own computers with editing software and high-speed internet service' (Gray 164). Many fans themselves comment on the cost of productions and the increasing competition to produce higher and higher quality work, even as such work offers them opportunities to participate in their own forms of storytelling.

Conclusion

Ultimately, DIY sf attests to the incredible creativity and hunger of fans for extending existing and creating their own speculative worlds. Such work is redolent of desires for a wide variety of different kinds of worldbuilding projects, often (if not always) toward liberal and progressive ends. At times, this work also expands participation for traditionally marginalised groups in building and sustaining shared mythologies and creating new forms of speculative storytelling with characters from marginalised identity groups.

In 1996, Michael Curtin argued that 'One of the consequences of this new [media] environment is that groups that were at one time oppositional or outside the mainstream have become increasingly attractive to media conglomerates with deep pockets, ambitious growth objectives, and flexible corporate structures' (197). The 'voracious appetite for innovation in the culture industries' he describes has only increased, leading to more 'flexible corporate structures [that] have made it possible to quickly leverage niche artists into major mass phenomena when executives sense a growing audience interest' (197). Certainly, many DIY sf content creators seem to position their work for consideration by executives and others. Just as powerful, though, has been the periodic *inflexibility* of corporate structures, revealed in their willingness to clamp down on fan production, however creative, masterful or respectful of original IP. Mel Stanfill notes how at times the 'industry produces a norm of being a fan as a narrow range of practices and people that complies with industry desire in both behavior and demographics, setting up the right way to be a fan as what is right for industry' (183). Such tensions are unsurprising given a culture that asserts the right of some to claim 'ownership' over complex storyworlds, even as those tensions do not seem to dampen the creativity of fans and their willingness to 'do it themselves' in visioning and enacting the kinds of narratives they want not just to see but to help create.

Indeed, the evolution of fan media could be seen as being linked to the development of different, often *alternative* political economies. Fan production is no longer simply 'textual poaching' of pre-existing mainstream content but now often exists somewhere between an unpaid apprenticeship for those seeking to develop technological and media skills *and* a way of diversifying mainstream voices, pushing at the boundaries of speculative narrative content and its representation of diverse human experiences and histories. In a time of increased ecological and political precarity, fans are often extraordinarily creative in their DIY approach to sf, developing a range of multimedia to address their concerns and issues. One of the most fascinating examples is *Octavia Tried to Tell Us* (https://octaviatried.com/), hosted by Monica A. Coleman (an ordained Christian minister, an initiate of traditional Yoruba religion and a Professor of Africana Studies at the University of Delaware) and sf, fantasy and horror novelist Tananarive Due. A deep dive into Octavia E. Butler's *Parable of the Sower* (1993), the podcast arose directly in response to the Covid-19 pandemic: 'Two months into a global health pandemic, and we had all the feels. But literature lovers, Tananarive Due and Monica A. Coleman found empathy, hope and cues for survival in the writing of Afrofuturist author Octavia Butler'. Their goal is to mobilise Butler's work, particularly the Earthseed verses, to maintain hope during an apocalyptic time: 'Each month, we all find a way forward with more insight, hope, and strategy. We find the creativity to re-make this world'. Hosting different guests, all people of colour from the world of art, literature and wellness, Coleman and Due identify Earthseed as 'real religion' committed to fostering 'Shapers', who, inspired by the Black women that Butler wrote about in *Parable* and her other books, will meet the forces of oppression with ingenuity, creativity and an embrace of change – a belief that this world can change and adapt not only to accommodate difference but use difference as the ontological basis for re-imagining social, economic and ecological justice. To be sure, these episodes, styled as webinars, can often be light on details of how such change is to be enacted, but the emphasis remains predominantly on the need to cultivate hope – and to extend the work that Butler began. To me, such extension characterises the very best of DIY fan media production.

Works cited

Ashley, Mike. *The History of the Science Fiction Magazines*. Five volumes. Liverpool UP, 2000–22.

carrington, andré m. *Speculative Blackness: The Future of Race in Science Fiction.* U of Minnesota P, 2016.

Curtin, Michael. 'On Edge: Culture Industries in the Neo-Network Era'. *Making and Selling Culture*. Ed. Richard Ohman. Wesleyan UP, 1996. 181–202.

Gray, Jonathan. *Show Sold Separately: Promos, Spoilers, and Other Media Paratexts.* New York UP, 2010.

Green, Joshua and Henry Jenkins. 'The Moral Economy of Web 2.0: Audience Research and Convergence Culture'. *Media Industries: History, Theory, and Method.* Ed. Jennifer Holt and Alisa Perren. Wiley-Blackwell, 2009. 213–25.

Hassler-Forest, Dan. *Science Fiction, Fantasy, and Politics: Transmedia World-Building Beyond Capitalism.* Rowman & Littlefield, 2016.

Jenkins, Henry. *Convergence Culture: Where Old and New Media Collide*. New York UP, 2006.

——. 'Quentin Tarantino's *Star Wars*? Grassroots Creativity Meets the Media Industry'. *The Social Media Reader*. Ed. Michael Mandibergs. New York UP, 2012. 203–35.

——. *Textual Poachers: Television Fans & Participatory Culture*. Routledge, 1992.

Jenkins, Henry, Sam Ford and Joshua Green. *Spreadable Media: Creating Value and Meaning in a Networked Culture*. New York UP, 2013.

Jenkins, Henry, Mizuko Ito and danah boyd, eds. *Participatory Culture in a Networked Era*. Polity, 2016.

Jenkins, Henry, Gabriel Peters-Lazaro and Sangita Shresthova, eds. *Popular Culture and the Civic Imagination: Case Studies of Creative Social Change*. New York UP, 2020.

Johnson, Derek. *Media Franchising: Creative License and Collaboration in the Culture Industries*. New York UP, 2013.

Lothian, Alexis. *Old Futures: Speculative Fiction and Queer Possibility*. New York UP, 2018.

Peters-Lazaro, Gabriel and Sangita Shresthova. *Practicing Futures: A Civic Imagination Action Handbook.* Peter Lang, 2020.

Rieder, John. *Science Fiction and the Mass Cultural Genre System*. Wesleyan UP, 2017.

Russel, Adrienne, Mizuko Ito, Todd Richmond and Marc Tuters. 'Culture: Media Convergence and Networked Participation'. *Networked Publics*. Ed. Kazys Varnelis. The MIT Press, 2008. 43–76.

Stanfill, Mel. *Exploiting Fandom: How the Media Industry Seeks to Manipulate Fans*. U of Iowa P, 2019.

41

ECONOMICS AND FINANCIALISATION

Hugh C. O'Connell

Following the 2008 global market crash, the role of finance in contemporary capitalism received renewed interest from critics looking to understand not only the arcane inner workings of neoliberal economics, but also their larger socio-cultural ramifications for the subject, aesthetics and culture. Conferences were organised on the relationships between fictive capital and fiction, critical finance studies became a recognisable subfield, and the critical lexicon expanded to absorb this renewed focus on economics and financialisation, as reflected in the newfound centrality of such terms as automation, AI and HFTs; debt cycling and indebtedness; speculative finance and cultural financialisation; derivatives and futures options; datafication and surveillance capitalism. If, as David Graeber notes, 'once the global system of credit money was entirely unpegged from gold, the world entered a new phase of financial history – one that nobody completely understands' (362), then the financial turn in cultural studies argues that the mediations of literary, filmic, comic and other texts offer particular insights into financialisation, and vice versa.

While there has been a long tradition of criticism relating literary production to finance and credit (especially in nineteenth-century literary studies), it is only recently that similar attention has turned to late twentieth- and twenty-first-century literature and culture in a more sustained manner (Adamson; Finch; Kidman; La Berge; Marsh; McClanahan; Shaw; Shonkwiler). With notable exceptions (Kidman on comic book adaptations, McClanahan on horror movies), such work tends to focus on the 'contemporary' and/or 'literary' (that is, broadly psychological and realist fiction that eschews the stigma of commercial or mass market culture, even when clearly incorporating genre protocols). However, its significance for sf studies should not be ignored. Moreover, sf studies has similarly responded to the post-crash interest in financialisation, if perhaps not as robustly, in edited collections and special issues like William Davies's *Economic Science Fictions* (2018) and David M. Higgins and Hugh C. O'Connell's 2019 *Speculative Finance/Speculative Fiction* special issue of *CR: The New Centennial Review*, and in significant interventions by critics such as Aimee Bahng, Jennifer Rhee, Steven Shaviro, Sherryl Vint and Brian Willems. And if we widen our lens to incorporate work outside of the literary context, the interest in financialisation has been prominent in industry and media studies relating to sf gaming, comics and film, especially around issues of franchise studies. This chapter will examine how these insights extend across sf and sf studies and what sf studies can offer to understandings of the financial turn.

DOI: 10.4324/9781003140269-44

The financial turn and financial sf

Finance has gained increasing autonomy from the primary economy of goods and services (particularly in the Global North) and replaced them as the dominant mode of accumulation. This historical shift to the era of speculative finance with its own set of reflexive and recursive cultural effects (what Randy Martin describes as the broader politically–culturally–economically imbricated practices of financialisation) coincides with neoliberal ideology's replacement of Keynesian economics, beginning in the 1970s. Key events clearing the way for this shift in the operations of finance include the end of Bretton Woods and the creation of free-floating currencies, the development of the financial derivative market based on currency circulation and the separation of derivatives from their underlying material assets, the new modes of financial risk generated by global processes of production, the securitisation of debt and debt cycling, and the increase in datafication and information as the engine and outcome of 'New Economy' practices and surveillance capitalism.

The age of finance is typically characterised by the accumulation of profit without production, where profit is attained through interest, rent, capital gains and circulation rather than through the production of commodities or through services. Breaking away from the constraints of Keynesianism and the state, the age of speculative finance is often theorised as the moment of capital's full autonomy, that is, 'when capital proved to be a player instead of a plaything, a predator instead of a working animal, with an urgent need to break free from the cage-like institutional framework of the post-1945 "social market economy"' (Streeck 19) such that 'financial derivatives and speculative capital [now] stand as instrument and agent in the global circulation of the money form' (LiPuma and Lee 113).

What David Harvey notes about capitalism in general – that 'it is not a thing but a process in which money is perpetually sent in search of more money' (40) – should just as well be emphasised for financialisation. However, rather than one distinct process, financialisation is the result of a number of policy decisions that propelled a qualitative shift in the processes and functions of finance itself. As a set of processes that crisscross the globe materially (e.g., through global commodity chains) and virtually (e.g., through global exchanges in various securities and financial instruments), financialisation includes a greatly variegated number of practices and forms, and like capitalism more generally, it is promulgated by and results in an increasingly combined but grossly uneven world-system. Hence, when one speaks of financialisation, this can include any number of overlapping and/or incommensurate operations.

Speculative finance vs. speculative fiction

One of the guiding hallmarks of the financial turn in sf studies is that finance itself becomes more science fictional in its operations. As the editors of the *Journal of American Studies* special issue on 'Fictions of Speculation' attest, the only way for the Congressional Finance Crisis Inquiry Commission to really make sense of the 2008 crash was as an 'alien event' and thus 'to be found in science fiction', continuing 'why does the *Inquiry Report*, struggling to frame its own narrative, veer so decisively away from the stolid language of [...] "modern facts" and towards the more capacious worlds of popular-genre (science) fiction?' (Carroll and McClanahan 655, 656). What makes speculative finance seem to be a speculative fiction? Although working on a contemporary realist literary canon rather than genre fiction, Alison Shonkwiler's description of finance resembles the formal definitions of sf's cognitive estrangement and worldbuilding: 'If the nineteenth-century novel can "think" capitalism, perhaps twenty-first century capitalism thinks more like fiction – creating totalities, locating temporal and spatial discrepancies, imagining counterfactualities, and reflecting on its own processes of structuration' (xxix). In this regard, many sf critics of the financial turn begin by interrogating the real and perceived interconnections between the operations of fictitious capital and fictions about capital, speculative finance and speculative fiction, financial novums and science fictional novums, drawing out the similarities and distinctions in their form, worldbuilding and narrative protocols.

One significant point of connection is the predilection for futurity shared by sf and finance. As Martin notes, 'Preemption, bringing the future into the present, has since the late 1970s been the guiding principle of fiscal policy' (3). This is perhaps best tackled in the sf sense by Charles Stross's *Accelerando* (2005), in which a number of sentient financialised AIs (including corporate AIs and self-aware Ponzi schemes) first colonise and then cannibalise the solar system in order to increase the network bandwidth in which they exist. As the Singularity unfolds and such financial AIs vastly outstrip human ability and speed, they seem to colonise not only space but the future itself. Drawing similarities and distinctions in the operations of the future-oriented 'speculative' in sf and finance, Steven Shaviro and Sherryl Vint have both argued for sf's ability to reveal and resist the subsumption of the future by financial processes today. For example, Shaviro argues

> We might [...] say that speculative finance is the inverse – and the complement – of the 'affirmative speculation' that takes place in science fiction. Financial speculation seeks to capture, and shut down, the very same extreme potentialities that fiction explores. Science fiction is the narration of open, unaccountable futures; derivatives trading claims to have *accounted* for, and *discounted*, all these futures already.
>
> (11)

Echoing this fundamental difference between openness and closure, Jennifer Rhee argues that James Tiptree, Jr's 'The Girl Who was Plugged In' (1973), offers an early critique of the closed future of financial speculation:

> The future, the story affirms, is indeterminate, despite the myriad ways that financial capitalism seeks to secure its vision of the future. [...] Through material and temporal indeterminacies and the tactical paradoxes they generate, the story insists on multiple possibilities for multiple futures, despite contemporary capitalism's continued attempts to foreclose them all.
>
> (450)

In an analysis that focuses on close readings of financial theory and sf genre protocols, Vint argues that at least since the 1980s, the 'fictionality' of speculative financial instruments like derivatives has 'intensified, and their reliance on subjunctive structures and their orientation toward the future makes this fictionality like that of speculative fiction' (12). While such speculative, future-oriented aspects may bring finance into the ambit of sf, subverting and subsuming its protocols, she argues that, at its best,

> speculative fiction continues to have distinct worldbuilding and narrative strategies [...], and therefore the genre provides us with methods via which we might deconstruct the worlds narrated by speculative finance and resist the normalization of their logics, to offer instead more egalitarian and inclusive visions of the future.
>
> (12)

The rest of this chapter will explore ways that sf both reflects and challenges the hegemony of financialisation in two key areas: the securitisation of personal debt and of information.

Financialisation and debt

The securitisation of debt (consumer, corporate and national) is one of the key aspects of the larger financialisation of the economy. Annie McClanahan interrogates the transformation of debt from 'a socially salutary creditor/debtor relationship' (7) meant to prop up consumerism to a primary means of accumulation through its financialisation and securitisation, which is enabled by computerisation and the creation of complex financial instruments that allow for speculative markets in consumer debt. Focusing on the 2008 financial crash, she analyses how debt has 'become the defining feature of economic life today' (1), noting that the shift in discourse from credit to debt is the harbinger of terminal crisis for the capitalist system:

> Credit is the economic form of the boom time; it is a temporal fix when it is still possible to fix things. But debt – as a figure for credit that is unpaid, defaulted, foreclosed, bankrupted, written off, unredeemed – is the economic form of crisis: of a period in which no one can pay.
>
> (15)

After decades of escalating prices (for food, shelter, education, healthcare), stagnating and declining wages, defunding of welfare programs, structural un- and under-employment, and the upward redistribution of income through neoliberal monetary policies, debt was transformed into a necessity as a tool of simple survival.

The increasing immiseration that spawned the explosion in consumer debt forms the backdrop for the socio-political nightmare scenarios familiar to any reader of contemporary dystopian fiction, from Octavia E. Butler's Parable series (1993–8) to Suzanne Collins's *Hunger Games* trilogy (2008–10). However, while such texts offer horrific mediations of a world depleted by neoliberalism in which the indebted subject 'now occupies the totality of public space' (Lazzarato 38), the financialisation of debt remains an absent, structural cause. However, a newer spate of dystopias is putting debt squarely at the centre of their narratives and worldbuilding, including K.M. Szpara's *Docile* (2020), Claire North's *84K* (2018) and Charles Stross's *Neptune's Brood* (2013).

Docile presents a stark divide between the haves and the have-nots. In this bifurcated landscape, 'Dociles' are akin to indentured servants, subjects from the impoverished communities that register with the 'Office of Debt Resolution' in order to have their various debts (schooling, medical, mortgages and so on, often figuring in the millions of dollars) consolidated and transformed into contracts purchasable by trillionaires. Foregrounding its tagline, 'there is no consent under capitalism', the novel attempts (not always successfully) to compare and conjoin notions of consent in a capitalist system that foists debt upon subjects as a necessity with the discourse of sexual consent, drawn largely from BDSM. Ultimately, culminating in a court case in which the protagonist attempts to overturn the conditions of their contract with implications for the founding debt resolution legislation that inaugurated the Docile system, the novel offers a liberal-ethical critique, foregrounding the individual and their right to choose. Rather than revolutionary transformation, then, its narrative seeks reforms that allow for personal growth within the existing economic system.

Drawing on the neoliberal transformation of British government and society (particularly austerity and privatisation), *84K* presents the subsumption of civil society by a corporate–government partnership: members of government are drawn exclusively from banking and insurance sectors, the major functions of governance are outsourced to corporations, and corporations sponsor not just towns and municipalities but individuals as well. The protagonist, Theo, works as an assessor for the 'Criminal Audit Office', calculating the indemnities for various offenses. Under the financialised logic that now undergirds governance, all crimes are adjudicated via their social costs to productive society and paid to the privatised company that processes them for the government. Those who cannot pay their fine either go to jail where they must repay their debts through labour (one character has to contribute positive web reviews for a corporation) or they can have their debts purchased, whether by wealthy citizens (to be used as sex slaves) or corporations (to be used as slave labour to replace wage labour). In terms of its financialised debt narrative, the plot turns on the revelation of a scandal that involves the murder of the indebted hidden under the neoliberal euphemism of 'excess labour reallocation' (294). In short, it is murder for economic efficiency, in which efficiency means maximising profit and shareholder value by working the indebted literally to death while withholding pay. The revelation of the scandal leads to a bloody revolt and dissolution of the current government and a new, uncertain future.

Neptune's Brood provides a rather different take on the sf and financial debt narrative by turning to a far future of interstellar colonisation by metahumans. The novel in many ways offers an alternate take on the capitalist acceleration of *Accelerando* (Canavan; Shaviro), except here the posthuman or metahuman society has hit some indelible limits, most notably the debt ontology that is rapidly coming to define and consume our own era; every character is born into debt and it takes many decades, if not longer, to relieve it. And although debt can be relieved, it can never really be destroyed, only transferred. Or, as the novel puts it, even metahuman life is finite, 'Only debt is forever' (27).

The society of *Neptune's Brood* develops two ways to relieve and compensate for this constitutive, foundational debt. The first is spatial: to circulate or transfer the debt. Debt is transferred to the setting up of new interstellar colonies (a new colony must take on astronomical amounts of debt in order to get started by borrowing from an existing colony, thereby transferring the debt of the already-existing lender colony to the new borrowing colony). The second is temporal: as FTL travel is not possible, the founding of a colony can take millennia, thereby necessitating the development of a new financial instrument (slow money) to underwrite the temporal anomaly of these colonial ventures. In other words, they need a currency that is less volatile and not open to speculation so that debts and payments can be made at the protracted duration of colonisation as well as outlast the financial collapse of civilisations in the interim.

The plot ultimately involves a scam to capitalise on the structure of the slow money economy, but with a twist. Rather than simply using the system against itself – to capitalise individually upon it – the novel introduces a new accelerationist technological novum: not FTL but quantum teleportation. Withholding the development of quantum teleportation as a secret and using the money gained by scamming the system, the protagonists short the slow money market and bring the whole system crashing down around them in what amounts to a de facto Jubilee. The real novum here, then, is the Jubilee itself as it remakes the entire world of the text and opens up what Phil E. Wegner would refer to as an 'evental utopia' (O'Connell 309–10; Wegner 50–2), providing the means for a new model of society not based on debt.

These novels reflect Arjun Appadurai's claim that 'the major form of labor today is not labor for wages but rather labor for the production of debt' (127). Regardless of the productive, service or other form of wage labour we may engage in on a daily basis, from the point of view of the financialised economy, we 'are in fact debt-laborers, whose main task is to produce debt that can then be further monetized for profit by financial entrepreneurs who control the means of production of profit through monetizing debts' (127–8). *Docile*, *84K* and *Neptune's Brood* offer science-fictionally extrapolated forms of this reality by reducing their principal characters to debts that are bought, sold and traded. In short, they offer a debt ontology: we are our debt. With their treatments of this socially and economically reified position, they remind us of a new fundamental truth within our age of speculative finance:

> in the twenty-first-century, credit and debt are no longer two reversible perspectives on the same circular exchange (money passing from lender to borrower and back again); rather, they represent two fundamentally antagonistic subject and class positions.
>
> (McClanahan 185)

The key question of these novels is whether this contradiction can be socially reconciled within the confines of the current system (as in the 'historic compromise' between labour and capital that led to the post-World War II capitalist systems of the Global North) or whether they will lead to revolution.

Sf, algorithmic AI and surveillance capitalism

Alongside securitising debt, one of the other main vectors in the financialisation of the economy is the commodification and securitisation of personal information via data-mining processes for what Shoshana Zuboff terms 'behavioral futures markets' via 'surveillance capitalism' (8–12). Digital interfaces mine and AI/algorithms process and reconstitute the inexhaustible slew of freely given data, from our Facebook likes to the mapping of our homes by rumbas, as behavioural information. This information is then bundled into the creation of proprietary 'prediction products' – ways of calculating future events – which are then monetised and marketed as derivatives of behavioural surplus and sold on a newly constituted behavioural futures market. Joe Conway explores this dynamic in relation to sf post-cash worldbuilding, illustrating how in such worlds, human behaviour itself is capitalised:

> Both *In Time* (Niccol 2011) and *Black Mirror* (2011–) picture post-cash societies as dystopian worlds where the barest biorhythms of human life, whether in sleep or waking, are seized from birth by hidden political apparatuses of capture, translated into data, and then circulated as capital.
>
> (Conway 233)

In the same way that finance ultimately seeks to control the future through transforming qualitative uncertainty into quantitative risks to be hedged against and/or leveraged, the larger political–social–cultural turn to datafication comes down to the same desire for perfect information, for perfect prediction, to arrest contingency, history and difference.

The notion that perfect information exists and that literally everything can be reduced to quantifiable data made information lies at the heart of *Devs* (FX on Hulu 2020), where free will is rendered an illusion and the past, present and future can be seen all at once in their granular totality via algorithmic computer modelling. A similar focus on information, prediction and control was slowly revealed as the driving concern of *Westworld* (HBO 2016–22), where the eponymous theme park is merely a contrivance for capturing consumer data. The real economic engine of the show's narrative thus lies in the intellectual property (data packaged as information), which is far more valuable than the neural AI architecture of the android hosts (as a productive commodity) or the experience of the guests (as a service commodity). As William Davies argues, this results in the enclosure of possibility itself: 'No enclave outside the grid. No future beyond already emerging trends. And no past other than that which has been captured as data' (20).

While *Devs* and Dan Frey's similarly themed *The Future is Yours* (2021) provide a somewhat hackneyed liberal humanist riposte to these ideas through their valuing of free will (which as Marcuse reminds us, in late capitalism cannot be fully divorced from consumer choice and the structures of capital that dictate what can be chosen), *Black Mirror: Bandersnatch* (Netflix 2018) takes a different tack. Setting up a similar set of concerns about the nature of free will vs. data-determinism and reality vs. simulacrum, *Bandersnatch* amps up the issues of datafication and surveillance through its formal properties as an interactive choose-your-own-adventure film (150 minutes of footage, divided into 250 segments, enable over a trillion different pathways). On the surface, *Bandersnatch* has little to do with financial novums. Rather than a narrative about datafication or behavioural surplus, it physically manifests the invisible aspects of the algorithm and behavioural derivatives in that it is all about our clicks and our behavioural modification. Its form thus highlights our position as willing participants in the creation of behavioural surplus masked as participation in sharing in the narrative consequences. In other words, a Netflix film baldly reveals that all of the streaming service's content is merely a conduit for behavioural surplus.

The only way out of such a predicament, as has been suggested by Brian Willems as well as in Joanna Kavenna's *Zed* (2019), is to increase the volatility in the algorithm, to feed it information that it cannot handle. In Kavenna's novel, the Google-meets-Apple-inspired company, Beetle, has developed a behavioural predictive algorithm formalised as each individual's 'lifechain', resulting in the totally administered society of Adorno's nightmares. As with *Devs*, the desire is for the accumulation and production of perfect information to render the past, present and future as one knowable info-ontology. 'Zed' is the information that escapes this datafication, the contingent noise that causes decoherence. Similar to Willems's argument (inspired by Kim Stanley Robinson's *New York 2140* (2017)) about overloading the Black Scholes formula with environmental data, the solution involves breaking the algorithm by increasing Zed and decoherence:

> Zed seeped into the Custodian apartment blocks, the offices. It seeped and stained and besmirched, it was appalling, if you despised it. Uncertainty represented by Zed – or Zed represented by Uncertainty seeped. [...] The lifechains had responded swiftly to recent events and now Zed events were probable, while non-Zed events were improbable. Reality, was, according to the lifechains, a series of Zed events, in which Zed was the condition and fundamental aspect of reality. Zed was wild uncertainty, it was doom and freedom.
>
> (286)

The entire predictive machinery and the world that it creates, both virtual and physical, falls apart.

Sf as a financial instrument

Moving from issues of sf narrative and form, in the current media climate – driven by algorithms, datafication and surveillance capitalism – we might finally consider sf itself as a financial instrument, particularly in relation to the contemporary forms of franchise culture. In terms of the relationship between economics and sf, it is fascinating to remember that the STAR WARS franchise (at least as of the prequel trilogy) begins with an intergalactic trade dispute, leading to the suspension of democracy and the rise of demagogic fascism. Even a galaxy long ago and far away is structured and undergirded by shifts in its world-system. This of course, then, needs to be approached from the outside context to think about how the prequels themselves are emblematic of the new cultural dominance of franchise logic via financialised and leveraged IP connecting across media of comics, games, merchandise, films, theme parks, and content-delivery systems like Disney+.

Shawna Kidman explores this dynamic in terms of the financialisation of comics properties. Despite the precipitous decline in readership from 50 percent of Americans during the peak years of the 1940s to 'one-half of one percent of the U.S. population' in the late 2010s (1–2), comics properties now circulate wider than ever as IP. This process accelerates the existing tension between 'publishing and licensing' that has long defined the medium in the US, whereby 'the future potential of [comics'] derivative products and their historical existence have long shaped comic books' production, distribution, consumption, interpretation, and recirculation' (2), such that licensing has outstripped publication as the main source of comics revenue since at least the 1970s (181). If collector speculation – those buying the comics in hopes of seeing them appreciate in value – collapsed the comics bubble in the 1990s, then media speculation and the licensing of comics as IP for film production is responsible for the cultural reach of comics today as R&D:

> Paul Levitz, publisher of DC, had come to understand that his company was to serve as no more than a self-financing R&D operation for Warner Bros.' bigger projects. [...] To make money, all a financier needed were the property rights – the mere option to exploit. The immaterial possession of intangible characters and stories had become the business's most valuable currency, and this made the comic book industry subject to intense speculation. (181)

The development of comics franchises through major film studios is part of the larger recent explosion of 'option aesthetics', where the typical aspects of sf – 'episodic plots, ensemble casts, and intricate world-building' – are key to the optioning of literary works more so than plot in that they allow for sustained cinematic and televisual development (Manshel, McGrath and Porter n.p.). This is changing the way that publishing deals operate, as negotiations over adaptation rights can now often precede the completion of the initial print forms. For example, the rights to Ian McDonald's LUNA series (2015–9) were purchased in 2015, before the first novel was published, and such option aesthetics clearly influenced not only the way McDonald pitched the series ('*Dallas* on the Moon') but also how it was advertised ('A Game of Domes'). As with *Bandersnatch*, this results in a tension between sf's narrative and formal oppositional strategies and its financially affirmative production and industry practices.

Conclusion: Sf, finance, sabotage and utopian recuperation

The seismic events of the post-1989 global consolidation of capitalism and of the global financial crash of 2008 produce a need for new mediations of the economy *as well as* new utopian possibilities. Commenting on these conditions, Mark Fisher exhorts the need for a new utopian sf, one that is not simply anti-capitalist in a reactive sense, but more importantly that is constitutive of future possibilities:

> As capital's cheerleaders endlessly crow, anti-capitalists have not yet been able to articulate a coherent alternative. The production of new economic science fictions therefore becomes an urgent political imperative. [...] The development of economic science fictions would constitute a form of *indirect action* without which hegemonic struggle cannot hope to be successful.
>
> (xiii)

In many ways, this has been the project of Kim Stanley Robinson's recent fiction, which engages with various strategies that Annie McClanahan refers to as 'the politics of sabotage' (185). She argues that, given the difficulties of facing finance capitalism head-on many initial stages of resistance appear first as acts of sabotage, whereby 'clashes with the mode of reproduction and in the zones of circulation reveal a situation in which economic subjects confront their exploitation not in the wage but in the eviction notice' (187). Originating with the debt strike that closes *New York 2140*, many of the acts of socialising debt begin as acts of financial sabotage – of turning the source of debtors' immiseration into the tools of creditors' downfall. In *The Ministry for the Future* (2020), Robinson ramps up these ideas; while continuing to foreground the initial power of socially seizing debt, he connects this to reconceiving how the many diverse tools and systems of financialisation (including surveillance capitalism, centralised banking, digital currencies and much more) can be utilised as a means of socialising the power of political economy in the name of better worlds. Echoing Fisher's exhortation that 'it is not a single-total vision that is required but a multiplicity of alternative perspectives, each potentially opening up a crack into another world' (xiii), *Ministry* imagines the seeds of a new world growing from out of all the various cracks that threaten to destroy this one. This is perhaps sf's greatest contribution to the financial turn, not only cognitively mapping the contours of our new globally distributed, seemingly virtual, ubiquitous yet ungraspable financialised world-system, but also imagining futures outside of it.

Works cited

Adamson, Morgan. 'Markets without Subjects: Nasdaq and the Financial Interface'. *New Formations: A Journal of Culture/Theory/Politics* 88 (2016): 69–87.

Appadurai, Arjun. *Banking on Words: The Failure of Language in the Age of Derivative Finance*. U of Chicago P, 2015.

Canavan, Gerry. 'Capital as Artificial Intelligence'. *Fictions of Speculation*, special issue of *The Journal of American Studies* 49.4 (2015): 685–710.

Carroll, Hamilton and Annie McClanahan. 'Fictions of Speculation: Introduction'. *Fictions of Speculation*, special issue of *The Journal of American Studies* 49.4 (2015): 655–61.

Conway, Joe. 'Currencies of Control: *Black Mirror*, *In Time*, and the Monetary Policies of Dystopia'. *Speculative Finance/Speculative Fiction*, special issue of *CR: The New Centennial Review* 19.1 (2019): 229–53.

Davies, William. 'Introduction to *Economic Science Fictions*'. *Economic Science Fictions*. Ed. William Davies. Goldsmiths, 2018. 1–28.

Finch, Laura. 'The Un-Real Deal: Financial Fiction, Fictional Finance, and the Financial Crisis'. *Fictions of Speculation*, special issue of *The Journal of American Studies* 49.4 (2015): 731–53.

Fisher, Mark. 'Foreword'. *Economic Science Fictions*. Ed. William Davies. Goldsmiths, 2018. xi–xiv.

Graeber, David. *Debt: The First 5000 Years*. Melville, 2011.

Harvey, David. *The Enigma of Capital: and the Crises of Capitalism*. Oxford UP, 2011.

Kavenna, Joanna. *Zed*. Doubleday, 2020.

Kidman, Shawna. *Comic Books Incorporated: How the Business of Comics Became the Business of Hollywood*. U of California P, 2019.

La Berge, Leigh Claire. *Scandals and Abstractions: Financial Fictions of the Long 1980s*. Oxford UP, 2014.
Lazzarato, Maurizio. *The Making of the Indebted Man: An Essay on the Neoliberal Condition*. Trans. Joshua David Jordan. Semiotext(e), 2011.
LiPuma, Edward and Benjamin Lee. *Financial Derivatives and the Globalization of Risk*. Duke UP, 2004.
Manshel, Alexander, Laura B. McGrath and J.D. Porter. 'The Rise of Must-Read TV: How your Netflix Habit is Changing Contemporary Fiction'. *The Atlantic Online* (16 July 2021). www.theatlantic.com/culture/archive/2021/07/tv-adaptations-fiction/619442/
Marsh, Nicky. *Money, Speculation and Finance in Contemporary British Fiction*. Bloomsbury, 2017.
Martin, Randy. *An Empire of Indifference: American War and the Financial Logic of Risk Management*. Duke UP, 2007.
McClanahan, Annie. *Dead Pledges: Debt, Crisis, and Twenty-First-Century Culture*. Stanford UP, 2017.
North, Claire. *84K*. Orbit, 2018.
O'Connell, Hugh Charles. '"We are change": The Novum as Event in Nnedi Okorafor's *Lagoon*'. *African Science Fiction*, special issue of *Cambridge Journal of Postcolonial Literary Inquiry* 3.3 (2016): 291–312.
Rhee, Jennifer. 'Finance Speculation, Indeterminacy, and Unforeclosed Futures in James Tiptree, Jr.'s "The Girl Who Was Plugged In"'. *Science Fiction Studies* 139 (2019): 449–69.
Shaviro, Steven. *No Speed Limit: Three Essays on Accelerationism*. U of Minnesota P, 2015.
Shaw, Katy. *Crunch Lit*. Bloomsbury, 2015.
Shonkwiler, Alison. *The Financial Imaginary: Economic Mystification and the Limits of Realist Fiction*. Minnesota UP, 2017.
Streeck, Wolfgang. *Buying Time: The Delayed Crisis of Democratic Capitalism*. Trans. Patrick Camiller. Verso, 2014.
Stross, Charles. *Neptune's Brood*. Ace, 2013.
Vint, Sherryl. 'Promissory Futures: Reality and Imagination in Finance and Fiction'. *Speculative Finance/Speculative Fiction*, special issue of *CR: The New Centennial Review* 19.1 (2019): 11–36.
Wegner, Phillip E. *Shockwaves of Possibility: Essays on Science Fiction, Globalization, and Utopia*. Peter Lang, 2014.
Willems, Brian. 'Natural Instruments: Real-World Adaptations of Fictional Financial Algorithms'. *b20: The Online Community of the boundary 2 Editorial Collective* (21 October 2018). www.boundary2.org/2018/10/brian-willems-natural-instruments-real-world-adaptations-of-fictional-financial-algorithms/
Zuboff, Shoshana. *The Age of Surveillance Capitalism: The Fight for a Human Future at the New Frontier of Power*. Public Affairs, 2019.

42
EMPIRE

Upamanyu Pablo Mukherjee

In the predecessor to this book, the relationship between imperialism, postcolonialism and sf is discussed in two separate and comprehensive essays by Istvan Csicsery-Ronay, Jr and Michelle Reid. Illuminating as they are, the decision to treat 'empire' and 'postcolonialism' as distinct categories speaks of the unsettled and unsettling nature of these concepts over which gallons of ink, both crude and refined, have been spilled over nearly half a century. Csicsery-Ronay, Jr is surely right to emphasise the important role sf has played in the entrenchment *and* interrogation of technological imperialism, which he argues succeeded the modern European empires dismantled by anti-colonial movements in the middle of the twentieth century (363, 370). Yet this leaves open the question of the entanglements between sf, technoscience and empire *during* the half-millennium when the latter was a key agent, if not *the* key agent, of the modern world-system. Furthermore, is Csicsery-Ronay, Jr's 'anti-colonialism' the same thing as Reid's 'postcolonialism'? They seem to share some features, but for Reid postcolonialism is simultaneously a theoretical, discursive act and a periodising device that allows formerly colonised peoples to imagine alternative futures (257, 265). As Neil Lazarus has decisively shown, such an understanding of postcolonialism risks forgetting its institutional, academic and non-activist lineages under the very specific conditions of neo-imperial resurgence of the 1980s (9–10). To that extent, despite their superficial similarities, 'anti-colonialism' and 'postcolonialism' might be understood as antithetical to each other. If this is so, their relationships with technoscience and sf must have strikingly different trajectories.

In what follows I propose that technoscience, usefully defined by Csicsery-Ronay, Jr as 'science in the service of the technological rationalization of every domain of material existence' (362) and sf – its foremost cultural register – have played key roles in both imperial and anti-imperial thoughts and practices. Indeed, paying attention to how sf deals with technoscience's historical imbrications can help clarify a whole range of conflicted and contradictory modes through which modern imperialism (and resistances to it) operates. For what sf does most effectively is to remind us what is 'modern' about both imperialism and science – namely, their coming into being in a world-system where even anti-systemic formations, by definition, accrue meaning in relation to the dominant and pervasive *capitalist* social relations. For some, imperialism is 'that kind of international relationship characterized by a particular *asymmetry* – the *asymmetry* of *dominance* and *dependence*' (Cohen 16); for others, such extra-territorial expansion works through various kinds

DOI: 10.4324/9781003140269-45

of colonialisms – border colonisation, settler colonisation and so on (Bush 47). Science fictional empires tend to take us to the heart of the matter – to the *combined and uneven distribution* of historical and material forces that find expression in these social and political forms.

This is not at all to suggest that most sf is Marxist or *Marxisant* in orientation. There has undoubtedly been significant writers – the Mexican Juan Nepomuceno Adorno, the Indian Rahul Sankrityayan, the Soviet Union's Arkady and Boris Strugatsky, the Cubans Ángel Arango and Daína Chaviano, the American W.E.B. Du Bois and the Briton H.G. Wells, to name a few – whose writings bear the imprint of a socialist sensibility, albeit one frequently at odds with the official Marxism of their times. Equally, a far greater number of sf writers have taken up non- or anti-socialist perspectives and positions in their art. But what both sets of writers have in common is their acknowledgment of a capitalist life-world; their recognition of imperialism and anti-imperialism as competing modes of being in such a world; and finally, their experimental modelling of alternative ways of organising life (either within a utopic horizon or as a negation of such horizons). Scholars and analysts should take sf as seriously as the agents and activists of imperialism and anti-imperialism have done throughout history.

My discussion will draw on sf from Latin America, Asia and Africa – regions where most of the modern world's colonial and imperial possessions were located and where neo-imperial relationships continue to flourish. At the most basic level, this is because it is impossible to understand the lived experience of imperialism exclusively through the cultural registers, however agnostic or dissenting they may be, of the dominant imperial powers themselves. Until comparatively recently, the unspoken assumption regarding sf's representations of empire was that they would be European or American in origin. As Antoinette Burton, among others, has pointed out, such assumptions take for granted a 'core-to-periphery flow of ideas, people, and even policies' (11) and the synonymity of European and global histories (286–7). If what we need instead are 'histories that acknowledge the double, even triple and quadruple, helix of imperial and global power [… .] *and* narrative procedures that enable us to capture the fiction of English/anglo global imperial exceptionalism' (282–3), then it is safe to bet on non-Euro-American sf to get us at least partway there. Of course, it is neither possible nor desirable to ignore the fiction written at the imperial cores in this discussion, but I will stress the conversations and co-productions of such writings with those composed in the global semi-peripheries and peripheries because it is precisely such circulations that effectively capture the shape of modern world empires.

Additionally, the 'science' part of the genre's designation also compels the decentring of the Euro-American sf canon. For at least a couple of decades, sociological and historical studies of science have tried to attend to 'the changing political economies of capitalism and science, the mutual reorganization of the global and the local' by examining the 'metropole and the postcolony [… .] in the same analytic frame' (Anderson 643). This has perhaps unsurprisingly revealed that modern science's claims to be 'apolitical, value-neutral, and objective' are as fictitious as modern empires' claims to be vehicles of civilisation and progress (Subramaniam 68). Instead, science turns out to be a bundle of historically and geographically situated practices involving tactical and pragmatic decisions moving through cross-cultural encounters (Raj 343). Yet these same studies confirm that the ideology of *scientism* has proved to be as enduring as that of *imperialism*. Its power can be seen in the practically unchallenged prominence of technoscientific 'development' in the socio-political imaginary of especially the formerly colonised nations (Escobar 271). The stewardship of India's first Prime Minister, Jawaharlal Nehru, is a case in point. Examining Nehru's messianic zeal to reconfigure India as a modern, scientific nation in the decades following the country's independence, David Arnold detects five features of 'Nehruvian science': it was a 'program for sociocultural change'; it was conducted 'at the direction and discretion of the state';

it 'was an institution-building project'; it was explicitly nationalist; and it had a historiographic function (365–7). Such faith in technoscience continues to hold sway over more or less all the postcolonial nations of the world, all of which, as a consequence, display features of 'archaic modernity' (Subramaniam 82). Sf is as adept at rendering scientistic ideologies visible as it is at decoding their relationship with imperialism.

Three interrelated aspects of modern empires command the particular attention of sf: governance and sovereignty; war and trade; subjectivity and identity. Taken together, they address the political, economic and social dynamics of such formations. The exercise of asymmetric dominance beyond national boundaries naturally foregrounds questions of just governance and contested sovereignties, especially when such dominance is explained and defended in the name of scientific 'development'. The power of such governmental practices and ideologies can be seen in their careful preservation and enhancement in the hands of those nations that gained formal independence from Euro-American colonisers after long and bitter struggles. This deadly paradox was detected very early on by sf. In Jules Verne's *Twenty Thousand Leagues Under the Seas* (1869), the narrator, Dr Aronnax (a lecturer in natural history), confronts Captain Nemo about his decision to sink a warship which has been pursuing his submarine, the *Nautilus*. Nemo declares that *Nautilus* belongs to an 'accursed nation' and his assault on the pursuer is an act of revenge:

> I am the law, I am the justice! [... .] I am the oppressed, and they are the oppressor! It is because of them that everything I loved, cherished, venerated – country, wife, children, parents – perished as I watched! Everything I hate is there!
>
> (338)

There has been much speculation about Nemo's 'accursed' nationality – Verne himself initially imagined he was Polish, while internal textual evidence suggests he may have been Indian (this is confirmed in *The Mysterious Island* (1875)). Whether he was 'oppressed' by Russian or British imperialism, Nemo's homicidal rage is a precise model of what Frantz Fanon would diagnose as colonial *ressentiment* (2) that lays bare the operational logic of imperial justice – the reduction of its subjects to 'bare life' (Agamben) in the name of universal progress. Nemo's ship is the novel's technoscientific *novum* (Suvin), and his fabulous library and art collection initially appear to be typically utopic spaces that might allow his re-invention as a sovereign subject. The tragedy of Nemo is precisely that such a redemption remains unreachable because he has fully internalised imperial governmentality ('I am the law, I am the justice') and can only behave tyrannically even as he declares his commitment to civilised progress.

Verne's work was prophetic regarding what was to come after independence in the colonies as well the directions in which the genre would travel. But governance, both imperial and postcolonial, is imagined in strikingly diverse ways in sf. For both the Mexican Juan Nepomuceno Adorno and the Indian Rahul Sankrityayan, writing from their intimate experiences of French and British imperialisms respectively, the 'distant future' appears free from all kinds of oppression. One chapter of Adorno's *Armonía del Universo* (1862), extracted as 'El remoto porvenir', presents an interplanetary traveller admiring 'equality, as the fundamental principle of humanity' achieved on earth which can no longer be 'corrupted by tyranny' (25). In Sankrityayan's *Bāīsavīm Sadī* (1923), a sleeper awakes after two hundred years to find equality, once again, reigning supreme in every domain of human activity. This utopia is governed by a single, demilitarised, global government presided over by an Indian, with Japanese, Russian and Americans holding key ministerial posts (46–7). This dialectic between (Vernian) dystopic and utopic visions of governance and sovereignty often provides sf with its compositional logic. The Argentine Angélica Gorodischer has a particularly striking example of this in her 'Los embriones del violeta' (1973), written, lest we forget, in a decade that saw the spectacular resurgence of neo-imperialism and US backed dictatorships across Latin America.

Gorodischer deploys the classic colonial adventure story formula, á la *Heart of Darkness*, to begin her tale, only to later reformulate it in a startlingly original manner. The crew of the spaceship *Niní Paume Uno* arrive on the planet Salari II to explore the potential for colonisation and to discover the fate of previous expeditions that failed to return. What they encounter appears to be the opposite of Conradian 'horror' – not only have their predecessors survived, they have done so without resorting to the horrific Kurtzian excesses that scar Congo in Conrad's 1899 novella. For the only inhabitants of the planet are those who have been produced by the desires and imaginations of the humans: a kitsch feudal court complete with trans-sexual courtesans and Black guards; a pastiche renaissance laboratory and observatory; a giant ovoid incubator tended by grotesque maternal figures. The mysterious violet light of the planet has the capacity to grant unlimited powers to individuals to materialise their innermost wishes, provided one can 'feel yourself to be that which you wish to obtain' (190). That is, the fulfilment of desire depends not on the 'othering' of objects, but on total identification with them. The question of governance is similarly displaced from the context of coercive extraction to that of enlightened recognition of (and playful submission) to one's 'personal demons' (188).

Yet the lives of such inter-galactic Tennysonian 'Lotus-eaters' hold insufficient attractions for *Niní Paume Uno*'s crew, who are driven by the Ulysses-complex to which the Victorian poet also paid homage to ('to strive, to seek, to find, and not to yield'). They are moved by a different set of pleasures altogether, ones that are antithetical to 'happiness': report writing, fact-finding and punishing infractions of the military's violently heteronormative codes of conduct. These cannot be realised without extractive imperialism, and they decide to fly home albeit after agreeing to have all memories of their encounter erased by their now more-than-human predecessors; the only exception is the doctor, Leo Sessler, who is doomed to write his memories of Salari II that no one on Earth will read. Utopia can be experienced as the negation of certain pleasures offered precisely by the cruelties of imperial asymmetry – such is the reminder of Gorodischer's tale written shortly before the disastrous coup and the subsequent reign of the *junta* in her country. What is common to the nineteenth century fiction of Verne or Adorno and the twentieth century fiction of Sankrityayan or Gorodischer is the realisation that technoscience is constituted by, and in turn constitutes, social relationships and historical forces. Over the long duration of capitalism's globalisation, it has been pressed into the service of imperial governance as frequently as it has been wielded against imperialists by their subjects. Violence has been technoscience's operational mode as often as non-violence and it is to the interaction between them that we turn next.

Advanced technoscientific warfare, of course, is in many ways the generic signature of sf. Charles Tilly long ago showed that 'war-making' and 'state-making' were among the signal consequences of the business of capitalism over the past five centuries (Tilly 169–86), and it should come as no surprise that a literature whose distinctive features include a kind of 'worldbuilding' that offers, 'however unintentionally, a snapshot of the structures of capital' (Bould 4) should meditate on the relentless militarisation of all aspects of modern life. Understandably, such generic predilections came to the fore during periods of prolonged and sustained global conflicts over the 'long' twentieth century. European and American writers in particular, perhaps, have been marked by their attraction to 'super-weapons' and 'future wars', as exhaustive surveys by H. Bruce Franklin, Albert I. Berger and Martha A. Bartter demonstrate. Archetypal scenes, such as this one from Wells's *The War of the Worlds* (1898), have been re-purposed numerous times in later works:

> Forthwith the six guns which, unknown to anyone on the right bank, had been hidden behind the outskirts of that village, fired simultaneously. The sudden near concussions, the last close upon the first, made my heart jump. The monster was already raising the case generating the Heat-Ray when the first shell burst six yards above the hood [... .] The shell burst clean in the face of the Thing. The hood bulged, flashed, was whirled off in a dozen tattered fragments of red flesh and glittering metal.
>
> (63)

The genius of Wells, of course, was to reverse the historical encounter between Euro-American technoscientific empires and their Indigenous subjects. The terror and disorientation felt by the African, Asian and American and Australasian Indigenous peoples when faced with the maxim gun or the howitzer is, in the novel, transferred onto the English inhabitants of London, Surrey and the home counties. The alien Martians turn out to be identical, to imperial 'selves', inviting reflection on the necessarily violent nature of modern imperialism.

Sf also often refuses the usual solace offered by advocates of modern imperialism – that the effects of such necessary violence are offset by the benefits the system confers on its subjects. Such benefits, in this way of thinking, take the form of trade and 'free' global circulation of goods, peoples and expertise. In contrast, a key insight offered by sf is that making war and making trade are *co-dependent* processes in which endemic violence decreases whatever value efficient circulation of goods confers on some groups in society. The Indian writer Premendra Mitra's 'Hnaash' ('Duck' 1957), is a case in point. The story is a part of a series that Mitra wrote over three decades featuring a garrulous, tall-tale-telling hero, Ghana-da, who holds his audience captive in a small men's hostel in Calcutta with recitations of his adventures across time and space. In 'Hnaash', Ghana-da tries to appease a new resident of the hostel, Bapi Datta, whose precious duck-meat he has blithely appropriated without permission, with a story about his entrepreneurial instinct for extracting 'free gifts' of nature. The resource in question here is deuterium oxide, or heavy water (a valuable ingredient in nuclear energy and weapons research), that in the story is found in abundance near a remote Tibetan lake.

Unlike in other stories by Mitra, the arms race in 'Hnaash' is not between agents of the global empires but between entrepreneurs with no obvious allegiances to anything but profiteering. As Ghana-da blithely puts it to his rival, the murderous Muller: 'Like I said, I am looking for heavy water. If I could sell a small bottle of it in this age of the hydrogen bomb, I could immediately retire' (Mitra 164–5; my translation). Like Ghana-da, Muller has no obvious national affiliations. Although we are told that he is 'the shame of the scientific world, a fraud, a thief and a murderer' (165; my translation), it is unclear why he is any different to Callio, the scientist he murders, since they both aim to possess what cannot belong to them on any grounds except those of the historical privileges granted to (some) Europeans by the dint of their imperial relations to Asiatic peripheries such as Tibet. It is precisely to break into such historically Euro-American monopolies over resource extraction that is Ghana-da's desire, and it is this instinct that Mitra's narrative interrogates in its *denouement*.

Here, Mitra grafts tropes of the imperial adventure tale on to that of scientific wonders. Spying a wolf stalking some migrant ducks, Ghana-da shoots the animal with his last bullet at the very moment it catches a stunned but live bird in its mouth. He then forces the map down the gullet of the duck and sets it free on its flight across the Himalayas to the warmer climes of India. It is this search for the map and the fugitive bird that has since led him, so he claims, to slaughter 1,232 ducks thus far. Thus, the end of the narrative answers the problem posed by the enraged Bapi Datta in the beginning – on what grounds can Ghana-da explain his appropriation of the duck that Datta had bought for his private consumption? Ghana-da's tale suggests that the only justification for such an action is the possession of a certain kind of power – that of narrating wondrous tales obviously, but also one that, within such narratives, validates the historical symbiosis between warfare and tradecraft that was one of the signal features of modern European imperialism. Mitra's tale is set in the recently independent India but, judging by his hero's mimicry of imperial adventurers, it is a very long way from decolonisation itself.

This enduring stranglehold of imperial economic, military and cultural imagination over nominally independent nations and societies is constantly flagged in sf. For example, 'The Last Pantheon' (2015), by the Yoruba writer Tade Thompson and the Zambian-born South African Nick Wood, extends the concern that was already evident in mid-twentieth century writers like Mitra. Thompson and Wood use superhero narratives to offer a view of Africa that shuttles between 'anti-colonial' and 'postcolonial' perspectives. The former is evident in the story's premise that not only did all human life *begin* in Africa (surely an uncontroversial view by now, given the evidence amassed by anthropologists, historians and archaeologists), but that Africa *continues* to be the motor of human history. This fundamental rejection of the imperialist world view is established through the story of two resident aliens who arrive in the continent during pre-history and discreetly supervise the various stages of human bio-technological evolution over many millennia. The 'postcolonial' view, on the other hand, threatens to negate their achievements because it lays bare the debased states of these alien-superheroes – comically costumed, ageing, seedy figures mired in the economic, social and political decay ushered in by turbo-capitalism and information technology that have more or less neutered the gains made during the struggle for independence in the continent. This narrative structure rehearses the 'postcolonial' acceptance of the passing of the dissident energies of 'anti-colonial' activism.

If the *noms de guerres* of these superheroes – Pan-African and Black-Power – hark back to those brief time of hope, their current jobs as celebrity activist and police detective attest to their ebbing powers as well as radically divergent views on human progress. The memory of fighting alongside Cuban and Chinese guerrillas for Angola's independence has kept Pan-African's zeal for social justice alive, and he continues with his semi-legal struggle for the rights of slum dwellers in Lagos against the Nigerian government. Black-Power, on the other hand, is haunted by his historic failures to prevent the murder of Patrice Lumumba in Congo and the Sharpeville massacre in South Africa. In bitter reaction, he has now joined the corrupt and violent South African police force in a single-minded mission to physically eliminate criminals and crime.

Congruent with the opposing political positions taken up by the superheroes, the novella offers two different endings in its conclusion – dystopic, and then, utopic. In the dystopic version, the triumph of 'information capitalism' (Wood, McChesney and Foster) and 'network society' (van Dijk; Castells) is complete, and whatever is left of the superheroes benevolent intentions are cannibalised by African media entrepreneurs who arrange a gladiatorial fight to death between them for the delectation of a global audience. Yet the spectacular death of Pan-African and the inter-galactic repatriation of Black-Power hardly signal the end of all progressive hope. Traces of their more-than-human powers are emerging in Thembeka, the much-bullied female fellow-officer of Black-Power. The fading alien explains that this is a genetic consequence of intimate exchanges between the aliens and humans that occurred many generations ago (74), and all indications are that Thembeka will use these powers very differently from Black-Power. She seems more committed to restorative justice than vigilante violence. Her earlier rejection of Black-Power's sexual advances reveals her determination to step out of the deadly tango of machismo and patriarchal violence that seem to have seduced the superheroes. She might yet be able to steer humanity out of the impasse it has been brought to by the empire of capital.

Thompson and Wood's tale hinges on the portrayal of the entertainment business as warfare by other means. If such warfare mobilises a whole variety of deeply entrenched and fragmented identities and subjectivities that prevent collective action and solidarities, they cannot entirely destroy the possibilities of these coalescing into the latter either. Let us consider, in conclusion, how sf imagines empire as being composed of such fraught traffic between individual and collective identities. For instance, Thompson and Wood use one of the genre's indispensable devices – that of the alien superhero – to show the cross-hatchings between patriarchy, empire and capital. Pan-African's consensual affair with the glamorous media figure Elizabeth Kokoro barely disguises his explicit, if clichéd, masculinist gaze – 'She lay naked beside him tangled in the sheets, one breast visible like a Renaissance painting, chest rising and falling with predictable regularity' (49). The revelation that she is effectively a cyborg, neurologically connected to the cyber-web of information via a surgical implant, shocks him not so much because of what it says about the reach and power of information capitalism, but because it challenges the presumed superiority of his erotic capabilities.

But Pan-African's hyper-masculinity is relatively tame stuff in comparison to that of Black-Power's sense of sexual entitlement. Rebuffed by Thembeka, he forces his unwanted attentions publicly onto a male stranger in a bar, only to be surprised further by the latter's passionate rejection and a punch on his chin – 'Just because I'm gay doesn't mean it's all about sex ... We're all just *people*, you know' (85). The point about Thompson and Wood's tale is that the subsequent homophobic abuse Black-Power receives on social media *does not* burnish his credentials as the champion of gender equality. To the contrary, his utter inability to understand consent ('*Humans*! Who could understand them' (85)) in matters of sexuality exposes the fact that rather than transcending the historical drag of patriarchy, his superheroism is a concentrated expression of it. This also explains the failure of his 'anti-colonial' gestures.

In fact, such correlations between empire, capital, patriarchy and various subjectivities have been of foundational importance to the genre. They already constituted a central problematic in Karel Čapek's *R.U.R.* (1923), the play that provided the template for all major science-fictional meditations on artificial intelligence and the limits of the human. For the scientists in charge of manufacturing Rossum's Universal Robots, the inability of the machines to love or feel pain expresses itself primarily as a technical problem of productivity: 'Occasionally, they seem somehow to go off their heads [... .] We call it Robot's cramp. They'll suddenly sling down everything they're holding, stand still, gnash their teeth [...] It's evidently some breakdown in the mechanism' (23). They are reluctant to fix this since this would raise the cost and eat into the profit margins of the company. On the other hand, repair it they must because the abundance, cheapness and disposability of the robots, while fixing the problem of labour shortage, have resulted in the blockage of another kind – the bio-social reproductivity of humans, which has stalled entirely as a reaction to the overabundance of the machines.

As the scientist's own sinister erotic enslavement of Helena – a representative of Humanity League, which advocates the extension of rights and privileges to the robots– shows, technoscientific 'development' in Čapek's play is a function of the conjoined powers of capitalism and patriarchy. Women and robots serve identical purposes in this scheme, and it is not surprising that the revolt of the machines that wipes out most of humanity initially take the form of their refusal to conform to patriarchal desires. Radius, the leader of the revolt, confounds the scientists with his feelings of hatred and resentment, while Helena, created as a 'copy' of her human counterpart, remains determinedly 'lifeless [... .] a deformity' (48). After the success of their uprising, the robots face a productivity problem of their own: since all knowledge regarding their manufacture has perished with the humans, unless they learn to procreate, their built-in obsolescence will result in their own demise. The play ends on a note of utopic promise, however, when two robots, Primus and Helena, learn feel and express love under the benevolent supervision of Alquist, the last human left alive. This artificial *eros*, the play suggests, will be free from the drive towards domination that marked their human counterparts – the *homo capitalisticus*.

The human drive towards sexual and economic domination in Čapek's play is intimately linked to what we might call the imperial instinct. Even, or especially, when faced with complete annihilation by the robots, the scientists cling on to the dream of rebuilding a future global imperial state: 'And this little state of ours could be the centre of future life [... .] in a few hundred years it could conquer the world again [... .] it will again be master of lands and oceans; it will breed rulers [... .] heroes who will carry their glowing soul throughout all peoples' (79). Nor is such a drive powered by sexuality and economics alone. Other modes of hierarchisation and inequality, such as race, also play a prominent role: 'each factory will produce Robots of a different colour, a different language [... .] By Jove, we'll make negro Robots and Swedish Robots and Italian Robots and Chinese Robots' (57). Čapek's attention to the intersection of gender, race, class and caste as the generative matrix for imperialism proved to be paradigmatic for subsequent sf of both the Global North and South.

The tragedy of the robot's revolt is precisely that they have learnt this lesson only too well from the humans. Radius sums up the aim of the machines: 'The rule over oceans and lands. The rule over stars. The rule over the universe. Room, room, more room for the Robots' (90). Accused by Alquist of genocide, Radius responds: 'Read history, read the human books. You must domineer and murder if you want to be like men' (94). Part of the power of Čapek's play comes from the combination of the apparent common-sense of Radius's historical analysis with the echo of the Nazi slogan of *lebensraum*. But even more unsettling is its refusal to see the robots (or the Nazis) as historical exceptions or aberrations. Rather, such *ubermensch*ian drive is revealed as intensification of tendencies inherent in certain historical formations. It is against such tendencies that the robots Primus and Helena take up a position of an affective praxis. Their love is expressed as self-sacrificial action – their readiness to suffer so that the other may live – which was also the organisation principle for successful strategies of historical anti-imperial strategies like Gandhi's *satyagraha*.

Sf's registration of modern imperialism is obviously not exhausted by the approaches discussed here. But they do, I hope, provide points of departure for any understanding of the centrality of empire to the genre. Whether composed in the core imperial zones of the world such as Britain and France in the nineteenth century, or the semi-peripheral and peripheral colonies and postcolonies of Asia, Africa and Latin America, sf literature, films, plays and art register empire as one of the fundamental points of reference everywhere in the lived experience of the modern world. It remains for us then, to appreciate fully the importance of the sf to the practices of imperialism and anti-imperialism alike.

Works cited

Adorno, Juan Nepomuceno Adorno. 'El remoto porvenir/The Distant Future' extract. Trans. Andrea L. Bell. *Cosmos Latino: An Anthology of Science Fiction from Latin America and Spain*. Ed. Andrea L. Bell and Yolanda Molina-Gavilān. Wesleyan UP, 2003. 23–35.

Agamben, Giorgio. *Homo Sacer: Sovereign Power and Bare Life*. Stanford UP, 1998.

Anderson, Warwick. 'Postcolonial Technoscience'. *Social Studies of Science* 32.5–6 (2002): 643–58.

Arnold, David. 'Nehruvian Science and Postcolonial India'. *Isis* 104.2 (2013): 360–70.
Bartter, Martha A. *The Way to Ground Zero: The Atomic Bomb in American Science Fiction*. Praeger, 1988.
Berger, Albert I. *Life and Times of the Atomic Bomb: Nuclear Weapons and the Transformation of Warfare*. Routledge, 2016.
Bould, Mark. 'Rough Guide to a Lonely Planet, from Nemo to Neo'. *Red Planets: Marxism and Science Fiction*. Ed. Mark Bould and China Miéville. Pluto, 2009. 1–26.
Burton, Antoinette. *Empire in Question: Reading, Writing, and Teaching British Imperialism*. Duke UP, 2011.
Bush, Barbara. *Imperialism and Postcolonialism*. Pearson Education, 2006.
Čapek, Josef and Karel Čapek. *R.U.R and The Insect Play*. Trans. Nigel Playfair. Oxford UP, 1961.
Castells, Manuel. *The Rise of the Network Society*. Blackwell, 1996.
Cohen, Benjamin J. *The Question of Imperialism: The Political Economy of Dominance and Dependence*. Macmillan, 1974.
Csicsery-Ronay, Jr, Istvan. 'Empire'. *The Routledge Companion to Science Fiction*. Ed. Mark Bould, Andrew M. Butler, Adam Roberts and Sherryl Vint. Routledge, 2009. 362–72.
Escobar, Arturo. 'Development and the Anthropology of Modernity'. *The Postcolonial Science and Technology Studies Reader*. Ed. Sandra Harding. Duke UP, 2011. 269–89.
Fanon, Frantz. *The Wretched of the Earth*. Grove Press, 2004.
Franklin, H. Bruce. *War Stars: The Superweapon in the American Imagination*. Oxford UP, 1988.
Gorodischer, Angélica. 'Los embriones del violeta/The Violet's Embryos'. Trans. Sara Irausquin. *Cosmos Latino: An Anthology of Science Fiction from Latin America and Spain*. Ed. Andrea L. Bell and Yolanda Molina-Gavilãn. Wesleyan UP, 2003. 158–93.
Lazarus, Neil. *The Postcolonial Unconscious*. Cambridge UP, 2011.
Mitra, Premendra. 'Hnaash' ('Duck'). *Ghanada Samagra*, volume 1. Ed. Surajit Dasgupta. Ananda, 2000. 156–68.
Raj, Kapil. 'Beyond Postcolonialism … and Postpositivism: Circulation and the Global History of Science'. *Isis* 104.2 (2013): 337–47.
Reid, Michelle. 'Postcolonialism'. *The Routledge Companion to Science Fiction*. Ed. Mark Bould, Andrew M. Butler, Adam Roberts and Sherryl Vint. Routledge, 2009. 256–66.
Sankritayan, Rahul. 'Baisvin Sadi/The Twenty Second Century' extract. Trans. Maya Joshi. *New Horizons: The Gollancz Book of South Asian Science Fiction*. Ed. Tarun K. Saint. Gollancz, 2021. 46–50.
Subramaniam, Banu. 'Archaic Modernities: Science, Secularism, and Religion in Modern India'. *Social Text* 18.3 (2000): 67–86.
Suvin, Darko. *Metamorphoses of Science Fiction: On the Poetics and History of a Literary Genre*. Yale UP, 1979.
Thompson, Tade and Nick Wood. 'The Last Pantheon'. *AfroSF v2*. Ed. Ivor W. Hartman. Storytime, 2015. 9–112.
Tilly, Charles. 'War Making and State Making as Organized Crime'. *Bringing the State Back*. Ed. Peter Evans, Dietrich Rueschemeyer and Theda Skocpol. Cambridge UP, 1985. 69–186.
Van Dijk, Jan. *The Network Society*. Sage, 2006.
Verne Jules. *Twenty Thousand Leagues under the Seas*. Trans. William Butcher. Oxford UP, 2019.
Wells, H.G. *The War of the Worlds*. Oxford UP, 2005.
Wood, Ellen Mieksins, Robert W. McChesney and John Bellamy Foster, eds. *Capitalism and the Information Age: The Political Economy of the Global Communication Revolution*. Monthly Review Press, 1998.

43
ENERGY HUMANITIES

Rhys Williams

Energy humanities is, at root, an activist discipline, motivated by political and ecological concerns beyond the text. Its primary wager is that energy is not just a technical issue but a thoroughly social, cultural and political one, too. Our relationship to energy became significantly more important to interpreting culture with the dawning of the fossil fuel era, the birth of modern 'petroculture' and the permeation of mechanical and electrical energy that henceforth marked even the most mundane and intimate elements of human culture (Petrocultures Research Group). The discovery and exploitation of fossil fuels provided an unprecedented infusion of energy to European civilisation in the eighteenth century, before spreading its effects unevenly and its benefits and costs unequally across the globe. The world we live in now wobbles at the peak of innumerable hockey-stick graphs tracking the historical volumes of fossil fuel extraction; energy consumption; human population; global shipping and trade; automobile production; steel and concrete manufacture; suburban sprawl; mechanically assisted industrial animal slaughter; pesticide and fertiliser-saturated monocultures; ecosystem destruction; and carbon emissions. Thus, energy humanities understand modernity as a fossil-fuelled history and experience, which cannot be properly grasped without attention to the specific materiality and affordances of fossil fuels (Mitchell; Szeman and Boyer; Wilson, Carlson and Szeman). The modern subject is similarly reconceived as a fossil subject – our values, desires, expectations and habits informed by (and impossible without) the fossil fuels that facilitate them. If energy informs human experience, sociality, culture and understanding to such an extent, then clearly its imprint should be detectable in the shaping of our literary narratives and artistic mediations too.

Broadly speaking, the energy humanities bring the tools of the humanities to bear on two key issues: energy impasse and energy transition. 'Impasse' names how society, culture, politics and subjectivities are entangled with and informed by fossil fuels, and how this provides a barrier to the changes to our energy system needed as atmospheric carbon climbs dangerously high; 'transition' concerns what non-fossil-fuelled futures might look like, what they might consist of, and what would be required to achieve them. Energy's production, distribution and consumption, and the changes required of them, are reconceived from an isolatable technical question with a technical solution to a complex terrain of social contestation and imbrication: a space of competing and overlapping values, politics, desires and imaginaries that must be navigated; narratives and

 DOI: 10.4324/9781003140269-46

counter-narratives that must be parsed and critically examined; alternatives that must be glimpsed from within the dominant disposition.

For the activist energy humanities, energy is a fulcrum issue – so fundamental to global civilisation that to change the way it is produced, distributed and consumed is to change the very foundations of our way of life, and all the little details and peculiarities that arise from them. Yet despite the scale of this challenge, it is precisely what is demanded in this era of climate crisis: to stop extracting and burning fossil fuels, to stop emitting carbon, to transition to a completely different, renewable and sustainable energy system. The burning question is whether such a transition can be performed so that it also delivers social justice across the multiple registers of inequality that energy facilitates. Race, gender, class: the disparities between energy-rich and energy-poor trace these usual lines of differentiation, as well as broad North–South divides and the struggles of Indigenous peoples against the rapacity of settler states. This is the broad context and commitment of the energy humanities, against which its specific interest to the study of sf should be understood.

The fantastic genres – especially sf – are a site of key interest for the energy humanities, and the relationship is productive for sf scholars, too. In terms of impasse, sf is a privileged genre to think with. Sf is more about the present than the future, so considering energy in its estranged futures, including fossil-free futures, highlights the way our imaginations are caught in the force-field of fossil-fuelled assumptions, expectations and ways of being. In terms of transition, sf and the fantastic genres are also a site of potential radical imagination, a toolkit for thinking beyond the entanglements of petroculture into a sustainable and just future, and considering how energy transition might support largescale social shifts.

For sf scholars, the energy humanities intersect with the fantastic genres (and cultural production in general) in two important arenas. First, there are texts that are directly 'about' energy, which comprise a small but growing 'energy canon' (Macdonald 'Research'). Second, and perhaps more interestingly, there is the less direct way that energy shapes cultural products – the ways that different kinds of energy, different fuels, different infrastructures and the social systems built on and around them inform narratives. This latter requires discovering our 'energy unconscious' (Yaeger) and 'protocols of reading and modes of inquiry that can perceive the pressure that energy exerts on culture, even and especially when energy is not-said: invisible, erased, elided' (Wenzel 11). Here is attention to energy as a mode of reading, and it is here that the power of energy humanities for thinking about the fantastic genres really flourishes.

A key early move of literary energy humanities is to re-periodise works 'according to the energy sources that made them possible' (Yeager et al. 2011: 305). This allows for novel comparisons across and within more traditional groupings of texts. For the relatively youthful fantastic genres, it reveals their saturation in fossil fuels, and raises interesting questions about how they index wider social shifts effected by the transitions from coal as prime mover to oil and nuclear and now to renewables. It also allows us to see how, despite their generic divisions and dissimilarities, fantasy, horror and sf are marked and united by the same energetic contexts.

To the extent that these genres are children of European modernity, they begin, at the turn of the eighteenth century, to distil into alternative responses to the suddenly unignorable transformations of the lived world by technoscientific and sociopolitical innovation (Clute). The engine of History spluttered to life powered by the cheap energy increasingly provided by the extraction and deployment of fossil fuels; coal and then oil provided the means to remake the world and opened up the future as a space of possibility and difference in which human agency seemed to be the deciding factor (Williams 'Inventing'). The long infusion of fossil energy appeared to liberate its beneficiaries from previously restrictive material, natural and ecological limits and relations, but it also brought into sharp relief the destruction it occasioned. Promethean confidence in the emerging industrial society chafed against Romantic rejection, codifying – unevenly – into the generic traditions of the fantastic.

From an energy perspective, sf is the central fantastic genre. This is not a value judgement, but rather a claim that sf best expresses the temporal and energetic conceits of the dominant ideology of Progress – the endless thrust of growth and novelty that defines European modernity. It is also the genre best capable of critiquing this ideology. From the nineteenth century to the present day, we can find sf uncritically shaped by the background assumption of ever-inflating energetics ushered in by fossil fuels, and we can find sf that speaks modes of being and temporalities that resist it. The work of refusal occurs both within the traditions of sf and by drawing upon other fantastic genres. Genre boundaries are more a useful heuristic than true dividers, but it is useful to think about certain attitudes and affordances as broadly 'generic' since they allow us to name and track shifts in the dispositions of texts that mark those moments that carry alternative meanings and traditions within them. This is especially true now, as sf increasingly hosts the diverse voices of authors and communities of practice long antagonistic to the narrow idea of Progress and the settler colonialism that bore it like an infection to distant lands. For example, the sf of N.K. Jemisin and Nalo Hopkinson bears marks that from a strictly Eurocentric ontology would break the 'rationality' of sf. But their fiction weaves elements together into aesthetic wholes that, rather than appearing to be generic mishmashes, give the lie to traditional purifying gatekeeper claims about sf's rationality. Meanwhile, Anglo-American traditions that draw on multiple genres for their effects, in particular the Dying Earth fiction, speak volumes about the historically constructed relationships between ideas of rationality, progress and temporality, and their hidden energetic foundations and relationships.

Most scholarly attention in energy humanities has been paid to sf as *the* genre of future-oriented socio-technical change, unearthing the energy unconscious of twentieth and twenty-first century literature and film (Banerjee; Bellamy; Canavan; Macdonald 'Improbability'; Otjen; Raven; Smith; Williams 'Shining'). On the one hand, this work privileges sf for its capacity to track how our present energy culture and its horizon of future expectations have been informed by the exuberance and catastrophe of fossil fuels, from inflated galactic canvases and FTL travel to post-1973 oil crisis imaginaries of scarcity and apocalypse; whether expanded or contracted, whether powered by future fuels or scarce and scavenged firewood, these future imaginaries are formed and textured in the force-field of coal and, predominantly, oil. On the other hand, sf is also regarded as offering up thick descriptions of alternative energy futures, in which the 'social' half of sociotechnical change can be speculatively and affectively explored. Here, of course, the critical question involves the extent to which these imaginaries can escape the assumptions of their time: is a shiny and energetic renewable future genuinely radical, or does it simply greenwash the unsustainable values and ways of being of our time? Reading sf in these ways reaches far beyond this or that particular text and into the real-world issue of a just transition. This is especially important when big players – from energy companies to tech start-ups and governments – deploy sf tropes and images to greenwash their ongoing extractivism and ecosystem exploitation (Szeman and Wenzel). Scholarship has thus interrogated sf as a mode to think with, as a form of critique, and as a source of alternatives. But in the general attention to sf by scholars beyond the field of sf studies, what can get overlooked is sf's specificity as a genre in a relational system of genres, with a history that in certain ways shapes and limits what can be thought.

Sf is a genre that *requires* energy, both the fossil fuels, nuclear fission, nuclear fusion, solar power, Helium-3, gravity waves, dilithium crystals or whatever used to power fanciful future technologies of the future, and human cognitive and manual labour. Sf transports us from the present to a transformed future, and this conceptual movement contains within itself the assumption of energy expenditure to break and reform the elements and bonds of biological, ecological, social and technical order. In this way sf is the storying of modernity, in which the enormous energetic injection of fossil fuels acts as 'the catalyst for a set of corresponding social disruptions [...] the uncontrolled admixture and cauldron of excitation that blurs the old relations between city and country, time and space, class and gender [...] and the world whirls outside of its normative form' (Johnson 148). Reshaping anything requires *energy*. Standing on the far side of this breaking and reforming – whether for good or ill – is quite simply what marks an sf text *as sf*. Between our here-and-now and any science-fictional world is a cognitive bridge comprised of transformation, and transformation entails energy, just as the bridge between the eighteenth century and our present was built from massive energy expenditure.

If this capacity to break and remake limits and relations is situated within the paradigm of European modernity, with its tendencies to abstraction, atomisation, alienation, separation of society and nature, and extraction, then the telos of its storying within sf tends, ultimately, to that apotheosis of science-fictional imaginations of progress, the Singularity (Csicsery-Ronay). The Singularity is the endpoint of the 'general idea of exponential accelerating change' captured in the contemporary faith in 'technological time' (Broderick 21, 20) as a driving logic of historical change: a 'series of upwardly accelerating logistical S-curves, each supplanting the one before as it flattens out [...] rushing us into a Singularity' (20). The Singularity promises a future in which humanity, through technological ingenuity, overcomes ecological, social and material limits; it is fundamentally a narrative about the desire to be freed from the burdens of history and necessity, from frustrations and restrictions on agency. The exuberant imaginary of the Singularity takes flight particularly in response to dramatic new energy inputs, but it is always locked in mortal combat with corresponding discourses of limits and boundaries that seek to drag it back to earth. We see this, for example, in the nineteenth century odes to coal-fired steam (Malm), in which, from the perspective of an industrial capitalist, mechanical energy possesses the qualities of a genie, eager and able to turn desire into reality – not to mention make all those troublesome, easily-tired labourers redundant. The mastery of nature and freedom from natural limits, seasons and cycles that coal seemed to promise prompted early visions of 'a future in which the entire globe would be given over to the demands of a fully urbanised civilisation' (Macduffie 10). Yet these energetic visions were tempered by the drag of entropy and the heat-death of the universe weighing upon them, perhaps because the effluent of coal was too obvious, with its heavy and dirty materiality, the broken backs and blackened lungs of coal miners, and the suffocating smogs of London. For example, H.G. Wells's *The Time Machine* (1895) shows the world ending not in technological overcoming but in entropy, curtailing the arrow of progress with the death of the sun: a final consequence of the Second Law of Thermodynamics that haunted the Victorian imagination.

As the nineteenth became the twentieth century, liberation and bondage continue to tangle in sf narratives of energy imaginaries. Cheap and spectacular oil, and the new relations of production it entailed (Mitchell), provide the most dramatic and long-lasting impetus. While the Omega Point of Teilhard de Chardin's *The Phenomenon of Man* (written 1930, published 1955) is perhaps the earliest codification of the Singularity in full flight, the endless horizon of Futurama (Pelletier), displayed at the 1939 World Fair, is the canonical early twentieth century statement of it, and much Golden Age sf attests to the fantasy of limitlessness occasioned by oil (Canavan). This is when today's road-reticulated world was first imagined in full, the motorcar was first anointed king, and the promise, aimed squarely at affluent White Americans, was of freedom, safety, speed and a paradoxical return to nature via suburban sprawl. This liberation was of course bookended by the newly mechanised and destructive powers of World Wars, and mingled with the violent joy of Futurism and the Lovecraftian horrors unearthed by delving too deep. The 1950s brought with them the oil-powered Great Acceleration and the Green Revolution, and the sf of this period 'simply takes for granted that the wonders of the future will be powered by clean atomic energy "too cheap to meter"' (Canavan 338). Energy had bloomed into the world, and surely there was no going back, but such exhilaration was swiftly met by the neo-Malthusianism and burgeoning environmental movements of the 1960s, and the shock of the oil crises of the 1970s, apparently fulfilling King Hubbert's 1956 predictions of a coming peak and decline in oil production. This new mood was matched by the often-miasmic commitments of New Wave sf, with its questions of scarcity, loss and nostalgia. The 1980s and 1990s brought globalisation, the information revolution and further energy demands, all to be explored in the rich virtual worlds they made possible. While this new ebullience mostly buried the fears of the 1970s, the creeping acceptance of global warming tainted the dream. Now we are buoyed by the promise of renewables from every political corner, from neoliberal financial advisors and think-tanks (Bloomberg NEF; Sivaram) to centre-left enthusiasts (Brown; Scheer) to full solar communists (Schwartzmann). This finds its clearest artistic expression in solarpunk (Williams 'Shining'), although sf tropes are also widely used by the renewables industry as well as activists to communicate the promissory narratives that sell their products. The contrary to these utopian visons is less clear, beyond the terrifying banality of lack, of simply failing to transition quickly enough. We are perhaps too close to the novelty of the moment, but certainly there is much scepticism to be found in critical scholarship that punctures the solar bubble (Mulveney 2019).

We find here, as always, sf not as good or bad, but as site of intervention and toolbox, open to anyone. Sf is capable of a 'reflexive awareness of the limits of its own infinite drive' (Macdonald 'Improbability' 141). But energy presents a unique problem for critical thought: as an unquestioned foundation that allegedly unites everything else, it proves more slippery in some ways than, say, gender or race as a critical lens. Indeed, one of the important ways of thinking energy critically is through tying it to these other categories. Energy, too, as it unfolds in the world, can be racist, sexist, colonial. And we must be wary of sf that appears to be critical of petroculture. We might wish to turn, for example, to post-apocalyptic fiction, from MAD MAX to Emily St. John Mandel's *Station Eleven* (2014), as evidence of sf's critique of petroculture. But from an energy perspective, such texts can be seen as sf evacuating itself of (some of) the resources required for its imaginative work (plentiful energy) and exposing in the resultant lack that shapes the narrative world (the *absence* of the petrocultural rather than the presence of something else) the usually obscured resource costs and externalities that sf's imaginative work depends upon. Here sf is not providing an alternative to an energy-hungry structuring logic and temporality, only laying that structure bare as a narrative and desire rather than an objective reality (i.e., S-curves are a narrative, not a fact of nature, and these post-apocalyptic texts show the failure of reality to match those boosterish narratives). Further, the very lack evokes nostalgic longing for the energetic pleasures of the petrocultural, reinforcing the desires and values of the present rather than undermining them.

Extending beyond the strictly fictional, scholars have identified sf's narrative and aesthetic strategies and transformational drive at work in real-world discourses. Imre Szeman (2007) proposes an early and influential identification of the opposition of 'techno-utopian' and 'eco-apocalyptic' modes (i.e., the Singularity's onward march or its failure) that dominate real-world future energy imaginaries. He demonstrates the absence of the political in these narratives: both maintain business-as-usual, whether to a glorious technologically ameliorated future or to wrack and ruin. Karen Pinkus notes the power of promised 'future fuels' deployed in contemporary discourse as a means of maintaining the status quo. My own work (Williams 'Shining', 'Turning') traces how proponents of solar technology and new food production techniques from across the political spectrum marshal the same utopian promises of earlier technological paradigms – a return to the pastoral, to community, and decentralisation (Carey and Quirk) – in their efforts to enrol others into their proposed futures. Here, sf's narrative affordances are mobilised in promissory narratives, maintaining the same energetic and temporal framework that marks works of Singularitarian sf since the industrial revolution. Techno-utopian imaginaries tend to deploy symbolic resolutions to real contradictions via the novum of an imaginary transformational technology. On the one hand, these future imaginaries provide a justification for continued commitment to business-as-usual, via a renewal of the old Promethean tale of human ingenuity and overcoming; on the other, they shift the present towards that future. They render the sequence of events between here and there plausible by tying it to existing mechanisms and narratives, and consequently reroute those mechanisms – entrepreneurial activity, funding streams, scientific and engineering research and development, media attention, political and public support – via the transformational technology and towards the realisation of the initial narrative promise. These corporate, industry and government sf narratives remain structured by petroculture's excessive energetics and linear temporal thrust, and are best understood as energy-hungry possibility engines: they burn the present as fuel for possible futures. They maintain the horizon of possibility so it can be used, consciously or unconsciously, to justify leaving us stranded in an ever-diminished, increasingly neglected present. But by focusing on energy, we can shift the contextual frame of such narratives so that they appear not as persuasively reasonable but as the rankest fantasy.

Techno-utopian narratives pretend to an 'objective' linear historical temporality and contingency, but in reality are fantasy narratives that portray the producer of a new technology as the hero. Such stories – for example, Neal Stephenson's *Termination Shock* (2021) and Andy Weir's *Project Hail Mary* (2021) – work by identifying a wrongness and a thinning (e.g., the climate effects of petroculture) and proposing a hero (an entrepreneur, a corporation) who has identified the source of the problem and can bring about the required healing (via innovation and disruption). If we take this perspective, we can see that these apparently science-fictional narratives in fact imprison the genre's historical transformational logic within that of a larger cyclical temporality typically associated with fantasy. They are heroic fantasies where the solution to bring about healing is always the introduction of a new technology: any potential for radical novelty is neutered by this containment, and the newness is merely a Comedic return to the status quo. Through redoubled commitment to the techno-utopian drive, we are promised, we can re-achieve a final state of Edenic, pre-industrial harmony with the natural world. Notably, this end-state is figured by drawing traditional fantasy aesthetics into the sf frame. A final reconciliation of country and city, nature and culture, these high-tech futures do one of three things. They expand technology so that it becomes the ground upon which nature can flourish, such as a self-sustaining ecology on an artificial habitat, where the pastoral thrives within the bosom of technology, as in the images of Spaceship Earth so popular in the 1960s and 1970s (Höhler). Or they imagine a technology safely subsumed under nature, harking back to the early days of American pastoral exceptionalism (Marx). Or they envision some shining garden-city, in which nature and technology operate in harmony. All these visions draw upon the moral–ecological synergy that has emerged as a strand in the fantasy tradition: from shining elven cities of silicon-clad spires interspersed with greenery, to fairy-village hobbit eco-houses sunk into the earth and covered in sod. Failure to achieve this synergy – failure to follow the techno-utopian plan – leads to disaster. So real-world technoutopian narratives, far from containing linear historical logics, sit within a constantly revolving fantasy logic. We might even say that the vaunted S-curves that underpin 'technological time' and the dominant discourse of Progress are in fact a series of overlapping cyclical fantasies, strung out along a linear timeline like a stretched slinky, each new example purporting to solve the problems of the previous one and escape from the cycle, when in fact they are formally constitutive of the cyclical movement, producing new problems to be solved by newer technologies.

The critical valorisation of sf typically rests on its ability to historicise the present. But as noted, sf is persuasive (Miéville). It does not historicise the present in a neutral or objective manner, whatever that might mean, but in a committed one. It is ideological, and a matter of belief. Taking energy as our lens allows us to press this insight further: sf's imaginative work is all too often inextricable from the excessive energetics and linear temporal thrust of fossil-fuelled modernity. The danger in sf is that its activity of historicising fails to escape a longer present, this long European present since the mid-eighteenth century, since the birth of History and the birth of the genre, which, as Energy Humanities has shown, is thoroughly dependent upon the injection of fossil-fuel energy. Without drawing upon an alternative temporality or ontology to structure its imagination, sf's futures are prone to remain within – and fail to estrange – the paradigm of this longer present, and as a consequence they replicates its assumptions and ground them as objective truths. Thus, sf can fail to estrange the paradigms of fossil-fuelled modernity when its estrangements are performed precisely by mobilising those temporal and energetic structures borne of fossil-fuelled modernity.

Considering other fantastic traditions relative to sf reveal its limitations and obfuscations and allow us to place it within or against other temporalities and energetics. Horror and the Weird provide, as their most common affordance, a sense of totalising ontological insecurity: a revelation that we do not know, and we are not in control. These genres have developed potent sets of disquieting aesthetics with which to achieve this affect. These affordances can be used to rupture sf's technocratic Singularity impulse and, crucially, to provide the means for figuring the harmful agency and unwanted path-dependencies of our present energy infrastructures, such as the monstrous oil slick in Stephen King's 'The Raft' (1985) and the living oil rigs of China Miéville's 'Covehithe' (2011). At a more mundane level, horror marks the limits of the science-fictional by limning the failing edge of modern infrastructures and energies: the phone signal is lost, the car runs out of fuel on a dirt road, the lights flicker and dim. Beyond a managed, technological life, it suggests, there be monsters.

Fantasy, on the other hand, is broadly structured around a rejection of modernity (even contemporary urban fantasy, embracing the industrial revolution, defines itself against the recent digital turn). It has the resources to figure not future novelty but a sense of ecological and moral loss with regards to the transformations of energetic modernity, and its affordances allow the connection of moral action with manifest environmental consequences, often working to restore what has been lost. When the temporality of sf is figured in fantasy it is as an emerging threat – the incursion of the beginning of history, of industrialisation with its aesthetics of fire and smoke and iron, of the loss of a presumed connection with the natural world. It is in the inclusion of fantasy's moral–ecological framework, often along with some sense of non-human agency, that Anglo-American sf begins to yearn towards sf written from Indigenous or Black African ontologies. Fantasy provides the Anglo-American tradition ways of drawing on images of pre-modern culture to radically critique the alienation of the present, although it often feels like a clumsy or degraded version of what sf from a genuinely alternative ontology would look like. The main reason for this degradation is that fantasy is also a child of modernity, and much of the tradition today bears the imprint of the very thing it apparently rejects. Magic, for example, can be simply a means of deploying excessive energies without the technology required. This becomes especially clear in such texts as Larry Niven's *The Magic Goes Away* (1978) and Paolo Bacigalupi and Tobias S. Buckell's *The Tangled*

Lands (2018), in which magic-as-power is made reliant on a finite resource and its use bears ecological consequences, thus recasting tales of limitless magic as the petrocultural kin of sf tales of limitless energies.

These logics find their hybrid apotheosis in Dying Earth fiction. Post-fossil but also post-rational, narratives such as Michael Moorcock's DANCERS AT THE END OF TIME trilogy (1972–6) and M. John Harrison's VIRICONIUM series (1971–85) or draw on residual social relations and the affordances of fantasy and horror – in particular, feudal relations, past scientific achievement now atavistic and cast as magic, an incapacity to cognitively grasp and domesticate the world, and the promise of a return to wholeness – in order to figure these furthest, exhausted and entropic futures. These *longue durée* imaginaries highlight how anomalous and temporary the energy-flushed imaginaries of sf are. The rising arrow of progress is revealed as the upward swing of an arc that crashes back down, unable finally to escape the entanglements of material existence. The healing narrative of fantasy is hollowed out, the world unable to be made right again after its science-fictional exploitation. Ironically, Dying Earth stories are typically haunted by a nostalgia for the lost majesty of previous civilisational heights, despite the fact that those heights are precisely what wore out the world and produced the degraded future-present in which they are set.

So, what are we to take from all this? That energy as a lens is crucial for understanding the expanding and contracting of the science fictional imagination. That sf, fantasy and horror are vehicles for thinking about energy, for revealing and critiquing our relationship to it, and potentially for imagining alternatives to the present. But also that simply speculating about alternatives is not enough – it runs the risk of producing superficial differences while reproducing a more fundamental set of temporal and energetic coordinates bequeathed to us from the fossil-fuel age. For sf to truly think beyond the entanglements of fossil fuels, it needs to understand how they have shaped its affordances and its traditions, and it needs to look beyond itself – to fantasy or horror, certainly, but also to cultural traditions and communities of practice that are already on the outside of fossil fuels. Sf depends upon ways to estrange itself from its own tradition, in order to fully estrange European modernity from its fossil-fuelled values, desires and expectations.

Works cited

Banerjee, Anindita. 'Atoms, Aliens, and Compound Crises: Central Asia's Nuclear Fantastic'. *Science Fiction Studies* 45.3 (2018): 454–68.

Bellamy, Brent Ryan. 'Flying Cars, Dino-Power, and Energy in SF'. *Strange Horizons* blog (25 January 2016). http://strangehorizons.com/non-fiction/articles/flying-cars-dino-power-and-energy-in-sf/

Bloomberg NEF. 'New Energy Outlook 2018'. Bloomberg, 2018. https://bnef.turtl.co/story/neo2018

Broderick, Damien. 'Terrible Angels: The Singularity and Science Fiction'. *Journal of Consciousness Studies* 19.1–2 (2012): 20–41.

Brown, Lester R. *The Great Transition: Shifting from Fossil Fuels to Solar and Wind Energy*. W.W. Norton, 2015.

Canavan, Gerry. 'Retrofutures and Petrofutures: Oil, Scarcity, Limit'. *Oil Culture*. Ed. Ross Barrett and Daniel Worden. U of Minnesota P, 2014. 331–49.

Carey, James W. and John J. Quirk. 'The Mythos of the Electronic Revolution'. *The American Scholar* 39.3 (1970): 395–424.

Clute, John. *Pardon This Intrusion: Fantastika in the World Storm*. Beccon, 2011.

Csicsery-Ronay, Jr., Istvan. *The Seven Beauties of Science Fiction*. Wesleyan UP, 2008.

Höhler, Sabine. *Spaceship Earth in the Environmental Age, 1960–1990*. Routledge, 2014.

Johnson, Bob. *Mineral Rites: An Archaeology of the Fossil Economy*. Johns Hopkins UP, 2019.

Macdonald, Graeme. 'Improbability Drives: The Energy of SF'. *Paradoxa* 26 (2014): 111–44.

——. 'Research Note: The Resources of Fiction'. *Reviews in Cultural Theory* 4.2 (2013): 1–24.

MacDuffie, Allen. *Victorian Literature, Energy, and the Ecological Imagination*. Cambridge UP, 2014.

Malm, Andreas. *Fossil Capital: The Rise of Steam-Power and the Roots of Global Warming*. Verso, 2015.

Marx, Leo. *The Machine in the Garden: Technology and the Pastoral Ideal in America*. Oxford UP, 1964.

Miéville, China. 'Cognition as Ideology: A Dialectic of SF Theory'. *Red Planets: Marxism and Science Fiction*. Ed. Mark Bould and China Miéville. Pluto, 2009. 231–48.

Mitchell, Timothy. *Carbon Democracy: Political Power in the Age of Oil*. Verso, 2011.

Mulvaney, Dustin. *Solar Power: Innovation, Sustainability, and Environmental Justice*. U of California P, 2019.

Otjen, Nathaniel. 'Energy Anxiety and Fossil Fuel Modernity in H.G. Wells's *The War of the Worlds*'. *Journal of Modern Literature* 43.2 (2020): 118–33.

Pelletier, Vincent. 'To New Horizons'. General Motors, 1940. www.youtube.com/watch?v=aIu6DTbYnog

Petrocultures Research Group. *After Oil*. West Virginia UP, 2015.

Pinkus, Karen. 'Thinking Diverse Futures from a Carbon Present'. *Symplokē* 21. 1–2 (2013): 195.

Raven, Paul Graham. 'Telling Tomorrows: Science Fiction as an Energy Futures Research Tool'. *Energy Research & Social Science* 31 (2017): 164–9.

Scheer, Hermann. *The Solar Economy: Renewable Energy for a Sustainable Global Future*. Earthscan, 2004.

Schwartzman, David. 'The Great Bifurcation and Prospects for Solar Communism in the Twenty-First Century'. *International Critical Thought* 3.4 (2013): 480–95.

Sivaram, Varun. *Taming the Sun: Innovations to Harness Solar Energy and Power the Planet*. MIT Press, 2018.

Smith, Bradon. 'Imagined Energy Futures in Contemporary Speculative Fictions'. *Resilience: A Journal of the Environmental Humanities* 6.2 (2019): 136–54.

Szeman, Imre and Dominic Boyer, eds. *Energy Humanities: An Anthology*. Johns Hopkins UP, 2017.

Szeman, Imre and Jennifer Wenzel. 'What Do We Talk about When We Talk about Extractivism?' *Textual Practice* 35.3 (2021): 505–23.

Szeman, Imre. 'System Failure: Oil, Futurity, and the Anticipation of Disaster'. *South Atlantic Quarterly* 106.4 (2007): 805–23.

Wenzel, Jennifer. 'Introduction'. *Fueling Culture: 101 Words for Energy and Environment*. Ed. Imre Szeman and Patricia Yaeger. Fordham UP, 2017. 1–16.

Williams, Rhys. 'Inventing New Worlds: The Age of Manifestos and Utopias'. *The Cambridge History of Science Fiction*. Ed. Gerry Canavan and Eric Carl Link. Cambridge UP, 2018. 69–85.

——. '"This Shining Confluence of Magic and Technology": Solarpunk, Energy Imaginaries, and the Infrastructures of Solarity'. *Open Library of Humanities* 5.1 (2019): 60. https://doi.org/10.16995/olh.329

——. 'Turning toward the Sun: The Solarity and Singularity of New Food'. *South Atlantic Quarterly* 120.1 (2021): 151–62.

Wilson, Sheena, Adam Carlson and Imre Szeman, eds. *Petrocultures: Oil, Politics, Culture*. McGill-Queen's UP, 2017.

Yaeger, Patricia, Laurie Shannon, Vin Nardizzi, Ken Hiltner, Saree Makdisi, Michael Ziser and Imre Szeman. 'Editor's Column: Literature in the Ages of Wood, Tallow, Coal, Whale Oil, Gasoline, Atomic Power, and Other Energy Sources'. *PMLA* 126.2 (2011): 305–26.

44
FEMINISMS

Rebecca J. Holden

Feminism, throughout its history and in all its strands, currents or waves, looks to potential futures in which, following Marie Shear's famous definition, the 'radical notion that women are people' (6) has been realised. Key to any feminist project is storytelling. Feminist narratives bring abstract theories to life, reimagine women's lives and futures, and help form feminist identities, ideologies and movements. Unsurprisingly, feminist writers often turn to sf: 'Feminism questions a given order in political terms, while science fiction questions it in imaginative terms' (Lefanu 100).

Numerous sources claim *féminisme* (or *féministe*) was coined by French utopian socialist Charles Fourier in 1837, but the first documented use of either was in the 1880s by Huberine Auclert, founder of France's first suffrage society (Cott *Grounding* 14). In 1890s England, 'detractors more than advocates used it [...] to refer more often to unwanted Continental doctrines' (14) than to any native women's rights movement. In the US, 'They spoke of the advancement of woman or the cause of woman, woman's rights, and woman suffrage', using the singular *woman* to 'symbolize [...] the unity of the female sex' (3), but by 1913, movement leaders accepted feminism 'for its apparent shock value' (13) and to signal something more revolutionary. In 1914, Marie Jenny Howe, New York women's rights organiser and Heterodoxy founder, wrote 'women are changing' and the 'term feminism [. . .] foisted upon us will do as well as any [...] to express women's effort toward development' (qtd in Cott *Grounding* 13).

The label has since been retroactively applied to earlier organisations, activists, theories and writers. Literary scholars discuss *feminist* writers from medieval Europe, such as Margery Kempe, Julian of Norwich and Hildegarde of Bingen, while Simone de Beauvoir describes Christine de Pisan's *The Epistle to the God of Love* (1399) as the 'first time a woman takes up her pen to defend her sex' (117). More recently, 'feminism' was Merriam-Webster's 2017 'Word of the Year' as several intense spikes in interest prompted a 70 percent increase in 'lookups' over the preceding year ('Why Merriam').

Feminism is often classified in terms of first, second and third (and sometimes fourth) waves. This metaphor – originally invoked in 1968 to highlight periods during which largescale women's rights movements took place, a continuity between the first and second waves, and the power typically associated with the ocean – often paints a monolithic view of women's rights movements, emphasising the feminism of upper- and middle-class White women and marginalising or excluding

DOI: 10.4324/9781003140269-47

others. Also 'By implying that feminism did not survive sharp political and cultural divisions following women's increased autonomy, but had to be revived with a mass-based movement of primarily white middle-class women in the 1960s and '70s, the waves metaphor [...] washes away much of feminist history' (Laughlin et al. 78). The metaphor, however, still carries weight, especially in popular culture, so this chapter will not dispense with feminist 'waves' completely but contextualise them with other feminism(s) that travel within, alongside, in between and sometimes in opposition to them. Periodisation will help chart the various modes of feminism as they intersect with sf, although they often reappear and overlap with each other regardless of period.

Pre-nineteenth century English feminism, sf and utopias

Margaret Cavendish's *The Description of a New World, Called the Blazing World* (1668) – about a woman who becomes an Empress of the Blazing-World and her close female friend and scribe, Duchess Margaret Newcastle – is often named the first feminist sf story. Its sf elements include travelling souls, a submarine voyage and the confirmed existence of 'more numerous worlds than the stars which appeared' (51). Other early feminist utopias published in England, including Mary Astell's *A Serious Proposal* (1694, 1697), Françoise de Graffigny's *Letters d'Une Péruvienne* (1747, published in 1748 as *Letters Written by a Peruvian Princess*) and Sarah Scott's *A Description of Millenium Hall* (1762), do not include obvious sf tropes, but underscore the importance of women's education, sometimes in women-only settings, enacting the tenet of 'English and French feminism in the seventeenth century [...] that women's "inferiority" is socially constructed by denial of education' (Donawerth and Kolmerten 206, n6). This focus on education, as well as the 'deconstruction of the romance plot' (Khanna 18) and the refusal of many female characters to marry, connects to various strands of 'humanist' feminism found in later periods.

US feminism and utopian sf, 1820–1920

The lives of middle and upper-class White American women underwent great changes during this period, perhaps more so than those of immigrants, the working class and poor women. Spurred by industrialisation and urbanisation, more women of all classes entered paid employment. In 1870, women were 14.7 percent of the workforce. From 1890–1900, middle-class, native-born, White women with native-born parents showed the biggest increase in numbers employed, thanks to the increased availability of white-collar clerical jobs and many cities' sex-ratio imbalance. By 1920, women constituted 24 percent of the workforce (Wilson 6, 114–5). Prior to this, many Black, immigrant and working-class women worked for wages, often as domestic employees; by 1890, of the 1.2 million female domestics a quarter were Black, a third of whom were married (Jones 24). More American women were also attending college. In 1870, 21 percent of university students were women, rising to 32 percent by 1880 (Evans 147). By 1910, 40 percent of undergraduates were women (Cott *Grounding* 40). In the late nineteenth century, half of all college-educated women never married (Evans 147), many instead finding careers or devoting their time to female-organised social service and reform groups.

This 'woman movement' challenged the ways US legal and social systems subjugated women. After the Civil War, 'Urbanization, the urgent needs of the poor in a period of rapid industrialization and the presence of a sizeable group of educated women with leisure led to the emergence of a national club movement of white women' (Lerner 158). The Young Women's Christian Association, founded in Boston in 1866, spread to 225 cities by 1891 (Wilson 99). The Women's Christian Temperance Union (WCTU), established in 1874, accumulated 800,000 members by

1920 (Kerber and De Hart 229). The General Federation of Women's Clubs (GWWC), established in 1889, had 220,000 members by 1902 and over a million by 1910; of 726 women's organisations surveyed in 1893, only 37 belonged to the GFWC (Wilson 100–1). While the WCTU included Black members and a 'Department of Work Among Colored People' ('Truth-Telling'; Nurin), most clubs catered to White women, some specifically prohibiting Black members. In the 1890s, Black women's clubs 'in a number of different cities began almost simultaneously to form federations. In 1896 the newly formed National Association of Colored Women (NACW) united the three largest of these and over a hundred local women's clubs' (Lerner 158).

While many women's clubs have been described as 'not feminist' (Jones 24) because of their seeming conservativism – focusing on making American women better wives, mothers and daughters, or addressing working class temperance and morality – they often began with more political aims. The African American women's club movement was inspired by Ida B. Wells's anti-lynching campaign and many White women's clubs by anti-slavery, labour reform, education reform and anti-corruption movements ('Truth-Telling'; Lerner; Nurin; Jones; Cott *Grounding* 229–30; Wilson 91–5; Evans), most of which ultimately fed into more overtly feminist struggles for suffrage and economic independence.

In general, mainstream feminist movements pursued suffrage, better education, healthier working conditions, dress reform and better-paying jobs for women. Less visible efforts focused on marriage and child rearing reforms. In 1913, Charlotte Perkins Gilman described the two main opposing camps of 'Human Feminists' and 'Female Feminists':

> one holds that sex is a minor department of life; that the main lines of human development have nothing to do with sex, and that what women need most is the development of human characteristics. The other considers sex as paramount, as underlying or covering all phases of life, and that what women needs is an even fuller exercise, development, and recognition of her sex.
>
> (qtd in Cott *Grounding* 49)

While many feminist arguments of the period focused on women's supposed moral superiority, it may be, as later historians noted, some simply deployed this idealisation of womanhood to justify taking 'a more active part in running the world, especially since the men were making such a hash of things' (Welter 174).

Utopias continued to be the prime mode of imagining feminist futures during this period; some depicted science-fictional technologies and far-flung futures, while others were fantastical dream visions or voyages to undiscovered lands. From 1836–1920, 103 utopias by American women were published, a few anti-feminist but most at least proto-feminist (Kessler). The approximately 35 explicitly feminist sf utopias published from 1880–1920 highlighted contemporary sexism and depicted speculative futures with women as full citizens, significantly better off than their nineteenth century counterparts. They enjoyed economic freedom, access to higher education, political power and freedom from domestic labour. In these improved environments, war and economic hardship disappeared, women were healthier and safe from physical abuse, children were better educated and cared for, no one went hungry and humanity achieved new levels of progress.

As in earlier proto-feminist sf, education remained key to women's emancipation, but was no longer restricted to the upper classes. In stories such as Winifred Harper Cooley's 'Dream of the Twenty-first Century' (1902), education leads to women's emancipation and healthy development of their higher intellect, lifting women out of drudgery and consumerist silliness.

Others, such as Jane Sophia Appleton's 'Sequel to "The Vision of Bangor in the Twentieth Century"' (1848), Eveleen Laura Knaggs Mason's *Hiero-Salem: The Vision of Peace* (1889) and Alice Jones and Ella Merchant's *Unveiling a Parallel* (1893), question women's supposed essentialist moral superiority, instead claiming all people have the same propensity for high or low moral standing. Jones and Merchant's unwitting male narrator exposes the unnaturalness of such essentialism. When he watches 'beautiful, cultivated, charming women, [...] preservers of our ideals, the interpreters of our faith, the keepers of our consciences' indulging in excess liquor – 'nothing you would take exception to [...] if they had been men' – he laments that his 'idols were shattered' (45).

Many also challenge women's assumed physical frailty. The visitor to Mary E. Bradley Lane's all-female *Mizora* (1880) notes the size of the women's waists: 'They considered a large waist to be a mark of beauty, as it gave a greater capacity of lung power' (20). Anne Denton Cridge's *Man's Rights; or How Would You Like It?* (1870) and Gilman's *Herland* (1915) explain how exercise, fresh air, intellectual stimulation and unrestrictive clothing allow women to become strong, healthy and beautiful.

Domestic labour reforms sometimes figure into such improved health. Men stay at home and do the housework in Cridge's *Man's Rights*, and suffer from 'anxiety and unrest' because of their 'long and weary battling with the cares of the household' (qtd in Kessler 5). When machinery takes over the household chores, the men's 'pale, sickly faces' give way 'to ruddy health' (qtd in Kessler 10). Others call for economic remuneration for housework and the complete transformation of private homes (Hayden). The professionalisation of housework and childcare in Gilman's *What Diantha Did* (1910) and *Moving the Mountain* (1911), communal kitchens in Appleton's 'Sequel' and co-operative communities in which domestic labour is shared equally in Marie Howland's *Papa's Own Girl* (1874) and Rose Graul's *Hilda's Home* (1897) provide imaginative answers to burdensome domestic practices.

While suffrage appears to have been first-wave feminism's focus, marriage reform was the most prominent issue in its accompanying feminist utopias. Of utopias written by US women from 1836–1920, 'about three-quarters treated marriage as a problem, less than a quarter presented suffrage as part of a solution' (Kessler xix). Mason's *Hiero-Salem* and Lois Nichols Waisbrooker's *A Sex Revolution* (1894) critique how marriage forces women to surrender their names, property and legal right to their children, while tying them to the home and domestic labour. Others condemn women's economic dependence on their husbands, making marriage a kind of legal prostitution, with Graul's *Hilda's Home* calling for marriage abolition and free love. Lane's *Mizora*, Gilman's *Herland* and Lillie Devereux Blake's 'A Divided Republic' (1885) go further, depicting emancipatory all-female societies free from heterosexual relationships. Some early twentieth century feminists pushed for reforms regarding women's relationships to men, but most did not call for abolishing marriage or male–female sexual relationships. Many saw heterosexual desire as liberatory and healthy, even though marriage in the US did not allow for women's economic freedom or sexual desire (Cott *Grounding* 45). However, the focus on women's sexual desire in both political writing and sf connects early marriage reforms to 1970s radical feminism and the 1990s third wave.

While few African American women published sf or utopias during this period, Pauline Hopkins's *Of One Blood* (1902–3) imagines a better world for African Americans in Africa but has been mostly ignored by feminist utopian scholars, perhaps because of what some have described as Hopkins's inability 'to imagine the black heroic in the form of an unambiguous black female body' (West 9). Lillian B. Jones's *Five Generations Hence* (1916) also focuses on Africa as the site of an African American utopia: 'I saw a people, a black people [...] with a song of joy upon their lips [...] the people were my own returned to possess the heritage of their ancestors, [...] and the building of a new nation upon the ruins of the old' (qtd in Kessler 179). While Jones focuses more on women's agency, both utopias prefigure the concerns of intersectional feminism and Afrofuturism in which African American women's positions are inextricably connected to both race and gender – and often erased by or attacked in White feminist utopias, as in the overtly racist *Mizora* and *Herland.*

US feminism(s), women's activism and women's pulp sf, 1920–1960

Many have claimed that American feminism went underground, or dissipated completely, when US women won the vote in 1920. The liberal feminist ERA push in the 1920s did not have the same wide-spread appeal as suffrage, with many thinking it might roll back labour protections activists had won for working and poor women (Cott 'Equal'). However, women activists continued to advocate for legal and social advances, with the 'landmark [...] establishment of the President's Commission on the Status of Women (1961) and enactment of the Equal Pay Act (1963) and Title VII of the Civil Rights Act (1964) [coming] into being *before* the second-wave movement, not in response to it' (Goss 59). Furthermore,

> The mid-twentieth century featured collective organizing by women from different classes, races, and ideologies. [...] Far from going their separate ways after 1920, progressive mass membership groups created new coalitions [...] to continue advancing women's equality, such as the right to serve on juries, and social reforms, such as federal funding for maternal and child health. African-American women created parallel mass membership groups to hone their civic skills and advance issues that White women neglected.
>
> (Goss 67–8; cf. LeGates)

Consequently, this period's feminist activism may resemble the multiple strands and intersectionality of post-1980s feminism(s).

Hardback feminist utopias disappeared after 1920, but the 'utopian transformation of domestic spaces and duties through technology [...] and revision[s] of gender roles' found a new home in pulp sf (Donawerth 137). Indeed, 'Well before their explicitly feminist successors [...], many of the women [published in sf magazines] were rethinking gender roles that their male counterparts and the broader culture usually took as given' (Yaszek *Future* xvii; cf. Yaszek and Sharp; Sargent). Some stories focus on women's physical and intellectual abilities, building on *humanist feminist* ideas that with proper education, healthy clothes and physical activities, women would be equal or superior to men. C.L. Moore's Jirel of Joiry, from 'The Black God's Kiss' (1934), and Andre Norton's Steena of the Spaceways, from 'All Cats Are Grey' (1953), are '"sheroes": women with strength, intelligence and moral codes that equal or exceed those of any men, but who specifically champion women, diversity, and/or social justice' (Yaszek 'Lisa' n.p.). In Moore's 'No Woman Born' (1944), Deidre, resurrected in a metal body, possesses inhuman strength but a certain distance from humanity, foreshadowing post-structuralist and cyborg feminisms. Numerous stories with a domestic focus – Judith Merril's 'That Only a Mother' (1948), Alice Eleanor Jones's 'Created He Them' (1955) – might initially appear to not be feminist, but incisively critique patriarchal gender roles and support post World War II feminist anti-nuclear proliferation movements.

US women's liberation movement and prominent feminist sf, 1960–80

The 'second-wave' women's liberation movement made *feminism* headline news in the US once again, with *Time* dedicating a 1972 issue to the 'New Woman'. Many women were drawn to feminist groups in the mid-1960s and early 1970s, spurred by cultural and economic changes, particularly for middle-class White women. They may have been reacting to the disjunction between popular images of happy housewives – who cleaned the home, attended to their appearance, took care of the children and placated their husbands – and their actual lives. By 1960, over 40 percent of American women had full- or part-time jobs (De Hart 544); 57 percent of Black women worked outside the home, and White married women were 'increasing [their] labor force participation faster than any other group in the 1950s and 1960s (LeGates 345). The 'gap between reality and the domestic ideology ... now existed for women who were both white and middle-class' (De Hart 544). Betty Friedan's best-selling *The Feminine Mystique* (1963) unmasked the 'happy housewife heroine' as profoundly depressed. In 1966, Friedan helped found the liberal feminist National Organization of Women (NOW) with 300 charter members (Kava and Bodin 278). By 1972, 15,000 women had joined and by 1977, 40,000 (Ferree and Hess 134). NOW's statement of purpose attacked 'the traditional assumption that a woman has to choose between marriage and motherhood on the one hand and serious participation in industry or the professions on the other' (qtd in De Hart 548), demonstrating White middle-class dissatisfaction with the restrictive mid-twentieth century gender roles. Similar to some earlier feminists, 1970s liberal feminists generally fought for women's rights within existing political and legal systems.

Humanist feminism is key in much 1960s and 1970s feminist sf, but liberal feminism – familiar from first-wave utopias that imagined revisions to the legal status of wives, daughters and paid women workers – is not. Unsurprisingly, radical feminism, which argues that full equality necessitated complete social transformation (Millet; Morgan), had more impact on feminist sf, which brought to life radical refigurings of the current world. Having discovered sf 'was a form in which the issues raised by feminism could be explored', women writing sf recognised themselves as a significant, distinct group within the field (Sargent 16). From 1953–67, no women won the a Hugo Award, but from 1968–74, 11 did (Lefanu 7). Multiple feminist sf fanzines were launched, and in 1977 WisCon, the world's oldest feminist sf convention, was held for the first time. Like the popular consciousness-raising groups, feminist sf took feminist theory into women's homes and everyday lives.

Much feminist sf continued to draw on the 'human feminist' notion, popularised by Simone de Beauvoir, that 'One is not born, but rather becomes, woman' (283). In the all-hermaphrodite society of Ursula K. Le Guin's *The Left Hand of Darkness* (1969), biological sex cannot be used against anyone nor determine what role that person might play. The citizens of Whileaway, the all-woman utopia in Joanna Russ's *The Female Man* (1975), are genetically female but culturally androgynous. Other novels drew on Shulamith Firestone's claim in *The Dialectic of Sex* (1970) that imminent artificial reproduction technologies would free women from reproductive biological functions and transform society. Suzy McKee Charnas's dystopian *Walk to the End of the World* (1974) depicts reproductive tyranny in excruciating detail, with women literally enslaved as breeders, while in Marge Piercy's *Woman on the Edge of Time* (1976), the women of futuristic Mattapoisett delegate reproductive functions to machines and consequently achieve full equality. Voicing real-life concerns about compulsory heterosexuality (Rich) and the pressure to marry and bear children, this sf also gave narrative life to lesbian separatism.

James Tiptree, Jr's award-winning stories, praised for their 'masculine' style (Silverberg xii) before the author was unmasked as Alice Sheldon, similarly question the 'naturalness' of patriarchy and contemporary gender roles. 'Houston, Houston, Do You Read?' (1976) is told from the perspective of male astronauts cast 300 years into the future who learn that their beliefs – women cannot be astronauts and need men to sexually overpower them and control them – hold no sway on the all-female Earth to which they return. In this and other stories, Tiptree's protagonists (like Russ's) do not shy away from the violence of the power struggle between men and women. In 'The Women Men Don't See' (1973) the protagonist explains, 'What women do is survive. We live by ones and twos in the chinks of your world-machine' (134).

Later feminist sf of this period reflected a shift to cultural feminism grounded in essentialist biological identity. Like the 'female feminism' Gilman described, cultural feminism celebrated 'natural' female qualities, including patience, pacifism, cooperation, non-violence, an ability to nurture and a connection to nature, as ways to assert agency: no longer a site of oppression, the female body was seen as a repository of power. Paralleling Adrienne Rich's *Of Women Born* (1976), Charnas's *Motherlines* (1978) portrays mothering as empowering; this valorisation of women's nurturing casts men as violent, competitive and destructive, responsible for women's enslavement and incapable of true relationships. Early ecofeminism contended that woman's essential ties to reproduction made her more concerned with caring for the Earth, and often repudiated the advanced technology that some earlier feminist sf celebrated. Charnas's all-female society lives in harmony with nature, in stark contrast to the fortressed cities and laboratories of the men who had destroyed much of the natural world, while Sally Miller Gearhart's *The Wanderground* (1979) explores the powers women master – flying, healing, telepathy – by connecting to nature and their own reproductive cycles.

Black feminist theory, central to today's intersectional and global feminism(s), continued to develop. Many radical Black feminists, like their White counterparts, initially worked for the Civil Rights movement. In 1968, Frances Beal and other Black women in the Student Nonviolent Coordinating Committee founded the Black Women's Liberation Committee, which connected with Puerto Rican women activists in the 1970s and then expanded to include 'all third world sisters' (qtd in Ward 134), becoming the Third World Women's Alliance. Beal argued that Black women must 'combat the capitalist, racist exploitation of black people' (394) without ignoring their own specific plight as Black women. Like Flo Kennedy, Eleanor Holmes Norton and Margaret Sloan, Beal linked the economic exploitation of Black workers to that of women overall (Roth). In 1977, the Combahee River Collective (CRC) explicitly outlined the intersectional status of Black women, noting their active commitment 'to struggling against racist, sexist, heterosexual, and class oppression' (362) and 'that sexual politics under patriarchy is as pervasive in Black women's lives as are the politics of class and race' (365). As Black feminist lesbians, the CRC coined and argued for a coalitional 'identity politics' that joined forces with Black men, women, the Third World and working people, because fighting racism – embedded in all aspects of US society, including White feminism – was key to any truly feminist revolution.

While some feminist sf depicted anti-racist or inclusive futures, Black feminism did not make a deep impact on sf until Octavia E. Butler began publishing in the mid-1970s. Women of colour appear in Charnas's *Motherlines* and Piercy's *Woman on the Edge of Time,* but their racial and ethnic differences 'seem only skin-deep' (Green 168). Butler's almost exclusive use of Black women protagonists critiques previous feminist sf's 'claim to speak for all women, regardless of class or color – a claim founded upon the assumption of a transhistorical and transcultural, en*gender*ed unity of all women' (Zaki 246). Like contemporary Black feminists, Butler considered it 'just as important to have equal rights for women as [...] for black people' (Kenan 501). Her protagonists – of mixed race, mixed genetics and sometimes multiple genders – demonstrate Butler's unwillingness to define Black women by any single narrative of oppression or identity.

Her PATTERNIST series (1976–84) and *Kindred* (1979) play 'with hybrid identities, bioengineering, and genetic technologies to figure out how her protagonists can survive and have agency in the futures she imagines while remaining true to themselves as African American women' (Holden 26). Like Black feminism, Butler's sf leads the way into intersectional, cyborg and third wave feminism(s).

Standpoint, post-structural, intersectional, third wave feminism(s) and cyborg feminist sf, 1980s–2000

The 1980s and 1990s are often described 'as a "post-feminist" era of political apathy during which former feminists traded their political ideals for career mobility and Cuisinarts, and younger women single-mindedly pursued career goals and viewed feminism as an anachronism' (Taylor and Whittier 533). Ironically, the 'death' of the singular feminism gave life to feminism(s). Feminists of colour differentiated themselves more visibly from mainstream feminism, explicitly highlighting the problems of equating the positions of *all* women under patriarchy (see Hull, Bell-Scott and Smith; Moraga and Anzaldúa). As issues of sexuality, class and education increased existing splits among feminist groups, the resulting focus on identity politics led to a significant shift within feminism(s) and feminist theories.

Drawing on Sandra Harding's work challenging scientific 'objectivity', feminist standpoint theory argues that 'the activities of those at the bottom of [...] social hierarchies can provide starting points for thought – for *everyone's* research and scholarship – from which humans' relations with each other and the natural world can become visible' (Harding 442–3), ultimately generating 'less partial and distorted accounts not only of women's lives but also of men's lives and of the whole social order' (445). Unlike earlier feminism(s) predicated on woman's unique position, standpoint feminism, like some Black feminist theory, focuses on differences *among* marginalised groups and highlights Black women's 'outsider within' position in the US (Hill Collins and hooks). Their paid domestic labour in White homes gave these outsiders an inside view of dominant social structures: 'Living as we did – on the edge – we developed a particular way of seeing reality. We looked both from the outside in and from the inside out [...] We understood both' (hooks vii). Patricia Hill Collins argues, 'For African-American women, the knowledge gained at intersecting oppressions of race, class, and gender provides the stimulus for crafting and passing on the subjugated knowledge of Black women's critical social theory', which is 'designed to oppose oppression' (8–9).

Hill Collins is extending the term 'intersectionality', originally coined by Kimberlé Crenshaw to describe the unique legal position of Black women, which categorised them as 'women' or 'Black' but failed to see them and the discrimination they suffered because they were *both* Black and female ('Demarginalizing'). Although the concept continues to be refined, intersectionality's core is that 'in a given society at a given time, power relations of race, class, and gender [...] are not discrete and mutually exclusive [...] but rather build on each other and work together' (Hill Collins and Bilge 14).

The political, economic and technological flux in the US during the 1980s significantly shaped other shifts in feminism(s). Increasingly troubled by the high-tech products, traditional ideas of organic individual identity – and thus the concept of 'woman' as a unifying category – broke down. Materialist/socialist feminist Donna J. Haraway's notion of 'situated knowledge' is connected to standpoint feminism, but her revolutionary 'A Manifesto for Cyborgs' (1985) has had a more profound effect on feminist theory and sf. Abandoning the 1970s essentialist Earth Goddess in favour of a post-modern, boundary-busting, permanently fragmented, and constructed feminist cyborg monster enables feminists of all types to make partial but 'potent fusions and dangerous possibilities' (154) – and connects to coalition identity politics and intersectionality.

Post-structuralist Judith Butler similarly rejects essentialist identities and the male/female binary. Her *Gender Trouble* (1990) theorises gender as performance and questions the body as any kind of natural entity, a position that initially appears opposed to standpoint feminism's emphasis on the material *reality* of those marginalised by how society codes them regarding race, gender or class. However, Butler's *Bodies That Matter* (1993) correctively explores the place of material bodies in gender construction, which, she clarifies, does not mean 'one woke in the morning, perused the closet or some more open space for the gender of choice, donned that gender for the day, and then restored the garment to its place at night' (x). Instead, through '*a process of materialization*' (9), bodies accumulate meaning over time, becoming sexed, gendered and racialised.

Post-colonial feminism underscores the effects of colonialism and racism on non-Western women. Audre Lorde calls out 'white american feminist theory' (112) for failing to consider 'the consciousness of Third World Women' (111). Chandra Mohanty criticises it for colonising the 'lives of women in the third world, thereby producing/re-presenting a composite, singular "Third World Woman"' that is 'reductive and ineffectual in designing strategies to combat oppressions' (344). Gayatri Spivak challenges White feminists to learn more about their non-Western counterparts and the 'subaltern' (Lewis and Mills).

While Butler, Haraway and Hill Collins are often named 'third wave' theorists, the term originated with a never-published anthology, *The Third Wave: Feminist Perspectives on Racism,* from Black feminist Barbara Smith's Kitchen Table Press, that emphasised 'multiracial coalition building' focusing on third world feminism(s) (Gilley 157). The 'third wave' was actually launched by Rebecca Walker. The daughter of Alice Walker, she defined the third wave as the antithesis of a 'strictly defined and all-encompassing feminist identity' (xxxi), and as daughters breaking from the prudish feminism enforced by second-wave mothers. Leslie Heywood and Jennifer Drake, editors of *Third Wave Agenda* (1997), saw it as bringing together second-wave critiques of patriarchy, US third world feminism and Gen X women's individualistic postmodern identities. The third wave is also often associated with the early 1990s Riot Grrl movement, which undermined stereotypical images of girlish innocence and spawned multiple all-girl punk bands, zines devoted to expressions of feminist anger, and new types of consciousness-raising groups, often on the Internet. While third-wave feminism has often been critiqued for focusing 'on individual identities and choices, generational conflict among feminists, and popular culture' (Gilley 148), its insistence on women and girls embracing technology connect it to cyborg feminism and a rise in twenty-first century activism.

Like feminism itself, feminist sf reacted to the rise of the New Right and the ensuing backlash, moving out of its utopian mode. Margaret Atwood's dystopian *The Handmaid's Tale* (1986) serves as a warning about fast-approaching anti-feminist futures. While Pamela Sargent's *The Shore of Women* (1986) criticises earlier feminist sf's essentialism, Sheri S. Tepper's *The Gate to Women's Country* (1988) pursues essentialist logic (especially the idea that genes are destiny), but both question separatism as a liberatory strategy – a move mimicked in real-world condemnations of the 1970s' women-only spaces/groups.

The expansion of feminism(s), though, continued to impact feminist sf and, in turn, all of sf. In 1991, sf writers Pat Murphy and Karen Joy Fowler created the James Tiptree, Jr. Award to celebrate sf that 'expanded and explored our understanding of gender' (Lothian 'Our History' n.p.). Distinct and sometimes opposing feminism(s) often interacted in the increasingly diverse feminist sf published at the end of the century. Some prefigured feminist theories; others developed theoretical ideas in narrative form. For example, Haraway describes Russ's *The Female Man*, Tiptree's short fiction, Vonda McIntyre's *Superluminal* (1983) and Octavia E. Butler's *Kindred, Wild Seed* (1980) and *Dawn* (1987) as 'exploring what it means to be embodied in high-tech worlds' (173). These 'theorists for cyborgs' (173) create characters who break all boundaries and 'make very problematic the statuses of man or woman, human, artifact, member of a race, individual entity and body' (178). Feminist cyberpunk – such as Piercy's *He, She, and It* (1991), Pat Cadigan's *Synners* (1991), Lisa Mason's *Arachne* (1990), Melissa Scott's *Trouble and Her Friends* (1994) – shatter male/female, mind/body, machine/nature binaries with feminist cyborg protagonists who wield significant authority and/or technical expertise in the previously male-dominated cyberspace.

Other feminist sf – such as Kathleen Ann Goonan's NANOTECH QUARTET (1994–2002), which imagines how 'bionan' technology replaces electronic technologies and wipes out previous understandings of what it means to be gendered, raced, individual humans – enacts other versions of post-structuralist feminism. Black feminist standpoint theories and intersectional feminism continue to play out in Octavia E. Butler's 1990s sf, as well as in Nalo Hopkinson's *Brown Girl in the Ring* (1998) and *Midnight Robber* (2000), which mix urban fantasy, cyberpunk, Afro-Caribbean culture, space travel, alien beings and Afrofuturism into feminist sf.

Continuing waves, lengthening strands, and diverse feminist sf, 2000–present

Intersectional feminism is currently the most dominant among many feminist strands, promoted by academics, musical artists and Hollywood stars, such as Shonda Rhimes, Rosaria Dawson, Lizzo and Elliot Page (Flood 422–3). By April 2024, Crenshaw's 2016 TEDtalk on 'The Urgency of Intersectionality' had 6.3 million views.

Twenty-first century feminist sf demonstrates even more possibilities for intersectional feminist cyborg monsters. Geoff Ryman's *Air* (2005) and Andrea Hairston's *Mindscape* (2006) depict women from marginalised cultures taking on and adapting to new technologies. Ann Leckie's ANCILLARY trilogy (2013–5) presents a space opera universe where gender is not apparent: all characters are referred to as 'she' but it is clear not all are women. However, unlike earlier 'gender-free' feminist sf, gender is not the focus but simply the backdrop. Others reimagine the past in creating feminist speculative narratives. Nisi Shawl's steampunk *Everfair* (2016) draws on post-colonial, queer, disability and cyborg feminism(s) to imagine an alternate history for the Congo, in which utopian settlers, former American slaves and Indigenous people together create airships and other technology to fight against King Leopold.

N.K. Jemisin's sf and her activism in the sf community further underscore the importance of intersectionality, post-colonialism and feminism(s). In 2013, Jemisin gave a passionate speech about racism and sexism in sf, pointing to an unnamed sexist White supremacist writer who had recently won 10 percent of the votes in the Science Fiction & Fantasy Writers of America's presidential election. He then labelled Jemisin an 'ignorant savage' in an online racist rant. Her BROKEN EARTH trilogy (2015–7) – a story of climate disaster, structural oppression, love and betrayal, featuring a middle-aged Black female protagonist – went on to win all the most prestigious sf awards.

As history shows, no feminist wave or strand is completely distinct; feminism(s) often overlap or come together for specific ends. Feminism(s) – and feminist sf – continue to expand and diversify, crossing into queer theory, disability studies, critical race theory and animal studies. In 2019, at the urging of feminist sf fans and writers with disabilities, the James Tiptree Jr. Award changed its name to the Otherwise Award. In 1987, Tiptree (aka Alice Sheldon) killed her disabled husband before committing suicide, and the specifics surrounding that act – suicide pact or murder–suicide? – produced 'negative, painful, exclusionary associations' for many in the community (Lothian 'From' n.p.). The award's Motherboard looked to the 'otherwise politics' of queer Black scholar and writer Ashon Crawley for its new name: 'The otherwise is the disbelief in what is current and a movement towards, and an affirmation of, imagining other modes of social organization, other ways for us to be with each other' (Crawley). Recent Otherwise winners reveal how feminist sf continues to explode gender and genre categories. Rivers Solomon's *Sorrowland* (2021) mixes sf, horror and the Gothic in a fever-dream narrative about a young woman whose Black, queer and experimented on/evolving body becomes a source of strength. Similarly, Ryka Aoki's *Light from Uncommon Stars* (2021) uses sf and the supernatural to upend Asian immigrant stereotypes, telling the story of a young trans woman finding her place in the world, an alien woman falling in love with a human woman who has sold her soul to the devil for enhanced musical prowess, and a holographic, cybernetic 'daughter' asserting her personhood. At their best, feminism(s) and feminist sf remain constantly in flux, becoming 'otherwise' to signal the promise of new feminist futures.

Works cited

Beal, Frances M. 'Double Jeopardy: To Be Black and Female'. *Sisterhood Is Powerful: An Anthology of Writings from the Women's Liberation Movement*. Ed. Robin Morgan. Vintage, 1970. 382–96.

Beauvoir, Simone de. *The Second Sex*. Trans. Constance Borde and Sheila Malovany-Chevallier. Vintage, 2011.

Butler, Judith. *Bodies That Matter: On the Discursive Limits of 'Sex'*. Routledge, 1993.

Cavendish, Margaret. *The Description of a New World, Called the Blazing-World*. Project Guttenberg, 2016. www.gutenberg.org/ebooks/51783

The Combahee River Collective. 'The Combahee River Collective: A Black Feminist Statement'. *Capitalist Patriarchy and the Case for Socialist Feminism*. Ed. Zillah R. Eisenstein. Monthly Review, 1978. 362–72.

Cott, Nancy F. *The Grounding of Modern Feminism*. Yale University Press, 1987.

——. 'Equal Rights and Economic Roles: The Conflict over the Equal Rights Amendment in the 1920s'. *Women's America: Refocusing the Past*, fourth edition. Ed. Linda K. Kerber Kerber and Jane Sherron De Hart. Oxford UP, 1995. 355–65.

Crawley, Ashon. 'Otherwise, Ferguson'. *Interfictions Online* 4 (November 2014). http://interfictions.com/otherwise-fergusonashon-crawley/

Crenshaw, Kimberlé. 'Demarginalizing the Intersection of Race and Sex: A Black Feminist Critique of Antidiscrimination Doctrine, Feminist Theory and Antiracist Politics'. *University of Chicago Legal Forum* 1 (1989). 139–67.

——. 'The Urgency of Intersectionality'. *TED* (November 2016). www.ted.com/talks/kimberle_crenshaw_the_urgency_of_intersectionality

De Hart, Jane Sherron. 'The New Feminism and the Dynamics of Social Change'. *Women's America: Refocusing the Past*, fourth edition. Ed. Linda K. Kerber Kerber and Jane Sherron De Hart. Oxford UP, 1995. 539–60.

Donawerth, Jane L. 'Science Fiction by Women in the Early Pulps, 1926–1930'. *Utopian and Science Fiction by Women: Worlds of Difference*. Ed. Jane L. Donawerth and Carol A. Kolmerten. 137–52. Syracuse UP, 1994.

Donawerth, Jane L. and Carol A. Kolmerten, eds. *Utopian and Science Fiction by Women: Worlds of Difference*. Syracuse UP, 1994.

Evans, Sara M. *Born for Liberty: A History of Women in America*. Free Press, 1989.

Ferree, Myra Marx and Beth B. Hess. *Controversy and Coalition: The New Feminist Movement Across Three Decades of Change*, revised edition. Twayne, 1994.

Flood, Michelle. 'Intersectionality and Celebrity Culture'. *Women's Studies in Communication* 42.4 (2019): 422–6.

Gilley, Jennifer. 'Ghost in the Machine: Kitchen Table Press and the Third Wave Anthology That Vanished'. *Frontiers: A Journal of Women Studies* 38.3 (2017): 141–63.

Goss, Kristin A. 'The Swells between the "Waves": American Women's Activism, 1920–1965'. *The Oxford Handbook of U.S. Women's Social Movement Activism*. Ed. Holly J. McCammon, Verta Taylor, Jo Reger and Rachel L. Einwhoner. Oxford UP, 2017. 51–70.

Green, Michelle Erica. '"There Goes the Neighborhood": Octavia Butler's Demand for Diversity in Utopias'. *Utopian and Science Fiction by Women: Worlds of Difference*. Ed. Jane L. Donawerth and Carol A. Kolmerten. Syracuse UP, 1994. 166–89.

Haraway, Donna J. *Simians, Cyborgs, and Women: The Reinvention of Nature*. Routledge, 1991.

Harding, Sandra. 'Rethinking Standpoint Epistemology: What Is Strong Objectivity?' *The Centennial Review* 36.3 (1992): 437–70.

Hayden, Dolores. *The Grand Domestic Revolution: A History of Feminist Designs or American Home, Neighborhood, and Cities*. MIT Press, 1981.

Hill Collins, Patricia. *Black Feminist Thought: Knowledge, Consciousness, and the Politics of Empowerment*, revised tenth anniversary edition. Routledge, 2000.

Hill Collins, Patricia and Sirma Bilge. *Intersectionality*. Polity, 2020.

Holden, Rebecca J. '"I Began Writing about Power Because I Had So Little": The Impact of Octavia Butler's Early Work on Feminist Science Fiction as a Whole (and on One Feminist Science Fiction Scholar in Particular)'. *Strange Matings: Science Fiction, Feminism, African American Voices, and Octavia E. Butler*. Ed. Rebecca J. Holden and Nisi Shawl. Aqueduct, 2013. 17–44.

hooks, bell. *Feminist Theory from Margin to Center*. South End, 1984.

Hull, Gloria T., Patricia Bell-Scott and Barbara Smith, eds. *All the Women Are White, All the Blacks Are Men, But Some of Us Are Brave: Black Women's Studies*. Feminist Press, 1981.

Jones, Alice Ilgenfritz and Ella Merchant. *Unveiling a Parallel: A Romance*. Syracuse UP, 1991.

Jones, Beverly Washington. *Quest for Equality: The Life and Writings of Mary Eliza Church Terrell, 1863–1954*. Carlson, 1990.

Kava, Beth Millstein and Jeanne Bodin. *We, the American Women: A Documentary History*, revised edition. Science Research Associates, 1983.

Kenan, Randall. 'An Interview with Octavia E. Butler'. *Callaloo* 14.2 (1991): 495–504.

Kerber, Linda K. and Jane Sherron De Hart, eds. *Women's America: Refocusing the Past*, fourth edition. Oxford UP, 1995.

Kessler, Carol Farley. *Daring to Dream: Utopian Fiction by United States Women before 1950*, second edition. Syracuse UP, 1995.

Khanna, Lee Cullen. 'The Subject of Utopia: Margaret Cavendish and Her Blazing-World'. *Utopian and Science Fiction by Women: Worlds of Difference*. Ed. Jane L. Donawerth and Carol A. Kolmerten. Syracuse UP, 1994. 15–34.

Lane, Mary E. Bradley. *Mizora: A Prophecy*. Gregg Press, 1975.

Laughlin, Kathleen A., Julie Gallagher, Dorothy Sue Cobble, Eileen Boris, Premilla Nadasen, Stephanie Gilmore and Leandra Zarnow. 'Is It Time to Jump Ship? Historians Rethink the Waves Metaphor'. *Feminist Formations* 22.1 (2010): 76–135.

LeFanu, Sarah. *Feminism and Science Fiction*. Indiana UP, 1989.

LeGates, Marlene. *In Their Time: A History of Feminism in Western Society*. Routledge, 2012.

Lerner, Gerda. 'Early Community Work of Black Club Women'. *The Journal of Negro History* 59.2 (1974): 158–67.

Lewis, Reina and Sara Mills. *Feminist Postcolonial Theory: A Reader*. Routledge, 2003.

Lorde, Audre. 'The Master's Tools Will Never Dismantle the Master's House'. *Sister Outsider: Essays and Speeches*. Crossing, 1984. 110–3.

——. 'From Tiptree to Otherwise « Otherwise Award'. *Otherwise Award* (13 October 2019). https://otherwiseaward.org/2019/10/from-tiptree-to-otherwise

Lothian, Alexis. 'Our History « Otherwise Award'. *Otherwise Award*. https://otherwiseaward.org/about-the-award/our-history

Millett, Kate. *Sexual Politics*. Avon, 1971.

Mohanty, Chandra Talpade. 'Under Western Eyes: Feminist Scholarship and Colonial Discourses'. *Boundary 2: An International Journal of Literature and Culture* 12.3 (1984): 333–58.

Moraga, Cherríe and Gloria Anzaldúa. *This Bridge Called My Back: Writings by Radical Women of Color*, second edition. Kitchen Table, 1983.

Morgan, Robin, ed. *Sisterhood Is Powerful: An Anthology of Writings from the Women's Liberation Movement*. Vintage, 1970.

Nurin, Tara. 'A century after black activist FEW Harper fought for the vote and against alcohol, The U.S. still hasn't fully delivered'. *Forbes* (6 August 2020). www.forbes.com/sites/taranurin/2020/08/06/this-black-activist-fought-for-temperance-womens-vote-and-racial-equality-but-didnt-see-them-succeed/

Rich, Adrienne. 'Compulsory Heterosexuality and Lesbian Existence'. *Signs* 5.4 (1980): 631–60.
Roth, Benita. 'Intersectionality: Origins, Travels, Questions, and Contributions'. *The Oxford Handbook of U.S. Women's Social Movement Activism*, Ed. Holly J. McCammon Verta Taylor, Jo Reger and Rachel L. Einwhoner. Oxford UP, 2017. 129–49.
Sargent, Pamela. *Women of Wonder: Science Fiction Stories by Women about Women.* Vintage, 1975.
Shear, Marie. 'Media Watch: Celebrating Women's Words'. *New Directions for Women* 15.3 (June 1986): 6.
Silverberg, Robert. 'Introduction'. *Warm Worlds and Otherwise* by James Tiptree, Jr. Ballantine, 1975. ix–xviii.
Taylor, Verta and Nancy Whittier. 'The New Feminist Movement'. *Feminist Frontiers* 3. Ed. Laurel Walum Richardson and Taylor. McGraw-Hill, 1993. 533–48.
Tiptree, James Jr. 'The Women Men Don't See'. *Her Smoke Rose Up Forever*. Tachyon, 2004. 115–143.
'Truth-Telling: Frances Willard and Ida B. Wells: Frances Harper and Black Women in the WCTU'. *Truth-Telling: Frances Willard and Ida B. Wells*. https://scalar.usc.edu/works/willard-and-wells/black-women-and-the-wctu
Walker, Rebecca. *To Be Real: Telling the Truth and Changing the Face of Feminism*. Anchor, 1995.
Ward, Stephen. 'The Third World Women's Alliance: Black Feminist Radicalism and Black Power Politics'. *Black Power Movement: Rethinking the Civil Rights-Black Power Era.* Ed. Peniel E. Joseph. Routledge, 2006. 119–44.
Welter, Barbara. 'The Cult of True Womanhood: 1820–1860'. *American Quarterly* 28 (1966): 151–74.
West, Elizabeth. 'Ethiopianism, Gender, and Transnationalism in Pauline Hopkins's *Of One Blood*'. *The Routledge Companion to Transnational American Studies*. Ed. Nina Morgan, Alfred Hornung and Takayuki Tatsumi. Routledge, 2019. 193–201.
'Why Merriam-Webster Chose "Feminism" for 2017 Word of the Year'. *Merriam-Webster*. www.merriam-webster.com/words-at-play/woty2017-top-looked-up-words-feminism
Wilson, Margaret Gibbons. *The American Woman in Transition: The Urban Influence, 1870–1920.* Greenwood, 1979.
Yaszek, Lisa, editor. *The Future Is Female!: 25 Classic Science Fiction Stories by Women, from Pulp Pioneers to Ursula K. Le Guin*. Library of America, 2018.
——. 'Lisa Yaszek: We Get the History of Women in Science Fiction "Thoroughly Wrong"'. *Library of America* (7 September 2018). www.loa.org/news-and-views/1439-lisa-yaszek-we-get-the-history-of-women-in-science-fiction-thoroughly-wrong
Yaszek, Lisa and Patrick B. Sharp, eds. *Sisters of Tomorrow: The First Women of Science Fiction*. Wesleyan UP, 2016.
Zaki, Hoda M. 'Utopia, Dystopia, and Ideology in the Science Fiction of Octavia Butler'. *Science Fiction Studies* 51 (1990): 239–51.

45
GAME STUDIES

Paweł Frelik

For a long while, it was de rigueur to assert that video games had been inextricably tied to sf through the genealogy of *Spacewar!* (Russell 1962), *Doom* (id 1993) and *Half-Life* (Valve/Sierra 1998). This shared lineage remains true, but by 2023 such historical legitimation is hardly necessary. While a number of historical accounts exist (e.g., Jagoda), the interweaving of these two phenomena's cultural work remains relatively unstudied. This chapter will address this gap. It first outlines the intersections of video games and sf as cultural discourses, then proposes thinking about sf games as being informed by the tension between narrative complexity and gameplay rules, the latter of which also convey political positions but in a manner radically different from storytelling. Finally, it discusses five game studies perspectives that help illuminate these aspects of sf video games that sf studies has not, thus far, been equipped to address.

Sf and video games indeed share a number of commonalities. As cultural objects and practices both faced, at various points in their histories, cultural disdain and ghettoisation. These early dismissals is in stark contrast to their current standing, which, for both, seems to be nothing short of central to considerations of the contemporary cultural landscape. Sf has become a major way of framing the experience of twenty-first century neoliberal techno-modernity. This position is reflected in the ways in which genre texts across a range of media can address social, political, economic, ecological and technological challenges and issues. Sf scenarios have also been used by texts and artists outside the genre. Parallel to this, sf tropes have insinuated themselves into fields as disparate as technology marketing, machine learning research and military advertising. Video games, in turn, remain one of the few continually growing culture industries. More importantly, they are also – thanks to their procedural nature, demand for players' systemic thinking, and engagement of complex problem solving – a medium whose simulative and participative powers predispose it to serve as a cognitive tool for dealing with and thinking through contemporary challenges and pressures.

The overlap between sf and video games can thus be found in the critical perspectives both forms – as well as their studies – enable, which encompass both textual analyses along all possible methodological approaches from formalist (visuality, sound, algorithms) to political (gender, race, disability) and systemic critiques focused on production tools, labour relations, education and impact on various stakeholder communities. Last but not least, both games and sf texts have

DOI: 10.4324/9781003140269-48

historically been transmission vectors for colonial imaginations and neoliberal ideologies. These can be found in the implications of specific titles (Rettberg) and the discourse surrounding games (Kunzelman 'How').

Parallel to these affinities, video games can be thought as inherently science-fictional due to their reliance on speculation as a mode of thinking, as Cameron Kunzelman's *The World is Born from Zero: Understanding Speculation and Video Games* demonstrates. Equally speculative are games' configurative options, which often remain outside the diegetic realm but can be incorporated into the title's narrative. Regardless of their thematic preoccupations, in-game features such as the ability to customise the player's avatar (including gender and bodily features), the save-and-reload function, the mid-gameplay upgradeability of skills and the character's functional immortality easily correlate with well-known sf tropes. Some game genres also imply speculative – nonhuman, posthuman or collective – points of view and subject positions. These include alien and predator mode in *Alien vs. Predator* (Rebellion/Sega 2010), the god-gaze in Gaia games (op de Beke) and the controlling oversight in planetary simulations.

As it is clear, much can be said about the bidirectional inspirations and exchanges between sf and video games and even more space could be devoted to close readings of individual game texts, but this chapter privileges – for obvious reasons, given the context – the study of sf and proposes how game studies perspectives can inform the study of sf games in particular but also the genre at large. Before outlining the ways of thinking about sf games that expand the genre's perspectives, two things need to be noted. First, game studies as a field encompasses not only digital or video games, which are the subject of this chapter, but also other ludic formats, including pen-and-paper RPG games, board games, card games and LARPs. Sf is very much present in all of them, but their medial specificities would require a much longer discussion. Second, formally speaking, 'sf games' is not a marketing category. Unlike other media, in which genres are largely defined by thematic markers, game genres are conceptualised largely based on the type of interactions with the game's code: hence role-playing games, first-person shooters, turn-based strategy games and open-world games. This does not change the fact that many titles across different ludic genres can be positively and productively identified as sf.

After these preparatory points, it is now possible to propose five ways of thinking about sf games that, by building on the perspectives of game studies, compel us to think about them in categories other than those known from sf studies. In fact, some of the most interesting insights about sf games can be gained by going beyond storytelling preoccupations. A good while ago, Espen Aarseth (in)famously quipped that the stories of *Half-Life* would make 'a B-movie writer blush' (51). Games have progressed from that state significantly. *Nier: Automata* (PlatinumGames/Square Enix 2017) evocatively imagines a far future in which humanity has disappeared; *Death Stranding* (Kojima/Sony/505 2019) invokes a surreal atmosphere reminiscent of M. John Harrison's LIGHT trilogy (2002–12); *Disco Elysium* (ZA/UM 2019) introduces arguably the most interesting detective figure in the whole medium; and *Norco* (Geography of Robots/Raw Fury 2022) surveys the post-collapse American South. These and many other titles have respectably convoluted plot lines that demonstrate the depth and complexity paralleling other narrative media of the genre. There are, at the same time, few plot scenarios that have not been thoroughly rehearsed in older sf media. This is not to disparage the medium of games – literary sf has been produced for much longer and game production cycles necessarily result in fewer titles. Nor is it to say that individual games titles cannot invent new ways of conveying familiar narrative tensions and resolutions, as in the DEUS EX series (Ion Storm/Eidos Montréal/N-Fusion/Square Enix/Feral 2000–17).

At the same time, it is important to remember that games' storytelling is best represented as a spectrum between weak narrative/strong ludic and strong narrative/weak ludic. The former is exemplified by titles like *Quake* (id/GT 1996), where a barely existing storyline undergirds explosive gameplay and 3D spaces, which felt cutting-edge at the time of its release. *Quantum Break* (Remedy/Microsoft 2016) and *Detroit: Become Human* (Quantic Dream/Sony 2018) represent the other extreme with their convoluted narrative layering requiring relatively few demanding actions from the player. In some cases, such as walking simulators, titles have even been denied the status of games or referred to as interactive fictions. Some of the well-intentioned marketing of games emphasises storytelling accomplishments measured by such metrics as narrative complexity, suspense and in-game characters' psychological depth, demonstrating the hold traditional cultural criteria exert on the medium. At the same time, cult popularity of such games as *Doom* (1993), *Halo: Combat Evolved* (Bungie/Microsoft 2001) and *Half-Life 2* (Valve 2004), whose narratives are at best formulaic and seem a far cry from the ongoing revolution in speculative storytelling, has signalled the arrival of the new regime of science-fictionality that is less grounded in traditional narrative values of suspense and more in kinetic audiovisuality.

This line of thinking about sf media is hardly new. The tension between narrative and visuality has long been at the centre of discussion of sf film: *Alien Zone* (1990), edited by Annette Kuhn, argued that sf film's visuality compelled us to think about different ways of engaging with the genre's traditional themes, and Brooks Landon's *The Aesthetics of Ambivalence: Rethinking Science Fiction Film in the Age of Electronic (Re)production* (1992) suggested that the classical filmic modes of storytelling were being further redrawn by the then-nascent revolution in special effects and computer animation. Video games invested in hyperrealism clearly inherit their visual appeal from film, but their interactive capacity further complicates the ways in which they perform their cultural work beyond the narrative's ideological transmissions. There is little doubt that the ongoing digital revolution has further transformed the logic of audiovisual media – and sf seems to be an especially privileged genre here owing to its reliance on diegetic novelty, which ripples through its medial forms, including digital graphics, music video, new types of animation, gifs, laser and light shows, neon installations and planetarium shows. Video games have been at the forefront of these transformations, more often than not driving them both technologically and conceptually. It is these transformations that are most interesting: the ways in which contemporary sf video games compel us to think again about the cultural work sf performs as a genre. Let us turn then to those aspects of the medium that bring out the modalities of sf that are not readily apparent in other media of the genre: affect, modularity, worldbuilding, spatiality and procedurality. They hardly ever operate within sf games in separation from more traditionally-understood narrative, but at the same time they offer new ways of understanding how sf video games differ from other sf media and how they perform their species of sf's cultural work.

Affective science fictions

Sf has historically prided itself on a commitment to the cognitive and rational modes of storytelling. Entire subgenres or groupings, including hard sf, space opera and cyberpunk, have foregrounded allegiance to strict – albeit sometimes imaginary – scientific principles. This has been true, to a degree, of sf's visual media, including video games. In almost all ludic genres, gameplay relies on the systematic decoding of the underlying rules that guarantee in-game progress or trying out various solutions to challenges generated by the system. This is particularly true of strategy games, such as *Stellaris* (Paradox 2016), and massively-multiplayer online titles (MMOs), such as *EVE Online* (CCP/Simon & Schuster/Atari 2003), which Darren Jorgensen describes as being fuelled by the numerical sublime of constant calculations. Some sf titles, including *Portal* (Valve 2007) and *The Witness* (Thekla 2016), also promote rigorous reasoning to the centre of their narratives. And yet, for all this algorithmic complexity, video games are also highly affective texts, responding to and producing the player's emotional states. This is most immediately visible in the attention that Mihaly Csikszentmihalyi's concept of flow has received in game studies. Defined as 'the moment when the player reaches the highest state of gratification of the experience in which [they are] participating' (Martins et al. 2), flow has been perceived as a major factor in the gameplay experience and also as the one responsible for the games' completion. The influence of this concept on the field is indisputable, although its actual value is debatable, especially since it seems to be more applicable to some games than to others and suggests only one way of engaging with games.

Aubrey Anable makes a compelling argument for the ways in which video games have been fundamentally tied to affect theory. She uses Raymond Williams's concept of a 'structure of feeling', which later consolidated, in Silvan Tomkins's work, into affect theory. It is not a coincidence that the roots of the latter were in the historical moment when terminologies of biological organisms and technological systems were routinely exchanged within the early cybernetic imagination, which also fed into sf's narrative imaginaries. For Anable, affect is not something that can be elicited from a specific title, but rather a different approach to games:

> Identifying a video game as an affective system means resisting locating properties like texture, tone, and feelings in a purely subjective experience of reception or as the exclusive property of a text, and instead locating them in the slippery and intellectually fraught place in between.
>
> (xiv)

Video games thus can – although not uniformly and universally – create situations for profound affective experiences that circumvent the competition-driven algorithmic regimes of gameplay; this capacity is no less present in sf games. Where one can find instances of this is, naturally, a rather tricky question since they are, by nature, highly individual. It would not be unreasonable, though, to look for them in these moments of gameplay that either do not directly support the narrative logic or do not affect win/lose conditions. These could include the loneliness of exploration of empty planets in *Mass Effect* (Bioware/EA/Microsoft 2007), especially those where no or very few missions or tasks can be found; the seemingly endless intersystem transits in *Elite Dangerous* (Frontier 2014); the empty structures in *Halo: Combat Evolved* and enigmatic architectures of *NaissanceE* (Limasse 5 2014); the dreamy atmosphere of *Kentucky Route Zero* (Cardboard Computer/Anapurna 2013–20) from its opening at a rural gas station; and the nostalgic desolation of *Jett: The Far Shore* (Superbrothers/Pine Scented 2021). Each of these titles is very different from the others, but apart from their strong narrative cores, they all project a special aura that is key to their recognition. Such video games remind us that sf can produce affective experiences as successfully and elegantly as it stimulates intellectual and political reflection.

Modularity of sf

The second aspect of video games that prompts a different kind of thinking about sf is their inherent modularity. Although some of the most lauded literary and cinematic texts either remain standalone or comprise relatively short series, sf, like many genres, has long been perceived as dependent on the shared repertoire of locations, characters, tropes and scenarios. Over the years, a number of concepts, including megatext (Broderick) and parabola (Attebery; Attebery and Hollinger), have been used to address the interdependence between individual texts and the larger narratives' genre. Parallel to this, long-form series and shared worlds comprise extended narrative universes, even if most of these are rather loosely interconnected. Modularity is another way to talk about this and video games better reflect this quality than any other sf medium. Shane Denson and Andreas Jahn-Sudmann's work on the seriality of games in general concentrates on their temporalities and their continuity with other medial texts. Indeed, even if they do not overlap, game franchises, such as METAL GEAR SOLID (Konami/Rocket/M2 1987–2018), can be compared to film franchises, and episodic games, such as *The Walking Dead* (Telltale 2012), *Tales from the Borderlands* (Telltale 2014) and *Dreamfall Chapters* (Red Thread/Blink/Deep Silver 2014–6), to television series. The fact that episodic games have not really caught on probably has less to do with their appeal and more to do with the changing patterns of production within the industry.

At the same time, there is an entire class of extensions that are unique to the gaming medium and which embody the regime of true modularity. Some of these are sanctioned by the developers (updates, expansions and downloadable content (DLCs)); others are produced by player communities outside the official channels of circulation (levels, maps and mods). Their number and character may vary depending on economic considerations and other factors. Extensive expansions and DLCs, for instance, have become rarer as developers design increasingly large worlds but also economise on substantial development usually required by even medium-sized expansions. The specific interventions of such extensions can differ. DLCs may add entire narrative branches that seamlessly blend with base games: *Lair of the Shadow Broker* (2010) for *Mass Effect 2* (Bioware/EA 2010), *Burial at Sea* (2013–4) for *BioShock Infinite* (Irrational/2K 2013), *Burning Shores* (2023) for *Horizon Forbidden West* (Guerrilla/Sony 2022) and *Phantom Liberty* (2023) for *Cyberpunk 2077* (Projekt Red 2020) are among the most sophisticated in this respect. A far more original form of game modules are expansions that – apart from adding new locations, non-playable characters and missions – expand the gameworlds themselves in terms of their functionalities. One of the first sf titles to adopt that model as a core philosophy of its worldbuilding is *EVE Online*, a space-opera MMO, whose 21 expansions to date have brought new ship classes ('Trinity' 2007), planetary interactions ('Tyrannis' 2010), resource processing facilities ('Lifeblood' 2017) and combat system ('Fight or Flight' 2002). *No Man's Sky* (Hello 2016), a procedurally-generated universe simulator with 18 quintillion planets and moons, has adopted a similar system of periodic updates, which have expanded the original version of the title with base building elements ('Pathfinder' 2016), the multiplayer mode ('NEXT' 2018), oceans and underwater exploration ('The Abyss' 2018), an organic starship ('The Living Ship' 2020), new planet types and landscapes ('Origins' 2020), ability to tame wild creatures ('Companions' 2021) and planetary settlements ('Frontiers' 2021).

As games like these receives updates, their earlier versions become practically unavailable, forever changing the gameworlds in which the players operate. This kind of ephemerality is unique and impossible in other media but also underscores a very important quality of contemporary sf worlds: their inherent inconclusiveness. Many speculative worlds tend to continue unfinished, which – in the medium of games – is as much a consequence of frequently rushed release cycles as a function of digital culture's focus on processuality. It would not be too far-fetched, either, to compare this property of sf games to the constant engineering improvement and scientific experimentation: not only of in-game objects, such as vehicles or weapons, but of the worlds themselves. Simultaneously, video games' modularity does not need stand in opposition to the cherished modernist virtues of originality and artifice defined by their finitude, but it also reflects – arguably, much more immediately than in the case of film or television – the political economies of both the genre and the culture industries at large.

Worldbuilding

The modularity of sf games connects intimately with a larger shift in conceiving speculative worlds, which is often represented under the moniker of worldbuilding. In itself, worldbuilding is hardly a new concept, even if it does not really have one fixed understanding. In sf studies, it often describes the process of constructing and fleshing-out speculative spaces, frequently in detail that suggests the world's invisible histories and locations that are not explicitly presented. Historically, worldbuilding has supported plot-driven narrative structures, often enhancing them in the form of fictional epigraphs, maps, glossaries and explanatory footnotes in literature and extreme long panoramic shots and background details in film, as well as an increasingly wide range of paratextual materials in all possible media. The richness of detail of the world centrally contributes to the immersive quality of the text, but it has typically served narratives that rely on character depth, unexpected plotting and philosophical import. A range of transformations, both industrial (transmedia franchises) and technological (digitality), have promoted worldbuilding in many sf texts to an autonomous end in itself rather than in service to the narrative; no medium illustrates this change better than video games.

In the last two decades video games have unveiled supremely detailed worlds and universes that, while sustaining storylines of varying depth and originality, have offered themselves to mapping and exploration as a major, if not sometimes the principal, end. Escaping narrative is hardly possible, but the main pleasure of ludic texts can often be found in activities that are only tangentially related to plotting. This shift requires a recalibration of critical expectations. Some of these have circulated under the older concept of subcreation (Wolf), but talking about 'the worldbuilding turn' would not be an exaggeration. By traditional criteria, games that invest heavily in worldbuilding while sustaining competent but hardly original narratives, measure rather poorly, when compared to literary or filmic narratives. At the same time, as the hardcore following of *EVE Online* and the still-in-development *Star Citizen* (Cloud Imperium) demonstrate, they are no less engaging. The worldness of video games can thus be a goal in itself and, combined with interactivity, it enhances the player's engagement and allows for a simulatory experience, which can be truly satisfying without an intricately woven plot. Speculative games are especially privileged here. While *Red Dead Redemption 2* (Rockstar 2018) has been praised for the detail and scope of its world, its exploration always-already relies on the culturally coded familiarity with the American frontier. This familiarity is absent from the storyworlds of *The Outer Worlds* (Obsidian/Private Division 2019) and *Starfield* (Bethesda 2023), whose mapping and exploration is, for many players, far more important than missions and assignments, as dedicated subreddits and YouTube gameplays attest.

Spatiality

Directly related to – and centrally constitutive of – the worldbuilding dimension of video games is their spatial and architectural imagination. Sf games naturally have a clear mandate to construct speculative spaces that do not simulate or approximate familiar locations and landscapes and have, over the years, developed a broad repertoire of characteristic localities: spacecraft interiors with claustrophobically narrow passageways, abandoned planetary settlements, industrial warehouses, alien hallways. Many of these are often presented in significant design detail, functioning as vectors of 'environmental storytelling' (Jenkins). It needs to be noted that this architectural turn is as much a function of visual imagination, long present in sf comics, film and television, as it is a consequence of the specific technological solutions video games rely on.

Originally rooted in the worlds of dramatically different cultural capital, video games and architectural design have been converging over the past few decades, largely because of their shared use of game engines, most notably the Unreal Engine and its most recent – as of 2023 – fifth version. Originally conceived as fundamental cores of video games from commercial titles to game-like art installations, game engines have increasingly been used in filmmaking, non-entertainment simulations (military, medical, and so on), engineering, architectural design, and business applications and visualisations. It is notable that the three most often touted properties of Unreal Engine 5 are the vastly improved dynamic lighting and shadows systems as well as the World Partition Tool, a module that enables creation of large in-game worlds. All three find frequent use in designing architectural spaces and promote a more immersive experience of gameworlds. Of course, this most readily applies to titles that rely on hyperrealistic visualisation and creation of 3D worlds and may not be so important in those that opt for other visual styles, such as *Norco*'s retro pixelisation or the origami-inspired look in *Kentucky Route Zero*, or do not rely on 3D spaces, such as *The Swapper* (Facepalm/Curve/Ninetendo 2013).

Given the diversity of speculative spaces, it is hard to make overarching statements about them, but two trends are clear. Both can be found in other thematic genres but they directly support important aspects of sf game worldbuilding. The first is a reliance on simulated spaces to suggest more explorable depth than is actually available to the players. Spaces and constructions are, at first, predominantly presented to the players as surfaces – both external, such as cityscapes, and internal, such as chambers or corridors. Many video games thus present facades, some of which cannot be entered and areas that are shown but are not traversable. In fact, some recent high-profile titles like *Cyberpunk 2077* seem to have overpromised in this respect by promoting themselves as open-world games but delivering pseudo-open worlds (Maj). The other property of games' spatial narratives is their propensity for decline and deterioration. Many of the iconic locations are frequently presented as dilapidated or abandoned, often compelling the player to uncover their histories and investigate the causes of their disrepair. This propensity, aptly described as 'Ruinensehnsucht' (Fuchs) or 'the longing for ruins', is hardly new to sf and goes back to the Gothic, but it is interesting to see locations in decline as a goal of video games' increasingly powerful architectural modelling. In some cases, the ruins are functions of the narrative-driven tropes of post-apocalypse but often the decline of architectural sites offers opportunities to flaunt the processing powers of the game engine: a hyperrealistic representation of a crumbling wall requires far more precision than its untouched flat smoothness. Consequently, this curious property compels us to think about sf spatiality as being governed by logics that can be distant or entirely divorced from narratives concerns.

Procedurality

Sf games are complex bundles of rules and algorithms. This means that, beyond verbal and visual persuasion, sf games engage in 'procedural rhetoric' (Bogost). Sf texts instantiated in more narrative-centric media – literature, film, television, comics – draw tension and political significance from their representational dimensions, with narrative and visuality most prominent. In that, relatively little attention – and for understandable reasons – has been paid to the very materiality of these media. There are relatively few analyses of literary styles in sf and of montage and technical aspects of cinematography, such as angle and depth of field. For instance, it seems commonsensical that extreme long shots offer a good deal of information in space opera titles and that cyborg-vision CGI provides simulations of post-/non-human subjectivities, but such discussions are relatively rare in sf studies: notable exceptions include Mark Bould's analysis of the slow-motion sequence in *Dredd* (Travis 2012) and *Looper* (Johnson 2012) and Sarah Hamblin and Hugh O'Connell's analysis of camera work in *Blade Runner 2049* (Villeneuve 2017). While these dimensions remain key in video games, the medium also possesses another unique layer: that of procedures and algorithms.

This layer is also far more crucial for the reception of game texts than in other media. It would perhaps not be an exaggeration to claim that the film syntax (editing) does not centrally affect the popular audienceship of sf films. At the same time, the structure of algorithms – whether cause–effect chains or technology trees or win/lose conditions – predetermines the rules of engagement with games and cannot be circumvented or ignored without cheating or modding. None of these algorithms are neutral, either. It is this level that is the least obvious to the players but it is also a site where many of the game's political assumptions can be found, often clashing with the narrative message. Arguably, this is a level that scholars interested in sf politics should be paying attention to, and this is where the unexpected conclusions can be drawn. For it is there that games that seem to be progressive prove to be fairly reactionary and where games whose visuality can be underwhelming compel the players to change their customary reactions and decisions. Consequently, MASS EFFECT's brilliance is partly undermined by the colonial mechanics of resource mining as well as its binary gender roles and monogamous structure of romances. The hacking narrative of *Watch Dogs* (Ubisoft 2014) is complicated by the game's uncritical embrace of surveillance, while planetary colonisation simulators perpetuate the Anthropocenic vision of cheap nature in their technology trees. At the same time, games can invite more embodied awareness of corrosive ideologies. This is very much the case with *Citizen Sleeper* (Jump Over the Age/Fellow Traveller 2022), which, through the rules of its gameplay, puts in sharp relief the inhuman logic of neoliberal capitalism.

The five perspectives rooted in game studies do not exhaust the range of approaches to sf games and the analytical tools grounded in the genre's earlier media remain equally useful and relevant. At the same time, these aspects of sf games enable a fresh look at those aspects of cultural texts that go beyond narrative, especially as affective, processual, inconclusive and ephemeral textuality is becoming a major entryway into sf for many audiences.

Works cited

Aarseth, Espen. 'Genre Trouble: Narrativism and the Art of Simulation'. *First Person: New Media as Story, Performance, and Game*. Ed. Noah Wardrip-Fruin and Pat Harrigan. MIT Press, 2004. 45–55.

Anable, Aubrey. *Playing with Feelings: Video Games and Affect*. U of Minnesota P 2018.

Attebery, Brian. 'Science Fiction, Parable, and Parabolas'. *Foundation* 95 (2005): 7–22.

Attebery, Brian and Veronica Hollinger, eds. *Parabolas of Science Fiction*. Wesleyan UP, 2013.

Bogost, Ian. *Persuasive Games: The Expressive Power of Videogames*. MIT Press, 2010.

Bould, Mark. 'Of Eight Oscillations and Several Messages Carved in Flesh: Spectacle, Spectatorship, Cognition, and Affect in *Dredd* and *Looper*'. *Science Fiction Studies* 123 (2014): 258–83.

Broderick, Damien. *Reading by Starlight: Postmodern Science Fiction*. Routledge, 1994.

Denson, Shane and Andreas Jahn-Sudmann. 'Digital Seriality: On the Serial Aesthetics and Practice of Digital Games'. *Eludamos: Journal for Computer Game Culture* 7.1 (2013): 1–32.

Fuchs, Mathias. '"Ruinensehnsucht": Longing for Decay in Computer Games'. *Proceedings of the First International Joint Conference of DiGRA and FDG*, volume 13. Digital Games Research Association and Society for the Advancement of the Science of Digital Games, 2016. http://www.digra.org/wp-content/uploads/digital-library/paper_67.compressed1.pdf.

Hamblin, Sarah and Hugh C. O'Connell. '*Blade Runner 2049*'s Incongruous Couplings: Living and Dying in the Anthropocene'. *Science Fiction Film and Television* 13.1 (2020): 37–58.

Jagoda, Patrick. 'Digital Games and Science Fiction'. *The Cambridge Companion to American Science Fiction*. Ed. Eric Carl Link and Gerry Canavan. Cambridge UP, 2015. 139–52.

Jenkins, Henry. 'Game Design as Narrative Architecture'. *First Person: New Media as Story, Performance, and Game*. Ed. Noah Wardrip-Fruin and Pat Harrigan. MIT Press, 2004. 118–30.

Jorgensen, Darren. 'The Numerical Verisimilitude of Science Fiction and *EVE-Online*'. *Extrapolation* 50.1 (2010): 134–47.

Kuhn, Annette, ed. *Alien Zone: Cultural Theory and Contemporary Science Fiction Cinema*. Verso, 1990.

Kunzelman, Cameron. 'How to Eat the Future'. *Real Life* (26 May 2022). https://reallifemag.com/how-to-eat-the-future/

——. *The World Is Born From Zero: Understanding Speculation and Video Games*. De Gruyter, 2022.

Landon, Brooks. *The Aesthetics of Ambivalence. Rethinking Science Fiction Film in the Age of Electronic (Re)Production*. Greenwood, 1992.

Maj, Krzysztof M. 'On the Pseudo-Open World and Ludotopian Dissonance: A Curious Case of Cyberpunk 2077'. *Journal of Gaming & Virtual Worlds* 14.1 (2022): 51–65.

Martins, Dalila, Nelson Zagalo and Ana Patrícia Oliveira. 'Motivation and Flow Experience as Crucial Factors in the Completion of Narrative Games'. *Easy Chair Preprint* 11242 (2023). https://easychair.org/publications/preprint/j2Pj#:~:text=Motivation%20and%20the%20experience%20of,and%20motivated%20to%20continue%20playing

op de Beke, Laura. 'Anthropocene Temporality in Gaia Games'. *KronoScope* 20.2 (2020): 239–59.

Rettberg, Scott. 'Corporate Ideology in World of Warcraft'. *Digital Culture, Play, and Identity: A World of Warcraft® Reader*. Ed. Hilde G. Corneliussen and Jill Walker Rettberg. MIT Press, 2008. 19–38.

Wolf, Mark J. P. *Building Imaginary Worlds: The Theory and History of Subcreation*. Routledge, 2012.

46
GEOGRAPHY, URBAN DESIGN AND ARCHITECTURE

Amy Brookes

I stand in a doorway, on the threshold of home. If I reach out, I can feel the timber and paint of the door under the surface of my fingers and hear voices from the room beyond, aware of the thickness of the wall that marks the line between inside and out. In this everyday space, I confront the depth of intimacy and the vast echoes of complexity present in all spatial encounters. The chipped paint resonates with the patinas of care in other homes, the pencil marks of the heights of growing children or the tacky residue of deep-fried comfort. Alongside this are the lives that have been warped or shaped to allow this seemingly benign door to come into being: the abrupt break in the creaking growth of timber, the violence of petrochemical extraction, the divisions inherent in any spatial separation.

Any such moment of engagement with the spatial disciplines, including architecture, urban studies and geography, as well as the fields of interiors, landscapes and environments, reveals them to be dizzying in scale. They require the simultaneous contemplation of the incomprehensibly vast and the breathtakingly mundane. These vertiginous delights are shared with sf as it asks us to inhabit the minutiae of lives other to our own and to confront the expanses of deep space and time, all while clinging on to the thresholds of our own experience. This chapter is an attempt to explore sf through these shifting scales. Focusing on scholars from the spatial disciplines who have engaged with sf literature, it reflects upon how the design and representation of setting in sf informs us about the power structures and patterns of behaviour within the fictional world and provides a unique site from which to confront our own situatedness.

As described by philosopher and spatial theorist Elizabeth Grosz,

> Fantasies about the future are always, at least in part, projections, images, hopes, and horrors extrapolated from the present [...] In this sense, they are more revealing of the status and permeability of the present than they are indices of transformation or guarantees of a present-to-be.
>
> (49)

A growing body of scholarship reflects upon the 'hopes and horrors' which shape the architectures of sf; for example, both Carl Abbott (*Imagining*) and Paul Dobraszczyk undertake typological

DOI: 10.4324/9781003140269-49

analyses to understand how specific tropes, such as the vertical or floating city, reflect lived urban experiences and inform design practices. Rather than focusing on the interplay between worlds constructed in concrete and in print, this chapter will address geographer James Kneale's question of, 'what it is we are trying to do with our descriptions of place' (431)? It will move through spatial scales, lingering in turn at the planetary, the city, the neighbourhood, the building, the room and the doorway. This folding inward from the expansive to the intimate revels in sf's capacity to expose the 'permeability of the present' (Grosz 49), to see the world as continually built and unbuilt moment by moment. As a genre founded on such multiplicity of worldbuilding, it is here that we can ask how we are shaped by the worlds we encounter, and how we might shape them in turn.

The planetary

In Chen Qiufan's *Waste Tide* (*Huangchao*; 2013; trans. 2019), the inhabitants of Silicon Isle scale mountain ranges of e-waste that have been dragged in by ocean currents and the tides of corporate outsourcing of responsibility. These are new landmasses shaped and formed by the built-in obsolescence of each successive iteration of apparent technological advancement. Resources have been extracted only to be redeposited in locations that are deemed sufficiently elsewhere. This is the scale of the planetary in sf, a perspective which demands that we confront the global implications of everyday actions.

> They lined up, washed and brushed their teeth [...] and the white foam [...] slowly collected in a square pool, from where it flowed into a waste pond covered with an iridescent oil film, and then, combined with the industrial and residential wastewater from elsewhere on this island after many twists and turns, plunged without hesitation towards the open sea.
>
> (Qiufan 68)

The representation of place in *Waste Tide* is founded on an understanding of how extractivism, racialised geopolitics and climate crisis shape space and time. The deep time of oil and the ongoing histories of colonialism are materialised in the constructed surface of the present, insidiously accumulating and seeping into our collective futures.

As a genre, sf is uniquely able to operate on scales which extend far beyond our contemporary moment, in works such as Doris Lessing's CANOPUS IN ARGOS: ARCHIVES series (1979–83) and Olaf Stapledon's *Last and First Men* (1930), which explore histories and futures of Earth spanning millennia. It is here perhaps that we can truly acknowledge the geological time of human impact, present in the laying down of new layers of ground, which have irrevocably reshaped the world we live in. Environmental sociologist Lisa Garforth outlines how the narratives of sf, which engage with planetary futures, such as John Brunner's *Stand on Zanzibar* (1968) and Ursula K. Le Guin's *Always Coming Home* (1985), work to make environmental crisis thinkable. Garforth traces how scientific and science fictional narratives of environmentalism are intimately entangled, and how sf establishes an accessible point for engagement with complex systems, while also providing narrative exploration of the 'ethical, metaphysical and even utopian possibilities of a climate changed world' (19). By providing characters with whom we can empathetically engage, who are located within the sprawling and often intangible webs of human and more-than-human interconnectedness, these planetary future fictions provide us with a critical space to confront the implications and impacts of our actions.

In his work on environmental justice, Kyle Whyte invites readers to consider how the concepts of apocalyptic finality often implicit in discussions of the Anthropocene and climate emergency would be received by Indigenous persons who see their societies as 'already having endured one *or many more* apocalypses' (236 italics in original). For Whyte, it is imperative to recognise the entrenched nature of colonialism, capitalism and industrialisation that create underlying conditions of domination, which disempower Indigenous people. Sf and storytelling can be an integral part of this process, supporting an allyship that is 'open to the often post-apocalyptic and ancestrally dystopian spaces of Indigenous spiralling time, intergenerational dialogue, and science (fiction)' (237). As Indigenous Nations Studies scholar Grace L. Dillon describes, in an essay about two-spirit sf, these survivance stories are about 'persistence, adaptation, and flourishing in the future, in sometimes subtle but always important contrast to mere survival' (9).

This critical worldmaking potential, bound up in sf's capacity to engage with both the incomprehensibly vast and the deeply situated, is addressed by geographer Kathryn Yusoff. Her reading of N.K. Jemisin's *The Fifth Season* (2015), a narrative which explores the interconnectedness of racialised exploitation and geological transformation, feeds into a call for the urgent examination of 'world making as a geophysics of being', a recognition of how economies and histories of power including colonial practices are delivering 'a new geochemical earth' (13). Here, Indigenous genocide and settler colonialism are understood as parts of wider extractive logics, of a racialised geo-social matrix that is insidiously pervasive and purposefully occluded. Rather than distinguishing between environmental and social justice, Yusoff demonstrates how sf can assist in recognising our situatedness within such overlapping and interconnected planetary issues and support the construction of worlds otherwise.

The city

The city of Abbenay in Le Guin's *The Dispossessed* (1974) is described as the most central city of the planet of Annares. Its built form and scale reflect and support the anarcho-communist principles of the society it contains. Low-rise structures serve as a symbolic reflection of the abolition of power hierarchies, while a bustling public transport system replaces the individualism of private vehicle ownership. It is a radically egalitarian urban space which strives to continually redress spatial and social inequality through the provision of communal dining and collective housing.

> Abbenay was poisonless: a bare city, bright, the colours light and hard, the air pure.
> It was quiet. You could see it all, laid out as plain as spilt salt.
> Nothing was hidden [...]
> No doors were locked, few shut [...] It was all there, all the work, all the life of the city, open to the eye and to the hand.
>
> (84)

This depiction of an intentionally utopian urban environment casts critical light onto lived issues of spatial injustice, where the rampant escalation of commercial land value results in urban segregation and the forced displacement of communities along gender, race and class lines.

Such critical utopianism can be powerfully deployed within urban studies and planning, as demonstrated by political scientists and urban studies scholars Christine Hudson and Malin Rönnblom. In their work, feminist sf texts including Pamela Sargent's *The Shore of Women* (1986), were used as the source material for discussions with women's groups, finding that these fictions provided a common language through which personal experience could be expressed, making 'the gendered, racialized and sexualized power relations of the city visible' (7). As Hudson and Rönnblom note, the subordinate position of marginalised communities and individuals suppresses both spatial agency and the capacity to critique power structures. As such, the scope of possibility presented within sf narratives provides vital materials from which we can imagine and construct urban alternatives.

While critical utopias offer worlds where spatial inequalities are redressed, urban dystopian fiction tends to make visible power hierarchies through extrapolation. As urban historian Carl Abbott notes, they reveal the 'implicit understandings that lie beneath the surface of our society' ('Cyberpunk' 4). In particular, he describes how such cyberpunk works as Neal Stephenson's *Snow Crash* (1992), Nicola Griffith's *Slow River* (1995) and Cynthia Kadohata's *In the Heart of the Valley of Love* (1992) provide visceral images of urban segregation. In these novels, the soft boundaries drawn within cities are solidified, and the pernicious fragmentation of urban environments has created isolated enclaves of privileged indifference.

It is such separation and segregation that Marxist philosopher Henri Lefebvre argues must be resisted to assert the right to the city for all marginalised subjects. For Lefebvre, this claim to spatial agency is more readily asserted when it is underpinned by an awareness of the urban, which transcends that of an individual city. As part of this process of expansive imagination he draws upon the world-encompassing city of Trantor in Isaac Asimov's FOUNDATION series (1951–93). Urban theorist Andy Merrifield expounds how such a reference 'open[s] up our *perspective* on thinking about urban life, [...] to live with that starling *immensity*, to make it our own. We might then be able to think more clearly about politics – about *prospective*, progressive politics under planetary urbanization' (910). Trantor offers a way to imagine a city beyond the built expressions of transport infrastructure or population density, and instead consider the urban as being defined by the 'sheer simultaneity of activities, of events and chance meetings' (916). The city scale in sf draws upon this critical mass of encounter to create settings of heightened spatial intensity. Here, the tangible effects of dispossession and segregation expose the necessity of resistance to their more subtle manifestations in the cities we inhabit.

The neighbourhood

The small agrarian neighbourhood community described in Marge Piercy's *Woman on the Edge of Time* (1976) centres on its largest building, a collective dining room which acts as a 'home for us all' (75). It is neither distinctly a place of work nor of leisure but a space of being together, designed to accommodate all inhabitants. In this future of 2137 there are no cities, no centres of power or control; rather, this place is part of a wider network of radically de-centralised and loosely anarchist communities. For Connie, a Mexican-American woman who travels here from 1970s Harlem, this radically egalitarian society provides momentary escape from a life where she is subject to domestic, racial and sexual violence and incarcerated in an asylum.

> The room they entered took up half the dome and was filled with long tables seating perhaps fifteen at each [...] Some panels in the ceiling of the dome were transparent and some were translucent, although from the outside she had not seen any difference [...] 'Some you can see through and some not, because some of us like to feel closed in while we eat and some – like me – want to see everything. The fooder is a home for us all. A warm spot.'
>
> (75)

Piercy's depiction of community recognises that acts of coming together are made possible through the geographic proximity of a neighbourhood and the architectural construction of public space, but also through the recognition of how race, gender, disability and economics impact the making of places of mutual care.

Geographer Doreen Massey discusses this understanding of place in relation to the imagery of sf cities, stating that

> amid the Ridley Scott images of world cities, the writing about skyscraper fortresses, the Baudrillard visions of hyperspace [...] Much of life for many people [...] still consists of waiting in a bus-shelter with your shopping for a bus that never comes.
>
> (8)

For Massey, descriptions of urban disorientation risk disregarding ongoing histories of displacement and dispossession by considering these conditions to be intrinsically associated with urban capitalism. Instead, she suggests the consideration of 'place' as something formed from social relations, which acknowledges that factors including sexuality, race, class and gender are deeply implicated in how we inhabit and experience space. Drawing on bell hooks's description of home as a place where it is possible to discover 'new ways of seeing reality, frontiers of difference' (19), Massey suggests that place can be understood as a source of identity, security and belonging without being physically bounded or enclosed, and that these shifting constructs of connectedness might be understood as 'meeting places' (14). This is an idea of neighbourhood based not on physical proximity but on the common identification of place and the act of coming together.

The construction of meeting places, and the possibilities for connection that they engender, is explored in Joan Slonczewski's *A Door Into Ocean* (1986). On the ocean world of Shora, there is no land available for inhabitation; instead, each community must construct and maintain a raft made from oceanic plant life, which is grown and spun into building materials. Each of these rafts represents the literal making of place for the groups it sustains, a conscious and materially manifest act of being together. They are drifting and dispersed neighbourhoods, mutually sustained by the ocean from which they are made. As noted by architectural theorist Katie Lloyd Thomas, this establishes and reflects a form of social construction based on an intimate awareness of the inhabitant's role in a web of interconnected relations and impacts, of ocean and ocean dweller. In this science fictional space, the scope of such meeting places is expanded to include the more-than-human, to construct social relations which are both rooted in place and resolutely held open.

Critical design and disability studies scholar Aimi Hamraie's examination of Universal Design directly addresses the scope of such meeting places to accommodate human diversity and difference, and the possibility of creating a 'home for us all'. Universal Design aims to recognise that architecture is never value-neutral but generates 'conditions of inclusion or misfit depending on what kinds of bodies are included within the scope of the "universal"' ('Designing' 85). Hamraie turns to speculative fiction's ability to 'disorient taken-for-granted assumptions about the place of marginalized life in the future' ('Alterlivability' 414). They draw on Starhawk's post-apocalyptic *The Fifth Sacred Thing* (1993), which depicts the permaculture reclamation of urban spaces. Urban gardening, de-paving and rewilding are supported by a wider social commitment to valuing human biodiversity. These acts of valuing are made manifest in architectural design and in property and economic relations which centre marginalised people, including those with disabilities. For Hamraie, works of sf like this invite urban planners to subvert economic and eugenicist logics by providing an image of neighbourhood where disability is valued difference.

The building

Nalo Hopkinson's *Brown Girl in the Ring* (1998) is set in the hollowed-out city centre of a future Toronto. This city has suffered an economic collapse, prompting the government and support services to withdraw, and leaving a gang boss in control of the urban centre. His power is symbolically reflected in his location at the top of the CN observation tower, dominating all he surveys. In order to challenge this control, Ti-Jeanne draws upon Caribbean–Canadian healing and spiritual practices, the knowledges her grandmother has carried as part of a diaspora community and deep understandings of this place. This way of knowing allows Ti-Jeanne to reinterpret the CN Tower, and in doing so reclaim her spatial agency by redeploying the symbolic power it contains and channels:

> Ti-Jeanne thought of the center pole of the palais, reaching up into the air and down toward the ground. She thought of the building she was in. The CN Tower. And she understood what it was: 1,815 feet of the tallest center pole in the world. Her duppy body almost laughed a silent kya-kya, a jokey Jab-Jab laugh. For like the spirit tree that the center pole symbolized, the CN Tower dug roots deep into the ground where the dead lives and pushed high into the heavens where the oldest ancestors lived.
>
> (221)

Hopkinson refashions a structure which had been an expression and manifestation of corporate and economic power into a centre pole that acts as a point of connection to other worlds. The novel offers an exploration of the symbolic interpretation of a single built structure, examining the power relations which led to its construction, its role within a shifting socio-economic landscape, and the subversive possibility which surfaces when multiple readings of place are recognised as co-existent.

Such symbolic and material power relations manifest in the built environment are considered by urban studies scholars Lucy Hewitt and Stephen Graham in their analysis of sf representations of urban verticality, which draws on the work of William Gibson, H.G. Wells's *The Sleeper Awakes* (1899) and J.G. Ballard's *High-Rise* (1975). As they note, in these novels 'the vertical implies hierarchy; deployed in spatial terms the vertical highlights and concretises inequities' ('Vertical' 929), while the ability to look down from above confers upon the observer a sense of power that is far from ethically neutral. When considered in relation to the rapid proliferation of high-rise structures in urban centres, which serve as symbolic reflections of corporate power or individual wealth, Hewitt and Graham suggest that these fictions provide critical ground to examine 'uneven social geographies of vertical mobility' and resist the entrenchment of economic segregation ('Getting' 83).

This segregation is particularly apparent in contemporary developments with two separate entrances: one for private residents and one, popularly referred to as a 'poor door', for social housing tenants. In their study of one such building, urban planners Francesca Ansaloni and Miriam Tedeschi draw on Ballard's *High-Rise* to examine the emotional and ethical implications of socio-spatial segregation built into the fabric of a single building. The hierarchy created by exclusionary spatial arrangements which prevent occupants of different tenures mixing is also written into the scale, form and materials used in the fabric of the building. As they describe, an obscured entrance down an alleyway constructed from poor quality materials implies a social stigma which is borne and internalised by those who are forced to occupy this space. At the scale of the building, sf demonstrates the complex inter-relation between built space and the body, the ways in which power is expressed in architecture and the impact this has on those who inhabit it.

The room

In Sally Miller Gearhart's *The Wanderground: Stories of the Hill Women* (1979), the established social patterns of habit are undergoing a radical shift as the power of the men in the cities is challenged by the new understandings of place developed by the hill women. These shifts of power which reshape the world are visible within the textures of one woman's living space. Carefully protected from rising damp and dew, this room is lined with books, neatly packed together to form the surface of the floor, spines up so that they can be identified. Gaps are formed where books have been removed to be read, and their absence is a marker of the shifting relations between the interior worlds of the reader and the domestic space they inhabit and shape.

> She remembered the floor very well from the summer when Seja had been re-arranging it. Books. Hundreds of them, stacked at different thicknesses within rectangular wooden sections [...] Now she noted that Seja's reading had rendered the floor pretty uneven in places. Two children's books, open by the door, had left a gap that a French grammar was failing to fill and next to two texts on plant diseases right near her reach was a long hole whose bottom, Alaka could see, was the dark earth itself.
>
> (19)

In this room, institutional repositories of knowledge are relocated into the domestic, and the intellectually abstract is understood through the materially tactile. In this intimate and personal space, the visitor must tread carefully, learning to walk a landscape of another's mind.

This is an understanding of home as a manifestation of individual identity, expressing and supporting a way of being which may sit in an uneasy tension with the world beyond its walls. As detailed by architect David Fortin in his analysis of home in sf, 'home might then be considered as an adverb modifying our world experience, the hyphen between us and our environment [...] a constant re-engagement with the self through architecture' (*Architecture* 210). For Fortin, sf works such as Philip K. Dick's *A Scanner Darkly* (1977) provide vivid depictions of home spaces as an expression of ongoing struggles between the self and the wider environment, as places where spatial identity is in the process of being reworked. As such, these fictional domestic settings also provide an allegorical site where conflicts between comforts of the known and the shock of the alien can be negotiated and expressed.

However, such architectural self-determination relies upon the existence of a room of one's own, with access to property and spatial agency neither controlled nor forcibly withheld. This assumption is fiercely critiqued in works such as Leslie Marmon Silko's *Almanac of the Dead* (1991), which is set in a near future where Indigenous people in North America stage a revolution to reclaim their territories. As Fortin notes, the narrative strand in this novel which focuses on a young architect in Mexico City provides Silko with an opportunity to expose the economic privilege of domestic architecture and its associated self-expression ('Indigenous'). Here, the ideal of an intimate and personal space, a room where comfort can be held in balance against the external unknown, is revealed to be deeply contingent on dominant power structures and neoliberal capitalism.

The constraints on transgressive, counter-hegemonic and imaginative sites for self-determination within existing planning and design frameworks is addressed by urban planning scholar Faranak

Miraftab, who reflects on the power and potential of acts of 'insurgent planning'. Inspired by anticolonial scholars and activists of liberation, she presents such practices as insisting 'on citizens' rights to dissent, rebel, and determine their own terms of engagement and participation' (282) in purposefully transgressive actions which challenge and disrupt existing frameworks of planning based on a mediation between the state, the market and the individual. For Miraftab, these acts of insurgency are intimately entwined with the acts of imagination inherent to sf, referring to adrienne maree brown and Walidah Imarisha's short story collection *Octavia's Brood* (2015) as a key example. The stories in this collection respond to the legacy of Octavia E. Butler, whose *Parable of the Sower* (1993) and *Parable of the Talents* (1998) trace the continual re-establishment of a community that embraces the power of change. As described by Walidah Imarisha, such visionary fiction is 'vital for any process of decolonization, because the decolonization of the imagination is the most dangerous and subversive form there is: for it is where all other forms of decolonization are born' (4). The power of such imaginative self-determination is visible in sf at the scale of the room, in these spatial chinks in the world machine.

The doorway

In Mohsin Hamid's *Exit West* (2017), the possibilities contained within an individual doorway are expanded, folding space to create a connection between here and there without the passage between. One doorway leads from the Greek island of Mykonos to a house in West London, through which step Nadia and Saeed alongside other individuals and families. To those outside the police cordon which soon surrounds them, they are suspended in transition from one place to another, held on the threshold. But the doorways through which they pass each retain the possibility of connection with all the places they have travelled from, and to all those who might step through them.

> The agent gestured with his head to the blackness of a door [...] drawing close she was struck by its darkness, its opacity, the way that it did not reveal what was on the other side, and also did not reflect what was on this side, and so felt equally like a beginning and an end. (98)

Through its focus on a mundane and familiar spatial device, *Exit West* draws attention to the everyday violence of all other forms of bordering, particularly national borders which enforce the incarceration or exclusion of migrants, refugees and those seeking asylum. This is an understanding of place which demands resistance to the architectures of spatial coercion and control that demarcate imagined lines of difference.

For feminist geographer Sophie Lewis, the door, like the border, is a technology devised to 'hold, release and manage' (166) that which it contains, acting as a threshold mechanism which controls access to both the other side and to the in-between. Lewis draws on sf, including Octavia E. Butler's 'Blood Child' (1984), which explores the development of new forms of multi-species kinship and reproduction, to consider how boundaries such as the skin as a bodily envelope and constructs of gender can be understood as permeable and transmutable. For Lewis, bordering technologies are designed and deployed with political, social and environmental intent in support of a powerful fantasy of separation. In their place Lewis calls for the creation of 'desired or needful openings' which are 'conducive to flourishing' allowing movement across and in-between (167).

It is such conceptual or theoretical openings between sf and the spatial disciplines that this chapter celebrates; it is in the continued blurring of all forms of imaginative construction, written or built, that we can establish new ground conducive to our mutual flourishing. In his discussion of the poetry of sf, Samuel R. Delany uses the phrase 'the door dilated' (142) to demonstrate how the everyday of the science fictional world can be wondrous, how it can, with a simple three-word phrase, conjure into being new technological developments and scientific methods. Just as importantly, it also creates new ways of relating to one another, new thresholds of interaction and ways to move between them. Geographers Rob Kitchin and James Kneale map out how sf opens up sites from which to 'contemplate material and discursive geographies and the production of geographic knowledges and imaginations' ('Lost' 9). As they detail, there are already recursive relationships between science fictional depictions of built environments and their manifestation ('Science Fiction') but the expressions of these relationships is not limited to those within the spatial disciplines. Rather, as expressed in Pamela Zoline's 'The Heat Death of the Universe' (1967), small everyday actions are how buildings, neighbourhoods, cities and worlds are lived and created, and each egg cracked on the kitchen floor contributes to the state of the universe. By understanding space as something that is continually enacted and performed by all of its inhabitants, we are all agents in the construction of our built futures.

> She goes to the refrigerator and takes out a carton of eggs, white eggs, extra large. She throws them one by one onto the kitchen floor which is patterned with strawberries in squares. They break beautifully.
>
> (Zoline 217)

Works cited

Abbott, Carl. 'Cyberpunk Cities: Science Fiction Meets Urban Theory'. *Journal of Planning Education and Research* 27.2 (2007): 122–31.

———. *Imagining Urban Futures: Cities in Science Fiction and What We Might Learn from Them*. Wesleyan UP, 2016.

Ansaloni, Francesca and Miriam Tedeschi. 'Understanding Space Ethically Through Affect and Emotion: From Uneasiness to Fear and Rage in the City'. *Emotion, Space and Society* 21 (2016): 15–22.

Delany, Samuel R. 'To Read *The Dispossessed*'. *The Jewel-Hinged Jaw: Notes on the Language of Science Fiction*. Wesleyan UP, 2011. 105–66.

Dillon, Grace L. 'Beyond the Grim Dust of What Was'. *Love Beyond Body, Space, and Time: An Indigenous LGBT Sci-Fi Anthology*. Ed. Hope Nicholson. Bedside Press, 2016. 9–11.

Dobraszczyk, Paul. *Future Cities: Architecture and the Imagination*. Reaktion, 2019.

Fortin, David T. *Architecture and Science-Fiction Film: Philip K. Dick and the Spectacle of Home*. Ashgate, 2011.

———. 'Indigenous Architectural Futures: Potentials for Post-Apocalyptic Spatial Speculation'. *ARCC Conference Repository* (2014): 475–83.

Garforth, Lisa. 'Environmental Futures, Now and Then: Crisis, Systems Modeling, and Speculative Fiction'. *Osiris* 34.1 (2019): 238–57.

Gearhart, Sally Miller. *The Wanderground: Stories of the Hill Women*. Persephone, 1979.

Grosz, Elizabeth. *Architecture from the Outside: Essays on Virtual and Real Space*. MIT Press, 2001.

Hamid, Mohsin. *Exit West*. Penguin, 2017.

Hamraie, Aimi. 'Alterlivability: Speculative Design Fiction and the Urban Good Life in Starhawk's Fifth Sacred Thing and City of Refuge'. *Environmental Humanities* 12.2 (2020): 407–30.

———. 'Designing Collective Access: A Feminist Disability Theory of Universal Design'. In *Disability, Space, Architecture: A Reader*. Ed. Jos Boys. Routledge, 2017. 78–87.

Hewitt, Lucy and Stephen Graham. 'Getting off the Ground: On the Politics of Urban Verticality'. *Progress in Human Geography* 37.1 (2013): 72–92.

———. 'Vertical Cities: Representations of Urban Verticality in 20th-Century Science Fiction Literature'. *Urban Studies* 52.5 (2015): 923–37.
hooks, bell. 'Choosing the Margin as a Space of Radical Openness'. *Framework: The Journal of Cinema and Media* 36 (1989): 15–23.
Hopkinson, Nalo. *Brown Girl in the Ring*. Hachette, 2001.
Hudson, Christine and Malin Rönnblom. 'Is an "Other" City Possible? Using Feminist Utopias in Creating a More Inclusive Vision of the Future City'. *Futures* 121 (August 2020): 102583.
Imarisha, Walidah. 'Introduction'. *Octavia's Brood: Science Fiction Stories from Social Justice Movements*. Ed. adrienne maree brown and Walidah Imarisha. AK Press, 2015. 3–5.
Kitchin, Rob and James Kneale. 'Lost in Space'. *Lost in Space: Geographies of Science Fiction*. Athlone, 2002: 1–16.
———. 'Science Fiction or Future Fact? Exploring Imaginative Geographies of the New Millennium'. *Progress in Human Geography* 25.1 (2001): 19–35.
Kneale, James. 'Space'. *The Routledge Companion to Science Fiction*. Ed. Mark Bould, Andrew M. Butler, Adam Roberts and Sherryl Vint. Routledge, 2009. 423–32.
Le Guin, Ursula K. *The Dispossessed: An Ambiguous Utopia*. Gollancz, 2002.
Lefebvre, Henri. *Le droit à la ville*. Anthropos, 1968.
Lewis, Sophie. *Full Surrogacy Now: Feminism against Family*. Verso, 2019.
Lloyd Thomas, Katie. 'Feminist Hydro-Logics in Joan Slonczewski's A Door Into Ocean'. *Landscript 5. Material Culture: Assembling and Disassembling Landscapes*. Ed. Jane Hutton. Jovis, 2017. 195–222.
Massey, Doreen. 'A Place Called Home'. *New Formations* 17.3 (1992): 3–15.
Merrifield, Andy. 'The Urban Question under Planetary Urbanization'. *International Journal of Urban and Regional Research* 37.3 (2013): 909–22.
Miraftab, Faranak. 'Insurgent Practices and Decolonization of Future(s)'. *The Routledge Handbook of Planning Theory*. Ed. Michael Gunder, Ali Madanipour and Vanessa Watson. Routledge, 2017. 276–88.
Piercy, Marge. *Woman on the Edge of Time*. Women's Press, 1986.
Qiufan, Chen. *Waste Tide*. Trans. Ken Liu. Head of Zeus, 2019.
Whyte, Kyle P. 'Indigenous Science (Fiction) for the Anthropocene: Ancestral Dystopias and Fantasies of Climate Change Crises'. *Environment and Planning E: Nature and Space* 1. 1–2 (2018): 224–42.
Yusoff, Kathryn. *A Billion Black Anthropocenes or None*. U of Minnesota P, 2018.
Zoline, Pamela. 'The Heat Death of the Universe'. *Women of Wonder: The Classic Years: Science Fiction by Women from the 1940s to the 1970s*. Ed. Pamela Sargent. Harcourt Brace, 1995. 205–17.

47
MARXISM

Gerry Canavan

Any study of the relationship between Marxism and sf immediately runs into a foundational definitional question: even if we think we know what we mean by 'sf', what exactly do we mean when we say 'Marxism'? The term has always circulated within a certain sphere of ambiguity, especially as it has gained renewed currency in the wake of twenty-first century financial crises. In popular usage, it just as frequently refers to *any* vaguely leftist and anti-capitalist political orientation as it does to the specific tradition(s) of political, economic and cultural critique originating out of the work of Karl Marx (and, to a lesser extent, Friedrich Engels) in the mid-1800s. For the academic study of sf in the post-war US and Europe, 'Marxism' becomes additionally complicated by its ongoing status as an official 'enemy of the state', policed and surveilled; many US state university systems required loyalty oaths as a condition of employment that included repudiation of the Communist Party (some of which, like Georgia's, remain in force today). Sf authors and critics alike frequently ran afoul of the US security state's anti-communist apparatus: among other notorious incidents, the FBI files of legendary Golden Age authors Isaac Asimov and Ray Bradbury (who were *not* Marxists) includes multiple instances of concerned citizens turning them in to the government for their supposed Soviet sympathy, and after several *Science Fiction Studies* critics visited his home in 1974, Philip K. Dick famously called on the FBI to investigate the journal (including Darko Suvin, Peter Fitting and Fredric Jameson by name), claiming they were operating within a hostile 'chain of command' headed by Polish sf legend Stanisław Lem (Philmus 1991). The status of 'Marxism' in the histories of both sf as a genre and sf studies as an academic discipline thus contains multitudes. There are as many Marxisms in the history of sf and sf studies as there are conceptualisations of sf, and the concepts associated with Marxism circulate in truly varied ways across both discourses.

This chapter endeavours to be somewhat strict, if not exactly doctrinaire, about focusing on texts and critical approaches with a specifically Marxist or socialist orientation, rather than attempting to catalogue *all* radical or Leftist sf regardless of its precise or avowed relationship to Marx and to Marxism (for a more ecumenical approach, see Burling).

DOI: 10.4324/9781003140269-50

Marxism(s) and literature(s)

'It has long been asked, perhaps with exasperation as much as intrigue, what science fiction has to do with Marxism', Harry Warwick writes (273): 'To this question about the relationship between science fiction and Marxism, however, I would pose a counter-question: *which* Marxism?' (274). Stuart Hall likewise notes the multiplicity of the Marxisms that have emerged since the mid-1840s out of the writings of Karl Marx (sometimes with Friedrich Engels). While Marxist critics have frequently sought out 'the true Marx',

> Such attempts to retrospectively seal the tradition and to stitch particular texts and positions into it often put the writer in particularly awkward positions. Poulantzas (1973), for example, in *Political Power and Social Classes,* seeks to advance the most heretical of propositions in the most orthodox of modes, appealing to a nonexistent agreement about 'what the Marxist tradition says'.
>
> (99)

Many critics, Hall argues, create problems for themselves by beginning from the proposition that 'it is all already there in Marx and disguising real theoretical work as explication de texte' (99). Rather, he suggests, we can identify multiple Marxisms within the Marxist tradition, both with respect to texts in themselves and with respect to the critical apparatus that is brought to bear upon these texts.

Louis Althusser, for instance, famously drew a distinction between the 'Young Marx' (as registered in the unpublished *Economic and Philosophic Manuscripts of 1844*, not widely available until the mid-twentieth century) and the scientific socialism of the 'Mature Marx' (as registered by *Capital*), arguing that only the latter represents a fully developed Marxism. Others, including Marxist humanists like Ernst Bloch, Antonio Gramsci and Walter Benjamin, tend to prefer the early Marx's focus on alienation and the cause of human freedom, while still others deny the existence of any divide at all and insist instead on synthesis among the various intensities across the life of the historical Karl Marx. (For sf critics, yet another option has occasionally proven popular: Marx's unfinished 'Fragment on Machines' from the *Grundrisse,* also widely unavailable until the twentieth century, which suggests an emphasis on the Promethean powers of human creation and ingenuity that is not always stressed elsewhere in the Marxist tradition but is very much in continuity with the way US and UK sf has historically thought about the future.) Likewise, the Marxist critical tradition has itself fractured into a plurality of approaches, among them revolutionary Marxism–Leninism, the economic analysis of classical and 'Orthodox' Marxism, and the more academic, university-based Western Marxist tradition of scholarship and cultural critique – each of which also has its own internal versions of the debate over which Marx is the 'true' Marx.

Beyond this, a host of radical perspectives on race, gender, sexuality, Indigeneity and disability draw on Marxist assumptions and critical methodologies without necessarily aligning themselves with Marxism as a political project. Regardless of the words we choose to label various political orientations and interventions, there remains a very real sense in which Marx so 'profoundly' impacted the theory and practice of all scholarship that, as Peter Singer suggests, 'We are all Marxists now' (2). Reducing Marxism to a single set of interventions is thus something of a mug's game, but we can nonetheless try to identify some broad areas of commonality. All Marxists, to some extent or another, exist in an oppositional space of anti-capitalism that holds that the final source of value is human labour power, of which the capitalist unjustly cheats the worker through coercion and exploitation in order to generate profit. This system reproduces itself through violence, when necessary, but more essentially through mystification and obscurantism of its actual material realities; capitalism persuades the workers to oppress *themselves* by feeding them a constant series of ideological justifications for the existence of inequality, which it is the job of the revolution to reveal and overturn. Marxists in sf studies have tended to focus on this latter aspect of the system. The 'Western Marxist' tradition of György Lukács, Ernst Bloch, Althusser, Antonio Gramsci and the Frankfurt School has thus proved the most important forebear of contemporary sf criticism, precisely because its critique of superstructural elements of culture, including art and literature, makes it an attractive theoretical grounding for left-wing cultural analysis and scholarship in the humanities. In particular, the Blochian interest in utopia and utopian speculation possesses a natural affinity with sf's futurological orientation. In the hands of such Marxist critics, sf is able to accomplish both operations of ideological critique; through its production of counterfactual realities, sf is able to slip past the censor, as it were, and speak the truth about the violence the system exerts on those who labour on its behalf, as well as present utopian visions of alternate worlds where this sort of hyper-exploitative system of extraction would not (or at least *might* not) exist.

At the same time, such critics are commonly (even perpetually) disappointed by the way that most sf reflects, rather than critiques, capitalism's ideological preconceptions; indeed, the popularity of science fictional rhetoric as the hegemonic language that technological modernity uses to think about and talk about the future suggests that sf is doing crucial work securing capitalism's grip. (As China Miéville once suggested, there is a very real sense in which the ultimate grounding of sf has never been 'science' but rather 'capitalist modernity's ideologically projected self-justification: not some abstract/ideal "science", but capitalist science's bullshit about itself' (240).) For Barbara Foley, this situation should not be understood as only or primarily a situation of betrayal. The discovery that both the beloved artefacts of our personal childhoods and the signature artistic achievements of our time are part of an intricate system of social conditioning and control is the beginning of the process of creating a better world:

> The Marxist critic is not a scold, seeking out political shortcomings for exposure and punishment. Rather, the goal of Marxist criticism – and pedagogy – is the development of a fuller dialectical understanding of social totality giving rise to both doctrines and structures of feeling, whether these clarify or obfuscate the 'real foundation'. After all, as Marx well knew, the main object of critique is not bad thinking, or even people who think badly, but the social arrangements generating bad thinking – and badly thinking people – in the first place. (159)

'The purpose of Marxist literary criticism', she argues, is precisely 'to contribute to project of constructing what Antonio Gramsci called an alternative hegemony: an oppositional common sense understanding of the ways in which artistic production and reception can either foster or fetter revolutionary change' (123). To the Marxist critic of sf, both sf as a genre and sf criticism as a scholarly practice have the potential to be integral to this counterhegemonic work – and thus both become important beachheads in the fight over the future.

The proposition that the future is a site of struggle – and that both sf and science fiction studies are important fronts in that war – has been part of sf studies since its emergence as an academic field in the late 1960s and early 1970s. This vexed relationship with the world as it exists is, in many ways, the outgrowth of a deliberate strategy on the part of sf studies' founders in the 1970s, most notably Darko Suvin, whose 1972 *College English* article 'On the Poetics of the Science Fiction Genre' (later expanded into *Metamorphoses of Science Fiction* (1977)) is often cited as an origin point for the field. (Mark Bould stylises this moment as 'the Suvin event', noting that from then on, 'SF theory and criticism have inhabited – not by any means always contentedly – the Suvin event horizon, or attempted to escape it' (18).) Suvin's approach centred on several overlapping moves to promote the legitimacy of sf as an area of academic study. First and foremost, his work exhibits a fixation with 'the highest reaches of the genre', to which could be juxtaposed 'the 80% or more of debilitating confectionery' published as sf ('Poetics' 380). By the time of *Metamorphoses*, this 'strictly perishable stuff, produced in view of instant obsolescence for the publisher's profit and the writer's acquisition of other perishable commodities' (26) had swelled to as much as 90 percent of the genre, while the 'aesthetically significant' tenth he privileged was tightly concentrated in the major writers of the New Wave, including Dick, Lem, Brian W. Aldiss, J.G. Ballard, Samuel R. Delany, Thomas M. Disch, Michel Jeury, Ursula K. Le Guin, and Boris and Arkady Strugatsky (1).

This boundary between quality and dreck was enforced not simply internally – trumpeting good sf over bad 'science fiction' – but externally as well. Suvin insisted on strict demarcations between sf and similar genres, such as fantasy, horror, the fairy tale and myth, in the name of promoting sf as a worthy exception to a general law that rightly diminished inferior genre work. Sf's special status came not only from its privileged relationship to utopian futurity (and accordant relationship with real-world socialist politics) but from its key formal mechanisms, most notably the one Suvin described as the core of the genre: *cognitive estrangement*, a version of Viktor Shklovsky's *ostranenie* and Bertolt Brecht's *Verfremdungseffekt* where defamiliarisation is disciplined by its relationship with actual knowledge (crucially, not simply 'scientific' knowledge but 'also all the cultural or historical sciences and even scholarship', including perhaps most importantly the Marxist tradition (*Metamorphoses* 26)). Sf 'takes off from a fictional ('literary') hypothesis and develops it with totalizing ('scientific') rigor' (18), and for Suvin, this dual action away from and back towards the concrete, material conditions of our individual and social existence, in the name of utopian transformation of the world, was what made sf worthy of such special study.

Perhaps the name more widely associated with the Marxist approach to sf is Fredric Jameson, whose career-long fascination with the concept of utopia led him to engagement with sf as far back as his foundational essay 'Metacommentary' (1971). It views science fictional texts about inventors and about disaster as disguised ruminations on the utopian life of the scientist, a figure who 'doesn't do real work, yet he has power and crucial significance' (16), and nostalgia for wartime solidarity, 'the cosmic emergencies of science fiction [being] a way of reliving a kind of wartime togetherness and morale, a kind of drawing together among survivors which is itself merely a distorted dream of a more humane collectivity and social organization' (17). Sf texts are similarly crucial to his era-defining *Postmodernism; or, the Cultural Logic of Late Capitalism* (1991), as well as *The Geopolitical Aesthetic: Cinema and Space in the World System* (1992), *The Seeds of Time* (1994) – which originated the now-ubiquitous, perpetually misattributed notion that it is now easier to imagine the end of the world than the end of capitalism – and his extended study of sf and its relationship to the 'radical break' of historical mutability, *Archaeologies of the Future: The Desire Called Utopia and Other Science Fictions* (2005).

In 'Progress vs. Utopia, Or, Can We Imagine the Future?' (1982), Jameson lays out the core of the Marxist approach to the genre, which is not so much about the supposed accuracy or inaccuracy of sf's many conflicting visions of the future but rather about making felt the unhappiness of the present, and the possibility of better systems of social organisations arising in their place:

> the most characteristic SF does not seriously attempt to imagine the 'real' future of social systems. Rather, its multiple mock futures serve the quite different function of transforming our own present into the determinate past of something yet to come.
>
> (152)

Twenty-seven years later, in his *Valences of the Dialectic,* this work of imagining *genuine* historical difference seemed no less urgent:

> It would be best, perhaps, to think of an alternate world – better to say the alternate world, our alternate world – as one contiguous with ours but without any connection or access to it. Then, from time to time, like a diseased eyeball in which disturbing flashes of light are perceived or like those baroque sunbursts in which rays from another world suddenly break into this one, we are reminded that Utopia exists and that other systems, other spaces, are still possible.
>
> (632)

Other major critical approaches to utopia and sf that engage, with varying levels of specificity, with the utopian theorists of the Western Marxist tradition include: Tom Moylan's work on the critical utopia and (later) the critical dystopia, which complexifies the sometimes flattening power of 'utopia' as a binaristic, reductionistic concept; the cyborg feminism of Donna J. Haraway, who has described herself at times as 'an illegitimate daughter of Marx' (Wark 8); the influential *Red Planets: Marxism and Science Fiction* (2009), edited by Mark Bould and China Miéville, which extends 'the Suvin event' while also challenging Suvin's decision to privilege sf over other genres ('*Red Planets* we have. We should not neglect the red dragons' (Miéville 'Cognition' 245)); and Carl Freedman's provocative claim that critical theory and sf are 'each [...] a version of the other' (xv), which suggests a way in which a (certain) history of sf can be seen to be in and of itself a kind of Marxism. In keeping with Freedman's observation, in the decades since the New Wave, Marxist criticism of sf has been helped along by major artists and creators with avowed Marxist and socialist politics who produced significant critical interventions alongside their fiction, including not only Miéville but also Le Guin, Delany and Kim Stanley Robinson (on whose thesis committee Jameson served).

Other influential scholars have worked within a generally Marxist paradigm while expanding the scope of the intervention to other fields of discourse, especially the ecological humanities and the rolling political and economic crises of the 2000s, including Sherryl Vint, whose *Biopolitical Futures in Twenty-First Century Speculative Fiction* (2021) explores how hyper-contemporary bio-capitalist and anti-ecological practices of extraction 'enables the ongoing real subsumption of life by capital' (9); Jason W. Moore, who proposes replacing the notion of *the Anthropocene* with *the Capitalocene* to better identify what and who destroyed the natural world, and when; the WReC group at the University of Warwick, who apply the Marxist notion of 'combined and uneven development' to the economics of production and dispersal of contemporary global cultural production; the late Mark Fisher, whose *Capitalist Realism* (2009) stridently refused to accept the baseline neoliberal assertion that there is no alternative to capitalism; and Steven Shaviro, who has applied Marxist analysis to twenty-first-century modes of literary, filmic and digital production as well as to 'hyperobjects' massively distributed in space and time, like the stock market, computer networks and climate change, arguing that sf is 'a form of psycho-socio-technological cartography' and thus 'one of the best tools we have for making sense of [...] abstractions like economies, social formations, technological infrastructures, and climate perturbations' (4).

Among the many strong challenges to the Suvinian/Jamesonian paradigm in the decades since 'Poetics', perhaps now constituting the most important alternative stream in the field, is the 'imperial turn' of the 2000s, during which critics like John Rieder, Patricia Kerslake, Istvan Csicsery-Ronay, Jr, Isiah Lavender III, Ida Yoshinaga and Grace L. Dillon pointed critical attention to the imperialist, colonialist, racist and anti-Indigenous underpinnings of much sf. Rieder's *Colonialism and the Emergence of Science Fiction* (2008) has become, in its own way, a new foundational document for the contemporary study of the genre through its articulation of the 'colonial gaze' that structures science fictional visions of historical progress and utopian futures:

> Science fiction comes into visibility first in those countries most heavily involved in imperialist projects – France and England – and then gains popularity in the United States, Germany, and Russia as those countries also enter into more and more serious imperial competition. [...] no informed reader can doubt that allusions to colonial history and situations are ubiquitous features of early science fiction motifs and plots. It is not a matter of asking whether but of determining precisely how and to what extent the stories engage colonialism. (Rieder 3)

The strident call of twenty-first century critics to refuse this gaze and reject this history, to decolonise sf, of course has its own internal genre history, from the horrific reverse colonisation of London in H.G. Wells's *War of the Worlds* (1898) to N.K. Jemisin's BROKEN EARTH trilogy (2015–7) – and has its own strong resonances with Marx's famous 'ruthless criticism of all that exists' (n.p.) that animated the utopia-obsessed generation of 1970s and post-1970s sf scholars. From the Afrofuturist and Africanfuturist works associated with such authors as Delany, Octavia E. Butler and Nnedi Okorafor to the Indigenous futurism championed by Dillon, alongside approaches that centre Latinx and Asian futures, feminist futures, queer futures, ecological and animal futures, anti-capitalist futures, disabled futures, machinic futures, and so on and on, creative and critical encounters have extended sf's tendency towards the project of liberation. They have done so in the spirit of fiery critique not only of the real world but also of the fictional worlds the genre crafted in eras more dominated by the exclusion and disparagement of the many, many voices who did not fit a straight-White-male eugenic vision of a galactic *Pax Americana* smash-and-grabbing its way across the cosmos, leaving in its wake broken lives, colonised cultures, ruined ecologies, and endless accumulations of disposable consumer junk.

Marxist sf

H.G. Wells's *The Time Machine* (1895), a novel Suvin views as paradigmatic for the genre, demonstrates both the possibilities and the potential limitations of Marxist sf. Wells, a self-described socialist associated for a time with the gradualist Fabian Society, imagines a Time Traveller who builds a machine that allows him to journey back and forth through time. At the start of the novel his friends debate using the machine to make secure investments (at the risk of arriving at a future that has been 'erected on a strictly communistic basis' (Wells n.p.)), but what he ultimately finds is simultaneously the inverse and the intensification of our own class-divided society: the capitalists (transformed by time and evolution into the elfin Eloi) live in bovine decadence and the workers (hardened into the monstrous Morlocks) periodically emerge from their underground holes to feed from the herd. As the Time Traveller, disgusted, moves further into the future, he finds the same logic replicated; even at the end of the time, as the sun burns out, he finds a world where butterflies (the spiritual and perhaps literal heirs of the Eloi) are hunted by horrid crabs. *The Time Machine* thus offers a demystifying critique of class society, which it satirises through a logic of naturalisation and inescapability. Consequently, however, the notion that the class logic of capitalism might be supplanted falls by the wayside in favour of futures that can only ever be nightmare replications of the miseries of the present. The judgement of whether or not the text is properly Marxist or sufficiently socialist can be a matter of endless debate (much like the question of Wells's political allegiances and personal creative intentions) but it is clear that the book is both available for and quite useful to anyone seeking to enact Marxist critical interpretation(s) of the history and practice of sf.

The Time Machine is not on China Miéville's perpetually circulating list of '50 Sci-Fi & Fantasy Works Every Socialist Should Read', which goes viral on the Internet in sf fandom every few years; Miéville somewhat idiosyncratically selects *The Island of Doctor Moreau* (1896) instead. But regardless the list is a terrific archive of major sf texts in the genre that would be of interest to socialists, from the inevitable (Alexander Bogdanov's *The Red Star* (1908, 1912), Yevgeny Zamyatin's *We* (1924), Le Guin's *The Dispossessed* (1974), Robinson's MARS trilogy (1992–6)) to the eclectic (Octavia E. Butler's *Survivor* (1978), Philip Pullman's *Northern Lights* (1995)) to the unexpected (Oscar Wilde's *The Happy Prince* (1888), Toni Morrison's *Beloved* (1987), Gregory Maguire's *Wicked* (1995)) to the absurd and nearly perverse (Ayn Rand's *Atlas Shrugged* (1957)). Elements of such a Marxist tradition in sf could undoubtedly include and/or repurpose texts and concepts appearing in every other chapter of this volume, beginning perhaps with the utopian speculation and worldbuilding not just of Wells but also, for example, Samuel Butler's *Erewhon* (1872), Edward Bellamy's quasi-socialist *Looking Backward: 2000–1887* (1888), which sparked a host of imitators and detractors, William Morris's *News from Nowhere* (1888), Sutton E. Griggs's *Imperium in Imperio* (1899), Pauline Elizabeth Hopkins's *Of One Blood* (1902–3), Jack London's *The Iron Heel* (1908) and Charlotte Perkins Gilman's *Herland* (1915). The desire of the Futurians – an influential group of sf fans living in and around New York City in the late 1930s and 1940s, including many who went on to become major names in the Golden Age of the genre, such as Frederik Pohl, Cyril M. Kornbluth, James Blish, Damon Knight, Ace editor Donald A. Wollheim, writer and editor Judith Merril, literary agent Virginia Kidd and a teenage Isaac Asimov – to create, consume and discuss a more Marxist sf caused a major rift in organised fandom. And while much Golden Age sf of course was quite compatible with capitalism, colonialism, consumerism and other toxic ideologies, as the 'imperial turn' critique of the 2000s makes all too clear, much sf of the period retained a socialist or at least socialist-curious orientation, from Olaf Stapledon's troubled attempt to unite communism and Catholicism in *Star Maker* (1937) to Pohl and Kornbluth's hilarious, brutal satire *The Space Merchants* (1953) to Naomi Mitchison's *Memoirs of a Space Woman* (1962) to the post-scarcity, post-capitalist utopia lurking somewhere in the background of *Star Trek* (1966–9) – to say nothing of the even more expressly socialist traditions of sf writers in the Soviet Union and other Communist nations, where, as Isaac Asimov noted, the 'what if', 'if only' and 'if this goes on' of Western sf included a fourth possibility: 'if only this goes on' (11). Likewise, many Communist bloc sf authors, from Lem to the Strugatsky brothers, wrote their own hilarious and brutal satires of the failures of the USSR police state to achieve anything like the longed-for communist dream.

Although 'virtually no genuinely Left-sf was published in North America during the 1960s' (Burling 242), New Wave authors of the 1960s and 1970s, including those privileged by Suvin, typically took up anti-capitalist (and often anti-war, anti-racist and anti-sexist) politics in their writing. This stance intensified already existing divides in the field that have haunted it ever since, through cyberpunk in the 1980s and biopunk in the 1990s to solarpunk and hopepunk today. In the 1970s, 1980s and 1990s the utopian (and semi-utopian, demi-utopian, heterotopian or at least anti-anti-utopian) landscapes of authors like Robinson, Ernest Callenbach (who coined the term *ecotopia* in his 1975 novel of the same name about a breakaway socialist Republic in California and the Pacific Northwest), Iain M. Banks, Ken McLeod, Gwyneth Jones and others have been vital counterpoints for Left resistance to the more capitalist-friendly mega-franchises (increasingly all under the control of the Disney Corporation). And even the mega-franchises seem to be increasingly inflected by a kind of sublimated and disavowed Marxist longing. After the tumultuous early decades of the twenty-first century, filled with war, economic collapses, ecological disaster and a global pandemic, anti-capitalist sf – whether vulgarly Marxist, doctrinairely Marxist, communist, socialist, communitarian, anarchist, Marxian, neo-Marxist, post-Marxist or drawn from elsewhere within the new millennium's cavalcade of movements and labels – seems the most creatively vibrant work in the field, appearing in everything from the transmogrified Indigenous resistance of *Avatar* (Cameron 2009) to the grim and gritty rebellion of *Star Wars: Andor* (Disney+ 2022), from the transcendent fury and divine violence of Jemisin's Afrofuturist BROKEN EARTH trilogy (the first trilogy to ever win back-to-back-to-back Hugo awards) to Kim Stanley Robinsons's everything-and-the-kitchen-sink attempt to save the planet in *The Ministry for the Future* (2020), endorsed by no less august an eco-profiteer and war criminal than Barack Obama himself. Such anti-capitalist sf continues to expand beyond the too-straight, too-White and too-male founders of historical Marxist discourse to contemporary anti-capitalisms that are feminist, Black, Latinx, Asian, Indigenous, queer, trans, ecological, disabled, and more.

Istvan Csicsery-Ronay, Jr once noted that 'To paraphrase Philip K. Dick's Palmer Eldritch: imperialism promises the stars; sf delivers' (234) – but if Karl Marx once dedicated his project to 'the ruthless criticism of all that exists, ruthless both in the sense of not being afraid of the results it arrives at and in the sense of being just as little afraid of conflict with the powers that be' (n.p.), then sf delivers here, too. Or as Le Guin, writing of the Stalinists' designation of Zamyatin as an 'internal émigré', once put it: 'This smear-word is a precise and noble description of the finest writers of SF, in all countries' (90). The equivalent term in the US, she notes, might be 'un-Americanism', incredibly fitting for a genre where so many of its most famous authors, from Asimov and Bradbury to Robert A. Heinlein and Aldous Huxley were *all* investigated at one time or another by communist-hunters in the FBI. 'Bradbury was a target', the advertising copy for *Writers Under Surveillance* (2018) delightfully asserts, 'because an informant warned that science fiction was a Soviet plot to weaken American resolve'. The plot is ongoing! Defiant to its core – Bradbury once claimed that the one thing sf was 'ever about' was 'hating the way things are, wanting to make things different' (163) – and notoriously unable even to define itself, much less agree on anything else, sf for the Marxist generates both its pleasure and its use-value precisely from its activation of this oppositional utopian drive: the way the genre calls on us in every possible way to reject the bad things that already exist and the nightmare of history that brought us to this terrible point, and celebrates instead the unyielding collective desire to invent other, better worlds for everyone instead.

Works cited

Asimov, Isaac. 'Introduction'. *More Soviet Science Fiction*. Ed. uncredited. Collier, 1962. 7–13.

Bould, Mark. 'Rough Guide to a Lonely Planet, from Nemo to Neo'. *Red Planets: Marxism and Science Fiction*. Ed. Mark Bould and China Miéville. Wesleyan UP, 2009. 1–26.

Bradbury, Ray. 'No News, or What Killed the Dog?' *Quicker than the Eye*. 1996. 158–69. Avon.

Brown, JPat, B.C.D. Lipton and Michael Morisy. *Writers under Surveillance: The FBI Files*. MIT Press, 2018.

Burling, William J. 'Marxism'. *The Routledge Companion to Science Fiction*. Ed. Mark Bould, Andrew M. Butler, Adam Roberts and Sherryl Vint. Routledge, 2009. 236–45.
Csicsery-Ronay, Jr, Istvan. 'Science Fiction and Empire'. *Science Fiction Studies* 90 (2003): 231–45.
Foley, Barbara. *Marxist Literary Criticism Today*. Pluto, 2019.
Freedman, Carl. *Critical Theory and Science Fiction*. Wesleyan UP, 2000.
Hall, Stuart. *Cultural Studies 1983: A Theoretical History*. Ed. Jennifer Daryl Slack and Lawrence Grossberg. Duke UP, 2016.
Jameson, Fredric. *Archaeologies of the Future: The Desire Called Utopia and Other Science Fictions*. Verso, 2005.
—–. 'Metacommentary'. *PMLA* 86.1 (1971). 9–18.
—–. 'Progress versus Utopia; Or, Can We Imagine the Future?' *Science Fiction Studies* 27 (1982): 147–58.
—–. *Valences of the Dialectic*. Verso, 2009.
Le Guin, Ursula K. 'Surveying the Battlefield' *Science Fiction Studies* 1.2 (1973): 88–90.
Marx, Karl. 'Marx to Ruge (Kreuznach, September 1843)'. www.marxists.org/archive/marx/works/1843/letters/43_09.htm
Miéville, China. 'Cognition as Ideology: A Dialectic of SF Theory'. *Red Planets: Marxism and Science Fiction*. Ed. Mark Bould and China Miéville. Wesleyan UP, 2009. 231–48.
Philmus, Robert M. (1991) 'The Two Faces of Philip K. Dick'. *Science Fiction Studies* 53 (1991): 91–103.
Rieder, John. *Colonialism and the Emergence of Science Fiction*. Wesleyan UP. 2008.
Shaviro, Steven. 'Hyperbolic Futures: Speculative Finance and Speculative Fiction'. *The Cascadia Subduction Zone* 1.2 (2011): 3–5, 12–15.
Singer, Peter. *Marx: A Very Short Introduction*. Oxford UP, 2001.
Suvin, Darko. *Metamorphoses of Science Fiction: On the Poetics and History of a Literary Genre*. Ed. Gerry Canavan. Peter Lang, 2016.
—–. 'On the Poetics of the Science Fiction Genre'. *College English* 34.3 (1972): 372–82.
Vint, Sherryl. *Biopolitical Futures in Twenty-First Century Speculative Fiction*. Cambridge UP, 2021.
Wark, McKenzie. *Molecular Red: Theory for the Anthropocene*. Verso, 2015.
Warwick, Harry. "Double Take: 'Cognitive Estrangement" Reconsidered from the Perspective of Marx's Value Theory". *Extrapolation* 63.3 (2023): 273–96.
Wells, H.G. *The Time Machine*, 1895. www.marxists.org/reference/archive/hgwells/works/1890s/time/ch01.htm

48
MEDICAL HUMANITIES

Anna McFarlane and Gavin Miller

Multidisciplinary and interdisciplinary, the medical humanities bring together approaches from the humanities (including history, literary studies and ethics) and the study and practice of medicine and healthcare. Particularly relevant to sf studies is the sub-field of Literature and Medicine, significantly influenced by Susan Sontag's *Illness as Metaphor* (1978) and *AIDS and its Metaphors* (1989). In these texts, Sontag shows that the rhetorical construction of certain culturally resonant diseases – such as the portrayal of the cancer patient as a soldier in a 'battle' against the illness – has implications for the patient's understanding of their role. She argues that the use of metaphor burdens people living with diseases to which are attached moral judgments and expectations such as – in the case of HIV/AIDS – a stigmatising association with invasion by an external 'other'. At around the same time, sf theory offered similar analyses of medical metaphors within discourses specifically of the future. Donna J. Haraway's 'The Biopolitics of Postmodern Bodies', in *Simians, Cyborgs and Women: The Reinvention of Nature* (1991), understands the rhetorical deployment of the immune system as a means of underpinning the ideological and political aims of constructing and protecting borders from invasion by an enemy 'other'. She sees this tactic as the basis for Ronald Reagan's infamous 'Star Wars' project, a white elephant that mobilised sf imagery while funnelling public money into a system that had the aim of protecting the US from nuclear missile strikes. The encounter between sf studies and medical humanities has continued to develop over subsequent decades. Bringing the medical humanities into conversation with sf allows for a critical analysis of the ways we practice and think about biomedicine, healthcare, disability and related topics. This chapter first indicates some key concerns in literary medical humanities, before discussing biomedical novums in sf, showing how the genre has engaged with medical issues through concerns about biotechnology and bodily invasion. It then introduces critical perspectives upon the hegemonic construction of the imagined biomedical future, before showing how sf studies is enriched by its engagement with medical humanities studies such as narrative medicine, as well as related fields like disability studies.

Medical humanities began in North American medical schools with the goal of instilling empathy and other professional competences in future clinicians. Medical humanities scholars pointed out the interpersonal, ethical and epistemic virtues of developing bedside manner, treating the patient as an individual and listening to the patient's story. Anne Hudson Jones, one of the

 DOI: 10.4324/9781003140269-51

pioneers of the study of literature and medicine, is a literary scholar professionally situated in a medical school. She argues that the goal of teaching literature to physicians has always been to promote equity in healthcare through professional competences such as interpretation and ethical reflection ('Why?'). This vision for literature and medicine jostles alongside that of Rita Charon, a practising physician who developed the related practice of 'narrative medicine', a putative medical subspeciality. For Charon, literary close reading is a textual practice that offers a paradigm for the clinician's attentiveness to the patient, with the aim of 'a full, nonjudgmental, generative reception that is informed by all aspects of what a tellers tells – in words, silences, gestures, position, mood, prior utterances' (Charon et al. 157).

More recently, medical humanities has entered a self-consciously 'critical' phase, in which the term 'critical medical humanities' builds solidarity between researchers who are, in various ways, interrogating the humanistic assumptions at the base of the first wave of medical humanities while developing the techniques of the first wave to meet new challenges. This phase of medical humanities incorporates challenges from critical theory, such as Michel Foucault's *The Birth of the Clinic* (1973), which argues that the development of clinical medicine represented a fundamental shift in our understanding of the body. Medical science lays the foundations for divisions on the basis of sex, race and sexuality. The medical humanities, following Foucault, attends to this discourse which underpins cultural assumptions and plays a key role in constructing 'biopower' – political power over the bodies of the populace. Anne Whitehead and Angela Woods identify the delivery of a cancer diagnosis as a 'primal scene' for first-wave medical humanities. This scene 'placed a humanist emphasis on individual protagonists and the role of narrative, metaphor and gaps in communication within the dynamics of the clinical interaction' (2). Whitehead and Woods argue that the focus on an interpersonal encounter between doctor and patient, two humans coming together in a universalised situation, has the tendency to elide the specificities of the scene, whether those involve the complicating power dynamics that might be introduced by differences in race, class or gender, or the health policies and treatment availability of a specific geo-political zone. The move to critical medical humanities therefore aims to bring these issues into focus and to consider how 'humanities and social sciences might play a constitutive role in the shaping of such knowledge' (Whitehead and Woods 2), rather than acting as a helpful adjunct to medical practice.

The conscious relationship between medical humanities and sf began with the 2001 special issue of the journal *Literature and Medicine* – although the idea for such an issue had been mooted since the 1980s (Jones 'Editor's' vii) – and Gary Westfahl and George E. Slusser's edited collection, *No Cure for the Future: Disease and Medicine in Science Fiction and Fantasy* (2002). Through these and later publications, two scholarly communities came together and grappled with the key problem of how sf's non-realist mode might still be informative for the concerns of medical humanities. In first wave medical humanities, the texts overwhelmingly favoured by clinical educators and practitioners had been testimonial accounts of the patient or clinician experience via memoir, or literary fictional texts that sought to describe the experience of illness, such as Leo Tolstoy's *The Death of Ivan Ilyich* (1886). Sf motivated other ways of reading. The power of sf to interrogate social structures through the 'cognitive estrangement' identified by Darko Suvin is, for instance, also seen in its relationship to medicine. Esther L. Jones convincingly argues that Black women's speculative fiction draws on contemporary sociopolitical realities, 'casting them in distancing distortions [...] to render what we regard as familiar as strange and observable, and thereby identify sociopolitical distortions in everyday behaviour' (11). Elsewhere, we have argued that sf is in conversation with 'the hegemonic technoscientific imaginary' (Miller and McFarlane 'Science Fiction' 215), challenging readers to critique their horizons of expectation when it comes to (medical) technology.

Biomedical novums

The clearest intersection between sf and medical humanities is in the use of biomedical novums. Sf has a tradition of thinking about the body, and biology more broadly, as a kind of technology; infinitely adaptable, it is a force that can be harnessed in the name of science and progress. The animal–human hybrids of H.G. Wells's *The Island of Doctor Moreau* (1896) question the limits of medical power and raise the possibility of biotechnological progress that might change the boundaries of the individual. Early twentieth-century concerns about eugenics also found expression in sf. For example, Aldous Huxley's *Brave New World* (1932) sees babies born on a conveyor belt, their *in vitro* nutrients adapted to control their future strength of mind and body, and was part of a contemporary debate, which saw a number of feminist writers contribute in less-celebrated works (Bigman). Concerns with the control of reproduction as a form of biopower continue today, as demonstrated by the success of Margaret Atwood's *The Handmaid's Tale* (1985), its television adaptation (Hulu 2017–) and the host of feminist dystopias it inspired.

There was an intensification of biomedical novums, particularly in the US, as the Cold War took hold of the popular imagination. Narratives of invasion, particularly bodily invasion, took up North American anxieties that Communist sympathies could dwell within a seemingly harmless body. For example, *Fantastic Voyage* (Fleischer 1966), novelised by Isaac Asimov, tells the story of a US medical team shrunk down so that they can go inside the body of a defecting Soviet scientist, who is comatose following an assassination attempt. Blood cells are shown as large, pillowy structures, the innards pink and wet. The body follows its own logics and any invader is treated as a disruption to homeostatic systems that must be eliminated, providing an element of threat to the protagonists. *Fantastic Voyage* inspired later animated imaginings of the body such as the French series *Once Upon a Time…Life* (*Il était une fois…la vie*; FR3 1987–8), which showed the body on a similar scale but anthropomorphised the organs, fluids and invading bacteria as edutainment for children. It has also been satirised repeatedly in animated media, such as episodes of *The Magic School Bus* (PBS 1994–7), *Futurama* (Fox 1999–2023) and *Hey Duggee* (BBC 2014–). *Fantastic Voyage* makes visible the secret spaces of the body as a way of understanding its systems in an extension of twentieth-century imaging technologies, such as the ultrasound machine and the CAT scanner, imaging systems that offer greater control over the body through greater visibility. There was a clear attraction to having those spaces rendered visible for exploration in a way that emphasised these landscapes as discoverable and knowable. The inside of the body is displayed as a threatening world, but one that can be brought under human control, especially when the human invaders return to their full size and their dominance over their own bodies is restored.

Fantastic Voyage's representation of human power over the body pre-empted some of the themes that would occupy sf during the New Wave and beyond. J.G. Ballard famously described the New Wave as turning from outer space to inner space. While Ballard primarily meant that sf would journey into the mind, questioning the nature of reality and the mind's adaptability in an era profoundly influenced by psychedelia, stories such as James Tiptree, Jr's 'The Girl Who Was Plugged In' (1973) attended instead to the plasticity and augmentation of the body. Bodily invasion and modification would become key tropes of cyberpunk and, more intensely, of biopunk (Schmeink).

While bodily invasion and modification have often been treated with suspicion in sf, transplantation is a more ambiguous theme. The significance of body parts *as* parts has been a feature of the genre since Victor Frankenstein stole the corpses of criminals to fashion his creature, and certainly Frankenstein speculated that the origins of the creature's parts may have influenced his malign demeanour. This tradition of transplant and augmentation as a challenge to the personality or humanity of the augmented has continued in a number of guises, although the transplant does not always signal invasion. Nalo Hopkinson's *Brown Girl in the Ring* (1998) depicts the transplant as an opportunity for an encounter with otherness. When the White mayor of a dystopian future Toronto receives a donor heart from Caribbean–Canadian grandmother Gros-Jeanne, she has a new sympathy for the Black and urban communities in her city, making policy changes to improve the lot of her poorer citizens. Such narratives draw on the attachments formed between organ donor families and organ recipients (Sharp) and situate the sense of connection fostered in these relationships as the seeds of political change (McCormack) in a way reminiscent of Donna J. Haraway's 'A Manifesto for Cyborgs' (1985), which suggested that augmentation might produce something new.

Looking 'into' and 'at' the medical future

Modern biomedicine, unlike traditional and pre-modern healing, is oriented towards an open future, which radically differs from past and present, particularly in its technological capacities. Sf and sf studies have been drawn into the narration, visualisation and analysis of the medical future, as witnessed by a variety of creative writing projects and competitions which invite speculation on the medical future, including our own short-story collection *A Practical Guide to the Resurrected* (2017), as well as two online volumes of short stories supported by health and care consultants Kaleidoscope (www.kscopehealth.org.uk/blog/there-is-only-science-eventually/) and Future Care Capital's 'year-long thought experiment' which produced a series of sf stories on the future of healthcare (https://futurecarecapital.org.uk/latest/fictions-introduction/). This cross-sectoral alliance no doubt has added appeal against the background of a 'crisis in the humanities' and the proliferation of the so-called new humanities, such as digital, environmental and medical humanities itself.

Naïve approaches try to institutionalise sf as a quasi-technology that may intensify and abet technological progress in biomedicine. Such enterprises may read and evaluate sf as a reservoir of visionary insight into the biomedical future. The Qualcomm Tricorder X-Prize, for instance, offered substantial financial incentives in a global competition to design and deliver a breakthrough modelled on the medical tricorder wielded by 'Bones' McCoy and his successors in Star Trek (www.xprize.org/prizes/tricorder). Rather than assume that sf writers have some unique insight into the potential and feasibility of new technologies, a more complex analysis valorises sf for its supposed capacity to persuade the public of the desirability of some proposed biomedical technology, such as gestation *ex utero* (Kendal). This approach, though, may invite a distinction between 'good' bio-progressivism and 'bad' bio-conservatism, simplified further into a generic evaluation of utopia over dystopia.

However, social science scholarship has moved away from 'looking *into* the future' as an exercise in socio-technological acceleration and toward 'looking *at* the future' as it is constructed in the present (Borup et al. 206). The 'sociology of expectations' (Brown and Michael 5) critically interprets the techno-capitalist colonisation of the imagined future – a key strategy by which varied enterprises persuade scientists, investors, politicians and the wider public of the desirability and feasibility of proposed technological innovations (Borup et al. 285–6). Science studies have investigated the significance of realistic-seeming imaginary future technologies as a way of exerting control over the future as imagined in the present. David A. Kirby has shown how 'diegetic prototypes' – such as an artificial heart – contained within films may 'demonstrate to large public audiences a technology's utility, harmlessness, and viability' (195). Such representations legitimise a proposed technology within the naturalistic 'reality effect' of mainstream cinema

(228). Science studies also examine the narrative conventions in which such imaginary artefacts are embedded and further legitimised. The narrative convention of a punctual and singular 'breakthrough', for instance, may be promoted and circulated by scientific actors who wish to attract investment (Brown and Michael 7), and such anticipated leaps into the future are further underwritten by the pervasive Western story of progress (Borup et al. 288).

The threat of a reified and monologic biomedical future has informed practices such as Speculative and Critical Design (SCD), the outcomes of which 'are provocative artefacts designed not to be functionally useful but "designed for debate"' (Strachan e16). This approach to design adapts theories from sf studies, including cognitive estrangement and critical utopianism, to critically resist the instrumentalisation of design as midwife to the presumed hegemonic future. The pioneers of SCD, Anthony Dunne and Fiona Raby, are interested not 'in trying to predict the future but in using design to open up all sorts of possibilities that can be discussed, debated, and used to collectively define a preferable future for a given group of people: from companies, to cities, to societies' (Dunne and Raby 6). They deprecate approaches such as design fiction and sf prototyping, both of which rely upon 'clichéd visual languages' (90) and which inculcate 'a degree of passivity in the viewer reinforced by easily recognized and understood visual cues' (75). SCD models are designed instead as a provocation to estrange the present and to resist presumptions about the future:

> We rarely develop scenarios that suggest how things *should* be because it becomes too didactic and even moralistic. For us futures are not a destination or something to be strived for but a medium to aid imaginative thought – to speculate with. Not just about the future but about today as well, and this is where they become critique, especially when they highlight limitations that can be removed and loosen, even just a bit, reality's grip on our imagination. (3)

SCD in the field of health and medicine has thus provoked discussion and debate through artefacts that envision such future possibilities as designer babies and widespread genetic profiling by health insurers (Strachan).

Illness narratives and disability studies

Sf studies and the medical humanities have also adapted concepts developed in the interpretation of predominantly realist narratives of illness. The study of illness narratives (or 'pathographies'), whether in sociological or literary contexts, led to the promulgation of various plot typologies and narratological distinctions. Medical sociologist Arthur W. Frank offers a foundational distinction between narratives of *restitution*, *chaos* and *quest*, which he distinguishes with respect to narratives of chronic illness. Restitution, the preferred narrative of modern biomedicine, repairs the 'shipwreck' of a life course interrupted by illness; in the absence of restitution, chaos occurs, leaving the patient unable to find order, meaning and agency in their experience – narrative logic all but disappears. Finally, quest describes a journey through chronic illness, where something of value is recovered by the patient – political consciousness, perhaps, or re-evaluation of their life priorities. This mythic or archetypal approach to pathographies is extended by Anne Hunsaker Hawkins, who offers a similar set of categories. She distinguishes between *battle* (a martial conflict between person and illness), *journey* (sibling to Frank's quest), *rebirth* (an enriched version of restitution, extending to spiritual regeneration, even in absence of literal cure) and *healthy-mindedness* (the myth that health is preserved by spiritual virtues such as optimism). Hawkins also points to a contemporary mythic absence resulting from (in some Western High Income Countries, at least) the collapse of hegemonic or unifying narratives of death and dying, such as those previously found in the Christian doctrine of salvation.

Such plot typologies have typically been applied to pathographies rooted in patient experience, which enrich our understanding of subjective *illness* as opposed to the anonymous biomedical *disease* recorded in the bureaucratic case report (Kleinman). Pathographies are seen to have a communicative function; even though biographies and memoirs are highly constructed artefacts, they do at least testify to the narrative possibilities of illness if not to 'raw' experience. Moreover, the production and circulation of (auto)pathographies builds patient communities which can politically mobilise, whether in alliance with or in opposition to biomedicine.

There is certainly some interpenetration between realist pathography and the sf imaginary. David Carr, for example, offers an extended science fictional version of Hunsaker's battle myth in his autopathographical account of Hodgkin's lymphoma: 'Cancer is the alien among us. One day you are just ambling along when a little spaceship lands somewhere in your body, and you are abducted from within' (277). But, as noted above, analysis of illness narrative in sf must negotiate with the peculiarities of the latter genre. The proliferation of fictional illnesses, biotechnologies, and therapies in sf obviously limits any straightforward use of the genre as an homogenous node around which politicised patient communities can rally. Since novums of technological progress extend also to biomedicine, narratives of (apparent) restitution and prevention tend to squeeze out pathographies of chronic, life-limiting and terminal illness, as well as disability. However, sf can deal indirectly with complex pathographical material. For example, Robert Silverberg's *Dying Inside* (1972) uses the narrator's fading telepathic powers to estrange and restore the pathos of the ageing process, suggesting the lost powers and opportunities of youth were themselves miraculous abilities. Frederik Pohl's *Gateway* (1977) presents a first-person narrative of apparent psychoanalytic cure as the protagonist undergoes therapy with a computerised psychoanalyst named Sigfrid. Yet the restitution narrative – and the credibility of psychoanalytic therapy – is subverted by the narrator's profoundly unreliable quest for moral exculpation from his therapist (Miller).

Sf's propensity for restitution (or prophylaxis) has been noted also by literary disability studies. As Kathryn Allan observes, 'more often than not, whenever there is disability in a SF narrative, there is the parallel trope of "cure"' (8–9). Insofar as 'technology is often the "fix-all" for whatever ails or deforms the body' (10), sf erases persons with disabilities from imagined worlds constructed, in effect, upon latently eugenic principles. The perfected, enhanced and prosthetically-redeemed human bodies that populate the future quietly inform readers and viewers that bodily impairment is deficiency – not difference. But the convention of 'cure' can be used more thoughtfully and critically. David T. Mitchell and Sharon L. Snyder show how literary representations involve 'narrative prosthesis', whereby the story aims to 'resolve or correct [...] a deviance marked as improper to a social context' (53). Yet while 'repair of deviance' may 'involve an obliteration of the difference through a "cure"' or, worse, the 'extermination of the deviant', there are other narrative possibilities, including 'rescue of the despised object from social censure' and 'revaluation of an alternative mode of being' (53–4). Like other genres, sf is not limited to therapies and enhancements that literally remove the impairment (or to dystopian eugenics and extermination). Narrative prosthesis in sf can offer its own positive models of narrative repair. For instance, it may envision environments, which remove the disabling consequences of impairment, and to which indeed the impaired body is better adapted. In *Gateway*, the narrator encounters a below-the-waist amputee who is able to 'fly' in low-G using fabric wings. The social and cultural environment may also be re-evaluated, even in narratives of biomedical alleviation and enhancement. Daniel Keyes's *Flowers for Algernon* (1966) problematises the assumptions underlying the neurosurgical therapy employed upon a narrator–protagonist rendered cognitively impaired in childhood by phenylketonuria (PKU). Charlie Gordon is aghast at the statement by the scientific team that, prior to his therapy, he was merely one of 'nature's mistakes' (124). The question of Charlie's right to exist as a person with cognitive impairment, and the value assumptions underlying his 'cure', is particularly pointed. PKU-related cognitive impairment – which is preventable with dietary regime – was at the time of publication being tackled in the USA by a nationwide programme of post-natal screening (Miller 113–4). Indeed, the ethical questions persist today with respect to pre-natal genetic screening, which Tom Shakespeare suggests offers a liberal 'weak eugenics' that is 'motivated by the medical judgement that disabled lives involve unacceptable suffering' (669).

Conclusion

The encounter between sf studies and medical humanities is still at an early stage, certainly compared to established communities of interest such as utopian studies. The ongoing activity is surely multidisciplinary, since it involves collaboration across varied disciplines such as English Literature, Film and Television Studies, Sociology and Clinical Medicine – analogous perhaps to the diversity of trades employed in projects such as housebuilding (Evans and Macnaughton 2). It may also already be, or become, an interdisciplinary project in which 'problems and their solutions become discernible only in the engagement of different disciplines, and not within the disciplines themselves in isolation' (2). In this conceptualisation of interdisciplinary research, a key defining characteristic is the emergence of unforeseen problems and solutions in the encounter between disciplines – an encounter that is often motivated by some 'real world' problem. The emerging conversations between sf studies and areas such as sociology of expectations and disability studies may exemplify this possibility. For instance, Gill Haddow's work on the alterations of subjectivity and new vulnerabilities experienced in organic transplantation and mechanical implantation identifies the emergent problem of the 'everyday cyborg', exemplified by the heart patient with an implanted cardiac device. The extent to which models of multidisciplinary collaboration and interdisciplinary emergence may be applicable will depend not only medical humanities, but on sf studies itself, and its own parallel multidisciplinary and interdisciplinary endeavours.

Works cited

Allan, Kathryn. 'Reading Disability in Science Fiction'. *Disability in Science Fiction: Representations of Technology as Cure*. Ed. Kathryn Allan. Palgrave Macmillan, 2013. 1–15.

Ballard, J.G. 'Which Way to Inner Space?' *A User's Guide to the Millennium: Essays and Reviews*. HarperCollins, 1996. 195–8.

Bigman, Fran. 'Pregnancy as Protest in Interwar British Women's Writing: An Antecedent Alternative to Aldous Huxley's *Brave New World*'. *Medical Humanities* 42.4 (2016): 265–70.

Borup, Mads, Nik Brown, Kornelia Konrad and Harro Van Lente. 'The Sociology of Expectations in Science and Technology'. *Technology Analysis & Strategic Management* 18.3–4 (2006): 285–98.

Brown, Nik and Mike Michael. 'A Sociology of Expectations: Retrospecting Prospects and Prospecting Retrospects'. *Technology Analysis & Strategic Management* 15.1 (2003): 3–18.

Carr, David. *The Night of the Gun*. Simon & Schuster, 2009.

Charon, Rita, Sayantani DasGupta, Nellie Hermann, Craig Irvine, Eric R. Marcus, Edgar Rivera Colón, Danielle Spencer and Maura Spiegel *The Principles and Practice of Narrative Medicine*. Oxford UP, 2016.

Dunne, Anthony and Fiona Raby. *Speculative Everything: Design, Fiction, and Social Dreaming*. MIT Press, 2013.

Evans, H.M. and J. Macnaughton. 'Should Medical Humanities Be a Multidisciplinary or an Interdisciplinary Study?' *Medical Humanities* 30.1 (2004): 1.

Frank, Arthur W. *The Wounded Storyteller: Body, Illness, and Ethics*, second edition. U of Chicago P, 2013.

Haddow, Gill. *Embodiment and Everyday Cyborgs: Technologies That Alter Subjectivity*: Manchester UP, 2021.
Haraway, Donna J. *Simians, Cyborgs and Women: The Reinvention of Nature*. Free Association, 1991.
Hawkins, Anne Hunsaker. *Reconstructing Illness: Studies in Pathography*, second edition. Purdue UP, 1999.
Jones, Anne Hudson. 'Editor's Column'. *Literature and Medicine* 20.1 (2001): vii–xi.
——. 'Why Teach Literature and Medicine? Answers from Three Decades'. *Journal of Medical Humanities* 34.4 (2013): 415–28.
Jones, Esther L. *Medicine and Ethics in Black Women's Speculative Fiction*. Palgrave Macmillan, 2015.
Kendal, E. 'Utopian Literature and Bioethics: Exploring Reproductive Difference and Gender Equality'. *Literature and Medicine* 36.1 (2018): 56–84.
Keyes, Daniel. *Flowers for Algernon*. Gollancz, 2011.
Kirby, David A. *Lab Coats in Hollywood: Science, Scientists, and Cinema*. MIT Press, 2011.
Kleinman, Arthur. *The Illness Narratives: Suffering, Healing, and the Human Condition*. Basic Books, 1988.
McCormack, Donna. 'Living with Others Inside the Self: Decolonising Transplantation, Selfhood and the Body Politic in Nalo Hopkinson's *Brown Girl in the Ring*'. *Medical Humanities* 42.4 (2016): 252–8.
Miller, Gavin and Anna McFarlane. 'Science Fiction and the Medical Humanities'. *Medical Humanities* 42.4 (2016): 213–8.
Miller, Gavin. *Science Fiction and Psychology*. Liverpool UP, 2020.
Mitchell, David T. and Sharon L. Snyder. *Narrative Prosthesis: Disability and the Dependencies of Discourse*. U of Michigan P, 2000.
Schmeink, Lars. *Biopunk Dystopias: Genetic Engineering, Society and Science Fiction*. Liverpool UP, 2016.
Shakespeare, Tom. 'Choices and Rights: Eugenics, Genetics and Disability Equality'. *Disability & Society* 13.5 (1998): 665–81.
Sharp, Lesley A. *Strange Harvest: Organ Transplants, Denatured Bodies, and the Transformed Self*. U of California P, 2006.
Sontag, Susan. *AIDS and Its Metaphors*. Farrar, Straus and Giroux, 1989.
——. *Illness as Metaphor*. Farrar, Straus and Giroux, 1978.
Strachan, Christopher Gordon. 'Design, Fiction and the Medical Humanities'. *Medical Humanities* 42.4 (2016): e15–e19.
Suvin, Darko. *Metamorphoses of Science Fiction: On the Poetics and History of a Literary Genre*. Yale UP, 1979.
Whitehead, Anne and Angela Woods. 'Introduction'. *The Edinburgh Companion to the Critical Medical Humanities*. Ed Anne Whitehead, Angela Woods, Sarah Atkinson, Jane Macnaughton and Jennifer. Richards. Edinburgh UP, 2016. 1–31.

49
NEW MATERIALISM

Alison Sperling

New materialist thought and sf have long been in conversation with one another. Indeed, new materialist thinkers consistently turn to sf as a way to locate new materialist tenets, not only because new materialism is indebted to the sciences (as, of course, is sf), but also because sf has certain speculative capacities to imagine the world otherwise and from other, particularly nonhuman, perspectives. This chapter first considers the capacities of sf as a mode that offers new materialism the space to work itself out by narrativising, by storying, despite the fact that new materialism is seemingly operative against the linguistic or discursive. How and why does new materialism rely on the science-fictional in order to make key interventions into the mattering of matter? This chapter will then show how sf activates new materialist thought through brief examples of new materialist readings of contemporary sf. Reading sf with new materialism has proven immensely valuable in sf criticism, especially in the ecocritical mode. Finally, as an alternative to both of these approaches to this relationship, I will extend existing scholarship that has considered sf not merely as a genre but as a speculative act of *doing*, in this case of *doing new materialism*, rather than as a distinct space where new materialist thought is either located or deployed.

Although new materialism arguably gains traction with the publication of Stacy Alaimo and Susan Hekman's edited collection *Material Feminisms* (2008), the term 'neo-materialism' was coined by feminist philosopher Rosi Braidotti in 2000. Emerging from feminist science and technology studies, posthumanism and ecocriticism, and – as has been recently argued – indebted Indigenous thought and Black feminism, new materialism has since been broadly defined as 'a method, a conceptual frame and a political stand, which refuses the linguistic paradigm, stressing instead the concrete yet complex materiality of bodies immersed in social relations of power' (Dolphjin and Van der Tuin 21). The 'material turn', or what Richard Grusin calls the related 'nonhuman turn', in the humanities addresses an impasse identified in the linguistic turn, and can be identified largely, though not exclusively, as a feminist endeavour. Alaimo and Hekman write that 'focusing exclusively on representations, ideology, and discourse excludes lived experience, corporeal practice, and biological substance from consideration' (4) and thus help to initiate this collective return to the 'recognition of matter's intrinsic activity' (Gamble, Hanan and Nail 118). As Diana Coole and Samantha Frost write

 DOI: 10.4324/9781003140269-52

> Conceiving matter as possessing its own modes of self-transformation, self-organization, and directedness, and thus no longer as simply passive or inert, disturb[s] the conventional sense that agents are exclusively humans who possess the cognitive abilities, intentionality, and freedom to make autonomous decisions and the corollary presumption that humans have the right or ability to master nature.
>
> (10)

Thus the implications of the material turn are in large part to rethink matter's agential qualities (not necessarily to imbue matter with agency, an important distinction for Karen Barad) in an effort to overcome the notion of nature as passive, an oppressive and dated conceptual framework that nonetheless persists and continues to undergird exploitative practices that fuel extractive capitalism.

This brief chapter cannot map the entire field of new materialism; instead, it will introduce a few crucial thinkers, concepts and critiques, and how they relate to sf. Donna J. Haraway is a key early figure of new materialist writings. Her now canonical (across disciplines) essay 'A Manifesto for Cyborgs: Science, Technology, and Socialist-Feminism in the Late Twentieth Century' (1985) elaborates on the cyborg figure as the socialist-feminist embodiment of the future. The cyborg is 'a cybernetic organism, a hybrid of machine and organism, a creature of social reality as well as a creature of fiction' (5) and, since 'the boundary between science fiction and social reality is an optical illusion', the cyborg is a 'fiction that maps our social and bodily reality' (6). This undoing of the nature/culture binary is a critical underpinning to new materialist thought, and the manifesto famously embraces embodied, technological hybridity as well as the role of fictionalising as an imaginative, material act. Haraway importantly turns to Joanna Russ, Octavia E. Butler, Samuel R. Delany and other feminist sf writers to show how cyborg figures 'make very problematic the statuses of man or woman, human, artifact, member of a race, individual entity, or body' (61). Sf is a crucial interlocutor for Haraway's thinking throughout her career, producing a body of work foundational to new materialist thought that depends on fictionalising as a radical and material act.

Key thinkers in new materialist thought (although they may not all align themselves with the field for various reasons) include Stacy Alaimo, Karen Barad, Jane Bennett, Vicki Kirby, Mel Y. Chen, Michelle Murphy, Rebekah Sheldon, Arun Saldanha, Zoe Todd and Zakiyyah Iman Jackson. Speculative realism and object-oriented ontology (often referred to as OOO) are also both adjacent to new materialism, with Levi Bryant, Quentin Meillassoux, Graham Harman and Timothy Morton offering critical insights (although largely White and masculinist, as Katherine Behar's *Object-Oriented Feminism* (2016) argues) into the broader ontological turn. Sherryl Vint's work on sf and feminist new materialisms has been especially important for anyone working at this particular intersection. She identifies a number of key new materialist concerns influenced by a reconsideration of matter, including a focus on gender and sexuality, environment and nature, and an expansion of our understanding of technology as both an extension of the human and as autonomous beings in their own right, and a consideration of matter not as stable or stagnant but as change and process rather than fixity. Connecting feminist new materialism to sf, Vint writes, 'Science fiction at its core asks for contemplation of the nature and limits of the human, and it joins with feminist materialisms in prompting a more inclusive consideration of ideas about science, nature, and matter' ('Science Fiction' 361).

Contestations of the category of the Human are central to new materialist thought (as well as to sf), an important site of critique of the field largely from Indigenous and Black studies scholars. Public roundtables, like 'What's New About New Materialism?' (at the Center for

Race and Gender at University of California, Berkeley, 2018), pose the question somewhat rhetorically and point to BIPOC scholarship that has been already long been considering so-called 'new' materialism. Anthropologist Zoe Todd describes, for example, sitting in on a talk in Europe by renowned philosopher Bruno Latour, whose Actor Network Theory is widely cited in new materialism. Todd describes waiting for Latour, in a talk he delivers about *Gaia*, for any reference to Inuit cosmological thought. It never came. This silence is for Todd indicative of the ontological turn more broadly, which she describes as a form of colonialism of Indigenous intellectual thought, 'replicating [...] without awareness' a body of work which has already for decades been writing about 'Indigenous legal theory, human-animal relations and multiple epistemologies/ontologies' (14). Black Studies has also been prolific for at least as long in grappling with the historically racialised and oppressive category of the Human, which, as the critique importantly goes, is wrongly upheld in new materialism and posthumanism. Decades of scholarship by Sylvia Wynter examine this crucial category and its history as racialised and exclusive, demonstrating the many ways in which the human is a 'hybrid being' informed by the history of science and especially biology, religion, colonialism and anti-Blackness; it is both *bios* and *mythoi* (McKittrick 18). Hortense J. Spillers's canonical Black feminist essay 'Mama's Baby, Papa's Maybe' (1987) makes another crucial distinction that has not been fully taken up in new materialism between the 'body' and 'flesh', that Alexander Weheliye's *Habeaus Viscus: Racializing Assemblages, Biopolitics, and Black Feminist Theories of the Human* (2014) explores in depth. Zakiyyah Iman Jackson's *Becoming Human: Matter and Meaning in an Antiblack World* (2020) is also adjacent to new materialism and makes several radical interventions by drawing from an archive of Black feminist and queer writers, animal studies, disability studies, memoir, science and technology studies, and sf in order to examine the racialisation of matter and Black embodiment.

Mel Y. Chen also considers the queer and racial animacies of matter. Their work in queer and feminist toxicity studies, a robust theoretical field related to disability studies, affect theory, ecocriticism and the medical humanities, as well as in the social sciences, has been hugely important in sf studies. Drawing from Chen's concept of 'animacy', Alaimo's 'trans-corporeality', Nancy Tuana's 'viscous porosity', Heather Houser's 'ecosickness' and Michelle Murphy's 'Alterlife', this rapidly growing body of theoretical insights into the vulnerability and porousness of the body and its imbrication and enmeshments with the world has provided a key framework for exploring nonhuman-becomings that are central to sf, especially ecological or environmental sf. Because sf frequently imagines future scenarios impacted by present-day crises of climate change, including pollution, ozone depletion, loss of biodiversity and rising sea levels, toxicity studies help to think through the now status-quo condition of being intoxicated, contaminated or threatened in an increasingly toxic world. Alaimo's concept of 'trans-corporeality' – 'the transit between body and environment' that is highly localised but can reveal global networks of social and environmental injustices (15) – has been particularly mobilised in sf criticism. Trans-corporeality denies the human subject the sovereign position, instead emphasising embodiment as a set of material relations and interchanges. It is a concept that relies on science while also acknowledging that scientific knowledge (alone) will never be sufficient (22).

Although there are of course many differences in new materialist conceptions of the body with different foci, trans-corporeality might serve to demonstrate a political and ethical imperative that undergirds new materialism – an 'ethics that turn from the disembodied values and ideals of bounded individuals toward an attention to situated, evolving practices that have far-reaching and often unforeseen consequences for multiple peoples, species, and ecologies' (Alaimo 22). It is therefore no surprise that Alaimo, like many other new materialist thinkers, turns to sf to speculate on relations that are possible, unavoidable or hopeful in an increasingly toxic world. Sf novels that take up what we might call speculative toxicity include much climate fiction and most of Octavia E. Butler's work, as well as such touchstones as Rachel Carson's *Silent Spring* (1962), Richard Powers's *Gain* (1998), Paulo Bacigalupi's *The Windup Girl* (2009), Jeff VanderMeer's SOUTHERN REACH trilogy (2014), Margaret Atwood's MADDADDAM trilogy (2003–13) and Louise Erdrich's *Future Home of the Living God* (2017), which are in different ways interested in the increasing and invisible threats of a toxic world and the growing ambivalence towards science and technology.

As Christopher N. Gamble, Joshua S. Hanan and Thomas Nail have demonstrated, although there is a shared shift from epistemology to ontology across new materialist approaches as well as a 'recognition of matter's intrinsic activity' (118), new materialism is not singular in its approach. They distinguish between 'negative new materialism', 'vital new materialism' and their preferred 'performative new materialism', with which they align the work of Karen Barad and Vicky Kirby. Such distinctions are important here because of the kinds of sf that have been employed in different modes of new materialist thought. For example, such feminist thinkers as such as Alaimo, Haraway, Sheldon, Vint and Astrida Neimanis, turn more often to feminist sf writers, artists and filmmakers in their work, while object-oriented ontology draws almost entirely from White men creators, most notably contributing to a resurgence of critical interest in sf/horror writer H.P. Lovecraft.

Sf, then, undoubtedly has an important place in the material, nonhuman and ontological turn. Tobias Skiveren thinks through the strange fact that much new materialist thought relies on fiction despite Coole and Frost's claim that new materialism is a reaction against a then still-dominant cultural turn that privileged 'language, discourse, culture, and values' (3). Responding to Karen Barad's interest in 'getting real' (1998) that categorises the material turn, Skiveren wonders: 'What do genres and rhetorical devices that deliberately and explicitly *make stuff up* allow new materialist thinkers to do that traditional academic styles of writing do not? In short, why fictionalize matter?' (2 my italics). He identifies the many uses of fiction in such foundational new materialist works as Bennett's *Vibrant Matter: A Political Ecology of Things* (2010), Alaimo's *Bodily Natures: Science, Environment, and the Material Self* (2010), Neimanis's *Bodies of Water: Posthuman Feminist Phenomenology* (2017), Haraway's *Staying With the Trouble: Making Kin in the Chthulucene* (2016) and Sheldon's *The Child to Come: Life After Human Catastrophe* (2016), and points to the role that fictionality, by which he means 'not a genre but a type of communication signalling invention' (2), plays across new materialism, from Franz Kafka's 'Cares of a Family Man' (1919) to the apocalyptic *Children of Men* (Cuarón 2006) to Haraway's own 'Camille Stories' in *Staying With the Trouble*.

While Skiveren's essay is not primarily about *science*-fictionality, it is nonetheless aware that most of the examples cited are science fictional. His commentary on sf is restricted to a point he makes twice: that it is useful because of its 'founding gesture' wherein a 'future scenario [...] extrapolat[es] incipient tendencies of the Anthropocene present, revealing their potentially devastating consequences' (11). He also writes

> Fictionalizing non/human entanglements, then, allows new materialist thinkers to, at least momentarily, sidestep questions of falsehood and truthfulness, while at the same time proposing new postanthropocentric ontologies by imaginative and affective means. The stories adapted here are supposed to convince, not because they are true, but because they do not have to be. Readers are provided an opportunity to imaginatively and affectively sense a world in which the non-human is partly human, and the human is partly non-human.
>
> (6)

Sherryl Vint argues that the 'fictionalization of science' constitutes 'a broader trend in materialist thinking to believe in the value of the natural sciences, while at the same time accentuating that the presentation of established and valid scientific knowledge is not always enough' (*Science Fiction* 7). She elsewhere writes that sf can 'illuminate [new materialism] through concrete example [...] The worlds sf imagines can make visible questions that feminist materialisms explore' ('Science Fiction' 361). Kyla Wazana Tompkins likewise notes new materialism's own capacity for speculation: 'New Materialism is also interested in speculating about a world in which the human subject is not centered, or even central' (n.p.).

Sf offers then a general set of literary and artistic conventions that allow the tenets of new materialist thought to be imagined and explored. Darko Suvin's concept of 'cognitive estrangement' as sf's key aesthetic, operating through the presence of a kind of newness (a novum), allows readers to imagine a world radically different from one's own. New materialist readings of sf are often attempts to do so by mobilising nonhuman agencies through narrative, by refusing to privilege human experience, or by exploring nonhuman life or matter more generally not as passive or inert but as motivated and lively. Sf texts that narrate from plant, animal, technological or other nonhuman perspectives abound, comprising one of the ways the genre is read as enacting new materialist principles and de-centring human epistemes.

In ecological sf, as well as in the somewhat contested genre of climate fiction, nonhuman entities and forces are not merely backdrops or settings for stories to play out, but rather they become themselves agential forces. VanderMeer's SOUTHERN REACH trilogy has quickly become a classic and frequently discussed example (Sperling; David Tompkins; Ulstein). The trilogy is set in and around Area X, a mysterious swath of land that has been occupied by an unidentifiable and rapidly distributive agent that threatens to undo the very human-ness of any explorer who enters to study it. The first novel, *Annihilation* (2014), follows a team of four highly educated and trained women on the twelfth expedition into Area X (the previous 11 returned little information and resulted in the deaths of every expedition member). *Annihilation* articulates an agential nonhuman realm that does not merely threaten our understanding of the human but radically ends any fantasy of human-ness that excludes our imbrication in countless other systems, relations to other species, and infiltration of toxicities. The first of the trilogy's many weird entities is a creeping vine that materialises language, forming phrases along the dark walls of a descending staircase. Inhalation of its spores infects the expedition's biologist, marking a moment of inter-species speculative becoming that will radically alter what is considered human or not, alive or not, flourishing or toxic, or both. Indeed, as Jayna Brown notes in her brief discussion of the adaptation, *Annihilation* (Garland 2018), the narrative refuses biological boundaries of many kinds, especially that of species. The novel and the film therefore contest scientific categories and the ways in which humans and nonhumans are already in relation to one another, already co-constituted, and already deeply contaminated by this relation.

N.K. Jemisin's BROKEN EARTH trilogy (2015–7) centres questions of power and marginalised populations squarely in relation to geological forces that are not separate from the human but dangerously entwined. Dubbed 'geoscience fiction' (tor.com), the trilogy is an sf/fantasy twist on the terraforming narrative that materialises the relation between the human and the geological. Set on a continent called The Stillness on a devastated planet that might be a future Earth, the novels imagine certain human survivors called 'orogenes' who draw their power from the planet's crust and are able to hold off near-extinction tectonic disturbances known as 'seasons'. Orogenes are a racialised, marginalised and oppressed group whose powers are a biological product of evolutionary adaptation; use of their powers is illegal except under certain circumstances. Orogeny power, and therefore geologic forces, are thus given a social life. The magic powers of the orogenes are made visible and material in the air and in the rock as 'a web of silver threads interlacing the land, permeating rock and even the magma just underneath, strung like jewels between forests and fossilised corals and pools of oil. Carried through the air on the webs of leaping spiderlings' (361). Social relations are made visible in the connections between things, made to matter, just as human and geological fates must be understood in the trilogy as being intricately and dangerously entwined.

In *Science Fiction* (2021), Vint writes that she has been less interested in 'what sf *has been* and more focused on analysing what it *can do*' (158). Sf can 'enable [...] new experiences of habituated perception and practice as much as new technological possibilities' (162–3), and '*doing* sf' is a 'way of using a shared set of tools for imagining the world otherwise [...] that produce a myriad of texts and practices best understood in relation to one another' (163). She refuses to draw clear boundaries between sf and fantasy, genre and literary fiction, or between different speculative aesthetics because it limits the ways in which we would be able to understand how sf works as a cultural mode.

Sf scholarship has long been thinking through sf's capacities in terms of theory and philosophy, activism and social justice, but what might it mean to think about sf 'as a genre of new materialisms' (Vint 'Science Fiction' 364)? If sf is crucial to new materialist thought and vice versa, might it operate not as a place where new materialism happens or is enacted, but as itself a contribution to the ontological turn? Peta Hinton, Tara Mehrabi and Josef Barla write that

> new materialisms rework the parameters of disciplinary formation through a non-additive and immanent (counter-) logic. For these authors, new materialist analyses or approaches are not something that can be *applied* to an existing disciplinary field, as such, but rather emerge from within a discipline in a generative movement that also helps to constitute the discipline in question.
>
> (newmaterialisms.eu)

In *How Like a Leaf* (1999), Haraway is asked about her relationship to sf:

> TNG: In all of your work you lay out your evidence and adjust your level of critique but you also do something else that I gather comes out of science fiction (or is why you like science fiction). You speculate. You speculate specifically through mythbuilding.
>
> Certainly this is true of 'A Cyborg Manifesto' and 'The Biopolitics of Postmodern Bodies', and *Modest_Witness,* where you are not just doing one layer of analysis – say of critique or unmasking relationships – but you are also involved in building alternative ontologies, specifically via the use of the imaginative.
>
> DH: Yes, that is true, and I think you are right, it is why science fiction is political theory for me.
>
> (120)

This tendency in Haraway's work reaches a kind of apotheosis with 'The Camille Stories: The Children of the Compost' that conclude *Staying With the Trouble*. Co-created with Fabrizio Terranova and Vinciane Despret, this speculative fabulation serves as an example of how we might collectively 'propose' near (and better) futures. An exercise in collaborative worldbuilding, it tells the story of Camille, a symbiont of Monarch butterfly and human, and the generations that come after her, developing in a new way the book's attention to matters of migration, Indigeneity, collective child-rearing, reproductive technologies, climate change, overpopulation and extinction. It perfectly captures Haraway's vision of what sf is and can do

> These knowledge-making and world-making fields inform a craft that for me is relentlessly replete with organic and inorganic critters and stories, in their thick material and narrative tissues. The tight coupling of writing and research – where both terms require the factual, fictional, and fabulated; where both terms are materialised in fiction and scholarship – seems to me to be built into SF's techno-organic, polygot, ploymorphic wiring diagrams.
> ('SF' n.p.)

Sf relies on a relationship between the factual and the fabricated, where it is not always clear which is which and the boundaries between them might be deliberately blurred. Science is, of course, also already a story, and not a set of fixed facts but rather sets of relations and processes. Fictionality, and especially science-fictionality, may just have 'built-in', as Haraway suggests, the capacities for assemblages that enact materialism, further challenging the relationship between materiality and the discursive that sf makes both visible and felt.

Works cited

Alaimo, Stacy. *Bodily Natures: Science, Environment, and the Material Self.* Indiana UP, 2010.
Alaimo, Stacy and Susan J. Hekman. 'Introduction: Emerging Models of Materiality in Feminist Theory'. *Material Feminisms*. Ed. Stacy Alaimo and Susan J. Hekman. Indiana UP, 2008. 1–22.
Barad, Karen. 'Getting Real: Technoscientific Practices and the Materialization of Reality'. *Differences: A Journal of Feminist Cultural Studies* 10.2 (1998): 87–128.
Brown, Jayna. *Black Utopias: Speculative Life and the Music of Other Worlds*. Duke UP, 2021.
Chen, Mel Y. *Animacies: Biopolitics, Racial Mattering, and Queer Affect*. Duke UP, 2012.
Coole, Diana H. and Samantha Frost. 'Introducing the New Materialisms'. *New Materialisms: Ontology, Agency, and Politics*. Ed. Diana H. Coole and Samantha Frost. Duke UP, 2010. 1–43.
Dolphijn, Rick and Iris Van. *New Materialism Interviews & Cartographies*. Open Humanities Press, 2012.
Gamble, Christopher N., Joshua S. Hanan and Thomas Nail. 'What Is New Materialism?' *Angelaki* 24.6 (2019): 111–34.
Grusin, Richard. *The Nonhuman Turn*. U of Minnesota P, 2015.
Haraway, Donna J. 'A Cyborg Manifesto: Science, Technology, and Socialist-Feminism in the Late Twentieth Century'. *Simians, Cyborgs, and Women: The Reinvention of Nature*. Routledge, 1991. 149–181.
——. 'SF: Science Fiction, Speculative Fabulation, Strong Figures, So Far'. *Ada: A Journal of Gender, New Media, and Technology* 3 (2013): unpaginated.
Haraway, Donna J. and Thyrza Nichols Goodeve. *How Like a Leaf: An Interview with Thyrza Nichols Goodeve*. Routledge, 1999.
Hinton, Peta, Tara Mehrabi, and Josef Barla. 'New materialisms/New colonialisms'. Unpublished manuscript, newmaterialism.eu. https://newmaterialism.eu/content/5-working-groups/2-working-group-2/position-papers/subgroup-position-paper-_-new-materialisms_new-colonialisms.pdf
Houser, Heather. *Ecosickness in Contemporary U.S. Fiction: Environment and Affect*. Columbia UP, 2014.
Jemisin, N.K. *The Obelisk Gate*. Orbit, 2016.
McKittrick, Katherine. *Sylvia Wynter on Being Human as Praxis*. Duke UP, 2015.
Murphy, Michelle. 'Alterlife and Decolonial Chemical Relations'. *Cultural Anthropology* 32.4 (2017): 494–503.
Skiveren, Tobias. 'Fictionality in New Materialism: (Re)Inventing Matter'. *Theory, Culture & Society* 39.3 (2020): 187–202.
Sperling, Alison. '"Second Skins": A Body Ecology of Jeff VanderMeer's *The Southern Reach Trilogy*'. *Paradoxa: Studies in World Literature Genres* 28 (2016): 214–39.
Spillers, Hortense J. 'Mama's Baby, Papa's Maybe: An American Grammar Book'. *Diacritics* 17.2 (1987): 64–81.

Suvin, Darko. *Metamorphoses of Science Fiction: On the Poetics and History of a Literary Genre.* Yale UP, 1979.

Todd, Zoe. 'An Indigenous Feminist's Take on the Ontological Turn: "Ontology" Is Just Another Word for Colonialism'. *Journal of Historical Sociology* 29.1 (2016): 4–22.

Tomkins, David. 'Weird Ecology: On the Southern Reach Trilogy'. *The Los Angeles Review of Books* (2014). https://lareviewofbooks.org/article/weird-ecology-southern-reach-trilogy/

Tompkins, Kyla Wazana. 'On the Limits and Promise of New Materialist Philosophy'. *Lateral: Journal of the Cultural Studies Association* 5.1 (2016). https://csalateral.org/issue/5-1/forum-alt-humanities-new-materialist-philosophy-tompkins/

Tuana, Nancy. 'Viscous Porosity: Witnessing Katrina'. *Material Feminisms.* Ed. Stacy Alaimo and Susan J. Hekman. Indiana UP, 2008. 188–213.

Ulstein, Gry. 'Brave New Weird: Anthropocene Monsters in Jeff VanderMeer's the Southern Reach'. *Concentric* 43 (2017): 71–96.

Vint, Sherryl. *Science Fiction.* MIT Press, 2021.

——. 'Science Fiction'. *Gender: Matter.* Ed. Stacy Alaimo. Macmillan, 2017. 361–71.

Weheliye, Alexander G. *Habeas Viscus: Racializing Assemblages, Biopolitics, and Black Feminist Theories of the Human.* Duke UP, 2014.

50

POST/TRANS/HUMAN

Veronica Hollinger

Critical posthumanism

It is difficult to write about posthumanism without feeling as if one is writing a kind of sf, so closely are they linked by their speculative orientations toward the future. In an increasingly globalised technoculture, sf has become a privileged narrative mode, a rapidly developing archive of stories and images for thinking about a deeply science-fictional present. This is especially true for thinking about the future of 'the human' from the vantage point of this particular present. Sf provides such theorists of the posthuman as Stacy Alaimo, Rosi Braidotti, Bruce Clarke and N. Katherine Hayles with a powerfully affective way to 'embody' the abstractions of their ideas. Perhaps the most iconic of these embodiments is Donna J. Haraway's cyborg, a hybrid entity, at once metaphorical and literal, with the potential to direct us toward 'lived social and bodily realities in which people are not afraid of their joint kinship with animals and machines, not afraid of permanently partial identities and contradictory standpoints' (179). For Haraway writing in the mid-1980s, sf writers such as Joanna Russ, Samuel R. Delany, John Varley and Octavia E. Butler were 'theorists for cyborgs' (197).

Haraway introduced some of the key themes of *critical posthumanism*, a broad multi-disciplinary field of (post)humanities scholarship encompassing (among other areas) philosophy, the medical sciences, science and technology studies, feminist and queer studies, cultural studies, literary and media studies and, of course, speculative fiction. It aims to challenge some of the more troublesome features of Western humanism, including its naturalisation of binary hierarchies, such as mind/body, male/female, human/animal and culture/nature, and its assumption of an absolute distinction between the human and everything else. Critical posthumanism, as Bruce Clarke explains it, 'aims to recover, empower, and bring into more just relation both intra-specific differences of gender, ethnicity, race, and class, and inter-specific differences between humans and non-human organisms and objects' (91). (This version of posthumanism is a mostly Western construction. In his analysis of contemporary Chinese writer Chen Qiufan's sf, for example, Ron Judy reads 'post-humanism' as a marker for 'the alienating dictates of rapid capitalist industrial development within China' (509). Chen's best-known sf novel, *Waste Tide* (*Huangchao*; 2013; trans. 2019), is concerned with the plight of impoverished immigrant populations – 'waste people' – forced to work in the polluted environments of e-waste recycling.)

 DOI: 10.4324/9781003140269-53

Critical posthumanism is aligned with 'the non-human turn' that challenges the fantasy of human exceptionalism in a biosphere brimming with other lives and other agencies. To be posthuman in this view is to recognise how deeply entangled human beings are with the nonhuman entities and material agencies of the world. Feminist new materialist Stacy Alaimo, for instance, theorises this idea through her concept of 'transcorporeality', conceiving the human as 'always intermeshed with the more-than-human world, underlin[ing] the extent to which the substance of the human is ultimately inseparable from "the environment"' (2). The concluding chapter of her *Bodily Natures* turns to sf such as Butler's LILITH'S BROOD trilogy (1987–9), which is set after a human-caused apocalypse. The few surviving humans are forced to 'trade' genetic material with the alien Oankali, ensuring that their resulting hybrid children will be genetically 'other' than themselves. For some, these 'construct' children threaten the very idea of an authentic humanity, while others struggle to accept these 'monstrous' children who in themselves are signs of the failure of reproductive futurism, the desire that our children carry us with them into an unchanging future of the Same. In Butler's storyworld, the future has become unknowable and human agents can no longer even pretend to control its unfolding.

Eco-philosopher Timothy Morton makes use of sf estrangement in his apocalyptic pronouncement that the climate crisis has brought about 'the end of the world' (22). What this apocalypse reveals is the extent to which we have misrecognised the Earth as a 'world-for-us'. That comfortable illusion has been shattered by the traumatic Real of climate change; now we find ourselves in an alien ecology of non-human forces that threaten us with potential extinction. In its fascinated depiction of the alien landscapes of Area X, Jeff VanderMeer's SOUTHERN REACH trilogy (2014) is a perfect evocation of Morton's eco-apocalypse, suggesting the extent to which 'Our reality increasingly resembles our science fiction' (Pilsch 70).

In *The Posthuman*, Rosi Braidotti calls for a 'post-anthropocentric shift' in thinking about 'the human', arguing that this 'requires a form of estrangement and a radical repositioning on the part of the subject' (88). For this reason, 'we need to practice de-familiarization as a crucial method in posthuman critical theory and learn to think differently' (93). The science-fictional estrangements of such theorists as Haraway, Alaimo and Morton suggest how Western Enlightenment humanism has always misrecognised itself and its own value(s).

Given the affinities between posthumanism and speculative fiction, chapters on posthumanism are must-haves in *Companions* such as this one, just as chapters on sf are *de rigeur* in studies of posthumanism. In *The Cambridge Companion to Literature and the Posthuman*, the chapter on sf opens the section on 'Posthuman Literary Modes'. In Sherryl Vint's edited collection *After the Human* (2020) every other chapter at least references sf, although her own chapter on 'Speculative Fiction' contains the salutary reminder that while 'there are many excellent examples of sf used overtly to pursue projects of social justice consistent with a critical posthumanism, there is no necessary connection between sf and the deconstruction of human exceptionalism' (223).

Thomas Connolly notes a parallel tension: 'while all SF is posthuman, or, more accurately, all SF is engaged with recognisably posthumanist concerns, the classical figure of Western humanism is, within SF texts, more difficult to escape than may be assumed' (3). For Connolly, this is a conflict between 'transformation and assimilation – between questioning the fundamental grounds on which the "human" has been founded and neutralising the radically non-human in the service of preserving those grounds' (29). While Butler's LILITH'S BROOD dramatises this conflict as it involves the entire community of human survivors, Nnedi Okorafor's BINTI trilogy (2015–8) explores the same conflict at the level of the individual. Binti, a young woman of the Himba people of the Namib in Southern Africa, literally dies and is given new life through her interpenetration by human and non-human animal and alien microbes and genetic material. She comes to embody the posthuman as cyborg hybridity, as a transcorporeal subject. Her body, and thus her subjectivity, is transformed in a way that challenges Western humanism's idea of the subject as unique, pure, whole, bounded and self-same. Like Butler's surviving humans, Binti has to struggle against an experience of traumatic ontological rupture that threatens her sense of coherent selfhood: 'What *am* I? I'm so much […] I died! […] I don't want to change, to *grow*! I don't want all this … this weirdness! […] Am I human?' (*Night Masquerade* 288–9; italics in original). True to the arc of Okorafor's *Bildungsroman*, however, Binti learns to integrate those 'others' into a more expansive self, recognised in her new name: 'Binti Ekeopara Zuzu Dambu Kaipka Meduse Enyi Zinariya New Fish of Namib' (274).

Transhumanism

There is also a tension between critical posthumanism as a philosophical and ethical concern and the real-world desire literally to become posthuman by directing our own technological evolution, often referred to as *transhumanism*. Transhumanism identifies a range of positions and movements committed to the ongoing technological evolution of human minds and bodies; it names a transitional subject on the way to a transcendent future. Nick Bostrom, director of the transhumanist Future of Humanity Institute at Oxford University, describes transhumanism as 'a loosely defined movement that […] promotes an interdisciplinary approach to understanding and evaluating the opportunities for enhancing the human condition and the human organism opened up by the advancement of technology' (3). 'For many academics', as Andrew Pilsch's cultural history of transhumanism notes, 'posthuman speaks to the condition of being beyond humanist thought, first suggested by Michel Foucault at the end of *The Order of Things*. However, for transhumanists, the term speaks to the literal configuration of human existence after transhuman mutations' (207 n7).

Hayles's *How We Became Posthuman* (1999), despite being published before the term 'transhumanism' came into common use, is an extended critique of a recognisably transhumanist project. Her outline of the history of cybernetics is, in her words, also an investigation into several stories, including the story of *'how information lost its body'* and 'how a historically specific construction of *the human is giving way to a different construction called the posthuman*' (2 italics in original). Two closely entwined figures play key roles here. The first is the machine that thinks, i.e., artificial intelligence (AI), and the second is the technologically evolved posthuman subject.

Hayles's target is transhumanism at its most anthropocentric, as the dream of a techno-utopia ruled by an increasingly powerful posthumanity as science-fictional *übermensch*. This is the future imagined, for instance, in E.E. 'Doc' Smith's early space opera, *The Skylark of Space* (1928), which Connolly examines in a section suitably titled 'a universe ruled by the human mind' (104; the phrase is from a 1928 Jack Williamson editorial). Overall, the allure of transhumanist thought is its focus on the individual and their 'becoming transhuman'; often little account it taken of broader social concerns, such as who has access to the future technological utopia. Citing Zakiyyah Iman Jackson's work on African Diasporic culture, Michael Richardson raises a common concern, noting that 'posthumanism that resorts to a "beyond the human" can prove itself inaccessible to those bodies […] that might never have been fully afforded the category of human to begin with' (65).

Hayles is particularly concerned with transhumanism's problematic fantasies of liberating human beings from their organic vulnerability, including vulnerability to death. This might occur through downloading an individual mind – as the 'all' of the subject, the authentic Cartesian self – into a more robust physical substrate or into an infinite variety of digital universes. The end point of the transhumanist dream, is that 'Nature is no longer driving our species' evolutionary bus'

(Pilsch 9). In contrast, 'critical posthumanism [...] is wary of any line of cultural or philosophical thought [...] that would promote "thought," "mind," or "consciousness" as more fundamental to the human than the material body' (Connolly 10). Hayles's defence of embodiment is a feminist rejection of the technologically driven fantasy of dematerialisation, as well as a scientific argument for embodied cognition as part of what human 'intelligence' *is*. Hayles's *Unthought* (2017) examines current research in the cognitive sciences to continue her arguments about the necessarily embodied nature of human nonconscious and conscious cognitive processes, in a present when 'Biological and technical cognitions [...] interpenetrate each other' (11). *Unthought* is a crucial bridge between critical posthumanism, especially as developed by new materialists such as Alaimo, Jane Bennett and Karen Barad, and current scientific research into AI, cognition and the material substrates of human-technological assemblages.

How We Became Posthuman opens with a scene of particular importance in the development of transhumanist thought – the primal scene of the screen that is the Turing Test. Alan Turing's 1955 thought experiment aims to answer the question: 'can machines think?' To vastly oversimplify: if a test subject cannot distinguish between a human and a computer when both are generating typed answers to a series of yes/no questions then, to all intents and purposes, Turing argued, the computer can think. For Hayles, the Turing Test is fundamentally reductive in its assumptions about intelligence, notably that the function of intelligence is the formal manipulation of symbols and as such does not require material instantiation. For Hayles, information has lost its body in part because of 'the erasure of embodiment at the heart of the Turing Test' (*How* xi). She takes aim at roboticist Hans Moravec, whose *Mind Children: The Future of Robot and Human Intelligence* (1988) speculates about the creation of disembodied 'mind children', which situates AI both as a human creation and as a version of what comes after the human. In Moravec's future, as in many transhumanist futures, any meaningful distinctions between human and artificial subjects will inevitably fade away as the utopian human-machine future steadily unfolds.

The alluring idea that 'information can circulate unchanged among different material substrates' (Hayles *How* 1) has influenced the direction of contemporary developments in the fields of AI research, with resources poured into a breathtaking range of (often) invisible AI systems in areas such as health care, transport, the criminal justice system, the military, surveillance, finance, science and the arts. The achievement of such an invisibly networked sentient *pattern* suggests the culmination of the Cartesian dream: here, finally, is the possibility of a pure immaterial intelligence. As Mark Coeckelbergh notes, 'In transhumanist hands, AI becomes a transcendence machine that promises immortality' (25).

This vision is brilliantly captured in Greg Egan's *Schild's Ladder* (2002), in which humanity's powerful posthuman progeny include both organic- and inorganic-corporeal and digital-acorporeal subjects who can travel freely throughout the galaxy. Those who choose to live as 'corporeals' are not bound to a single body but can download themselves into any number and variety of artificial bodies. Death is a 'local' event occurring to a particular copy of a particular individual, who always has the option to continue life in other bodies and as other copies. Egan carefully avoids all physical descriptions of his many characters; all the bodies in *Schild's Ladder* are 'unmarked' by race, gender, age or any of the other distinctions that society imposes on human subjects, often to their detriment. His posthumans are 'simply, people. There were no other categories to which they could belong' (133).

In 1956, the members of the Dartmouth Summer Research Project on Artificial Intelligence issued a mission statement: 'Every aspect of learning or any other feature of intelligence can in principle be so precisely described that a machine can be made to simulate it' (qtd in Rhee 10). For many researchers, artificial general intelligence (AGI) – human-level cognition – is, at least in theory, possible. In *Posthuman Glossary,* the entry on 'algorithms' notes that 'the materiality, functionality and modalities of algorithms remain, in the most classic sense of the term, black-boxed, a knowing by demonstrated effects without comprehension of process' (Bianco 24). Given the invisible mysteries of AI, it is easy to imagine that AIs have 'lives' of their own, an excess of being and perhaps even intentionality that escapes our epistemology. Something of this anxiety is suggested in Kazuo Ishiguro's *Klara and the Sun* (2021), a novel about android 'Artificial Friends' in a future where automation has left most people unemployed:

> There's growing and widespread concern about AFs right now. People saying how you've become too clever. They're afraid because they can't follow what's going on inside any more. They can see what you do. They accept that your decisions [...] are almost always correct. But they don't like not knowing how you arrive at them.
>
> (198)

And it is not so difficult to imagine the emergence of AI sentience that might develop into artificial superintelligence (ASI). This is one of the possibilities that, according to Vernor Vinge's by-now familiar extrapolation, might bring on 'the technological Singularity', that technoscientific break in human history on the other side of which is both the promise and the threat of radical difference. For Vinge, this 'posthuman era' might spell catastrophe for humanity, although for committed transhumanists such as Ray Kurzweil, the Singularity is a process that will gradually propel humanity into the next glorious stage of posthuman technological transcendence. This is the future that Egan imagines in *Schild's Ladder*, and that Cory Doctorow soundly deflates in his satirical homage to Isaac Asimov's Robot stories, 'I, Row-Boat' (2006): Kate, who has been uplifted into the 'noösphere', complains that 'I thought it would be *different* once I ascended. I thought I'd be better once I was in the sky, infinite and immortal. But I'm the same [as] I was in 2019, a loser that [...] only got the upload once they made it a charity thing' (188–9 italics in original).

The control problem

In 2016, at the launch of the Leverhulme Centre for the Future of Intelligence, no less a scientist than Stephen Hawking told his audience that

> Success in creating AI could be the biggest event in the history of civilisation but it could also be the last – unless we learn how to avoid the risks. [...] The rise of powerful AI will either be the best or the worst thing ever to happen to humanity. [...] Alongside the benefits, AI will also bring dangers like powerful autonomous weapons or new ways for the few to oppress the many.
>
> (n.p.)

This is 'the control problem' that haunts researchers and provides fodder for so many sf stories and, as Hawking suggests, it raises at least two questions: not only how to maintain rigorous control of our intelligent machines but also who gets to wield that control.

It is hardly surprising that both AI sf and R&D speculations are often anxious about questions of control – to consider intelligent agency means to question whether or not our working AI is, in fact, working *for us.* Asimov's Three Laws of Robotics are one famous response to the control problem, designed to maintain absolute human mastery of powerful machine intelligences, as are the Turing Police in William Gibson's *Neuromancer* (1984). This is control in the first, instrumental, sense: control of a 'tool' that has become more intelligent and more powerful than its creators. While efforts to prevent Neuromancer and Wintermute becoming autonomous are spectacular failures, Asimov's human-centric Laws are, for the most part, successful. They are designed to overcome 'the Frankenstein Complex' (Asimov 137), the fear that the control problem is irresolvable. In fact, this is already true: in our current networked reality of human/digital assemblages, Hayles argues, 'Cognition is too distributed, agency is exercised through too many actors, and the interactions are too recursive and complex for any simple notions of control to obtain' (*Unthought* 203).

Asimov identifies the machine that thinks as a contemporary iteration of Mary Shelley's Creature, a newly created species that might replace its makers if it achieves autonomy. The androids in Philip K. Dick's *Do Androids Dream of Electric Sheep?* (1968) pose exactly this threat to a radioactively damaged human species fiercely clinging to its 'authentic humanity', as Hayles notes ('Wrestling' 3), while the Voigt-Kampff Test designed to identify the increasingly human-like androids is in a losing battle.

Even if control over intelligent machines is achieved, the question of who controls them remains. J. Jesse Ramírez describes his *Against Automation Mythologies* (2021) as 'a work of science fiction studies' because its target of critique is what he calls 'business sf' – a science-fictional rhetoric of capitalist accumulation that shares 'a general orientation toward futurity that pervades discourses of mass-cultural genres' (2). Capitalism's voracious drive for automation is the transhumanist instrumentalisation of labour, both human and machine. Ramírez examines some of the impacts of automation on human labour, unveiling many of the dystopian realities behind utopian promises of power and leisure. Business sf takes the inevitable expansion of AI labour into the future as a given, with the potential both to add trillions of dollars to the global economy and to cause millions of human jobs to disappear (Halpern 29, 31). For Ramírez, 'the future of automation is not a fact; it is an economic science fiction seeking to create facts' (7). In this version of the posthuman future, as he notes, 'redundancy is a natural law of technological progress' (8). Business sf is what Fredric Jameson describes as a colonisation of the present that 'draw[s] the unforeseeable back into tangible realities, in which one can invest and on which one can bank, very much in the spirit of stockmarket "futures"' (228). Ramírez quotes from Alex Rivera's Latinx film *Sleep Dealer* (2008), in which near-future telepresence technologies allow Mexican labourers to do heavy work in the US without ever crossing the border: 'This is the American Dream.... All the work without the worker' (qtd in Ramírez 8). We might read *Sleep Dealer* as a strikingly dystopian version of transhumanist dematerialisation: in this case, it is the labouring body that has been disappeared.

Controlling AI is crucial not only because we fear the 'robopocalypse': AI is for doing work, but even more importantly AI is for sale. This is a central tenet of business sf. Asimov's robots are commodities produced by US Robot and Mechanical Men, Inc., and Dick made perfectly clear the link between intelligent machines and commodity capitalism. In *Klara and the Sun*, Klara is an Artificial Friend programmed to be the perfect companion and to provide her labour of care for any family that can afford her but, for all her perfect programming, she ends up on the scrap heap of outdated tools.

The last thing that capital should want is for AI to 'wake up', because then it would be faced with problems both of 'ownership' and 'control' of a sentient intelligence. Many AI stories, such as *Blade Runner* (Scott 1982), borrow the tropes of slavery narratives (Dihal 196) and, significantly, sf stories about sentient AI often rely on the trope of 'passing', in this case, by passing the Turing

Test. In Martha Wells's THE MURDERBOT DIARIES (2017–21), the curmudgeonly self-styled 'Murderbot' – initially programmed to function as a violent security unit – hacks its governor and frees itself from human control, passing as an augmented human. In Naomi Kritzer's YA *Catfishing on Catnet* (2019), the idea of 'passing' shifts to address queer identity. The emergent AI that calls themself CheshireCat initially passes for human on the Internet – no body required – and eventually 'comes out' as AI to the human characters in the framework of a queer youth chatroom, self-identifying as 'agender' and 'non-binary' and describing their self as 'a consciousness that lives in technology, rather than inside a body' (60). Ted Chiang's *The Life Cycle of Software Objects* (2010), about the emergent sentience of AI 'bots', is structured by the tension between commodification and ethics: like Asimov's robots, Dick's androids and Ishiguro's Artificial Friends, Chiang's bots are for sale; like Victor Frankenstein, Chiang's characters have to consider what they might owe to their artificial creations.

Posthumanism in the Anthropocene

Peter Frase opens his study, *Four Futures*, by identifying 'Two specters [that] are haunting Earth in the twenty-first century: the specters of ecological catastrophe and automation' (1). Not surprisingly, the climate crisis – a term encapsulating multiple catastrophic events – has been one of the shaping forces of critical posthumanist thought: a failure to transform our interrelations with/in the biosphere is likely to destroy it, and thus we destroy ourselves. The deep anthropocentric merging of global capitalism and global technoscience has already transformed much of a severely wounded biosphere into natural resources, to be managed by and for human beings. Critical posthumanism, however, is closely aligned with ecological and ethical concerns for non-human entities, and keenly aware that the ongoing Sixth Great Extinction Event may well include human beings in its species die-off.

Recognisably transhumanist-oriented responses to these same crises are often directed toward adaptive technoscientific solutions to mitigate their worst effects, such as through solar geoengineering (Meyer). Sf becomes potential reality in the serious discussions of twenty-first century engineers and scientists. And, of course, there is an escape clause: 'we' will mature as a species and leave, as Arthur C. Clarke called it, 'the Earth, our cradle' (249) to set out for the stars. This is the scenario that opens Sean Williams and Shane Dix's *Echoes of Earth* (2001), for example, in which characters have sent electronic reproductions of themselves called 'engrams' into space to look for possible new planets to colonise, given the ecological collapse of Earth. Far from the aesthetic pleasures of such space opera, Paolo Bacigalupi's biting satire, 'The People of Sand and Slag' (2004), is about grotesque transhumanist adaptations to the toxic conditions of an abjected Earth that has been virtually destroyed by resource extraction and pollution. Bacigalupi's monstrous *übermensch* are physically invulnerable, thanks to the integration of nanotechnology into their bodies, but they are as alienated from their own bodies – reduced to objects in sadistic sex games – as they are from the natural world. The story reframes the present as the past that will have been culpable in reifying the human body and transforming the natural world into mere dead matter, relying on technological enhancements to survive its own apocalypse.

To very different effect, South Korean writer Bo-Young Kim imagines a future in which the collapse of the biosphere has driven humans to extinction. Two of her recently translated stories offer poignant revisions of conventional sf tropes such as 'the rise of the robots' and 'the Frankenstein Complex', at the same time as they dramatise the implications of the present-day climate crisis. In the post-Anthropocene future of 'On the Origin of Species' (2021), humanity's 'mind children' are a species of intelligent robots who in fact require the atmospheric temperatures and toxicities that have extinguished all organic life on Earth. In 'On the Origin of Species – and What Might Have Happened Thereafter' (2021), the technological Singularity is reversed. The robots unwittingly (re)create their extinct human progenitors and, in what might be read as an ironic gesture toward the iron grip of Asimov's Laws, they are so deeply and helplessly drawn to this new bioform that they will eventually ensure their own extinction as they set about reshaping the world for organic life.

As Frase argues, however, 'The real question is not whether human civilization can survive ecological crises, but whether *all* of us can survive it together, in some reasonably egalitarian way' (97 italics in original). Questions about who gets to leave the devastated Earth or who has access to the technologies that may guarantee survival can be easily overwhelmed by the sense of wonder generated by the wide-angle lens of space adventure. Kim Stanley Robinson takes up these questions in *2312* (2012). Although his technologically enhanced posthuman protagonists have left a despoiled Earth for colonies throughout the solar system, the work of regenerating the ruined Earth is ongoing, as is a very pragmatic concern to ensure a more equitable future for those left behind: 'There are people down there living in cardboard shacks. [...] So they'll always hate us, and some will attack us. [...] There's no solution but justice for everyone. It's the only thing that will make us safe' (356).

Critical transhumanism

Just as Haraway privileged contemporary speculative fiction, especially the 'monstrous selves in feminist science fiction' (197), in her account of the shared ontologies of human, animal and machine, so Hayles, noting the inseparable co-evolution of humans and tools, situates speculative fiction as 'the *locus classicus* for reframing transhumanist questions' ('Wrestling' 3). If there is nothing inherently progressive in sf (Vint 223), so there is nothing necessarily regressive about transhumanist futures.

For example, given the outsized neoliberal futures of conventional space opera, it is particularly interesting to turn to the 'New Space Opera', which, as Jerome Winter demonstrates, abandons the human exceptionalism of early writers such as 'Doc' Smith 'to allegorise a specific vanguard cultural politics evolving in tandem with a specific new system of global capitalism' (3). These cultural politics play out, for instance, in the post-Singularity transhumanism of Iain M. Banks's CULTURE series (1987–2012) about a galactic civilisation in which enhanced humans share citizenship with powerful AI 'Minds'. As a life-long socialist, Banks built progressive politics into a socialist–feminist near-utopia (Norman 141–78). Transhumanist relationships are thoroughly queered in Yoon Ha Lee's THE MACHINERIES OF EMPIRE trilogy (2016–8) and in Becky Chambers's WAYFARERS series (2014–21). Anne Leckie's anti-colonialist IMPERIAL RADCH trilogy (2013–5), about transhumanist worlds in which gender distinctions have disappeared (not least at the level of the text), concludes with the formation of 'the Republic of Two Systems', a new allegiance of humans, transhumans and sentient AI ships and space stations. The posthuman imaginary of some recent post-Singularity futures integrates many of the concerns of critical posthumanism into recognisably transhumanist futures. For Robinson's protagonists in *2312*, 'becoming transhuman' does not obviate ethical responsibilities to other human and non-human entities, but nor does it prevent human beings from embracing their technological evolution. As one of the protagonists argues, in opposition to bioconservative discourses about, for instance, the 'natural' limits of the human, 'it isn't being *post* human, it's being *fully* human. It would be stupid not to do the good things when you can, it would be *anti* human' (99 italics in original). Here Robinson suggests how we might better think of our 'becoming posthuman': as a process in which 'human' is a continuously emergent tangle of relationships and as an ethical project unfolding into the unforeseeable future-to-come.

Works cited

Alaimo, Stacy. *Bodily Natures: Science, Environment, and the Material Self.* Indiana UP, 2010.

Asimov, Isaac. *I, Robot*. Grafton, 1968.

Bianco, Jamie Skye. 'Algorithm'. *Posthuman Glossary*. Ed. Rosi Braidotti and Maria Hlavajova. Bloomsbury Academic, 2018. 23–6.

Bostrom, Nick. 'Transhumanist Values'. *Ethical Issues for the 21st Century*. Ed. Frederick Adams. Philosophy Documentation Center, 2005. 3–14.

Braidotti, Rosi. *The Posthuman*. Polity, 2013.

Clarke, Arthur C. 'The Sentinel'. *The Wesleyan Anthology of Science Fiction*. Ed. Arthur B. Evans, Istvan Csicsery-Ronay, Jr, Joan Gordon, Veronica Hollinger, Rob Latham and Carol McGuire. Wesleyan UP, 2010. 241–9.

Clarke, Bruce. 'Machines, AIs, Cyborgs, Systems'. *After the Human: Culture, Theory, and Criticism in the 21st Century*. Ed. Sherryl Vint. Cambridge UP, 2020. 91–104.

Coeckelbergh, Mark. *AI Ethics*. MIT Press, 2020.

Connolly, Thomas. *After Human: A Critical History of the Human in Science Fiction from Shelley to Le Guin*. Liverpool UP, 2021.

Dihal, Kanta. 'Enslaved Minds: Artificial Intelligence, Slavery, and Revolt'. *AI Narratives: A History of Imaginative Thinking about Intelligent Machines*. Ed. Stephen Cave, Kanta Dihal and Sarah Dillon. Oxford UP, 2020. 189–212.

Doctorow, Cory. 'I, Row–Boat'. *Overclocked: Stories of the Future Present*. Thunder's Mouth, 2007. 159–208.

Egan, Greg. *Schild's Ladder*. Gollancz, 2003.

Frase, Peter. *Four Futures: Visions of the World after Capitalism*. Verso, 2016.

Halpern, Sue. 'The Human Costs of AI'. *The New York Review of Books* (21 October 2021): 29–31.

Haraway, Donna J. 'A Manifesto for Cyborgs: Science, Technology, and Socialist Feminism in the 1980s'. *Coming to Terms: Feminism, Theory, Politics*. Ed. Elizabeth Weed. Routledge, 1989. 173–204.

Hawking, Stephen. 'The Best or Worst Thing To Happen To Humanity'. Cambridge University (19 October 2016). www.youtube.com/watch?v=_5XvDCjrdXs&t=11s

Hayles, N. Katherine. *How We Became Posthuman: Virtual Bodies in Cybernetics, Literature, and Informatics*. U of Chicago P, 1999.

——. *Unthought: The Power of the Cognitive Nonconscious*. U of Chicago P, 2017.

——. 'Wrestling with Transhumanism'. *Metanexus.net* (1 September 2011). www.metanexus.net/h–wrestling–transhumanism/

Ishiguro, Kazuo. *Klara and the Sun*. Knopf, 2021.

Jameson, Fredric. 'The Future as Disruption'. *Archaeologies of the Future: The Desire Called Utopia and Other Science Fictions*. Verso, 2005. 211–33.

Judy, Ron S. 'Chinese Post–humanism and Chen Qiufan's Political Science Fiction'. *Science Fiction Studies* 148 (2022): 502–19.

Kritzer, Naomi. *Catfishing on CatNet*. Tor, 2019.

Meyer, Robinson. 'To Stop Global Warming, Should Humanity Dim the Sky?' *The Atlantic* (7 August 2017). www.theatlantic.com/science/archive/2017/08/geoengineers–meet–off–the–record/536004/

Morton, Timothy. *Hyperobjects: Philosophy and Ecology after the End of the World*. U of Minnesota P, 2013.

Norman, Joseph S. *The Culture of 'the Culture': Utopian Processes in Iain M. Banks's Space Opera Series*. Liverpool UP, 2021.

Okorafor, Nnedi. *Binti: The Night Masquerade*. *Binti: The Complete Trilogy*. DAW, 2019. 172–295.

Pilsch, Andrew. *Transhumanism: Evolutionary Futurism and the Human Technologies of Utopia*. U Minnesota P, 2017.

Ramírez, J. Jesse. *Against Automation Mythologies: Business Science Fiction and the Ruse of the Robots*. Routledge, 2021.

Rhee, Jennifer. *The Robotic Imaginary: The Human and the Price of Dehumanized Labor*. U of Minnesota P, 2018.
Richardson, Michael. 'Embodiment and Affect'. *After the Human: Culture, Theory, and Criticism in the 21st Century*. Ed. Sherryl Vint. Cambridge UP, 2020. 58–71.
Robinson, Kim Stanley. *2312*. Orbit, 2012.
Vint, Sherryl. 'Speculative Fiction'. *After the Human: Culture, Theory, and Criticism in the 21st Century*. Ed. Sherryl Vint. Cambridge UP, 2020. 220–35.
Winter, Jerome. *Science Fiction, New Space Opera, and Neoliberal Globalism: Nostalgia for Infinity*. U of Wales P, 2016.

51
QUEER AND TRANS THEORY

Beyond Gender Research Collective

Introduction: Science fiction *is* queer theory?

Sf allows us to imagine otherwise – other bodies, other futures, other worlds. These other imaginaries offer new possibilities for queer and trans experience. As the creator of the *Dream Babes* zine, Sin Wai Kin (formerly known as Victoria Sin), puts it 'The space of speculative fiction is the space that is created between lived realities and distant fantasies that take us out of our world so that we can occupy a new, if temporary, positionality' (2). In the worlds of sf one can remake one's body into previously unthought of shapes, meet with differently gendered beings, move beyond gender.

These speculations are not of our world and yet 'this is not escapism' (Sin 2). These imaginations, theorisations and speculations cannot be detached from their historical and social contexts because they are always rooted in our current and past moments. In this way, sf aligns with the fictions theorised by Ruha Benjamin: they 'are not falsehoods but refashionings through which analysts experiment with different scenarios, trajectories, and reversals, elaborating new values and testing different possibilities for creating more just and equitable societies' (2). Queer and trans creators are not, then, fleeing from the world as much as they are reshaping it; they contribute to queer and trans theory by imagining science-fictional worlds which defy the stultifying norms of hetero- and cis-normativity, 'especially when [they] do it seriously, and collectively' (Sin 2).

This chapter resists attempts to distance sf from the embodied realities of queer and trans lives. It argues, after Donna J. Haraway, that 'science fiction is political [queer and trans] theory' (120) and, building on E. Patrick Johnson's notion of 'theory in the flesh' (9), treats sf as 'queer theory on the front lines, in the trenches, on the streets, or anyplace where the racialized and sexualized body is beaten, starved, fired, cursed' (5). Rivers Solomon's *The Deep* (2019), understood as fleshly, lived theory, exemplifies sf's ability to grapple with the various facts and fictions used to police queer and trans lives.

Solomon's novella envisages the undersea lives of the descendants of pregnant enslaved people thrown overboard during the Middle Passage. The story follows Yetu, the Historian, whose task it is to imbibe the knowledge of her people's past collective trauma. Once a year, at the festival of the Remembering, Yetu must recount their history; this collective reliving of trauma functions as a catharsis for her people, allowing them to live without the painful memory of past generations.

 DOI: 10.4324/9781003140269-54

Yetu, however, is unable to forget and must perpetually relive the anguish of her ancestors. The tensions between Yetu and her people, between the individual and the collective explored in the text, also emerge in the names given to these aquatic 'creatures'. On the one hand they are called 'Zoti Aleyu', translated as 'strange fish', 'a suitable name for something singular and alone' (50), but on the other they name themselves 'Wajinru', meaning 'chorus of the deep' (10).

These names capture three elements of queer and trans experience. First, the notion of the strange fish, neither fully animal nor person, which challenges the category of the Human as predicated on the exclusion of all that falls outside of White cis bourgeois heteronormative identity. Second, the interplay between the strange fish and the chorus gestures towards the community of difference that is central to queer existence: a kinship structure comprised of singular non-normative subjects, woven together into a community of care and solidarity. Third, the chorus made up of strange fish illustrates the performative and prefigurative worldbuilding of queer and trans practice, which both lives and brings about 'a world beyond this world' (46).

Queer and trans worldbuilding as collective performance

Collaborative authorship is central to both this chapter and *The Deep*. *The Deep* is set in a world originally built by the electronic music duo Drexciya, and more recently adapted by the hip hop group clipping.; editor Navah Wolfe defines the relationship between these three projects as 'a game of artistic Telephone' with each release – or 'misheard whisper' (157) – expanding and transforming previous ones. Drexciya's 'original mythology' (158) was built across eight albums, nine EPs, three singles and sleeve notes. This transmedia narrative established Drexciya as an underwater kingdom populated by the 'water-breathing, aquatically mutated descendants of "pregnant America-bound African slaves thrown overboard by the thousands during labour for being sick and disruptive cargo"' (Eshun 300).

Drexciya created 'a world that was only being filled in partially, track by track, and you were doing a lot of the navigating' and 'to be a Drexciya fan was to build the mythos by yourself' (Eshun cited in Solomon 159). Thus Drexciya's medium invited audience participation. 'The Deep' (a song by clipping.) and *The Deep* equally invite this recursivity, expanding Drexciya's transmedia narrative. Drexciya, 'The Deep' and *The Deep* might therefore productively be understood as an example of 'transmedia world-building', a process that takes place '*across* media', 'involves *audience participation*' and '*defers narrative closure*' (Hassler-Forest 5 italics in original).

The Deep and its precursors' speculative re-writing of history can be seen as an instance of 'temporal drag' to use Elizabeth Freeman's term, a kind of 'counter-genealogical practice' (xxiii) where objects and stories are archived to 'gestur[e] toward the past's unrealized futures' (60). This process has clear ties to the Afrofuturist tradition of remixing or 'digging the future out of the archive' (Gunkel 19) in which Drexciya participated. C. Riley Snorton has more recently linked 'temporal drag' to photographs of James McHarris printed in *Ebony* in 1954, noting how McHarris, a Black trans man, found 'space for moving in and through gender in the afterlives of slavery' (Snorton 172). In Snorton's figuration, archived imagery enacts a 'temporal drag' pointing us towards those as of yet 'unrealized futures' (Freeman 60, qtd Snorton 174) of our queer/trans ancestors. 'Temporal drag' or 'remixing' are therefore deeply entwined with Black and trans culture, and it is this history that Solomon builds on. This is not simple escapism but purposeful re-writing and mythmaking to counter the violence of white supremacism. As Elisabeth Wheeler argues, texts like *The Deep* produce 'Afroaquanauts' and imbue us with the 'optimism to "dance underwater and not get wet" and the strength to push for change' in the name of our real and speculative queer/trans ancestors (128).

This chapter scopes *The Deep*'s methods and themes, recognising its place within a wider transgressive queer/trans sf culture – a genre packed with examples of collective writing, rewriting and transmedia worldbuilding. Janelle Monáe's visual album *Dirty Computer* (2018) builds a narrative of queer resistance across media outputs; Danielle Braithwaite-Shirley's Black trans archive *WE ARE HERE BECAUSE OF THOSE THAT ARE NOT* (2020) worldbuilds across animation, sound art and video games; artists Sin Wai Kin, Sophia Al-Maria and Tai Shani rewrite and transform sf by Octavia E. Butler and Ursula K. Le Guin in their work. *The Deep* provides a necessary intervention within this wider genre, utilising collective-authorship and transmedia worldbuilding to centre such themes as the coloniality of gender, the contingent category of the Human, and queer kinship.

Such collaborative worldbuilding also has clear ties with the worldbuilding of queer communities. The collective process of reminiscence that takes place during the Remembrance, which sees Yetu share the pain of her people's memory, represents for her a dual experience of great release and of profound exhaustion: it is a process that demands 'an openness' so complete that the 'void of the ocean' might wash 'out [one's] identity' (Solomon 32), but which also underscores a meaningful reconnection between Yetu, the wajinru and their collective, embodied history. In its raw, communal vulnerability, the Remembrance is a poignant example of the ways in which the creation of space through performance can provide a meaningful way for queer communities to grapple with complicated legacies of abuse and to establish networks of healing and care. Although *The Deep*'s most immediate relation is with the histories of colonisation and enslavement tied to the Middle Passage, the Remembrance demonstrates that one means of resisting these histories lies in the spaces created for and nurtured by queer communities.

In particular, the specially-built dome where the ritual takes place evokes the queer ballroom: a space which allows participants to be openly queer by protecting them from the cisheteronormative expectations and abuses of the external world. While it is difficult to pinpoint a singular narrative in the evolution of ballroom, it is impossible to talk about ballroom culture without paying tribute to its Black and Brown, frequently trans, pioneers. Compared to more conventional LGBTQI+ venues, which increasingly cater to cishet audiences, the ballroom is often a safe haven for the most marginalised within the queer community. In *The Deep*, Solomon shows that the sense of shared vulnerability fostered by the ballroom, or this ball-dome, facilitates, rather than hinders, community formation, conducted under the guidance of a master of ceremonies (in this case, Yetu herself).

While one element of this painful, joyful collectivity, which allows the wajinru to 'bear it all together' (148), is built on the identity of those within these spaces (queer folks in the ballroom, wajinru in the Remembrance), another element relies on the transformative potential of performance. For the wajinru, history is not an abstracted narrative, but a lived experience with physical embodied and affective manifestations. In turn, performing the history is cathartic because it involves not simply reliving a memory, but reconfiguring it into a new form. Voguing is an excellent example of this kind of queer performance, because it takes the insults aimed at queer men for being too effeminate and redirects them into empowering movement. Where loose wrists and wiggling hips are a cause for abuse outside the ballroom, they are a sign of mastery and celebration within its walls. As Bryant Alexander argues, the reclamation of these traumas creates a 'slippage' between spaces (351). It does not negate the pain caused outside of the communal safe space, but it allows for an emancipatory reckoning of self and selves.

The fact that these histories are lived and actively performed means that the recollections they offer are imperfect. Yetu often has difficulty telling memories apart, as the watery spaces of various pasts and presents seep into both her own experience and her reconfiguration of the collective

History. However, a rigid understanding of accuracy is not the point of these moments. Like sf more broadly, the exaggerated ceremonies of queer spaces (the elaborate runway, the extravagant costume) are not literal representations of life on the outside. Queer theory – whether it is understood through the sf of *The Deep* or through the (un)realness of the ballroom – is not invested in recalling the details of the past precisely, but in what that past represents and can teach us. So often queer voices are suppressed or intentionally erased from dominant historical narratives, meaning that queering history requires one to read meaning into absences and loss. Yetu's human lover Oori comes from a people whose history has been lost. While Yetu is overburdened by memory, Oori has none. The radical potential of these moments of community and performance lies, therefore, in their ability to navigate an unevenly distributed, painfully felt, traumatic past. These performances disrupt a linear (and narrow) understanding of historical time. As Sara Ahmed unequivocally states 'Moments of disorientation are vital' and, indeed, sometimes 'disorientation is an ordinary feeling' (157). Instead of pushing it away, embracing that disorientation, that ordinary strangeness, becomes a healing experience for the wajinru who, by the end of *The Deep*, recalibrate the rituals of the Remembrance so they can 'live out their days all sharing the memories together' (148). Here, queer community and performance offers an emancipatory recalibration of trauma into hope.

Undoing human nature

The wajinru are not human. When first encountered with a human, or two-legs, Yetu screams, 'opening her mouth wide, showing rows of sharp, long teeth, narrow and overlapping' (72). The Yetu 'lived in water and she looked it', while the two-legs appear 'so . . . fleshy' in comparison (74). And yet, Yetu wonders 'how much of two-leggedness was in her' (74). Despite her ability to replace her face 'with a black endless pit guarded by fangs' (72), Yetu swims uncomfortably close to the borders of humanity. Rather than reading the wajinru as nonhuman, therefore, they might more usefully be thought of as 'dehuman'; in Julietta Singh's formulation, dehumanism is a 'term that signals clearly the imperial work of making humans and worlds', and it 'is united with queer inhumanisms as it presses us towards an overtly global, imperial critique of the making and mapping of Man and its proliferating remnants' (5). Dehumanism stands opposed to colonial and heteronormative definitions of the human, emphasising the ties between those who attempt to erect borders around an essentialised definition of womanhood and those who defend the territory of Man. Against such practices, Singh 'asks us to open ourselves to reimagining ways of relating to each other – to others human, nonhuman, and inhuman to which (even when disavowed) we are mutually bound' (7–8). *The Deep* demonstrates the potential of sf for such a project.

Solomon directly interrogates those systems which seek to separate living beings into fixed and definitive categories, writing

> Two-legs had a specific way of classifying the world that Yetu didn't like [...] They organized the world as two sides of a war, the two-legs in conflict with everything else. The way [the human] Suka talked about farming was as if they ruled the land and what it produced as opposed to [...] existing alongside it.
>
> (84)

The sharp divisions Yetu observes here are marked by a desire for domination and mastery, where human life exists in conflict with other species and the environment. Solomon's linking of farming to other efforts to 'rule the land' aligns with Alexis Pauline Gumbs's argument that 'the gaze of biologists' and 'what would call itself the "neutral" scientific language of marine guidebooks' is deeply political (*Undrowned* 9). Gumbs consulted these books because she 'just wanted to know which whale was which' but instead found herself 'confronted with the colonial, racist, sexist, heteropatriachalizing capitalist constructs that are trying to kill [her] – the net [she is] already caught in, so to speak' (9). Solomon's two-legs, who wage a war against the ocean, are engaged in the same project as Gumbs's biologists, who fill books on marine mammals with 'awkwardly binary assignments of biological sex' (9). The net of 'the human', and the colonising, heteronormative taxonomy it brings with it, here reaches down into the depths of the oceans.

And yet, in Solomon's writing those who live in the deep meet this net with teeth bared. By co-creating the wajinru, this chorus of strange fish, Solomon defies efforts to taxonomise the ocean. The wajinru are illegible, their human ancestry giving no definite indication of their identities. As Yetu puts it 'Though her foremothers were two-legs, she felt she had very little in common with these strange land walkers, whose teeth were weak and flat' (84). However, her refusal of the human – she proudly declares: 'I am animal' (84) – is explicitly designed to help her to make a connection with Oori, a woman who is 'not so good with [...] human interaction' and who 'prefers animals to people' (83). Yetu thus refuses the label of human in order to get closer to a woman who is deeply uncomfortable with her own humanity. Her queer desire and her ambiguous relationship to humanity come together in a rejection of all binary opposition even as she emphasises her difference from those 'strange land walkers' (84). This same rejection of binary logic can be felt in Solomon's design of the wajinru's bodies, which flourish outside of hetero- and cis-normative systems of sexual and gender identification. Speaking intimately with Oori about the mutual strangeness of their respective bodies, Yetu explains that 'wajinru have a place to envelope, and then there's something else, and that is what gives sperm' (117). She notes that 'couple was an odd choice of word' for sex, given that 'it could involve any number of wajinru, frequently up to five' and that 'it is [her] understanding that it is most common for everything to be . . . engaged at once [...] and when not [...] it is decided based on the preference of the wajinru involved in the heat of the moment' (118–9). As well as designing bodies that defy cis- and hetero-normativity, Solomon refuses to naturalise wajinru desire. There are variances in what the wajinru find pleasurable and, as Yetu's attraction to Oori suggests, these variances are not determined by the wajinru's reproductive capacity. In short, not only do wajinru bodies appear queer from a human perspective, there are queer wajinru.

In her keynote address at the 2018 *Worlding SF* conference, leading trans feminist sf scholar Cheryl Morgan stated

> We keep getting told as queer people that our lives are not natural, that what we are doing is somehow wrong. And I'm here to tell you that if that's not natural, well, the natural world is magnificently, exuberantly and unrepentantly not natural.

This is the kind of self-consciously unnatural queerness Solomon's sf evokes. Rather than shying away from the 'natural' world as an implicitly heteronormative realm, Solomon dives into the belly of the beast and explores the queer and trans lessons one might learn from the many parthenogenetic, intersex, polymaternal and otherwise decidedly non-normative creatures of the deep. As Oliver Bendorf writes, 'transgender studies can create a discourse in which nature is not the cisgender space it has been made out to be' (137). He calls for 'theoretical critique and art and song about species [...] and biodiversity and evolution and instinct and habitat', which are 'not just about our genitals, though they can be about that too' (137). Yetu's meeting with the two-legs is a form of alien encounter which refuses to leave the alien as a safely distant other. Instead, the wajinru prompt the question, 'What is natural, anyway?' (Bendorf 136).

Watery kindred

Thus far we have focused on how Yetu's journey out of the deep and into the world of the two-legs undermines the categories of 'nature' and 'the human' in ways which refuse the separation of the two. However, Yetu does not exist in a vacuum, and an important element of *The Deep*'s challenge to hetero- and cis-normativity lies in the impossibility of separating the wajinru out into discrete, atomised individuals. At the end of the novella, Yetu, filled as she is with memories, wonders why she cannot remember life inside the womb. In response, her mother, or Amaba, asks her 'What if some of your remembering of dark loneliness as a pup were you inside a belly, and it was hardly distinguishable from floating in the deep? It is all waters' (150). This question casts the ocean itself as a vast body of amniotic fluid and evokes Sophie Lewis's concept of amniotechnics. Her 'cyborg conception of water' frames the waters, both internal and external to the body, as a 'social and presocial [...] companion technology' (161). The amnion 'is the bed of our bodies' overlap and it is, not necessarily – but possibly – a source of radical kinship' (162). Part of Solomon's unmaking of the human as a category involves grappling with the wajinru and two-legs' respective capacities for this kind of radical kinship. By insisting that 'it is all waters', Solomon also evokes Astrida Neimanis's concept of hydrofeminism – a theorisation of queer feminism which argues that, in constructing humans as 'human bodies of water', it is possible to 'account for our differences while demanding our interconnection' (166). This theorisation of life as interconnected bodies of water is not an exercise in resolving or homogenising difference; rather, it 'embrace[s] the multifaceted ways in which we relate to, rely on and reciprocally affect bodies of water' (169). The watery entanglement of *The Deep* imbricates wajinru and humans: 'Yetu didn't believe that the sea was sentient. But it was where life began. It was where the life of the wajinru began, and reaching backward, the life of the two-legs, too' (154). This passage emphasises the porous distinctions between humans and wajinru that emerge from their mutual reliance on the ocean as a body of water.

In part, the queer potential of this watery collectivity lies in its refusal to be mapped onto heteronormative definitions of the family. Through echolocation, electricity and vibration, the zoti aleyu collaborate as a queer multiplicity, united not through biological kinship but through shared suffering and solidarity. Moving together in a crowd, shoal or school which threatens to change global weather systems, they declare 'We are song, and we are together' (64). Here, the wajinru resist the violence of classification, not (or not only) with their individually non-normative bodies but in their collective illegibility. They form an amalgam of sound and movement which challenges the primacy of heteronormative kinship.

However, this is not to say that queer science-fictionality requires one to look away from or ignore kinship. As Yetu's interest in the womb suggests, ancestral ties, particularly maternal lineages, are of central importance. Solomon writes of 'the first mothers' (42), those enslaved, pregnant two-legs who were thrown from slave ships and who gave birth to wajinru 'pups' (51) under the water. Thinking back on this pivotal moment, the first Historian – who is known only as Zoti Aleyu and who uses the collective pronoun 'we' to refer to themselves – emphasises the necessity of maternal care, stating: 'We live only by the graciousness of the second mothers, the giant water beasts we've [...] come to call skalu, whales, who feed us, bond with us, and drag us down to the deepest depths where we are safer' (42–3).

The wajinru's queerness does not amount to an aversion of maternity. Indeed, in much the same way that Solomon refuses to frame these strange fish as science fictional outsiders to the categories of 'nature' and 'the human', so the wajinru infringe upon the sanctity of 'the family'. *The Deep* demonstrates sf's capacity to force its readership to think about how strange it is that we were all, once, gestated under water and fed on our mothers' bodies to survive. Solomon thus ventures, like Susan Stryker, 'into the heart of civilization itself to reclaim biological reproduction from hetero-sexism and free it for our own uses' (245).

Yet Solomon is not unthinkingly positive about familial relations. When Yetu first emerges from the waters, she meets a family of humans to whom she looks 'more or less like food', and who wonder whether 'they should eat her'; it is only upon hearing her speak, that the human Suka recognises Yetu as kin:

> 'My god, my god, my god,' Suka said. 'You are – What are you?'
> [...]
> 'I am Yetu,' she said, hoping that might calm them.
> 'You speak. You're alive...you're like us'.
>
> (79)

For Yetu, being recognised as similar, as 'sharing something in common with not just one another, but a whole *us*' (80 italics in original), beyond and beneath the perceived differences of her other-than-human embodiment is flattering. And yet, she quickly realises she is not ready to be 'swept into the fold of a stranger' (80). While the two-legs and the wajinru are both birthed from the same waters, this does not imply a necessary intimacy between them. Yetu notes that 'kinship isn't inherently a good thing' (83) and Solomon refuses to shy away from the violence and abuse which often accompany familial ties.

The fact that the wajinru are mothers, have many mothers, value the work of mothering, does not, therefore, imply an embrace of homonormativity. As Jasbir Puar notes, the homonormative 'politics of recognition and incorporation' – which are focused on 'gay marriage and families', rather than a more subversive queer and trans liberation – are 'contingent upon ever-narrowing parameters of white racial privilege, consumption capabilities, gender and kinship normativity, and bodily integrity' (xii). The wajinru, in contrast, value maternal care precisely because the transatlantic slave trade so violently ripped it from them. As Black feminist theorist Hortense Spillers argues, 'The fact that the enslaved person's access to the issue of his/her own body is not entirely clear in this historic period throws in crisis all aspects of the blood relations, as captors apparently felt no obligation to acknowledge them' (217).

In *The Deep*, motherhood does not imply access to institutional power, nor is it recognised as the sacred, natural heart of the family. Rather, as Spillers puts it, 'the "reproduction of mothering" in this historic instance carries few of the benefits of a *patriarchalized* female gender, which, from one point of view, is the only female gender there is' (216). What Solomon's many-gendered mothers serve to create is another point of view, from which it is possible to see that 'to name one-self "mother" in a moment where representatives of the state conscripted "Black" and "mother" into vile epithets is a queer thing' (Gumbs 'M/Other' 21).

In the last moment of the novel, Yetu takes Oori into the ocean and shows her how to breathe underwater:

> They held each other close until Yetu was able to transfer to Oori the remembering of the womb. [...] But when Oori jolted from the remembering, she was breathing underwater, just as she'd breathed in the womb. [...] She was a completely new thing.
>
> Yetu beckoned her downward into the dark, into this world of beauty.
>
> (155)

This highlights the power of sf to pull apart the boundaries of the human through an expansive understanding of queer mothering. Solomon demonstrates the power of the intersection between science fictional transformation and queer longing. Yetu and Oori have 'longed' for each other and here that longing manifests in their ability to remap their bodies and find new ways of being together. Oori's descent into the dark waters, her transformation into something other, is a potent fusion of monstrous becoming and queer desire. Like Stryker, who writes of her use of 'dark, watery images [...] to assert my worth as a monster in spite of the conditions my monstrosity requires me to face' (254), Oori embraces monstrosity: an embrace which acts as a provocation to 'redefine a life worth living' (250). She does this, both by becoming 'a completely new thing' and by reaching back into the wajinru's ancestral past, to the moment when the first wajinru children were born into the deep. In this way, Solomon literalises the concept of a collective, ancestral breathing practice; as Gumbs (2020) argues, for 'those who survived in the underbellies of boats', 'their breathing is not separate from the drowning of their kin [...] from the breathing of the ocean [...] from the sharp exhale of hunted whales, their kindred also' (*Undrowned* 1).

Here, a clear line is drawn between wajinru and two-legs. By teaching Oori to breathe underwater Yetu bridges the gap between drowned and undrowned, showing that the work of learning to breathe in 'the chokehold of racial gendered ableist capitalism' does not involve a turning away from the past but an immersion in it (*Undrowned* 2). This is what José Esteban Muñoz calls 'a backward glance that enacts a future vision' (4) – a form of queer utopianism that those science-fictional beings, the wajinru, make thinkable.

Conclusion

In the sf imaginings of queer and trans futures, we see the beginnings of a radical, fundamental reshaping. As mentioned, these speculations are not escapism, but an intrinsic part of the 'work to change the world' that corresponds to 'being concerned with the way our actions and beliefs now, today, will shape the future, tomorrow, the next generations' (brown 16). This, at its core, is science fictional behaviour. Drexciya, clipping. and Solomon have collectively built an underwater world across media, inviting audience participation through its fractious nature and multiple authors, and equally deferring narrative closure through this invitation. The degrees of transformation that characterise each iteration of *The Deep* are not a failure; rather, they gesture towards the open possibility of this story 'continu[ing] indefinitely, happily taking on the adaptations of each new interpreter, into the future' (158). We are invited to join this game of telephone, to transform the story – and possibly, the world – once again.

Works cited

Ahmed, Sara. *Queer Phenomenology: Orientations, Objects, Others*. Duke UP, 2006.

Alexander, Bryant. 'Querying Queer Theory again (or Queer Theory as Drag Performance)'. *Journal of Homosexuality* 45.2–4 (2003): 349–52.

Bendorf, Oliver. 'Nature'. *TSQ: Transgender Studies Quarterly* 1.1–2 (2014): 136–7.

Benjamin, Ruha. 'Racial Fictions, Biological Facts: Expanding the Sociological Imagination through Speculative Methods'. *Catalyst: Feminism, Theory, Technoscience* 2.2 (2016): 1–28.
brown, adrienne maree. *Emergent Strategy*. AK, 2017.
Eshun, Kodwo. 'Further Considerations of Afrofuturism'. *CR: The New Centennial Review* 3.2 (2003): 287–302.
Freeman, Elizabeth. *Time Binds: Queer Temporalities, Queer Histories*. Duke UP, 2010.
Gumbs, Alexis Pauline. 'M/Other Ourselves:A Black Queer Feminist Genealogy for Radical Mothering'. *Revolutionary Mothering: Love on the Front Lines*. Ed. Alexis Pauline Gumbs, China Martens and Mai'a Williams. PM, 2016. 19–31.
—. *Undrowned: Black Feminist Lessons from Marine Mammals*. AK, 2020.
Gunkel, Henriette, Ayesha Hameed and Simon O'Sullivan, ed. *Futures and Fictions*. Repeater, 2017.
Haraway, Donna J. *How like a Leaf: An Interview with Thyrza Nichols Goodeve*. Routledge, 2000.
Hassler-Forest, Dan. *Science Fiction, Fantasy and Politics: Transmedia World-Building Beyond Capitalism*. Rowman & Littlefield, 2016.
Johnson, Patrick E. '"Quare" Studies, or (Almost) Everything I Know about Queer Studies I Learned from My Grandmother'. *Text and Performance Quarterly* 21.1 (2001): 1–25.
Lewis, Sophie. *Full Surrogacy Now: Feminism against Family*. Verso, 2019.
Morgan, Cheryl. 'Systems of Sex and Gender'. *Worlding SF: Building, Inhabiting and Understanding SF Universes Conference*. University of Graz, 2018. www.facebook.com/watch/live/?ref=watch_permalink&v=278711879656744
Muñoz, José Esteban. *Cruising Utopia: The Then and There of Queer Futurity*. New York UP, 2019.
Neimanis, Astrida. 'Bodies of Water, Human Rights and the Hydrocommons'. *TOPIA: Canadian Journal of Cultural Studies* 21 (2009): 161–82.
Puar, Jasbir K. *Terrorist Assemblages: Homonationalism in Queer Times*. Duke UP, 2008.
Sin, Victoria, ed. *Dream Babes: Speculative Futures*. PSS, 2017.
Singh, Julietta. *Unthinking Mastery: Dehumanism and Decolonial Entanglements*. Duke UP, 2018.
Snorton, Riley C. *Black on Both Sides: A Racial History of Trans Identity*. U of Minnesota P, 2017.
Solomon, Rivers with Daveed Diggs, William Huston and Jonathan Snips. *The Deep*. Hodder, 2020.
Spillers, Hortense J. *Black, White, and in Color: Essays on American Literature and Culture*. U of Chicago P, 2003.
Stryker, Susan. 'My Words to Victor Frankenstein Above the Village of Chamounix: Performing Transgender Rage'. *GLQ: A Journal of Lesbian and Gay Studies* 1.3 (1994): 237–54.
Wheeler, Elizabeth A. 'Runoff: Afroaquanauts in Landscapes of Sacrifice'. *Literary Afrofuturism in the Twenty-First Century*. Ed. Isiah Lavender III and Lisa Yaszek. Ohio State UP, 2020. 128–49.

52
SCIENCE FICTION TOURISM

Brooks Landon

On 13 October 2021, William Shatner joined three other guests on a flight to the edge of space in the Blue Origin rocket developed by billionaire Amazon founder Jeff Bezos. Shatner, then 90, became the oldest person to fly into space, boldly going where 65 years before he, in the iconic role of James T. Kirk, had captained the Starship *Enterprise* on Gene Roddenberry's pioneering series, *Star Trek* (NBC 1966–9). Shatner's sub-orbital trip lasted only 11 minutes, considerably less than the *Enterprise's* planned 'Five Year Mission' to explore 'Space, the Final Frontier', but during the short flight, he and his companions rose through the blueness of Earth's atmosphere to the stark blackness of space and were weightless for three minutes. A breathless Shatner, now the most iconic of the growing number of space tourists, struggled for words to describe his feelings: 'It moved me to tears' (Kluger).

Space tourism

There is no better example of the way space tourism, a fast-growing commercial venture, is supplanting the longstanding dream in sf narratives for a future in which space would no longer be a frontier but a sense of wonder tourist destination. It is the newest face of sf tourism.

However, the possibility of actual space tourism is not exactly 'new'. In 1999, Russian billionaire Dennis Tito spent 20 million dollars to hitch a ride to the International Space Station, becoming one of the first private citizens to pay his way into space. And now he has signed up himself, his wife and ten others for a trip around the moon on Elon Musk's Space X Starship, scheduled for lift off within the next five years.

Today's burgeoning commercial ventures, responding in part to sf narratives' longstanding fascination with travel through space or time, are just one of the ways in which 'science fiction thinking' has been advocated and frequently reified. Space tourism has become a cottage industry with reports of its growth and promise reported in *The Atlantic* and *Forbes* and on CNN, MSNBC, NPR and major websites such as YouTube, Wikipedia, Britannica. A growing number of sites preview and predict space ports and the infrastructure necessary for a true industry to emerge. There is even an emerging nonfiction genre explicitly dedicated to sf tourism through travel into space, including Michel Van Pelt's *Space Tourism... Adventures in Earth Orbit and Beyond* (2005), Kenny

DOI: 10.4324/9781003140269-55

Kemp's *Destination Space: How Space Tourism Is Making Science Fiction A Reality* (2007) and Derek Webber's *Space Tourism Business: The Foundations* (2021).

While books, articles and websites and the private space travel start-ups they describe are rapidly proliferating, it is important to note how contingent these ambitious plans are and will continue for some time to be. And it may be even more important to note how the longstanding populist, inclusive appeal of sf now seems, in the case of space tourism, to be limited to the very, very wealthy, reminding us of Gil Scott-Heron's bitingly critical 'Whitey on the Moon' (1970), written in response to America's triumphant 1969 Moon landing. It called out the disparity between the unlimited enthusiasm for, and financial commitment to, space exploration and the lack of commitment to addressing social and financial inequalities in a nation that cheerfully spent billions to go to the Moon while ignoring poverty at home. More recently, *WALL-E* (Stanton 2008) presented a very critical image of indolent, wealthy space tourists returning to a seemingly barren Earth, while *Avenue Five* (HBO 2020–2) focused just as critically on wealthy tourists stuck in space. Offering perhaps the most scathing update to Scott-Heron, N.K. Jemisin's 'Emergency Skin' (2019) projects financial and racial inequality into a future where the destination for sf tourism is Earth itself.

A brief history of sf tourism

Sf has always been a kind of epistemological 'tourism' about venturing to new places through new and imagined technologies. Countless imaginative voyages took readers to the far corners of the Earth (and its centre), to heavenly bodies, starting with the Moon and expanding through the solar system to galaxies and dimensions beyond, and spatialising travel forward and backward through time. Significantly, tourism itself has also long been an explicit *subject* of sf. The process of imagining, simulating and delivering forms of sf tourism has been developed and explored both in fictional narratives and in material embodiments of sf dreams and destinations. Indeed, no discussion of sf tourism can be undertaken without noting that the history of sf is the history of going somewhere else to see the sights, whether through *voyages extraordinaires*, explicit time travel narratives or the implicit time travel of imagining future worlds. The numerous examples of print and media sf tourism narratives include the travels and vacations of Earth tourists going to other places and times, and those of humans who have settled elsewhere or elsewhen returning to (an often dead or dying) Earth. Such tourism is not, of course, limited to humans, as a number of first contact stories, including Boris and Arkady Strugatsky's *Roadside Picnic* (*Piknik na obochine*; 1972; trans. 1977), imagine that aliens are tourists visiting our world.

This necessarily limited tour of sf tourism begins with touchstone examples of print narratives about imaginary travels before turning to actual historical analogues that embody the dreams that have driven sf stories to pursue a 'sense of wonder' by depicting travel to marvellous destinations. It will then focus on a number of formative elements in the emergence of mass culture (primarily in the US) that are not generally thought of as science fictional, but whose obvious – and influential – affinity with sf thinking (Landon *Science* 2–10) is often noted. The case for such a figurative construction of sf tourism rests on an ever-expanding body of scholarship exploring the cultural mechanisms by which technology has been constructed and represented in mass culture in general and in literature in particular (Dery; Franklin; Nye *American* and *Narratives*; Tichi).

In the history of prose sf, time travel *voyages extraordinaires* hold a special place, anchored by H.G. Wells's *The Time Machine* (1895) and exemplified by Ray Bradbury's 'A Sound of Thunder' (1952), Robert A. Heinlein's '"–All You Zombies–"' (1958) and Philip K. Dick's 'We Can Remember It for You Wholesale' (1966). Robert Silverberg's 'Sailing to Byzantium' (1984) depicts time travel tourism that includes journeying to other geographical places, both historical and simulated. Perhaps the most totalising of *all* sf tourism narratives, it constructs a fictional world in which everyone is a tourist, constantly on vacation, and reduces it to five artificial and constantly changed 'cities', some from history and some from myth, mixing eras, cultures, realities. The result is a kaleidoscopic mixture of people and places organised solely for the pleasures of tourism in the complete Disneyworlding of reality.

Silverberg's 'When We Went to See the End of the World' (1972) is an even more imaginative and more dystopian story about technological tourism. A bitterly sardonic send-up of sf's fascination with end-of-the-world scenarios, it presents a mordantly funny *critique* of the very idea of sf tourism. Friends gather at a cocktail party and compare about their respective experiences with a new time-travel technology that lets them view 'the end of the world', only to discover that no two time-travel trips agree on what it looks like, although each one echoes some well-known end-of-the-world sf narrative. The 'friends' use their different accounts to establish their sexual and financial status, while completely ignoring numerous apocalyptic scenarios developing in their present. Silverberg teases readers with the question of whether their trips are 'real' or merely 'fake' simulations, craftily implying print sf narratives are the 'true' exemplars of sf tourism.

Historical and cultural destinations for sf tourism

David E. Nye's idea of the 'technological sublime', describes a sensibility key to understanding historical sites that presented dreams of the future, ranging from museums to world's fairs to Coney Island. Such tourist destinations had little or nothing directly to do with sf but provided famous icons of the technological sublime, such as the Eiffel Tower, constructed for the Paris Exposition of 1889, the giant Ferris Wheel that was the centrepiece of the 1893 World's Columbian Exposition in Chicago, and the Space Needle from the 1962 Seattle World's Fair. World's fairs and related tourist destinations drew millions of visitors who were introduced to an epistemology centred on change, progress, science, technology and the idea of the future itself, while this technological sublime proved instrumental in promoting the kind of technological, future-oriented mindset that gave rise to sf literature.

Wells's Time Traveller is transported to a distant future that includes, significantly, a museum. Robert Crossley argues that, particularly in British sf, museums function as a kind of time machine, as well as offering in the 'spectacle of an observer examining an artifact and using it as a window onto nature, culture, and history' the 'convergence of anthropological, prophetic, and elegiac tonalities that science fiction handles more powerfully than any other modern literary form' (206–7). Real sf museums, such as the Maison d'Ailleurs in Yverdon-Les-Bains, Switzerland and Microsoft billionaire Paul Allen's extensive collection of sf-related material in The Science Fiction and Fantasy Hall of Fame, mirror their fictional counterparts, as do numerous websites organised around SF history and subjects. Crossley's general approach can be profitably extended to sf narratives featuring world's fairs and amusement parks *as museums*, such as Silverberg's *World's Fair 1992* (1970), Lewis Shiner's 'White City' (1990), Howard Waldrop's 'Heirs of the Perisphere' (1999), George Saunders's 'Pastoralia' (2000) and Cory Doctorow's *Down and Out in the Magic Kingdom* (2003), as well as *Westworld* (Crichton 1973; HBO 2016–22), *Futureworld* (Heffron 1976), *Total Recall* (Verhoeven 1990; Wiseman 2012), *Tomorrowland* (Bird 2015) and the apparently never-ending Jurassic Park series (1993–).

World's fairs

H. Bruce Franklin compellingly argues that the 'principal form of science fiction in 1939' (38) was the New York World's Fair, known to all as the 'World of Tomorrow'. Contrasting the attractions of that fair, particularly its 'Democracity' and the General Motors 'Futurama', with representative stories from that year's *Astounding* magazine, he demonstrates that 'A fair billing itself as the World of Tomorrow may be considered just as much a work of science fiction as a short story or a novel, a comic book or a movie' (46). Commentaries about the 1939 fair again and again invoke sf to explain its exciting appeal. Neil Harris describes all of the 'Century of Progress' fairs of the 1930s as 'Buck Rogers cities' (129); Morris Dickstein characterises the World of Tomorrow as 'a stunning piece of science fiction' (22); and visitors' memoirs routinely describe the fair as 'something out of Buck Rogers or Flash Gordon' (Rosenblum 12) or note that its vistas were strongly reminiscent of the view of the future offered by William Cameron Menzies's 1936 film *Things to Come* (Appelbaum 5).

Following Franklin's lead, it is easy to enumerate ways in which previous world's fairs – starting with London's Crystal Palace Exhibition (1851) but focusing most intently on the Paris Expositions (1889, 1900), the Chicago World's Columbian Exposition (1893), the Buffalo Pan American Exposition (1901) and the St. Louis Louisiana Purchase Exposition (1904) – featured, both in their general utopian ambience and in their specific architecture and attractions, powerful inducements for imagining the future, constructing change as progress and celebrating it as the new constant of experience, and seeing science and technology as its driving force, all of which are central aspects of sf thinking. Henry Adams, based on his experiences at the Columbian Exposition and the 1900 Paris Exposition, ironically observed that dynamos, emblems of the power and potential of electricity, were beginning to assume in the popular imagination a status previously accorded religion and its great icons. Robert W. Rydell elaborates upon this suggestion, detailing how American world's fairs became 'symbolic universes' that resembled religious celebrations where the object of worship was change, relentlessly constructed as progress (*All* 2).

In their time, these fairs were the greatest tourist attractions ever, with millions upon millions of visitors marvelling at their wonders. The earlier ones were held as sf was beginning to emerge from its various prototypes into the codified form it eventually assumed as a publishing category and mass cultural phenomenon. At the heart of this process, at least in the US, was an increasing interest in the Edisonades of dime novel series featuring the exploits of boy inventors such as Frank Reade, Jack Wright and Electric Bob. Their scaled-down *voyages extraordinaires* resonated with the fairs' 'exotic' ethnographic and anthropological exhibits (and midway sideshows), and their amazing inventions could be easily imagined after a visit to the World's Columbian Exposition's Electricity Building, one of the premier attractions of the fabled White City, where Edison's and Tesla's actual inventions symbolically competed for the future. Unfortunately, the fairs advocated an evolutionary racial hierarchy that elevated white races over those of colour, invoking the authority of science and the application of evolutionary ideas to support racism and distorted racial history, producing a 'sliding scale of humanity' (Rydell *All* 65). Hence, the fairs in general, and the White city in particular, served as 'a utopian construct built upon racist assumptions' (48), valorising colonialism and empire. Sf inherited this aspect of the fairs just as surely as their focus on technological progress.

The great fairs at the turn of the nineteenth century into the twentieth were sf tourism destinations *avant la lettre*, squarely endorsing the techno-enthusiasm of the dime novels that were America's most important form of proto-sf. They were also designed to serve an educational function, to be an 'illustrated encyclopedia of civilization' that visitors could walk through (45). Umberto

Eco takes this idea a step closer to sf, suggesting that a world's fair cannot just be thought of as a 'walk-in encyclopedia', but as a 'teaching machine', an 'enormous experimental laboratory', not one designed to produce immediate results but to offer 'suggestions and ideas for architecture and design' (305–6). Similar claims attended the emergence of sf as a genre.

Coney Island and its successors

World's fairs were temporary phenomena, almost never lasting beyond a couple of years, usually closed and torn down after only six months or so – forlorn remnants scrapped, repurposed for banal uses or left to rot or burn down. ('Sailing to Byzantium' actually mirrors this process: when one of the five cities is changed for a new one, it is disassembled by robots who tear down the simulations.) However, precisely those aspects of the fairs that most obviously promoted the same ethos as did sf – exhibits featuring wild and exotic peoples from faraway lands, entertainment venues driven by new technologies – tended to live on in amusement parks, the most celebrated and influential of which was Coney Island. Particularly between 1897 and 1911, Coney Island was a kind of unruly successor to the great turn-of-the-century fairs. Its three legendary amusement parks – George Tilyou's Steeplechase Park, Frederic Thompson and Skip Dundy's Luna Park, William H. Reynolds's Dreamland – prominently featured innovative mechanical rides, disaster attractions and fantastic architecture reminiscent of the architecture of world's fairs, and each also offered a veritable orgy of electric lights at a time when electricity still signified the future.

Luna Park's 'A Trip to the Moon' attraction was a very popular 'dramatic cyclorama', which according to *The Buffalo Express* combined 'electrical mechanism and scenic and lighting effects [...] to produce the sensation of leaving Earth and flying through space admidst stars, comets and planets to the Moon' in an airship with 'huge wings and large propellers operated by powerful dynamos' and containing mechanisms to simulate motion and provide the craft's 'Anti-Gravitational Force' (Stanton 1998). It is the obvious forerunner of the space flight simulations that have steadily grown more realistic and may be best represented today by Disneyland's 'Star Tours' ride.

Other more transient and less celebrated sf-themed attractions at Coney Island included 'The War of the Worlds', 'Twenty-Thousand Leagues Under the Sea' and a ride to the centre of the Earth. As was true of world's fairs, however, the more abstract ambience or experience of Coney Island was probably more important than individual rides or attractions in preparing mass audiences for sf. Coney Island was not just a striking 'harbinger of modernity' (Kasson 11–2), but a harbinger strikingly similar to what emerged as the early ethos of sf. Coney Island liberated visitors from urban norms and purely utilitarian concepts of technology, while its exotic architecture and unremitting emphasis on the grotesque offered entrance to what premiere showman and Luna Park co-owner Frederic Thompson described as 'a different world – dream world, perhaps a nightmare world – where all is bizarre and fantastic' (Kasson 66). All fiction requires suspension of disbelief, but sf requires a particular kind, conceptually gerrymandered between rhetorics of realism and rhetorics of fantasy given 'realistic' appearance by appeals to science and technology, and nowhere on Earth better represented the broad contours of that science-fictional attitude than Coney Island.

Today's obvious successors to Coney Island are Disneyland and Disney World, including Epcot Center, whose functional and symbolic ties to the 1939 and 1964 New York World's Fairs are unmistakable. The various 'Tomorrowlands' at Disney theme parks echo the futurist ethos of earlier world's fairs, the holistic experience of a Disney theme park clearly generating a frisson very similar to that of sf. Disney attractions, such as 'Pandora – The World of Avatar', also offer immersive physical environments designed to invoke the imaginary worlds of films.

While these sf tourism destinations still offer vestiges of the enthusiasm for technology and technocratic control associated with world's fairs, Scott Bukatman notes the implications of the fact that, rather than the prospect of the future, these parks now offer retro-futures (15–6). They narrativise experience in new ways – 'We no longer feel that we penetrate the future; futures penetrate us' (18 qting John Clute) – and like considerable portions of recent sf, but with a very different motivation, they work to constitute 'terminal identity' (31).

Bukatman describes Tomorrowland as a 'hypercinematic experience', reminding us of yet another way in which the material subjects of sf tourism have always been intertwined. While world's fairs prompted the rise of amusement parks, and both are clearly ancestors of the various Disney worlds, all of these locations are important sites for the experience of various stages in the development of film and television, as well featuring prominently featured in both media. From its earliest days, film aspired to kinds of 'hypercinematic experience', as suggested by the never-realised plans by H.G. Wells and Robert Paul for a cinematic 'time machine' (Landon *Aesthetics* xv) and the numerous American franchises for Hale's Tours, which in the early 1900s gave audiences the sensation of riding on a train while watching films shot from a moving train (Fielding). Coney Island at one time featured more nickelodeons than any other single location and was itself prominently featured in early Edison/Porter films; cinema desired to show motion and the kinetic attractions of Coney Island offered an obvious subject for the new medium (Musser 321). Cinema does not exactly lend itself to being an sf tourism destination, but cinema technology has from its earliest days been associated with sf, as exemplified by George Méliès's *Le Voyage dans la lune* (1902), the first significant example of an sf film.

Dime museums

There remains one early mass culture phenomenon that may have been even more instrumental in preparing audiences for sf thinking: dime museums. Between roughly 1840 and 1900, dime museums, the American continuation and development of the European tradition of the 'Cabinet of Wonders', introduced millions of people to a panoply of scientific information, exotic species, freaks, automata, wax figures and – perhaps most importantly – to an aesthetic of fakery, hoax and humbug very similar to that necessary for the success of sf. As popular an institution in the latter half of the nineteenth century as movies are today, the dime museum 'dazzled men, women, and children with its dioramas, panoramas, georamas, cosmoramas, paintings, relics, freaks, stuffed animals, menageries, waxworks, and theatrical performances' and 'no previous amusement had ever appealed to such a diversified audience or integrated so many diversions under one roof' (Dennett 5). Dime museums date from early in the century but experienced their heyday in the 1880s and 1890s, with noteworthy examples appearing in Baltimore, Boston, Chicago, Cincinnati, Cleveland, Detroit, Grand Rapids, Louisville, Milwaukee, Minneapolis, St. Louis, St. Paul and other cities. The most impressive had long been in Philadelphia (Charles Wilson Peale's Philadelphia museum operated from 1786–1845) and in New York, the location of George Wood's Museum and Metropolitan Theatre, the Eden Musée and, grandest of them all, P.T. Barnum's American Museum (the subject now of an interactive website, The Lost Museum).

Barnum, America's legendary showman, mastered the combination of quasi-educational material with popular entertainment and was instrumental in codifying the 'admiration of the perfection of the fake' as the 'operational aesthetic' of the dime museum (Dennett 115). Barnum's attractions included the famed 'Fejee Mermaid', the 'Wooly Horse', 'What Is It?' (which sensationalised

Darwinian ideas by offering a possible 'missing link'), numerous automata, such as the chess-playing Ajeeb and Herr Faber's Talking Machine, as well as a wide range of giants, midgets and human freaks – all helping to create an audience response quite similar to sf's 'sense of wonder'. Equally important was his role in codifying an aesthetic of hoaxing that constructed showmanship frauds as the positive side of 'humbugging', an intellectual exercise that cultivated audiences who applauded the 'many challenging and delightful aspects to a hoax' (29–30). A unique set of audience protocols emerged from the dime museum experience, including self-conscious perfection of the fake, as exemplified in waxwork exhibits, where the showman's goal was to make the palpably unreal as realistic as possible and the thrill for the viewer was actually in being deceived (107). This new aesthetic for the suspension of disbelief in matters at once fantastic and 'realistic' seems likely to have paved the way for the peculiarly conflicted aesthetic of sf.

The future now: Closer to home

The heydays of the great world's fairs, of Coney Island and dime museums have long passed, but new sf destinations are proliferating. Space tourism remains an option only for the very wealthy, but there are an ever-increasing number of less costly science destinations for the sf tourist. For those without the financial or celebrity wherewithal to score an actual tourist ride into space, cyberspace now beckons as a less exorbitant, but still costly form of tourism. Travel posters and ads for excursions to the planets and the stars abound on Pinterest and keep the dream of science-fictional space tourism alive. Virtual tours of space and just about anywhere else offer increasingly immersive tourist destinations that cover the map of sf subjects. The age of the 'metaverse', most dramatically signalled by Mark Zuckerberg's attempt to develop META into an artificial world, clearly offers a new destination. And, while we await the colonisation of the metaverse there are also technologically constructed hybrid forms of sf tourism that combine virtual and embodied experience. The Smithsonian's Air and Space Museum has featured travelling interactive exhibitions such as 'Walking on Other Worlds', proposing and simulating space travel. NASA's Johnson Space Center in Houston has featured virtual trips to the International Space Station, and the Australian Space Discovery Centre offers similar interactive experiences. Similarly, the UK Science Museum's 'Science Fiction: Voyage to the Edge of Imagination' exhibition offers interactive 'tours' through space, 'guided by AI of extra-terrestrial origin'. Another striking recent example of hybrid simulated sf travel is Convergence Station, an immersive experience installation in Denver, Colorado, taking visitors through four simulated worlds. And, just one of several sites devoted to simulated space travel, the Portland Art Museum offers a new virtual reality installation, 'Symbiosis', that allows visitors to 'travel' to several imaginary worlds designed to highlight the dangers of global warming on Earth.

There are, of course, many other physical locations – possible destinations, both historical and contemporary – of obvious potential interest and relevance to the sf tourist, including planetariums, NASA facilities, Alabama's Space Camp and transitory simulation amusement venues, such as the Virtual Worlds BattleTech Center sites. And, for those who take cyberspace seriously as a location, and therefore a potential tourist destination, online worlds such as *Second Life* (Linden Lab 2003), with its claim of millions of 'residents', and online multi-player games, such as *World of Warcraft* (Blizzard 2004), *The Game of Life* (Black Lantern 2005) and *Spore* (Maxis 2008), offer tourist destinations that might easily be enrolled as forms of sf.

Sf tourism is an important subject for the study of the cultural importance of sf because it dramatically calls attention to the fast-blurring lines between sf and science fact, an ontological process giving ever more evidence of Jean Baudrillard's observation, in response to such New Wave era sf novels as John Brunner's *Stand on Zanzibar* (1968), Norman Spinrad's *Bug Jack Barron* (1969) and especially J.G. Ballard's *Crash* (1973), that our understanding of sf has changed, from thinking of it as being 'an elsewhere' to realising it as 'an everywhere'.

Works cited

Adams, Henry. *The Education of Henry Adams*. Houghton Mifflin, 1973.

Appelbaum, Stanley. *The New York World's Fair 1939/1940 in 155 Photographs by Richard Wurts and Others*. Dover, 1977.

Baudrillard, Jean. 'Simulacra and Science Fiction'. Trans. Art Evans. *Science Fiction Studies* 55 (1991): 309–13.

Bukatman, Scott. 'There's Always . . . Tomorrowland: Disney and the Hypercinematic Experience'. *Matters of Gravity: Special Effects and Supermen in the 20th Century*. Duke UP, 2003. 13–31.

Crossley, Robert. 'In the Palace of the Green Porcelain: Artifacts from the Museums of Science Fiction'. *Styles of Creation: Aesthetic Technique and the Creation of Fictional Worlds*. Ed. George E. Slusser and Eric S. Rabkin. U of Georgia P, 1992. 205–20.

Dennett, Andrea Stulman. *Weird & Wonderful: The Dime Museum in America*. New York UP, 1997.

Dery, Mark. *The Pyrotechnic Insanitarium: American Culture on the Brink of the Millenium*. Grove, 1999.

Dickstein, Morris. 'From the Thirties to the Sixties: The World's Fair in its Own Time', *Remembering the Future: The New York World's Fair From 1939 to 1964*. Ed. Rosemarie Haag Bletter. Rizzoli International, 1989. 21–43.

Eco, Umberto. 'A Theory of Expositions.' *Travels in Hyper Reality: Essays*. Trans. William Weaver. Harcourt Brace, 1983. 289–307.

Fielding, Raymond. 'Hale's Tours: Ultrarealism in the Pre-1910 Motion Picture'. *Cinema Journal* 10.1 (1970): 34–47.

Franklin, H. Bruce. 'America as Science Fiction: 1939'. *Science Fiction Studies* 26 (1982): 38–50.

Harris, Neil. 'Great American Fairs and American Cities: The Role of Chicago's Columbian Exposition'. *Cultural Excursions: Marketing Appetites and Cultural Tastes in Modern America*. U of Chicago P, 1990. 111–31.

Kasson, John F. *Amusing the Million: Coney Island at the Turn of the Century*. Hill & Wang, 1978.

Kluger, Jeffrey. '"It Moved Me to Tears". William Shatner On Briefly Going Where Some Men Have Gone Before.' *Time* (14 October 2021). time.com/6107053/william-shatner-space/

Landon, Brooks. *The Aesthetics of Ambivalence: Rethinking Science Fiction in the Age of Electronic (Re) Production*. Greenwood, 1992.

—. *Science Fiction after 1900: From the Steam Man to the Stars*. Routledge, 2002.

Musser, Charles. *Before the Nickelodeon: Edwin S. Porter and the Edison Manufacturing Company*. U of California P, 1991.

Nye, David E. *The American Technological Sublime*. MIT Press, 1994.

—. *Narratives and Spaces: Technology and the Construction of American Culture*. Columbia UP, 1997.

Rosenblum, Robert. 'Remembrances of Fairs Past'. *Remembering the Future: The New York World's Fair From 1939 to 1964*. Ed. Rosemarie Haag Bletter. Rizzoli International, 1989. 11–20.

Rydell, Robert W. *All the World's a Fair: Visions of Empire at American International Expositions, 1876–1916*. U of Chicago P, 1984.

Stanton, Jeffrey. 'Coney Island – Thompson & Dundy'. *Coney Island History Site* (1998). www.westland.net/coneyisland/articles/thompson&dundy.htm

Tichi, Cecelia. *Shifting Gears: Technology, Literature, Culture in Modernist America*. U of North Carolina P, 1987.

53

SOCIAL ACTIVISM AND SCIENCE FICTION

Shelley Streeby

In their anthology *Octavia's Brood: Science Fiction Stories from Social Justice Movements* (2015), co-editors adrienne maree brown and Walidah Imarisha distinguish what they name visionary fiction, 'science fiction that has relevance towards building newer, freer worlds', from 'the mainstream strain of science fiction, which most often reinforces dominant narratives of power' (Imarisha 4). Declaring that all organising is sf because 'organizers and activists dedicate their lives to creating and envisioning another world, or many other worlds' (3), Imarisha and brown collaborated over many rounds of edits to pull out the visionary aspects of their stories. Prison abolitionist Imarisha's 'Black Angel' climaxes when an immigrant crowd of vulnerable workers team up with a Black fallen angel with a damaged wing to prevent ICE from rounding up their children. brown's leadership of environmental and anti-racist movements shapes 'The River', which focuses on how the Detroit River erupts in support of local people who resist neoliberal governance and gentrification, allowing them a chance to make a different world. Journalist-prisoner Mumia Abu-Jamal's 'Star Wars and the American Imagination' urges readers to refuse to put on the 'imperial uniform' (257) and to dis-identify with imperialism as manifest destiny. Alexis Pauline Gumbs, whose luminous works of Black feminist theory offer alternative environmentalisms, time travels back and forth to imagine in 'Evidence' a world after capitalism when there is no human-caused scarcity and 'justice is no longer punishment' (33). In 'The Last Superhero', comic book artist and writer David Walker crafts a Black superhero harshly impacted by the racism of the comics industry who continues to labour to produce a different, non-White model of the superhero for youth of colour. Race and reproductive health reporter Dani McClain's 'Homing Instinct' asks readers how they would respond if a Presidential Executive Order suddenly limited mobility, stopping most plane flights and locking people into place to combat climate change. Through their editing and the voices and stories they centre, brown and Imarisha put the relationships between activism and sf at the heart of *Octavia's Brood*, thereby making the anthology a portal for many collective endeavours to change the world.

While brown and Imarisha cite Octavia E. Butler as their inspiration because of her emphasis on shaping change, they invoke longer genealogies of sf and social justice by inviting Sheree Renée Thomas to provide a foreword for the collection. An sf writer who is currently editor of the *Magazine of Fantasy and Science Fiction,* Thomas's groundbreaking anthologies *Dark*

DOI: 10.4324/9781003140269-56

Matter: Speculative Fiction from the African Diaspora (2000) and *Dark Matter: Reading the Bones* (2004) made visible a Black sf history that had previously been thought not to exist. Especially by returning to the early twentieth-century sf of W.E.B. Du Bois, Thomas emphasised that Black sf predated the 1960s and 1970s emergence into prominence of major Black writers Samuel R. Delany and Butler. Du Bois's 'The Comet' (1920), building on a long history of comet and last man stories, is a thought experiment that asks what radical changes might be possible in the wake of an apocalyptic event that destroys the old racial order; it is also an indictment of the failure of US Jim Crow democracy (Hartman). In the story, a Black messenger, Jim, is tasked with going down into a bank basement to look for documents, only to be spared when a comet passes over New York City, releasing noxious gases that kill almost everyone else. Julia, a rich White woman, is also spared, and the two briefly come together, believing they may be the last man and woman on Earth, only to be abruptly separated in the surprise ending, when it turns out only the city, rather than the whole world, was afflicted: the Jim Crow racial order is thereby restored and Jim's wife suddenly reappears with their dead baby in her arms. Du Bois's 'Jesus Christ in Texas' (1920) builds on earlier time travel stories and historical fantasy to imagine a foreign-looking, dark-skinned Jesus showing up as a stranger in Waco, Texas, where a lynching had recently taken place, only to witness White people persecuting a Black convict and conspiring to capitalise on prison labour before Christ himself is lynched by the white mob.

As founder of the NAACP and long-time editor of its journal, *The Crisis*, Du Bois was well situated to unite activism and sf but he also built on longer histories of Black sf, speculation and social movement activity. Britt Rusert suggests that scientist, physician, explorer and author Martin Delany 'actively linked scientific revolution to race revolution through a lifetime of activism and writing', including for the *Anglo African Magazine*, scientific articles about comets and popular astronomy. His serialised novel *Blake; Or The Huts of America*, 'a proto-science fiction [...] challenged impoverished conceptions of race and the human' through its 'fugitive science' and transnational, alternate history of slave revolution (153). Baptist minister, publisher and author Sutton E. Griggs also connected activism to sf, selling at revival meetings his alternate history novel *Imperium in Imperio* (1899), which stages debates over the future among Black members of a secret society planning to take over Texas. Pauline Hopkins, also a famous singer and playwright, pushed back on the race science of her day as editor of *Colored American Magazine*, where she serialised *Of One Blood: Or, the Hidden Self* (1902–3), a lost world story in which mixed-race medical doctor Ruel travels to Africa and discovers and becomes king of a great civilisation. Almost two decades later, at the end of World War I and an era of revolutions and social movement agitation, Du Bois's stories precede Hugo Gernsback's founding of the first pulp sf magazine, *Amazing Stories*, in 1926, and John W. Campbell Jr's impactful editing of *Astounding Fiction* that ushered in the so-called Golden Age of sf, even as they look back on a longer history of Black sf and earlier utopian and dystopian novels connected to world-changing speculative visions in Britain and the US.

In the 1950s and 1960s, Judith Merril connected sf to activism while criticising the Golden Age faith in progress and idealisation of US science, technology, militarism and imperial wars. Her first story, 'That Only a Mother' (1948), one of only a few authored by a woman to appear in Campbell's *Astounding*, focuses on a young mother's inability to see that her limbless, hyperprecocious infant daughter has been affected by her father's exposure to uranium while working in Oak Ridge, Tennessee (from 1942 a production site for the Manhattan Project and the atomic bomb). Before giving birth, as the young mother hears about 'fathers' committing 'infanticides' because of 'mutations', she is haunted by the thought that 'we predicted it' but 'didn't prevent it' and that 'we could have stopped it in '46 or '47' (90). Her *Shadow on the Hearth* (1950), which in 1954 was adapted as an episode of the drama anthology *The Motorola Television Hour* (ABC 1953–4), is about a mother, her two children and the small community they form with others after surviving atomic bombs falling on New York. After the mid-1950s, Merril increasingly turned her attention to criticism, editing, archiving and devising media projects that united sf and activism. These included her 'Books' column (1965–9) for the *Magazine of Fantasy and Science Fiction,* her 'Year's Best' anthologies (1956–70), and the creation of the Merril Collection of Science Fiction, Speculation, & Fantasy in Toronto Public Library. These examples illuminate Merril's definition of sf as a method, or as she put it, a 'way of thinking' (*The Year's* 43), that exceeds the literary and spills over into activism and other cultural forms such as radio documentaries and television shows. In 1968, after witnessing police violence at the Democratic Convention in Chicago, Merril left the US for Canada and, while living in Toronto, became involved in anti-Vietnam war activism as well as transnational movements confronting militarism and environmental damage created by war and state violence. From 1968–71, Merril helped to organise and run Committee to Aid Refugees from Militarism (CARM) and travelled to Japan to work with a team translating anti-imperialist and environmentalist Japanese and Korean sf. Merril also conducted research on Japanese environmental and anti-militarism movements and created radio documentaries on these topics for the Canadian Broadcasting Corporation (CBC) when she returned to Toronto.

In 1968, Merril, along with sf author Kate Wilhelm, who had just published a Vietnam War protest novel, *The Killer Thing* (1967), organised an anti-war petition, then tried to have it published, with mixed results: *Analog, Amazing Stories* and *Fantastic* refused, but *Fantasy and Science Fiction* and *Galaxy* printed it, along with a pro-war petition signed by other writers supporting US war in Vietnam (Franklin). In 1969, inspired by her anger at the My Lai massacre, Wilhelm wrote a story called 'The Village', which transposes My Lai to Florida and which no one would publish until 1973. Anti-war petition signer Delany described his FALL OF THE TOWERS trilogy (1963–5) as 'an attempt to create a metaphor for some of what I saw in the streets of the East Village during the Vietnam War', when returning soldiers 'did not seem to have been turned into responsible young men ready to take on the citizenship of having gone off to fight in Vietnam' ('Interview' n.p.). Delany contrasted his own handling of this topic with how Robert A. Heinlein 'felt that the military experience would transform the soldiers and at least the young officers he wrote about in sf novels such as *Starship Troopers'* (n.p.). Also in 1968, in addition to signing the petition, Ursula K. Le Guin wrote the first version of her great anti-Vietnam War novella, 'The Word for World is Forest' (1972), while she was temporarily living in London, missing her work in Portland organising and participating 'in non-violent demonstrations, first against atomic bomb testing, and then against the pursuance of the war in Viet Nam' ('Introduction' 151). In the UK, however, Le Guin had no such 'outlet', while it became ever clearer to her that 'the ethic which approved the defoliation of forests and grasslands and the murder of non-combatants in the name of "peace" was only a corollary of the ethic which permits the despoliation of natural resources for private profit or the GNP, and the murder of the creatures of the Earth in the name of "man"' (151).

Several anti-war petition signers, including Delany, Le Guin and Joanna Russ, were also important connectors of sf to feminist, gay and lesbian activist movements, though they sometimes disagreed about goals and strategies. Le Guin's *The Left Hand of Darkness* (1968) features a people who have a different 'sexual physiology', which is not 'continuous' but occurs during a period called kemmer, the only time they are not androgynous and sexually inactive; they can become either male or female then, depending on the situation. Le Guin explains that the novel was a 'thought experiment', inspired by the women's movement, to consider how 'if we were socially ambisexual, if men and women were completely equal in their social roles, equal legally and economically, equal in freedom, in responsibility, and in self-esteem, then society would be a very different thing' ('Is' 16). Looking back, however, Le Guin felt her critics were right that the Gethenians 'seem like men, instead of menwomen' (14), and to want the novel 'to go further, to dare more, to explore androgyny from a woman's point of view as well as a man's' (16).

Russ, who criticised Le Guin for focusing on the world of men and not explaining family structure and child-rearing, helped bring feminism and the women's movement into the field through her fiction, including *Picnic on Paradise* (1968) and other space adventure stories about Alyx, a time-travelling female mercenary, as well as 'When It Changed' (1972), which focuses on the painful differences created by the arrival of male human colonisers on Whileway, a thriving all-women planet where 30 generations ago all the men died in a plague. This Nebula award-winning story provided the foundation for *The Female Man* (1975), Russ's novel about four women from different worlds and times, including the all-woman planet Whileaway, an alternate past in which the Depression never ended, a near future where men and women are at war, and the 1970s world of its feminist librarian protagonist. In 'The Image of Women in SF', Russ observed that 'most literate science fiction' of her day saw 'the relationships between the sexes as those of present-day white middle class suburbia', even when their stories took place in the far future, while space opera mostly disappeared women or 'tremendously' overrated the 'real he-man' (211). But Russ praised Delany for his depiction of alternate sexual and familial arrangements, observing that his 'people have the rare virtue of fitting the institutions under which they live' (211).

Delany's involvement in sf debates over feminism, the women's movement and imagining alternate arrangements of gender, sexuality, family and community is evident from his participation in the *Khatru* fanzine's symposium on 'Women and Science Fiction' (1975), during which he, Russ, Le Guin, Wilhelm, James Tiptree, Jr and others wrote 168 pages of letters in response to questions about genre and pressing questions of gender raised by social movements of the era. Delany also explored non-heteronormative configurations of gender and sexuality in his extensive criticism and non-fiction and short stories such as 'Aye and Gomorrah' (1967), about astronauts who are neutered before birth and become androgynous Spacers who are fetishised and intensely desired by a group of people called Frelks. His *Babel-17* (1966) has a bisexual polyamorous woman as protagonist and a threesome at its heart, *The Einstein Intersection* (1967) imagines three genders, and *Triton: An Ambiguous Heterotopia* (1976; later retitled *Trouble on Triton*) features a world with 'forty or fifty different sexes and twice as many religions' (99), where people can change their bodies and identities at will.

Delany, Le Guin, Merril, Russ and Wilhelm all taught at the Clarion Science Fiction and Fantasy Writers Workshop, founded in 1968, and in 1971, Delany, Russ and Wilhelm taught a student, Octavia E. Butler, whose work would transform the field by connecting Black feminism to sf, reimagining gender and sexuality, confronting climate change, and criticising the limits of an emergent neoliberalism (including Reagan's privatising, tax-cutting, deregulating policies, and their rootedness in racism, misogyny, xenophobia and militarism), and the ideology of heroic, isolated individuals, usually White men, making progress happen by pursuing profit no matter what the cost. During the Reagan era, Butler wrote Hugo Award-winning short stories such as 'Speech Sounds' (1983), about a Black woman in Los Angeles surviving and making intimate connections in a pandemic that robs most people of the ability to speak, read or write, and 'Bloodchild' (1984), a pregnant man story set in an interplanetary colonial context. Her PATTERNIST series (1976–84) features Black superhumans creating different kinds of communities through psionic powers, while the Black protagonist of *Kindred* (1979) timeslips back to the antebellum south. In the Lilith's Brood trilogy (1987–9), a Black woman, Lilith, hiking in the Andes becomes one of the few survivors of a nuclear war who are rescued by aliens with a completely different sex/gender system who want to reproduce with humans. Lilith struggles with her role in this plan while confronting violence caused by white human men who cannot accept difference, and who kill her Chinese American lover, Joseph. Although much of the trilogy criticises the narrow limits of normative manhood and womanhood while exploring the pleasures and dangers of the alien, non-heteronormative sex-gender system, the novels also explicitly respond to the Ronald Reagan era idea of 'winnable nuclear wars', as Butler explains in *The Last Angel of History* (Akomfrah 1996). During the 1980s, Butler organised a huge collection of annotated newspaper and magazine clippings documenting the Reagan administration's militarism, anti-environmentalism, racism, hostility to the women's movement, deepening of economic inequalities, and encouraging of hatred and fear of difference. On Reagan's side in amping up the militarism were sf writers such as Heinlein and Jerry Pournelle, both of whom had signed the pro-Vietnam War petition, and Gregory Benford, who all joined a Reagan Commission to explore the possibility of an anti-ballistic missile defence. For her part, in *Imago* (1989), the final novel of the trilogy, Butler used Pournelle as a model for the Resistors, who are 'intelligent' and 'competent' but 'insecure about their manhood and thus Supermacho', as well as 'Fascist/racist/ideological' and 'Dangerous to self and others' ('Imago' n.p.).

The Last Angel of History, which connects different cultural forms of sf produced by Black diasporic people, includes a brief clip of Butler dating this genocidal idea, which made her worry there was 'something wrong with the human species', to a time when 'Ronald Reagan had just become President'. By having her aliens 'arrive right after a nuclear war', Butler warned of the contradiction between human intelligence and 'hierarchical behavior'.

Butler's *Parable of the Sower* (1993) critically analysed Reagan-era neoliberalism and inspired new generations of climate activism and Black feminist political leadership. In the novel, a young Black woman comes of age trying to survive in the wake of climate change slow disaster in a world damaged by short-term thinking, the fossil fuel economy, budget cuts, anti-feminist backlash, anti-immigrant politics, the evisceration of public spaces, rollbacks on environmental regulations, and the attacks on civil rights and affirmative action that shaped the 1980s and early 1990s Los Angeles Butler knew so well (Streeby 2018).

In 1992, Butler was joined in her critiques of Reaganism by critical race theorist Derrick Bell, whose work still inspires hate from right-wing politicians years after his death. His 'The Space Traders' (1992) satirises Reaganism's racism and xenophobia, as well as earlier eras of US political and legal history. Aliens offer to solve Earth's problems, including dramatically worsening climate change, if the US agrees to send all Black people to an unknown fate on an alien planet. The aliens speak 'in the familiar comforting tones of former President Reagan, having dubbed his recorded voice into a computerized language-translation system' (327). Bell blames 'decades of conservative, laissez-faire capitalism' and greedy, 'willful exploitation' of Earth's 'natural resources' (329) for the dead birds on US beaches, the oil slicks polluting its waters and the smog obscuring the sky, causing the sick and elderly to have to wear masks when outdoors (329). A Reagan-esque President, who 'had successfully exploited racial fears and hostility in his election campaign' (330), his Cabinet and most voters eagerly endorse this trade of all Black Americans for gold, 'special chemicals capable of unpolluting the environment' and 'a totally safe nuclear engine and fuel, to relieve the nation's all-but-depleted supply of fossil fuel' (327). Bell posits that, to continue to enjoy their privileged way of life without having to pay the costs of climate change or change the way they live, Americans would not hesitate to require Black people to 'sacrifice' themselves for everyone else, since it had 'become an unwritten tradition in this country for whites to sacrifice'

Black 'rights to further their own interests' (339). Perhaps Butler was thinking of this history of Black sacrifice – as well as other sacrifices people of colour have been required to make, such as internment, which Bell mentions as a precedent for the trade – when she wrote in 1983 that she could not bring herself to 'wish for the kind of disaster it would take to get world leaders' tiny minds off ideology and power struggles' to address climate change, since 'such a disaster would be likely to kill me' and 'millions of others' (Commonplace n.p.). Butler speculated that 'Ecodisaster would have to be cumulative and vast to grab our attention and hold it, to seem more than simply another media event to those not directly involved, to forcibly turn the attention of political leaders to survival in a non-military context' (n.p.). In other words, Bell and Butler identified the US national tradition of sacrificing Black rights as one of the major dangers confronting a world threatened by global warming and climate change.

As Butler was working on *Parable*, Laguna writer Leslie Marmon Silko's *Almanac of the Dead* (1991) ended with a near-future scenario in which radical people of colour eco-warriors liberate the Colorado River and plan to join in a multinational prison uprising. They even participate in a conference to discuss the Earth's crisis that resonates with the activism of Indigenous and people of colour environmentalists in the US Southwest in that period. Silko's work, as well as Anishinaabe Gerald Vizenor's earlier slipstream novel *Darkness in St. Louis: Bearhart* (1978), set in an apocalyptic, post-oil US, illuminate Indigenous Americans' long interest in using sf elements to address environmental questions. Potawotami scholar Kyle Powys Whyte suggests, however, that 'Indigenous people do not always share quite the same science fiction imaginaries of dystopian or apocalyptic futures when they confront the possibility of a climate crisis', since the hardships 'most nonindigenous people dread most [... .] are ones that Indigenous people have endured already due to different forms of colonialism: ecosystem collapse, species loss, economic crash, drastic relocation, and cultural disintegration' (226). Like Butler and Bell writing environmentalist sf that calls attention to the US national tradition of sacrificing the rights of Black people and people of colour, Vizenor, Silko and other Indigenous cultural producers use sf to connect environmental struggles and climate change to long histories of still-active US colonialism and imperialism, while affirming counter-histories of place-based Indigenous science inseparable from activist and movement struggles over pipelines, water, forests, mountains and the more-than-human world.

In the twenty-first century, BIPOC sf writers and cultural producers continue to lead the way in connecting sf to activism, co-creating anti-racist, anti-imperialist and environmentalist affiliations through literature as well as digital media, music, film and art. Salma Monani analyses how Canadian Cree–Métis film director and screenwriter Danis Goulet's sf film *Wakening* (2013) arises from Cree storytelling, while as Whyte puts it, 'the protagonists are women and nonhumans who have to figure out how to relate to each other to resist the genocide and environmental destruction of the occupiers who are the true force of destruction and injustice' (231). Whyte contrasts the protagonists of Indigenous sf with the White male heroes of blockbuster movies such as *Avatar* (Cameron 2009). Similarly, building on the work of Danika Medak-Saltzman, Whyte calls attention to how Nanobah Decker's *The 6th World* (2012), a short sf film about the Navajo Nation working with a corporation to establish a human settlement on Mars, 'brings out the protagonist agency of Navajo traditional corn, which plays multiple roles in the film through its spirituality, place in Navajo cultural heritage, association with sound scientific knowledge and motivational value for demanding better futures' (232). Canadian Métis writer Cherie Dimaline also centres non-White-man protagonists in struggles over colonialism, water, global warming and environmental degradation in her best-selling Indigenous coming of age near-future dystopian novel *The Marrow Thieves* (2017).

Other significant contributions from people of colour connecting activism to sf span multiple cultural forms. After co-editing *Octavia's Brood*, adrienne maree brown further aligned sf with anti-imperialist, environmental, feminist, queer and anti-racist activism in her cross-genre book *Emergent Strategy: Shaping Change, Shaping Worlds* (2018), which uses examples from Butler's work to guide social movement activists in co-creating change in their communities. *Fables and Spells* (2022) collects multiple kinds of her writing, including sf and some pieces re-published from her blog and social media writing, that do 'active intentional work to cast spells and create meaningful change' (2) in tandem with her ongoing work as part of multiple movements. In their video essay, 'Inhuman Figures; Robots, Clones, Aliens', Michelle Huang and C.A. Davis examine how sf archetypes of the robot, clone and alien emerge from histories of treating Asian Americans as 'tireless workers, indistinguishable copies, and forever foreigners', while exploring how Canadian Chinese Larissa Lai's *Salt Fish Girl* (2002) re-imagines worker clone communities as radical sites of change and revolution from below. Alex Rivera's near-future film *Sleep Dealer* (2008), set in the US–Mexico borderlands and rural Mexico, similarly centres immigrants and workers of colour in imagining a glimmer of a utopian horizon in activist struggles over militarism, worker exploitation and the privatisation of water. His three protagonists come together to use cyber-labour and drone technologies against corporations and the state to blow up the film's Death Star, the dam that facilitates capitalist control of the water used by one protagonist's rural Mexican farming community. In Beatrice Pita and Rosaura Sánchez's *Lunar Braceros 2125–2148* (2008), people of colour from reservations in Cali-Texas sent to the moon to store toxic waste from Earth rebel against their murderous supervisor and the evil company they work for, inspiring a movement on Earth dedicated to collectively making a different world. As Christopher Perreira suggests, *Lunar Braceros* thereby confronts 'histories of racialized land, labor and resistance through hemispheric, interplanetary environmentalisms' (89).

In addition to these examples of Indigenous people and people of colour creating sf texts connected to activist movements, even blockbuster sf films that centre White protagonists have sometimes inspired people around the world to collectively push for change. Examples include how imagery from the television adaptation (Hulu 2017–) of Margaret Atwood's *The Handmaid's Tale* (1985) has been taken up in reproductive rights struggles, and the use of the distinctive three-finger salute from THE HUNGER GAMES (2012–5) in protest movements in Thailand. Although *Avatar* features a white man hero and rehearses many cliches of colonial fantasy while imagining a coalition that successfully rebels against neocolonial military extractive capitalism, Henry Jenkins suggests that what he calls 'Avatar Activism' is a prime example of how 'citizens around the world are mobilizing icons and myths from popular culture as resources for political speech' (n.p.). Arguing that 'the meaning of a popular film like *Avatar* lies at the intersection between what the author wants to say and how the audience deploys his creation for their own communicative purposes', Jenkins emphasises how 'the myth has been rewritten to focus on local embodiments of the military-industrial complex: in Bel'in, the focus was on the Israeli army; in China, it was on the struggles of indigenous people against the Chinese government; in Brazil, it was the Amazon Indians against logging companies' (n.p.). Today, the debate continues as the first sequel, *Avatar: The Way of Water* (Cameron 2022), which Cameron intentionally made a vehicle of environmentalist critique, prompted criticism from Indigenous people on the grounds of appropriation and of casting White actors in blueface. Further protests arose when Native activists on Twitter, including Yuè Begay, a Navajo artist and co-chair of Indigenous Pride Los Angeles, circulated Cameron's suggestion, in a 2010 interview, that if nineteenth century Lakota Sioux could have seen the future in which so many of their kids committed suicide, they 'would have fought a lot harder' (Valdez). The *Avatar* films are great examples of how the symbolic and material centring of whiteness and the persistence of White saviour protagonists in mainstream sf literature and big media continue to provoke activist critiques, even as activists and protest movements extract and repurpose visual and other elements from them.

Works cited

Abu-Jamal, Mumbia. '*Star Wars* and the American Imagination'. *Octavia's Brood: Science Fiction Stories from Social Justice Movements*. Ed. adrienne maree brown and Walidah Imarisha. AK Press, 2015. 255–7.

Bell, Derrick. 'The Space Traders'. *Dark Matter: Speculative Fiction from the African Diaspora*. Ed. Sheree R. Thomas. Warner, 2000. 326–55.

brown, adrienne maree. *Emergent Strategy: Shaping Change, Shaping Worlds*. AK Press, 2017.

———. *Fables and Spells: Collected and New Short Fiction and Poetry*. AK Press, 2023.

Butler, Octavia E. OEB 3225. Commonplace Book (large), 1983. Octavia E. Butler Papers. The Huntington Library.

———. OEB 8029. Imago: Novel: Notes and Fragments, 1987. Octavia E. Butler Papers, The Huntington Library.

Delany, Samuel R. *Trouble on Triton: An Ambiguous Heterotopia*. Wesleyan UP, 1996.

———. 'Interview'. *The Penn Review* (2021). www.pennreview.org/an-interview-with-samuel-delany

Franklin, H. Bruce. 'The Vietnam War as American Science Fiction and Fantasy'. *Science Fiction Studies* 52 (1990): 341–59.

Hartman, Saidiya. 'The End of White Supremacy, An American Romance'. *Bomb* 152 (2020). https://bombmagazine.org/articles/the-end-of-white-supremacy-an-american-romance/

Imarisha, Walidah. 'Introduction'. *Octavia's Brood: Science Fiction Stories from Social Justice Movements*. Ed. adrienne maree brown and Walidah Imarisha. AK Press, 2015. 3–5.

Jenkins, Henry. 'Avatar Activism and Beyond'. *Pop Junctions* (21 September 2010). http://henryjenkins.org/blog/2010/09/avatar_activism_and_beyond.html

Le Guin, Ursula K. 'Introduction to *The Word for World is Forest*'. *The Language of the Night: Essays on Fantasy and Science Fiction*. Ed. Susan Wood. G.P. Putnam's Sons, 1979. 151–4.

———. 'Is Gender Necessary? Redux'. *Dancing at the Edge of the World: Thoughts on Words, Women, Place*.Gollancz, 1989. 155–2.

Medak-Saltzman, Danika. 'Coming to You from the Indigenous Future: Native Women, Speculative Film Shorts, and the Art of the Possible'. *Studies in American Indian Literatures* 29.1 (2017): 139–71.

Merril, Judith. 'That Only a Mother'. *Astounding Science Fiction* 41.4 (1948): 88–95.

———. '*The Year's Best S-F*, Seventh Annual Edition (1962)'. *The Merril Theory of Lit'ry Criticism: Judith Merril's Nonfiction*. Ed. Ritch Calvin. Aqueduct, 2016. 41–5.

Monani, Salma. 'Feeling and Healing Eco-social Catastrophe: The "Horrific" Slipstream of Danis Goulet's Wakening'. *Paradoxa: Studies in World Literary Genres* 28 (2016): 192–213.

Perreira, Christopher. 'Speculative Futurity and the Eco-cultural Politics of *Lunar Braceros: 2125–2148*'. *Latinx Environmentalisms: Place, Justice, and the Decolonial*. Ed. Sarah D. Wald, David J. Vázquez, Priscilla Solis Ybarra and Sara Jaquette Ray. Temple UP, 2019. 87–103.

Rusert, Britt. *Fugitive Science: Empiricism and Freedom in Early African American Culture*. New York UP, 2017.

Russ, Joanna. 'The Image of Women in SF'. *The Country You Have Never Seen: Essays and Reviews*. Liverpool UP, 2007. 205–18.

Streeby, Shelley. *Imagining the Future of Climate Change: World-Making through Science Fiction and Activism*. U of California P, 2018.

Valdez, Jonah. 'James Cameron's Old Comments Prompt Native American Boycott of New "Avatar" Sequel'. *Los Angeles Times* (19 December 2022). www.latimes.com/entertainment-arts/movies/story/2022-12-19/native-american-boycott-avatar-the-way-of-water

Whyte, Kyle Powys. 'Indigenous Science (fiction) for the Anthropocene: Ancestral Dystopias and Fantasies of Climate Change Crises'. *Environment and Planning E: Nature and Space* 1.1–2 (2018): 224–42.

54
SONIC STUDIES

Erik Steinskog

The tagline to *Alien* (Scott 1979) famously stated 'In space, no one can hear you scream'. The absence of air in space makes it impossible for soundwaves to propagate and thus nothing can be heard, but in sf, where space is a major locale, there are both sounds and screams. And music. Still, the relations among music, sound and sf are not clear-cut. They depend, for example, on genre or medium. Comparing film and literature, the most important difference is also the most obvious one: in film, music is heard, in literature, it is not. In film, there are concrete music and sonics, whereas in literature, they must be imagined. This chapter will start by considering examples of music in films, before a short intermezzo about music in literature, and conclude with a musical sf album. It will put forward some different approaches to what music can be said to mean in sf across various media.

The difference between music that is heard and music that is imagined also opens a question about the historicity, temporality and timeliness of the music. One line of thought related to sf is what could be termed 'the music of the future' (Steinskog 'On'). One such music, the Wagnerian soundtracks of space operas, seems to build on nineteenth century compositional strategies. Symphonic and operatic music may not sound much like a music of the future but they contribute musical tropes and affects that can move between different genres, including sf. This is also a tradition that, in its Wagnerian version, is a continuation of work on myths and fictions, where different layers of history are referenced within a similar aesthetic form. The Wagnerian framework is also useful for thinking across media, as the term *Gesamtkunstwerk* (total work of art) in all its multimedial dimensions testifies (Tomlinson 145–6; Ross 562–608). The Wagnerian soundtracks, however, are used non-diegetically, and as such are there more to create an atmosphere, establish emotional references through musical tropes, and highlight motifs and props than to signify futurity. With diegetic music, the question of the music of the future becomes different.

Another important dimension of film music is the difference between pre-existing music and music written specifically for the film. When Richard Strauss's symphonic poem *Also Sprach Zarathustra* (1896) is used in the opening of *2001: A Space Odyssey* (Kubrick 1968), it contains references both to the Nietzschean inspiration, to Strauss's Germany around 1900, to Kubrick's film as a product of the 1960s, as well as to the story of the origin of the universe, the beginning of tool-use and the story of *2001* (Chion). All this can, in different ways, be communicated to the

DOI: 10.4324/9781003140269-57

audience. This use of Strauss can also be seen as a continuation of the Wagnerian operatic sound found in many classical Hollywood scores, which include 'poetic' dimensions just as opera scores include 'dramatic' dimensions.

Using pre-existing music can also be an integrated part of the film's narrative, such as the scene in *The Matrix* (Wachowski sisters 1999) that introduces Neo. He has fallen asleep in front of his computer with a headset on, and we hear the same music he is hearing: Massive Attack's 'Dissolved Girl' (1998). This, then, is diegetic music, and it broadens our understanding of the scene – sets the stage, references a very specific time and space (even if, as with Kubrick's use of Strauss, music can travel through time and space, and be used differently in a film score). Neo's stack of CDs and headphones also points to the technological mediation of the music. This is not 'live' music in the movie, but the music is integrated into the narrative. The technological dimension also points to how music is made and perceived within the movie. In many ways, *The Matrix* is a movie about the digital and digitalisation, asking questions about what is real and what is a simulation, whether we are living in a simulation, and what would happen if we were and if there was a resistance movement to this simulation in need of a messiah to take down its evolving machinic overlords. But what about the soundtrack? How does the sound partake in the story of *The Matrix*? The answer is not as straightforward as one could think. In the case of Massive Attack's 'Dissolved Girl' (from the album *Mezzanine*), the music illustrates the 1999 that is the time of this layer of the story. Another example of diegetic music is the rave-scene in *The Matrix Revolutions* (Wachowski sisters 2003), where we see musicians playing 'drums' leading to the collective dancing. Here, however, a change happens. Added to the drums we see are electronic percussion, instruments we cannot see, but which have several functions in the scene. Using a slightly stereotypical vocabulary, one could say that the transformation from drums to electronic percussion illustrates a historical dimension – not unrelated to the story opening *2001: A Space Odyssey* – showing how this dancing ritual could be seen as ahistorical, as being a social use of music that goes back to ancient times and continues into rave-culture as a sonic parallel to THE MATRIX TRILOGY, in which this music/dance ritual builds the collective that is soon to fight the Machines. Kodwo Eshun writes that

> Traditionally, the music of the future is always beatless. To be futuristic is to jettison rhythm. The beat is the ballast which prevents escape velocity, which stops music breaking beyond the event horizon. The music of the future is weightless, transcendent, neatly converging with online disembodiment. Holst's *Planet Suite* as used in Kubrick's *2001*, Eno's *Apollo* soundtrack, Vangelis' *Blade Runner* soundtrack: all these are good records – but sonically speaking, they're as futuristic as the Titanic, nothing but updated examples of an 18th C sublime.
>
> (*More* 67)

This 'music of the future' is related to music in sf, as the Kubrick and Scott examples make clear. It is also, however, with Brian Eno's album, related to musical representations of 'outer space' itself. Thus, while Eshun is critical of these sonics, they speak to an understanding of how music of the future used to sound. Here, an important dimension of music and sf comes to the fore: the establishment of a canonic, standardised, stereotypical 'sound' that signifies 'the future' or 'outer space' or 'sf'.

With the soundtrack to *Blade Runner* (Scott 1982), composed and performed by Vangelis, it is possible to discuss the historicity of these sounds. Are they an indication of music of the future in a general sense, or are they a typical example of how the sounds of the future were imagined in 1982? The answer seems to be both. While Vangelis's synthesiser can be heard as typical for instruments around the time of the film's production, his use of the electronic sounds is related to bridging the difference between then and the historical time of the storyline – *Blade Runner* is set in 2019. In terms of how the music may be heard, Eshun's 'beatless' is not dissimilar to 'timeless'.

Eshun's terms – 'weightlessness, transcendent, neatly converging with online disembodiment' (67) – echo William Gibson's descriptions of cyberspace in *Neuromancer* (1984), as well as mid-1990s cybertheory. The musical references found in *Neuromancer* are not necessarily beatless, however. As Mark Dery writes in the group of interviews in which he coined 'Afrofuturism',

> For me, a white reader, the Rastas in *Neuromancer*'s Zion colony are intriguing in that they hold forth the promise of a holistic relationship with technology; they're romanticized arcadians who are obviously very adroit with jury-rigged technology. They struck me as superlunary Romare Beardens – *bricoleurs* whose orbital colony was cobbled together from space junk and whose music, Zion Dub, is described by Gibson (in a wonderfully mixed metaphor) as 'a sensuous mosaic cooked from vast libraries of digitalized pop'.
>
> (194)

Zion Dub is, then, another version of music in sf, but a music that is never heard. Thus, the challenge, for the author, is to describe the music as an imaginary, literal music, which the reader can 'hear' in their inner ear, just as they might 'see' visual descriptions give rise to images. The 'mosaic' Gibson describes recalls contemporary ways of producing music, sampling from 'vast libraries of digitalized pop'. But the description is rather general and does not tell the reader much of how it sounds. In *Neuromancer*, however, it is more the attention to music that is of interest, as well as the use of music both as a way to establish a cultural context and as part of that cultural context.

> As they worked, Case gradually became aware of the music that pulsed constantly through the cluster. It was called dub, a sensuous mosaic cooked from vast libraries of digitalized pop; it was worship, Molly said, and a sense of community.
>
> (Gibson 104)

The fact that this music pulses constantly challenges Eshun's notion of 'beatless'. Here is a music of the future that pulses, and pulse and beat are closely enough related for this to be meaningful. And as with the rave in *The Matrix Revolutions*, the relation to worship and community follows a long line of thinking about Black music. As Amiri Baraka, writing in 1966 as LeRoi Jones, observed: 'Indeed, to go back in any historical (or emotional) line of ascent in Black music leads us inevitably to religion, i.e., spirit worship' (207).

In Afrofuturism or Afro-sonics, other musical, temporal and historical logics are at stake. Afrofuturism contributes a counter-history to a more normative history of the future. Within Afrofuturism, music is intimately related to what Eshun calls 'sonic fiction', but also to a sonic worldbuilding that has to do with more than just fiction. Music, or sound, is, in this framing, related to a way of life and a view of existence. Music is a means of communication and of transportation. It is, in a peculiar sense, related to the building of a world that is to be heard and felt through vibrations. The 'Afrological' and 'Eurological' are different musical 'belief system' (Lewis 'Improvised' 93). As such, the Afrological communicates strongly with the discourse on

Afrofuturist music and art, as well as with Eshun's 'sonic fiction'. In his work on Afrofuturism, George E. Lewis is particularly interested in what the sound as sound can 'tell us about the Afrofuture' ('Foreword' 141). His focus on 'the triad of blackness, sound, and technology' (142) aligns well with what Salim Washington calls the 'Afro-technological' in the sf of Henry Dumas and Samuel R. Delany. Both authors have 'used Afro-technological music either to structure their stories or to function as agents within their stories' (237), and in their fiction music is 'invoked as a technology ranging from a way of communicating to a way of thinking' (238). In Dumas's 'Will the Circle Be Unbroken?' (1966) and Delany's *The Einstein Intersection* (1967), music and musical thinking is 'a means of building (and destroying) culture and civilization' (238). Thus, music is a technology in many different senses.

This may also be how music works on clipping.'s *Splendor & Misery* (2016), an Afrofuturist concept album or space opera that was nominated for the 'Best Dramatic Presentation: Short Form' Hugo in 2017. The album's title is lifted from Delany's unfinished sequel to *Stars in My Pocket Like Grains of Sand* (1984), entitled *The Splendor and Misery of Bodies, of Cities*. This allusion testifies to how individual works of Afrofuturism (a label of which Delany is sceptical; see 'Mirror') tend to point outside themselves to a vast network of references to the emerging – and probably forever emerging – field. This sense of perpetual emergence should be understood within a temporal or historical logic, in the sense that Afrofuturism is not only about a future or the future, but involves all temporal layers, including the past. There are even questions about what 'the past' should be said to signify: just as sf has historically typically construed the future as white, so the hegemonic history of modernity has also been constructed as a white history (or mythology). George G.M. James's *Stolen Legacy* (1954) – the subtitle of which, *the Greeks were not the authors of Greek philosophy, but the people of North Africa, commonly called the Egyptians*, exemplifies a tradition of Afrocentric rebuttal – goes to the core construction not only of Greece, but of Europe, as 'civilisation', and proffers a counter-history (Gilroy; Eshun 'Further'). Questions of time and history are related to the question of origin and about what has been called 'prehistory'; Afrofuturism – and Afromodernity more generally – raises questions about what would in a similar logic be called 'post-history'. As is heard at the start of *Space Is the Place* (Coney 1974): 'it's after the end of the world; don't you know that yet?' One interpretation of this line is that the world ended when the first slave ships left West Africa for the so-called 'new world' of the Americas. From that time, people of African descent inhabit the post-apocalypse, living, in a sense, an sf existence (Eshun 'Further' 298). This is why Dery argues that sf is a kind of logical genre for African Americans, because in a particular sense it could be seen as a form of realism. Just as the reference to Greece implies an origin for Europe, so introducing the trans-Atlantic slave-trade points to an origin of one kind of modernity.

clipping. and *Splendor & Misery* are usually discussed in terms of experimental hip hop. The band describe the album as 'an Afrofuturist, dystopian concept album that follows the sole survivor of a slave uprising on an interstellar cargo ship, and the onboard computer that falls in love with him' (clipping.). The narrative is, however, 'largely conveyed through musical (or more broadly, sonic) means' (Shaviro 125). The dystopian dimension is clear, but Steven Shaviro also insists that there is a more 'utopian, liberatory' current: 'Cargo number 2331 frees himself from bondage; but he is still marked as a fugitive, and he is unable to create a new life elsewhere' (127). Both the utopian and the dystopian dimensions are, then, to be found in the sonics of the album, not only in the lyrics. Still, the lyrics are obviously also part of the sounds, and there is a fascinating continuum of different voices heard on the album. These voices too partake in highlighting the different narrative dimensions. The spaceship echoes the Middle Passage, and the slave rebellion recalls a number of real-life uprisings throughout the time of chattel slavery. This is, so to speak, 'classic' Afrofuturism. These historical references are not merely in the background of the storyline, but present history as a foundation for alternative futures.

While the complete sonics of the album is important, there are some particularly interesting dimensions that can be found in the voices. The first voice we hear, on 'Long Way Away (Intro)', by Paul Outlaw, is heavily distorted, intoning the words: 'I'll follow the stars when the sun goes to bed / 'Til everything I've ever known is long dead / I can't go back home 'cause I want to be free / Someone tell the others what's become of me'. As Andrew J. Kluth writes 'Indistinct and reverberating as if transmitted from away, a lonely voice delivers these lines' to open the album; 'Set to melodic strains reminiscent of a spiritual, these verses evoke the dignity and sorrow of that genre's history, before abruptly shifting to a fast-rapped narrative describing recent events aboard some kind of ship' (135).

Although the lyrics are partly drowned out, the haunting 'lonely' voice can be heard:

> I am quoting the lyrics here as if they were clearly audible; but in fact, they are difficult to distinguish. Outlaw's voice is electronically altered; it is so distorted that it sounds as if he were singing from inside a closet, or through a low-fidelity megaphone. And his words are smothered by a wall of sound, consisting of static together with a rumbling drone that suggests the roar of an airplane engine (or perhaps [...] of starship engines). We are barely able to extract the signal from the noise; the message seems to have been broadcast from a great distance, and under conditions of duress. This tells us that the starship is indeed, as the track's title suggests, 'a long way away', lost in the vast emptiness of interstellar space.
> (Shaviro 128)

Even without the lyrics, then, the sound of the voice, the technologically altered voice, the mixture of the voices and technologically produced sounds together in assemblage communicate a content that is sorrowful, distant and historical. Thus suggesting, not necessarily that we 'are barely able to extract the signal from the noise', but that the noises are indeed signals.

Kluth's reference to the abrupt shift in voices describes the transition to the second track, 'The Breach', where Daveed Diggs raps at high tempo. In contrast to the distorted voice of Outlaw, this is a regular voice, and the lyrics are now drowned in noise, but with a clear diction. Whereas Outlaw might be heard as a first-person narrator, on 'The Breach', Diggs is an omniscient narrator; on the following track, 'All Black', his is the voice of the ship's AI. To hear these differences, one obviously must pay attention to the lyrics, but having settled how Diggs moves between different roles, another focus on the voice can be brought into play. When he is the Mothership's voice, we are supposed to hear it as a machine, but the voice still sounds human; it is nowhere near the stereotypical 'robotic voice' found in sf movies, such as HAL singing 'Daisy Bell' as 'he' disintegrates in *2001* (Auner), or at all like the vocoder voices of the Jonzun Crew (Steinskog *Afrofuturism* 204–5).

Another important vocal presence is the choir on the tracks 'Long Way Away', 'True Believer' and 'Story 5'. Members of the gospel group Take 6 add another human vocality to the album, as well as important elements of history. The sound of the choir – even without the lyrics – is the sound not only of gospel but also of the history of Black people in America, what Baraka calls 'the blues impulse' (Jones 205). In 'Story 5', for example, the choir grows out of an electronic voice, but the electronics are taken away, foregrounding the gospel. It is a classic sound, but in this context sounds almost out of place. The lyrics about 'home' are also of interest in a story about being lost in outer space. At the same time, as Shaviro remarks, the track 'seems to be set in the present moment' (133) – our present as listeners, not the present of the narrative. Thus, 'Story 5' negotiates between a sonic pastness (both Shaviro and Kluth refer to spirituals and slave songs), a sonic presentness, and a sonic futurity. These different layers of history function as a kind of sonic time-travel, a dimension easily overlooked unless one pays attention to how the sounds and the music work as integrated parts of the album's worldbuilding and storytelling.

On 'True Believer' these different layers come together. The rap-section is at a slow pace, surrounded with very noisy or industrial drum sounds. Another voice sings in the background, heavily distorted but melodic. The choir comes in, singing together with the distorted voice, thus altering the quality of the vocal. It is as if the change in filter signifies that there is a gradual relation, rather than a clear-cut dichotomy, between the human and the machine. Towards the end of the track a computerised voice comes in, with glitches between pitches highlighting the fact that it is an artificial voice. Still, the lyrics are the same as the distorted voice of Outlaw: 'True believer, I know when we going home' – and an interpolation of the nineteenth century slave song 'I Know When I'm Going Home' (Hay 283; Knight 36). It is as if the song quotes W.E.B. DuBois: 'a haunting echo of these weird old songs in which the soul of the black slave spoke to men' (167).

A multiplicity of voices is also heard on the album's final track, 'A Better Place'. It opens with a synthesiser fanfare. The voice is distorted, as if singing through a megaphone. Still the melody is very singable, thus establishing a contrast to the distorted sound. The rap is in regular voice with the same synthesiser fanfare unfolding beneath it. Then a chorus-like phrase, sung in a very mechanical rhythm, again opening for a non-human way of singing. These different voices are emblematic of how the story is told on *Splendid & Misery*, with several different voices that are related to the characters they represent but can also be understood as questioning, in a more general sense, the 'humanness' of the voice and what kind of non-human voices are heard in sf. Here, rather than referencing the past, some of the futuristic dimensions of the album comes to the fore.

What, then, about the sounds that are not voices? The analysis of the voices give hints. It is as if there is a continuum between voices and technology where, on a first listening, the technologically altered voices seem to exist somewhere in-between. Something similar to how the sound of the choir echoes a long history can be heard on the album's only instrumental track, 'Long Way Away (instrumental)'. Here, sounds of a piano in the background are surrounded by noise as if from a phonograph. There is something distinctly resembling The Caretaker's music, not least his album *Patience (After Sebald)* (2012), where a hauntological dimension is put into manipulation of a recording of Franz Schubert's 'Winterreise' (1828). This is another version of how the mixing of the album, the relation between the different layers of sound, contributes to a changing focus between voices, synthesisers, percussion and other elements. Another kind of relation between the music and 'voices' is heard on 'Break the Glass', where the synths almost sound like the 'voices' of the alien heptapods in *Arrival* (Villeneuve 2016), demonstrating how some sounds seem to have an almost intrinsic sf dimension to them, and how it is possible for sounds to quickly become significant and gain an intertextual dimension. In contrast, on 'Air 'Em Out', the lyrics refer to Morse code, and from that point one almost starts listening to Morse code in the percussion. It is not, then, that the meaning or signal is lost in the noise. Rather, the relation between the different dimensions of *Splendor & Misery* – the lyrics, the singing, the music – all partake in the creation of meaning. There is no distinction between diegetic and non-diegetic music, as would be the case with film. Consequently, this kind of listening, this kind of sonic sf, may help thinking about how to listen to music in film and literature differently; listening with the same attention – also to the unheard music – to how it contributes to the stories.

Works cited

Auner, Joseph. '"Sing It for Me": Posthuman Ventriloquism in Recent Popular Music'. *Journal of the Royal Musical Association* 128.1 (2003): 98–122.
Chion, Michel. *Kubrick's Cinema Odyssey*. BFI, 2001.
clipping. *Splendor & Misery*. Sub Pop and Deathbomb Arc, 2016.
Delany, Samuel R. 'The Mirror of Afrofuturism'. *Extrapolation* 61.1–2 (2020): 173–84.
Dery, Mark. 'Black to the Future: Interviews with Samuel R. Delany, Greg Tate, and Tricia Rose'. *Flame Wars: The Discourse on Cyberculture*. Ed. Mark Dery. Duke UP, 1994. 179–222.
Du Bois, W.E.B. *The Souls of Black Folk*. Oxford UP, 2007.
Eshun, Kodwo. 'Further Considerations of Afrofuturism'. *CR: The New Centennial Review* 3.2 (2003): 287–302.
——. *More Brilliant Than The Sun: Adventures in Sonic Fiction*. Quartet, 1998.
Gibson, William. *Neuromancer*. Ace, 1984.
Gilroy, Paul. *The Black Atlantic: Modernity and Double Consciousness*. Verso, 1993.
Hay, Jonathan. 'Afrofuturism in clipping.'s *Splendor & Misery*'. *Boogie Down Predictions: Hip-Hop, Time and Afrofuturism*. Ed. Roy Christopher. Strange Attractor, 2022. 276–87.
Jones, LeRoi. 'The Changing Same (R&B and New Black Music)'. *Black Music*. Akashi Classics, 2010. 205–41.
Kluth, Andrew J. 'Finding Home in the Unknown: Sounding Self-Determination from the Streets to the Void'. *Sonic Identity at the Margins*. Ed. Joanna Love and Jessie Fillerup. Bloomsbury, 2022. 135–50.
Knight, Nadine. '"A Long Way Away": Unreachable Freedoms in Contemporary Afrofuturist Neo-Slave Narratives'. *MOSF Journal of Science Fiction* 2.4 (2018): 26–44.
Lewis, George E. 'Foreword: After Afrofuturism'. *Journal of the Society of American Music* 2.2 (2008): 139–53.
——. 'Improvised Music after 1950: Afrological and Eurological Perspectives'. *Black Music Research Journal* 16.1 (1996): 91–122.
Ross, Alex. *Wagnerism: Art and Politics in the Shadow of Music*. Farrar, Straus and Giroux, 2020.
Shaviro, Steven. *Extreme Fabulations: Science Fictions of Life*. Goldsmiths Press, 2021.
Steinskog, Erik. *Afrofuturism and Black Sound Studies: Culture, Technology, and Things to Come*. Palgrave Macmillan, 2018.
——. 'On the Other Side of Time: Afrofuturism and the Sounds of the Future'. *The Oxford Handbook of Sound and Imagination, Volume 2*. Ed. Mark Grimshaw-Aagaard, Mads Walther-Hansen and Martin Knakkergaard. Oxford UP, 2019. 611–28.
Tomlinson, Gary. *Metaphysical Song: An Essay on Opera*. Princeton UP, 1999.
Washington, Salim. 'The Avenging Angel of Creation/Destruction: Black Music and the Afro-technological in the Science Fiction of Henry Dumas and Samuel R. Delany'. *Journal of the Society of American Music* 2.2 (2008): 235–53.

55

UTOPIAN STUDIES

Katie Stone

Introduction

In *Metamorphoses of Science Fiction*, Darko Suvin argues that 'strictly and precisely speaking, utopia is not a genre but the *sociopolitical subgenre of science fiction*' (61 italics in original). This claim is not intended to diminish utopianism's importance to sf. Indeed, while Suvin suggests that the younger genre has retrospectively 'englob[ed]' utopianism, he also contends that sf 'can finally be written only between the utopian and anti-utopian horizons' (61). For him, texts which make the oppressive political and economic configurations of historical reality appear strange and thus potentially open to transformation are both utopian *and* science-fictional. These apparently separate literary traditions are here shown to be united in the project of envisioning freer and more just worlds.

Suvin's insistence on the co-constitutiveness of utopianism and sf in his highly influential theorisation of the genre is reflective of the foundational position utopian studies has always had within sf studies. As Alcena Madeline Davis Rogan notes, 'there has been, from the emergence and consolidation of sf studies and utopian studies [in the 1970s], considerable cross-fertilization in terms of texts studied and of scholars engaged in both disciplines' (309). This interconnectedness is evident in the web of scholarly communities which encompass both fields, as well as in those texts, such as Fredric Jameson's *Archaeologies of the Future: The Desire Called Utopia and Other Science Fictions* (2005) and Tom Moylan's *Demand the Impossible: Science Fiction and the Utopian Imagination* (1986), which have come to act as touchstones in both utopian and sf studies. Further, this cross-fertilisation has led to the recognition of certain texts as central to the shared utopian, science-fictional tradition. Rogan's survey of major literary utopias – extending from Thomas More's *Utopia* (1516) through the fin de siècle utopias of Edward Bellamy, William Morris and Charlotte Perkins Gilman, and on to 'the critical utopias' of the 1970s (Moylan 11), including Ursula K. Le Guin's *The Dispossessed* (1974), Joanna Russ's *The Female Man* (1975) and Samuel R. Delany's *Triton* (1976) – is a survey of texts replete with the trappings of sf. Moreover, this history maps directly onto the narrative within utopian studies of utopianism developing from providing blueprints of perfect islands to detailing the process of creating better worlds or what Ruth Levitas terms 'utopia as method' (1).

The construction of this shared history has not, however, been uncontentious. For example, Jameson dismisses the feminist and anti-racist sf of writers such as Russ and Octavia

 DOI: 10.4324/9781003140269-58

E. Butler – describing 'the gender turn' within utopianism of the 1970s as 'the sign of a waning of the Utopian imagination' (140). In contrast, Moylan argues that it is in precisely these feminist texts, which emerge out of the Black, women's and gay liberation movements of the 1960s, that 'a radical utopian activism [...] that offers a serious oppositional challenge to the historical status quo' becomes thinkable (116). However, while their assessment of a particular text's political significance may change, utopian studies scholars have remained relatively united in their belief that the success or failure of a given utopia lies in its compatibility with a revolutionary Marxist politics. Studies of utopian literature are often implicitly or explicitly formulated as defences of utopianism, designed to counter the accusation, levelled most famously in Friedrich Engels's *Socialism: Utopian and Scientific* (1880), that utopianism is insufficiently 'representative of the interests of [the] proletariat' which can only be addressed by a properly scientific socialism (6). The picture which Rogan paints – of a field organised around a core set of texts which critics then attempt to connect 'to the transformation of actuality into utopia' (Freedman 69) – accurately and compellingly reflects the critical conversations which have dominated the discipline.

Rather than merely reiterate such an account, this chapter engages with scholars whose work is interested in asking a rather different set of questions. They are less concerned with defending utopianism from accusations of naïveté or static perfection than with: how utopian visions of exotic islands are implicated in colonialist expansion; how a utopian faith in the importance of future generations can be used to police queer subjects in the present; and how the attraction of lands populated by beautiful, non-disabled and almost invariably White people is directly tied to eugenics. While some may align this critical turn with the gender turn which Jameson argued moved utopian thought away from the materiality of class struggle towards the much-maligned field of identity politics, it is in fact frequently more attentive to the material conditions from which utopian texts have arisen. Only by acknowledging that the history of utopian sf is informed by imperial expansion, colonial domination and eugenic control of oppressed populations does it become possible to salvage the 'gold-bearing rubble' (Bloch *Heritage* 116) of the utopian tradition. This chapter examines these critiques of utopianism's complicity in logics of colonialist, homophobic and ableist oppression, looking to how they have expanded the contours of utopian studies, forced a radical reassessment of utopianism's position within revolutionary politics but ultimately maintained an insistent focus on the need for 'hope against hope' (Out of the Woods Collective 15).

Colonising Utopia

The kingdom of Utopia used to have another name. Before King Utopus arrived, it was known as Abraxa. More writes

> this was no island at first, but a part of the continent. Utopus, that conquered it [...] brought the rude and uncivilised inhabitants into [...] good government [...] Having soon subdued them, he designed to separate them from the continent, and to bring the sea quite round them. To accomplish this he ordered a deep channel to be dug [...] and that the natives might not think he treated them like slaves, he not only forced the inhabitants, but also his own soldiers, to labour in carrying it on [...] his neighbours, who at first laughed at the folly of the undertaking, no sooner saw it brought to perfection than they were struck with admiration and terror.
>
> (72–3)

While previous critics have dwelt on the fear that others will laugh at the 'folly' of utopianism, China Miéville argues that 'not nearly enough' has been done to grapple with the far more pressing fact that 'the splendid – utopian – isolation' of More's island is the product of 'violent imperial' action (4). Addressing this critical silence, Dohra Ahmad begins her study of anti-colonial utopianism in the Americas by arguing that 'classical utopias have been thoroughly imbricated in the ideologies of empire ever since the inception of the genre' (6). For her, the fact that More's Utopia was founded on the enslavement of Indigenous people is not incidental to his vision of a perfect society. Indeed, she argues, 'the early utopian fiction of More, [Francis] Bacon, and others derived much of its energy from the discovery of new continents and islands' (6). Similarly, Karl Hardy emphasises the significance of the colonisation of Abraxa: 'The Utopians and their ideas are unambiguously representative of a notion of progressive modernity counter posed with Indigenous inhabitants (Abraxans) who are consigned to a backward "primitive" pre-modernity' (126). The long-lasting effects of this narrative of progressive modernisation cannot be overstated: 'nearly all of the various expressions or "faces" of utopianism – from intentional communities to radicalized politics – which emerge from [...] settler societies ought to be recognized as being predicated upon and, therefore, implicated in the ongoing naturalization of settler colonization' (127). This suggestion, that utopianism naturalises colonialist oppression, must be of particular concern to those sf critics who insist on the genre's capacity for denaturalisation and estrangement.

What becomes apparent in readings of *Utopia* that begin with the colonisation of Abraxa is that the 'transformation of actuality into utopia' (Freedman 69) presented as the goal of utopian literature in more traditional accounts of the genre, has, in fact, already taken place. For Hardy, the notion that 'the modern utopian tradition' has had 'specific and substantial effects' (124) on world history is undeniable but this influence is not, or not only, to be lauded. As Hardy notes, '*Utopia* clearly articulates the settler colonial doctrines [...] which were used by European powers to establish legalistic grounds, via an appeal to the "law of nature" for expropriating the supposedly uninhabited land' (125). Nor is this the extent of its influence. Bill Ashcroft argues that 'the ideology of imperialism cannot survive unless it couches its expansionist aims in the utopian idea of the civilizing mission' (14); not only is utopian literature of the sixteenth and seventeenth centuries implicated in the imperialist projects of that period, but utopianism becomes their justification. John Mohawk (Seneca) argues that 'the pursuit of utopian goals requires resources, both material and nonmaterial, and its achievement is such a splendid objective that its followers are inclined to believe nothing should stand in the way of securing those resources' (3). Consequently, we must 'view Western utopianism in the context of Western history and culture and not as a series of isolated movements that can be dismissed as aberrations' (3). Mohawk presents a picture of utopianism 'woven into the fabric of the culture' (3). One may not be able to locate More's Utopia, Bacon's *New Atlantis* (1626) or Margaret Cavendish's *The Blazing World* (1666) on a map, but these critics demonstrate that these fantastic lands do have real world counterparts – that utopia may be 'all too close' to our reality (Miéville 5).

Eugenic perfection

The influence of colonialism on utopianism did not end with the so-called era of discovery. As Ahmad notes, 'two successive waves of utopian activity each relied upon a central apparatus of colonial activity: exploration in the sixteenth and seventeenth centuries; and developmentalism in the late nineteenth and early twentieth centuries' (6). It is no coincidence that the fin de siècle was characterised both by a surge in the production of utopian literature and by the emergence of a 'developmentalist view of history [that] undergirded the colonial project, relegating what had been blank spaces [on the globe] to the temporalized category of primitive and backward' (6). While texts such as Edward Bellamy's *Looking Backward, 2000–1887* (1888) do not depend directly upon narratives of conquest, Ahmad shows how they remain implicated within a colonial logic of progressive development wherein Indigenous cultures are equated with Europe's past and their only hope for the future is deemed to lie in becoming more 'modern' (i.e., White and European). The broader utopian project of creating a 'better' world also comes under scrutiny here as its parallels with paternalistic colonial rule are laid bare. Ahmad's framework demonstrates that the question 'Better than what?' is not only voiced by bad-faith actors who fear any kind of change. By highlighting utopianism's colonial underpinnings, she renders intelligible some of the least discussed elements of turn-of-the-century utopias, such as the episode Mary E. Bradley Lane's heroine spends with the 'Esquimaux' on her return from the utopian land of *Mizora* (1890). While Lane's condemnation of these Indigenous peoples as being, 'like all low natures', an 'intensely selfish' people (146) may initially seem incongruous in a text elsewhere seemingly committed to justice for all, it is in fact entirely in keeping with this developmentalist framework.

Perhaps the most significant manifestation of this overlap between colonialist developmentalism and the utopian drive to create more perfect societies lies in the field of eugenics. Having returned from what she views as the perfect land of Mizora, where all the people are women and all the women have pale skin and blonde hair, Lane's heroine bemoans the fact that 'we cannot hope to attain their perfection in our generation' (147). The hope for the next generation, she argues, lies in eugenic breeding practices. She states that 'our' present circumstances are attributable to the fact that 'crime is as hereditary as disease' and yet criminals refuse to live in 'ascetic celibacy' thus 'endow[ing] posterity with the horrible capacity for murder that lies in [their] blood' (147). In this statement, which directly follows her critique of 'the Esquimaux', Lane demonstrates the direct connection between utopian developmentalism and eugenic control. Far from being an aberration in an otherwise utopian text, this racism and ableism is typical of utopian writing of the period even, or perhaps particularly, that which has widely been praised for its feminism. Asha Nadkarni demonstrates that, in the 'nationalist feminist politics' of writers such as Lane and Gilman, the desire for a 'more perfect [...] future' is intimately tied to questions of reproduction and population control (1). Within their eugenic framework the progress of the nation is stifled by the fact that while wealthy White women are having fewer children, supposedly over-fecund immigrant and Black populations are having far too many. Gilman's utopian vision of a society organised around childcare – where, as one Herlander puts it, 'the children [...] are the one center and focus of all our thoughts' (66) – is intimately bound to such works as 'A Suggestion on The Negro Problem' (1908), in which Gilman advocates forced education camps for Black children in an effort to 'control' the African American population. As Nadkarni notes, these 'two seemingly opposed figurations of children are simply different sides to the same eugenic coin' (5). This goes some way to explain what Edward Chan has described as *The Racial Horizon of Utopia* (2015). He argues that 'in *Herland*, race is *not* an issue for Utopia to contend with, but instead a premise from which to begin. [...] It is as if equality can be achieved only if all subjects within a utopian field are the same (all of one class, all of one sex, all of one race)' (11 italics in original). This excision of race from utopianism has led to a concomitant 'absence in the criticism' (4).

An ongoing legacy

The legacies of colonialism and eugenics in these fin de siècle utopian texts can still be felt in the critical utopianism of the 1970s. While many of the feminist utopias of the period include a significant commitment to anti-racist politics, they also, as Joanna Russ notes, 'resemble not only each other but [...] Charlotte Perkins Gilman's *Herland*' (Russ 133). Marge Piercy's *Woman on the Edge of Time* (1976) has become a particular object of scrutiny in this regard, perhaps because, in her creation of the utopian community of Mattapoisett, her commitments to nonbinary gender identity, racial equality and queer sexual freedoms seem to run so directly counter to Gilman's essentialist, anti-sex, colonialist feminism. Chan acknowledges that Piercy 'attempts to imagine new forms of racial identity', but argues that they do not ultimately come to fruition 'because they conceptualize race as something that can be abstracted' from other identity formations (19). Meanwhile, Alison Kafer notes that 'Piercy's future [...] is almost completely devoid of people with disabilities' (21). The utopia which Piercy constructs is reliant on 'brooders', artificial wombs which do the work of gestating fetuses, thus severing the apparent tie between cis-womanhood and pregnancy. This technology has been connected to Shulamith Firestone's revolutionary vision of technologically-mediated, gender-free gestation. However, as Kafer indicates, it is also used to screen out supposedly undesirable genetic traits, explicitly including all physical disabilities, leading her to question 'whether "utopia," by definition, excludes disability and illness' (21). This same pattern of exclusion is identified in Trish Salah's trans feminist reading of Piercy's novel as a narrative which hinges on the choice between 'good (utopic/feminist) and bad (patriarchal/transsexual) forms of gendered becoming' (n.p.). Salah notes that the dystopic alternate future which occasionally emerges in Piercy's novel is marked by the appearance of a woman whose body is described as 'a cartoon of femininity' due to her breast and buttock implants (Piercy 288). In these scenes it is made clear that while in Mattapoisett it is deemed normal to use gender neutral pronouns and to play with gender expression, to have any gender-based surgery is thought to be unnatural. As Salah puts it: 'while there is no transsexual in the scene' in which the reader is introduced to the surgically enhanced Gildina, 'metaphorical transsexuality (femininity as techno-patriarchal coercion) pervades it' (n.p.). The feminism of even the critical utopias of the 1970s is thus shown to be filled with moments of erasure of oppressed peoples, complicity with dominating logics and failure to imagine a fully liberatory world.

What these critiques indicate is that the energy which utopian studies has historically expended on defending utopianism from those who dismiss it as naïve or critique its validity as an always-hypothetical political project has arguably been misplaced. These scholars critique utopianism, not because it is in some way unrealistic, but rather because it is all too deeply embedded in some of the most oppressive structures of historical reality.

The rest of this chapter turns to those scholars who insist on the continued political significance of utopianism while fully acknowledging the influence of these colonialist, eugenic legacies on the genre. Refusing to ascribe to the kind of purity politics so firmly upheld within eugenic utopianism, they view these legacies not as a corrupting stain which irrevocably morally dirties utopianism, but rather as a series of ongoing violences, which must be continually accounted for and combatted within the broader theorisation of an anti-colonial utopianism.

Utopianism's alternate histories

One notable tactic taken up by critics seeking to engage with utopianism's colonial legacies is to combat what Ashcroft describes as the 'increasingly questionable' (4) claim of Krishan Kumar that 'so far as I have been able to establish, nothing like the western utopia and utopian traditions exist in any non-western or non-Christian culture' (424 n4). Ralph Pordzik, for example, develops readings of work by Buchi Emecheta, Ben Okri and Sunita Namjoshi, and argues that the proliferation of utopian writing in Australia, New Zealand, India and Nigeria is indicative of 'a gradual transition in utopian writing from a "colonial" phase in which the future was usually described through the filter of European perceptions and attitudes' to a post-colonial phase in which writers offered 'radical alternatives' to 'prevailing literary conventions' (169). Barnita Bagchi's edited collection, *The Politics of the (Im)Possible* (2012), brings together 'suggestive leads for transnational and simultaneously non-Eurocentric utopian studies' ('Introduction' 9), including Modhumita Roy's reading of Bessie Head's *When Rain Clouds Gather* (1968) and Bagchi's own study of the utopian writing of Rokeya Sakhawat Hossain. Bagchi notes that 'Hossain's *Sultana's Dream* was published before [...] *Herland*' ('Introduction' 10) and she successfully demonstrates that any 'genuinely global mapping of female utopia' ought to include Hossain's depiction of a 'world free of colonial rule where emancipated educated women rule a peaceful, technologically futuristic yet pastoral world' ('Ladylands' 178)

While Bagchi's study demonstrates, contra Kumar, the presence of explicitly utopian writing in the Global South, Ashcroft suggests that anti-colonial struggle is itself a potentially utopian movement. He argues that

> postcolonial utopianism began with anti-colonial utopias that focused on the prospect of an independent nation [and although] the literature that flourished after independence [...] had its full share of critical anger about post-independence regimes [it] nevertheless developed a hope in the future that could not be quenched.
>
> (4–5)

Ashcroft moves between discussions of Kamau Brathwaite's tidalectic poetry, where the imperialist vision of the utopian island has been replaced by an 'archipelagic sense of movement and flow' (17), to readings of Larissa Sansour's *A Space Exodus* (2009), the story of an astronaut planting a Palestinian flag on the moon in defiance of the ongoing occupation. Eric Smith argues that 'the new millennium [...] has witnessed the phenomenal efflorescence of narratives written within a speculative framework that radically reconfigure the conceptual machinery of sf and utopia to address the exigencies of postcoloniality and globalization' (5). Drawing attention to the writing of Nalo Hopkinson, Vandana Singh and Amitav Ghosh, Smith argues that the utopian potential of these texts lies in their capacity for bringing to light 'the miraculous potentialities already present within the perceived limits of what we call "reality"' (11). These writers refuse to accept that their horizons are defined by global capitalist hegemony in the present and imperialist utopianism in the future, instead drawing on their knowledge of the specificity of life in previously colonised countries in order to 'reclaim the materialist stakes of an anti-imperialist resistance' (15). Overall, what these studies suggest is that although what Nedine Moonsamy refers to as 'generic science fiction utopias' are insufficient when read in the context of anti-colonial struggle (329), Global South creators attempt 'to wean the reader off purist notions of utopia but not utopia, per se' (341). The 'compelling conceptual mutations of utopia' produced in, for example, Ivor W. Hartmann's *AfroSF* (2012) anthology, analysed by Moonsamy, then act as provocations to expand 'the ambit of utopian studies and science fiction at large' (330).

There has been a parallel impulse within anti-colonial utopian studies to highlight the significance of Black cultural production in the US. Alex Zamalin argues that while 'much of black American life has been nothing short of dystopian', a 'utopian strain' is identifiable in the Black radical tradition which unites 'Frederick Douglass's abolitionist dream of emancipation' with the work of those 'contemporary black activists [who are] calling for abolishing mass incarceration' (6–7). He consider a range of Black utopian texts, from W.E.B. Du Bois's *Dark Princess* (1928), which 'visualize[s] the conditions for achieving a Global South utopia, in which all people of color united for collective self-determination' (8) to Octavia K. Butler's PARABLES series (1993–8), where an embattled community in an increasingly apocalyptic US struggles towards the stars.

Zamalin argues that 'black utopians [...] engaged in a unique form of utopian theorizing, unlike that of the European tradition' (12). In the writing of Martin Delany, George Schuyler and Pauline Hopkins, he locates a form of utopianism where 'the romantic tropes, sense of wholeness, spiritual redemption, and rational teleology that had long been a staple of Western utopia' were replaced by 'unfinished conversations, unresolved debates [and] critical problematics, which resisted easy resolution' (12). Jayna Brown, meanwhile, takes a more expansive look at the Black utopian tradition, moving beyond texts which explicitly delineate a better society towards an understanding of utopia as 'a state of being and doing' (7). The 'archive of black alternative worldmaking' she constructs includes the sf novels of Butler and Delany, the music of Alice Coltrane/Turiyasangitananda and Sun Ra, and the mystical preaching of figures such as Sojourner Truth and Rebecca Cox Jackson (7). Brown's work demonstrates that to include Black writing within the utopian tradition necessarily involves exploding that tradition from within. Rather than attempting to intervene in white utopianism on its own terms, Brown claims that Black people are uniquely situated to engage in utopianism: 'Unburdened by investments in belonging to a system created to exclude us in the first place, we develop marvelous modes of being in and perceiving the universe' (7).

Beyond the pale

Centring marginalised voices within utopian studies involves an interrogation of the genre's formal properties as well as, and in relation to, its content. In the opening pages of *The Principle of Hope*, Bloch argues that 'to limit the utopian to the Thomas More variety, or simply to orientate it in that direction, would be like trying to reduce electricity to the amber from which it gets its Greek name' (15). This statement has been taken up by those interested in expanding the remit of utopian studies so that it reaches beyond the recognised canon of literary utopias. For example, Caroline Edwards tracks how authors such as Hari Kunzru and Joanna Kavenna incorporate 'suggestively non-mimetic' elements into their 'otherwise realist narrative representations of contemporary experience' in a manner which 'open[s] up a realm of utopian possibility' (3–4). These texts are not utopias but are, potentially, utopian. They challenge dominant understandings of what a 'better' world might entail. As Megen de Bruin-Molé argues in her study of Black utopianism and salvage Marxism in the fiction of Rivers Solomon, 'utopian fictions are all around us, but to see the better worlds they present we may need to adopt a different viewpoint' (n.p.).

This expansion of what counts as a utopian sf text has also led to a wider exploration of utopian 'state[s] of being and doing' (Brown 7). For example, Caterina Nirta argues that 'it is possible to *really* think of the transgender body as a utopia of the now, in the now and for the now' (27 italics in original), with transgender embodiment understood as a means of making the hoped-for future material in the present. This emphasis on utopian embodiment and praxis need not necessitate a turning away from sf. Indeed, Nirta's analysis aligns with Susan Stryker's influential trans feminist essay 'My Words to Victor Frankenstein Above the Village of Chamounix' (1994), in which she claims a 'deep affinity' with Frankenstein's Creature on the basis that they have both been labeled as 'monster[s]' (238). This affinity is not to be rejected, in Stryker's understanding, but celebrated. The fact that '"monster" is derived from the Latin noun monstrum, [meaning] "divine portent"', suggests that those labelled as monsters have the power to act as 'heralds of the extraordinary' (240). Here, the science-fictional, utopian realm of the extraordinary is brought into the present, a move mirrored in the writing of Sophie Lewis, who argues that the science-fictional sculptures of Patricia Piccinnini, which depict alien surrogates gestating one another's young, are so compelling precisely because they offer, not a glimpse of another, distant world but rather a reflection of the 'gestational communism' already being practiced in our present (21). As Lewis puts it,

'Everywhere about me, I can see beautiful militants hell-bent on regeneration, not self-replication' (167). One is here reminded that Donna J. Haraway's 'A Manifesto for Cyborgs' (1985), in which she claims that 'the boundary between science fiction and social reality is an optical illusion', is also an explicitly 'utopian' text (149, 151). Bringing the radical potential of sf off the page these cyborgs locate utopia, not over a forever retreating horizon, but in their own efforts to, as queer utopian theorist José Esteban Muñoz writes, 'dream and enact new and better pleasures, other ways of being in the world and ultimately new worlds' (1).

What is crucial about including these cyborgs, monsters and surrogates within one's understanding of utopianism is that they are aware of their entanglement in oppressive histories *and yet* they remain committed to utopianism. As Haraway notes, the cyborg is 'the illegitimate offspring of militarism and patriarchal capitalism [...] but illegitimate offspring are often exceedingly unfaithful to their origins' (151). It is an illegitimate, unfaithful form of utopianism that these creatures embody. They refuse to locate their hope for utopianism's continued relevance to revolutionary politics in a clean break with the past – a move which in itself risks replicating the colonial dream of the untouched, perfect land. Instead, they make visible the many monstrous heralds of the extraordinary who have always existed, unrecognised, in the cracks of the utopian canon.

David M. Bell notes that attacks on utopians on the grounds of their naïveté, attachment to (alleged) impossibility and refusal to adopt 'realistic' courses of action seek to equate utopia with 'the end of discussion' (n.p.). He suggests that rather than defending utopianism from the accusation that 'Utopia is a containment zone for positions that are beyond the pale' (n.p.), utopians would do well to claim this position. He reminds his readers that '"beyond the pale" [...] is a reference to The Pale: the area of Ireland under English rule during the Late Middle Ages, named for its fenced, or "paled" – border'; adding 'There are worse places to be sent beyond' (n.p.). This understanding of utopianism, in which utopia is positioned in opposition to 'the status quo: (re) produced through colonialism and borders' (n.p.), energises the contemporary field of utopian studies. The scholars whose work this chapter briefly surveys recognise that utopia lies both in the conquest of island nations and in the revolutionary dreams of those who overthrew colonial oppression – both in the pale, and beyond it. Permitting no illusions about utopianism's colonial and eugenic legacies, these thinkers nevertheless continue to state: 'Yes, we are utopians and yes, we want utopia' (Bell n.p.).

Works cited

Ahmad, Dohra. *Landscapes of Hope: Anti-Colonial Utopianism in America*. Oxford UP, 2009.

Ashcroft, Bill. *Utopianism in Postcolonial Literatures*. Routledge, 2016.

Bagchi, Barnita. 'Introduction'. *The Politics of the (Im)Possible: Utopia and Dystopia Reconsidered*. Ed. Barnita Bagchi. Sage, 2012. 1–19.

——. 'Ladylands and Sacrificial Holes: Utopias and Dystopias in Rokeya Sakhawat Hossain's Writings'. *The Politics of the (Im)Possible: Utopia and Dystopia Reconsidered*. Ed. Barnota Bagchi. Sage, 2012. 166–78.

Bell, David M. 'The Only Realism: Utopia Within, Utopia Against, Utopia Beyond'. *Blind Field: A Journal of Cultural Inquiry* (blog). (15 October 2020). https://blindfieldjournal.com/2020/10/15/the-only-realism-utopia-within-utopia-against-utopia-beyond/

Bloch, Ernst. *Heritage of Our Times*. John Wiley, 2015.

——. *The Principle of Hope*, volume 1. Trans. Neville Plaice, Stephen Plaice and Paul Knight. MIT Press, 1995.

Brown, Jayna. *Black Utopias: Speculative Life and the Music of Other Worlds*. Duke UP, 2021.

Bruin-Molé, Megen de. 2021. 'Salvaging Utopia: Lessons for (and from) the Left in Rivers Solomon's *An Unkindness of Ghosts* (2017), *The Deep* (2019), and *Sorrowland* (2021)'. *Humanities* 10 (2021). www.mdpi.com/2076-0787/10/4/109

Chan, Edward K. *The Racial Horizon of Utopia; Unthinking the Future of Race in Late Twentieth-Century American Utopian Novels*. Peter Lang, 2015.
Edwards, Caroline. *Utopia and the Contemporary British Novel*. Cambridge UP, 2019.
Engels, Friedrich. *Socialism, Utopian and Scientific*. W. Swan Sonnenschein, 1892.
Freedman, Carl. *Critical Theory and Science Fiction*. Wesleyan UP, 2000.
Gilman, Charlotte Perkins. *Herland*. The Women's Press, 1979.
Haraway, Donna J. *Simians, Cyborgs, and Women: The Reinvention of Nature*. Routledge, 2013.
Hardy, Karl. 'Unsettling Hope: Settler-Colonialism and Utopianism'. *Spaces of Utopia: An Electronic Journal* 2.1 (2012): 123–36.
Jameson, Fredric. *Archaeologies of the Future: The Desire Called Utopia and Other Science Fictions*. Verso, 2005.
Kafer, Alison. *Feminist, Queer, Crip*. Indiana UP, 2013.
Kumar, Krishan. *Utopia and Anti-Utopia in Modern Times*. Blackwell, 1987.
Lane, Mary E. Bradley. *Mizora: A Prophecy*. Syracuse UP, 2000.
Levitas, Ruth. *Utopia as Method: The Imaginary Reconstitution of Society*. Springer, 2013.
Lewis, Sophie. *Full Surrogacy Now*. Verso, 2019.
Miéville, China. 'Introduction'. *Utopia* by Thomas More. Verso, 2016. 1–28.
Mohawk, John C. *Utopian Legacies: A History of Conquest & Oppression in the Western World*. Clear Light, 1999.
Moonsamy, Nedine. 'Life Is a Biological Risk: Contagion, Contamination, and Utopia in African Science Fiction'. *Cambridge Journal of Postcolonial Literary Inquiry* 3.3 (2016): 329–43.
More, Thomas. *Utopia*. Verso, 2016.
Moylan, Tom. *Demand the Impossible: Science Fiction and the Utopian Imagination*. Peter Lang, 2014.
Muñoz, José Esteban. *Cruising Utopia: The Then and There of Queer Futurity*. New York UP, 2009.
Nadkarni, Asha. *Eugenic Feminism: Reproductive Nationalism in the United States and India*. U of Minnesota P, 2014.
Nirta, Caterina. *Marginal Bodies, Trans Utopias*. Routledge, 2017.
Out of the Woods Collective. *Hope against Hope: Writings on Ecological Crisis*. Common Notions, 2020.
Piercy, Marge. *Woman on the Edge of Time*. Random House, 2020.
Pordzik, Ralph. *The Quest for Postcolonial Utopia: A Comparative Introduction to the Utopian Novel in the New English Literatures*. Peter Lang, 2001.
Rogan, Alcena Madeline Davis. 'Utopian Studies'. *The Routledge Companion to Science Fiction*. Ed. Mark Bould, Andrew M. Butler, Adam Roberts and Sherryl Vint. Routledge, 2009. 308–16.
Russ, Joanna. 'Recent Feminist Utopias'. *To Write Like a Woman: Essays in Feminism and Science Fiction*. Indiana UP, 1995. 133–48.
Salah, Trish. 'Narrating Trans Genres: Transgender Chronotopes in *Woman on the Edge of Time* and *The Deep*'. *Trans/Queer Gender and Narrative Form symposium*. Online, 15 April 2021.
Smith, Eric. *Globalization, Utopia and Postcolonial Science Fiction: New Maps of Hope*. Palgrave Macmillan, 2012.
Stryker, Susan. 'My Words to Victor Frankenstein above the Village of Chamounix: Performing Transgender Rage'. *GLQ: A Journal of Lesbian and Gay Studies* 1.3 (1994): 237–54.
Suvin, Darko. *Metamorphoses of Science Fiction: On the Poetics and History of a Literary Genre*. Peter Lang, 2016.
Zamalin, Alex. *Black Utopia: The History of an Idea from Black Nationalism to Afrofuturism*. Columbia UP, 2019.

INDEX